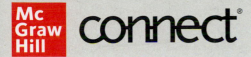 

Instructors: Student Success Starts with You

Tools to enhance your unique voice

Want to build your own course? No problem. Prefer to use our turnkey, prebuilt course? Easy. Want to make changes throughout the semester? Sure. And you'll save time with Connect's auto-grading too.

65%
Less Time Grading

Laptop: McGraw Hill; Woman/dog: George Doyle/Getty Images

Study made personal

Incorporate adaptive study resources like SmartBook® 2.0 into your course and help your students be better prepared in less time. Learn more about the powerful personalized learning experience available in SmartBook 2.0 at **www.mheducation.com/highered/connect/smartbook**

Affordable solutions, added value

Make technology work for you with LMS integration for single sign-on access, mobile access to the digital textbook, and reports to quickly show you how each of your students is doing. And with our Inclusive Access program you can provide all these tools at a discount to your students. Ask your McGraw Hill representative for more information.

Padlock: Jobalou/Getty Images

Solutions for your challenges

A product isn't a solution. Real solutions are affordable, reliable, and come with training and ongoing support when you need it and how you want it. Visit **www.supportateverystep.com** for videos and resources both you and your students can use throughout the semester.

Checkmark: Jobalou/Getty Images

Students: Get Learning that Fits You

Effective tools for efficient studying

Connect is designed to make you more productive with simple, flexible, intuitive tools that maximize your study time and meet your individual learning needs. Get learning that works for you with Connect.

Study anytime, anywhere

Download the free ReadAnywhere app and access your online eBook or SmartBook 2.0 assignments when it's convenient, even if you're offline. And since the app automatically syncs with your eBook and SmartBook 2.0 assignments in Connect, all of your work is available every time you open it. Find out more at **www.mheducation.com/readanywhere**

"I really liked this app—it made it easy to study when you don't have your textbook in front of you."

- Jordan Cunningham, Eastern Washington University

Calendar: owattaphotos/Getty Images

Everything you need in one place

Your Connect course has everything you need—whether reading on your digital eBook or completing assignments for class, Connect makes it easy to get your work done.

Learning for everyone

McGraw Hill works directly with Accessibility Services Departments and faculty to meet the learning needs of all students. Please contact your Accessibility Services Office and ask them to email accessibility@mheducation.com, or visit **www.mheducation.com/about/accessibility** for more information.

WE THE PEOPLE

AN INTRODUCTION TO AMERICAN GOVERNMENT

FOURTEENTH EDITION

THOMAS E. PATTERSON

Bradlee Professor of Government and the Press
John F. Kennedy School of Government
Harvard University

WE THE PEOPLE: AN INTRODUCTION TO AMERICAN GOVERNMENT,
FOURTEENTH EDITION

Published by McGraw Hill Education, 2 Penn Plaza, New York, NY 10121. Copyright © 2022 by McGraw Hill Education. All rights reserved. Printed in the United States of America. Previous editions © 2019, 2017, and 2015. No part of this publication may be reproduced or distributed in any form or by any means, or stored in a database or retrieval system, without the prior written consent of McGraw Hill Education, including, but not limited to, in any network or other electronic storage or transmission, or broadcast for distance learning.

Some ancillaries, including electronic and print components, may not be available to customers outside the United States.

This book is printed on acid-free paper.

1 2 3 4 5 6 7 8 9 LCR 26 25 24 23 22 21

ISBN 978-1-260-24292-8 (bound edition)
MHID 1-260-24292-7 (bound edition)
ISBN 978-1-260-39591-4 (loose-leaf edition)
MHID 1-260-39591-X (loose-leaf edition)

Senior Portofolio Manager: *Jason Seitz*
Product Development Manager: *Dawn Groundwater*
Senior Product Developer: *Sarah Colwell*
Marketing Manager: *Michael Gedatus*
Content Project Managers: *Rick Hecker, George Theofanopoulos*
Buyer: *Sandy Ludovissy*
Design: *Matt Diamond*
Content Licensing Specialist: *Lori Hancock*
Cover Image: *Sean Pavone/Shutterstock*
Compositor: *Aptara®, Inc.*

All credits appearing on page or at the end of the book are considered to be an extension of the copyright page.

Library of Congress Cataloging-in-Publication Data

Names: Patterson, Thomas E., author.
Title: We the people : an introduction to American government / Thomas E.
  Patterson, Bradlee Professor of Government and the Press, John F. Kennedy School
  of Government, Harvard University.
Description: Fourteenth edition. | New York, NY : McGraw Hill Education, [2022] |
  Includes index.
Identifiers: LCCN 2020031872 | ISBN 9781260242928 (hardcover) | ISBN
  9781260395914 (spiral bound) | ISBN 9781260395891 (ebook) | ISBN
  9781260395945 (ebook other)
Subjects: LCSH: United States–Politics and government–Textbooks.
Classification: LCC JK276 .P38 2022 | DDC 320.473–dc23 LC record available at
  https://lccn.loc.gov/2020031872

The Internet addresses listed in the text were accurate at the time of publication. The inclusion of a website does not indicate an endorsement by the authors or McGraw Hill Education, and McGraw Hill Education does not guarantee the accuracy of the information presented at these sites.

mheducation.com/highered

To My Son and Daughter,
Alex and Leigh

ABOUT THE AUTHOR

Thomas E. Patterson is Bradlee Professor of Government and the Press in the John F. Kennedy School of Government at Harvard University. He was previously Distinguished Professor of Political Science in the Maxwell School of Citizenship at Syracuse University. Raised in a small Minnesota town near the Iowa and South Dakota borders, he attended South Dakota State University as an undergraduate and served in the U.S. Army Special Forces in Vietnam before enrolling at the University of Minnesota, where he received his PhD in 1971.

Since then, he has regularly taught introductory American government. In 2013, he was chosen as teacher of the year and adviser of the year by Harvard University's Kennedy School of Government students, the first time a member of its faculty has received both awards in the same year.

He has authored numerous books and articles, which focus mainly on elections, the media, political parties, and citizenship. His recent book, *How America Lost Its Mind* (2019), charts the causes and consequences of the rapid rise in misinformation. Another book, *Informing the News* (2013), examines the need for news that is more trustworthy and relevant. An earlier book, *The Vanishing Voter* (2002), describes and explains the long-term decline in voter participation. His book *Out of Order* (1994) received national attention when President Clinton urged every politician and journalist to read it. In 2002, *Out of Order* received the American Political Science Association's Graber Award for the best book of the past decade in political communication. Another of Patterson's books, *The Mass Media Election* (1980), received a Choice award as Outstanding Academic Title, 1980–1981. Patterson's first book, *The Unseeing Eye* (1976), was selected by the American Association for Public Opinion Research as one of the 50 most influential books of the past half century in the field of public opinion. His current project is a pair of books, one on the problems facing the Republican Party, the other on the problems facing the Democratic Party.

His research has been funded by major grants from the National Science Foundation, the Markle Foundation, the Smith-Richardson Foundation, the Ford Foundation, the Knight Foundation, The Carnegie Corporation, and the Pew Charitable Trusts.

CONTENTS

CHAPTER THREE

FEDERALISM: FORGING A NATION   59

CHAPTER SIX

PUBLIC OPINION AND POLITICAL SOCIALIZATION: SHAPING THE PEOPLE'S VOICE

CHAPTER SEVEN

CHAPTER EIGHT

CHAPTER ELEVEN

CONGRESS: BALANCING NATIONAL GOALS AND LOCAL INTERESTS

CHAPTER FOURTEEN

THE FEDERAL JUDICIAL SYSTEM: APPLYING THE LAW

CHAPTER SEVENTEEN

FOREIGN POLICY: PROTECTING THE AMERICAN WAY   501

A LETTER FROM THE AUTHOR

Anyone who writes an introductory program on American government faces the challenge of explaining a wide range of subjects. One way is to pile fact upon fact and list upon list. It's a common approach to textbook writing, but it turns politics into a pretty dry subject. Politics doesn't have to be dry, and it certainly doesn't have to be dull. Politics has all the elements of drama plus the added feature of affecting the everyday lives of real people.

My goal has been to make this text the most readable one available. Rather than piling fact upon fact, the program relies on narrative. A narrative program weaves together theory, information, and examples in order to bring out key facts and ideas. The response to this approach has been gratifying. As a previous edition was being prepared, I received the following note from a longtime instructor:

> I read this book in about three days, cover to cover. . . . I have never seen a better basic government/politics textbook. I think reading standard textbooks is "boring" (to use a favorite student word), but this one overcomes that. Dr. Patterson has managed to do something that I heretofore thought could not be done.

While writing, I regularly reminded myself that the readers are citizens as well as students. For this reason, the text encourages "critical thinking," by which I mean the process through which an individual determines what can reasonably be believed and then applies reason and information to reach a thoughtful conclusion. Each chapter has five boxes that ask you to "think critically." Two of these—the "How the U.S. Differs" box and the "How the 50 States Differ" box—ask you to think critically about differences in governing systems. A third box—"Party Polarization"—asks you to critically analyze differences in the Republican and Democratic Parties. A fourth box—"Case Study"—discusses a political event and then asks you to analyze the outcome. The final box—"Fake or Fact?"—asks you to critically assess a factual claim. These various boxes are based on the idea that critical thinking is a skill that can be nurtured and, once acquired, can make you a more responsible citizen, whether in casting a vote, forming an opinion about a public policy, or contributing to a political cause.

Improving your ability to think critically is a primary goal of this text. If the only result of reading the text was to increase your factual knowledge of

American government, I would judge it a failure. As Albert Einstein once noted, "The value of a college education is not the learning of many facts but the training of the mind to think." Political science courses, like those in other social science and humanities disciplines, should help students hone their critical thinking skills. As I indicated, the five boxes in each chapter are designed for this purpose. So, too, is the "Critical Thinking Zone" at the end of each chapter. This feature asks you to make use of the chapter's information through the application of the three skills—conceptualizing, synthesizing, and analyzing—that are the foundation of critical thinking.

The well-being of a democracy rests on its citizens. Nevertheless, aside from voting, we seldom ask what citizenship requires of each of us. Each chapter includes two ways in which you as a citizen can strengthen your community and your country.

Finally, in this program I have attempted to present American government through the analytical lens of political science, but in a way that captures the vivid world of real-life politics. Only a tiny fraction of students in the introductory course are enrolled because they plan an academic career in political science. Most students take it because they have an interest in politics or because they are required to do so. I have sought to write a book that will deepen your political interest if you are the first type of student, and spark an interest in politics if you are the second type.

We the People has been in use in college classrooms for more than two decades. During this time, the program has been adopted at more than 1,000 colleges and universities. I am extremely grateful to all who have used it and particularly indebted to the many instructors and students who have sent me suggestions on how to strengthen it. For this edition, I owe a deep thanks to Chris Worden of Sierra College, who provided a host of thoughtful and constructive ideas. If you have ideas you would like to share, please contact me at thomas_patterson@harvard.edu.

Thomas E. Patterson

PREFACE

RELEVANCY AND READABILITY TO ENGAGE TODAY'S STUDENT

Tom Patterson's *We the People* is a **concise** approach to American government, emphasizing **critical thinking** through questions and examples **relevant** to today's students. This exceptionally **readable** text provides opportunities to **engage** with the political process through tools that help students **learn how to think about politics**, utilizing digital resources that connect students with the material in a **personalized** way.

BETTER DATA, SMARTER REVISION, IMPROVED RESULTS

Students helped inform the revision strategy:

STEP 1. Over the course of a few years, data points showing concepts that caused students the most difficulty were collected anonymously from McGraw Hill Education's Connect® American Government's SmartBook 2.0 for *We the People.*

STEP 2. The data from SmartBook 2.0 were provided to the author in the form of a *heat map*, which graphically illustrated "hot spots" in the text where student comprehension was less complete than elsewhere (see the image to the right).

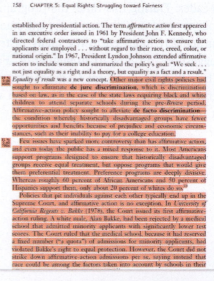

STEP 3. For this edition, the author used the *heat map* data to refine the content and heighten student comprehension. Additional quiz questions and assignable activities were created for use in Connect American Government to further strengthen student learning.

RESULT: Because the *heat map* gave the author empirically based feedback at the paragraph and even sentence level, he was able to develop the new edition using precise student data that pinpointed concepts that caused students the most difficulty.

Heat map data also inform the activities and assessments in Connect American Government, McGraw Hill Education's assignable and accessible learning platform. Where the heat map data indicate that students struggled with specific learning objectives or concepts, we created Connect assets—Concept Clips, Applied Critical Thinking (ACT), and Newsflash current event activities—to provide another avenue for students to learn and master the content.

SMARTBOOK®

SmartBook 2.0 creates a personalized reading experience by highlighting significant concepts that a student needs to learn at a particular point in the course. This ensures that every minute spent with SmartBook 2.0 productively contributes to student learning. The reading experience continuously adapts by highlighting content based on what the student knows and doesn't know. Real-time reports quickly identify the concepts that require more attention from individual students—or the entire class. SmartBook 2.0 detects the content a student is most likely to forget and displays it to improve retention.

Writing Assignment

McGraw Hill's new Writing Assignment Plus tool delivers a learning experience that improves students' written communication skills and conceptual understanding with every assignment. Assign, monitor, and provide feedback on writing more efficiently and grade your assignments within McGraw Hill Connect®. Writing Assignment Plus gives you time-saving tools with a just-in-time basic writing and originality checker.

Features include

- Grammar/writing checking with McGraw Hill learning resources
- Originality checker with McGraw Hill learning resources
- Writing stats
- Rubric building and scoring
- Ability to assign draft and final deadline milestones
- Tablet ready and tools for all learners

INFORMING AND ENGAGING STUDENTS ON POLITICAL CONCEPTS

Using Connect American Government, students can learn the course material more deeply and study more effectively than ever before.

At the *remember* and *understand* levels of Bloom's taxonomy, **Concept Clips** help students break down key concepts in American government. Using easy-to-understand audio narration, visual cues, and colorful animations, Concept Clips provide a step-by-step presentation that aids in student retention. Topics include Federalists and Antifederalists, What Is Devolution?, and Who Participates. In addition, several skills-based clips equip students for work within and outside the classroom, covering topics such as How to Read a Court Case, How to Understand Charts and Graphs, and How to Avoid Plagiarism.

Also at the *remember* and *understand* levels of Bloom's taxonomy, **Newsflash** ties current news stories to key American government concepts and learning objectives. After evaluating a related news story, students are assessed on their ability to connect it to the course content. An example is the impact of the COVID-19 coronavirus on the U.S. economy.

Our new **Podcast Assignments** also deepen students' understanding of real-life politics. These assignments allow you to bring discussion and debate to your courses through the storytelling power of actual podcasts.

At the *apply, analyze,* and *evaluate* levels of Bloom's taxonomy, **critical thinking activities** allow students to engage with the political process and learn by doing.

- Quiz: What Is Your Political Ideology?
- Poll: Americans' Confidence in the Police
- Research: Find Your Senator
- Infographic: Compare the Courts

Practice Government, McGraw Hill's educational game focused on the American political system, is fully integrated inside Connect American Government! A set of focused introductory missions is paired with auto-grade and critical thinking.

Instructor Resources

We the People includes the following instructor resources.

Instructor's manual. The instructor's manual provides a wide variety of tools and resources for presenting the course, including learning objectives and ideas for lectures and discussions.

Test bank. By increasing the rigor of the test bank development process, McGraw Hill has raised the bar for student assessment. Each question has been tagged for level of difficulty, Bloom's taxonomy, and topic coverage. Organized by chapter, the questions are designed to test factual, conceptual, and higher-order thinking.

Test Builder. New to this edition and available within Connect, Test Builder is a cloud-based tool that enables instructors to format tests that can be printed and administered within a Learning Management System. Test Builder offers a modern, streamlined interface for easy content configuration that matches course needs without requiring a download.

Test Builder enables instructors to

- Access all test bank content from a particular title
- Easily pinpoint the most relevant content through robust filtering options
- Manipulate the order of questions or scramble questions and/or answers
- Pin questions to a specific location within a test
- Determine their preferred treatment of algorithmic questions
- Choose the layout and spacing
- Add instructions and configure default settings

PowerPoint. The PowerPoint presentations highlight the key points of the chapter and include supporting visuals. All slides are WCAG compliant.

Remote proctoring. New remote proctoring and browser-locking capabilities are seamlessly integrated within Connect to offer more control over the integrity of online assessments. Instructors can enable security options that restrict browser activity, monitor student use, and verify the identity of each student. Instant and detailed reporting gives instructors an at-a-glance view of potential concerns, thereby avoiding personal bias while fostering evidence-based claims.

CONTENT CHANGES

In addition to the 2020 election results, thorough updates of the data and figures throughout the text, new and updated boxed features (*Fake or Fact?*, *Case Study, How the U.S. Differs, How the 50 States Differ*, and *Party Polarization*), and fresh, new photographs and other images, a new feature in every chapter— *Citizen Action!*—helps students to think of themselves as active participants in the American political process. The three types of *Citizen Action!* sidebars encourage students to (1) improve their understanding of how our government works through reading, reflecting, and research ("Getting Ready"); (2) participate in the public arena by contacting representatives, making contributions, doing service, volunteering, or interning ("Getting Involved"); and (3) reflect on their duty as informed and active citizens ("Taking Responsibility").

Finally, *We the People*, 14th edition, includes the following specific chapter-by-chapter changes:

Chapter 1, Critical Thinking and Political Culture: Becoming a Responsible Citizen

- New introduction focused on how misinformation impacts public opinion, discussing how misinformation in the wake of the COVID-19 coronavirus resulted in unnecessary loss of life
- Thoroughly revised and clarified discussion of critical thinking in the "Learning to Think Critically" section
- Revised and updated "How the U.S. Differs" box, "A Nation of Immigrants," in the "Political Culture: Americans' Enduring Beliefs" section
- Revised and updated "Case Study" box, "Social Welfare Policy," in the "Politics and Power in America" section

Chapter 2, Constitutional Democracy: Promoting Liberty and Self-Government

- New "Fake or Fact?" box, "Is the President Above the Law?" in the "Protecting Liberty: Limited Government" section
- Discussion of two key 2020 Supreme Court rulings, *Trump v. Vance* and *Trump v. Mazers,* that limit the president's ability to withhold information relevant to congressional and legal investigations
- New "How the 50 States Differ" box, "Choosing the President," in the "Providing for Representative Government" section

Chapter 3, Federalism: Forging a Nation

- Thoroughly updated "Fake or Fact?" box, "Do States Have Final Authority over Marijuana Laws?," in the "Federalism: National and State Sovereignty" section
- New "Case Study" box, "Federalism and the COVID-19 Response," in the "Contemporary Federalism (Since 1937)" section

Chapter 4, Civil Liberties: Protecting Individual Rights

- Revised and updated "How the U.S. Differs" box, "Civil Liberties," in "The Bill of Rights, the Fourteenth Amendment, and Selective Incorporation" section
- Coverage, in the "Freedom of Religion" section, of the Supreme Court's important 2020 *Espinoza v. Montana Department of Revenue* ruling that held, if a state provides scholarships for students attending secular private schools, it must also make them available to those attending religious schools
- Discussion of the significant 2020 *June Medical Services v. Russo* Supreme Court decision striking down a Louisiana law requiring abortion providers to have hospital admitting privileges in "The Right to Privacy" section
- Coverage of the landmark 2020 *Ramos v. Louisiana* Supreme Court decision extending the constitutional protection of a unanimous jury verdict in cases of serious crime to state courts in the "Rights of Persons Accused of Crimes" section

Chapter 5, Equal Rights: Struggling toward Fairness

- In "The Struggle for Equality" section, the 2020 Supreme Court decision invalidating the Trump administration's rescinding of the Deferred Action for Childhood Arrivals (DACA) program, which protects undocumented immigrants brought into the country as young children from deportation
- New discussion of the landmark 2020 Supreme Court decision extending the 1964 Civil Rights Act's ban on workplace sex discrimination to include LGBT Americans in "The Struggle for Equality" section
- New coverage of disparity by race of death rates from the COVID-19 coronavirus in the "Discrimination: Superficial Differences, Deep Divisions" section

Chapter 6, Public Opinion and Political Socialization: Shaping the People's Voice

- Thoroughly revised and updated "Case Study" box, "Gun Control," in "The Measurement of Public Opinion" section

- Analysis of how Americans responded to the advice of public officials and health care experts on how to protect themselves from the threat posed by the COVID-19 coronavirus
- New Glossary term, *identity politics*, in the "Frames of Reference" section
- Assessment of why Americans, early in the pandemic, underestimated the threat posed by the COVID-19 coronavirus

Chapter 7, Political Participation: Activating the Popular Will

- New "How the U.S. Differs" box, "Voter Turnout," in the "Voter Participation" section
- Expanded discussion of the depressive effect of voter registration laws in the "Voter Participation" section
- New "Fake or Fact?" box, "Is Illegal Voting Widespread?," in the "Voter Participation" section
- New Glossary term, *political interest*, in the "Voter Participation" section
- Revised "Party Polarization" box, "Party Identification and Voter Turnout," in the "Voter Participation" section
- Discussion of the expanded Black Lives Matter movement in the wake of the George Floyd killing, in the "Unconventional Activism" section
- New "Case Study" box, "The Rise and Fall of Occupy Wall Street," in the "Unconventional Activism" section

Chapter 8, Political Parties, Candidates, and Campaigns: Defining the Voters' Choice

- Analysis of the impact of young adult voters in the "Electoral and Party Systems" section, with accompanying new figure, "Vote of Adults 18–29 Years of Age in the 2000–2020 Presidential Elections"
- Trump-Biden 2020 presidential election debates in the "Parties and Candidates in the Campaign" section
- New "Fake or Fact?" box, "Do Republicans and Democrats Understand Each Other?," in the "Parties, Candidates, and the Public's Influence" section

Chapter 9, Interest Groups: Organizing for Influence

- Thoroughly revised introduction clarifying how loopholes allow lobbying expenditures to go unchecked and how the narrow focus of interest groups can trump the interests of society as a whole
- Revised "How the U.S. Differs" box, "A Nation of Joiners," in "The Interest-Group System" section
- New discussion of the 2017 Tax Cut and Jobs Act and how it reflected the power of business interest groups in "The Interest-Group System" section
- Discussion of how the change to Democratic control of the House of Representatives in 2019 shifted focus from business to labor lobbyists in the "Inside Lobbying" section

Chapter 10, The News Media and the Internet: Communicating Politics

- New introduction discussing widely varying media reactions to Donald Trump's COVID-19 policy response
- Assessment of the media's response to the COVID-19 outbreak in "The Media: Content and Functions" section
- New Glossary term, *priming*, in "The Media: Content and Functions" section
- New Glossary term, *low-choice media system*, in the "Media Audiences and Effects" section

Chapter 11, Congress: Balancing National Goals and Local Interests

- New chapter introduction focused on the COVID-19 stimulus bill as an example of the dual nature of Congress
- Expanded discussion of how Congress members' preoccupation with reelection affects their decisions in the "Congress as a Career" section
- Results and implications of the 2020 U.S. House and Senate elections
- Expanded discussion of the roles of congressional party leaders in the "Parties and Party Leadership" section
- Updated "How the 50 States Differ: Women in the State Legislatures" box in the "Parties and Party Leadership" section
- New "Case Study" box, "Leadership Styles of Women in Congress," in the "Congress's Policymaking Role" section
- Discussion of congressional grants-in-aid to the states in the wake of the COVID-19 pandemic in the "Congress's Policymaking Role" section

Chapter 12, The Presidency: Leading the Nation

- New chapter introduction reflecting the results of the 2020 presidential election
- New introduction to—and new title for—the "Origins of the Modern Presidency" section (formerly "Foundations of the Modern Presidency"), which summarizes the formal and informal boundaries to becoming president
- Expanded discussion of the various roles of the president in the "Origins of the Modern Presidency" section
- New Glossary terms in the "Origins of the Modern Presidency" section: *chief executive, commander in chief, chief diplomat, head of state, chief legislator*, and *limited presidency theory*.
- New "Case Study" box, "Presidential Nominating Campaigns," in the "Origins of the Modern Presidency" section (which replaces the "Choosing the President" section from the previous edition)
- New introduction to the "Staffing the Presidency" section, which discusses how staffing has changed greatly over the course of history, and revised sub-sections "The Executive Office of the President" (with

expanded discussion of the National Security Council), "The Vice
President" (reflecting the results of the 2020 presidential election), and
"The Cabinet and Agency Appointees" (with expanded discussion of the
close links between the president and the departments of State and
Defense)

- New Glossary term, *Executive Office of the Presidency (EOP)*, in the "Staffing
  the Presidency" section
- New discussion of Vice President Mike Pence's role heading the COVID-19
  task force in the "Staffing the Presidency" section
- New section, "Bridging the Power Gap," focusing on presidents' efforts to
  overcome barriers to presidential action imposed by separation of executive
  and legislative power
- New subsections in the "Bridging the Gap" section discussing how the
  president can bridge the gap between powers by being an agenda setter
  (using the bully pulpit), garnering public support (the permanent campaign), asserting the roles of chief legislator and party leader, and going
  it alone (pushing the limits of formal authority via executive order, executive
  agreements, and military force)
- New subsections in the "Bridging the Gap" section focused on the steps
  Congress can take to curb presidential power, such as impeachment
  (includes discussion of President Trump's impeachment)
- New Glossary terms in the "Bridging the Gap" section: *bully pulpit, permanent campaign, presidential veto, party leader, executive order*, and *execu-
  tive agreement*
- New "Fake or Fact?" box, "Are the News Media Politically Biased?," in
  the "Bridging the Gap" section
- New "How the 50 States Differ" box, "The Permanent Campaign," in the
  "Bridging the Gap" section
- Revised and newly titled "Factors in Presidential Success" section (formerly
  "Factors in Presidential Leadership"), with revised and updated discussion
  within the subsections "The Force of Circumstance," "The Stage of the
  President's Term," "The Nature of the Issue: Foreign or Domestic," and
  "The Makeup of Congress" (formerly "Relations with Congress")

Chapter 13, The Federal Bureaucracy: Administering the Government

- New discussion of the federal bureaucracy's uneven response to the
  COVID-19 outbreak in the chapter introduction
- New "Case Study" box, "Control of Bureaucratic Agencies" focusing on
  the 2020 Supreme Court ruling on the president's authority to remove
  the head of a federal agency in the "Democracy and Bureaucratic
  Accountability" section

Chapter 14, The Federal Judicial System: Applying the Law

- New "How the U.S. Differs" box, "Supreme Court Justices' Term of Office," in "The Federal Judicial System" section
- New discussion of ripeness, mootness, and standing as factors in the Supreme Court's decision whether to hear a case, in "The Federal Judicial System" section
- New Glossary terms, *per curiam opinion* and *rule of four*, in "The Federal Judicial System" section
- In the "Federal Court Appointees" section, new discussions of the death of Ruth Bader Ginsburg and the controversial rush to confirm her replacement, how the abolishment of using the filibuster to block Supreme Court nominations has affected the makeup of the Court, and how the demographics of the Supreme Court have changed in recent decades.
- New "Fake or Fact?" box, "Are Federal Judges Biased?," in "The Nature of Judicial Decision Making" section
- Discussion of the Supreme Court's landmark 2020 decision in *Bostock v Clayton County,* in "The Nature of Judicial Decision Making" section
- Updated "Case Study" box, "*Citizens United v. Federal Election Commission* (2010)," in the "Judicial Power and Democratic Government" section

Chapter 15, Economic and Environmental Policy: Contributing to Prosperity

- New chapter introduction focused on the economic policy response to the COVID-19 coronavirus outbreak.
- New "Fake or Fact?" box, "Is Weather an Indicator of Climate Change?," in the "Government as Protector of the Environment" section
- Discussion of the $500 billion set aside in the 2020 coronavirus stimulus bill for business firms in the "Government as Promoter of Economic Interests" section

Chapter 16, Income, Welfare, and Education Policy: Providing for Personal Security

- New "Fake or Fact?" box, "Does Welfare Create Dependency?," in the "Welfare Politics and Policies" section, including discussion of job loss as a result of the COVID-19 coronavirus

Chapter 17, Foreign Policy: Protecting the American Way

- Insertion of the "Case Study" box "Invasion of Iraq" into the "U.S. Foreign and Defense Policy since World War II" section
- New Glossary term, *hard power,* in the "U.S. Foreign and Defense Policy since World War II" section
- New "Fake or Fact?" box, "Would Eliminating Foreign Aid Balance the Budget?," in "The Economic Dimension of National Security Policy" section

ACKNOWLEDGMENTS

Nearly two decades ago, when planning the first edition of *We the People,* my editor and I concluded that it would be enormously helpful if a way could be found to bring into each chapter the judgment of those political scientists who teach the introductory course year in and year out. Thus, in addition to soliciting general reviews from a select number of expert scholars, we sent each chapter to faculty members at U.S. colleges and universities of all types—public and private, large and small, two-year and four-year. These political scientists had years of experience teaching the introductory course, and they provided countless good ideas.

I decided to use that same review process for this edition. The response was gratifying and extraordinarily helpful. The reviewers' suggestions led to important changes in every chapter and, in the case of one chapter, led me to rewrite it from front to back. I'm extremely grateful to each and all of them:

Noemi Alexander, *California Baptist University*
Milan Andrejevich, *Ivy Tech Community College, South Bend*
Yan Bai, *Grand Rapids Community College*
Tiffany Boehm, *Lake Michigan College*
Todd Bradley, *Indiana University, Kokomo*
Colette Carter, *Colorado State University, Pueblo*
Douglas Clouatre, *Mid-Plains Community College*
Kevin Coakley, *Palm Beach State College, Belle Glade*
Frank Colucci, *Purdue University Northwest*
Magfirah Dahlan-Taylor, *Craven Community College*
Anthony Daniels, *University of Toledo*
Elsa Dias, *Pikes Peak Community College*
G. Denise Dupree, *Southern University of Shreveport*
Amanda Cook Fesperman, *Illinois Valley Community College*
Russell Fox, *Friends University*
Nicholas Giordano, *Suffolk County Community College*
George Hale, *Kutztown University of Pennsylvania*
Phillip Hardy, *Benedictine University, Lisle*
Matthew Harrigan, *Santa Clara University*
Ron Keller, *Lincoln College*
Megan Kerr, *Owens Community College*
Richard Keifer, *Waubonsee Community College*
Elizabeth Klages, *Normandale Community College*

Scott LaDeur, *North Central Michigan College*
Jill Lane, *North Seattle College*
Dedric Lee, *Jefferson College*
Derek Mosley, *Meridian Community College*
Chad Mueller, *Northwest Vista College*
Carolyn Myers, *Southwestern Illinois College*
Kevin Navratil, *Moraine Valley Community College*
Bobby Pace, *Community College of Aurora*
Erin Richards, *Cascadia College*
Jason Roberts, *Quincy College*
Jamie Roughton, *Greenville Technical College*
Andrew Sanders, *Texas A&M University, San Antonio*
Erich Saphir, *Pima Community College, West*
Jeff Schultz, *Luzerne County Community College*
Becky Sims, *South Georgia State College*
Zack Sullivan, *Inver Hills Community College*
Gary Timm, *Northeast Community College, Norfolk*
Austin Trantham, *Jacksonville University*
Tony Wiley, *Dodge City Community College*
Amanda Wintersieck, *Virginia Commonwealth University*
Mary Young-Marcks, *Southwestern Michigan College*

I also want to thank those at McGraw-Hill Education who contributed to the 14th edition: Jason Seitz, Dawn Groundwater, Rick Hecker, Danielle Bennett, Ann Marie Jannette, and Rasheite Calhoun, as well as product developer Bruce Cantley, copyeditor Debra DeBord, and photo researcher Nichole Nalenz at Aptara. At Harvard, I had the dedicated support of Kevin Wren.

Thomas E. Patterson

WE THE PEOPLE

CRITICAL THINKING AND POLITICAL CULTURE: BECOMING A RESPONSIBLE CITIZEN

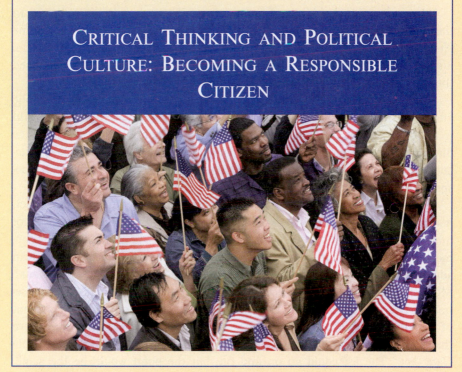

sirtravelalot/Shutterstock

66 The worth of the state, in the long run, is the worth of the individuals composing it. 99

JOHN STUART MILL[1]

In the span of a few months, the death toll had surpassed the number of Americans killed in the Korean war, the Vietnam war, the Afghan war, and the Iraq war combined. No part of the country was spared, although the toll was much higher in metropolitan areas and nursing homes. Public officials and health experts warned Americans to take strict measures to avoid contracting the COVID-19 coronavirus. Unlike the flu, there was no vaccine to protect them nor did they have any natural immunity from previous exposure. COVID-19 was a novel virus, one never before seen in people.

Most Americans responded to the pandemic by limiting their social contact, covering their faces when going out, and washing their hands thoroughly after they did. These measures saved tens of thousands of lives. Yet lives were lost because some Americans held beliefs that were at odds with the facts. More than a third of Americans were convinced that COVID-19 was no more deadly than the seasonal flu and many of them ignored social distancing, increasing the likelihood that they, and those around them, would contract the disease.[2]

Years ago, journalist Walter Lippmann noted that people respond, not to the world as it actually is, but to the world as they think it is. Given that some Americans believed that the coronavirus was no more dangerous than the flu, it's not surprising that they behaved in a carefree way. But their belief increased the risk to themselves and others.

Some amount of misinformation is to be expected. The world of public affairs is large and complex, and most of what people believe about that world is a result of what they hear from others rather than what they experience directly. In that context, it's not surprising that some people will make inaccurate judgments about the nature of the world. What's alarming is the widespread nature of such beliefs.

Misinformation is now at its highest level in the history of polling.[3] In fact, it's hard to find a leading issue on which large numbers of Americans are not misinformed. Russian meddling in our elections has been thoroughly documented by U.S. intelligence agencies and, yet, one out of every four American adults—roughly 60 million in all—deny that Russia has interfered in our elections.[4] More than two-thirds of Americans falsely believe that middle-income households pay a greater portion of their income in taxes than do the top 1 percent of income-earning households.[5] More than half of Americans falsely believe that illegal immigrants are entitled to free medical care under the Affordable Care Act.[6] The list could go on and on, but the point would be the same. Many Americans hold opinions that are wildly at odds with reality.

Misinformation has its comic side. In one poll, 10 percent of respondents thought that Judith Sheindlin ("Judge Judy") holds a seat on the Supreme Court.[7] But the grim side is alarming. Democracy is at risk when misinformation

A healthy democracy depends on citizen participation but also requires that this participation be informed and thoughtful. (Alexandros Michailidis/Shutterstock)

is widespread. If large numbers of citizens are misinformed and base their behavior and opinions on what they think is true, effective governing is difficult to achieve. Theodore Sorensen, who was a policy aide to President John F. Kennedy, put his finger on the problem when he said, "To decide, you first have to know."[8]

LEARNING TO THINK CRITICALLY

A goal of this book is to help students to think critically about politics. Critical thinking is not the mere act of voicing an opinion about a current issue or development. **Critical thinking** is the process of forming an opinion after weighing the relevant facts. Opinions not reached in this way are incomplete at best, perhaps even wildly wrong.[9] Of course, it's not enough to have a grasp of the facts. Critical thinking also requires citizens to recognize how their interests and values are affected by a choice they face. Citizens differ in what they cherish and what they need and can reasonably arrive at different opinions even when they share the same facts. But misinformation is a barrier to sound judgment. Most Americans believe, for example, that foreign aid accounts for 20 percent or more of the federal budget, which has led some of them to believe that eliminating foreign aid would balance the federal budget. In reality, less than 1 percent of the federal budget is spent on foreign aid and, even if it was eliminated, the budget deficit would still be huge.[10]

Unlike an authoritarian regime that requires people to think in a certain way or risk punishment, a democracy lets people decide for themselves what to think, and how much effort to put into it. Citizens can choose to engage in wild thinking, but they have only themselves to blame when things go wrong.[11] Many Americans, for example, supported the U.S. invasion of Iraq in 2003 on a belief that Iraq was no match for the U.S. military and that the war would end within a few weeks.[12] It's now two decades later and U.S. forces are still in Iraq trying to quell the ethnic and religious strife unleashed by the American invasion. If a two-decades-long war would have been hard to predict, the notion that the conflict would end quickly was wishful thinking, not critical thinking.

Obstacles to Critical Thinking

The obstacles to critical thinking have increased in recent decades. Our media system has changed markedly, as first cable and then the Internet expanded our sources of information. Many of the newer sources are not to be trusted. Some talk-show hosts and bloggers care little about the accuracy of the claims they make. They routinely slant or invent information to suit their purpose while burying contradictory facts. Much of the misinformation about COVID-19 originated on partisan talk shows, including the claim that it was no more dangerous

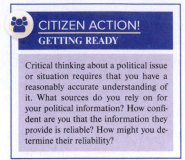

CITIZEN ACTION!
GETTING READY

Critical thinking about a political issue or situation requires that you have a reasonably accurate understanding of it. What sources do you rely on for your political information? How confident are you that the information they provide is reliable? How might you determine their reliability?

than the flu and that it was a "hoax" created to discredit the Trump administration.[13]

Nor can political leaders always be counted on to tell the truth. During the Vietnam conflict, Presidents Lyndon Johnson and Richard Nixon told Americans that the conflict was going well when, in fact, it was going poorly. Nevertheless, the public at an earlier time was less tolerant of deceptive claims, and leaders were less inclined to make them.

In recent years, as our politics has become more heated and divisive, we've become more tolerant of leaders who slant the facts, and they've become more willing to do so.[14] Many of our leaders claim, for example, that free trade is the reason that America has lost millions of manufacturing jobs. Free trade has, in fact, contributed to the job loss, but it's far from being the main source. Seven of every eight lost jobs are due to automation, the replacement of workers with machines.[15]

Our mental habits can also lead us to hold false beliefs. In *Thinking Fast and Slow,* Nobel laureate Daniel Kahneman notes that we often accept explanations based on what we'd like to believe rather than what the evidence shows.[16] We also engage in what behavioral scientists Gordon Pennycook and David Rand call "cognitive laziness."[17] Rather than studying a claim, we often judge its accuracy on the basis of who's saying it or whether we've heard it before.

What Political Science Can Contribute to Critical Thinking

This text will not try to tell you *what* to think politically. There is no correct way of thinking when it comes to the "what" of politics. People differ in their political values and interests and thereby differ in their political views.

Instead, this text will help you learn *how* to think critically by providing you with analytical tools that can sharpen your understanding of American politics. The tools are derived from **political science**—the systematic study of government and politics. Political science has developed largely through the work of scholars, but political practitioners and writers have also contributed. One of America's foremost political scientists was the chief architect of the U.S. Constitution and later a president. Even today, James Madison's *Federalist* essays on constitutional design are masterpieces of political science.

As a discipline, political science is descriptive and analytical—that is, it attempts to depict and explain politics. This effort takes place through various frameworks, including rational choice theory, institutional analysis, historical reasoning, behavioral studies, legal reasoning, and cultural analysis. Political science provides knowledge and analytical tools that can increase citizens' ability to think critically:

- Reliable information about how the U.S. political system operates
- Systematic generalizations about major tendencies in American politics
- Terms and concepts that highlight key aspects of politics

Like any skill, critical thinking is developed through practice. For this reason, each of the text's chapters includes boxes that ask you to think critically. Some boxes deal with perennial questions, such as the nature of the president's war powers. Other boxes ask you to think critically by having you compare politics in the United States and in your state with politics in other nations and states. Still other boxes present cases of actual events and ask you to analyze them. Other boxes provide information and ask you to assess whether a claim is fake or fact. Finally, some boxes deal with current controversies, including the rising level of party polarization in America.

POLITICAL CULTURE: AMERICANS' ENDURING BELIEFS

An understanding of U.S. politics properly begins with an assessment of the nation's political culture. Every country has its **political culture**—the widely shared and deep-seated beliefs of its people about politics.[18] These beliefs derive from the country's traditions and help define the relationship of citizens to their government and to each other.

Although every country has a distinctive political culture, the United States, as the British writer James Bryce observed, is a special case.[19] Americans' beliefs are the basis of their national identity. Other people take their identity from the common ancestry that led them gradually to gather under one flag. Thus, long before there was a France, Germany, or Japan, there were French, German, and Japanese people, each a kinship group united through ancestry. Not so for Americans. They are a multitude of people from different lands— England, Germany, Ireland, Africa, Italy, Poland, Mexico, and China, to name just a few (see "How the U.S. Differs"). Americans are linked not by a shared ancestry but by allegiance to a common set of ideals. The French writer Alexis de Tocqueville was among the first to recognize that shared beliefs were Americans' common bond. "Habits of the heart" was how he described their attachment to them.

HOW THE U.S. DIFFERS

CRITICAL THINKING THROUGH COMPARISONS

A Nation of Immigrants

Americans trace their roots to every country on earth, which has led the United States to be called a "nation of immigrants." Even today, one in every seven Americans is an immigrant. If the children of immigrants are included, the figure is one in four.

Elsewhere, as the accompanying chart illustrates, there is typically a single ethnic group that makes up a majority of the population. Ninety-eight percent of the residents of Japan are ethnically Japanese. In Italy, 92 percent are ethnically Italian. In Germany and Great Britain, roughly 80 percent have a shared ethnicity. Not so for Americans. The largest ethnic group in the United States is German Americans, who constitute 14 percent of the population. Mexican Americans at 11 percent and Irish Americans at 10 percent are the second and third largest ethnic groups. America's great diversity is reflected in the Latin phrase *E Pluribus Unum* (one out of many) that appears on the official Seal of the United States.

Largest ethnic group, as a percentage of total population.

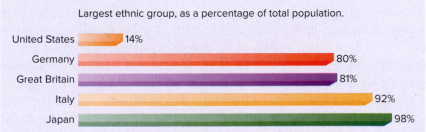

Source: Compiled by the author from various sources.

Q: How might more recent U.S. immigrants differ from those who came to the United States earlier in its history?

A: The great majority of early immigrants to America came from Europe, in part because of restrictions on immigrants from other parts of the world. Legislation enacted in 1965 eased restrictions on immigration from Latin America and Asia, and most immigrants since then have come from these regions.

America's core ideals are rooted in the European heritage of the first white settlers. They arrived during the Enlightenment period, when people were awakening to the idea of individual progress, which could be pursued more fully in the open society of the New World than in the Old World, where kings and nobles claimed special privileges and owned most of the land. Ultimately, the colonists overturned the European way of governing. The American Revolution was the first successful large-scale rebellion in human history, driven largely by the desire to create a radically different form of society.[20] In the words of the Declaration of Independence,

> We hold these truths to be self-evident, that all men are created equal; that they are endowed by their Creator with certain unalienable rights; that among these are life, liberty, and the pursuit of happiness. That, to secure these rights, governments are instituted among men, deriving their just powers from the consent of the governed; that, whenever any form of government becomes destructive of these ends, it is the right of the people to alter or to abolish it, and to institute a new government, laying its foundation on such principles, and organizing its powers in such form, as to them shall seem most likely to effect their safety and happiness.

Those words are now familiar, but they were revolutionary at the time. And a decade later, when the U.S. Constitution was written, the break with the old way of governing was complete. The highest authority would not be a king but a written document that defined the lawful powers of government and the rights of citizens.

Core Values: Liberty, Individualism, Equality, and Self-Government

An understanding of America's cultural ideals begins with recognition that the individual is paramount. Government is secondary. Its role is to serve the people, as opposed to a system where people are subservient to government. No clearer statement of this principle exists than the Declaration of Independence's reference to "unalienable rights"—freedoms that belong to each and every citizen and that cannot lawfully be taken away by government.

Liberty, individualism, equality, and self-government are widely regarded as America's core political ideals. **Liberty** is the principle that individuals should be free to act and think as they choose, provided they do not infringe unreasonably on the freedom and well-being of others.[21] Political liberty was nearly a birthright for early Americans. They did not have to accept the European system of absolute government when greater personal liberty was as close as the next area of unsettled land. Religious sentiments also entered into the thinking of the early Americans. Many of them had fled Europe to escape religious persecution and came to look upon religious freedom as part of a broader set of rights, including freedom of speech. Unsurprisingly, these early Americans were determined, when forming their own government, to protect their liberty. The Declaration of Independence rings with the proclamation that people are entitled to "life, liberty, and the pursuit of happiness." The preamble to the Constitution declares that the U.S. government was founded to secure "the Blessings of Liberty to ourselves and our Posterity."

Early Americans also enjoyed unprecedented economic opportunity. Unlike Europe, America had no hereditary nobility that owned virtually all the land. The New World's great distance from Europe and its vast stretches of open territory gave ordinary people the chance to own property, provided they were willing to work hard enough to make it a success. Out of this experience grew a sense of self-reliance and a culture of "rugged individualism." **Individualism** is a commitment to personal initiative and self-sufficiency. Observers from Tocqueville onward have seen fit to note that liberty in America, as in no other country, is tied to a desire for economic independence. Americans' chief aim, wrote Tocqueville, "is to remain their own masters."[22]

A third American political ideal is **equality**—the notion that all individuals are equal in their moral worth and thereby entitled to equal treatment under

Americans' cultural beliefs are rooted in America's historical development. The challenges and opportunities of settling the nation's vast space contributed to beliefs in individualism, liberty, equality, and self-government. Pictured here is a general store that served a small town during the period of westward expansion. Notice that the store also served as the local post office. (Atmosphere1/Shutterstock)

the law. Europe's rigid system of aristocratic privilege was unenforceable in frontier America. It was this natural sense of personal equality that Thomas Jefferson expressed so forcefully in the Declaration of Independence: "We hold these truths to be self-evident, that all men are created equal." However, equality has always been America's most elusive ideal. Even Jefferson professed not to know its exact meaning. A slave owner, Jefferson distinguished between free citizens, who were entitled to equal rights, and slaves, who were not. After slavery was abolished, Americans continued to argue over the meaning of equality, and the debate continues today. Does equality require that wealth and opportunity be widely shared? Or does it merely require that artificial barriers to advancement be removed? Despite differing opinions about such questions, an insistence on equality is a distinctive feature of the American experience. Americans, said Bryce, reject "the very notion" that some people might be "better" than others merely because of birth or position.[23]

America's fourth great political ideal is **self-government**—the principle that the people are the ultimate source of governing authority and should have a voice in their governing. Americans' belief in self-government formed in colonial America. The Old World was an ocean away, and European governments had no option but to give the American colonies a degree of self-determination. Out of this experience came the vision of a self-governing nation that led tens of thousands of ordinary farmers, merchants, and tradespeople to risk their lives fighting the British during the American Revolution. "Governments," the Declaration of Independence proclaims, "deriv[e] their just powers from the consent of the governed." The Constitution of the United States begins with the words "We the People." Etched in a corridor of the Capitol in Washington, D.C., are the words Alexander Hamilton spoke when asked about the foundation of the nation's government: "Here, sir, the people govern."

The Limits and Power of Americans' Ideals

America's cultural beliefs are idealistic. They hold out the promise of a government of high purpose, in which power is widely shared and used for the common good, and where individuals are free, independent, and equal under the law.

Yet high ideals do not come with a guarantee that people will live up to them. The clearest proof of that in the American case is the human tragedy that began nearly four centuries ago and continues today. In 1619, the first Black slaves were brought in chains to America. Slavery lasted 250 years. Slaves worked in the fields from dawn to dark (from "can see, 'til can't"), in both the heat of summer and the cold of winter. The Civil War brought an end to slavery but not to racial oppression. Slavery was followed by the Jim Crow era of legal segregation. Black citizens in the South were forbidden by law to use

The largest stain on America's founding principles is the nation's treatment of its Black citizens. For more than two centuries, they were bought and sold as slaves and, after being freed by the Civil War, were denied equal citizenship throughout the South. That tragic legacy continues today, as evidenced by high levels of poverty among African Americans, who are also more likely to be victims of police misconduct. Shown here are demonstrators protesting the killing of an unarmed and handcuffed Black man, George Floyd, by Minneapolis police in 2020. (Tverdokhlib/Shutterstock)

the same schools, hospitals, restaurants, and restrooms as white citizens. Those who spoke out against this system were subjected to beatings, firebombings, rapes, and murder—hundreds of African Americans were lynched in the early 1900s by white vigilantes. Today, African Americans have equal rights under the law, but, in fact, they are far from equal. Compared with white children, Black children are twice as likely to live in poverty and to die in infancy.[24] There have always been two Americas, one for whites and one for Blacks.

Despite the lofty claim that "all men are created equal," equality has never been an American birthright. In 1882, Congress suspended Chinese immigration on the assumption that the Chinese were an inferior people. Calvin Coolidge in 1923 asked Congress for a permanent ban on Chinese immigration, saying that people "who do not want to be partakers of the American spirit ought not to settle in America."[25] Not to be outdone, California enacted legislation prohibiting individuals of Japanese descent from purchasing property in the state. Not until 1965 was discrimination against the Chinese, Japanese, and other Asians eliminated from U.S. immigration laws. For more on America's conflicted relationship with immigrants, see "Fake or Fact? Do Immigrants Commit More Crimes?"

FAKE or FACT

Detecting Misinformation

Do Immigrants Commit More Crimes?

America is portrayed as a nation that opens its arms to immigrants. At the base of the Statue of Liberty are the words of Emma Lazarus's oft-cited poem, "Give me your tired, your poor, your huddled masses yearning to breathe free."

Everett Historical/Shutterstock

Yet many Americans have opposed the entry of immigrants, particularly those of a different religious or ethnic background. In the mid-1800s, Catholic immigrants from Ireland and Germany were widely reviled by Protestants already here. In the late 1800s and early 1900s, hostility was directed at new arrivals from southern and eastern Europe—Italians, Greeks, Poles, Hungarians, Jews, Russians, and others. In 1924, Congress passed a law that largely halted immigration from southern and eastern Europe. Earlier, Congress had closed the door on immigrants from Asia.

An argument heard in those earlier periods and being heard again today is that immigrants pose a threat to public safety. A Pew Research Center poll found that Americans, by a ratio of seven to one, believe that immigrants are more likely than native-born Americans to commit crimes.[26]

Is that claim fact, or is it fake?

There has been substantial research on the issue, including recent studies by the National Academy of Sciences and the conservative Cato Institute. The studies have found that immigrants are more law abiding than are native-born Americans. The 2017 Cato Institute study, for example, found that immigrants are 69 percent less likely to be incarcerated than are the native born. That's true also of illegal immigrants, who are 44 percent less likely than the native born to have been convicted of crime and imprisoned.[27]

America's callous treatment of some groups is not among the stories that the American people like to tell about themselves. A University of Virginia survey found that American adults are far more likely to want children to be taught about the nation's achievements than about its shortcomings. For example, more than four out of five of those surveyed said children should be taught that "with hard work and perseverance anyone can succeed in America," while less than three in five said the same about teaching children of the nation's "cruel mistreatment of Blacks and American Indians." Selective memory can be found among all peoples, but the tendency to recast history is perhaps exaggerated in the American case because Americans' beliefs are so idealistic. How could a nation that proclaims "all men are created equal" have barred the Chinese, enslaved Blacks, declared wives to be the "property" of their husbands,[28] and killed Indians in order to take their land?

Although America's ideals obviously do not determine exactly what people will do, they are far from empty promises. If racial, gender, ethnic, and other forms of intolerance constitute the nation's sorriest chapter, the centuries-old struggle of Americans to build a more equal society is among its finest. Few nations have battled so relentlessly against the insidious discrimination that stems from superficial human differences such as the color of one's skin. The abolition and suffrage movements of the 1800s and the more recent civil rights movements of Black Americans, women, Hispanics, and the LGBTQ community testify to Americans' persistent effort to build a more equal society. In 1848, at the first-ever national convention on women's rights, the delegates issued the Declaration of Sentiments, which read in part: "We hold these truths to be self-evident: that all men and women are created equal." A century later, speaking at the Lincoln Memorial at the peak of the Black civil rights movement, Martin Luther King Jr. said, "'We hold these truths to be self-evident, that all men are created equal.'"[29]

Americans' determination to build a more equal society can also be seen in its public education system. In the early 1800s, the United States pioneered the idea of a free public education for children—this at a time when education in Europe was reserved for children of the wealthy. Even today, the United States spends more heavily on public education than do European countries. Compared with Great Britain or France, for example, the United States spends about 30 percent more per pupil annually on its primary and secondary schools. The United States also has the world's most elaborate system of higher education, which includes roughly 4,000 two-year and four-year institutions. Although some of America's youth do not have a realistic chance of attending college, the nation's college system is a relatively open one. Nearly a third of Americans over the age of 25 have a college degree, which ranks second only to Canada worldwide. Even the American states with the lowest proportion of college graduates have a higher percentage of residents with a bachelor's degree than does the typical European country (see "How the 50 States Differ").

HOW THE 50 STATES DIFFER

CRITICAL THINKING THROUGH COMPARISONS

A College Education

Reflecting their belief in individualism and equality, Americans have developed the world's largest college system—comprising roughly 4,000 institutions. According to U.S. Census Bureau figures, about one in three Americans over the age of 25 is a college graduate. Even the lowest-ranking state—West Virginia, with one in five—has a higher percentage of college graduates than do most European countries.

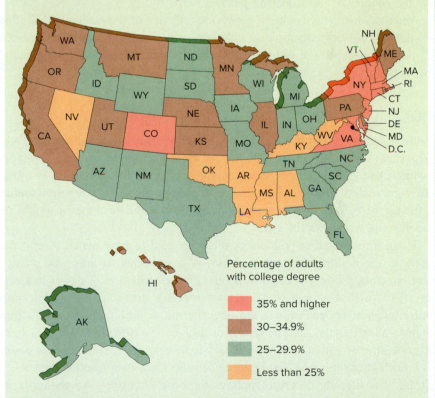

Percentage of adults with college degree

- 35% and higher
- 30–34.9%
- 25–29.9%
- Less than 25%

Q: Why do the northeastern states have a higher percentage of adults with college degrees?

A: The northeastern states are wealthier and more urbanized than most states. Accordingly, young people in these states can better afford the costs of college and are more likely to pursue careers that require a college degree.

The principle of self-government has also shaped American society. No country holds as many elections as does the United States, or has anywhere near as many publicly elected officials. There are roughly a half million American elected officials, everyone from the president of the United States to the local council member. The United States is also nearly the only country to use primary elections as the means of choosing party nominees.

The principles of liberty and individualism have also shaped American society. Few people have pursued their individual rights—ranging from freedom of expression to fair-trial protections—as relentlessly as have Americans. And there are few countries where individualism is as deeply ingrained as in the United States (see "Case Study: Social Welfare Policy" in the next section). Political analysts William Watts and Lloyd Free described the United States as "the country of individualism *par excellence.*"[30]

America's distinctive cultural beliefs are only one of the elements that affect the nation's politics, as subsequent chapters will show. The rest of this chapter introduces concepts and distinctions that are basic to a systematic understanding of politics.

POLITICS AND POWER IN AMERICA

Political scientist Harold Lasswell described politics as a conflict over "who gets what, when, and how."[31] Politics would be a simple matter if everyone thought alike and could have everything they pleased. But people do not think alike, and society's resources are limited. Conflict is the inevitable result. **Politics** is the means by which society settles its conflicts and determines who gets the benefits and who pays the costs.

Those who prevail in political conflicts are said to have **power**, a term that refers to the ability of persons, groups, or institutions to influence political developments.[32] Power is basic to politics. The distribution of power in a society affects who wins and who loses when policy decisions are made. Those with enough power can raise or cut taxes, permit or prohibit abortions, impose or relax trade barriers, and make war or declare peace. With so much at stake, it is not surprising that Americans, like people elsewhere, seek political power.

French philosopher Michel Foucault called politics "war by other means,"[33] a phrase that literally describes politics in some countries. An **authoritarian government** is one that openly represses its political opponents, mostly through intimidation and prohibitions on free expression but sometimes by brutalizing opposition leaders. Such regimes are backed by the country's police and armed forces, forego free and fair elections, and exert tight control over the media. The authoritarian regime in China, for example, blocks Facebook, Twitter, YouTube, and other outlets—including those within the country—that convey messages contrary to what the Chinese government wants its people to hear.[34]

Politics in Action

Social Welfare Policy

Americans' cultural beliefs distinguish them to a degree even from citizens of other Western democracies. Americans' belief in individualism is an example. Although a belief in self-reliance is common in Europe as well, it is more pronounced in the American case, as can be seen from the most recent Pew Research Center Global Attitudes survey. Respondents in four European countries and the United States were asked which was more important: that people have freedom from government "to pursue life's goals" or that government should guarantee that "nobody is in need." As can be seen in the chart, Americans were much less likely than Europeans to say that it was more important for government to see that "nobody is in need."

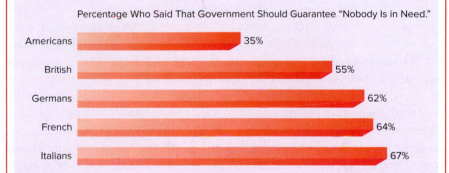

Percentage Who Said That Government Should Guarantee "Nobody Is in Need."

Americans	35%
British	55%
Germans	62%
French	64%
Italians	67%

The extent to which a people embrace individualism affects their country's social welfare policies. Although the United States has a higher poverty rate than do European countries, it spends less money per capita on programs for the poor. Americans are not necessarily less sympathetic toward the poor. Compared with Europeans, they are twice as likely to donate to charities. But Americans are less inclined than Europeans to support welfare policies that could relieve people of the responsibility to take care of themselves.

Q: Can you think of another public policy where the U.S. and Europe differ as a result of the emphasis their citizens place on individualism?

ASK YOURSELF: Which public policy affects how much of what you earn through your job goes to you and how much of it goes to the government?

The United States operates by a different standard. It has three basic "systems" designed to keep government in check. These systems—democracy, constitutionalism, and a free market—determine which side will prevail when conflict occurs, as well as what is off limits to the winning side (see Table 1-1). These systems will be examined in depth in later chapters, but a brief description of each system is useful at this point.

A Democratic System

The word *democracy* comes from the Greek words *demos,* meaning "the people," and *kratis,* meaning "to rule." In simple terms, **democracy** is a form of government in which the people govern, either directly or through elected representatives. A democracy is thus different from an *oligarchy* (in which control rests with a small group, such as top-ranking military officers or a few wealthy families) and from an *autocracy* (in which control rests with a single individual, such as a king or dictator).

In practice, democracy has come to mean majority rule through the free and open election of representatives. More direct forms of democracy exist, such as town meetings in which citizens vote directly on issues affecting them, but the impracticality of such an arrangement in a large society has made majority rule through elections the operative form of democratic government, including that of the United States (see Chapter 2).

Majoritarianism is the term used to describe situations in which political leaders act on behalf of the majority.[35] In the American case, majoritarianism occurs primarily through the competition between the Republican and Democratic Parties (see "Party Polarization: Rising Level of Party Conflict"). In the 2020 presidential campaign, for instance, Republican nominee Donald Trump

table 1-1	GOVERNING SYSTEMS AND POLITICAL POWER
System	**Description and Implications**
Democratic system	A system of majority rule through elections; empowers majorities (majoritarianism), groups (pluralism), and officials (authority)
Constitutional system	A system based on rule of law, including legal protections for individuals; empowers individuals by enabling them to claim their rights in court (legal action)
Free market system	An economic system that centers on the transactions between private parties; empowers business firms (corporate power) and the wealthy (elitism)

PARTY POLARIZATION

Conflicting Ideas

Rising Level of Party Conflict

Conflict between America's two major parties—the Republicans and the Democrats—has intensified in recent decades. Partisan divisions have surfaced on nearly every major issue, and the fights have been bitter and prolonged, so much so that the term **party (partisan) polarization** is used to describe today's politics. Subsequent chapters will examine various aspects of this polarization, but two things can be noted at the outset: The situation is different than it was a few decades ago but is not unprecedented.

A high level of bipartisanship—cooperation between the parties—marked the period from the end of World War II in 1945 until the late 1960s. Leaders and voters of both parties agreed on the need to contain Soviet communism. In addition, Republican leaders had largely abandoned their effort to turn back the New Deal policies of Democratic president Franklin Roosevelt, which had given the federal government a larger role in economic security (for example, the Social Security program) and economic regulation (for example, oversight of the stock market).

During much of the nation's earlier history, however, Americans disagreed strongly over policy and, in the case of the Civil War, took their fight to the battlefield. In fact, periods of bipartisanship are the exception rather than the rule. President George Washington's first years in office, the so-called Era of Good Feeling in the early 1800s, and the World War I and World War II periods are among the few times when party conflict was relatively mild.

Q: Do you see any contradiction in the fact that Americans share a common set of ideals and yet often find themselves on opposite sides when it comes to party politics?

and Democratic nominee Joe Biden differed sharply in their positions on immigration, health care, the environment, and other major policy issues, giving voters a choice about the direction of national policy.

However, majoritarianism has its limits. The public as a whole takes an interest in only a few of the hundreds of policy decisions that officials make each year (see Chapter 6). Even if they wanted to, party leaders would have difficulty getting the majority to pay attention to most issues. Accordingly, most policies are formulated in response to the groups with a direct interest in the issue. Farmers, for example, have more influence over agricultural subsidies than do other Americans, even though these subsidies affect them, including the price that they pay for food. Some political scientists, like Yale's Robert Dahl, argue that democracies more often operate as pluralistic (multi-interest) systems than as majoritarian systems.[36] **Pluralism** holds that, on most issues, the preference of the special interest largely determines what government does (see Chapter 9).

A democratic system also bestows another form of power. Although officials are empowered by the majority, they also exercise power in their own right as a result of the positions they hold. When President Trump decided in 2017 to withdraw the United States from the Paris Agreement on climate change, he did so despite polls showing that two-thirds of Americans wanted the United States to honor its commitment.[37] In making the decision, Trump was exercising his constitutional authority as chief executive. Such grants are a special kind of power. **Authority** is the recognized right of officials to exercise power. Members of Congress, judges, and bureaucrats, as well as the president, routinely make authoritative decisions, only some of which are aligned with what the majority or a special interest would prefer.

Authority is the recognized right of officials to exercise power. The president of the United States exercises authority through the powers granted the executive by the Constitution, just as do members of Congress and other public officials. Pictured here during a State of the Union address is President Donald Trump. Standing behind him are Vice President Mike Pence and House Speaker Nancy Pelosi. (Official White House Photo by Shealah Craighead)

A Constitutional System

In a democracy, the votes of the majority prevail over those of the minority. If this principle were unlimited, the majority could treat the minority in any manner of its choosing, including depriving it of its liberty and property. As unrealistic as this possibility might seem, it preoccupied the writers of the U.S. Constitution. The history of democracies was filled with examples of majority tyranny, and the nation's early experience was no exception. In 1786, debtors had gained control of Rhode Island's legislature and made paper money a legal means of paying debts, even though contracts called for payment in gold. Creditors were then hunted down and held captive in public places so that debtors could come and pay them in full with worthless paper money. A Boston newspaper wrote that Rhode Island ought to be renamed Rogue Island.

To guard against oppressive majorities, the writers of the Constitution devised an elaborate system of checks and balances, dividing authority among the legislative, executive, and judicial branches so that each branch could check the power of the others (see Chapter 2). The Bill of Rights was added to the Constitution a few years later as a further check on the majority. For example, Congress was prohibited from enacting laws that abridge freedom of speech, press, or religion. These limits reflect the principle of **constitutionalism**—the idea that there are lawful restrictions on government's power. Officials are obliged to act within the limits of the law, which include the protection of individual rights.

The Bill of Rights in combination with an independent judiciary and a firm attachment to private property have made **legal action**—the use of the courts as a means of asserting rights and interests—a channel through which ordinary citizens exercise power. Americans have an expansive view of their rights and turn more readily to the courts to make their claims than do people elsewhere (see Chapters 4 and 5).[38] A handwritten note by a penniless convict, for example, triggered the U.S. Supreme Court's landmark *Gideon v. Wainwright* ruling.[39] Clarence Gideon had been made to stand trial in Florida without the aid of a lawyer for breaking into a pool hall. When he appealed his conviction, the Supreme Court concluded that his constitutional right to counsel had been violated. The ruling established a new policy: If the accused is too poor to hire a lawyer, the government must provide one.

A Free-Market System

Politics is not confined to the halls of government. Many of society's costs and benefits are allocated through the private sector,

CITIZEN ACTION!
GETTING READY

Although citizen action involves many skills, none is more important than communication. It is through words that we voice our opinions, try to persuade others, and negotiate our differences. Few situations provide greater opportunity to develop your ability to speak and write effectively than does the college classroom. Make use of the opportunity it offers.

although economic systems differ in the degree of privatization. Under *communism,* which characterized the former Soviet Union and is practiced most fully today in North Korea, the government owns most or all major industries and takes responsibility for overall management of the economy, including production quotas, supply points, and pricing. Under *socialism,* as it is practiced today in Sweden and other countries, government does not attempt to manage the overall economy but owns a number of major industries and guarantees every individual a minimal standard of living. In contrast, a **free-market system** operates mainly on private transactions. Firms are largely free to make their own production, distribution, and pricing decisions, and individuals depend largely on themselves for economic security.

The U.S. economy is chiefly a free-market system. It has millions of small businesses, as well as a corporate sector that includes large firms such as Google, Ford, and Bank of America. **Corporate power**–the influence of business firms on public policy–has been a defining feature of American politics since the late 1800s. Corporate power can be seen today in the fact that roughly two-thirds of all lobbyists in the nation's capital represent business firms, which also contribute

As C. Wright Mills and other theorists have noted, corporate elites must be taken into account in assessing how power in America is distributed and used. The influence of the nation's major corporations goes beyond the workplace. Through advertising and public relations efforts, they seek to build public support for the private enterprise system. (Library of Congress Prints & Photographs Division [LC-DIG-fsa-8a05460])

heavily to political candidates. Corporate power can also be seen in the workplace, where U.S. firms have greater control over wages and working conditions than do firms in other Western democracies. The annual income of a minimum-wage worker, for instance, is roughly $15,000 in the United States, compared with roughly $21,000 in Germany and $22,500 in France.[40]

Economic power is also the foundation of **elitism**, which refers to the power exercised by well-positioned and highly influential individuals.[41] Sociologist C. Wright Mills concluded that corporate elites, operating behind the scenes, have greater control over economic policy than do elected officials.[42] Some scholars contend that Mills overstated the power of elites while overlooking the fact that some elites are motivated to serve society's interests as well as their own.[43] Few scholars, however, dispute the claim that corporate elites have more political power in America than they do in most other Western democracies.

Who Governs?

This text's perspective is that a full explanation of American politics requires an accounting of all these forms of power—as exercised by the majority, interest groups, elites, corporations, individuals through legal action, and those in positions of governing authority. In fact, a defining characteristic of American politics is the widespread sharing of power. Few nations have as many competing interests and institutions as does the United States.

THE TEXT'S ORGANIZATION

America's constitutional system defines how power is to be obtained and exercised. This system is the focus of the next few chapters, which examine how, in theory and practice, the Constitution defines the institutions of governments and the rights of individuals. The discussion then shifts to the political role of citizens and of the intermediaries that enable citizens to act together and connect them to government. These subjects are explored in chapters on public opinion, political participation, political parties, interest groups, and the news media. The functioning of governing officials is then addressed in chapters on the nation's elective institutions—the Congress and the presidency—and its appointive institutions—the federal bureaucracy and the federal courts. These chapters describe how these institutions are structured but aim chiefly to explain how their actions are affected by internal and external factors, as well as by the constitutional system in which they operate.

Throughout the text, but particularly in the concluding chapters, attention is given to **public policies**, which are the decisions of government to pursue particular courses of action. No aspect of a nation's politics is more revealing of how it is governed than are its policies—everything from how it chooses to educate its children to how it chooses to use its military power.

Underlying the text's discussion of American politics and policy is the recognition of how difficult it is to govern effectively and how important it is to try. It cannot be said too often that the issue of governing is the most difficult issue facing a democratic society. It also cannot be said too often that governing is a quest rather than a resolved issue. Political scientist E. E. Schattschneider said it clearly: "In the course of centuries, there has come a great deal of agreement about what democracy is, but nobody has a monopoly on it and the last word has not been spoken."[44]

SUMMARY

Critical thinking is the careful gathering and sifting of information in the process of forming knowledgeable views of political developments. Critical thinking is a key to responsible citizenship, but many citizens avoid it by virtue of paying scant attention to politics. The tools of political science can contribute to the critical thinking process.

The United States is a nation that was formed on a set of ideals. Liberty, individualism, equality, and self-government are foremost among these ideals. These ideals became Americans' common bond and today are the basis of their political culture. Although imperfect in practice, these ideals have influenced what generations of Americans have sought to achieve politically.

Politics is the process by which it is determined whose values and interests will prevail in society. The basis of politics is conflict over scarce resources and competing values. Those who have power win out in this conflict and are able to control governing authority and policy choices. In the United States, no one faction controls all power and policy. Majorities govern on some issues, while other issues are dominated by groups, elites, corporations, individuals through legal action, or officials who hold public office.

Politics in the United States plays out through rules of the game that include democracy, constitutionalism, and free markets. Democracy is rule by the people, which in practice refers to a representative system of government in which the people rule through their elected officials. *Constitutionalism* refers to rules that limit the rightful power of government over citizens. A free-market system assigns private parties the dominant role in determining how economic costs and benefits are allocated.

CRITICAL THINKING ZONE

KEY TERMS

authoritarian government (*p. 14*)
authority (*p. 18*)
constitutionalism (*p. 19*)
corporate power (*p. 20*)
critical thinking (*p. 3*)
democracy (*p. 16*)
elitism (*p. 21*)
equality (*p. 8*)
free-market system (*p. 20*)
individualism (*p. 8*)
legal action (*p. 19*)

liberty (*p. 7*)
majoritarianism (*p. 16*)
party (partisan) polarization (*p. 17*)
pluralism (*p. 18*)
political culture (*p. 5*)
political science (*p. 4*)
politics (*p. 14*)
power (*p. 14*)
public policies (*p. 22*)
self-government (*p. 9*)

APPLYING THE ELEMENTS OF CRITICAL THINKING

Conceptualizing: Distinguish between political power (generally) and authority (as a special kind of political power).

Synthesizing: Contrast the American political culture with that of most Western democracies. What in the American experience has led its people to derive their national identity from a set of shared political ideals?

Analyzing: Explain the types of power that result from each of America's major systems of governing—democracy, constitutionalism, and a free market.

EXTRA CREDIT

A Book Worth Reading: Gordon S. Wood, *The Idea of America: Reflections on the Birth of the United States* (New York: Penguin Press, 2011). A perceptive book by a Pulitzer Prize–winning historian, it explores the ideals, such as liberty and equality, that powered the American Revolution.

CONSTITUTIONAL DEMOCRACY: PROMOTING LIBERTY AND SELF-GOVERNMENT

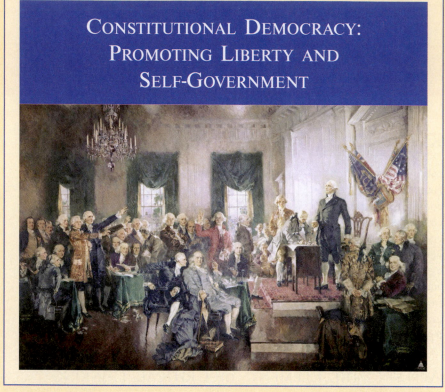

Architect of the Capitol

❝ Why has government been instituted at all? Because the passions of man will not conform to the dictates of reason and justice, without constraint. ❞

ALEXANDER HAMILTON[1]

On November 7, 2020, Joe Biden stepped to the stage for the first time as president-elect of the United States. Earlier in the day, narrow victories in Arizona and Pennsylvania had taken him past the 270 electoral votes needed for victory. Biden began his speech by thanking his family and all those who had worked hard to make his victory possible. He then invoked America's long-standing ideals. "Americans," he said, "have called on us to marshal the forces of decency and the forces of fairness." He made an appeal for unity and a commitment to common purpose. "There has never been anything we haven't been able to do when we've done it together."

Biden, who had earlier served in the U.S. Senate and as Barack Obama's vice president, concluded his speech by acknowledging the sacrifices of earlier Americans and invoking the nation's standing in the world. He vowed to make America "respected around the world" for its commitment to freedom and as a country where people of all races and religions could succeed. "At our best," he said, "America is a beacon for the globe." He reminded Americans that deeds, not words, define who we are as a nation and a people. "We lead not by the example of our power," he said, "but by the power of our example."

The ideas that guided Biden's speech would have been familiar to any generation of Americans. The same ideas have been invoked when Americans have gone to war, declared peace, celebrated national holidays, launched major policy initiatives, and asserted new rights.[2] The ideas expressed in Biden's speech were the same ones that shaped the speeches of George Washington and Abraham Lincoln, Susan B. Anthony, Franklin D. Roosevelt, Martin Luther King Jr., and Ronald Reagan.

The ideas were there at the nation's beginning, when Thomas Jefferson put them into words in the Declaration of Independence. They had been nurtured by the colonial experience in the New World, which offered the settlers a

Pictured here is Joe Biden. He narrowly won the 2020 presidential election over incumbent Donald Trump. Four of the last five presidential elections have been decided by the outcome in fewer than a handful of states. The 2008 campaign, where Barack Obama easily defeated John McCain, is the lone exception. Biden was also involved in the 2008 campaign, having been selected by Obama to be his vice-presidential running mate. (Sean Rayford, Getty Images)

degree of liberty, equality, and self-government unimaginable in Europe. When the Revolutionary War settled the issue of American independence in the colonists' favor, they faced the question of how to turn their ideals into a system of government. The Constitution of the United States became the instrument of that goal. The framers of the Constitution sought to create a **limited government**—one that is subject to strict legal limits on the uses of power so that it would not endanger the people's liberty. They also sought to establish a system of **representative government**—one in which the people would govern through the selection of their representatives.

The challenge facing the framers was that limited government and representative government can conflict. Representative government requires that the majority, through its elected representatives, has the power to rule. However, limited government requires that the majority's power stop at the point where it infringes on the lawful rights and interests of the minority. This consideration led the framers to craft a constitution that provides for majority rule but has built-in restrictions on the power of the majority and its elected representatives.

This chapter describes how the principles of representative government and limited government are embodied in the Constitution and explains the tension between them. It also indicates how these principles have been modified in practice in the course of American history. This chapter presents the following main points:

• *America during the colonial period developed traditions of limited government and representative government.* These traditions were rooted in governing practices, political theory, and cultural values.

• *The Constitution provides for limited government mainly by defining lawful powers and by dividing those powers among competing institutions.* The Constitution, with its Bill of Rights, also prohibits government from infringing on individual rights. Judicial review is an additional safeguard.

• *The Constitution in its original form provided for representative government mainly through indirect methods of electing representatives.* The framers' theory of representative government was based on the notion that political power must be separated from immediate popular influences if sound policies are to result.

• *The idea of popular government—in which the majority's desires have a more direct and immediate impact on governing officials—has gained strength since the nation's beginning.* Originally, the House of Representatives was the only institution subject to direct vote of the people. This mechanism has been extended to other institutions and, through primary elections, even to the nomination of candidates for public office.

BEFORE THE CONSTITUTION: THE COLONIAL AND REVOLUTIONARY EXPERIENCES

Early Americans' admiration for limited government stemmed from their British heritage. Unlike other European governments of the time, Britain did not have an absolute monarchy. Parliament was an independent body with lawmaking power and local representation. Many of the colonial charters conferred upon Americans "the rights of Englishmen," which included, for example, the right to trial by jury. The colonies also had experience in self-government. Each colony had an elected representative assembly.

The American Revolution was partly a rebellion against Britain's failure to uphold the colonies' established traditions. After the French and Indian War (1754–1763), during which colonists fought alongside British soldiers to drive the French out of the western territories, the British government for the first time imposed heavy taxes on the colonies. The war with France, which was also waged in Europe, had created a budget crisis in Britain. Taxing the colonies was a way to reduce the debt, so Parliament levied a stamp tax on colonial newspapers and business documents. The colonists were not represented in Parliament, and they objected to the tax. "No taxation without representation" was their rallying cry.

In 1774, the colonists met in Philadelphia at the First Continental Congress to formulate their demands on Britain. They asked for their own councils for the imposition of taxes, an end to the British military occupation, and a guarantee of trial by local juries. (British authorities had resorted to shipping "troublemakers" to London for trial.) King George III rejected their demands, and British troops and Massachusetts minutemen clashed at Lexington and Concord on April 19, 1775. Eight colonists died on the Lexington green in what became known as "the shot heard 'round the world." The American Revolution had begun.

The Declaration of Independence

Although British policies were the immediate cause of the American Revolution, ideas about the proper form of government also fueled the rebellion.[3] Building on the writings of Thomas Hobbes,[4] John Locke claimed that government is founded on a **social contract**. Locke asserted that people living in a state of nature enjoy certain **inalienable (natural) rights**, including those of life, liberty, and property, which are threatened by individuals who steal, kill, and otherwise act without regard for others. To protect against such individuals, people agree among themselves to form a government (the social contract). They submit to

Pictured here is the stamp that led to a revolution. In 1765, the British Parliament passed the Stamp Act, which required all legal documents and publications in the American colonies to carry a tax stamp, which cost a penny. The colonies had no representatives in the Parliament, which led to the rallying cry "No taxation without representation." Although another decade would pass before the Revolutionary War broke out, the Stamp Act marked the start of hostilities between Britain and the colonies. (Smithsonian National Postal Museum)

the government's authority in return for the protection it can provide, but in doing so they retain their natural rights, which the government is obliged to respect. If it fails to do so, Locke contended, people can rightfully rebel against it.[5]

Thomas Jefferson declared that Locke "was one of the three greatest men that ever lived, without exception." Jefferson paraphrased Locke's ideas in passages of the Declaration of Independence, including those asserting that "all men are created equal," that they are entitled to "life, liberty, and the pursuit of happiness," that governments derive "their just powers from the consent of the governed," and that "it is the right of the people to alter or abolish" a tyrannical government. The Declaration was a call to revolution

John Adams, Roger Sherman, Robert Livingston, Thomas Jefferson, and Benjamin Franklin present their draft of the Declaration of Independence to the Continental Congress. Jefferson (tallest of the three men standing directly in front of the desk) was its principal author. Jefferson's bold declaration that "all men are created equal" was contradicted by the fact that he, like several of the signers, was a lifelong slaveholder. (John Parrot/Stocktrek Images/Getty Images)

rather than a framework for a new form of government, but the ideas it contained—liberty, equality, individual rights, self-government, lawful powers—became the basis, 11 years later, for the Constitution of the United States. (The Declaration of Independence and the Constitution are reprinted in their entirety in this book's appendixes.)

The Articles of Confederation

A **constitution** is the fundamental law that defines how a government will legitimately operate—the method for choosing its leaders, the institutions through which these leaders will work, the procedures they must follow in making policy, and the powers they can lawfully exercise. The U.S. Constitution is exactly such a law; it is the highest law of the land. Its provisions define how power is to be acquired and how it can be used.

The first government of the United States, however, was based not on the Constitution but on the Articles of Confederation. The Articles, which were adopted during the Revolutionary War, created a very weak national government that was subordinate to the states. Under the Articles, each state retained its full "sovereignty, freedom, and independence." The colonies had always been governed separately, and their people considered themselves Virginians, New Yorkers, Pennsylvanians, and so on as much as they thought of themselves as Americans. Moreover, they were wary of creating a powerful central government. The American Revolution was a rebellion against the arbitrary policies of King George III, and Americans were in no mood to replace him with a powerful national authority of their own making.

Under the Articles of Confederation, the national government had no judiciary and no independent executive. All authority was vested in the Congress, but it was largely a creature of the states. Each of the 13 states had one vote in Congress, and each state appointed its congressional representatives and paid their salary. Legislation could be enacted only if 9 of the 13 state delegations agreed to it. The rule for constitutional amendments was even more imposing. The Articles of Confederation could be amended only if all states agreed.

The Articles prohibited Congress from levying taxes, so it had to ask the states for money. It was slow to arrive, if it arrived at all. During one period, Congress requested $12 million from the states but received only $3 million. By 1786, the national government was so desperate for funds that it sold the navy's ships and cut the army to less than 1,000 soldiers—this at a time when Britain had an army in Canada and Spain had one in Florida. Congress was also prohibited from regulating the states' trade policies, so it was powerless to forge a national economy. Free to do as they wanted, states enacted trade policies designed to protect their manufacturers from competitors in nearby states. Connecticut, for example, placed a higher tariff on goods produced in neighboring Massachusetts than on the same goods manufactured in England.

The American states had stayed together out of necessity during the Revolutionary War. They would have lost to the British if each state had tried to fend for itself. Once the war ended, however, the states felt free to go their separate ways. In a melancholy letter to Thomas Jefferson, George Washington wondered whether the United States deserved to be called "a nation."

A Nation Dissolving

In late 1785 at his Mount Vernon home, Washington met with leaders of Virginia and Maryland to secure an agreement between the two states on commercial use of the Potomac River. During the meeting, they decided on the desirability of a commerce policy binding on all the states, which would require an amendment to the Articles of Confederation.

A revolt in western Massachusetts added urgency to the situation. A ragtag army of 2,000 farmers armed with pitchforks marched on county courthouses to prevent foreclosures on their land. Many of the farmers were veterans of the Revolutionary War; their leader, Daniel Shays, had been a captain in the

American army. They had been given assurances during the Revolution that their land, which sat unused because they were away at war, would not be confiscated for unpaid debts and taxes. They were also promised the back pay owed to them for their military service. (Congress had run out of money during the Revolution.) Instead, they received no back pay, and heavy new taxes were levied on their farms. Many farmers faced not only losing their property but also being sent to prison for unpaid debts.

Shays' Rebellion frightened wealthy interests, who called on the governor of Massachusetts to put down the revolt. He in turn asked Congress for help, but it had no army to send. Although Shays' Rebellion was quashed by a private militia hired by wealthy merchants, the rebellion exposed the weaknesses of the national government, which prompted Virginia and Maryland to invite the other 11 states to meet in Annapolis to propose amendments to the Articles of Confederation. Only 5 states sent delegates to the Annapolis Convention, which meant no formal steps could be taken. However, James Madison and Alexander Hamilton convinced the delegates to adopt a resolution calling for a constitutional convention. Congress agreed and called for it to be held in Philadelphia. Congress placed a restriction on the convention: It was to meet for "the sole and express purpose of revising the Articles of Confederation."

NEGOTIATING TOWARD A CONSTITUTION

The delegates to the Philadelphia constitutional convention ignored the instructions of Congress, choosing instead to write an entirely new constitution. Prominent delegates (among them George Washington, Benjamin Franklin, and James Madison) were determined from the outset to create a stronger central government. They had come to understand the foolishness of the idea that small government is always the best form of government. The lesson of the Articles of Confederation was that government must have the power that it needs to carry out its responsibilities.

The Great Compromise: A Two-Chamber Congress

Debate at the constitutional convention of 1787 began over a plan put forward by the Virginia delegation, which was dominated by strong nationalists. The **Virginia Plan** (also called the *large-state plan*) included separate judicial and executive branches, as well as a two-chamber Congress that would have supreme authority in all areas "in which the separate states are incompetent," particularly defense and interstate trade. Members of the lower chamber would be chosen by the voters, while members of the upper chamber would be selected by members of the lower chamber from lists of nominees provided by their respective state legislatures. In both chambers, the heavily populated states would have more representatives than would the lightly populated ones. Small states such as Delaware and Rhode Island would be allowed only one representative in the lower chamber, while large states such as Massachusetts and Virginia would have more than a dozen.

The Virginia Plan was sharply attacked by delegates from the smaller states. They rallied around a proposal made by New Jersey's William Paterson. The **New Jersey Plan** (also called the *small-state plan*) called for a stronger national government than that provided for by the Articles of Confederation. It would have the power to tax and to regulate commerce among the states. In most other respects, however, the Articles would remain in effect. Congress would have a single chamber in which each state, large or small, would have a single vote.

The debate over the two plans dragged on for weeks before the delegates reached what is now known as the **Great Compromise**. It provided for a bicameral (two-chamber) Congress. One chamber, the House of Representatives, would be apportioned on the basis of population. States with larger populations would have more House members than states with smaller populations, although each state would have at least one representative. The other chamber, the Senate, would be apportioned on the basis of an equal number of senators (two) for each state. This compromise was critical. The small states would have refused to join a union in which their vote was always weaker than that of large states, a fact reflected in Article V of the Constitution: "No state, without its consent, shall be deprived of its equal suffrage in the Senate."

The Three-Fifths Compromise: Issues of Slavery and Trade

Differences between the interests of northern states and southern states forced a second major compromise, this time over issues of slavery and trade. The South's delegates were concerned that northern representatives in Congress would tax or even bar the importation of slaves. A decade earlier, at the insistence of southern states, a statement critical of slavery had been deleted from Jefferson's initial draft of the Declaration of Independence, and southern delegates to the Philadelphia convention were determined to block attempts to use the new constitution as a device for ending slavery.

The southern delegates were also concerned that the North, which included more states and had a larger population, would use its numerical majority in the House and Senate to enact tax policies harmful to the South. Most of the nation's manufacturing was based in the North, and, if Congress sought to protect it by placing a heavy tax (tariff) on manufactured products imported from Europe, the higher cost of these imports would be borne by the South, which was more dependent on them. If Congress also imposed a heavy tariff on the export of agricultural goods, which would make them more expensive and therefore less attractive to foreign buyers, the South would again bear most of the tax burden because it provided most of the agricultural goods shipped abroad, such as cotton and tobacco.

After extended debate, a compromise was reached. Congress would have the authority to tax imports but not exports, and it would be prohibited until 1808 from passing laws to end the slave trade. However, the most controversial trade-off was the so-called **Three-Fifths Compromise**, which was proposed by Madison, who was a slaveholder. For purposes of apportionment of taxes and seats in the U.S. House of Representatives, each slave was to count as less than a full person. Northern delegates had argued against the counting of slaves because they did not have legal rights. Southern delegates wanted to count them as full persons for purposes of apportioning House seats (which would have the effect of increasing the number of southern representatives) and to count them as nonpersons for purposes of apportioning taxes (which would have the effect of decreasing the amount of federal taxes levied on the southern states). The delegates finally settled on a compromise that included both taxation and apportionment but counted each slave as three-fifths of a person, which was the ratio necessary to give the southern states nearly half of the House seats. If slaves had not been counted at all, the southern states would have had only about a third of the House seats.

These compromises have led critics to claim that the framers of the Constitution were proponents of slavery. Some of them were, but most of the delegates were deeply troubled by it, recognizing the stark contrast between slavery and the nation's professed commitment to liberty and equality. "It is inconsistent with the principles of the Revolution," said Maryland's Luther Martin.[6] Benjamin Franklin and Alexander Hamilton were among the delegates who were members of antislavery organizations.

Nevertheless, the southern states' dependence on slavery was a reality that had to be confronted if there was to be a union of the states. The northern states had few slaves, whereas the South's economy was based on slavery (see Figure 2-1). John Rutledge of South Carolina asked during the convention debate whether the North regarded southerners as "fools." Southern delegates insisted that their states would form a separate union rather than join one that banned slavery.

A Strategy for Ratification

The compromises over slavery and the structure of the Congress took up most of the four months that the convention was in session. Some of the other issues were subject to remarkably little debate. Decisions on the structure of

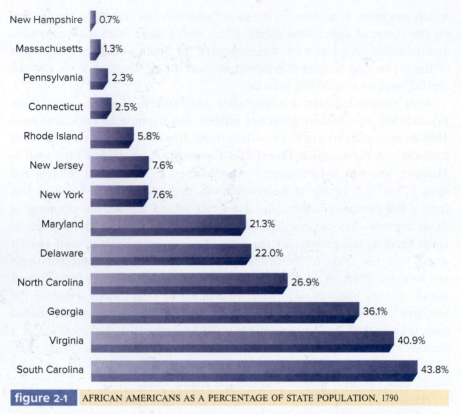

New Hampshire	0.7%
Massachusetts	1.3%
Pennsylvania	2.3%
Connecticut	2.5%
Rhode Island	5.8%
New Jersey	7.6%
New York	7.6%
Maryland	21.3%
Delaware	22.0%
North Carolina	26.9%
Georgia	36.1%
Virginia	40.9%
South Carolina	43.8%

figure 2-1 AFRICAN AMERICANS AS A PERCENTAGE OF STATE POPULATION, 1790

At the time of the writing of the Constitution, African Americans (most of whom were slaves) were concentrated in the southern states. (*Source:* U.S. Census Bureau.)

the federal judiciary and bureaucracy, for example, were largely delegated to Congress. The presidency was an exception. The delegates briefly considered but then abandoned the idea of a multiple executive, concluding that executive power should be entrusted to a single individual to avoid the paralysis and in-fighting that could ensue if executive power were divided. But it took more than 60 votes for the delegates to reach agreement on how the president would be chosen, Along the way, proposals to have the president elected directly by the people, by vote of Congress, or by the state legislatures were defeated. The delegates finally settled on the use of electors to chose the president, with each state having electors equal to its representation in Congress and having control over how its electors would be chosen,

The last issue to be decided was a process for ratifying the proposed constitution. The delegates recognized that their work would amount to nothing if the states did not adopt the new constitution. In authorizing the Philadelphia convention, Congress had stated that any proposed change in the Articles of

Confederation would have to be "agreed to in Congress" and then "confirmed by [all] the states." In a bold move, the delegates ignored Congress's directive and created their own ratification process. The document was to be submitted to the states, where it would become law if approved by at least 9 states in special ratifying conventions of popularly elected delegates. It was a masterful strategy. There was little hope that all 13 state legislatures would approve the Constitution, but 9 states through conventions might be persuaded to ratify it. Indeed, North Carolina and Rhode Island were steadfastly opposed to the new union and did not ratify the Constitution until the other 11 states had ratified it and had begun the process of forming the new government (see "Party Polarization: Fight over the Ratification of the Constitution").

The Ratification Debate

The debate over ratification was historic. The **Anti-Federalists** (as opponents of the Constitution were labeled) raised arguments that still echo in American politics. They claimed that the national government would be too powerful and would threaten self-government in the separate states and the liberty of the people. Many Americans had an innate distrust of centralized power and worried that the people's liberty could be eclipsed as easily by a distant American government as it had been by the British king.

The fact that the Constitution contained no bill of rights heightened this concern. Did its absence indicate that the central government would be free to define for itself what the people's rights would be? Patrick Henry expressed outrage at the omission, saying, "The necessity of a Bill of Rights appears to be greater in this government than ever it was in any government before."

The Anti-Federalists worried that the national government would fall under the control of a political elite. They admired state governments for having legislatures in which the members were not greatly different in wealth from the voters who elected them. New York's Melancton Smith argued that such representatives were "more competent" than "those of a superior class" whose concerns were far removed from the reality of most people's lives. "I am convinced," Smith said, that members of Congress will become "the natural aristocracy of the country. . . . The government will fall into the hands of the few and the great. This will be a government of repression."[7]

The presidency was another source of contention. The office of chief executive did not exist under the Articles of Confederation, and some worried that it would degenerate into an American monarchy. The fact that the president would be chosen by electors appointed by the states (the Electoral College) lessened but did not eliminate this concern.

PARTY POLARIZATION

Conflicting Ideas

Fight over the Ratification of the Constitution

The intense partisanship that typifies today's politics also marked the debate over the Constitution's ratification. Angry exchanges took place between proponents of a stronger national government and those arguing for a state-centered union. Although the pro-Constitution side won easily in most states, the balloting in New York and Virginia was so close that it took the promise of a bill of rights to secure the votes for ratification. North Carolina and Rhode Island (the latter had refused even to send delegates to the Philadelphia convention) initially rejected the Constitution, ratifying it only after the other states began to form a union without them. Here is the breakdown of the ratifying vote in each state:

State	Date of Ratification	Vote Totals
Delaware	December 7, 1787	30 for, 0 against
Pennsylvania	December 12, 1787	46 for, 23 against
New Jersey	December 18, 1787	38 for, 0 against
Georgia	January 2, 1788	26 for, 0 against
Connecticut	January 9, 1788	128 for, 40 against
Massachusetts	February 6, 1788	187 for, 168 against
Maryland	April 28, 1788	63 for, 11 against
South Carolina	May 23, 1788	149 for, 73 against
New Hampshire	June 21, 1788	57 for, 47 against
Virginia	June 25, 1788	89 for, 79 against
New York	July 26, 1788	30 for, 27 against
North Carolina	November 21, 1789	194 for, 77 against
Rhode Island	May 29, 1790	34 for, 32 against

Q: If historians are correct in concluding that the American public as a whole was evenly split over ratification of the Constitution, why might the pro-Constitution side have prevailed in so many states and so easily in some states?

A: State and local governments were in charge of selecting the delegates to the state ratifying conventions. For the most part, they chose prominent leaders to serve as delegates, with the result that wealthy merchants, large landholders, and top public officials dominated the conventions. They were more supportive of the Constitution than were small farmers, craftspeople, and shopkeepers.

The Anti-Federalists acknowledged the need for more economic cooperation between the states and for a stronger common defense, but they opposed the creation of a strong national government as the mechanism, arguing that a revision of the Articles of Confederation could accomplish these goals without the risk of establishing an overly powerful central government. (The Anti-Federalist argument is discussed further in Chapter 3.)

The **Federalists** (as the Constitution's supporters called themselves) responded with a strong case of their own. Their arguments were set forth by James Madison and Alexander Hamilton, who along with John Jay wrote a series of essays (*The Federalist Papers*) that were published in a New York City newspaper under the pen name Publius. Madison and Hamilton argued that the government of the Constitution would correct the defects of the Articles; it would have the power necessary to forge a secure and prosperous union. At the same time, because of restrictions on its powers, the new government would endanger neither the states nor personal liberty. In *Federalist* Nos. 47, 48, 49, 50, and 51, for example, Madison explained how the separation of national institutions was designed to control the power of the federal government. (The Federalist argument is discussed further in Chapter 3.)

Whether the ratification debate changed many minds is unclear. Historical evidence suggests, however, that a majority of ordinary Americans opposed the Constitution's ratification. But their voice in the state ratifying conventions was smaller than that of wealthier interests, which favored the change. The pro-ratification forces were also strengthened by the assumption that George Washington, the country's most trusted and popular leader, would become the first president. In the view of historians, this assumption, and the fact that Washington had presided over the Philadelphia convention, tipped the balance in favor of ratification.

Delaware was the first state to ratify the Constitution, and Connecticut, Georgia, and New Jersey soon followed, an indication that the Great Compromise had satisfied some of the small states. In the early summer of 1788, New Hampshire became the ninth state to ratify. The Constitution was law. But neither Virginia nor New York had ratified it, and a stable union without the two states was almost unthinkable. As large in area as many European countries, Virginia and New York conceivably could have survived as independent nations. In fact, they nearly did choose a separate path. In both states, the Constitution passed only after Federalists promised to amend it to include a bill of rights.

James Bryce, a noted British scholar and politician, ranked America's Constitution as its greatest contribution to the practice of government. The Constitution offered the world a new model of government in which a written document defining the government's lawful powers was a higher authority than the dictates of any political leader or institution.

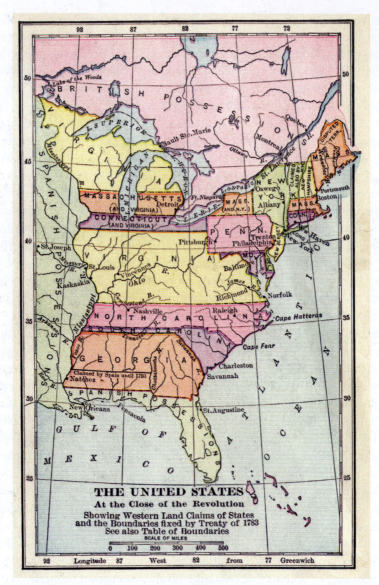

New York and Virginia voted narrowly in favor of ratification of the Constitution. They were the key to whether the United States could survive as a nation. New York and Virginia were each large enough and wealthy enough to be independent nations. If they had chosen that path, the United States would have been split into three parts—New England, mid-Atlantic, and southern. It's doubtful that the nation would have lasted for long in that form. (North Wind Picture Archives/Alamy Stock Photo)

The Framers' Goals

One of the framers' primary goals was the creation of a national government strong enough to meet the nation's needs, particularly in the areas of defense

table 2-1	PRIMARY GOALS OF THE FRAMERS OF THE CONSTITUTION

1. *Strong government:* a government strong enough to meet the nation's needs—an objective sought through substantial grants of power to the federal government in areas such as defense and commerce
2. *Federal government:* a government that would not threaten the existence of the separate states—an objective sought through federalism and through a Congress tied to the states through elections
3. *Limited government:* a government that would not threaten liberty—an objective sought through an elaborate system of checks and balances
4. *Representative government:* a government based on popular consent—an objective sought through provisions for the direct and indirect election of public officials

and commerce (see Table 2-1). Another basic goal was to preserve the states as governing entities. Accordingly, the framers established a system of government (federalism) in which power is divided between the national government and the states. Federalism is discussed at length in Chapter 3, which also explains how the Constitution laid the foundation for a strong national government.

The framers' two other major goals were, first, to establish a national government that was restricted in its lawful uses of power (limited government) and, second, to create a national government that gave the people a voice in governing (representative government). These goals are the focus of the rest of this chapter.

PROTECTING LIBERTY: LIMITED GOVERNMENT

The framers of the Constitution sought a national government that could act decisively, but not one that would act irresponsibly. History had taught them to mistrust unrestricted majority rule. In times of stress or danger, popular majorities had often acted recklessly, trampling on the liberty of others. In fact, the preservation of **liberty**—the principle that individuals should be free to act and think as they choose, provided they do not infringe unreasonably on the freedom and well-being of others—was the framer's main goal. Americans enjoyed an unparalleled level of personal freedom as a result of their open society, and the framers were determined that it not be sacrificed to either European-style monarchy or mob-driven democracy.

Government's threat to liberty was inherent in its coercive power. Government's unique feature is that it alone can legally arrest, imprison, or even kill people who violate its directives. Force is not the only basis by which government maintains order but, without it, lawless individuals would prey on innocent people.

The dilemma is that government itself can use force to intimidate or brutalize its opponents. "It is a melancholy reflection," James Madison wrote to Thomas Jefferson shortly after the Constitution's ratification, "that liberty should be equally exposed to danger whether the government has too much or too little power."[8]

Grants and Denials of Power

The framers chose to limit the national government in part by confining its scope to constitutional **grants of power** (see Table 2-2). Congress's lawmaking powers are specifically listed in Article I, Section 8, of the Constitution. Seventeen in number, these listed powers include the powers to tax, establish an army and navy, declare war, regulate commerce among the states, create a national currency, and borrow money. Powers *not* granted to the government by the Constitution are in theory denied to it. In a period when other governments had unrestricted powers, this limitation was remarkable.

The framers also used **denials of power** as a means to limit government, prohibiting certain practices that European rulers had routinely used to oppress political opponents. The French king, for example, could imprison a subject without charge for an indefinite period. The U.S. Constitution prohibits such action. Citizens have the right to be brought before a judge under a writ of habeas corpus for a determination of the legality of keeping them in jail. The

table 2-2	CONSTITUTIONAL PROVISIONS FOR LIMITED GOVERNMENT
Mechanism	**Purpose**
Grants of power	Powers granted to the national government; accordingly, powers not granted it are denied it unless necessary and proper to carry out granted powers
Separated institutions	Division of national government's power among three power-sharing branches, each of which acts as a check on the powers of the other two
Federalism	Division of political authority between national government and the states, enabling the people to appeal to one authority if their rights and interests are not respected by the other authority
Denials of power	Powers expressly denied to the national and state governments by the Constitution
Bill of Rights	First 10 amendments to the Constitution, which specify rights of citizens that the national government must respect
Judicial review	Power of courts to declare governmental action null and void when it violates the Constitution
Elections	Power of voters to remove officials from office

Constitution also forbids Congress and the states from passing ex post facto laws, under which citizens can be prosecuted for acts that were legal at the time they were committed.

Although not strictly a further denial of power, the framers made the Constitution difficult to amend, thereby making it hard for those in office to increase their power by changing the rules. An amendment could be proposed only by a two-thirds majority in both chambers of Congress or by a national constitutional convention called by two-thirds of the state legislatures. A proposed amendment would then become law only if ratified by three-fourths of state legislatures or state conventions.*

Using Power to Offset Power

Although the framers believed that grants and denials of power could act as controls on government, they had no illusion that written words alone would suffice. As a consequence, they sought to limit government by dividing its powers among separate branches.[9]

Decades earlier, French theorist Montesquieu had argued that the power of government could be controlled by dividing it among separate branches rather than investing it entirely in a single individual or institution. His concept of a **separation of powers** was widely admired in America, and, when the states drafted new constitutions after the start of the Revolutionary War, they built their governments around the ideal. Pennsylvania was an exception, and its experience only seemed to prove the necessity of separated powers. Unrestrained by an independent judiciary or executive, Pennsylvania's all-powerful legislature ignored basic rights and freedoms: Quakers were disenfranchised for their religious beliefs, conscientious objectors to the Revolutionary War were prosecuted, and the right of trial by jury was eliminated.

In *Federalist* No. 10, Madison asked why governments often act according to the interests of overbearing majorities rather than according to principles of justice. He attributed the problem to "the mischiefs of faction." People, he argued, are divided into opposing religious, geographic, ethnic, economic, and other factions. These divisions are natural and desirable in that free people have a right to their personal opinions and interests. However, if a faction gains full power, it will seek to use government to advance itself at the expense of all others. (*Federalist* No. 10 is widely regarded as the finest political essay ever written by an American.)

---

*During the nation's history, every amendment has been proposed by Congress and only one amendment—the Twenty-First, which repealed the prohibition on alcohol—was ratified by state conventions. The others were ratified by state legislatures. This imposing process has worked as the framers intended. Except for the ten Bill of Rights amendments, which were ratified shortly after establishment of the national government, only seventeen amendments have been added to the Constitution.

Out of this concern came the framers' special contribution to the doctrine of the separation of powers. They did not believe that it would be enough, as Montesquieu had proposed, to divide the government's authority strictly along institutional lines, granting all legislative power to the legislature, all judicial power to the courts, and all executive power to the president. This total separation would make it too easy for a single faction to exploit a particular type of political power. A faction that controlled the legislature, for example, could enact laws ruinous to other interests. A safer system would be one in which each branch had the capacity to check the power of the others.[10]

Separated Institutions Sharing Power: Checks and Balances

Political scientist Richard Neustadt devised the term **separated institutions sharing power** to describe the framers' governing system.[11] The separate branches are interlocked in such a way that an elaborate system of **checks and balances** is created (see Figure 2-2). No institution can act decisively without the support or acquiescence of the other institutions. Legislative, executive, and judicial powers in the American system are divided in such a way that they overlap: Each of the three branches of government checks the others' powers and balances those powers with powers of its own.

Shared Legislative Powers   Under the Constitution, Congress has legislative authority, but that power is partly shared with the other branches and thus is checked by them. The president can veto acts of Congress, recommend legislation, and call special sessions of Congress. The president also has the power to execute—and thereby interpret—the laws that Congress makes.

The Supreme Court has the power to interpret acts of Congress that are disputed in legal cases. The Court also has the power of judicial review: It can declare laws of Congress void when it finds that they are not in accord with the Constitution.

Within Congress, there is a further check on legislative power: For legislation to be passed, a majority in each chamber of Congress is required. Thus, the Senate and the House of Representatives can block each other from acting.

Shared Executive Powers   Executive power is vested in the president but is constrained by legislative and judicial checks. The president's power to make treaties and appoint high-ranking officials, for example, is subject to Senate approval. Congress also has the power to impeach and remove the president from office. In practical terms, Congress's greatest checks on executive action are its lawmaking and appropriations powers. The executive branch cannot act without laws that authorize its activities or without the money that pays for these activities.

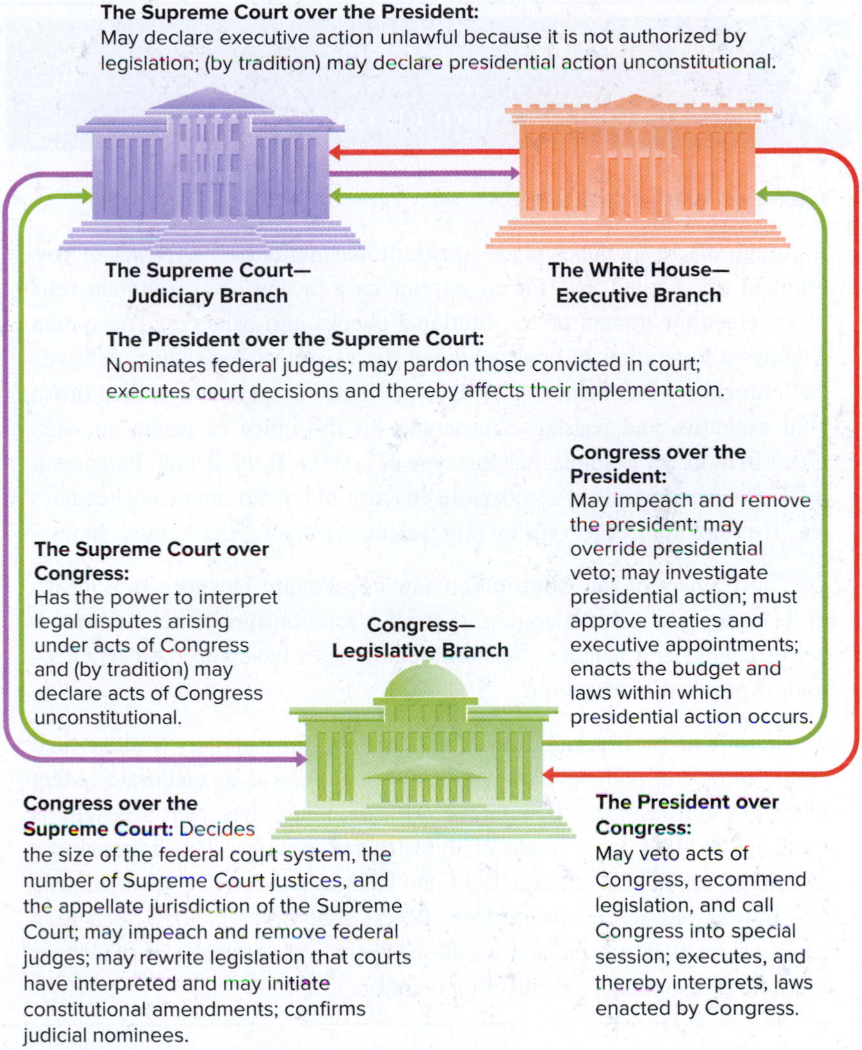

The Supreme Court over the President:
May declare executive action unlawful because it is not authorized by legislation; (by tradition) may declare presidential action unconstitutional.

The Supreme Court—
Judiciary Branch

The White House—
Executive Branch

The President over the Supreme Court:
Nominates federal judges; may pardon those convicted in court; executes court decisions and thereby affects their implementation.

Congress over the President:
May impeach and remove the president; may override presidential veto; may investigate presidential action; must approve treaties and executive appointments; enacts the budget and laws within which presidential action occurs.

The Supreme Court over Congress:
Has the power to interpret legal disputes arising under acts of Congress and (by tradition) may declare acts of Congress unconstitutional.

Congress—
Legislative Branch

Congress over the Supreme Court: Decides the size of the federal court system, the number of Supreme Court justices, and the appellate jurisdiction of the Supreme Court; may impeach and remove federal judges; may rewrite legislation that courts have interpreted and may initiate constitutional amendments; confirms judicial nominees.

The President over Congress:
May veto acts of Congress, recommend legislation, and call Congress into special session; executes, and thereby interprets, laws enacted by Congress.

figure 2-2   SEPARATE BRANCHES SHARING POWER

The U.S. Constitution separates power among the legislative, executive, and judicial branches but assigns each branch part of the power of the other two branches so that it can act as a check on their power. (*Source:* Richard Neustadt, *Presidential Power,* New York: Macmillan, 1986, 33.)

The judiciary's major check on the presidency is its power to declare an action unlawful because it is not authorized by the laws that the executive claims to be implementing.

Shared Judicial Powers   Judicial power rests with the Supreme Court and with lower federal courts, which are subject to checks by the other branches

HOW THE U.S. DIFFERS

CRITICAL THINKING THROUGH COMPARISONS

Checks and Balances

Although all democracies place constitutional limits on the power of government, the United States is an extreme case in that its government rests on an elaborate system of constitutional checks and balances. The system employs a separation of powers among the executive, legislative, and judicial branches. Most democracies have parliamentary systems, which invest both executive and legislative leadership in the office of prime minister. Great Britain, for example, has this type of system. If the British Parliament under the prime minister's leadership enacts a bill, it automatically becomes law. It is not subject to veto by a president, as it is in the United States.

Q: The framers of the Constitution saw checks and balances as a means of fostering political moderation. Is there a relationship between the number of checks and balances Western democracies have and their tendency toward political moderation?

A: There is no clear relationship. Great Britain, for example, is often cited as an example of political moderation, although it lacks an elaborate system of checks and balances. By contrast, Mexico, which has such a system, is often held up as an example of unrestrained politics. This fragmentary evidence does not mean that checks and balances are ineffective in controlling power, but the evidence does suggest that other factors, such as a country's political norms and traditions, must also be taken into account in a full explanation of political moderation.

of the federal government. Congress is empowered to establish the size of the federal court system, to restrict the Supreme Court's appellate jurisdiction in some circumstances, and to impeach and remove federal judges from office. More important, Congress can rewrite legislation that the courts have misinterpreted and can initiate amendments when it disagrees with court rulings on constitutional issues.

The president has the power to appoint federal judges with the consent of the Senate and to pardon persons convicted in the courts. The president also is responsible for executing court decisions, a function that provides opportunities to influence the way rulings are carried out.

The Bill of Rights

Although the delegates to the Philadelphia convention discussed the possibility of placing a list of individual rights (such as freedom of speech and the right to a fair trial) in the Constitution, they ultimately decided that such a list was unnecessary because of the doctrine of expressed powers: Government could not lawfully engage in actions, such as the suppression of speech, that were

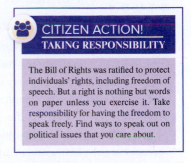

CITIZEN ACTION!
TAKING RESPONSIBILITY

The Bill of Rights was ratified to protect individuals' rights, including freedom of speech. But a right is nothing but words on paper unless you exercise it. Take responsibility for having the freedom to speak freely. Find ways to speak out on political issues that you care about.

not authorized by the Constitution. Moreover, the delegates argued that a bill of rights was undesirable because government might feel free to disregard any right that was inadvertently left off the list or that might emerge in the future.

These arguments failed to convince those who wanted a bill of rights. They worried that the Constitution, unlike the Articles of Confederation, granted the federal government direct authority over individual citizens and yet did not contain a list of their rights. "A bill of rights," Jefferson argued, "is what the people are entitled to against every government on earth, general or particular, and what no just government should refuse or rest on inference." Jefferson had included a bill of rights in the constitution he wrote for Virginia at the outbreak of the Revolutionary War, and all but four states had followed Virginia's example.

Ultimately, the demand for a bill of rights led to its addition to the Constitution. Madison himself introduced a series of amendments during the First Congress, 10 of which were quickly ratified by the states. Called the **Bill of Rights**, the 10 amendments include free-expression rights such as freedom of speech and fair trial protections such as the right to an attorney. (Individual rights are discussed in Chapter 4.)

The Bill of Rights is a precise expression of the concept of limited government. In consenting to be governed, the people agree to accept the authority of government in certain areas but not in others; the people's constitutional rights cannot lawfully be denied by government.*

————

*Although the Bill of Rights lists specific rights, the framers worried that rights not on the list might later emerge. To protect such rights, the framers included the Ninth Amendment in the Bill of Rights. It says that the "enumeration in the Constitution, of certain rights, shall not be construed to deny or disparage others retained by the people." Nevertheless, the Supreme Court has never relied solely on the Ninth Amendment to establish a new right, which confirms the foresight of those who demanded a list of rights. Without such a list, government might have denied Americans their basic rights and been allowed to do so by the Supreme Court.

Politics in Action

The Watergate Scandal

On a June night in 1972, a security guard at the Watergate complex in Washington, D.C. noticed that the latch on the door to the Democratic Party's national headquarters had been taped open.

He called police, who caught five men inside who were in the process of installing hidden microphones in the phones and ceilings. As it turned out, the men had links to President Richard Nixon's reelection campaign. The Watergate break-in was part of a large effort—including the stealing of documents—aimed at ensuring Nixon's reelection. Nixon denied

National Archives and Records Administration (NLRN-WHPO-E2678-14)

knowledge of the wrongdoing but was incriminated when tape-recorded Oval Office conversations revealed otherwise. Nixon withheld the tapes from Congress until the Supreme Court, which included four Nixon appointees, unanimously ruled that he was required to do so. The content of the tapes led the House of Representatives to begin impeachment proceedings, which prompted Nixon to resign his office, becoming the first and only president to do so.

Despite holding what is often called "the most powerful office on earth," Nixon was powerless to stop Congress and the Supreme Court from doing their duty under the Constitution. The framers of the Constitution had established them as separate and independent branches, and they upheld their constitutional obligation.

Q: Can you think of situations in which the separation of powers might not be effective in holding powerful officials accountable when they engage in criminal or unconstitutional action?

ASK YOURSELF: Have there been situations in which all three branches of government have agreed that unconstitutional action was required? (In this context, you might consider the forced internment of Japanese Americans during World War II.) What about the case in which one political party controls both the presidency and Congress? (In the Watergate case, President Nixon was a Republican, and Democrats controlled the House and the Senate.)

Judicial Review

The writers of the Constitution both empowered and limited government. But who was to decide whether officials were operating within the limits of their constitutional powers? The framers did not specifically entrust this power to a particular branch of government, although they did grant the Supreme Court the authority to decide on "all cases arising under this Constitution." Moreover, at the ratifying conventions of at least 8 of the 13 states, it was claimed that the judiciary would have the power to nullify actions that violated the Constitution.[12]

Nevertheless, because the Constitution did not explicitly grant the judiciary this authority, the principle of judicial review had to be established in practice. The opportunity arose with an incident that occurred after the presidential election of 1800, in which John Adams, running as the Federalist Party nominee, lost his bid for a second term after a bitter campaign against Jefferson, who was the nominee of the Democratic-Republican Party (the forerunner of today's Democratic Party). Between November 1800, when Jefferson was elected, and March 1801, when he was inaugurated, the Federalist-controlled Congress created 59 additional lower-court judgeships, enabling Adams to appoint loyal Federalists to the positions before he left office. However, Adams's term expired before his secretary of state could deliver the judicial commissions to all the appointees. Without this authorization, an appointee could not take office. Knowing this, Jefferson told his secretary of state, James Madison, not to deliver the commissions. William Marbury was one of those who did not receive his commission, and he asked the Supreme Court to issue a writ of mandamus (a court order directing an official to perform a specific act) that would force Madison to deliver it.

In *Marbury v. Madison* (1803), which many analysts regard as the most important constitutional ruling in the nation's history, the Supreme Court established the power of **judicial review**. Chief Justice John Marshall wrote the *Marbury* opinion, which declared that Marbury had a legal right to his commission but which also said that the Court lacked the authority to issue him a writ of mandamus. Congress had passed legislation in 1789 to give the Court this power, but the Court said the law was invalid because it expanded the Court's authority beyond what the Constitution specified[13]—that is, the power of the judiciary to decide whether a government official or institution has acted within the limits of the Constitution and, if not, to declare its action null and void. (Not every court case involves judicial review. It refers only to rulings on whether government has acted within the boundaries of its constitutional power.)

Marshall's decision was ingenious because it asserted the power of judicial review without creating the possibility of its rejection by either the executive or

Detecting Misinformation

Is the President "Above the Law"?

The U.S. constitutional system is premised on the idea that the law is the nation's highest authority and that Americans are equal under the law. But is the president an exception? During the congressional investigation of whether his 2016 presidential campaign benefited from Russian meddling and then again during impeachment proceedings in the House of Repre-

Jonathan Ernst/Pool/Getty Images

sentatives, President Donald Trump blocked current and former members of his administration from responding to House subpoenas and from turning over documents to House investigative committees. Trump claimed that, as president, he had "absolute immunity" from congressional oversight. In addition, when the Manhattan district attorney's office subpoenaed Trump's tax returns and other records in a criminal investigation, his lawyers argued that a sitting President enjoys absolute immunity from state criminal proceedings.

Is that fact, or is it fake?

The U.S. Justice Department holds that a sitting president cannot be indicted because such legal action would divert the president's time and attention from the duties of office. This protection ends when the president leaves office, meaning a former president could be indicted for crimes committed in office or earlier. While in office, impeachment and removal from office is, in the Justice Department's view, the only remedy for severe presidential wrongdoing.

At the same time, the president does not have absolute authority to refuse to comply with legal or congressional proceedings. In Nixon v. United States, the Supreme Court held that "executive privilege"—the president's right to protect from Congress the privacy of personal conversations—does not extend to criminal activity. That principle was broadened to include legal proceedings in

Continued

a key 2020 ruling, Trump v. Vance, that centered on the Manhattan district attorney's criminal probe. The Supreme Court said: "In our system of government, as this Court has often stated, no one is above the law." In a second 2020 ruling, Trump v. Mazars, the Court held that the president does not have the power to unilaterally reject congressional requests for information. If a president had that power, the Court said, Congress "would be unable to legislate wisely or effectively." Yet, the Court also placed limits on Congress's access to such information, saying that the requested information must serve a "valid legislative purpose."[14]

the legislative branch. In declaring that Marbury had a right to his commission, the Court in effect said that President Jefferson had failed in his constitutional duty to execute the laws faithfully. However, because it did not order Jefferson to deliver the commission, he was deprived of the opportunity to disobey the Court's ruling. At the same time, the Court rebuked Congress for passing legislation that exceeded its constitutional authority. But Congress also had no way to retaliate. It could not force the Court to accept the power to issue writs of mandamus if the Court itself refused to issue them.

PROVIDING FOR REPRESENTATIVE GOVERNMENT

The framers believed that citizens required a voice in their governing but worried that the majority could become inflamed by a passionate issue or fiery demagogue and trample on the rights of the minority. The framers' fear of **tyranny of the majority** was not unfounded. In reviewing the history of popular democracies, James Madison concluded that they "have ever been spectacles of turbulence and contention; have ever been found incompatible with personal security or the rights of property; and have in general been as short in their lives as they have been violent in their deaths."

Democracy versus Republic

No form of representative government can eliminate the possibility of majority tyranny, but the framers believed that the risk would be greatly reduced by creating a republican government as opposed to a democratic one.[15] Today, the terms *democracy, republic,* and *representative government* are often used interchangeably to refer to a system of government in which political power rests with the people through their ability to choose representatives in free and fair elections. To the writers of the Constitution, however, a democracy and a republic were different forms of government.

By the term **democracy**, the framers meant a government in which the majority, either directly or through its representatives, has full power. The law is whatever the majority declares it to be. If the majority decides to rule in the interest of all, it has the power to do so. However, if the majority decides instead to trample on the rights and interests of the minority, it has the power to do that as well.

By the term **republic**, the framers meant a government that has limits on its power. The people have rights that are beyond the reach of government, guaranteed by a constitution and protected through properly structured institutions. Governing institutions are designed in ways that require competing interests to compromise and that protect the rights of the minority. The majority has power, but its power is subject to constitutional and institutional limits.

Limited Popular Rule

The framers saw the separation of powers and other constitutional restraints on national power as hallmarks of a republican form of government. In addition, they devised a system of representation that placed most federal officials beyond the direct control of the voters (see Table 2-3).

The House of Representatives was the only institution that would be based on direct popular election—its members would be elected to serve for two years by a vote of the people. Frequent and direct election of House members was intended to make government responsive to the concerns of popular majorities.

U.S. senators would be appointed by the legislatures of the states they represented. Because state legislators were popularly elected, the people would be choosing their senators indirectly. Every two years, a third of the senators would be appointed to 6-year terms. The Senate, by virtue of the less frequent and indirect election of its members, was expected to be less responsive to popular pressure and thereby serve as a check on the House.

table 2-3 | METHODS OF CHOOSING FEDERAL OFFICIALS

Office	Method of Selection	Term of Service
President	Electoral College	4 years
U.S. senator	State legislature, changed in 1913 to popular election	6 years (one-third of senators' terms expire every 2 years)
U.S. representative	Popular election	2 years
Federal judge	Nominated by president, approved by Senate	Indefinite (subject to "good behavior")

Presidential selection was an issue of considerable debate at the Philadelphia convention. Direct election of the president was twice proposed and twice rejected because it would link executive power directly to popular majorities. The framers finally chose to have the president selected by the votes of electors (the so-called **Electoral College**). Each state would have the same number of **electoral votes** as it had members in Congress and could select its electors by a method of its choosing. The president would serve four years and be eligible for reelection.

The framers decided that federal judges and justices would be appointed rather than elected. They would be nominated by the president and confirmed if approved by a Senate majority. Once confirmed, they would "hold their offices during good behavior." In effect, they would be allowed to hold office for life unless they committed a crime. The judiciary was an unelected institution that would uphold the rule of law and serve as a check on the elected branches of government.[16]

These differing methods of selecting national officeholders would not prevent a determined majority from achieving unchecked power, but control could not be quickly acquired. Unlike the House of Representatives, institutions such as the Senate, presidency, and judiciary would not yield to an impassioned majority in a single election. The delay would reduce the chance that government would degenerate into mob rule driven by momentary passions.

Altering the Constitution: More Power to the People

The framers' conception of representative government was at odds with what the average American in 1787 would have expected.[17] Self-government was the promise that had led tens of thousands of ordinary farmers, merchants, and tradesmen to risk their lives fighting the British in the American Revolution. The state governments had kept that promise. Every state but South Carolina held annual legislative elections, and several states also chose their governors through direct annual election.

Not long after ratification of the Constitution, Americans began to challenge the Constitution's restrictions on majority rule, an effort that would extend into the early 1900s.

Jeffersonian Democracy: A Revolution of the Spirit   Thomas Jefferson was among the prominent Americans who questioned the Constitution's limited provisions for self-government. In a letter to Madison, he objected to its system of representation, voicing the Anti-Federalists' fear that federal officials would lose touch with the people and ignore their interests. His concern intensified when John Adams became president after Washington's retirement. Under Adams, the national government increasingly favored the nation's wealthy interests. Adams publicly stated that the Constitution was designed for a governing elite and hinted that he might use force to suppress dissent.[18] Jefferson asked whether Adams, with the aid of the army, intended to deprive ordinary people of their rights. Jefferson challenged Adams in the next presidential election and, upon defeating him, hailed his victory as the "Revolution of 1800."

Although Jefferson was a champion of the common people, he had no clear vision of how a popular government might work in practice. He saw Congress, not the presidency, as the place where the people would be most fully represented.[19] He also had no illusions about the ability of a largely uneducated population to play a substantial governing role and feared what would happen if the people were incited to rise up against the rich. Jeffersonian democracy was mostly a revolution of the spirit. Jefferson taught Americans to look on national government institutions as belonging to all, not just to the privileged few.[20]

Jacksonian Democracy: Linking the People and the Presidency   Not until the election of Andrew Jackson in 1828 did the nation have a powerful president who was willing and able to involve the public more fully in government. Jackson carried out the constitutional revolution that Jeffersonian democracy had foreshadowed.

Jackson recognized that the president was the only official who could legitimately claim to represent the people as a whole. Unlike members of Congress, who were elected from separate states and districts, the president was chosen by the whole of the country. Yet the president's claim to popular leadership was weakened by the fact that the president was chosen by electors rather than by direct vote of the people. To tie the presidency more closely to the people, Jackson pressured Congress for a constitutional amendment that would authorize the president's election by popular vote. Failing in that effort, he urged the states to award their electoral votes to the candidate who won the state's popular vote. Soon thereafter, nearly all states adopted this method. This arrangement, still in effect, places the selection of the president in the voters' hands in most elections. The candidate who gets the most popular votes nationally is also likely to finish first in enough states to win a majority of the electoral votes. Since Jackson's time, four candidates—Rutherford B. Hayes in 1876, Benjamin Harrison in 1888, George W. Bush in 2000, and Donald Trump in 2016—have won the presidency after losing the popular vote (see "How the 50 States Differ").

The Progressive Era of the early 1900s brought another wave of democratic reforms. The Progressives sought to weaken the influence of large corporations and political party bosses by placing power more directly in the hands of voters.[21] Progressive reforms at the state and local levels included the *initiative*. In some states, if citizens are able to gather enough signatures on a petition

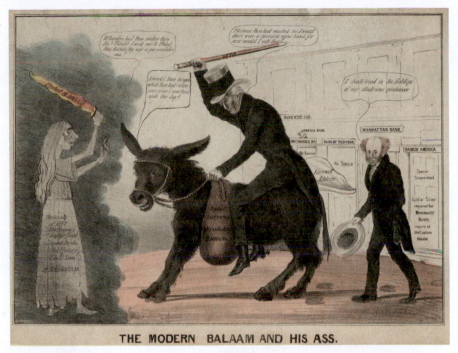

THE MODERN BALAAM AND HIS ASS.

Andrew Jackson revolutionized American politics by appealing to the "common man." He sought to reduce the power of the banks, fought for eliminating the property requirement for voting, argued for tying electoral votes to the popular vote, and appointed ordinary citizens to public office. This 1837 lithograph is the first time the donkey was used to symbolize the Democratic Party. It has been the party's symbol ever since. (Library of Congress Prints & Photographs Division [LC-DIG-ppmsca-15775])

for a proposed change in the law, the proposal is placed on the ballot where it becomes law if a majority of voters support it.

The Progressives also instigated changes in federal elections. One change was the direct election of U.S. senators, who before the ratification of the Seventeenth Amendment in 1913 were chosen by state legislatures and were widely perceived as tools of big business (the Senate was nicknamed the "Millionaires' Club"). Senators who stood to lose their seats in a direct popular vote had blocked earlier attempts to amend the Constitution. However, as a result of several developments, including revelations that several senators owed their seats to corporate bribes, the Senate was finally persuaded to back the amendment.

A second change brought about by the Progressive movement was the **primary election** (also called the *direct primary*), which gives ordinary voters the power to select party nominees. By 1920, nearly all states had adopted the primary election as the means of choosing nominees for the Senate and House of Representatives.

HOW THE 50 STATES DIFFER

POLITICAL THINKING THROUGH COMPARISONS

Choosing the President

The Constitution assigns the election of the president to electors chosen by the states, with each state having electors equal in number to its U.S. senators and representatives. Voters have an indirect voice in the selection. Each state, except for Maine and Nebraska, awards all of its electoral votes to the candidate who wins the state's popular vote—the so-called **unit rule**. This arrangement usually results in the election of the candidate who wins the national popular vote, but not always. In 2016, although Donald Trump lost the national popular vote to Hillary Clinton by almost 3 million votes, he prevailed in the Electoral College by winning in Pennsylvania, Michigan, and Wisconsin by a total of less than 100,000 votes, giving him a 304–227 edge in electoral votes.

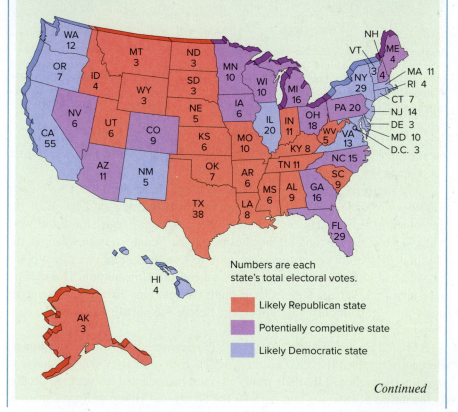

Numbers are each state's total electoral votes.

🟥 Likely Republican state

🟪 Potentially competitive state

🟦 Likely Democratic state

Continued

Even though the popular vote winner usually also wins an electoral vote majority, the unit rule diminishes the role of some voters. Because of the unit rule, presidential candidates focus on the competitive states—those that conceivably could be won by either party. During the general election, candidates campaign heavily in these states while largely ignoring the states that are solidly Republican or Democratic. The accompanying map is based on estimates of which states at the moment are potentially competitive in a closely contested presidential election.

Q: What might justify keeping the electoral college system? Would you favor instead a system where the president is chosen by direct vote of the people? Are there states that might be largely ignored by the candidates in a popular vote system? Finally, thinking about your state only, would it get more or less attention from presidential candidates than it does now if a popular vote system was adopted?

Some states also used the primary election method to elect their delegates to the national conventions that choose the parties' presidential nominees. Such a process is called an *indirect primary* because the voters are not choosing the nominees directly (as they do in House and Senate races) but rather are choosing delegates who in turn select the presidential nominees. However, the Progressives were unable to convince most states to adopt presidential primaries, which meant that party leaders continued to control a majority of the convention delegates. That process was reformed after the 1968 presidential election. Ever since, all states have selected their convention delegates through either a primary election or an **open party caucus** (where voters meet and discuss the candidates before voting). Today it is the voters in state primaries and open caucuses who choose the Democratic and Republican presidential nominees. (A half-dozen states use the caucus system and the rest choose their delegates through a primary election.)

The Progressive Era spawned attacks on the framers. A prominent critic was historian Charles S. Beard. In *An Economic Interpretation of the Constitution*, Beard argued that the Constitution's elaborate system of institutions was designed to protect the wealthy.[22] Beard noted that the framers were nearly all men of wealth and that property interests were often discussed during debate at the Philadelphia convention. Beard's thesis has some truth to it, but the framers were not opposed to representative government. They sought to balance the need for self-government with the need for limited government. Convinced that unchecked majority rule could devolve into tyranny, the framers devised institutions that were responsive to majority opinion without being captive to it.

CONSTITUTIONAL DEMOCRACY TODAY

The type of government created in the United States in 1787 is accurately described as a **constitutional democratic republic**. It is constitutional in its requirement that power gained through elections be exercised in accordance with law and with due respect for individual rights; democratic in its provisions for majority influence through elections; and a republic in its multiple institutions (presidency, Congress, and the courts), each of which checks the power of the others.[23]

By some standards, the American system of today is a model of *representative government*.[24] The United States schedules the election of its larger legislative chamber (the House of Representatives) and its chief executive more frequently than does any other democracy. In addition, it is the only major democracy to rely extensively on primary elections rather than party organizations for the selection of party nominees. The principle of direct popular election to office, which the writers of the Constitution regarded as a method to be used sparingly, has been extended further in the United States than anywhere else.

By other standards, however, the U.S. system is less democratic than that of some democracies. In the United States, popular majorities must work against the barriers to power devised by the framers—divided branches, staggered terms of office, and separate constituencies. In fact, the link between an electoral majority and a governing majority is less direct in the American system than in many democratic systems. In the European parliamentary democracies, for example, legislative and executive power is not divided, is not subject to close check by the judiciary, and is acquired through the winning of a legislative majority in a single national election. The framers' vision was a different one, dominated by a concern with liberty and therefore with controls on political power. It was a response to the experiences they took with them to Philadelphia in the summer of 1787.

CITIZEN ACTION!
GETTING INVOLVED

The United States holds more elections for more offices than does any other democracy, which gives citizens abundant opportunities to participate. Why not you? Consider volunteering for the campaign of a candidate who represents your interests and values.

SUMMARY

The Constitution of the United States is a reflection of the colonial and revolutionary experiences of the early Americans. Freedom from abusive government was a reason for the colonies' revolt against British rule, but the English tradition also provided ideas about government, power, and freedom that were expressed in the Constitution and, earlier, in the Declaration of Independence.

The Constitution was designed in part to provide for a limited government in which political power would be confined to proper uses. The framers wanted to ensure that the government they were creating would not itself be a threat to freedom. To this end, they confined the national government to expressly granted powers and denied it certain specific powers. Other prohibitions on government were later added to the Constitution in the form of stated guarantees of individual liberties in the Bill of Rights. The most significant constitutional provision for limited government, however, was a separation of powers among the three branches. The powers given to each branch enable it to act as a check on the exercise of power by the other two, an arrangement that, during the nation's history, has served as a barrier to abuses of power.

The Constitution, however, made no mention of how the powers and limits of government were to be judged in practice. In its historic ruling in *Marbury v. Madison*, the Supreme Court assumed the authority to review the constitutionality of legislative and executive actions and to declare them unconstitutional and thus invalid.

The framers of the Constitution, respecting the idea of self-government but distrusting popular majorities, devised a system of government that they felt would temper popular opinion and slow its momentum so that the public's "true interest" (which includes a regard for the rights and interests of the minority) would guide public policy. Different methods were advanced for selecting the president, the members of the House and the Senate, and federal judges as a means of insulating political power against momentary majorities.

Since the adoption of the Constitution, the public gradually has assumed more direct control of its representatives, particularly through measures that affect the way officeholders are chosen. Presidential popular voting (linked to the Electoral College), direct election of senators, and primary elections are among the devices aimed at strengthening the majority's influence. These developments are rooted in the idea, deeply held by ordinary Americans, that the people must have substantial direct influence over their representatives if government is to serve their interests.

CRITICAL THINKING ZONE

KEY TERMS

Anti-Federalists (*p. 35*)
Bill of Rights (*p. 45*)
checks and balances (*p. 42*)
constitution (*p. 29*)

constitutional democratic republic (*p. 56*)
democracy (*p. 50*)
denials of power (*p. 40*)
Electoral College (*p. 51*)

electoral votes (*p. 51*)
Federalists (*p. 37*)
grants of power (*p. 40*)
Great Compromise (*p. 32*)
inalienable (natural) rights (*p. 27*)
judicial review (*p. 47*)
liberty (*p. 39*)
limited government (*p. 26*)
New Jersey Plan (*p. 32*)
open party caucus (*p. 55*)

primary election (direct primary) (*p. 53*)
representative government (*p. 26*)
republic (*p. 50*)
separated institutions sharing power (*p. 42*)
separation of powers (*p. 41*)
social contract (*p. 27*)
Three-Fifths Compromise (*p. 33*)
tyranny of the majority (*p. 49*)
unit rule (*p. 54*)
Virginia Plan (*p. 31*)

APPLYING THE ELEMENTS OF CRITICAL THINKING

Conceptualizing: Define the concept of judicial review. How does a court decision involving judicial review differ from an ordinary court decision, such as a ruling in a case involving robbery?

Synthesizing: Contrast the original system for electing federal officials with the system of today, noting in each case how voters acquired a more direct voice in the election process than was originally the case.

Analyzing: Why is it more accurate to say that the United States has a system of "separated institutions sharing power" rather than a system of "separated powers"? Provide examples of how shared power can act to check and balance the power of each institution.

EXTRA CREDIT

A Book Worth Reading: Danielle Allen, *Our Declaration* (New York: Liveright, 2014). An award-winning book that claims the Declaration of Independence is a powerful argument for political equality.

A Website Worth Visiting: www.archives.gov The National Archives is the repository of America's important documents. Its site includes an in-depth history of the writing of the Declaration of Independence.

FEDERALISM: FORGING A NATION

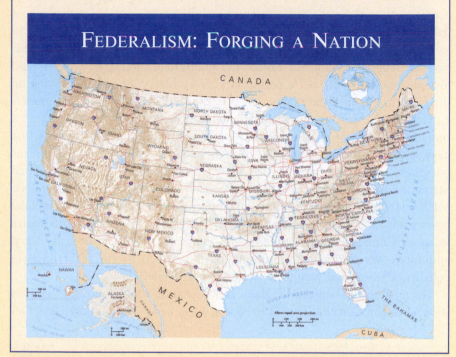

National Atlas of the United States/U.S. Geological Survey/U.S. Department of the Interior

> **66** The question of the relation of the states to the federal government is the cardinal question of our Constitutional system. It cannot be settled by the opinion of one generation, because it is a question of growth, and each successive stage of our political and economic development gives it a new aspect, makes it a new question. **99**
>
> WOODROW WILSON[1]

On his fourth day as president of the United States, Donald Trump issued sweeping directives aimed at deporting undocumented immigrants. Citing federal control over immigration, Trump ordered an increase in the number of immigration enforcement officers, expanded the list of targeted classes of deportees, and established an expedited process for deporting those who were apprehended. Trump asked state and local officials for help in identifying undocumented aliens and, when detaining such individuals, to hold them until federal officials could arrive to take them into custody.

Some states and cities cooperated with the Trump administration, but others declared themselves "sanctuaries" for undocumented immigrants. They instructed their officials not to cooperate with federal immigration officers, citing a Supreme Court ruling that says state and local officials cannot be "commandeered" by the federal government to assist in the enforcement of federal policy.[2] Trump then threatened to withhold federal grants-in-aid to sanctuary cities and states. In turn, they cited a Supreme Court ruling that says the federal government cannot use grants-in-aid to "coerce" states and localities into carrying out a particular action unless Congress, in setting up the grant program, listed that action as a condition for receipt of the grant.[3]

The conflict surrounding the Trump administration's deportation policy is one of thousands of disagreements over the course of American history that have hinged on whether national or state authority will prevail. Americans possess what amounts to dual citizenship: They are citizens both of the United States and of the state where they reside. The American political system is a *federal system,* in which constitutional authority is divided between a national government and state governments. Each government is assumed to derive its powers directly from the people and therefore to have sovereignty (final authority) over the policy responsibilities assigned to it. The federal system consists of states and nation, separate yet indivisible.[4]

The relationship between the states and the nation was the most contentious issue when the Constitution was written and has been a contentious issue ever

Early in his presidency, Donald Trump issued orders aimed at increasing the deportation of undocumented immigrants. A number of cities and states refused to cooperate in the federal effort, declaring themselves to be sanctuaries for the undocumented. The resulting conflict between federal power, on the one hand, and state and local power, on the other, is but one of many such episodes over the course of the nation's history. (wildpixel/Getty Images)

since. One of these disputes, the Civil War, nearly led to the dissolution of the United States. This chapter examines federalism—its creation through the Constitution, its evolution during the nation's history, and its current status. This chapter presents the following main points:

- *The power of government must be equal to its responsibilities.* The Constitution was needed because the nation's preceding system (under the Articles of Confederation) was too weak to accomplish its expected goals, particularly those of a strong defense and an integrated economy.

- *Federalism—the Constitution's division of governing authority between two levels, nation and states—was the result of political bargaining.* Federalism was not a theoretical principle, but rather a compromise made necessary in 1787 by the prior existence of the states.

- *Federalism is not a fixed principle for allocating power between the national and state governments, but rather a principle that has changed over time in response to political needs and partisan ideology.* Federalism has passed through several distinct stages in the course of the nation's history.

- *Contemporary federalism tilts toward national authority, reflecting the increased interdependence of American society.*

FEDERALISM: NATIONAL AND STATE SOVEREIGNTY

At the time of the writing of the Constitution, some of America's top leaders were dead set against the creation of a stronger national government. When rumors began to circulate that the Philadelphia convention was devising such a government, Virginia's Patrick Henry said that he "smelt a rat." His fears were confirmed when he obtained a copy of the draft constitution. "Who authorized them," he asked, "to speak the language of 'We, the People,' instead of 'We, the States'?"

The question of "people versus states" was precipitated by the failure of the Articles of Confederation. It had created a union of the states, and they alone had authority over citizens (see Chapter 2). The national government could not tax or conscript citizens, nor could it regulate their economic activities. Its directives applied only to the states, and they often ignored them. Georgia and North Carolina, for example, contributed no money at all to the national treasury between 1781 and 1786, and the federal government had no way to force them to pay. The only feasible solution to this problem was to give the federal government direct authority over the people. If individuals are ordered to pay

"GIVE ME LIBERTY, OR GIVE ME DEATH !"

PATRICK HENRY delivering his great speech on the Rights of the Colonies, before the Virginia Assembly

Patrick Henry was a leading figure in the American Revolution ("Give me liberty or give me death!"). He later opposed ratification of the Constitution on grounds that the national government should be a union of states and not also a union of people. (Library of Congress Prints & Photographs Division [LC-USZC2-2452])

taxes, most of them will do so rather than accept the alternative—imprisonment or confiscation of their property.

At the same time, the writers of the Constitution wanted to preserve the states. The states had their own constitutions and a governing history extending back to the colonial era. Although their residents thought of themselves as Americans, many of them identified more strongly with their states. When Virginia's George Mason said that he would never agree to a constitution that abolished the states, he was speaking for nearly all of the delegates.

These two realities—the need to preserve the states and the need for a national government with direct authority over the people—led the framers to invent an entirely new system of government. Until this point in history, **sovereignty** (supreme and final governing authority) had been regarded as indivisible. By definition, a government cannot be sovereign if it can be overruled by another government. Nevertheless, the framers divided sovereignty between the national government and the states, a system now known as **federalism**. Each level—the national government and the state governments—directly governs the residents within its assigned territory. Each level has authority that is not subject to the other's approval. And each level is constitutionally protected. The national government cannot abolish a state, and the states cannot abolish the national government.

In 1787, nations elsewhere in the world were governed by a **unitary system**, in which sovereignty is vested solely in the national government (see "How the U.S. Differs"). Local or regional governments in a unitary system do not have sovereignty. They have authority only to the degree that it is granted by the national government, which can also withdraw any such grant. (This situation applies to America's local governments. They are not sovereign, but instead derive their authority from their respective state governments, which can, though it rarely occurs, even choose to abolish a local unit of government.)

HOW THE U.S. DIFFERS

CRITICAL THINKING THROUGH COMPARISONS

Federal Systems

Federalism involves the division of sovereignty between a national government and subnational (state) governments. The United States established the first federal system, and about two dozen countries today have one. Most countries have instead a unitary system, which vests sovereignty solely in the national government.

In federal systems, the national legislature has two chambers—one apportioned by population (as in the case of the U.S. House of Representatives) and the other by geographic area (as in the case of the U.S. Senate). The U.S. Senate is a pure federal institution in the sense that each state has the same number of senators. In some federal systems, including Germany's and Canada's, the states are not equally represented even in the legislative chamber apportioned on the basis of geography rather than population.

Q: Federal systems have a two-chamber legislature, whereas some unitary systems have only one chamber. Why the difference?

A: In a unitary system, there is no constitutional need for a second legislative chamber based on geographic subdivisions (states), as is the case with a federal system.

Federalism is also different from a **confederacy**, which was the type of government that existed under the Articles of Confederation. In a confederacy, the states alone are sovereign. They decide the authority, even the continuing existence, of the central government. Confederacies have been rare in human history, but the government of the Articles was not the first. The ancient Greek city-states and medieval Europe's Hanseatic League were of this type. (Despite its name, the Confederate States of America—the South's Civil War government—had a federal constitution rather than a confederate one. Sovereignty was divided between the central and state governments.)

The federal system established in 1787 divides the responsibilities of government between the nation and the states (see Figure 3-1). The system gives states the power to address local issues in ways of their choosing; for example, they have primary responsibility for public education and police protection. The national government, by contrast, is responsible for matters of national scope, such as military defense and the currency. The national and state governments also have some concurrent powers (that is, powers exercised over the same policy areas). Each of them has, for example, the power to raise taxes and borrow money.

The Argument for Federalism

The strongest argument for federalism in 1787 was that it would correct the defects in the Articles. Two of the defects were particularly troublesome: The national government had neither the power to tax nor the power to regulate commerce among the states. Without money from taxes, the national government lacked the financial means to maintain an army strong enough to prevent

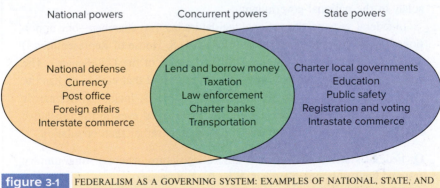

National powers   Concurrent powers   State powers

National defense	Lend and borrow money	Charter local governments
Currency	Taxation	Education
Post office	Law enforcement	Public safety
Foreign affairs	Charter banks	Registration and voting
Interstate commerce	Transportation	Intrastate commerce

figure 3-1   FEDERALISM AS A GOVERNING SYSTEM: EXAMPLES OF NATIONAL, STATE, AND CONCURRENT POWERS

The American federal system divides sovereignty between a national government and the state governments. Each is constitutionally protected in its existence and authority, although their powers overlap somewhat, even in areas granted to one level (for example, the federal government has a role in education policy).

encroachment by European powers or to maintain a navy strong enough to protect America's merchant ships from harassment and attack by pirates and foreign navies. Also, without the ability to regulate commerce, the national government could neither promote the general economy nor prevent trade wars between the states. New York and New Jersey were among the states that imposed taxes on goods shipped into their state from other states.

Although it is sometimes claimed that "the government which governs least is the government that governs best," the Articles proved otherwise. The problems with the too-weak national government were severe: public disorder, economic chaos, and an inadequate defense. Although the problems were apparent to all, many Americans in 1787 feared that a strong central government would eventually swallow up the states. One of the Anti-Federalists (as opponents of the Constitution were called) worried that the states would eventually "have power over little else than yoking hogs or determining the width of cart wheels."[5]

The challenge of providing a response to the Anti-Federalists fell to James Madison and Alexander Hamilton. During the ratification debate, they argued in a series of essays (the *Federalist Papers*) that a federal system would protect liberty and moderate the power of government.

Protecting Liberty   Although theorists such as John Locke and Montesquieu had not proposed a division of power between national and local authorities as a means of protecting liberty, the framers argued that federalism was a part of the system of checks and balances.[6] Alexander Hamilton wrote in *Federalist* No. 28 that the American people could shift their loyalties back and forth between the national and state governments in order to keep each under control. "If [the people's] rights are invaded by either," Hamilton wrote, "they can make use of the other as the instrument of redress."

Moderating the Power of Government   To the Anti-Federalists, the sacrifice of the states' power to the nation was unwise. They argued that a distant national government could never serve the people's interests as well as the states could. The Anti-Federalists claimed that the state governments would be more likely to protect liberty and self-government. To support their case, they turned to French theorist Montesquieu, who had claimed that a small republic is more likely than a large one to serve people's interests because it is in closer touch with the people.

In *Federalist* No. 10, James Madison took issue with this claim. He argued that whether a government serves the common good is a function not of its size but of the range of interests that share political power. The problem with a small republic, Madison said, is that it can have a dominant faction—whether it be landholders, financiers, an impoverished majority, or some other group—that is strong enough to control government and use it for selfish purposes.

A large republic is less likely to have an all-powerful faction. If financiers are strong in one area of a large republic, they are likely to be weaker elsewhere. The same will be true of farmers, merchants, laborers, and other groups. Madison argued that a large republic would make it more difficult for a single group to gain full control, which would force groups to share in the exercise of power. In making this claim, Madison was arguing not for central authority but for limited government, which he believed would result if power was widely shared. "Extend the sphere," said Madison, "and you take in a greater variety of parties and interests; you make it less probable that a majority of the whole will have a common motive to invade the rights of other citizens."

The Powers of the Nation and the States

The U.S. Constitution addresses the lawful authority of the national government, which is provided through *enumerated and implied powers.* Authority that is not granted to the national government is left—or "reserved"—to the states. Thus, the states have *reserved powers.*

Enumerated Powers and the Supremacy Clause   Article I of the Constitution grants to Congress 17 **enumerated (expressed) powers**. These powers were intended to establish a government strong enough to forge a union that was secure in its defense and stable in its economy. For example, Congress's power to regulate commerce among the states, to create a national currency, and to borrow money would provide the foundation for a sound national economy. Its power to tax, combined with its authority to establish an army and navy and to declare war, would enable it to provide for the common defense.

In addition, the Constitution prohibits the states from actions that would encroach on national powers. Article I, Section 10, prohibits the states from making treaties with other nations, raising armies, waging war, printing money, or entering into commercial agreements with other states without the approval of Congress.

The writers of the Constitution recognized that the lawful exercise of national authority would at times conflict with the laws of the states (see "Fake or Fact? Do States Have Final Authority over Marijuana Laws?"). In such instances, national law would prevail. Article VI of the Constitution grants this dominance in the **supremacy clause**, which provides that "the laws of the United States . . . shall be the supreme law of the land."

Implied Powers: The Necessary and Proper Clause   The writers of the Constitution recognized that government, if it was to be effective, had to be capable of responding to change. A weakness of the Articles was that the national government was prohibited from exercising powers not expressly granted it, which limited its ability to meet the country's changing needs after the end of the Revolutionary War.

Detecting Misinformation

Do States Have Final Authority over Marijuana Laws?

Nearly a fourth of the states have authorized the recreational use of marijuana, and other states have downgraded marijuana possession in limited amounts from a felony to a misdemeanor or citation. Additional states allow marijuana's use for medical purposes, although the medical conditions that qualify vary from one state to the next. From these examples, it would appear that states have final authority over the regulation of marijuana use.

Syda Productions/Shutterstock

Is that claim fact, or is it fake?

States have final authority over marijuana use only in a limited respect. State courts have held that, if the state has decriminalized marijuana, an individual cannot be convicted in state court for possession or use of marijuana that complies with state law—for example, possession of an amount of marijuana that does not exceed the state limit. On the other hand, marijuana use and possession are prohibited by federal law. The U.S. government classifies marijuana as an illegal controlled substance, and the Supreme Court in Gonzales v. Raich (2005) upheld that classification as a valid exercise of Congress's commerce power. Because of the Constitution's supremacy clause, federal law supersedes conflicting state law. Accordingly, residents of a state that has legalized marijuana could be charged with violating federal law. However, the federal government seldom pursues cases of marijuana use and possession where an individual is in compliance with state law. Law enforcement officers have leeway in deciding which criminal offenses will get their attention. Federal officials view personal marijuana use as a low priority relative to other types of federal crime.

To avoid this problem with the new government, the framers included in Article I of the Constitution the **"necessary and proper" clause** or, as it later came to be known, the *elastic clause*. It gives Congress the power "to make all laws which shall be necessary and proper for carrying into execution the foregoing [enumerated] powers." This clause gives the national government **implied powers**: powers that are not listed in the Constitution but that are related to the exercise of listed powers.

Reserved Powers: The States' Authority   The supremacy and "necessary and proper" clauses were worrisome to the Anti-Federalists. The two clauses stoked their fear of an overly powerful national government because they provided a constitutional basis for expanding federal authority. Such concerns led them to demand a constitutional amendment that would protect states' rights and interests. Ratified in 1791 as the Tenth Amendment to the Constitution, it reads "The powers not delegated to the United States by the Constitution, nor prohibited by it to the States, are reserved to the States." The states' powers under the U.S. Constitution are thus called **reserved powers**.

At the time of ratification, the Tenth Amendment was seen as strong protection of the states. It turned out to be something less. The logic of the Constitution is that the states control only those policies not controlled by the federal government. As a result, the constitutional issue in federal–state disputes is the limits on federal power. If an action is within the lawful power of the federal government, it's permissible. If it's outside the federal government's lawful power, it's not. This feature of the Constitution has enabled the national government to intrude on policy areas initially reserved to the states. Over time, there has been a **nationalization** of America's federal system—a gradual shift in power from the states to the national government.[7] During the course of the nation's history, the pendulum of power has sometimes swung toward the states and sometimes toward the national government but, overall, the national government has gained power relative to the states, as later sections of this chapter will show.

FEDERALISM IN HISTORICAL PERSPECTIVE

Since ratification of the Constitution over two centuries ago, no aspect of it has provoked more frequent or bitter conflict than federalism. By establishing two levels of sovereign authority, the Constitution created two centers of power and ambition, each of which was sure to claim disputed areas as belonging to it. Ambiguities in the Constitution have also contributed to conflict between the nation and the states. For example, the document does not specify the dividing line between *inter*state commerce (which the national government is empowered to regulate) and *intra*state commerce (which is reserved for regulation by the states).

Not surprisingly, federalism's development has been determined less by the words
of the Constitution than by the strength of
the contending interests and the country's
changing needs. Federalism can be viewed as
having progressed through three historical
eras, each of which has involved a different
relationship between the nation and the
states. At the same time, each era has ended
with a national government that was stronger than at the start of the era.

CITIZEN ACTION!
GETTING READY

History can inform citizenship. You
can strengthen your understanding of
history through reading but also by
visiting historical sites. Search out historical sites in your area. You're likely
to be surprised by how close you are to
places where history was made.

An Indestructible Union (1789–1865)

The issue during the first era—which lasted from the time the Constitution
went into effect (1789) until the end of the Civil War (1865)—was the Union's
survival. Given America's state-centered history before the Constitution, it was
inevitable that the states would dispute national policies that threatened their
interests.

The Nationalist View: McCulloch v. Maryland   An early dispute over
federalism arose when President George Washington's secretary of the treasury, Alexander Hamilton, proposed that Congress establish a national bank.
Hamilton and his supporters claimed that, because the federal government had
constitutional authority to regulate currency, it had the "implied power" to
establish a national bank. Thomas Jefferson, Washington's secretary of state,
opposed the bank on the grounds that its activities would enrich the wealthy
at the expense of ordinary people. Jefferson claimed the bank was unlawful
because the Constitution did not expressly authorize it. Jefferson said, "I consider the foundation of the Constitution as laid on this ground that 'all powers
not delegated to the United States by the Constitution, nor prohibited by it to
the states, are preserved to the states or to the people.'"

Hamilton's argument prevailed, and Congress in 1791 established the First
Bank of the United States, granting it a 20-year charter. Although Congress
did not renew the bank's charter when it expired in 1811, Congress decided
in 1816 to establish the Second Bank of the United States. State and local
banks did not want competition from a national bank and sought protection
from their state legislatures. Several states, including Maryland, levied taxes
on the national bank's operations within their borders, hoping to drive it out
of existence by making it unprofitable. James McCulloch, who was in charge
of the Maryland branch of the national bank, refused to pay the Maryland tax
and the resulting dispute was heard by the Supreme Court.

Born in the West Indies and orphaned as a child, Alexander Hamilton was the most influential of the early American leaders who did not serve as president. As secretary of treasury in the Washington administration, he was the architect of the nation's early economic policies. He created a system of tariffs, established a national bank, encouraged manufacturing, and promoted trade among the states and with Europe. Hamilton's policies provided the foundation for America's economic prosperity. A French diplomat called Hamilton the greatest leader of his era, ranking him ahead of even Washington and Napoleon. This portrait was painted by John Trumbull, a contemporary of Hamilton, who was called "The Painter of the Revolution." (Yale University Art Gallery)

The chief justice of the Supreme Court, John Marshall, was a nationalist, and in *McCulloch v. Maryland* (1819) the Court ruled decisively in favor of national authority. It was reasonable to infer, Marshall concluded, that a government with powers to tax, borrow money, and regulate commerce could establish a bank in order to exercise those powers effectively. Marshall's argument was a clear statement of *implied powers*—the idea that, through the "necessary and proper" clause, the national government's powers extend beyond a narrow interpretation of its enumerated powers.

Marshall's ruling also addressed the meaning of the Constitution's supremacy clause. The state of Maryland had argued that, even if the national government had the authority to establish a bank, a state had the authority to tax it. The Supreme Court rejected Maryland's position, concluding that valid national law overrides conflicting state law. Because the national government had the power to create the bank, it also could protect the bank from state actions, such as taxation, that might destroy it.[8]

The *McCulloch* decision served as precedent for later rulings in support of national power. In *Gibbons v. Ogden* (1824), for example, the Marshall-led Court rejected a New York law granting one of its residents a monopoly on a ferry that operated between New York and New Jersey, concluding that New York had encroached on Congress's power to regulate commerce among the states. The Court asserted that Congress's commerce power was not limited to trade between the states, but to all aspects of that trade, including the transportation of goods. The power over commerce, the Court said, "is vested in Congress as absolutely as it would be in a single government."[9]

Marshall's opinions asserted that legitimate uses of national power took precedence over state authority and that the "necessary and proper" clause and the commerce clause were broad grants of power to the national government. As a nationalist, Marshall provided a legal basis for expanding federal power in ways that fostered the development of the United States as a nation rather than as a collection of states. As Justice Oliver Wendell Holmes Jr. noted a century later, the Union could not have survived if each state had been allowed to decide for itself which national laws it would obey.[10]

The States' Rights View: The Dred Scott Decision   Although John Marshall's rulings strengthened national authority, the issue of slavery posed a growing threat to the Union's survival. Westward expansion and immigration into the northern states were tilting power in Congress toward the free states, which increasingly signaled their determination to outlaw slavery at some future time. Fearing the possibility, southern leaders did what others have done throughout American history: They developed a constitutional interpretation that suited their goal. John C. Calhoun declared that the United States was founded upon a "compact" between the states. The national government, he said, was "a government of states . . . not a government of individuals."[11] This line of reasoning led Calhoun to his famed "doctrine of nullification," which declared that a state has the constitutional right to nullify a national law.

In 1832, South Carolina invoked the doctrine, declaring "null and void" a national tariff law that favored northern interests. President Andrew Jackson called South Carolina's action "incompatible with the existence of the Union," a position that gained strength when Congress gave Jackson the authority to take military action against South Carolina. The state backed down after Congress agreed to changes in the tariff act. The dispute foreshadowed the Civil War, a confrontation of far greater consequence. Although war would not break out for another three decades, the dispute over states' rights was intensifying.

The Supreme Court's infamous *Dred Scott* decision (1857), written by Chief Justice Roger Taney, an ardent states'-rights advocate, inflamed the dispute.

Dred Scott, a slave who had lived in the North for four years, applied for his freedom when his master died, citing a federal law—the Missouri Compromise of 1820—that made slavery illegal in a free state or territory. The Supreme Court ruled against Scott, claiming that slaves were not citizens and therefore had no right to have their case heard in federal court. The Court also invalidated the Missouri Compromise by holding that slaves were property, not people. Accordingly, since the Constitution prohibited Congress from interfering with owners' property rights, Congress lacked the power to outlaw slavery in any state.[12]

The Taney Court's decision provoked outrage in the North and contributed to a sectional split in the nation's majority party, the Democrats. In 1860, the Democratic Party's northern and southern wings nominated different candidates for the presidency, which split the Democratic vote, enabling the Republican candidate, Abraham Lincoln, to win the presidency with only 40 percent of the popular vote. Lincoln had campaigned on a platform that called not for an immediate end to slavery but for its gradual abolition through payments to slaveholders. Nevertheless, southern states saw Lincoln's election as a threat

The American Civil War was the deadliest conflict the world had yet known. Ten percent of fighting-age men died in the four-year war, and an additional 15 percent were wounded. The death toll was 618,000, which exceeds the combined total of American war dead in World War I, World War II, the Korean War, and the Vietnam War. Shown here is a portion of the Gettysburg National Cemetery. It was on this site that Abraham Lincoln gave his Gettysburg Address a few days after a battle in which 50,000 Union and Confederate soldiers were killed or wounded. (Bob Pool/Shutterstock)

to their way of life. By the time Lincoln took office, seven southern states, led by South Carolina, had left the Union. Four more states followed. In justifying his decision to wage war on the South, Lincoln said, "The Union is older than the states." In 1865, the superior strength of the Union army settled by force the question of whether national authority is binding on the states.

Dual Federalism and Laissez-Faire Capitalism (1865–1937)

Although the North's victory in the Civil War preserved the Union, new challenges to federalism were surfacing. Constitutional doctrine held that certain policy areas, such as interstate commerce and defense, belonged exclusively to the national government, whereas other policy areas, such as public health and intrastate commerce, belonged exclusively to the states. This doctrine, known as **dual federalism**, was based on the idea that a precise separation of national and state authority was both possible and desirable. "The power which one possesses," said the Supreme Court, "the other does not."[13]

American society, however, was in the midst of changes that raised questions about the suitability of dual federalism as a governing concept. The Industrial Revolution had given rise to large business firms, which were using their economic power to dominate markets and exploit workers. Government was the logical counterforce to this economic power. Which level of government—state or national—would regulate business?

Dual federalism became a barrier to an effective response by either level of government. From the 1860s through the 1930s, the Supreme Court held firm to the idea that a sharp dividing line existed between national and state authority and that neither level of government would be allowed to substantially regulate business. The era of dual federalism was characterized by business supremacy in commerce policy.

The Fourteenth Amendment and State Discretion   Ratified after the Civil War, the Fourteenth Amendment was intended to protect the newly freed slaves from discriminatory action by state governments. A state was prohibited from depriving "any person of life, liberty, or property without due process of law," from denying "any person within its jurisdiction the equal protection of the laws," and from abridging "the privileges or immunities of citizens of the United States."

Supreme Court rulings in subsequent decades, however, undermined the Fourteenth Amendment's promise of liberty and equality for all. In 1873, for example, the Court held that the Fourteenth Amendment did not substantially limit the power of the states to determine the rights to which their residents were entitled.[14] Then, in *Plessy v. Ferguson* (1896), the Court issued its infamous "separate but equal" ruling. A Black man, Homer Adolph Plessy, had been convicted of violating a Louisiana law that required white and Black citizens to ride in separate railroad cars. The Supreme Court upheld his conviction, concluding that state governments could force Blacks to use separate facilities as long as the facilities were "equal" in quality to those reserved for use by whites. "If one race be inferior to the other socially," the Court argued, "the Constitution of the United States cannot put them on the same plane." The lone dissenting justice in the case, John Marshall Harlan, had harsh words for his colleagues: "Our Constitution is color-blind and neither knows nor tolerates classes among citizens. . . . The thin disguise of 'equal' accommodations . . . will not mislead anyone nor atone for the wrong this day done."[15]

With its *Plessy* decision, the Supreme Court endorsed government-based racial segregation in the South. Black children were forced into separate public schools that had few teachers. Public hospitals for Blacks had few doctors and almost no medical supplies. The *Plessy* ruling had become a justification for the separate and *unequal* treatment of Black Americans.[16]

Judicial Protection of Business   After the Civil War, the Supreme Court also gave nearly free rein to business. A majority of the Court's justices favored laissez-faire capitalism (which holds that business should be "allowed to act" without interference) and interpreted the Constitution in ways that limited government's ability to regulate business activity. In 1886, for example, the Court decided that corporations were "persons" within the meaning of the Fourteenth Amendment, and thereby were protected from substantial regulation by the states.[17] In other words, a constitutional amendment that had been enacted to protect newly freed slaves from being treated as second-class persons was ignored for that purpose but used instead to protect fictitious persons—business corporations.

The Court also weakened the national government's regulatory power by narrowly interpreting its commerce power. The Constitution's **commerce clause** says that Congress shall have the power "to regulate commerce" among the states. However, the clause does not spell out the economic activities included in the grant of power. When the federal government invoked the Sherman Antitrust Act (1890) in an attempt to break up the monopoly on the manufacture of sugar (a single company controlled 98 percent of it), the Supreme Court blocked the action, claiming that interstate commerce covered only the "transportation" of goods, not their "manufacture."[18] Manufacturing was deemed part of intrastate commerce and thus, according to the dual federalism doctrine, subject to state regulation only. However, because the Court had previously ruled that the states' regulatory powers were limited by the Fourteenth Amendment, the states were largely prohibited from regulating manufacturing.

Although some business regulation was subsequently allowed, the Court remained an obstacle to efforts to curb business practices. An example is the case of *Hammer v. Dagenhart* (1918), which arose from a 1916 federal law that prohibited the interstate shipment of goods produced by child labor. The law had public support in that factory owners were exploiting children, working them for long hours at low pay. Nevertheless, the Court invalidated the law, ruling that the Tenth Amendment gave the states, and not the federal government, the power to regulate factory practices.[19] However, in an earlier case, *Lochner v. New York* (1905), the Court had blocked states from regulating labor practices, concluding that such action violated factory owners' property rights.[20]

In effect, the Court had voided the principle of self-government. Neither the people's representatives in Congress nor those in the state legislatures were allowed to regulate business. America's corporations, with the Supreme Court as their protector, had control over economic policy.[21]

National Authority Prevails   The Democratic Party, with its working-class base, attacked the Court's position, and its candidates increasingly called for greater regulation of business and more rights for labor. Progressive Republicans such as Theodore Roosevelt also fought against uncontrolled business power, but the Republican Party as a whole was ideologically committed to unregulated markets and to a small role for the federal government. Accordingly, when the Great Depression began in 1929, Republican president Herbert Hoover refused at first to use federal authority to put people back to work. Adhering to his party's free-market philosophy, Hoover argued that the economy would quickly rebound on its own and that government intervention would only delay the recovery.

In the 1932 election, voters elected as president the Democratic candidate, Franklin D. Roosevelt, who recognized that the economy had become a national one. More than 10 million workers (compared to 1 million in 1860) were employed by industry, whose products were marketed throughout the nation. Urban workers typically were dependent on landlords for their housing, on farmers and grocers for their food, and on corporations for their jobs. Farmers were more independent, but they, too, were increasingly a part of a larger economic network. Farmers' income depended on market prices and shipping and equipment costs.[22] Economic interdependence meant that, when the Great Depression hit in 1929, its effects could not be contained. At the height of the Depression, a fourth of the nation's workers were jobless.

The states had responsibility for helping the poor, but they were nearly penniless because of declining tax revenues and the high demand for welfare

The Great Depression cost a fourth of workers their jobs. States lacked the resources to meet the needs of the unemployed and the national government stepped in, resulting in a permanent shift of power within the American federal system. Shown here is a soup kitchen in Chicago set up to feed the unemployed. This kitchen was opened and funded by Chicago mob boss Al Capone as a way to enhance his public image. (Everett Historical/Shutterstock)

assistance. Franklin Roosevelt's New Deal programs were designed to ease the hardship. The 1933 National Industrial Recovery Act (NIRA), for example, established a federal jobs program and enabled major industries to coordinate their production decisions. Economic conservatives opposed such programs, accusing Roosevelt of leading the country into socialism. They found an ally in the Supreme Court. In *Schechter Poultry Corp. v. United States* (1935), just as it had done in previous New Deal cases, the Supreme Court in a 5–4 ruling declared the NIRA to be unconstitutional.[23]

Frustrated by the Court's rulings, Roosevelt in 1937 sought to exploit the fact that the Constitution gives Congress the power to determine the number of Supreme Court justices. Although the number had stayed at nine justices for seven decades, there was no constitutional barrier to increasing the number, which, in fact, had been altered several times in the nation's early years. Roosevelt asked Congress to pass legislation that would allow a president to nominate a new justice whenever a seated member passed the age of 70½. Since some of the justices had already reached that age, the legislation would enable Roosevelt to appoint enough new justices to swing the Court to his side. Congress hesitated to do so, but the attempt ended with the "switch in time that saved nine." For reasons that have never been fully clear, Justice Owen Roberts switched sides on New Deal cases, giving the president a 5–4 majority on the Court.

Within months, the Court upheld the 1935 National Labor Relations Act, which gave employees the right to organize and bargain collectively.[24] In passing the legislation, Congress claimed that disputes between labor and management disrupted the nation's economy and therefore could be regulated through the commerce clause. In upholding the act, the Supreme Court endorsed Congress's reasoning.[25] In a subsequent ruling, the Court declared that Congress's commerce power is "as broad as the needs of the nation."[26] Congress would be allowed to regulate *all* aspects of commerce.

The Supreme Court had finally acknowledged the obvious: that an industrial economy is not confined by state boundaries and must be subject to national regulation. It was a principle that business also increasingly accepted. The nation's banking industry, for example, was saved from almost complete collapse in the 1930s by the creation of a federal regulatory agency, the Federal Deposit Insurance Corporation (FDIC). By insuring depositors' savings against loss, the FDIC stopped the panic withdrawals that had already forced thousands of the nation's banks to close.

During the 1930s, the Supreme Court also loosened its restrictions on Congress's taxing and spending power. In *United States v. Butler* (1936), the Court held that the Constitution's taxing and spending clause confers a grant of power that is "limited only by the requirement that it shall be exercised to provide for the general welfare of the United States."[27] General welfare is a very broad category, so broad, in fact, that Congress has used its spending power to involve itself in policy areas traditionally controlled by the states, as will be explained later in the chapter.[28]

CONTEMPORARY FEDERALISM (SINCE 1937)

Since the 1930s, relations between the nation and the states have changed so fully that dual federalism is no longer an accurate description of the American system. An understanding of today's federalism requires the recognition of two countervailing developments. The larger trend is a long-term *expansion* of national authority, which began in the 1930s and continues to this day. The national government now operates in many policy areas that were once almost exclusively within the control of states and localities. The national government does not dominate in these policy areas, but it does play a significant role.

Many of the federal initiatives trace to the 1960s as part of President Lyndon Johnson's Great Society program. A Democrat in the mold of Franklin Roosevelt, Johnson believed that federal power should be used to assist the economically disadvantaged. However, unlike Roosevelt's New Deal, which dealt mostly with the economy, Johnson's Great Society dealt mostly with social welfare issues, which have an indirect constitutional basis. The Constitution does not grant Congress the power to regulate "social welfare." However, Congress may tax and spend for that purpose, which was the basis of the Great Society. Johnson's presidency was marked by dozens of new federal assistance grants to states for programs in health care, public housing, nutrition, public assistance, urban development, education, and other policy areas traditionally reserved to states and localities. Johnson's initiatives were both creative and coercive: creative in the large number of new federal programs and coercive in the restrictions placed on states and localities as a condition of their receipt of federal funds.

A smaller and more recent development is the attempt to "pass down" authority from the national level to the state and local levels in selected areas. Known as *devolution,* this development peaked in the 1990s. Although it has since receded, devolution remains a component of contemporary federalism, as is discussed later in the chapter.

Interdependency and Intergovernmental Relations

Interdependency is a reason national authority has increased substantially. Modern systems of transportation, commerce, and communication transcend local and state boundaries. These systems are national—and even international—in scope, which means that problems affecting Americans living in one part of the country will affect Americans living elsewhere. This situation has required Washington to assume a larger policy role. National problems typically require a national policy solution.

Interdependency has also encouraged national, state, and local policymakers to work together to solve policy problems (see Case Study: Federalism and the Covid-19 Response). This collaborative effort has been described as **cooperative federalism**.[29] The difference between the older dual federalism and cooperative federalism has been likened to the difference between a layer cake, whose levels are separate, and a marble cake, whose levels flow together.[30]

Cooperative federalism is based on shared policy responsibilities rather than sharply divided ones. An example is the Medicaid program, which was created in 1965 as part of President Johnson's Great Society initiative and provides health care for the poor. The Medicaid program is jointly funded by the national and state governments, operates within eligibility standards set by the national government, and gives states some latitude in determining recipient eligibility and benefits. The Medicaid program is not an isolated example. Literally hundreds of policy programs today are run jointly by the national and state governments. In many cases, local governments are also involved. These programs have the following characteristics:

- Jointly funded by the national and state governments (and sometimes by local governments)
- Jointly administered, with the states and localities providing most of the direct service to recipients and a national agency providing general administration
- Jointly determined, with both state and national governments (and sometimes local governments) having a say in eligibility and benefit levels and with federal regulations, such as those prohibiting discrimination, imposing a degree of uniformity on state and local efforts

Cooperative federalism should not be interpreted to mean that the states are powerless and dependent.[31] States have retained most of their traditional authority in areas such as education, health, public safety, and roadways. In the area of public schools, for example, states determine the length of the school year, teachers' qualifications, and graduation requirements. Nevertheless, the federal government's involvement in policy areas traditionally reserved for the states has increased its policy influence and diminished state-to-state policy differences.

Government Revenues and Intergovernmental Relations

The interdependency of American society—the fact that developments in one area affect what happens elsewhere—is one of three major reasons the federal government's policy role has expanded greatly since the early 20th century. A second reason is that Americans expect government to assist with their problems. Whenever an area of the country has been hit by a natural disaster, for example, its residents have sought relief from Washington. Moreover, whenever a federal program, such as student loans or farm supports, has been established, its recipients have fought to keep it. As a result, federal programs rarely end, while new ones get added each year. A third reason is the federal government's superior taxing capacity. States and localities are in a competitive situation with regard to taxation.

CASE STUDY

Politics in Action

Federalism and the COVID-19 Response

Both levels of America's federal government responded when the COVID-19 coronavirus pandemic struck in 2020. The fed-

©McGraw-Hill Education

eral government's Center for Disease Control (CDC) assessed disease "hotspots" and developed guidelines for first responders, whereas the Department of Health and Human Services spearheaded efforts to develop a vaccine. President Trump held press conferences to announce the latest developments in the federal government's response. Governors directed efforts in their states, using their health emergency powers to determine which businesses and other entities had to close and when they would be allowed to reopen.

If federal and state officials worked together, the relationship was not always smooth. Some governors were upset by the federal government's delayed response to the crisis and by President Trump's refusal to use his full powers under the Defense Production Act to require firms to produce the equipment that healthcare providers needed to protect themselves and treat the surge in patients. In turn, federal officials were unhappy with some governors for responding too slowly to the crisis and with others for actions deemed overly aggressive and harmful to the economy.

President Trump and the state governors all gave themselves high marks for handling the crisis. Americans were more discerning. A survey of 22,000 Americans found that respondents in all 50 states gave their governor a higher mark for responding to the crisis than they gave to President Trump. On average, governors had an approval rating of 66 percent, compared with 44 percent for President Trump. But state residents did not uniformly approve of their governor's response. Slightly more than 80 percent of Ohio and Kentucky residents approved of their governor's response, which were the two highest ratings. The lowest approval ratings, just under 50 percent, went to the governors of South Dakota and Hawaii.[32]

Q: Do you think the response to the COVID-19 would have been more or less effective if the United States had a unitary system of government, where sovereignty is vested solely in the national government, instead of a federal system of government, where it's vested in the national and state governments?

ASK YOURSELF: What would have been the advantages and disadvantages if the national government had possessed full authority to direct the response to the pandemic? What were the advantages and disadvantages of the fact that governors in the U.S. system had the authority to make decisions fitted to what they saw as their state's particular needs?

A state with high corporate and personal income taxes will lose firms and people to states with lower taxes. By contrast, firms and people are less likely to move to another country in search of lower taxes. The result is that the federal government raises more tax revenue than do all 50 states and the thousands of local governments combined (see Figure 3-2).

Fiscal Federalism   The federal government's revenue-raising advantage has made money a basis for relations between the national government and the states and localities. **Fiscal federalism** refers to the expenditure of federal funds on programs run, in part, through state and local governments.[33] The federal government provides some or all of the money through **grants-in-aid** (cash payments) to states and localities, which then administer the programs. The pattern of federal assistance to states and localities is shown in Figure 3-3. Federal grants-in-aid have increased dramatically since the mid-1950s. Roughly one in every five dollars spent by local and state governments in recent decades has been raised not by them but by the federal government in Washington (see "How the 50 States Differ").

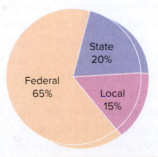

figure 3-2   FEDERAL, STATE, AND LOCAL SHARES OF GOVERNMENT TAX REVENUE

The federal government raises more tax revenues than do all state and local governments combined. (*Source:* Tax Policy Center, 2020)

Billions of dollars (in constant 2005 dollars)

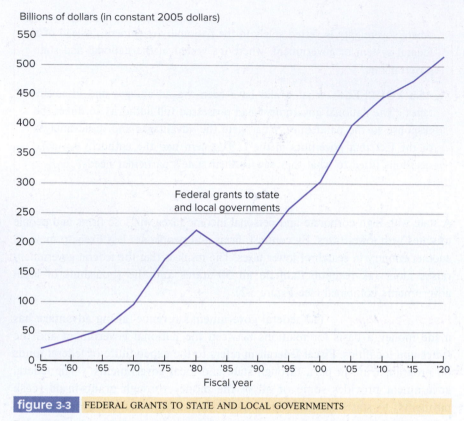

figure 3-3   FEDERAL GRANTS TO STATE AND LOCAL GOVERNMENTS

Federal aid to states and localities has increased dramatically since the 1950s. (*Source:* Office of Management and Budget (OMB), FY2021). Figures are based on constant (2005) dollars to control for effects of inflation. Figure for each year shown in graph is the average per year for previous five years.

Cash grants to states and localities increase Washington's policy influence. State and local governments can reject a grant-in-aid, but, if they accept it, they must spend it in the way specified by Congress. Money designated for a school lunch program, for example, cannot be used for school construction or teachers' salaries. Also, because most grants require states to contribute matching funds, the federal programs, in effect, determine how states will allocate some of their own tax dollars.

Nevertheless, federal grants-in-aid serve the policy interests of state and local officials. Although they complain that federal grants contain too many restrictions and infringe too much on their authority, most of them are eager to have the money because it permits them to offer services they could not otherwise afford. In 2019, for example, Congress passed a transportation bill that granted billions of dollars to states and localities to improve their roadways and mass transit systems.

HOW THE 50 STATES DIFFER

CRITICAL THINKING THROUGH COMPARISONS

Federal Grants-in-Aid to the States

Federal assistance accounts for a significant share of general state revenue, but the variation is considerable. Mississippi, which gets 42 percent of its general revenue from the federal government, is at one extreme. Virginia, at 21 percent, is at the other extreme.

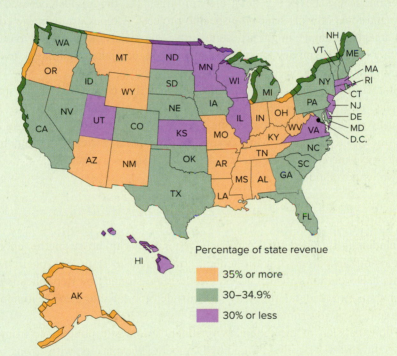

Percentage of state revenue

- 35% or more
- 30–34.9%
- 30% or less

Source: U.S. Census Bureau, 2020.

Q: What might explain why some states rely more heavily on federal grants than other states?

A: Many federal grants are designed to assist low-income people, and states that have higher poverty rates tend to rely more heavily on federal grants. States with a large land area and a small population also rely more heavily on grants as a result, for example, of their highway and rural development needs.

Said one observer about federal grants, "For governors, it's free money—they get the benefits and they don't have to pay the costs of raising the revenues."[34]

Categorical and Block Grants　State and local governments receive two major types of assistance—categorical grants and block grants—which differ in the degree to which Washington restricts their use. **Categorical grants**, the more restrictive type, can be used only for a designated activity. An example is Medicaid funds. The funds must be used to provide medical care to lower-income individuals. The funds can't be diverted to other health-related activities, such as the training of medical students. **Block grants** are less restrictive. The federal government specifies the general area in which the funds must be used, but state and local officials select the specific projects. A block grant in the education area, for example, might give state and local officials the authority to decide whether to use the money for school construction, computer equipment, teacher training, or some other education-related activity.

State and local officials prefer federal money that comes with fewer strings attached and thus favor block grants. In contrast, members of Congress have typically preferred categorical grants because Congress has more control over how the money is spent. Most grants are of the categorical type, but block grants have increased in frequency since the 1980s as a result of a movement known as devolution.

Devolution

Devolution is the idea that American federalism can be strengthened by a partial shift in power from the federal government to state and local governments.[35] Devolution rests on a belief—held more strongly by Republicans than Democrats—that federal authority has intruded too far into areas belonging to state and local governments.

The expansion of the federal government's domestic policy role from the 1930s onward was largely initiated by Democratic lawmakers, with strong backing from the public. The New Deal and Great Society programs had broad public support at the outset. However, public support for federal domestic spending declined after the 1960s. Some of the programs, particularly those providing welfare benefits to the poor, were widely seen as too costly, too bureaucratic, and too lax—there was a widespread perception that many welfare recipients were getting benefits they neither needed nor deserved. Republican leaders increasingly questioned the effectiveness of the programs, a position that meshed with the party's ideology of lower taxes and local control.

Upon taking office in 1981, Republican president Ronald Reagan proposed a "new federalism" that would give more control to states and localities. In

This familiar sign illustrates the power of fiscal federalism. In half the states until the 1980s, persons younger than 21 could legally buy alcohol. The policy changed when Congress enacted legislation requiring states to set the drinking age at 21 in order to receive their full allotment of federal highway funds. Although the states complained, the financial stakes were too high for them to keep a lower age limit. (Vitezslav Valka/Alamy Stock Photo)

issuing an executive order to initiate the change, Reagan said, "Federalism is rooted in the knowledge that our political liberties are best assured by limiting the size and scope of national government." Reagan advocated the use of block grants as opposed to categorical grants and prohibited federal agencies from submitting to Congress legislative proposals that would "regulate the states in ways that would interfere" with their "traditional governmental functions."

The Republican Revolution   When the Republican Party scored a decisive victory in the 1994 congressional elections, Speaker of the House Newt Gingrich declared that "1960s-style federalism is dead." Republican lawmakers proposed to cut some federal programs, but, even more, they sought to devolve power to the state and local levels. The Republican-controlled Congress grouped a number of categorical grants into block grants in order to give states more control over how the federal money was spent. Congressional Republicans also passed legislation to reduce *unfunded mandates*—federal programs that require action by states or localities but don't provide enough funds to pay for it. The Clean Air Act of 1963, for example, required states to comply with national air quality standards but did not provide them with all of the funds necessary to implement their plans.

However, the largest change occurred when the Republican-controlled Congress enacted the sweeping 1996 Welfare Reform Act. Opinion polls at the time indicated that a majority of Americans felt that government was spending too much on welfare and that too many welfare recipients were abusing the system. The Welfare Reform Act tightened spending and eligibility. The legislation's key element, the Temporary Assistance for Needy Families (TANF)

In the 1990s, some policy responsibilities were shifted from the federal government to the states, a policy called devolution. The trend stalled after 2000 for several reasons, including the terrorist attacks of September 11, 2001, which required a national response. Included was a larger role for the federal government in domestic security. Shown here is a scene familiar to air travelers. Federal officers rather than state or local police are in charge of screening airline passengers. (David R. Frazier Photolibrary, Inc.)

block grant, ended the decades-old federal program that granted cash assistance to poor families with children. TANF restricts a family's eligibility for federal assistance to five years and gives states wide latitude in setting benefit levels. TANF also provides funds to enable states to develop training programs that have the goal of moving people off welfare and into jobs. (TANF and other aspects of the 1996 welfare reform legislation are discussed further in later chapters.*)

The Continuing Issue of National Power Proponents of devolution had some success but were unable to substantially shift power back to the states or stop the flow of power to the federal government. After the terrorist attacks

---

*The Supreme Court played a role in devolution by retreating somewhat from its New Deal-era ruling that Congress's commerce power is "as broad as the needs of the nation." In *United States v. Lopez* (1995), the Court cited the Tenth Amendment in striking down a federal law banning the possession of guns within a thousand feet of a school. The Court ruled that the ban had "nothing to do with commerce, or any sort of economic activity." The Court then applied the Eleventh Amendment (which protects a state from being sued in federal court by a private citizen without its consent) to limit Congress's authority. In *Kimmel v. Board of Regents* (2000), the Court held that state government employees cannot sue their state for violating federal age-discrimination policies. The Court ruled that states have the authority to decide the retirement age of their own employees.

Conflicting Ideas

The Power of the Federal Government

Although the Republican and Democratic Parties have had opposing views on the power of the federal government since the 1930s, the gap has widened in recent years. Republicans have sought to roll back federal power, resisted at nearly every turn by Democrats. A recent example is the health care reform act that the Democrat-controlled Congress enacted in 2010 and that Republican lawmakers have since sought to overturn.

Differing opinions on federal power are not confined to lawmakers. As indicated by the accompanying graph, Americans who identify with the Republican Party are far more likely than Democratic identifiers to believe that the federal government "has too much power."

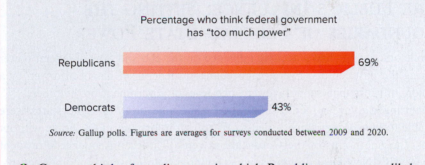

Percentage who think federal government has "too much power"

Republicans   69%
Democrats   43%

Source: Gallup polls. Figures are averages for surveys conducted between 2009 and 2020.

Q: Can you think of a policy area in which Republicans are more likely than Democrats to support higher federal spending?

on New York and Washington on September 11, 2001, there was an expansion of federal authority, including creation of the Department of Homeland Security, a cabinet-level federal agency with policing and emergency responsibilities traditionally belonging to states and localities. It was established during the presidency of George W. Bush, a Republican.

Then, in 2010, the Democrat-controlled Congress enacted the Affordable Care Act (ACA), which is one of the largest expansions of federal authority since the 1960s. Among its provisions is the requirement that business firms of a certain size provide their employees with health insurance or pay a penalty. In its original form, it also required individuals to have insurance or pay a penalty, but the Republican-controlled Congress removed that provision in 2017. Before the ACA was enacted, states controlled health insurance, regulating everything from the coverage plans that insurance companies could offer to the rates they could charge.

The partisan fight over the scope of federal power will continue, but one thing is certain: American federalism is, and will remain, a vastly different system than it was before the 1930s. The demands of contemporary life—a complex and integrated economy, a public that is insistent on its rights and reliant on government services, and a global environment filled with challenges and opportunities—have combined to give the federal government a bigger role in federal-state relations. The change can be seen even in the structure of the federal government. Five cabinet departments—Health and Human Services, Housing and Urban Development, Transportation, Education, and Homeland Security—were created after the 1930s to administer federal programs in policy areas traditionally reserved to the states.

THE PUBLIC'S INFLUENCE: SETTING THE BOUNDARIES OF FEDERAL-STATE POWER

Public opinion has had a decisive influence on the ebb and flow of federal power during the past century. Every major change in federalism has been driven by a major shift in public support toward one level of government or the other.

During the Great Depression, when it became clear that the states were unable to help, Americans turned to Washington for relief. For people without jobs, the fine points of the Constitution were of little consequence. President Roosevelt's New Deal programs, which offered both jobs and income security, were a radical departure from the past but quickly gained public favor. A 1936 Gallup poll indicated, for example, that 61 percent of Americans supported Roosevelt's Social Security program, whereas only 27 percent opposed it.[36] The second great wave of federal social programs—Lyndon Johnson's Great Society—was also driven by public demands. Income and education levels had risen dramatically after World War II, and Americans wanted more and better services from government.[37] When the states were slow to respond, Americans pressured federal officials to act. The Medicare and Medicaid programs, which provide health care for individuals who are elderly and poor, respectively, are examples of the Johnson administration's response. A 1965 Gallup poll indicated that two-thirds of Americans approved of federal involvement in the provision of medical care, despite the fact that health was traditionally the states' responsibility.

CITIZEN ACTION!
GETTING INVOLVED

Under America's federal system, all levels of government have policy authority. Consider doing a part-time internship with your local government. You will come to better understand how your community is governed and will gain valuable work experience.

Public opinion was also behind the rollback of federal authority in the 1990s. Polls showed that a majority of Americans had come to believe that the federal government had become too large and intrusive. Americans' dissatisfaction with federal programs and spending provided the springboard for the Republican takeover of Congress in the 1994 midterm elections, which led to policies aimed at devolving power to the states, including the widely popular 1996 Welfare Reform Act.[38]

The public's role in determining the boundaries between federal and state power would come as no surprise to the framers of the Constitution. For them, federalism was a pragmatic issue, one to be decided by the nation's needs rather than by inflexible rules. Alexander Hamilton and James Madison predicted as much when they said that Americans would look to whichever level of government was more responsive to their needs. Indeed, each succeeding generation of Americans has seen fit to devise a balance of federal and state power suited to the demands of their era.

SUMMARY

A leading feature of the American political system is its division of authority between a national government and state governments. The first U.S. government, established by the Articles of Confederation, was essentially a union of the states.

In establishing the basis for a stronger national government, the U.S. Constitution also made provision for safeguarding state interests. The result was the creation of a federal system (federalism) in which sovereignty was vested in both national and state governments. The Constitution enumerates the general powers of the national government and grants it implied powers through the "necessary and proper" clause. Other powers are reserved to the states by the Tenth Amendment.

From 1789 to 1865, the nation's survival was at issue. The states found it convenient at times to argue that their sovereignty took precedence over national authority. In the end, it took the Civil War to cement the idea that the United States was a union of people, not of states. From 1865 to 1937, federalism reflected the doctrine that certain policy areas were the exclusive responsibility of the national government, whereas responsibility in other policy areas belonged exclusively to the states. This constitutional position validated the laissez-faire doctrine that big business was largely beyond governmental control. It also allowed the states to discriminate against African Americans in their public policies. Federalism in a form recognizable today began to emerge in the 1930s.

In the areas of commerce, taxation, spending, civil rights, and civil liberties, among others, the federal government now plays an important role, one that is the inevitable consequence of the increasing complexity of American society and the interdependence of its people. National, state, and local officials now work closely together to solve the nation's problems, a situation known as cooperative federalism. Grants-in-aid from Washington to the states and localities have been the chief instrument of national influence. States and localities have received billions in federal assistance; in accepting federal money, they also have accepted both federal restrictions on its use and the national policy priorities that underlie the granting of the money.

Throughout the nation's history, the public, through its demands on government, has influenced the boundaries between federal and state power. The expansions of federal authority in the 1930s and the 1960s, for example, were driven by Americans' increased need for government assistance, whereas the devolutionary trend of the 1990s was sparked by Americans' sense that a rollback in federal power was desirable.

CRITICAL THINKING ZONE

KEY TERMS

block grants (*p. 84*)
categorical grants (*p. 84*)
commerce clause (*p. 74*)
confederacy (*p. 64*)
cooperative federalism (*p. 78*)
devolution (*p. 84*)
dual federalism (*p. 73*)
enumerated (expressed) powers (*p. 66*)
federalism (*p. 62*)

fiscal federalism (*p. 81*)
grants-in-aid (*p. 81*)
implied powers (*p. 68*)
nationalization (*p. 68*)
"necessary and proper" clause (*p. 68*)
reserved powers (*p. 68*)
sovereignty (*p. 62*)
supremacy clause (*p. 66*)
unitary system (*p. 63*)

APPLYING THE ELEMENTS OF CRITICAL THINKING

Conceptualizing: Distinguish among a federal system, a unitary system, and a confederacy. What circumstances led the framers of the Constitution to create a federal system?

Synthesizing: Contrast dual federalism and cooperative federalism. Is the distinction between a layer cake and a marble cake helpful in understanding the difference between dual federalism and cooperative federalism?

Analyzing: How have the federal government's superior taxing policy and the economic interdependency of the American states contributed over time to a larger policy role for the national government? What role have federal grants-in-aid played in the expansion of federal authority?

Extra Credit

A Book Worth Reading: Ron Chernow, *Alexander Hamilton* (New York: Penguin, 2005). Written by a Pulitzer Prize-winning historian, this biography examines the life of Alexander Hamilton, including the role of his economic policies in America's development.

A Website Worth Visiting: http://avalon.law.yale.edu/subject_menus/fed.asp. This Yale Law School site includes a documentary record of the *Federalist Papers,* the Annapolis convention, the Articles of Confederation, the Madison debates, and the U.S. Constitution.

CIVIL LIBERTIES: PROTECTING INDIVIDUAL RIGHTS

boyphare/Shutterstock

> **"** A bill of rights is what the people are entitled to against every government on earth, general or particular, and what no just government should refuse, or rest on inference. **"**
>
> THOMAS JEFFERSON[1]

Without a warrant from a judge, the police and the FBI had secretly attached a GPS tracking device to Antoine Jones's car and knew exactly where it was at any time of the day or night. For a month, they monitored the car's every turn. They subsequently arrested Jones on charges of conspiracy to sell drugs. The evidence obtained through the tracking device helped prosecutors convict him, and he was sentenced to life in prison.

Jones appealed his conviction and won a temporary victory when a federal appellate court—noting that individuals are protected by the Fourth Amendment from "unreasonable searches and seizures"—concluded that the officers should have sought a warrant from a judge, who would have decided whether they had sufficient cause to justify a search of Jones's possessions, much less the placing of a tracking device on his car.

In a unanimous 9-0 vote, the Supreme Court in *United States v. Jones* (2012) sided with Jones. The Court rejected the government's argument that attaching a small device to a car's undercarriage was too trivial an act to constitute an "unreasonable search." The government had also claimed that anyone driving a car on public streets can expect to be monitored, even continuously in some circumstances—after all, police had legally been "tailing" suspects for decades. The Court rejected those arguments, though the justices disagreed on exactly why the Constitution prohibits what the officers had done. Five justices said that the Fourth Amendment's protection of "persons, houses, papers, and effects" reasonably extends to private property such as an automobile. For them, the fact that the officers had placed a tracking device on the suspect's property without a warrant invalidated the evidence. Four justices went further, saying that the officers' actions intruded not only on the suspect's property rights but also on his "reasonable expectation of privacy." At its core, they said, the Fourth Amendment "protects people, not places."[2]

As the case illustrates, issues of individual rights have become increasingly complex. The framers of the Constitution could not possibly have envisioned a time when technology would have enabled authorities to track people's locations electronically. The framers understood that authorities would sometimes be tempted to snoop on people, which is why they wrote the Fourth Amendment. At the same time, the amendment protects Americans not from *all* searches but from *unreasonable* searches. The public would be unsafe if law officials could never track a suspect. However, citizens would forfeit their privacy if police could track at will anyone of their choosing. The challenge for a civil society is to establish a level of police authority that meets the demands of public safety without infringing unduly on personal freedom. The balance point, however, is always subject to dispute. In this case, the Supreme Court sided with the accused. In other cases, it has sided with law enforcement officials.

This chapter examines issues of **civil liberties**—specific individual rights, such as the right to a fair trial, that are constitutionally protected against infringement by government. Although the term *civil liberties* is sometimes used interchangeably with the term *civil rights,* they differ. Civil rights (which will be examined in Chapter 5) are a question of whether members of differing groups—racial, sexual, religious, and the like—are treated equally by government and, in some cases, by private parties. By contrast, civil liberties are individual rights, such as freedom of speech and the press. Civil liberties are the subject of this chapter, which focuses on these points:

- *Freedom of expression is the most basic of democratic rights, but, like all rights, it is not unlimited.*

- *"Due process of law" refers to legal protections (primarily procedural safeguards) designed to ensure that individual rights are respected by government.*
- *Over the course of the nation's history, Americans' civil liberties have been expanded in law and been more fully protected by the courts.* Of special significance has been the Supreme Court's use of the Fourteenth Amendment to protect individual rights from action by state and local governments.
- *Individual rights are constantly being weighed against the collective interests of society.* All political institutions are involved in this process, as is public opinion, but the judiciary plays a central role and is the institution that is typically most protective of civil liberties.

THE BILL OF RIGHTS, THE FOURTEENTH AMENDMENT, AND SELECTIVE INCORPORATION

As was explained in Chapter 2, the Constitution's failure to enumerate individual freedoms led to demands for the **Bill of Rights**. Ratified in 1791, these first 10 amendments to the Constitution provide a set of rights that the federal government is obliged to protect. Among them are the freedoms of speech, press, assembly, and religion (First Amendment); the right to bear arms (Second Amendment); protection against unreasonable search and seizure (Fourth Amendment); protection against self-incrimination and double jeopardy (Fifth Amendment); the right to a jury trial, to an attorney, and to confront witnesses (Sixth Amendment); and protection against cruel and unusual punishment (Eighth Amendment).

At the time the Bill of Rights was adopted, it applied only to action by the federal government and not to action by the states, a position the Supreme Court affirmed a few decades later.[3] Today, however, most of the rights contained in the Bill of Rights are also protected from action by the state governments, a development resulting from adoption of the Fourteenth Amendment shortly after the Civil War.

When the war ended, several southern states enacted laws that denied newly freed slaves their rights, including the right to own property and to travel freely. Congress responded by passing a constitutional amendment that, if ratified, would protect their rights. The former Confederate states, with the exception of Tennessee, refused to ratify it. Congress then passed the Reconstruction Act, which placed the southern states under military rule until they did so. In 1868, the Fourteenth Amendment was ratified. It includes a **due process clause** that says "No State shall . . . deprive any person of life, liberty, or property, without due process of law."

Initially, the Supreme Court largely ignored the due process clause, allowing states to decide for themselves what rights their residents would have. In 1925, however, the Court changed course by invoking the Fourteenth Amendment in a case involving state government. Although the Court upheld a New York law that made it illegal to advocate the violent overthrow of the U.S. government, it ruled in *Gitlow v. New York* that states do not have total control over what their residents can legally say. The Court said, "For present purposes we may and do assume that freedom of speech and of the press— which are protected by the First Amendment from abridgement by Congress— are among the fundamental personal rights and 'liberties' protected by the due process clause of the Fourteenth Amendment from impairment by the states."[4]

The ruling marked a fundamental shift in constitutional doctrine. In essence, the Court had concluded that a right protected by the Bill of Rights from action by the federal government was now also protected from action by state governments. Shortly thereafter, in a series of cases, the Court applied the new doctrine to other First Amendment rights. The Court invalidated state laws restricting expression in the areas of speech (*Fiske v. Kansas*), press (*Near v. Minnesota*), religion (*Hamilton v. Regents, University of California*), and assembly and petition (*DeJonge v. Oregon*).[5] The *Near* decision is the best known of these rulings. Jay Near was the publisher of a Minneapolis weekly newspaper that regularly made defamatory statements about Blacks, Jews, Catholics, and labor union leaders. His paper was closed down on the basis of a Minnesota law banning "malicious, scandalous, or defamatory" publications. Near appealed to the Supreme Court, which ruled in his favor, saying that the Minnesota law was "the essence of censorship."[6]

Three decades later, the Supreme Court extended the principle to include the rights of the criminally accused. The breakthrough case was *Mapp v. Ohio* (1961). Police had forcibly entered the home of Dollree Mapp, saying they had a tip she was harboring a fugitive. They didn't find the suspect but handcuffed her, anyway, and rummaged through her possessions, where they found obscene photographs. Mapp was convicted of violating an Ohio law prohibiting the possession of pornographic material. The Supreme Court overturned her conviction, ruling that police had acted unconstitutionally, citing the Fourth Amendment prohibition on unreasonable searches and seizures. The Court held that evidence acquired through an unconstitutional search cannot be used to obtain a conviction in state courts.[7]

During the 1960s, the Court also ruled that defendants in state criminal proceedings must be provided a lawyer in felony cases if they cannot afford to hire one,[8] cannot be compelled to testify against themselves,[9] have the right to remain silent and to have legal counsel at the time of arrest,[10] have the right to confront witnesses who testify against them,[11] must be granted a speedy trial,[12] have the right to a jury trial in criminal proceedings,[13] and cannot be subjected to double jeopardy.[14]

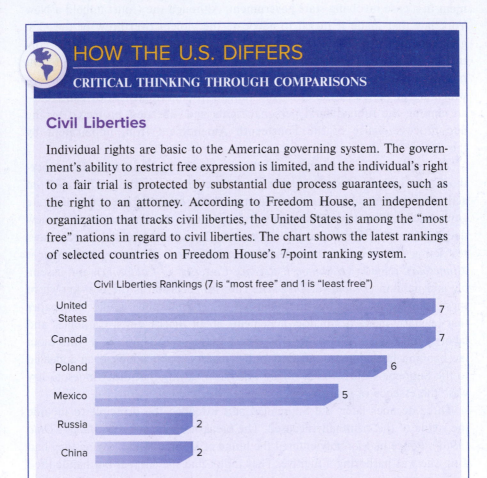

HOW THE U.S. DIFFERS

CRITICAL THINKING THROUGH COMPARISONS

Civil Liberties

Individual rights are basic to the American governing system. The government's ability to restrict free expression is limited, and the individual's right to a fair trial is protected by substantial due process guarantees, such as the right to an attorney. According to Freedom House, an independent organization that tracks civil liberties, the United States is among the "most free" nations in regard to civil liberties. The chart shows the latest rankings of selected countries on Freedom House's 7-point ranking system.

Civil Liberties Rankings (7 is "most free" and 1 is "least free")

United States	7
Canada	7
Poland	6
Mexico	5
Russia	2
China	2

Q: In addition to civil liberties, Freedom House ranks countries on "democratic rights," which include the right to vote and participate in free and fair elections. On this ranking, the U.S. receives a 6, which places it below Canada and several other democracies, all of which receive a 7. Why do you think the U.S. does not get the highest score on "democratic rights"?

A: Freedom House concludes that voter ID laws and other such policies effectively deprive some U.S. citizens of their right to vote and that excessive partisan gerrymandering makes elections in the U.S. less fair than those in some democracies.

In these various rulings, the Court was applying what came to be called the doctrine of **selective incorporation**—the use of the Fourteenth Amendment to apply selected provisions of the Bill of Rights to the states. In its *Mapp* ruling, for example, the Court incorporated the Fourth Amendment protection against unreasonable search and seizure into the Fourteenth Amendment, thereby protecting it from infringement by states and localities. (The incorporation process is selective in that the Supreme Court has chosen to protect some Bill of Rights guarantees, but not others, from state action. Even today, for example, the Seventh Amendment right to a jury trial in civil cases is not required of the states.)

Selective incorporation through the Fourteenth Amendment's due process clause has been of utmost importance. Because states and localities bear most of the responsibility for maintaining public order and safety, they are the authorities most likely to act in ways that infringe on people's rights. If they were allowed to determine for themselves what these rights mean in practice—for example, how far local police can go in interrogating suspects—Americans' rights would be at risk or, in some locations, ignored. As it stands, nearly all freedoms in the Bill of Rights are now national rights and under the protection of the federal courts.

In the sections that follow, the law and practice of Americans' civil liberties will be examined, starting with rights protected by the First Amendment.

FREEDOM OF EXPRESSION

The First Amendment provides for **freedom of expression**—the right of individual Americans to communicate ideas of their choosing (see Table 4-1). Some forms of expression are not protected by the First Amendment because

table 4-1	BILL OF RIGHTS: A SELECTED LIST OF FIRST AMENDMENT PROTECTIONS
First Amendment	
Speech: You are free to say almost anything except that which is obscene, slanders another person, or has a high probability of inciting others to take imminent lawless action.	
Press: You are free to write or publish almost anything except that which is obscene, libels another person, seriously endangers military action or national security, or has a high probability of inciting others to take imminent lawless action.	
Assembly: You are free to assemble, although government may regulate the time and place for reasons of public convenience and safety, provided such regulations are applied evenhandedly to all groups.	
Religion: You are protected from having the religious beliefs of others imposed on you, and you are free to believe what you like.	

the courts have concluded that they fall outside the civic realm. Some forms of "commercial speech" are of this type. For example, pharmaceutical companies in their public advertising are required by law to disclose the harmful side effects of drugs. Obscene forms of sexual expression—child pornography, as an example—also do not have First Amendment protection.*

The First Amendment had an inauspicious beginning. Although the First Amendment prohibits Congress from abridging freedom of expression, Congress ignored the restriction in passing the Sedition Act of 1798, which made it a crime to print newspaper stories critical of the president or other top national officials. Thomas Jefferson called the Sedition Act an "alarming infraction" of the Constitution and, upon replacing John Adams as president in 1801, pardoned those who had been convicted under it. However, the Sedition Act was not ruled on by the Supreme Court, which left open the question of whether Congress has the power to restrict free expression and, if so, how far its power extends.

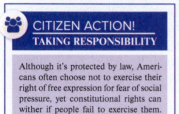

CITIZEN ACTION!
TAKING RESPONSIBILITY

Although it's protected by law, Americans often choose not to exercise their right of free expression for fear of social pressure, yet constitutional rights can wither if people fail to exercise them. Think of an issue that you care about but that is unpopular in your college or community. Consider writing a letter on the issue to the editor of your college or local newspaper.

Today, free expression is vigorously protected by the courts. Like other rights, it is not absolute in practice. Free expression does not entitle individuals to say whatever they want to whomever they want. Free expression can be denied, for example, if it endangers national security, wrongly damages the reputation of others, or deprives others of their basic rights. Nevertheless, in nearly every situation Americans can freely express their political views without fear of government interference or retribution.

Free Speech

Until the 20th century, free expression was rarely at issue in the United States. However, as the country began to get enmeshed in world affairs and face threats from abroad, the government started to restrict expression that it believed was a danger to national security. One of the first restrictions was the 1917 Espionage Act, which prohibited forms of dissent that could harm the nation's effort in World War I.

This legislation became the object of the first-ever Supreme Court free-expression ruling. In *Schenck v. United States* (1919), the Supreme Court upheld the conviction of defendants who had distributed leaflets urging draft-age men to refuse

---

*Although the Supreme Court has categorically excluded child pornography from First Amendment protection, it has struggled otherwise to develop a legal test for determining whether sexual material is obscene. It has said that such material must be of a "particularly offensive type" and must be perceived as such by a "reasonable person," but in practice the Court has had trouble applying that standard, or any other, in determining the sexually explicit material that adults are not allowed to produce, see, or possess.

induction into the military service. Writing for a unanimous Court, Justice Oliver Wendell Holmes upheld the constitutionality of the Espionage Act, saying that Congress had the authority to restrict expression that posed "a clear and present danger" to the nation's security. In a famous passage, Holmes argued that not even the First Amendment would permit a person to falsely yell "Fire!" in a crowded theater and create a panic that could kill or injure innocent people.[15]

Although the *Schenck* decision upheld a law that limited free expression, it also established a constitutional standard—the **clear-and-present-danger test**— for determining when government could legally do so. To meet the test, the government has to demonstrate that spoken or written expression presents a clear and present danger before it can prohibit the expression. (The use of a "test" to judge the limits of government's authority is a common practice of the Supreme Court.)

In the early 1950s, the Court applied the clear-and-present-danger test in upholding the convictions of 11 members of the U.S. Communist Party who had been prosecuted under a federal law (the Smith Act of 1940) that made it illegal to advocate the forceful overthrow of the U.S. government.[16] The Court concluded that "the gravity of the 'evil' . . . justifies such invasion of free speech as necessary to avoid the danger."

By the late 1950s, Americans had come to realize that fears of a communist takeover of the U.S. government were unfounded. The Supreme Court abruptly switched its position, concluding that words alone were not a threat to the nation's security.[17] Ever since, it has held that national security must be clearly and substantially endangered before government can lawfully prohibit citizens from speaking out. Because the spoken word rarely poses that kind of threat, Americans are largely free to say what they want about politics. Over the past six decades, which includes the Vietnam and Iraq Wars, not a single individual has been convicted solely for criticizing the government's war policies. (Some dissenters have been found guilty on other grounds, such as destroying property or assaulting a police officer.)

In addition to curbing the federal government's attempts to limit free speech, the Supreme Court has moved to protect speech from actions by the states. A defining case was *Brandenburg v. Ohio* (1969). In a speech at a Ku Klux Klan rally, Clarence Brandenburg said that "revenge" might have to be taken if the national government "continues to suppress the white Caucasian race." He was convicted under an Ohio law, but the Supreme Court overturned the conviction, saying a state cannot prohibit speech that advocates the unlawful use of force unless it meets a two-part test: First, the speech must be "directed at inciting or producing imminent lawless action" and, second, it must be "likely to produce such action."[18] This test—the likelihood of **imminent lawless action**—is an imposing barrier to any government attempt to restrict speech. It is extremely rare for words alone to lead others to engage in rioting or other immediate forms of lawless action.

The imminent lawless action test gives Americans the freedom to express nearly any political opinion they want, including "hate speech." In a unanimous 1992 opinion, the Court struck down a St. Paul, Minnesota, ordinance making it a crime to engage in speech likely to arouse "anger or alarm" on the basis of "race, color, creed, religion or gender." The Court said that the First Amendment prohibits government from "silencing speech on the basis of its content."[19] (This protection of hate *speech* does not extend to hate *crimes,* such as assault, motivated by racial or other prejudice. A Wisconsin law that allowed lengthier sentences for hate crimes was challenged as a violation of the First Amendment. In a unanimous 1993 opinion, the Court said that the law was aimed not at free speech but at "conduct unprotected by the First Amendment."[20])

Few cases illustrate more clearly the extent to which Americans are free to speak their minds than does *Snyder v. Phelps* (2011). Pastor Fred Phelps of the Westboro Baptist Church (WBC) led a protest demonstration at the funeral of Matthew Snyder, a U.S. Marine killed in Iraq. Like its protests at other military funerals, WBC's protest at Snyder's funeral service was directed at what the WBC claims is America's tolerance of gays and lesbians. Displaying signs such as "Fag troops" and "Thank God for dead soldiers," the protesters were otherwise orderly and stayed three blocks away from the memorial service.

Despite the inflammatory nature of their signs and slogans, which members of the Westboro Baptist Church have displayed at numerous military funerals and other events, the Supreme Court has ruled that their actions are protected by the First Amendment. (Enigma/Alamy Stock Photo)

Detecting Misinformation

Do You Have a Right to Speak Freely on Campus?

Eric Crama/Shutterstock

The Supreme Court holds that there are substantial limits on government's ability to restrict free expression. Government is not allowed to regulate the content of speech—your opinion has as much protection as anyone else's. At many colleges, both public and private, there have been instances when students have sought to prevent invited speakers from delivering a talk because they disagreed with what the speaker represented or was likely to say. Some students have assumed that their right of free expression includes the right to shout down or disrupt a speaker with whom they disagree.

Is that claim fact, or is it fake?

Students have substantial free-speech rights, but they're not as broad as in some situations. The Supreme Court has ruled that speech in a school setting can be limited if it is disruptive of "the educational mission." Moreover, students are governed by their college's code of conduct. Speech that violates the code is not typically protected. Students who violate it can be subject to disciplinary action by their college, though they have due process rights, including the right to be informed of the charge and the basis for it, as well as an opportunity to contest it. Finally, even free-speech rights that are protected in a campus setting do not extend to hostile actions. It is permissible for you to voice your disagreement with the opinions of others but not to physically threaten them.

Snyder's father sued the WBC for "emotional distress" and was awarded $5 million in a federal trial. In an 8-1 decision, the Supreme Court overturned the award, holding that WBC's protest, although "hurtful," was protected by the First Amendment.[21]

The Supreme Court's protection of **symbolic speech** (action, not words) has been nearly as strong as its protection of verbal speech. In 1989, for example, the Court ruled that the symbolic burning of the American flag is a lawful form of expression. The ruling came in the case of Gregory Lee Johnson, who had set fire to a flag outside the hall in Dallas where the 1984 Republican National Convention was being held. The Supreme Court rejected the state of Texas's argument that flag burning is, in every instance, an imminent danger to public safety. "If there is a bedrock principle underlying the First Amendment," the Court said, "it is that the Government may not prohibit the expression of an idea simply because society finds the idea itself offensive or disagreeable."[22]

In general, the Supreme Court has held that government regulation of the *content* of a message is unconstitutional. In the flag-burning case, for example, Texas was regulating the content of the message—contempt for the flag and the principles it represents. Texas could not have been regulating the act itself in that the Texas government's own method of disposing of worn-out flags is to burn them.

Free Assembly

In a key case involving freedom of assembly, the U.S. Supreme Court in 1977 upheld a lower-court ruling against local ordinances of Skokie, Illinois, that had been invoked to prevent a parade there by the American Nazi Party.[23] Skokie had a large Jewish population, including survivors of Nazi Germany's concentration camps. The Supreme Court held that the right of free assembly takes precedence over the mere *possibility* that the exercise of that right might have undesirable consequences. Before government can lawfully prevent a speech or rally, it must demonstrate that the event will likely cause harm and must show that it lacks an alternative way (such as assigning extra police officers to control the crowd) to prevent the harm from happening.

The Supreme Court has recognized that freedom of speech and assembly may conflict with the routines of daily life. Accordingly, individuals do not have the right to hold a public rally at a busy intersection during rush hour or the right to turn up the volume on loudspeakers to the point that they can be heard from miles away. The Court allows public officials to regulate the time, place, and conditions of public assembly, provided the regulations are reasonable and are applied fairly to all groups, whatever their issue.[24]

Press Freedom and Libel Law

Freedom of the press also receives strong judicial protection. In *New York Times Co. v. United States* (1971), the Court ruled that the *Times*'s publication of the "Pentagon Papers" (secret government documents revealing that officials had deceived the public about aspects of the Vietnam War) could not be blocked by the government, which claimed that publication would harm the war effort. The documents had been obtained illegally by antiwar activists, who gave them to the *Times*. The Court ruled that "any system of prior restraints" on the press is unconstitutional unless the government can provide a compelling reason the material should not be published.[25]

The unacceptability of **prior restraint**—government prohibition of speech or publication before it occurs—is basic to the current doctrine of press freedom. The Supreme Court has said that attempts by government to prevent expression carry "a 'heavy presumption' against its constitutionality."[26] One exception is wartime reporting; in some circumstances, the government can censor news reports that contain information that could compromise a military operation or risk the lives of American troops.

The constitutional right of free expression is not a legal license to avoid responsibility for the consequences of what is said or written. Although news outlets and individuals cannot ordinarily be stopped from speaking out, they can be held responsible for the impact of what they say. If false information harmful to a person's reputation is published (**libel**) or spoken (**slander**), the injured party can sue for damages. Nevertheless, slander and libel laws in the United States are based on the assumption that society has an interest in encouraging news organizations and citizens to express themselves freely. Accordingly, public officials can be criticized nearly at will without fear that the writer or speaker will have to pay them damages for slander or libel. (The courts are less protective of the writer or speaker when allegations are made about a private citizen. What is said about private individuals is considered to be less basic to the democratic process than what is said about public officials.)

The Supreme Court has held that factually accurate statements, no matter how damaging to a public official's reputation, are a protected form of expression.[27] Even false statements enjoy considerable legal protection. In *New York Times Co. v. Sullivan* (1964), the Supreme Court overruled an Alabama state court that had found the *New York Times* guilty of libel for publishing an advertisement that claimed Alabama officials had mistreated civil rights activists. Although only some of the allegations were true, the Supreme Court backed the *Times,* saying that libel of a public official requires proof of actual malice, which is defined as a knowing or reckless disregard for the truth.[28] It is hard to prove that a news outlet recklessly or knowingly published a false accusation. In fact, no federal official has won a libel judgment against a news outlet in the more than five decades since the *Sullivan* ruling.

FREEDOM OF RELIGION

Free religious expression is the forerunner of free political expression, at least within the English tradition of limited government. England's Glorious, or Bloodless, Revolution of 1689 resulted in the Act of Toleration, which gave members of Protestant sects the right to worship freely and publicly. The First Amendment reflects this tradition; it protects religious freedom, as well as political expression.

In regard to religion, the First Amendment reads "Congress shall make no law respecting an establishment of religion, or prohibiting the free exercise thereof." Two clauses are contained in those words, one referring to the "establishment of religion" (the establishment clause) and the other referring to the "free exercise" of religion (the free-exercise clause).

The Establishment Clause

The **establishment clause** has been interpreted by the Supreme Court to mean that government may not favor one religion over another or support religion over no religion. (This position contrasts with that of a country such as England, where Anglicanism is the official, or "established," state religion, though no religion is prohibited.)

To this end, the Court has largely prohibited religious practices in public schools. A leading case was *Engel v. Vitale* (1962), which held that the establishment clause prohibits the reciting of prayers in public schools.[29] A year later, the Court struck down Bible readings in public schools.[30] Efforts to bring religion into the schools in less direct ways have also been invalidated. For example, an Alabama law attempted to circumvent the prayer ruling by permitting public schools to set aside one minute each day for silent prayer or meditation. In 1985, the Court declared the law unconstitutional, saying that "government must pursue a course of complete neutrality toward religion."[31]

Families have different beliefs about religion, which is a reason the Supreme Court has blocked schools from imposing particular religious beliefs on children, who are more susceptible than adults to what those in authority tell them is true. The Court has been less strict about the expression of religious messages in other contexts. Congress and state legislatures, for example, open their sessions with a prayer, which the Court accepts as a long-standing tradition.

The Court also takes tradition into account in determining whether religious displays on public property will be allowed. Because of the prominence of religion in American life, many public buildings display religious symbols. For instance, a statue of Moses holding the Ten Commandments stands in the rotunda of the Library of Congress building, which opened in 1897. Legal challenges to such displays have rarely succeeded.[32] In contrast, the Supreme Court in 2005 ordered the removal of displays of the Ten Commandments on the walls of two Kentucky courthouses. The displays were recent and had initially hung alone on the courtroom walls. Only after county officials were sued did they place a few historical displays alongside the religious ones. The Supreme Court concluded that the officials had a religious purpose in mind when they erected the displays and had to remove them.[33]

Although the Court can be said to have applied the *wall-of-separation doctrine* (a strict separation of church and state) in these rulings, it has also relied upon what is called the *accommodation doctrine*. This doctrine allows government to aid religious activity if no preference is shown toward a particular religion and if the assistance is of a nonreligious nature. In applying the doctrine, the Court at times has used a test articulated in *Lemon v. Kurtzman* (1971), a case involving state funding of the salaries of religious school instructors who teach secular subjects, such as math and English. In its ruling, the Court articulated a three-point test that has come to be known as the **Lemon test**. Government policy must meet all three conditions for it to be lawful: First, the policy must have a nonreligious purpose; second, its primary effect must be one that neither advances nor inhibits religion; third, the policy must not foster "an excessive government entanglement with religion."[34]

In the *Lemon* case, the Court held that state funding of the salaries of religious school teachers failed the test. The Court concluded that such payments involve "excessive government entanglement with religion" because an instructor, even though teaching a subject such as math or science, could use the classroom as a time to engage in religious teaching. In contrast, the Court in another case allowed states to pay for math, science, and other secular textbooks used in church-affiliated schools, concluding that the textbooks contained little if any religious content.[35]

The Supreme Court departed from its wall-of-separation doctrine in a 2020 ruling that invalidated a Montana law that denied scholarship funds for students attending religious schools but granted them to those attending secular private schools. Writing for the majority in a 5-4 decision, Chief Justice John Roberts said, "A state need not subsidize private education. But once a state decides to do so, it cannot disqualify some private schools solely because they are religious." In her dissent, Justice Sonia Sotomayor said the majority opinion "weakens this country's longstanding commitment to a separation of church and state beneficial to both."[36]

The Free-Exercise Clause

The First and Fourteenth Amendments also prohibit government interference with the free exercise of religion. The **free-exercise clause** has been interpreted to mean that Americans are free to hold religious beliefs of their choosing. However, Americans are not completely free to act on their beliefs. The Supreme Court has allowed government interference when the exercise of religious beliefs conflicts with otherwise valid law. An example is court-ordered medical care for gravely ill children whose parents have denied them treatment on religious grounds.

In a key free-exercise decision (*Burwell v. Hobby Lobby Stores*), the Supreme Court in 2014 held that "closely held" companies (those with only a few owners) are not required to include contraceptives in their employees' health insurance coverage if the owners object on religious grounds,. The case stemmed from the 2010 Affordable Care Act, which required companies that provide employee health insurance to include contraceptives. The Court's majority said the requirement violates the owners' free-exercise rights if the use of contraceptives violates their religious beliefs. A 2020 Supreme Court ruling expanded the number of employers and religious groups that can deny contraceptive coverage because of "religious and conscientious objections."[37]

In a 2018 ruling, *Masterpiece Cakeshop v. Colorado Civil Rights Commission*, the Supreme Court sided with a bakery that had refused to provide a wedding cake for the marriage of a same-sex couple, concluding that the civil rights commission had violated the baker's free-exercise rights by showing religious hostility toward him in its deliberations. The Court chose not to issue a broad ruling on the intersection of antidiscrimination laws and the free exercise of religion, thus leaving open the question of how far a business can go in invoking religious freedom as a reason for denial of goods or services.[38]

The free exercise of religion can clash with the prohibition on the establishment of religion, and the Supreme Court in these instances is forced to choose between them. In 1987, for example, the Court overturned a Louisiana law that required creationism (the Bible's account of how God created life in seven days about 10,000 years ago) to be taught along with the theory of evolution (the scientific account of how life evolved over millions of years) in public school science courses. The Court held that creationism is a religious doctrine, not a scientific theory, and that its inclusion in public school curricula violates the establishment clause by promoting a religious belief.[39] Many Christians believe in creationism, and some of them see the Court's ruling as a violation of the free-exercise clause because it forces students who believe in creationism to study a version of creation—evolution—that contradicts their religious beliefs.

A Pew Research Center survey found that about one in five Americans believe that life was created by God in its present form about 10,000 years ago. Some Americans believe that their version (creationism) of human origin should be taught in public school science classes where the theory of evolution is taught. The Supreme Court has rejected that position, holding that creationism is a religious doctrine and that teaching it in public schools would violate the First Amendment ban on the establishment of religion. Shown here is artwork depicting Adam and Eve, who creationists believe were the first humans. The artwork is located at the Basilica of the Most Holy Annunciation in Florence, Italy. (Conde/Shutterstock)

THE RIGHT TO BEAR ARMS

The Second Amendment to the Constitution says, "A well regulated Militia, being necessary to the security of a free State, the right of the people to keep and bear Arms shall not be infringed." The amendment is widely understood to prevent the federal government from abolishing state militias (such as National Guard units), but there has been disagreement over whether the amendment also gives individuals the right to possess weapons outside their use in military service.

Remarkably, more than two centuries passed before the Supreme Court addressed the issue of how the Second Amendment was to be interpreted. In *District of Columbia v. Heller* (2008), the Court said that "the Second Amendment protects an individual right to possess a firearm unconnected with service in a militia, and to use that arm for traditionally lawful purposes, such as self-defense within the home." The ruling struck down a District of Columbia law that had banned the possession of handguns, but not rifles or shotguns, within the district's boundaries. Writing for the 5–4 majority, Justice Antonin Scalia said that the justices were "aware of the problem of handgun violence in this country." However, Scalia concluded, "The enshrinement of constitutional rights necessarily takes certain policy choices off the table. These include the

The Supreme Court has ruled that gun ownership is protected by the Second Amendment but has not said how far that protection extends. (Ryan Rodrick Beiler/Shutterstock)

absolute prohibition of handguns held and used for self-defense in the home."[40] In a sharply worded dissent, Justice John Paul Stevens said the majority had devised a ruling that fit its partisan agenda rather than what the framers intended. Stevens declared, "When each word in the text is given full effect, the Amendment is most naturally read to secure to the people a right to use and possess arms in conjunction with service in a well-regulated militia. So far as it appears, no more than that was contemplated by its drafters."

The District of Columbia is federal territory, so the *Heller* ruling applied only to the federal government. However, in a 2010 decision, *McDonald v. Chicago,* the Supreme Court, through selective incorporation, applied the same standard to state and local governments in striking down a Chicago ordinance that banned handgun possession.[41] In this and the *Heller* ruling, the Court did not prohibit all gun restrictions, such as bans on gun ownership by former felons. However, the Court did not list all of the allowable restrictions, leaving the issue to be determined in future cases.

THE RIGHT OF PRIVACY

Until the 1960s, Americans' constitutional rights were confined largely to those listed in the Bill of Rights. This situation prevailed despite the Ninth Amendment, which reads "The enumeration of the Constitution, of certain rights, shall not be construed to deny or disparage others retained by the people." In 1965, however, the Supreme Court added to the list of individual rights, declaring that Americans have "a right of privacy." This judgment derived from the case of *Griswold v. Connecticut,* which challenged a state law prohibiting the use of condoms and other birth control devices, even by married couples. The Supreme Court struck down the law, concluding that a state has no business dictating a married couple's method of birth control. Rather than invoking the Ninth Amendment, the Court's majority reasoned that the freedoms in the Bill of Rights imply an underlying **right of privacy**. The Court held that individuals have a "zone of [personal] privacy" that government cannot lawfully invade.[42]

Although the right of privacy has not been applied broadly by the Supreme Court, it has been invoked in two major areas—a woman's right to choose an abortion and consensual relations among same-sex adults.

Abortion

The right of privacy was the basis for the Supreme Court's ruling in *Roe v. Wade* (1973), which gave women full freedom to choose abortion during the first three months of pregnancy. In overturning a Texas law banning abortion except to save the life of the mother, the Court said that the right of privacy is "broad enough to encompass a woman's decision whether or not to terminate her pregnancy."[43]

The *Roe* decision provoked sharply different responses that continue to this day (see "Party Polarization: Pro-Life Versus Pro-Choice"). Although failing in their attempts to get a constitutional amendment that would ban abortion, anti-abortion activists have succeeded in limiting access to abortion. They persuaded the Missouri legislature to pass a law that prohibits abortions from being performed in the state's publicly funded medical facilities, a policy that the Supreme Court upheld in *Webster v. Reproductive Health Services* (1989).[44] Then, in *Planned Parenthood v. Casey* (1992), the Court upheld a Pennsylvania law that requires a minor to have parental or judicial consent before obtaining an abortion. The Court said that such restrictions are constitutional as as long as they do not impose an "undue burden" on the woman.[45] The Court has also upheld a complete ban on what is termed a partial-birth abortion on grounds that it does not impose an undue burden on women. The ban was contained in a bill enacted by Congress in 2007, which provides for a fine and prison term for a physician who performs an abortion when the mother is giving birth, even if her life or health is in danger. That ruling drew a sharp dissent from Justice Ruth Bader Ginsberg, who was the only woman on the Supreme Court at the time. She argued that the ruling put women's lives and health at risk.[46]

Conflicting Ideas

Pro-Life Versus Pro-Choice

Since the Supreme Court ruled in *Roe v. Wade* (1973) that a woman has a constitutional right to choose abortion, every Republican Party national platform has expressed opposition to abortion. In the same period, every Democratic Party national platform has had a pro-choice plank. A sharp divide over the abortion issue also exists between self-identified Democratic and Republican voters, as the following graph shows.

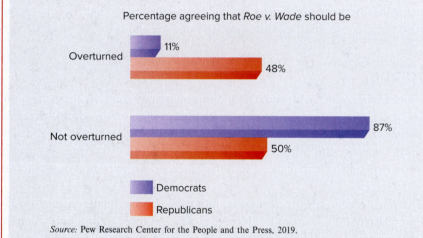

Percentage agreeing that *Roe v. Wade* should be

Overturned — 11% / 48%

Not overturned — 87% / 50%

Democrats
Republicans

Source: Pew Research Center for the People and the Press, 2019.

Q: Do you think there is a "middle ground" that could bring Republicans and Democrats together on the abortion issue? Or is the moral and political divide over the issue so great that no compromise is possible?

On the other hand, the Supreme Court in 2020 struck down a Louisiana law that would have required abortion providers to have admitting privileges at a hospital within 30 miles of the abortion clinic. Because abortions rarely have complications, physicians at abortion clinics seldom seek admitting privileges, which in any case can be denied by the local hospital. The Louisiana law would effectively have forced two of the state's three abortion clinics to close. In its 5-4 decision in *June Medical Services v. Russo*, the Supreme Court invalidated the law on grounds that it imposed an undue burden on women seeking an abortion.[47]

Consensual Sexual Relations Between Same-Sex Adults

Although the Supreme Court's 1965 *Griswold* ruling on contraceptive use was widely said to have taken "government out of people's bedrooms," an exception remained. Every state prohibited sexual relations between consenting adults of the same sex. Over the next two decades, many states eliminated this prohibition and others stopped enforcing it. Nevertheless, in a 1986 Georgia case, *Bowers v. Hardwick,* the Supreme Court held that the right of privacy did not extend to consensual sexual relations between adults of the same sex.[48]

Less than two decades later, the Supreme Court reversed its position, ruling by 6–3 in *Lawrence v. Texas* (2003) that sodomy laws violate "the right of privacy" implied by the grant of liberty in the Fourteenth Amendment's due process clause.[49] The Court held that states cannot lawfully ban sexual relations between consenting same-sex adults. (In 2015, the Supreme Court legalized marriage for same-sex couples, a subject discussed in Chapter 5.)

RIGHTS OF PERSONS ACCUSED OF CRIMES

Due process refers to legal protections that have been established to preserve the rights of individuals. The most significant of these protections is **procedural due process**; the term refers primarily to procedures that authorities must follow before a person can lawfully be punished for an offense.

No system of justice is foolproof. Even in the most careful systems, innocent people have been wrongly accused, convicted, and punished with imprisonment or death. But the scrupulous application of procedural safeguards, such as a defendant's right to legal counsel, greatly increases the likelihood of a fair trial. "The history of liberty has largely been the history of the observance of procedural guarantees," said Justice Felix Frankfurter in *McNabb v. United States* (1943).[50]

The U.S. Constitution offers procedural safeguards designed to protect a person from wrongful arrest, conviction, and punishment. The Fifth and Fourteenth Amendments provide generally that no person can be deprived of life, liberty, or property without due process of law. Specific procedural protections for the accused are listed in the Fourth, Fifth, Sixth, and Eighth Amendments.[51] (See Table 4-2.)

Suspicion Phase: Unreasonable Search and Seizure

In 1766, Parliamentary leader William Pitt forcefully expressed a principle of English common law: "The poorest man may, in his cottage, bid defiance to all the forces of the Crown. It may be frail; its roof may shake; the wind may blow through it; the rain may enter; but the King of England may not enter;

table 4-2	BILL OF RIGHTS: A SELECTED LIST OF DUE PROCESS PROTECTIONS
Fourth Amendment	**Sixth Amendment**
Search and seizure: You are protected from unreasonable searches and seizures, although you forfeit that right if you knowingly waive it. **Arrest:** You are protected from arrest unless authorities have probable cause to believe that you have committed a crime.	**Counsel:** You have a right to be represented by an attorney and can demand to speak first with an attorney before responding to questions from law enforcement officials. **Prompt and reasonable proceedings:** You have a right to be arraigned promptly, to be informed of the charges, to confront witnesses, and to have a speedy and open trial by an impartial jury.
Fifth Amendment	**Eighth Amendment**
Self-incrimination: You are protected against self-incrimination, which means that you have the right to remain silent and to be protected against coercion by law enforcement officials. **Double jeopardy:** You cannot be tried twice for the same crime if the first trial results in acquittal. **Due process:** You cannot be deprived of life, liberty, or property without proper legal proceedings.	**Bail:** You are protected against excessive bail or fines. **Cruel and unusual punishment:** You are protected from cruel and unusual punishment, although this provision does not protect you from the death penalty or from a long prison term for a minor offense.

all his force dares not cross the threshold."[52] In the period immediately preceding the American Revolution, few things provoked more anger among the colonists than Britain's disregard for the sanctity of the home. British soldiers regularly forced their way into colonists' houses, looking for documents or other evidence of anti-British activity.

The Fourth Amendment was included in the Bill of Rights to prohibit such actions by the U.S. government. The Fourth Amendment reads "The right of the people to be secure in their persons, houses, papers, and effects, against unreasonable searches and seizures, shall not be violated, and no Warrants shall issue, but upon probable cause, supported by Oath or affirmation, and particularly describing the place to be searched, and the persons or things to be seized."

The Fourth Amendment protects individuals against arbitrary police action. Although a person caught in the act of a crime can be arrested (seized) and searched for weapons and incriminating evidence, the police ordinarily cannot search an individual merely on the basis of suspicion. In such instances, they have to convince a judge that they have "probable cause" (sufficient evidence) to believe that a suspect is engaged in criminal activity. If the judge concludes that the evidence is strong enough, the police will be granted a search warrant. The Supreme Court has also held that police must have a search warrant to investigate a suspect using modern technology, such as a listening or thermal-imaging device.[53]

In a unanimous 2014 decision, the Supreme Court delivered what many legal experts consider a landmark ruling. At issue were two cases, one from California and the other from Massachusetts, in which police, without a warrant, searched a suspect's cell phone after an arrest. In each case, they found information implicating the suspect. In *Riley v. California* and *United States v. Wurie,* the Court noted that, although police upon making an arrest can normally search a suspect and seize relevant physical items (such as weapons or drugs), cell phones and similar electronic devices are different in kind in that they contain large amounts of personal information (see "Case Study: *Riley v. California* (2014)"). The Court noted that "a cell phone search would typically expose to the government far more than the most exhaustive search of a house." The Court acknowledged that its ruling would make the work of police more difficult but said the protection of Americans' constitutional rights took priority. "We cannot deny that our decision today will have an impact on the ability of law enforcement to combat crime," said the Court. "Privacy comes at a cost."[54]

C A S E
STUDY

Politics in Action

Riley v. California (2014)

The Fourth Amendment says "The right of the people to be secure in their persons, homes, papers, and effects, against unreasonable searches and seizures, shall not be violated." However, the Constitution does not distinguish between "unreasonable" search and seizure, which is prohibited, and "reasonable" search and seizure, which is permitted.

The Supreme Court addressed that issue in a key 2014 case, *Riley v. California*. David Riley had been pulled over by San Diego

Photographs in the Carol M. Highsmith Archive, Library of Congress, Prints and Photographs Division.

Continued

police in 2009 for having an expired vehicle registration tag. As it turned out, he also had a suspended driver's license, which, under California law, requires the vehicle to be towed. In such instances, officers must list the vehicle's contents to prevent the owner from later claiming that property had been stolen from it. In doing the inventory, police found two loaded handguns hidden under the vehicle's hood. Riley was a known gang member, and having a loaded handgun in a car is a criminal offense in California. Police arrested Riley, took his cell phone, and downloaded information from it that implicated him in a gang shooting. He was convicted of the shooting.

Riley appealed his conviction, arguing that police had violated his right to protection against unreasonable search and seizure. In a 9–0 ruling, the Supreme Court ruled in Riley's favor. The Court noted that cell phones and similar electronic devices can contain a significant amount of personal information. The Court said that to equate such devices to physical objects such as weapons "is like saying a ride on horseback is materially indistinguishable from a flight to the moon." The Court likened a cell phone to a home, saying that both contain large amounts of personal information. Since police cannot normally search a person's home without getting a search warrant from a judge, a warrant is also required in *most* circumstances before a cell phone search. Police had failed to seek a warrant in Riley's case, and the Supreme Court held that the evidence gathered from his cell phone could not be used against him at trial.

Q: Do you agree with the Court's reasoning in the *Riley* case? Can you think of circumstances in which police could lawfully search a suspect's cell phone without first getting a warrant?

ASK YOURSELF: Is a suspect's cell phone fundamentally different in kind from physical items, such as drugs, found on a suspect? What about a situation in which police have solid reason to believe the suspect's cell phone has information that could prevent an imminent criminal act by the suspect's accomplices, such as a terrorist attack or bank robbery? Would a warrantless search be legal in that type of situation?

The Supreme Court extended digital-age search and seizure protection in *Carpenter v. United States* (2018). At issue was a warrantless search in which police obtained from a suspect's cell phone provider a record of the locations from which he had placed calls. The locations matched those where the individual was suspected of having committed crimes, which contributed to his conviction. In a 5–4 decision, the Court held that government violates the Fourth Amendment when it obtains records of the physical locations of a cell phone without a search warrant.

The Supreme Court allows warrantless searches in some circumstances. For example, the Court has generally given school administrators wide latitude to search students for drugs and weapons on the grounds that school administrators bear responsibility for the safety of other students.[55] The Court has also held, for example, that police roadblocks to check drivers for signs of intoxication are legal as long as the action is systematic and not arbitrary (for example, stopping only young drivers would be unconstitutional, whereas stopping all drivers is acceptable). The Court justified this decision by saying that roadblocks serve an important highway safety objective.[56] However, the Court prohibits police roadblocks to check for drugs. The Court has held that narcotics roadblocks serve a general law enforcement purpose rather than one specific to highway safety and thereby violate the Fourth Amendment's requirement that police must have suspicion of wrongdoing before they can search an individual's auto.[57]

Arrest Phase: Protection Against Self-Incrimination

The Fifth Amendment says, in part, that an individual cannot "be compelled in any criminal case to be a witness against himself." This provision is designed to protect individuals from the age-old practice of coerced confession. Trickery, torture, and the threat of an extra-long prison sentence can lead people to confess to crimes they did not commit.

At the time of arrest, police cannot legally begin their interrogation, even a preliminary one,[58] until the suspect has been warned that his or her words can be used as evidence. This warning requirement emerged from *Miranda v. Arizona* (1966), which centered on Ernesto Miranda's confession to kidnapping and rape during police questioning. The Supreme Court overturned his conviction on the grounds that police had not informed him of his right to remain silent and to have legal assistance. The Court reasoned that suspects have a right to know their rights.[59] The Court's ruling led to the formulation of the "Miranda warning" that police are now required to read to suspects: "You have the right to remain silent. . . . Anything you say can and will be used against you in a court of law. . . . You have the right to an attorney." (Ernesto Miranda was subsequently retried and convicted on the basis of evidence other than his confession.)

Trial Phase: The Right to a Fair Trial

The right to a fair trial is basic to any reasonable notion of justice. If the trial process is arbitrary or biased against the defendant, justice is denied. It is

MIRANDA WARNING

1. YOU HAVE THE RIGHT TO REMAIN SILENT.

2. ANYTHING YOU SAY CAN AND WILL BE USED AGAINST YOU IN A COURT OF LAW.

3. YOU HAVE THE RIGHT TO TALK TO A LAWYER AND HAVE HIM PRESENT WITH YOU WHILE YOU ARE BEING QUESTIONED.

4. IF YOU CANNOT AFFORD TO HIRE A LAWYER. ONE WILL BE APPOINTED TO REPRESENT YOU BEFORE ANY QUESTIONING IF YOU WISH.

5. YOU CAN DECIDE AT ANY TIME TO EXERCISE THESE RIGHTS AND NOT ANSWER ANY QUESTIONS OR MAKE ANY STATEMENTS.

WAIVER

DO YOU UNDERSTAND EACH OF THESE RIGHTS I HAVE EXPLAINED TO YOU? HAVING THESE RIGHTS IN MIND. DO YOU WISH TO TALK TO US NOW?

Shown here is a reproduction of the Miranda warning card that FBI agents carry. Agents are required in most instances to read suspects their rights before interrogating them. The Miranda warning includes the Fifth Amendment right to remain silent and the Sixth Amendment right to have an attorney.

sometimes said the American justice system is based on the principle that it is better to let one hundred guilty parties go free than to convict one innocent person. The system does not actually work that way. Once a person has been charged with a crime, prosecutors work to get a conviction. Defendants in such instances have fair-trial guarantees that are intended to protect them from wrongful conviction.

Legal Counsel and Impartial Jury   Under the Fifth Amendment, suspects charged with a *federal* crime cannot be tried unless indicted by a grand jury. The grand jury hears the prosecution's evidence and decides whether it is strong enough to allow the government to try the suspect. (This protection has not been incorporated into the Fourteenth Amendment. As a result, states are not required to use grand juries, although roughly half of them do so. In the rest of the states, the prosecutor usually decides whether to proceed with a trial.)

The Sixth Amendment provides a right to legal counsel before and during trial. But what if a person cannot afford a lawyer? For most of the nation's history, poor people had no choice but to defend themselves. Then, in *Johnson v. Zerbst* (1938), the Supreme Court held that criminal defendants in federal cases must be provided a lawyer at government expense if they cannot afford one.[60] The Court extended this requirement to include state cases with its ruling in *Gideon v. Wainwright* (1963). This case centered on Clarence Gideon, who had been convicted in a Florida court of breaking into a pool hall. He had asked for a lawyer, but the trial judge denied the request, forcing Gideon to act as his own attorney. He appealed his conviction, and the Supreme Court overturned it on grounds that he did not have adequate legal counsel.[61]

(In his retrial, a Florida jury found Gideon not guilty. His lawyer was able to show that other men had committed the crime and then lied to say Gideon had done it.)

Criminal defendants also have the right to a speedy trial and to confront witnesses against them. At the federal level and sometimes at the state level, they have a right to jury trial, which is to be heard by an "impartial jury." The Court has ruled that a jury's impartiality in capital cases can be compromised if the prosecution stacks a jury by using peremptory challenges to remove from the jury anyone who expresses doubt about the appropriateness of the death penalty. To allow that practice, the Court ruled, is to virtually guarantee "a verdict of death" by a "hanging jury."[62] The jury's racial makeup can also be an issue, a concern that dates to a period in the South when Blacks accused of crimes against whites were tried by all-white juries, which invariably returned a guilty verdict. The Supreme Court outlawed the stacking of juries by race in 1968, but, though rare, it still happens. In 2019, the Supreme Court ordered the retrial of a Black defendant in a murder case where a Mississippi district attorney had eliminated 41 of 42 potential Black jurors for whom he was allowed a peremptory challenge.[63]

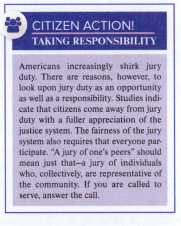

CITIZEN ACTION!
TAKING RESPONSIBILITY

Americans increasingly shirk jury duty. There are reasons, however, to look upon jury duty as an opportunity as well as a responsibility. Studies indicate that citizens come away from jury duty with a fuller appreciation of the justice system. The fairness of the jury system also requires that everyone participate. "A jury of one's peers" should mean just that—a jury of individuals who, collectively, are representative of the community. If you are called to serve, answer the call.

The Supreme Court recently further strengthened the right to a fair jury trial. The Sixth Amendment requires a unanimous jury verdict in federal cases but the Supreme Court had not applied the same rule to state cases until *Ramos v. Louisiana* (2020), when it held that the 14th Amendment's equal protection clause requires a unanimous jury for serious offenses. In a 6-3 ruling, the Court traced the practice of non-unanimous state juries "to the rise of the Ku Klux Klan and efforts to dilute the influence of racial and ethnic and religious minorities [on jury decisions]."[64]

An issue in some trials is the admissibility of evidence obtained in violation of the defendant's rights. The **exclusionary rule** bars the use of such evidence in some circumstances. The rule was formulated on a limited basis in a 1914 Supreme Court decision and was devised to deter police from violating people's rights. If police know that illegally obtained evidence will be inadmissible in court, they presumably will be less inclined to obtain it. As the Court wrote in *Weeks v. United States* (1914), "The tendency of those who execute the criminal laws of the country to obtain convictions by means of unlawful searches and enforced confessions . . . should find no sanction in the judgment of the courts."[65]

The Exclusionary Rule   In the 1960s, the liberal-dominated Supreme Court expanded the exclusionary rule to the point that illegally obtained evidence was almost never admissible in court. Opponents accused the Court of "coddling criminals," and the appointment of more conservative justices to the Court led to the creation of exceptions to the exclusionary rule. One such exception is called the *good faith exception*, which holds that otherwise inadmissible evidence can be used in trial if police honestly believed they were following proper procedures, as when they obtain a search warrant that later turns out to have been faulty.[66] A second instance in which tainted evidence can be admitted is the *inevitable discovery exception*. It holds that, even if incriminating evidence is wrongly obtained, it can be used if it would have inevitably been discovered by lawful means.[67] A third instance is the *plain view exception*, which holds that evidence found in plain sight is admissible even when the evidence relates to an infraction other than the one for which the individual was stopped, as when a driver is pulled over for speeding and the officer spots illegal drugs on the back seat.[68]

As some observers see it, the Court has weakened the exclusionary rule almost to the point where it applies only to extreme forms of police misconduct. Some Court rulings would support that contention. On the other hand, recent rulings on cell phones and tracking devices indicate that the Court is unwilling to give police broad latitude in the use of modern technology, recognizing that the exclusionary rule can easily be applied in ways that abridge constitutional rights.

Sentencing Phase: Cruel and Unusual Punishment

Most issues of criminal justice involve *procedural* due process. However, adherence to proper procedures does not necessarily produce reasonable outcomes. The Eighth Amendment was designed to address this issue. It prohibits "cruel and unusual punishment" of those convicted of a crime. The Supreme Court has applied several tests in determining whether punishment is cruel and unusual, including whether it is "disproportionate to the offence," violates "fundamental standards of good conscience and fairness," and is "unnecessarily cruel."

However, the Supreme Court has typically let Congress and the state legislatures determine the appropriate penalties for crime (see "How the 50 States Differ"). For example, the Court upheld a conviction under California's "three strikes and you're out" law that sent a twice previously convicted felon to prison for life without parole for shoplifting videotapes worth $100.[69]

At the same time, the Supreme Court has recently employed the Eighth Amendment's "cruel and unusual punishment" clause to ban the death penalty for juveniles and the mentally ill and to ban life sentences without parole for juveniles.[70]

HOW THE 50 STATES DIFFER

CRITICAL THINKING THROUGH COMPARISONS

Incarceration Rates

Most crimes in the United States are governed by state law rather than federal law, and states differ widely in their crime rates and sentencing practices. As a result, there is wide variation in the size of state prison populations. Oklahoma has the highest incarceration rate: 1,310 inmates for every 100,000 adults. Vermont has the lowest rate: 380 inmates per 100,000 adults.

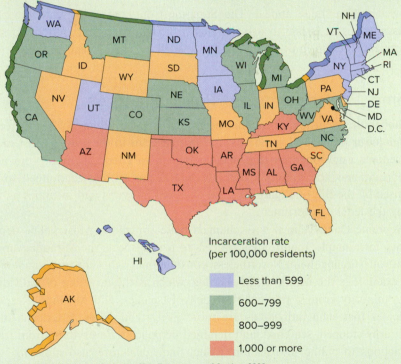

Incarceration rate
(per 100,000 residents)

- Less than 599
- 600–799
- 800–999
- 1,000 or more

Source: Office of Justice Statistics, U.S. Department of Justice, 2020

Q: What do many of the low-incarceration states have in common?

A: Most of them rank high on levels of education and income. Studies indicate that individuals who are college educated and those with higher incomes are less likely than others to engage in crime and, if convicted, less likely to receive a lengthy sentence.

Appeal: One Chance, Usually

The Constitution does not guarantee an appeal after conviction, but the federal government and all states permit at least one appeal. The Supreme Court has ruled that the appeal process cannot discriminate against poor defendants. At a minimum, government must provide indigent convicts with the legal resources to file a first appeal.[71]

Prisoners who believe their constitutional rights have been violated by state officials can appeal their conviction to a federal court. With a few exceptions, the Supreme Court has held that prisoners have the right to have their appeal heard in federal court unless they had "deliberately bypassed" the opportunity to first make their appeal in state courts.[72] Under a law enacted in 1996 to prevent inmates from filing frivolous and multiple appeals, they typically are allowed only a single appeal. The Supreme Court has ruled that, except in unusual cases, it is fair to ask inmates to first pursue their options in state courts and then to limit themselves to a single federal appeal.[73]

Crime, Punishment, and Police Practices

Although the exclusionary rule has been weakened, there has not been a return to the lower procedural standards that existed prior to the 1960s. Most of the precedents established in that decade remain in effect, including the most important one: the principle that procedural protections guaranteed to the accused by the Bill of Rights must be observed by states and localities as well as by the federal government.

Supreme Court rulings have changed police practices. Most police departments, for example, require their officers to read suspects the Miranda warning before questioning them. Nevertheless, constitutional rights are applied unevenly. An example is the use of *racial profiling,* which is the targeting of individuals from minority groups, particularly Blacks, Hispanics, and Muslims. Research indicates that such individuals are more likely than other Americans to be arbitrarily stopped, searched, and detained by police on everything from traffic infractions to public intoxication.[74] Such individuals are also more likely to become victims of police violence, an issue that became front-page news in 2020 when George Floyd, an unarmed Black man, was killed by four Minneapolis police officers while handcuffed and lying face down in the street. Floyd's killing sparked nationwide protests against police brutality that were reminiscent of the protests that occurred in 2014 after an unarmed Black teenager, Michael Brown, was shot to death by a police officer in Ferguson, Missouri. Brown's killing sparked "Black Lives Matter"—a movement aimed at ending racial disparities in police practices (see Chapter 7).

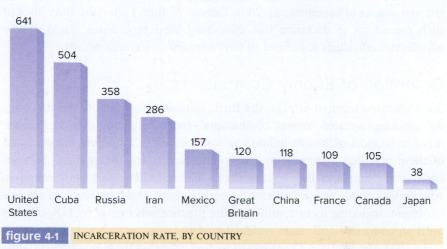

Incarceration rates (per 100,000 inhabitants)

641	504	358	286	157	120	118	109	105	38
United States	Cuba	Russia	Iran	Mexico	Great Britain	China	France	Canada	Japan

figure 4-1   INCARCERATION RATE, BY COUNTRY

The United States is the world leader in terms of the number of people it places behind bars. More than half of the people in U.S. prisons were convicted of nonviolent offenses, such as drug use or property theft. (*Source:* International Centre for Prison Studies, 2020.)

Sentencing policies are also an issue. Political candidates who are "tough on crime" are popular with some voters, which led state legislatures in the 1990s to enact stiffer penalties for crime while limiting the ability of judges to reduce sentences for nonviolent crimes committed by first-time offenders. As a result, the number of prison inmates more than doubled after the 1990s. In fact, on a per-capita basis, the United States has the largest prison population in the world (see Figure 4-1). Cuba is the only country that's even close to the United States in terms of the percentage of its citizens who are behind bars.

The human and financial cost of keeping so many people in prison has prompted some states to change their sentencing laws and implement early-release programs, primarily for those convicted of nonviolent, drug-related offenses. Some states have even set up treatment programs as an alternative to prison for some drug-related offenses, a policy that's in line with the practice of many Western democracies.

RIGHTS AND THE WAR ON TERRORISM

In time of war, the courts have upheld government policies that would not be permitted in peacetime.[75] After the Japanese attack on Pearl Harbor in 1941, for example, President Franklin D. Roosevelt ordered the forced relocation of tens of thousands of Japanese Americans living on the West Coast to detention camps in Arizona, Utah, and other inland locations. Congress endorsed the policy, and the Supreme Court upheld it in *Korematsu v. United States* (1944).[76] After the terrorist attacks of September 11, 2001, George W. Bush's administration invoked such precedents in declaring that customary legal protections would not be afforded to individuals it deemed to have engaged in terrorist activity.

Detention of Enemy Combatants

Soon after the terrorist attacks, the Bush administration announced its policy for handling captured "enemy combatants"—individuals judged to be engaged in, or in support of, hostile military actions against U.S. military forces. Some of these prisoners were sent to a detention facility created at the U.S. naval base at Guantánamo Bay on the tip of Cuba. Others were imprisoned in Afghanistan, Iraq, and elsewhere. Some prisoners were subjected to abusive treatment, including torture, although the practice was denied by U.S. officials until photographic and other evidence surfaced.

In 2004, the Supreme Court issued its first ruling on these practices, holding that the Guantánamo Bay detainees had the right to challenge their detention in court. The Court reasoned that the naval base, although in Cuba, is on land leased to the United States and therefore under the jurisdiction of U.S. courts.[77] In a second 2004 case, the Court ruled that one of the Guantánamo Bay detainees, who was a U.S. citizen by virtue of having been born in the United States although raised in Saudi Arabia, had the right to be heard in U.S. courts. The Court said that the government has a legitimate interest in detaining individuals who pose a threat to the nation's security but argued that "an unchecked system of detention carries the potential to become a means of oppression and abuse of others who do not present that sort of threat."[78]

Two years later, the Supreme Court issued its sharpest rebuke of the Bush administration's detention policies. In a ruling nearly unprecedented in its challenge to a president's wartime authority, the Court held that the detainees were protected both by the U.S. Uniform Code of Military Justice and by the Geneva Conventions. At issue was the Bush administration's use of secret military tribunals to try detainees. In *Hamdan v. Rumsfeld* (2006), the Court ruled that the tribunals were unlawful because they did not provide even minimal protections of detainees' rights, including the right to see the evidence against them. The Court said that the detainees were entitled to trial by a court that upholds rights "which are recognized as indispensable by civilized peoples."[79]

Surveillance of Suspected Terrorists

After the September 11 terrorist attacks, Congress passed the USA Patriot Act, which gave the government additional tools for combating terrorism, including expanded surveillance power. The National Security Agency (NSA) launched a program that collected Americans' phone records as a means of detecting activity that might be terrorist-related. If a pattern of phone calls or e-mails suggested the possibility of terrorist activity, NSA had to obtain a warrant from a federal judge before it could eavesdrop on a person's actual conversations.

The NSA program became public in 2013 when Edward Snowden, an NSA contractor, leaked documents about the program to the press. The documents showed that NSA had collected data on nearly every call made by Americans and had actually listened in on the calls of some foreign leaders, including German chancellor Angela Merkel.

The NSA program was challenged in court and a federal appellate court ruled it unlawful, not on grounds that it violated the Fourth Amendment protection against unreasonable search and seizure but because it had not been explicitly authorized by Congress. In 2015, after heated debate and a close vote in the Senate, Congress passed legislation authorizing the program while placing limits on it. For example, the legislation requires phone data to

Major national security threats can lead government to take actions that intrude on citizens' liberties. The war on terrorism is particularly challenging because the threat is not confined to overseas areas but includes the U.S. homeland. Concern about terrorist attacks on U.S. soil is the basis for the NSA's surveillance program, which collects data on Americans' phone calls and e-mails, particularly when the other party is elsewhere in the world. The courts have upheld the constitutionality of the program because NSA, although it collects data on communication traffic, must have a court warrant to examine the actual content of any message. Nevertheless, the NSA program involves a level of personal surveillance beyond anything Americans experienced in the past. (Morakot Kawinchan/Shutterstock)

be stored with telecommunications companies rather than with NSA and to be available to NSA only if it obtains a warrant. In 2018, Congress reauthorized the program, extending it for a period of six years.

THE COURTS AND A FREE SOCIETY

The United States was founded on the idea that individuals have an innate right to liberty—to speak their minds, to worship freely, to be secure in their homes and persons, and to be assured of a fair trial. Americans embrace these freedoms in the abstract. In particular situations, however, many Americans think otherwise. A 2010 CNN survey found, for example, that more than two in five Americans think that individuals arrested by police on suspicion of terrorism should not be read their Miranda rights.

The judiciary is not isolated from the public mood. Judges inevitably must balance society's need for security and public order against the rights of the individual. Nevertheless, relative to elected officials, police officers, or the general public, judges are more protective of individual rights. How far the courts will go in protecting a person's rights depends on the facts of the case, the existing status of the law, prevailing social needs, and the personal views of the judges (see Chapter 14). Nevertheless, most judges and justices regard the protection of individual rights as their constitutional duty, which is the way the framers saw it. The Bill of Rights was created to transform the abstract idea that individuals have a right to life, liberty, and happiness into a set of specified constitutional rights, thereby bringing them under the protection of courts of law.[80]

SUMMARY

The Bill of Rights was added to the Constitution shortly after its ratification. These amendments guarantee certain political, procedural, and property rights against infringement by the national government.

The guarantees embodied in the Bill of Rights originally applied only to the national government. Under the principle of selective incorporation of these guarantees into the Fourteenth Amendment, the courts extended them to state governments, though the process was slow and uneven. In the 1920s and 1930s, First Amendment guarantees of freedom of expression were given protection from infringement by the states. The states continued to have wide discretion in criminal proceedings until the early 1960s, when most of the fair-trial rights in the Bill of Rights were given federal protection.

Freedom of expression is the most basic of democratic rights. People are not free unless they can freely express their views. Nevertheless, free expression may conflict with the nation's security needs during times of war and insurrection. The courts at times have allowed government to limit expression substantially for purposes of national security. In recent decades, however, the courts have protected a wide range of free expression in the areas of speech, press, and religion. They have also established a right of privacy, which in some areas, such as abortion, remains a source of controversy and judicial action.

Due process of law refers to legal protections that have been established to preserve individual rights. The most significant form of these protections consists of procedures designed to ensure that an individual's rights are upheld (for example, the right of an accused person to have an attorney present during police interrogation). A major controversy in this area is the breadth of the exclusionary rule, which bars illegally obtained evidence from being used in trials.

The war on terrorism that began after the attacks on September 11, 2001, has raised new issues of civil liberties, including the detention of enemy combatants, the use of harsh interrogation techniques, and warrantless surveillance. The Supreme Court has not ruled on all such issues but has generally held that the president's war-making power does not include the authority to disregard provisions of statutory law, treaties (the Geneva Conventions), and the Constitution.

Civil liberties are not absolute but must be judged in the context of other considerations (such as national security or public safety) and against one another when different rights conflict. The judicial branch of government, particularly the Supreme Court, has taken on much of the responsibility for protecting and interpreting individual rights. The Court's positions have changed with time and conditions, but the Court is typically more protective of civil liberties than are elected officials or popular majorities.

CRITICAL THINKING ZONE

KEY TERMS

Bill of Rights (*p. 94*)

civil liberties (*p. 93*)

clear-and-present-danger test (*p. 99*)

due process clause (*p. 94*)

establishment clause (*p. 104*)

exclusionary rule (*p. 117*)

freedom of expression (*p. 97*)

free-exercise clause (*p. 106*)

imminent lawless action (*p. 99*)

Lemon test (*p. 105*)

libel (*p. 103*)

prior restraint (*p. 103*)

procedural due process (*p. 111*)

right of privacy (*p. 109*)

selective incorporation (*p. 97*)

slander (*p. 103*)

symbolic speech (*p. 102*)

APPLYING THE ELEMENTS OF CRITICAL THINKING

Conceptualizing: Distinguish between the establishment clause and the free-exercise clause of the First Amendment. To which one does the *Lemon* test apply, and what are the components of that test?

Synthesizing: Assume that an individual has been arrested and is eventually brought to trial. Identify the procedural due process rights that the individual has at each step in the legal process. How might the exclusionary rule affect the outcome?

Analyzing: What is the process of selective incorporation, and why is it important to the rights Americans have today?

EXTRA CREDIT

A Book Worth Reading: Anthony Lewis, *Gideon's Trumpet: How One Man, a Poor Prisoner, Took His Case to the Supreme Court—and Changed the Law of the United States* (New York: Vintage, 1964). Written by a two-time Pulitzer Prize winner, this best-selling book recounts the story of how James Earl Gideon got the Supreme Court to accept his case, which led to a constitutional ruling requiring government to provide the poor with legal counsel.

A Website Worth Visiting: www.sentencingproject.org/ The Sentencing Project works on issues and policies relating to criminal justice reform.

EQUAL RIGHTS: STRUGGLING TOWARD FAIRNESS

Mark Wilson/Getty Images

> ❝ The assertion that 'all men are created equal' was of no practical use in effecting our separation from Great Britain, and it was placed in the Declaration not for that, but for future use. ❞
>
> ABRAHAM LINCOLN[1]

The Urban Institute paired up a large number of male college students. The students in each pair had similar majors, grades, work records, speech patterns, and physical builds. The students then responded to hundreds of classified job advertisements in Chicago and Washington, D.C. Within each pair, one type consistently got more interview invitations and job offers than the other type. What was the difference in the two types? In each pair, one of the students was white and the other was Black. The white students were far more likely than the Black students to get interviews and jobs. As the Urban Institute study concluded, "The level of reverse discrimination [favoring Blacks over whites] that we found was limited, was certainly far lower than many might have been led to fear, and was swamped by the extent of discrimination against black job applicants."[2]

The Urban Institute study suggests why some Americans still struggle for equality. Although Americans have equal rights in theory, they are not now equal, nor have they ever been. African Americans, women, Hispanic Americans, individuals with disabilities, Jews, Native Americans, Catholics, Mormons, Asian Americans, LGBTQ people, and others have been victims of discrimination in fact and in law.

This chapter focuses on **equal rights (civil rights)**—the right of every person to equal protection under the laws and equal access to society's opportunities and public facilities. As Chapter 4 explained, *civil liberties* are specific *individual* rights, such as freedom of speech, that are protected from infringement by government. Equal rights, or civil rights, are a question of whether individual members of particular *groups,* such as racial, gender, or ethnic groups, are treated equally by government and, in some instances, by private parties.

Although the law refers to the rights of individuals first and to those of groups in a secondary and derivative way, this chapter concentrates on groups because the history of civil rights has been largely one of group claims to equality. The catchphrase of nearly every group's claim to a more equal standing in American society has been "equality under the law." When secure in their legal rights, people are positioned to pursue equality in other arenas, such as the economic sector. This chapter examines the major laws relating to equality and the conditions that led to their adoption. The chapter concludes with a brief look at some of the continuing challenges facing America's historically disadvantaged groups. The chapter emphasizes these points:

- *Americans have attained substantial equality under the law.* In purely legal terms, although not always in practice, they have equal protection under the laws, equal access to accommodations and housing, and an equal right to vote.

- *Legal equality for all Americans has not resulted in de facto equality.* African Americans, women, Hispanic Americans, and other traditionally disadvantaged groups have a disproportionately small share of America's opportunities and benefits. However, the issue of what, if anything, government should do to deal with this problem is a major source of contention.

- *Disadvantaged groups have had to struggle for equal rights.* African Americans, women, Native Americans, Hispanic Americans, Asian Americans, and a number of other groups have had to fight for their rights in order to achieve a fuller measure of equality.

EQUALITY THROUGH LAW

Equality has always been the least developed of America's founding concepts. Not even Thomas Jefferson, who wrote the words, believed that a precise meaning could be given to the claim of the Declaration of Independence that "all men are created equal."[3] Nevertheless, the promise contained in that phrase has placed history on the side of those seeking greater equality. Every civil rights movement, from suffrage for males

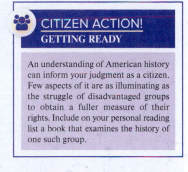

CITIZEN ACTION!
GETTING READY

An understanding of American history can inform your judgment as a citizen. Few aspects of it are as illuminating as the struggle of disadvantaged groups to obtain a fuller measure of their rights. Include on your personal reading list a book that examines the history of one such group.

without property in the 1830s to LGBTQ rights today, has derived moral strength from the nation's pledge of equality for all. Those efforts have led to policies that have made Americans more equal in law.

The Fourteenth Amendment: Equal Protection

Ratified in 1868 after the Civil War, the Fourteenth Amendment declares that no state shall "deny to any person within its jurisdiction the equal protection of the laws." The **equal-protection clause** was designed to require states to treat their residents equally, but the Supreme Court at first refused to interpret it that way. As discussed in Chapter 3, the Court in *Plessy v. Ferguson* (1896) ruled that "separate" public facilities for Black citizens did not violate the Constitution as long as the facilities were "equal."[4] The *Plessy* decision became a justification for the separate and *unequal* treatment of African Americans. Black children were forced, for example, to attend separate schools that rarely had libraries or enough teachers.

These practices were challenged through legal action, but not until the late 1930s did the Supreme Court begin to respond. In a first ruling, the Court held that Blacks must be allowed to use public facilities reserved for whites in cases where the states had not created separate facilities. When Oklahoma, which had no law school for Blacks, was ordered to admit Ada Sipuel as a law student in 1949, it created a separate law school for her—she sat alone in a roped-off corridor of the state capitol building. The white students, meanwhile, continued to meet at the University of Oklahoma's law school in Norman, 20 miles away. The Supreme Court then ordered the law school to admit her to regular classes. The law school did so but roped off her seat from the rest of the class and stenciled the word *colored* on it. In her memoir, Sipuel wrote that, although law school administrators did not try to help her, several law students did assist, including those who gave her notes from the classes she missed while sitting alone at the capitol building.[5]

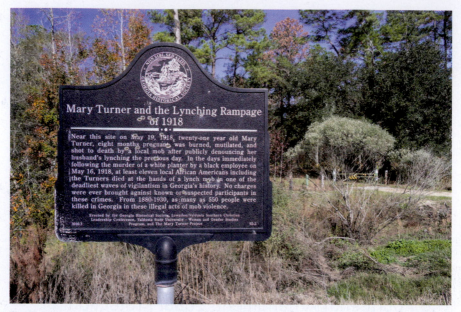

The Jim Crow era of racial segregation in the South was marked not only by racially segregated schools and other public facilities but also by violence against Black citizens who spoke against racial injustice. Nearly 3,500 Black citizens were lynched by white mobs. The Equal Justice Initiative has recently sponsored the installations of markers to remind Americans of this stain on their history. Shown here is a sign marking the spot in Hahira, Georgia, where 21-year-old Mary Turner was brutally murdered in 1918 by a local mob after publicly denouncing her husband's lynching. The pock marks on the sign are from bullets recently fired at it, presumably by individuals who harbor the same racial hatred that drove the lynching of Black citizens. (Jen Wolf/Shutterstock)

Segregation in the Schools   Substantial judicial intervention on behalf of African Americans finally occurred in 1954 with *Brown v. Board of Education of Topeka* (see "Case Study: *Brown v. Board of Education* (1954)"). The case began when Linda Carol Brown, a Black child in Topeka, Kansas, was denied admission to an all-white elementary school that she passed every day on her way to her all-Black school, which was nearly a mile farther away. In a unanimous decision, the Court invoked the Fourteenth Amendment's equal-protection clause, declaring that racial segregation of public schools "generates [among Black children] a feeling of inferiority as to their status in the community that may affect their hearts and minds in a way unlikely ever to be undone. . . . Separate educational facilities are inherently unequal."[6]

Although the *Brown* decision banned forced segregation in the public schools, it did not require states to take active steps to integrate their schools. Most children attended neighborhood schools, and, because most residential neighborhoods were racially segregated, so were the schools.

Politics in Action

Brown v. Board of Education (1954)

The Fourteenth Amendment, ratified after the Civil War to protect newly freed slaves, declared that no state shall "deny to any person within its jurisdiction the equal protection of the laws." Nevertheless, southern states soon established a two-race system. Black residents were prohibited from using the same public schools, hospitals, and other facilities as white residents. In 1896, the Supreme Court held that separate facilities for whites and Blacks were legal as long as they were

Library of Congress, Prints and Photographs Division [LC-USF34-046235-D]

"equal," ignoring both the intent of the Constitution and the fact that facilities reserved for Blacks were vastly inferior.

The South's two-race system crumbled when the Supreme Court in 1954 voided the policy of separate public schools. In its unanimous decision in *Brown v. Board of Education*, the Court said, "Separate educational facilities are inherently unequal [and violate] the equal protection of the laws guaranteed by the Fourteenth Amendment."

A 1954 Gallup poll indicated that most southern whites opposed the *Brown* decision, and billboards were erected along southern roadways that called for the impeachment of Chief Justice Earl Warren. In the so-called Southern Manifesto, southern members of Congress urged their state governments to "resist forced integration by any lawful means." Rioting broke out in 1957 when Arkansas's governor called out the state's National Guard to prevent Black students from entering Little Rock's high school. They achieved entry only after President Dwight D. Eisenhower used his power as commander in chief to place the Arkansas National Guard under federal control.

The Supreme Court's *Brown v. Board of Education* decision became precedent for rulings that, over the years, have extended equal protection to other groups. Indeed, *Brown* is widely regarded as one of the Supreme Court's most important decisions, ranking alongside such rulings as *Marbury v. Madison* (1803), *McCulloch v. Maryland* (1819), *Schenck v. United States* (1919), and *Mapp v. Ohio* (1961).

Continued

Q: What is the major limit on the Fourteenth Amendment as a means of preventing discrimination?

ASK YOURSELF: Who is prohibited by the Fourteenth Amendment from discriminating against individuals on the basis of their race, creed, or ethnicity? Who is not? If an individual is denied service in a restaurant because of race, creed, or ethnicity, is that person entitled to sue the owner on grounds that his or her Fourteenth Amendment rights have been violated? Why or why not?

Even as late as 15 years after *Brown,* 95 percent of Black children were attending schools that were mostly or entirely Black.

In *Swann v. Charlotte-Mecklenburg County Board of Education* (1971), the Supreme Court upheld the busing of children out of their neighborhoods for the purpose of achieving racially integrated schools.[7] Forced busing produced angry demonstrations in Charlotte, Detroit, Boston, and dozens of other cities, and the policy had mixed results. Studies found that busing improved school children's racial attitudes and improved minority children's performance on standardized tests without diminishing the performance of white classmates.[8] But the policy forced many children to spend long hours each day riding buses to and from school. Busing also contributed to white flight to the suburbs, which were protected by a 1974 Supreme Court decision that prohibited busing across school district lines except where district boundaries had been deliberately drawn to keep the races apart.[9] The declining number of white students in city schools made it harder, even with the use of busing, to create racially balanced classrooms. In a 2007 decision involving the Seattle and Louisville school systems, the Supreme Court effectively ended forced busing, ruling that it violated the equal-protection rights of students who were required to attend a distant school.[10]

As a result of white flight to private and suburban schools and the end of racial busing, America's schools have become less racially diverse. In fact, America's schools are now more racially segregated than they were when busing started.[11]

Judicial Tests of Equal Protection   The Fourteenth Amendment's equal-protection clause does not require government to treat all groups or classes of people equally in all circumstances. The judiciary allows inequalities that are "reasonably" related to a legitimate government interest. In applying this **reasonable-basis test**, the courts require government only to show that a particular law is reasonable. For example, 21-year-olds can legally drink alcohol but 20-year-olds cannot. The courts have held that the goal of reducing fatalities from alcohol-related accidents involving young drivers is a valid reason for imposing an age limit on the purchase and consumption of alcohol.

The reasonable-basis test does not apply to racial or ethnic classifications (see Table 5-1). The Supreme Court's position is that race and national origin are **suspect classifications**—in other words, laws that classify people differently on the basis of their race or ethnicity are assumed to have discrimination as their purpose. Any law that treats people differently because of race or ethnicity is subject to the **strict-scrutiny test**, which presumes that the law is unconstitutional unless government can provide a compelling reason for it.

Although the notion of suspect classifications was implicit in earlier cases, including *Brown,* the Court did not use those words until *Loving v. Virginia* (1967). The state of Virginia had a law that prohibited white residents from marrying a person of a different race. When Richard Loving, a white man, and Mildred Jeter, a woman of African American and Native American descent, went to Washington, D.C., to get married and then returned home to Virginia, police invaded their home and arrested them. The state of Virginia claimed that its ban on interracial marriage did not violate the equal-protection clause because the penalty for the offense—a prison sentence of one to five years—was the same for both the white and the nonwhite spouse. The Supreme Court ruled otherwise, saying that the Virginia law was "subversive of the principle of equality at the heart of the Fourteenth Amendment." The Court concluded that the law was based solely on "invidious racial discrimination" and that any such "classification" was unconstitutional.[12]

table 5-1	LEVELS OF COURT REVIEW FOR LAWS THAT TREAT AMERICANS DIFFERENTLY	
Test	**Application**	**Standard Used**
Strict scrutiny	Race, ethnicity	Suspect category—assumed unconstitutional in the absence of an overwhelming justification
Intermediate scrutiny	Gender	Almost suspect category—assumed unconstitutional unless the law serves a clearly compelling and justified purpose
Reasonable basis	Other categories (such as age and income)	Not suspect category—assumed constitutional unless no sound rationale for the law can be provided

When women began to assert their rights more forcefully in the 1970s, some observers thought the Supreme Court would expand the scope of strict scrutiny to include gender. Instead, the Court held that men and women can be treated differently if the policy in question is "substantially related" to the achievement of "important governmental objectives."[13] The Court thus placed gender classifications in an intermediate (or almost suspect) category. Gender classifications were to be scrutinized more closely than some others (for example, income or age) but were constitutionally valid if government could clearly show why men and women should be treated differently. In *Rostker v. Goldberg* (1980), the Court upheld such a classification, ruling that the male-only draft registration law served the important objective of excluding women from *involuntary* combat duty.[14]

Since then, however, the Supreme Court has struck down nearly every gender-based law it has reviewed. A leading case is *United States v. Virginia* (1996), in

The Supreme Court has ruled that government cannot treat men and women differently in law unless it has a compelling justification for doing so. One such law excludes women from being drafted involuntarily into the military, although they can volunteer for military duty. Shown here is a woman soldier who is part of a U.S. Army Ranger unit. (NEstudio/Shutterstock)

which the Court invalidated the male-only admissions policy of Virginia Military Institute (VMI), a 157-year-old state-supported college. In its ruling, the Court said that Virginia had failed to provide an "exceedingly persuasive" argument for its policy.[15]

FAKE or FACT   Detecting Misinformation

Is Justice Color Blind?

Over the past half-century, the United States has made progress in upholding the ideal of "equal justice under the law."

Supreme Court rulings based on the Fourteenth Amendment's due process and equal-protection clauses have boosted the legal standing of Black Americans and other historically disadvantaged groups. But does the reality of daily life match the legal gains? Most Black Americans say no.

Michael Matthews/Police Images/Alamy Stock Photo

An NBC poll found, for example, that only 12 percent of Blacks believe that their community's police officers treat white and Blacks equally.[16]

Is that claim fact, or is it fake?

Although there are communities where police treat white and Black residents equally, research indicates that the pattern is atypical. Studies show that Black residents are more likely than white residents to be ticketed or arrested for engaging in the same acts.[17] They are also more likely to be convicted and receive a stiffer sentence when charged with comparable crimes. A U.S. Department of Justice study found that, among persons convicted of drug crimes in state courts, half of the Black defendants received a prison sentence, compared with a third of the white defendants.[18] Moreover, as a study of 2013–2019 police killings revealed, unarmed Black persons are 30 percent more likely to be killed by police than unarmed white persons.[19] The unprovoked killing by Minneapolis police of George Floyd, an unarmed and handcuffed Black man, sparked nationwide protests in 2020.

The Civil Rights Act of 1964

The Fourteenth Amendment prohibits discrimination by government but not by private parties. As a result, for a long period in American history, private employers could freely discriminate in their hiring practices, and owners of restaurants, hotels, theaters, and other public accommodations could legally bar Black people from entering. That changed with passage of the 1964 Civil Rights Act. Based on Congress's power to regulate commerce, the legislation entitles all persons to equal access to public accommodations. The legislation also bars discrimination on the basis of race, color, religion, sex, or national origin in the hiring, promotion, and wages of employees of medium-size and large firms. A few forms of job discrimination are still lawful under the Civil Rights Act. For example, a church-related school can take religion into account in hiring teachers.

The Civil Rights Act proved effective in reducing discrimination in access to public accommodations because it's fairly easy to prove discrimination when a person is denied service at a restaurant or hotel that has available space. The act proved less effective in the area of job discrimination, where it's harder to prove that an individual has been the victim of discrimination. This situation led to the creation of affirmative action programs, discussed in a later section.

The Voting Rights Act of 1965

Although ratification of the Fifteenth Amendment in 1870 granted Black Americans the right to vote, southern whites invented an array of devices, such as whites-only primaries, poll taxes, and literacy tests, to keep Blacks from registering and voting. In the mid-1940s, for example, there were only 2,500 registered Black voters in the entire state of Mississippi, even though its Black population numbered half a million.[20]

Racial barriers to voting began to crumble in the mid-1940s when the Supreme Court declared that whites-only primary elections were unconstitutional.[21] Ratification of the Twenty-Fourth Amendment in 1964 outlawed the poll tax, which was a fee that an individual had to pay in order to register to vote. The Supreme Court subsequently banned the use of literacy tests as a condition for being allowed to register to vote.[22]

Nevertheless, the major policy change was the Voting Rights Act of 1965, which prohibited discrimination in voting and registration. The legislation empowered federal agents to register voters in states and localities with a history of voter discrimination. The Voting Rights Act had an immediate impact on Black participation. In the ensuing presidential election, Black turnout in the South jumped by 20 percentage points.

The Voting Rights Act is still in place but has been weakened. In *Shelby County v. Holder* (2013), the Supreme Court invalidated the provision (Section 4) of the

Voting Rights Act that included the formula for determining which states and counties were subject to federal oversight. The formula included factors such as an area's use of various devices keep Black citizens from voting. Designated states and counties were required by the preclearance provision (Section 5) of the Voting Rights Act to obtain permission from federal officials before they made changes—such as redrawing electoral districts or altering registration require-ments—that might adversely affect a minority group. In its *Shelby County* decision, the Court's majority held that the formula for identifying the states and counties subject to federal oversight was based on "obsolete statistics" and that Congress had to update it before it could be applied.[23]

Congress has not done so, with the result that no state or county needs federal permission to change its voting process. Once changes are made, how-ever, they can be challenged as discriminatory. In 2017, the Supreme Court struck down the boundaries of two North Carolina congressional districts on grounds they had been drawn to reduce the power of Black voters.[24]

The Civil Rights Act of 1968

In 1968, Congress passed civil rights legislation designed to prohibit discrim-ination in housing. A building owner cannot refuse to sell or rent housing because of a person's race, religion, ethnicity, or sex. An exception is allowed for owners of small, multifamily dwellings who reside on the premises.

Despite legal prohibitions on discrimination, housing in America remains highly segregated. Only a third of African Americans live in a neighborhood that is mostly white. One reason is that the annual income of most Black families is substantially below that of most white families. Another reason is banking practices. At one time, banks contributed to housing segregation by *redlining*—refusing to grant mortgage loans in certain neighborhoods, typically those with large Black populations. Since buyers could not get a mortgage, homeowners had to lower the selling price to sell their home. As home values dropped, white families increasingly left these neighborhoods, which increased the percentage of Black families living there. The 1968 Civil Rights Act prohib-its redlining, but many of the segregated neighborhoods it helped create still exist. Moreover, although discriminatory lending practices are now prohibited by law, studies indicate that Hispanics and African Americans still have more difficulty obtaining mortgages than do white applicants with the same income.[25]

Affirmative Action

Changes in the law seldom have large or immediate effects on how people behave. Although the 1964 Civil Rights Act prohibited job discrimination on the basis of race, color, religion, sex, or national origin, many employers continued to favor white male employees. Other employers maintained employment procedures that kept women and minorities at a disadvantage. Membership in many union locals, for example, was handed down from father to son. Moreover, the Civil Rights Act did not require employers to prove that their employment practices were fair. Instead, the burden of proof was on the woman or minority-group member who was denied a job. It was costly and usually difficult for an individual to prove in court that gender or race was the reason for not being hired or promoted. Moreover, a victory in court applied only to the individual in question; it did not help other women and minorities faced with job discrimination.

Affirmative action programs were devised as a remedy for such problems. **Affirmative action** refers to deliberate efforts to provide full and equal opportunities in employment, education, and other areas for members of traditionally disadvantaged groups. Affirmative action applies only to organizations—such as universities, agencies, and construction firms—that receive federal funding or contracts. These organizations are required to establish programs designed to ensure that all applicants are treated fairly. They also bear a burden of proof. If an organization grants a disproportionate share of opportunities to white males, it must show that the pattern is the result of necessity (such as the nature of the job or the locally available labor pool) and not the result of systematic discrimination.

Equality of result, which was the aim of affirmative action, was a new concept. Other major civil rights policies had sought to eliminate **de jure discrimination**, which is discrimination based on law, as in the case of state laws requiring Black and white children to attend separate schools during the pre-*Brown* period. Affirmative action policy sought to alleviate **de facto discrimination**—the condition whereby historically disadvantaged groups have fewer opportunities because of prejudice and financial constraints.

Few issues have sparked more controversy than has affirmative action, and even today the public has a mixed response to it. Most Americans support programs designed to ensure that historically disadvantaged groups receive equal treatment but oppose programs that would give them preferential treatment. A Gallup poll found, for example, that only 4 percent of white Americans believe race and ethnicity should be a "major factor" in college admission decisions, while 67 percent say race and ethnicity should count "not at all" in such decisions.[26]

Policies that pit individuals against each other over jobs, college admissions, and the like typically end up in the Supreme Court, and affirmative action is no exception. In *Regents of the University of California v. Bakke* (1978), the Court issued its first affirmative action ruling, holding that a California medical school had violated the equal-protection rights of Alan Bakke, a white male applicant, by reserving a fixed number of admissions ("a quota") for minority applicants. In doing so, it did not invalidate affirmative action per se. The Court said that race can be among the factors that colleges take into consideration to create a diverse student body but that colleges cannot use quotas as a means of admitting minority students.[27]

The Court later narrowed the scope of affirmative action. In the key case of *Adarand v. Peña* (1995), for example, the Court invalidated a federal policy that had reserved 10 percent of federally funded construction projects for minority-owned firms. The Court held that such firms cannot benefit from the fact that minority-owned firms had been discriminated against in the past.[28]

Opponents of affirmative action thought that the *Adarand* decision might lead the Supreme Court to eventually abolish it. However, in *Grutter v. Bollinger* (2003), the Court upheld the University of Michigan law school's admissions policy, which took into account race (along with other factors such as work experience and extracurricular activities) in admissions decisions. The Court concluded that Michigan's program was being applied sensibly and that it fostered Michigan's "compelling interest in obtaining the educational benefits that flow from a diverse student body."[29]

The Court reaffirmed that position in 2016 in *Fisher v. University of Texas*. At issue was the university's policy for admitting students who were not in the top 10 percent of their Texas high school graduating class. Whereas applicants at the top of their class were admitted automatically, other applicants were admitted or rejected based on a "holistic" evaluation that included their high school grades, standardized test scores, and other factors, including extracurricular activities, special skills (such as musical talent or athletic ability), and race or ethnicity. The Supreme Court held that the university's use of race and ethnicity as factors in admissions decisions was permissible, noting that it served the university's compelling interest in creating a diverse student body while noting that it was narrowly tailored in that it gave only a slight advantage to minority students. The Court said that "considerable deference is owed to a university in defining those intangible characteristics, like student body diversity, that are central to its identity and educational mission."[30]

The Michigan and Texas cases clarified the test that the Supreme Court applies in affirmative action cases. For affirmative action to be upheld, it must, first, serve a "compelling governmental interest." A diverse student body, for example, can be justified because it enhances understanding and fosters tolerance, which are central to a university's educational mission. Second, to be upheld, affirmative action must be "narrowly tailored" to achieve the desired goal. What this means, in effect, is that overly broad actions cannot be justified. That part of the test was what led the Supreme Court to strike down the

In 2016, the Supreme Court ruled on a key affirmative action case involving the University of Texas at Austin (pictured here). The case centered on the university's discretionary admissions policy, which, in addition to academic achievement, was based on such things as athletic ability, extracurricular activities, musical talent, and ethnic and racial background. The University of Texas case was not unprecedented. Several key affirmative action rulings have centered on college admissions policies, including the first ever affirmative action ruling, *Regents of the University of California v. Bakke* (1978). (dszc/Getty Images)

10 percent rule for government contracts. The awarding of contracts to minority firms merely because other such firms had been discriminated against in the past was not narrowly tailored to fit the current situation.

THE STRUGGLE FOR EQUALITY

American history indicates that disadvantaged groups have never achieved greater equality without a struggle.[31] The policies that protect these groups today are the result of sustained political action that forced entrenched interests to relinquish or share their privileged status. Progress has been made toward a more equal America, but civil rights problems involve deeply rooted conditions, habits, and prejudices. The following discussion describes the struggles these groups faced historically and some of the struggles they face today.

Black Americans

The impetus behind the 1964 Civil Rights Act was the black civil rights movement. Without it, the legislation would have come later and possibly have been less sweeping.

During World War II, African American soldiers fought against Nazi racism, only to return to an America where racial discrimination was legal and oppressive.[32] Demands for change intensified after an incident in Montgomery, Alabama, on December 1, 1955. Upon leaving work that day, Rosa Parks boarded a bus for home, taking her seat as required by law in the section reserved for Blacks. When all the seats for white passengers were occupied, the bus driver ordered Parks to give her seat to a white passenger. She refused and was arrested. A young pastor at a local Baptist church, Dr. Martin Luther King Jr., led a boycott of Montgomery's bus system, which spread to other cities. The Black civil rights movement was under way and would continue for more than a decade. A peak moment occurred in 1963 with the March on Washington for Jobs and Freedom, which attracted 250,000 marchers, one of the largest gatherings in the capital's history. In a riveting speech to the massive crowd, King expressed his dream of a better America, one where people are judged by the quality of their personal character rather than by the color of their skin.[33]

The momentum of the March on Washington carried over into Congress, where major civil rights legislation was languishing in House committee. Although opponents employed every possible legislative maneuver in an effort to block it, it finally cleared the House the following February. Senate maneuvering and debate—including a 55-day filibuster—took another four months. Finally, in early July, President Lyndon Johnson signed into law the Civil Rights Act of 1964.

Martin Luther King Jr.'s dream of an equal society for Black Americans remains elusive.[34] Poverty is a persistent problem in the Black community, affecting everyone from the very old to the very young. The median net worth of households headed by retired Black people is less than $20,000, compared with roughly $200,000 for retired white people. Among adults of employment age, the jobless rate of African Americans is twice that of white Americans.

Black children are particularly disadvantaged. Roughly 35 percent of them live below the government-defined poverty line, compared with about 12 percent of white children. In addition, more than half of Black children grow up in a single-parent family, and about 1 in 10 grow up in a home where neither parent is present. Children who grow up in a single-parent household are much more likely to have inadequate nutrition, not finish high school, not attend college, be unemployed as an adult, and spend time in prison.[35]

African Americans have made substantial progress in winning elective office. Although the percentage of Black elected officials is still far below the proportion of African Americans in the population, it has risen in recent decades.[36] There are now roughly 400 Black mayors and 40 Black members of

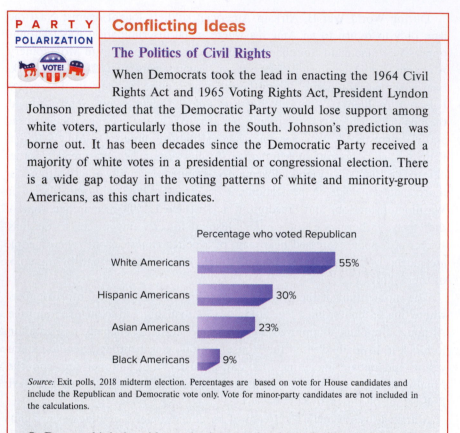

PARTY POLARIZATION

Conflicting Ideas

The Politics of Civil Rights

When Democrats took the lead in enacting the 1964 Civil Rights Act and 1965 Voting Rights Act, President Lyndon Johnson predicted that the Democratic Party would lose support among white voters, particularly those in the South. Johnson's prediction was borne out. It has been decades since the Democratic Party received a majority of white votes in a presidential or congressional election. There is a wide gap today in the voting patterns of white and minority-group Americans, as this chart indicates.

Percentage who voted Republican

White Americans 55%
Hispanic Americans 30%
Asian Americans 23%
Black Americans 9%

Source: Exit polls, 2018 midterm election. Percentages are based on vote for House candidates and include the Republican and Democratic vote only. Vote for minor-party candidates are not included in the calculations.

Q: Do you think the wide gap in the party loyalties of whites and minority-group members makes it easier or harder for Republicans and Democrats to bridge their other differences?

Congress. Barack Obama's election to the presidency in 2008 marked the first time an African American was chosen to fill the nation's highest office.

Women

The Black civil rights movement inspired other disadvantaged groups to demand their rights, of whom women were the most vocal and successful.

The United States carried over from English common law a political disregard for women, forbidding them to vote, hold public office, or serve on juries.[37] Upon marriage, a woman essentially lost her identity as an individual and could not own and dispose of property without her husband's consent. Even a wife's body was not fully hers. A wife's adultery was declared by the Supreme Court in 1904 to be a violation of the husband's property rights.[38]

The first large and well-organized attempt to promote women's rights came in 1848 in Seneca Falls, New York. Lucretia Mott and Elizabeth Cady Stanton had been barred from the main floor of an antislavery convention and decided to organize a women's rights convention. Thereafter, the struggle for women's rights became closely aligned with the abolitionist movement. However, when Congress wrote the Fifteenth Amendment after the Civil War, women were excluded. The amendment said only that the right to vote could not be abridged on account of race or color. Not until passage of the Nineteenth Amendment in 1920 did women acquire the right to vote.

The Nineteenth Amendment's ratification led to demands for a constitutional amendment granting equal rights to women. Congress rejected the proposal but, in 1972, approved the Equal Rights Amendment (ERA) and submitted it to the states for ratification.[39] The ERA failed by three states to receive the required three-fourths majority within the time limit specified by Congress.* However, women did succeed in other efforts to obtain equal treatment.

Historically disadvantaged groups awoke in the mid-20th century to their second-class status and pressed for change. Pictured here is a women's rights march that took place in Washington in 1970. The women's rights movement helped prompt legislation that prohibits sexual discrimination in areas such as employment and financial credit. (Library of Congress, Prints & Photographs Division [LC-U9- 23117-25])

---

*Since the deadline has passed, which was in 1982, three additional states have ratified the ERA. The most recent was Virginia in 2020, which has led advocates to challenge Congress's ability to put a time limit on ratification. An additional complication is that four states that had ratified the ERA have since rescinded it. Neither of these issues has been fully addressed by the Supreme Court, which leaves open the question of the ERA's ratification.

Among the congressional measures enacted were the Equal Pay Act of 1963, which prohibits sex discrimination in salary and wages by some categories of employers; Title IX of the Education Amendment of 1972, which prohibits sex discrimination in education; and the Equal Credit Act of 1974, which prohibits sex discrimination in the granting of financial credit.

In recent decades, increasing numbers of women have entered the job market. They are six times more likely today than a half-century ago to work outside the home and have made inroads in male-dominated occupations. For example, roughly half of all graduating lawyers and physicians are women. The change in women's work status is also reflected in general education statistics. A few decades ago, more men than women were enrolled in college. Today, the reverse is true. A recent U.S. Education Department report showed that women are ahead of men in more than just college enrollment; they are also more likely on average to complete their degree, do so in a shorter period, and get better grades.[40]

Nevertheless, women have not achieved job equality. Women increasingly hold managerial positions, but, as they rise through the ranks, they can encounter the so-called glass ceiling, which is the invisible but nonetheless real barrier that some women face when firms pick their top executives. Of the 500 largest U.S. corporations, only about 5 percent are headed by women. Women also earn less than men: The average hourly pay for full-time female employees is about 82 percent of that for full-time male employees. Many of the jobs traditionally held by women, such as office assistant, pay less than many of the jobs traditionally held by men, such as truck driver. Women's groups have had only limited success in persuading governments and firms to institute *comparable worth policies* that give women and men equal hourly pay for jobs that require a similar level of training and education.[41]

Women gained a major victory in the workplace in 1993 when Congress passed the Family and Medical Leave Act. It provides for up to 12 weeks of unpaid leave for employees to care for a new baby or a seriously ill family member. Upon return from leave, the employee ordinarily must be given the original or an equivalent job position with equivalent pay and benefits. These provisions apply to men as well as women, but women were the instigating force behind the legislation and are the primary beneficiaries because they usually bear most of the responsibility for newborn or sick family members.

Most single-parent families are headed by women, and about one in four of these families live below the poverty line, which is five times the level of two-parent families (see Figure 5-1). The situation has been described as "the feminization of poverty." Especially vulnerable are single-parent families headed by women who work in a nonprofessional field. Women without a college education or special skills often cannot find jobs that pay significantly more than the child-care expenses they incur if they work outside the home.

figure 5-1 PERCENTAGE OF FAMILIES LIVING IN POVERTY, BY FAMILY COMPOSITION

Poverty is more than five times higher among female-headed households than among two-parent households. (*Source:* U.S. Census Bureau, 2020)

Women have made major gains in the area of political office. In 1981, Sandra Day O'Connor became the first female Supreme Court justice. When the Democratic Party chose Geraldine Ferraro as its 1984 vice presidential nominee, she became the first woman to run on a major party's national ticket. In 2016, Hillary Clinton, as the Democratic presidential nominee, became the first woman to head the ticket. Kamala Harris's election as vice president in 2020 made her the first woman to hold the nation's second highest office. Nevertheless, women are still a long way from attaining political parity.[42] Women hold only a fourth of congressional seats (see "How the U.S. Differs").

Hispanic Americans

Hispanic Americans—that is, people of Spanish-speaking background—are one of the nation's oldest ethnic groups. Hispanics helped colonize California, Texas, Florida, New Mexico, and Arizona before those areas were annexed by the United States. Nevertheless, most Hispanics are immigrants or the children or grandchildren of immigrants.

Hispanics are the nation's largest racial or ethnic minority group. More than 50 million Hispanics live in the United States—twice the number of two decades ago. They have emigrated to the United States primarily from Mexico and the Caribbean islands, mainly Cuba and Puerto Rico. About half of all Hispanics in the United States were born in Mexico or claim a Mexican ancestry. Hispanics are concentrated in their states of entry. Florida, New York, and New Jersey have large numbers of Caribbean Hispanics, whereas California, Texas, Arizona, and New Mexico have many Mexican immigrants. Hispanics, mostly of Mexican descent, constitute more than half of the population of Los Angeles.

An early civil rights action by Hispanics occurred in California in the late 1960s, when Hispanic farm laborers, most of whom were migrant workers, went on strike over labor rights. Migrants were working long hours for low pay, were living in shacks without electricity or plumbing, and were unwelcome in many local schools and hospitals. Farm owners at first refused to bargain with the workers, but a well-organized national boycott of California grapes and lettuce forced the state to pass a law giving migrant workers the right to bargain collectively.

HOW THE U.S. DIFFERS

CRITICAL THINKING THROUGH COMPARISONS

Women's Representation in National Legislatures

Women today hold far more congressional seats than at earlier times in American history, but they are still far from achieving parity with men. Moreover, the United States ranks substantially below European democracies in terms of the percentage of women lawmakers, as the chart indicates.

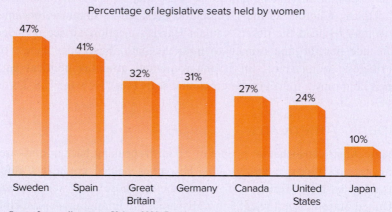

Percentage of legislative seats held by women

Sweden	Spain	Great Britain	Germany	Canada	United States	Japan
47%	41%	32%	31%	27%	24%	10%

Source: Inter-parliamentary Union, 2020. Based on seats in the single or lower legislative chamber, which is the House of Representatives in the case of the United States.

Q: How might differences in the U.S. and European electoral systems contribute to differences in the number of women legislators? (Most European democracies rely on a proportional representation system, where the parties get seats in proportion to the number of votes they receive in the election. In contrast, U.S. candidates are elected singly in legislative districts.)

A: In a proportional representation system, each party lists its candidates in priority order before the election. By placing women high on its list, a party can ensure that they will receive a certain proportion of the legislative seats that it wins in an election. In contrast, the U.S. system rests on the preferences of voters in individual contests, which makes it harder for a political party to control who gets its legislative seats. (The proportional and single-member district systems are explained more fully in Chapter 8.)

The strikes were led by Cesar Chavez, who had grown up in a Mexican American migrant family. Chavez's tactics were copied with less success in other states, including Texas.[43]

Recent Hispanic civil rights action has centered on undocumented immigrants, individuals who have entered the country illegally or stayed after their visa expired. Estimates of the number of undocumented immigrants run as high as 12 million people, most of whom are Hispanic. Although polls show that most Americans favor providing them a path to citizenship,[44] they've periodically been the target of heightened legislative or law enforcement efforts aimed at their deportation. Such efforts have been resisted by the Hispanic community and, in some instances, have sparked mass demonstrations.

Hispanics make up the largest proportion of "Dreamers," who are undocumented immigrants brought into the country as young children. Several attempts in Congress to grant them legal status have been unsuccessful and, in 2012, the Obama administration established the Deferred Action for Childhood Arrivals program (DACA) to protect them from deportation. The Trump administration rescinded the program but, in a 2020 ruling, the Supreme Court invalidated the action, saying that the Trump administration had not, as required by law, provided an adequate justification for its policy.[45]

President Donald Trump sought a border wall running the length of the U.S.–Mexico border to control illegal immigration and expanded efforts to detain and deport undocumented immigrants. Polls indicated that a large majority of Hispanic Americans opposed the policies. (a katz/Shutterstock)

Hispanics' average annual income is substantially below the national average, but the effect is buffered somewhat by Hispanics' family structure. Compared with Black Americans, Hispanics are nearly twice as likely to live in a two-parent family, often a two-income family. As a result, fewer Hispanic than Black families live below the poverty line. Health researchers have concluded that family structure helps account for the fact that Hispanics are healthier and have a longer life expectancy than would be predicted on the basis of their education and income levels.

More than 4,000 Hispanic Americans hold public office. Hispanics have been elected to statewide office in several states, including New Mexico and Arizona, and nearly three dozen Hispanic Americans currently serve in the House of Representatives. In 2009, Sonia Sotomayor was appointed to serve on the U.S. Supreme Court, becoming the first Hispanic to do so. In 2016, Senators Marco Rubio and Ted Cruz were top contenders for the Republican presidential nomination—the first time any Hispanic had achieve that level of success. At present, only about half of all Hispanics are registered to vote, limiting the group's political power. Nevertheless, the sheer size of the Hispanic population in states such as Texas, Florida, and California will make the group a potent political force in the years to come (see Chapter 8).

Native Americans

When white settlers first arrived, an estimated 5 to 10 million Native Americans lived in what is now the United States. By 1900, they numbered less than a million. In the whole of recorded history, no people had suffered such a steep population decline in such a short period. Smallpox and other diseases brought by white settlers took the heaviest toll, but wars and massacres also contributed. Until Congress changed the policy in 1924, Native Americans by law were denied citizenship, which meant they lacked even the power to vote.

At first, Native Americans were not part of the 1960s civil rights movement. That changed in 1972 when Native American leaders organized the "Trail of Broken Treaties," a caravan that journeyed from California to Washington, D.C., to protest federal policy. The next year, armed Native Americans took control of the village of Wounded Knee on a Sioux reservation in South Dakota. Over the next two months, they exchanged sporadic gunfire with U.S. marshals, leaving 2 Native Americans dead and 1 marshal paralyzed. Eight decades earlier at Wounded Knee, U.S. cavalry had shot to death 300 unarmed Sioux men, women, and children.

In 1974, Congress passed legislation that granted Native Americans living on reservations greater control over federal programs affecting them. Six years earlier, Congress had enacted the Indian Civil Rights Act, which gives Native Americans on reservations constitutional guarantees similar to those held by other Americans.

HOW THE 50 STATES DIFFER

CRITICAL THINKING THROUGH COMPARISONS

Minority-Group Populations in the States

Black Americans, Hispanics, and Asian Americans constitute about 40 percent of the U.S. population; by 2050, they will constitute a majority. Minorities are already in the majority in Hawaii, California, New Mexico, and Texas. States in the upper Midwest have the smallest minority-group populations.

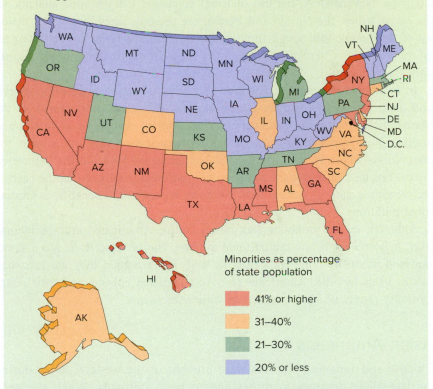

Minorities as percentage of state population

- 41% or higher
- 31–40%
- 21–30%
- 20% or less

Q: What factors might explain the high proportion of minorities in some states?

A: Southern states have large Black populations, a legacy of slavery. Southwestern states owe their large minority populations to their proximity to the Mexican border, which has been a major point of entry for immigrants from Mexico and Central and South America. In the North, the more heavily industrialized states tend to have larger minority populations than the more rural states. During the 20th century, large numbers of Black Americans left the South for jobs in northern cities (the so-called Great Migration).

Full-blooded Native Americans, including Alaska Natives, currently number more than 2 million, about half of whom live on or close to reservations set aside for them by the federal government. State governments have no direct authority over federal reservations, and the federal government's authority is defined by the terms of its treaty with each tribe. U.S. policy toward the reservations has varied over time, but the current policy is aimed at fostering self-government and economic self-sufficiency.[46]

Preservation of Native American culture is another policy goal. At an earlier time, English was required of Native American children in schools run by the Bureau of Indian Affairs. They can now be taught in their native language. Nevertheless, the use of tribal languages has declined sharply. Of the larger tribes, the Navajo and Pueblo are the only ones in which a majority of the people still speak their native language at home. Ninety percent or more of the Cherokee, Chippewa, Creek, Iroquois, and Lumbee speak only English.

In recent years, a number of tribes have erected gaming casinos on reservation land. One of the world's largest casinos, Foxwoods, is operated by the Mashantucket Pequots in Connecticut. Casinos have brought economic opportunities. The employment level of Native Americans living on or near the reservations where casinos are located has increased by a fourth.[47] However, the casinos have also brought controversy—traditionalists argue that the casinos are creating a gaming culture that, whatever its economic benefits, is eroding tribal traditions.[48]

Although casino gambling has raised Native Americans' average income level, it is still far below the national average. Native Americans are a disadvantaged group by other indicators as well. For example, they are less than half as likely as other Americans to have completed college, and their infant mortality rate is nearly twice that of white Americans.[49]

Asian Americans

Chinese and Japanese laborers were brought to the western states during the late 1800s to work in mines and to build railroads. When the need for their labor declined, Congress in 1892 suspended Asian immigration on grounds that Asians were inferior people. Over the next seven decades, laws and informal arrangements blocked the entry of people from most Asian countries, including China and Japan. In 1965, as part of its broader civil rights agenda, Congress lifted restrictions on Asian immigration. Strict limits on Hispanic immigration were also lifted at this time, and, since then, most immigrants have come from Latin America and Asia (see Figure 5-2).

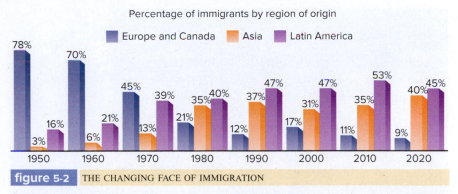

Percentage of immigrants by region of origin

■ Europe and Canada   ■ Asia   ■ Latin America

| figure 5-2 | THE CHANGING FACE OF IMMIGRATION |

Until 1965, immigration laws were biased in favor of European immigrants. The laws enacted in 1965 increased the proportion of immigrants from Asia and Latin America. Percentages are totals for each decade; for example, the 2020 figures are for the 2011–2020 period. (*Source:* U.S. Immigration and Naturalization Service, 2020)

Asian Americans were not active to any great extent in the civil rights movement, but their rights were expanded by the 1964 Civil Rights Act and other policies enacted in response to the efforts of other groups. However, in *Lau v. Nichols* (1974), a case initiated by a Chinese American family, the Supreme Court ruled unanimously that placing public school children for whom English is a second language in regular classrooms without special assistance violates the Civil Rights Act because it denies them the opportunity to obtain a proper education.[50] The Court did not mandate bilingual instruction, but the *Lau* decision prompted many schools to implement it.

Asian Americans are the nation's fastest growing ethnic group and now number about 18 million, or roughly 6 percent of the total U.S. population. Most Asian Americans live on the West Coast, particularly in California. China, Japan, Korea, India, Vietnam, and the Philippines are the ancestral homes of most Asian Americans.

Asian Americans are an upwardly mobile group.[51] Most Asian cultures emphasize family-based self-reliance, which, in the American context, includes educational achievement as a means of getting ahead. Asian Americans now make up a disproportionately large share of students at the nation's top universities, which base admission primarily on high school grades and standardized test scores.[52]

Asian Americans have the highest percentage of two-parent families of any racial group, which, in combination with educational attainment, has led to their emergence in the past two decades as the group with the highest median family income. The median Asian American family's income exceeds

Asian Americans have faced discrimination throughout their history. During World War II, for example, Japanese Americans living on the West Coast were relocated to inland detention camps on grounds they might assist America's enemy, Japan. Ironically, Japanese Americans were allowed to fight in Europe and made up the entirety of the U.S. Army's 442nd Regimental Combat Team. The 442nd became the most decorated unit of its size, not just in World War II but in the entire history of the U.S. Army. Twenty-one of its soldiers won the Congressional Medal of Honor—the nation's highest award for valor. (National Archives and Records Administration (26-G-3422))

$60,000, which is about $10,000 more than that of the median non-Hispanic white family and almost double that of the median Black or Hispanic family.

Nevertheless, Asian Americans are underrepresented in certain areas of the workplace. According to U.S. government figures, Asian Americans account for about 5 percent of professionals and technicians. However, they have not attained a proportionate share of top business positions; they hold less than 3 percent of managerial jobs. They hold a larger proportion of such positions in the tech sector, but, even there, they are underrepresented relative to the number of Asian Americans who work in that sector.[53]

Asian Americans are also underrepresented politically, even by comparison with Hispanics and Blacks.[54] Only a dozen Asian Americans currently serve in Congress. Nevertheless, the election of Kamala Harris as vice president in 2020 was a breakthrough for Asian Americans. She is of black and South Asian descent.

Other Disadvantaged Groups

The Civil Rights Act of 1964 classified women and minorities as legally protected groups, which has made it easier for them to pursue their claims in federal court. Other disadvantaged groups do not have the same degree of legal protection but have benefited from particular policies. For example, the Age Discrimination Act of 1975 and the Age Discrimination in Employment Act of 1967 prohibit discrimination against older workers in hiring for jobs in which age is not a critical factor in job performance. More recently, mandatory retirement ages for most jobs have been eliminated by law. Nevertheless, the courts have given government and employers some leeway in establishing age-based policies.[55] Forced retirement for reasons of age is permissible if justified by the nature of a particular job or the performance of a particular employee. Commercial airline pilots, for instance, are required by law to retire at 65 years of age and must pass a rigorous physical examination to continue flying after they reach the age of 60.

Individuals with disabilities also have legal protections. In 1990, for example, Congress passed the Americans with Disabilities Act, which grants employment and other protections to this group. Government agencies are required, for instance, to take reasonable steps, such as installing access ramps, to make public buildings and services available to those with disabilities.[56] Earlier, through the Education for All Handicapped Children Act of 1975, Congress required that schools provide all children, however severe their disability, with a free and appropriate education. Before the legislation, 4 million children with disabilities were getting either no education or an inappropriate one (for example, a blind child who is not taught braille).

No disadvantaged group has gained more legal protection recently than has the LGBTQ community. In 2004, Massachusetts became the first state to permit same-sex marriage. The effort spread to other states, and in *Obergefell v. Hodges* (2015) the Supreme Court expanded the right to include all states, holding that bans on same-sex marriage violated the Fourteenth Amendment's guarantees of equal protection and due process.[57]

Public opinion was a driving force behind the change. Rarely in the history of polling has public opinion on a major issue changed so dramatically and so quickly as in the case of same-sex marriage (see Figure 5-3). In the 1990s, less than 30 percent of Americans expressed support for same-sex marriage.

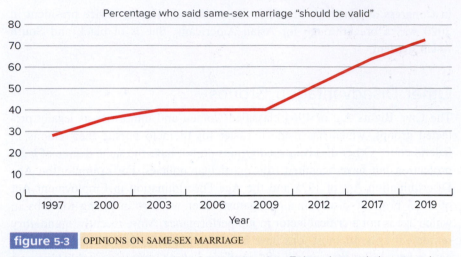

Percentage who said same-sex marriage "should be valid"

figure 5-3   OPINIONS ON SAME-SEX MARRIAGE

Twenty years ago, most Americans opposed same-sex marriage. Today, a large majority support it. (*Source:* Gallup poll, 2019)

Today, more than 70 percent do so. The support level is particularly high among younger adults—more than three-fourths of them say same-sex couples should be allowed to marry. Within all age groups, however, the support level has risen substantially. Among Americans over 65 years of age, for example, more than two in every five now approve of same-sex marriage, which is three times as many as favored it in the 1990s.

Nevertheless, job discrimination against gay and transgender workers was legal in many states. In 2020, the Supreme Court ruled on the question of whether the ban on sexual discrimination in the 1964 Civil Rights Act includes a ban on sexual orientation. In a 6-3 decision, the Court concluded that it did. Speaking for the majority, Justice Neil Gorsuch wrote, "An individual's homosexuality or transgender status is not relevant to employment decisions. That's because it is impossible to discriminate against a person for being homosexual or transgender without discriminating against that individual based on sex."[58]

Other groups could have been discussed in this section. The United States has a long history of religious discrimination, targeted at various times against Catholics, Jews, Mormons, Muslims, various Protestant sects, and others. Numerous ethnic groups, including the Irish, Italians, and Poles, have likewise faced severe discrimination. Space precludes a fuller discussion of discrimination in America, but there is no hiding the fact that equality has been America's most elusive ideal.

DISCRIMINATION: SUPERFICIAL DIFFERENCES, DEEP DIVISIONS

In 1944, Swedish sociologist Gunnar Myrdal gained fame for his book *An American Dilemma*, whose title referred to deep-rooted inequality in a country that idealizes equality.[59] Myrdal concluded that there were two Americas, one inhabited by its whites and one inhabited by its minorities. Few recent developments illustrate more clearly the two Americas than does the COVID-19 pandemic. Compared with white Americans, Black Americans were more than twice as likely to die from the disease, a reflection of their higher housing density, more limited access to quality medical care, and higher incidence of poverty-related comorbidity factors, including hypertension, obesity and diabetes.[60]

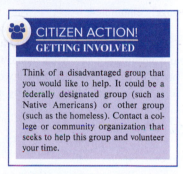

CITIZEN ACTION!
GETTING INVOLVED

Think of a disadvantaged group that you would like to help. It could be a federally designated group (such as Native Americans) or other group (such as the homeless). Contact a college or community organization that seeks to help this group and volunteer your time.

Myrdal called discrimination "America's curse." He could have broadened the generalization. Discrimination is civilization's curse, as is clear from the thousands of ethnic, national, and religious conflicts that have marred human history. But America carries a special responsibility because of its high ideals. In the words of Abraham Lincoln, the United States is a nation "dedicated to the proposition that all men are created equal."

SUMMARY

During the past half-century, the United States has undergone a revolution in the legal status of its traditionally disadvantaged groups, including African Americans, women, Native Americans, Hispanic Americans, and Asian Americans. Such groups are now provided equal protection under the law in areas such as education, employment, and voting. Discrimination by race, sex, and ethnicity has not been eliminated from American life, but it is no longer substantially backed by the force of law. This advance was achieved against strong resistance from established interests, which only begrudgingly and slowly responded to demands for equality in law.

Traditionally disadvantaged Americans have achieved fuller equality primarily as a result of their struggle for greater rights. The Supreme Court has been an instrument of change for disadvantaged groups. Its ruling in *Brown v. Board of Education* (1954), in which racial segregation in public schools was declared a violation of the Fourteenth Amendment's equal-protection clause, was a major breakthrough in equal rights. Through its affirmative action and other rulings, such as those providing equal access to the vote, the Court has also mandated the active promotion of social, political, and economic equality. However, because civil rights policy involves large issues concerned with social values and the distribution of society's opportunities and benefits, civil rights have also been advanced through legislative and administrative action. The history of civil rights includes landmark legislation, such as the 1964 Civil Rights Act and the 1965 Voting Rights Act.

In more recent decades, civil rights issues have receded from the prominence they had during the 1960s. The scope of affirmative action programs has narrowed, and the use of forced busing to achieve racial integration in America's public schools has been largely eliminated.

The legal gains of disadvantaged groups over the past half-century have not been fully matched by material gains. Although progress in areas such as education, income, and health care has been made, it has often been slow and incomplete. Tradition, prejudice, and the sheer difficulty of social, economic, and political progress stand as formidable obstacles to achieving a more equal America.

CRITICAL THINKING ZONE

KEY TERMS

affirmative action (*p. 138*)
de facto discrimination (*p. 138*)
de jure discrimination (*p. 138*)
equal-protection clause (*p. 129*)

equal rights (civil rights) (*p. 128*)
reasonable-basis test (*p. 132*)
strict-scrutiny test (*p. 133*)
suspect classifications (*p. 133*)

APPLYING THE ELEMENTS OF CRITICAL THINKING

Conceptualizing: Distinguish between de jure discrimination and de facto discrimination. Why is the latter form of discrimination more difficult to overcome?

Synthesizing: Using material in this chapter and the previous one, contrast the Fourteenth Amendment's due process clause with its equal-protection clause. What level of government in America's federal system is governed by the two clauses?

Analyzing: What role have political movements played in securing the legal rights of disadvantaged groups?

EXTRA CREDIT

A Book Worth Reading: Ta-Nehisi Coates, *Between the World and Me* (New York: Spiegel & Grau, 2015). Winner of the 2015 National Book Award for Nonfiction, the book recounts the history of violence directed at Black Americans.

A Website Worth Visiting: **www.cawp.rutgers.edu** The Center for American Women and Politics at Rutgers University tracks women's political participation. Its website has state-by-state information on the subject.

6
CHAPTER

PUBLIC OPINION AND POLITICAL SOCIALIZATION: SHAPING THE PEOPLE'S VOICE

Hisham Ibrahim/Getty Images

" Towering over Presidents and [Congress] . . . public opinion stands out, in the United States, as the great source of power, the master of servants who tremble before it. "

JAMES BRYCE[1]

On the afternoon of February 14, 2018, a gunman walked into Marjory Stoneman Douglas High School in Parkland, Florida, and opened fire, killing 14 students and 3 staff members, as well as wounding more than a dozen others. It was the eighth school shooting in less than two months, and the deadliest since the massacre of 26 children and teachers at Connecticut's Sandy Hook Elementary School in 2012.

The Parkland shooting brought calls for stricter gun control but, unlike earlier shootings, the response was sustained. The surviving Marjory Stoneman Douglas High School students demanded that lawmakers take action to stop school violence. They went on television to voice their concerns, held public demonstrations, and traveled to Washington and their state capital to pressure lawmakers. Polls showed a rise in support for gun control measures. Two-thirds of Americans said there should be a ban on assault rifles—the type of weapon used in the Parkland shooting. More than 90 percent wanted tighter background checks on gun buyers.[2] Nevertheless, few changes occurred. Congress took no action. That was also true of most state legislatures, although some states, including Florida, responded with policies such as "red flag" laws that give law enforcement officers the authority to temporarily take firearms from individuals deemed likely to harm other people or themselves.

Gun control is a telling example of the influence of public opinion on government. Public opinion is not something that public officials can ignore, but it is also not something that forces them to take a specific course of action. They have considerable freedom in deciding whether to act and what action to take if they do act.

Students from Marjory Stoneman Douglas High School in Parkland, Florida, spoke in support of gun control after 14 of their classmates and 3 staff members were shot to death by a former student. Their efforts placed pressure on lawmakers to address the problem of gun violence in America's schools. (Shawn Thew/EPA-EFE/Shutterstock)

This chapter discusses public opinion and its influence on U.S. politics. In this text, **public opinion** is defined as the politically relevant opinions held by ordinary citizens that they express openly. That expression can be verbal, as when citizens voice an opinion to a neighbor or respond to a question asked in an opinion poll. But public opinion can also take other forms—for example, participating in a protest demonstration or casting a vote in an election. The key point is that people's private thoughts become public opinion when they are revealed to others.

A major theme of the chapter is that public opinion is a powerful yet inexact force.[3] The policies of the U.S. government cannot be understood apart from public opinion; at the same time, public opinion is not a precise determinant of public policies. The chapter makes the following main points:

- *Public opinion consists of those views held by ordinary citizens that are openly expressed.* Public officials have various means of gauging public opinion but increasingly use public opinion polls for this purpose.

- *Public opinion is characterized by its direction (whether people hold a pro or con position on an issue), its intensity (how strongly people feel about their issue position), and its salience (how high a particular issue ranks in people's minds relative to other issues).*

- *The process by which individuals acquire their political opinions is called political socialization.* This process begins during childhood, when, through family and school, people acquire many of their basic political values and beliefs. Socialization continues into adulthood, during which time the news media, peers, and political leaders are important influences.

- *Americans' political opinions are shaped by several frames of reference, including partisanship, ideology, and group attachments.*

- *Public opinion has an important influence on government but ordinarily does not determine exactly what officials will do.*

THE MEASUREMENT OF PUBLIC OPINION

President Woodrow Wilson said that he had spent much of his adult life in government and yet had never seen "a government." What Wilson was saying, in effect, was that government is a system of relationships. A government is not tangible in the way that a building is. So it is with public opinion. No one has ever seen "a public opinion," and thus it cannot be measured directly. It must be assessed indirectly.

Election returns are a traditional method for assessing public opinion. Politicians routinely draw conclusions about what citizens are thinking by studying how they vote. Letters to the editor in newspapers and the size of crowds at mass demonstrations are among the other means of judging public opinion. All these indicators are useful guides for policymakers. Each of them, however, is a limited guide to what the public as a whole is thinking. Election returns indicate how many votes each party or candidate received but do not indicate why voters acted as they did. As for letter writers and demonstrators, research indicates that their opinions are more intense and often more extreme than those of most citizens.[4]

Public Opinion Polls

Today, opinion polls (also known as opinion surveys) are the primary method for estimating public sentiment.[5] In a **public opinion poll**, a relatively few individuals—the **sample**—are interviewed in order to estimate the opinions of a whole **population**, such as the residents of a city or country.

How is it possible to measure the thinking of a large population on the basis of a relatively small sample of that population? How can interviews with, say, 1,000 Americans provide a reliable estimate of what millions of them are thinking? The answer is found in the laws of probability. Consider a hypothetical example of a huge jar filled with a million marbles, half of them red and half of them blue. If a blindfolded person reaches into the jar, the probability of selecting a marble of a given color is 50–50. And, if 1,000 marbles are chosen in this random way, it is likely that about half of them will be red and about half will be blue. Opinion sampling works in the same way. If respondents are chosen at random from a population, their opinions will approximate those of the population as a whole.

Random selection is the key to scientific polling, which is theoretically based on *probability sampling*—a sample in which each individual in the population has a known probability of being chosen at random for inclusion. Individuals do not step forward to be interviewed; they are selected at random to be part of the sample. A scientific poll is thereby different from an Internet survey that invites visitors to a site to participate. Any such survey is biased because it includes only individuals who use the Internet, who happen for one reason or another to visit the particular site, and who have the time and inclination to complete the survey.

The science of polling is such that the size of the sample, as opposed to the size of the population, is the key to the poll's accuracy. Although it might be assumed that a much larger sample would be required to poll accurately the people of the United States as opposed to, say, the residents of Georgia or San Antonio, the sample requirements are nearly the same. Consider again the example of a huge jar filled with marbles, half of them red and half of them blue. If

1,000 marbles were randomly selected, about half would be red and about half would be blue, regardless of whether the jar held 1 million, 10 million, or 100 million marbles. By contrast, the size of the sample—the number of marbles selected—would matter. If only 10 marbles were drawn, it could happen that 5 would be of each color but, then again, it would not be unusual for 6 or 7 of them to have the same color. In fact, the odds are about 1 in 20 that 8 or more would be the same color. However, if 1,000 marbles were drawn, it's highly unlikely that 600 or more of the marbles would be of the same color. In fact, the odds of drawing 600 of the same color would be about 1 in 100,000.

The accuracy of a poll is expressed in terms of **sampling error**—the error that results from using a sample to estimate the population. A sample provides an estimate of what the population is thinking, and sampling error is a measure of how accurate that estimate is likely to be. As would be expected, the larger the sample, the smaller the sampling error. A sample of 1,000 respondents would be expected to be more accurate than one of 200 respondents if the surveys were otherwise conducted in the same way.

Sampling error is usually expressed as a plus-or-minus percentage. For example, a properly drawn sample of 1,000 individuals has a sampling error of roughly plus or minus 3 percent. Thus, if 55 percent of a sample of 1,000 respondents say they intend to vote for the Republican presidential candidate, there is a high probability that between 52 and 58 percent (55 percent plus or minus 3 percent) of all voters actually plan to vote Republican. It should be noted that, if the poll had found that the candidates were separated by one percentage point, it would be statistically incorrect to claim that one of them is "leading." The one-point difference in their support is smaller than the poll's three-point sampling error.

Opinion Dimensions

In studying public opinion, scholars and pollsters focus on attributes of people's opinions. One attribute is **direction**—whether people have a pro or con position on a topic. A 2020 poll, for example, asked respondents whether marijuana use should be made legal. Fifty-eight percent of the respondents said it should be made legal and 27 percent said it should not.[6]

A second attribute of people's opinions is **intensity**—how strongly people feel about their opinion on a topic. Studies have regularly found, for example, a difference in intensity on the gun control issue.[7] Although a larger number of Americans favor tightening controls on guns, those opposed to such controls feel more strongly about the issue and are more likely to say they will only vote for candidates who share their view (see "Case Study: Gun Control").

Politics in Action

Gun Control

The United States has more gun-related deaths per capita than nearly any country, which has led to calls for increased gun control. Some federal laws have been enacted, such as those banning gun sales to felons and the mentally ill, but the U.S. has less gun control than other Western democracies. In fact, despite dozens of recent mass shootings, including ones that have taken place in schools, Congress has not passed a major gun control law in more than two decades.

Zoonar GmbH/Alamy Stock Photo

What's the nature of public opinion on gun control, and how might it help explain Congress's inaction? In terms of the *direction* of public opinion, Americans are split on the issue, although a majority favors stricter gun control laws. In terms of *intensity,* gun rights advocates tend to be more committed to their position than are gun control advocates. Those who favor gun rights are far more likely than those who favor gun control to give money or contact a public official in an effort to influence gun policy.[8] Finally, in terms of *saliency,* gun control usually ranks low on the public's list of top issues. In most Gallup polls over the past two decades, 1 percent of respondents or fewer have named gun violence when asked what they regarded as the nation's "most important problem."

Q: How might the attributes of public opinion—its direction, intensity, and salience—help explain why Congress has not taken decisive action to curb gun violence?

ASK YOURSELF: What's the significance of the fact that those who oppose gun control have more intense opinions and are more likely to act on them? Does the relatively low salience of the issue give lawmakers leeway in terms of deciding whether to take action?

People's opinions differ in important ways, one of which is intensity. On virtually every issue, some people feel more strongly about it than do others. Politicians are typically more attentive to intense opinions than to lightly held ones, knowing that those who hold intense views are more likely to act on them. (Andrius Repsys/Shutterstock)

A third opinion attribute is **salience**—how important people think an issue is relative to other issues. Salience is related to intensity; the more strongly people feel about an issue, the more likely they are to think that it's important. But the two attributes are not identical. An individual might, for example, have an intense opinion about genetically modified food but see it as less salient than an issue such as unemployment. In polls, salience is typically measured by asking respondents what they regard as the top issues.

Problems with Polls

Although polls are the most widely used method for assessing public opinion, they are not without flaws. One problem is that pollsters rarely have a list of all individuals in the population from which to sample. An expedient alternative is a sample based on telephone numbers. Pollsters use computers to randomly pick telephone numbers (now also including cell phone numbers), which are dialed by interviewers to reach households. Within each of these households, a respondent is then randomly selected. Because the computer is as likely to pick one telephone number as any other, a sample selected in this way is assumed to be representative of the whole population.

Detecting Misinformation

Can the Polls Be Trusted?

In the 2020 presidential election, pollsters predicted that Joe Biden would win the national popular margin by a wider margin than proved to be the case, which prompted Donald Trump to accuse pollsters of deliberately falsifying the results. Four years earlier, although Hillary Clinton had more popular votes nationally than Trump, the margin was smaller than the polls had predicted. After Trump won the 2016 election by getting more

Bettmann/Getty Images

electoral votes than Clinton, he ridiculed the polls, tweeting that they were not to be trusted—"fake polls."

Is that claim fact, or is it fake?

In 2016 and 2020, the final national polls of Gallup and other established organizations underestimated Trump's voter support by roughly 2 percentage points on average. Nevertheless, their estimates of the national popular vote were within sampling error of the actual results both times. Only once have the established national polls been way off the mark, and it happened during the early years of polling. In 1948, a Gallup poll taken several weeks before the election showed Harry Truman trailing badly. Gallup stopped polling at that point in the campaign and missed a late shift in the vote that carried Truman to a four-point victory.

Typically, the least-accurate presidential election polls are those conducted at the state level. Some of the state-level polls are conducted by organizations with limited experience in election polling. In 2016, for example, some of them overestimated Hillary Clinton's vote because they failed to adjust the results for the fact that they had oversampled Democratic-leaning respondents. Resources are also a problem for some state polls. The sponsors lack the money to contact a large sample of respondents using live interviewers, which is the norm for established national polling organizations. Some state polls even resort to less reliable methods like robocalls. In short, not all polls are equal. The most accurate ones are conducted by experienced professionals who apply rigorous methodological standards.

Nevertheless, some Americans do not have phones, and many of those who are called will not be home or refuse to participate. Such factors reduce the accuracy of telephone polling. Indeed, pollsters are concerned about the future of telephone polling. The refusal rate has increased sharply in recent decades.

The accuracy of polling is also diminished when respondents are asked about issues with which they are not familiar. Although many respondents will answer the question anyway in order not to appear uninformed, their responses cannot be regarded as valid. Scholars label such responses "nonopinions." In other instances, respondents will have an opinion but choose to hide it. Respondents are not always truthful, for example, when it comes to expressing opinions that relate to race, gender, or ethnicity. A recent study that compared poll results and online behavior, for example, concluded that racism is far more prevalent in the United States than opinion polls indicate.[9]

Question wording can also affect poll results. A recent poll, for example, used a variety of questions to measure Americans' opinions on immigration policy. When respondents were asked whether "ties to family members in the United States" should be taken into account in deciding whom to admit, 60 percent said it should be. When they were then asked whether "professional or academic achievement" should factor in, 54 percent said yes. Responses to those two questions would suggest that Americans place family ties ahead of achievement as an immigration criterion. However, when respondents were asked later in the same poll whether immigration policy should place "greater emphasis on an applicant's job skills over their ties to family members," 56 percent agreed, while 42 percent disagreed, suggesting that Americans place achievement ahead of family ties as a criterion.[10]

Despite such issues, polls remain the best available indicator of people's opinions. If the questions are worded carefully and proper procedures are followed, polls can capture what the public is thinking on the issues and events of the moment.

POLITICAL SOCIALIZATION: THE ORIGINS OF AMERICANS' OPINIONS

Although public opinion is a response to current issues, personalities, and events, it has deeper origins. Public opinion is affected by citizens' prior attitudes, such as how they feel about the political parties and what they think is the proper role of government. Citizens' prior attitudes are acquired through a learning process called **political socialization**. Just as language, a religion, or an athletic skill is acquired through a learning process, so are people's political orientations.

Broadly speaking, the process of political socialization has two distinguishing characteristics. First, although socialization continues throughout life, most people's political outlook is influenced by childhood learning. Basic ideas about whether the Democratic Party or the Republican Party is the better party, for example, are often formed uncritically in childhood, in much the same way that belief in the superiority of a particular religion—typically, the religion of one's parents—is acquired.

A second characteristic of political socialization is that it is a cumulative process. Early learning affects later learning because people's prior beliefs serve as a psychological screen through which new information is filtered. When watching a presidential debate, for example, Republicans and Democrats are looking at the same event but seeing different ones. When their party's candidate is speaking, they tend to see sincerity and strength. When the other party's candidate is talking, they tend to see evasion and weakness. There's rarely been a presidential debate where Republicans or Democrats thought that their party's candidate had lost the debate.[11]

The political socialization process takes place through **agents of socialization**. They can be divided into primary and secondary agents. *Primary agents* interact closely and regularly with the individual, usually early in life, as in the case of the family. *Secondary agents* have a less intimate connection with the individual and are usually more important later in life, as in the case of work associates. It is helpful to consider briefly how various primary and secondary agents affect political learning.

Primary Socializing Agents: Family, School, and Religion

The family is a powerful primary agent because it has a near-monopoly on the attention of a young child, who trusts what a parent says. By the time children reach adulthood, many of the beliefs and values that will stay with them throughout life are firmly in place. Indeed, as sociologist Herbert Hyman concluded from his research, "Foremost among agencies of socialization into politics is the family."[12] Many adults are Republicans or Democrats today almost solely because their parents backed that party. They can give all sorts of reasons for preferring their party to the other, but the reasons came later in life.[13]

Like the family, schools have an influence on children's basic political beliefs. Teachers at the elementary level particularly praise the country's political institutions and mark the birthdays of national heroes such as George Washington, Abraham Lincoln, and Martin Luther King Jr.[14] U.S. schools are more instrumental in building support for the nation and its cultural beliefs

Grade school is a primary agent of political socialization, serving to introduce students to American ideals, customs, and historical heroes. (Jill Braaten/McGraw-Hill)

than are the schools in most other democracies. The Pledge of Allegiance, which is recited daily at the start of classes in many American schools, has no equivalent in Europe. Schools there do not open the day by asking students to pledge loyalty to their nation.

Religious organizations are also a powerful childhood socializing agent. Although many American children do not experience religion or do so only fleetingly, others attend religious services regularly. Scholars have not studied the influence of religion on childhood political socialization as closely as they have studied the influence of families or schools.[15] Nevertheless, religion can have a formative influence on children's attitudes, including beliefs about society's obligations to the poor and the unborn.

Secondary Socializing Agents: Peers, Media, Leaders, and Events

With age, additional socializing agents come into play. An individual's peers—friends, neighbors, coworkers, and the like—become sources of opinion. Research indicates that many individuals are unwilling to deviate too far politically from what their peers think. In *The Spiral of Silence,* Elisabeth Noelle-Neumann showed that individuals tend to withhold opinions that conflict with those of the people around them. If nearly everyone in a group favors legalizing same-sex marriage, for example, a person who believes otherwise is likely to remain silent. As a result, the group's dominant opinion will appear to be more widely held than it actually is, which can persuade those with lightly held opinions to adopt the group opinion as their own.[16]

The mass media are also a powerful socializing agent. Politics for the average citizen is a secondhand affair, observed mainly through the media rather than directly. In the words of journalist Walter Lippmann, "the pictures in our heads of the world outside" owe substantially to how that world is portrayed for us by the media.[17] Heavy exposure to crime on television, for example, can lead people to believe that their community is less safe than it actually is.[18]

Individuals in positions of authority are also sources of opinion. Few developments illustrate that type of response more clearly than how Americans reacted to the advice of public officials and health care experts on how to protect themselves from the threat posed by the COVID-19 coronavirus. They responded by engaging in social distancing and foregoing unnecessary travel outside the home. Traffic and air pollution dropped to their lowest levels in decades.[19]

Finally, no accounting of the political socialization process would be complete without considering the impact of major events. The Great Depression, World War II, the Vietnam War, and the 2001 terrorist attacks are examples of events that had a lasting influence on Americans' opinions. Younger citizens were particularly affected. Their opinions are generally not as deeply rooted, which heightens their response to disruptive events.[20] Slow, long-term developments can also produce changes in people's political views. Over the past few decades, for example, partisanship has intensified to the point that Democratic and Republican lawmakers fight over nearly every issue. Each party has usually been strong enough to block the other from acting and rarely strong enough to act decisively on its own. Urgent policy problems have worsened for lack of government action. In the words of one scholar, the U.S. political system "has become appallingly dysfunctional."[21] The situation has affected Americans' pride in their democracy. As recently as 2002, 9 of every 10 Americans said they were proud "of the way democracy works in America."[22] Now, less than 7 in 10 Americans feel that way.[23] (See "How the U.S. Differs" for more on the subject of national pride.)

HOW THE U.S. DIFFERS

CRITICAL THINKING THROUGH COMPARISONS

National Pride

Political socialization in the United States is not the rigid program of indoctrination imposed by some countries on their people. Nevertheless, Americans are told of their country's greatness in many ways, everything from the Pledge of Allegiance that American children recite at the beginning of the school day to the flying of the flag on American homes and businesses. Such practices are uncommon in other democracies. At the same time, as the accompanying figure indicates, Americans' pride in their nation has been declining in response to rising partisan hostility, policy deadlock in Washington, wage stagnation, and other factors.

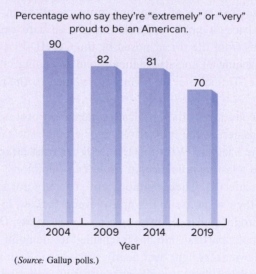

Percentage who say they're "extremely" or "very" proud to be an American.

(*Source:* Gallup polls.)

Q: Why might words and symbols of the nation's greatness be more important to Americans than to people of most countries? Why might the recent decline in Americans' pride in their political system be a worrying development?

A: The unifying bond in most countries is a common ancestral heritage. The French and Chinese, for example, have ancestral ties that go back centuries. In contrast, Americans come from many different countries and depend on national symbols and ceremonies as their unifying bond. When Americans' sense of being "one people" weakens, they can slip into selfishness and the scapegoating of those with whom they differ.

FRAMES OF REFERENCE: HOW AMERICANS THINK POLITICALLY

Through the socialization process, citizens acquire frames of reference that are important for two reasons. First, they provide an indication of how people think politically. Second, when citizens share a frame of reference, they find it easier to work together. The opinions of millions of Americans would mean almost nothing if each citizen had opinions that differed from those of all others. In contrast, if enough people have the same frame of reference, they may find reason to act together for political purposes.

The subject of how Americans think politically fills entire books. Briefly discussed here are three of the major frames of reference through which Americans evaluate political developments: party identification, political ideology, and group orientation. Subsequent chapters (particularly Chapters 7, 8, 11, and 12) will discuss them in greater detail.

Party Identification

Party identification refers to a person's sense of loyalty to a political party. Party identification is not formal membership in a party but rather an emotional attachment to it—the feeling that "I am a Democrat" or "I am a Republican." Scholars and pollsters typically have measured party identification with a question of the following type: "Generally speaking, do you think of yourself as a Republican, a Democrat, an independent, or what?" Most adults call themselves either Democrats or Republicans (see Figure 6-1). Even most of those who call themselves independents are not truly independent. When independents are asked if they lean toward the Republican or Democratic Party, about two in every three say they lean toward one of the parties. Most of them vote in the direction they lean. In fact, they are nearly as likely to support their preferred party's candidates as are voters who call themselves Republicans or Democrats.

Many Americans grow up thinking of themselves as Republicans or Democrats and remain that way throughout their adult lives, even when changes in their personal lives might reasonably lead them to switch to the other party.[24] That's clearly not true of everyone, but massive shifts in Americans' party identification are relatively rare and typically occur in response to disruptive events.[25] During the Great Depression, for example, Franklin Roosevelt's New Deal prompted large numbers of Republicans to switch their loyalty to the Democratic Party. Younger adults accounted for most of those who switched. Older adults tend to have firmer party loyalties and to be less responsive than younger adults to the issues and candidates of the moment.

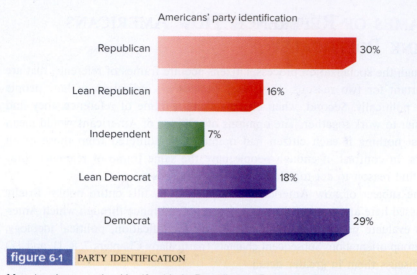

Americans' party identification

Republican — 30%

Lean Republican — 16%

Independent — 7%

Lean Democrat — 18%

Democrat — 29%

figure 6-1   PARTY IDENTIFICATION

Most Americans say they identify with the Republican or Democratic Party. Among those who call themselves independents, most say they "lean" toward a party and typically vote for that party's candidates. (*Source:* Gallup poll, March 2020)

For most people, partisanship is not blind faith in their party. Although they typically support their party's candidates, their party loyalty usually has its roots in policy. The Democratic Party, for example, has promoted the nation's social welfare and civil rights policies, whereas the Republican Party has spearheaded the nation's pro-business and tax reduction policies. The fact that most minority-group members are Democrats and most people in business are Republicans is hardly a coincidence.[26]

In the everyday world of politics, no source of opinion divides Americans more clearly than does their partisanship. On nearly every major issue, Republicans and Democrats have conflicting opinions (see Figure 6-2). A recent Pew Research Center poll found, for example, that Democrats are more likely than Republicans to see climate change and income inequality as major policy problems, whereas Republicans are more likely than Democrats to think that terrorism and illegal immigration are major problems.

Political Ideology

During the 20th century, the broad ideologies—communism, fascism, and socialism—that captured the loyalty of many Europeans proved to be of little interest to most Americans. But political ideology doesn't have to take an extreme form, as it did in the case of Soviet communism or German fascism. Conceptually,

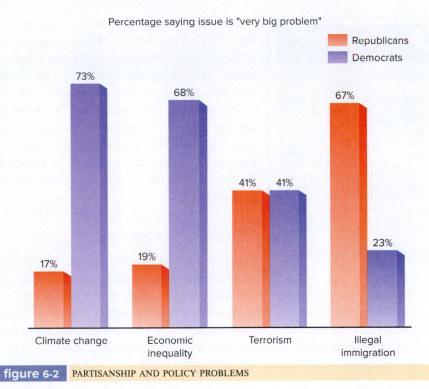

Percentage saying issue is "very big problem"

Republicans
Democrats

Climate change — 73%, 17%
Economic inequality — 68%, 19%
Terrorism — 41%, 41%
Illegal immigration — 67%, 23%

figure 6-2   PARTISANSHIP AND POLICY PROBLEMS

Republicans and Democrats differ in their opinions on the nation's top policy problems. (*Source:* Pew Research Center poll, 2019)

ideology refers to a general belief about the role and purpose of government.* Some Americans believe, for instance, that government should use its power to help people who are economically disadvantaged. Such individuals can be labeled **economic liberals**. Other Americans believe that the government should leave the distribution of economic benefits largely to the workings of the free market. They can be described as **economic conservatives**. Americans differ also in their views on government's role in regard to social and cultural issues, such as abortion and the legalization of marijuana. **Cultural (social) liberals** would leave lifestyle choices to the individual. In contrast, **cultural (social) conservatives** would use government to promote traditional values—for example, through laws banning abortion.

----

*Some scholars define ideology in a stricter way, arguing that it can be said to exist only when an individual has a consistent pattern of opinions across a broad range of specific issues. By this definition, most Americans don't have an ideology. This conception is analytically useful in some situations, but it blunts the discussion of general belief tendencies in the public as a whole, which is the purpose here.

CITIZEN ACTION!
GETTING READY

"Know thyself" was a basic tenet of Socrates' notion of citizenship. If you think of yourself as a liberal or conservative, what do you mean by that label? How do you feel about the proper role of government in helping people meet their economic needs? About the proper role of government in upholding traditional values? As defined by political scientists, conservatives are those who think government should not play a large role in helping people meet their economic needs but believe government should act to uphold traditional values, such as those stemming from traditional religious beliefs. Liberals are those who hold the opposite views.

Although it is sometimes said that liberals believe in big government, while conservatives believe in small government, this claim is inaccurate, as the foregoing discussion would indicate. Conservatives prefer a smaller role for government on economic issues but want to use the power of government to uphold cultural traditions. The reverse is true of liberals. Each group wants government to be active or inactive, depending on which approach serves its policy goals.*

Group Orientations

Many Americans see politics through group attachments. Their identity or self-interest is tied to a group, and they respond accordingly when a policy issue arises that affects it. Issues surrounding social security, for example, usually evoke a stronger response from senior citizens than from younger adults. Later chapters examine group tendencies more fully, but it is useful here to describe briefly a few groupings—religion, economic class, region, race and ethnicity, gender, and age.

Religion   Religious beliefs have long been a source of solidarity among group members and a source of conflict with outsiders. As Catholics came to America in large numbers in the 19th and early 20th centuries, they faced hostility from the Protestant majority. Religious hatred sparked the rebirth of the Ku Klux Klan, which resurrected itself in the early 1900s as anti-Catholic, as well as anti-Jewish, anti-Mormon, and anti-Black. At the Klan's peak in the 1920s, one in every six Protestant adult males was a Klan member.[27] It took the nation's all-out effort in World War II to convince the Protestant majority that Catholics weren't their enemy.

Today, Catholics, Protestants, and Jews hold similar opinions on many policy issues. Nevertheless, important religious differences remain, although the alignment shifts as the issue shifts.[28] Fundamentalist Protestants and Roman Catholics are more likely than mainline Protestants and Jews to oppose

---

*There is no logical reason, of course, why an economic liberal also has to be a cultural liberal. Although most economic liberals are also cultural liberals, some are not. The term *populist* (although some analysts prefer the term communitarian) is used to describe an individual who is an economic liberal and a cultural conservative. Similarly, some economic conservatives are cultural liberals. They believe government should refrain from undue intervention in the economic marketplace and in people's private lives. The term *libertarian* is used to characterize someone with this set of beliefs.

legalized abortion, a split that partly reflects differing religious beliefs about whether human life begins at conception or later in the development of the fetus. Religious beliefs also affect opinions on poverty programs. Support for such programs is higher among Catholics and Jews than among Protestants. An obligation to help the poor is a basic tenet of Catholic and Jewish teachings, whereas self-reliance is a basic tenet of the teachings of many Protestant denominations.

The strongest religious group in today's politics is the so-called religious right, which consists mostly of white evangelical Protestants (see "Party Polarization: Religion and Politics"). Their opinions on social issues differ sharply from those of the public as a whole. A 2020 Associated Press poll found, for example, that white evangelicals are twice as likely as other Americans to oppose gay rights and abortion rights.[29]

Economic Class   Economic class has always been a weaker force in the United States than in Europe. Friedrich Engles, who was Karl Marx's closest associate, accurately predicted that socialism, which was sweeping through Europe at the time, would fail to develop deep roots in America. Engels said

---

P A R T Y   Conflicting Ideas
POLARIZATION

Religion and Politics

A source of division for a long period of American politics, religious differences resurfaced as a dividing line in the 1970s, fueled by the abortion issue and later by issues such as same-sex marriage. Today, religious observance and partisanship are closely linked. Americans who attend church regularly are far more likely to vote Republican, as the accompanying figure indicates.

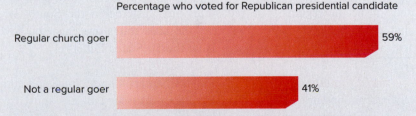

Percentage who voted for Republican presidential candidate

Regular church goer — 59%

Not a regular goer — 41%

(*Source:* Exit polls; figures are averages for the 2000 through 2020 presidential elections.)

Q: Overall, how large a role do you think religious beliefs should play in elections and in determining national policy?

that American workers lacked a deep class consciousness, believing instead that they could make it on their own.

Nevertheless, economic class does influence Americans' opinions on some issues. For example, lower-income Americans are more likely to support government-provided health care, while higher-income Americans are more likely to favor business deregulation.

An obstacle to class-based politics in the United States, particularly among those of lower income, is that they have different ideas about how to get ahead economically. Support for collective bargaining, for example, is higher among factory workers than among small farmers, white-collar workers, and workers in the skilled crafts, even though the average income of these groups is similar. Class-based action is also blunted by racial and ethnic differences. In *Strangers in Their Own Land*, Arlie Russell Hochschild describes how working-class whites see themselves as having waited patiently in line for a piece of the American Dream, only to see working-class minorities and immigrants cut the line, ushered there by affirmative action and other policy initiatives.[30] Working-class whites are better off economically than minorities, but many of them feel that they're being held back so that minorities can get ahead.[31] The interplay of class and opinion is examined more closely in Chapter 9, which discusses interest groups.

Region   For a lengthy period in U.S. history, region was the defining issue of American politics. The North and South were deeply divided over questions of race and states' rights, which persisted for a century after their bitter civil war.

Racial progress has shrunk the regional divide, as has the relocation to the South of millions of Americans from less conservative parts of the country. Nevertheless, regional differences have persisted on some issues, including social welfare and civil rights. The differences are large enough that "red states" (Republican bastions) and "blue states" (Democratic bastions) are concentrated in specific regions. The red states are clustered in the South, Great Plains, and Rocky Mountains, whereas the blue states are clustered in the Northeast and the West Coast (see "How the 50 States Differ").

Race and Ethnicity   As was discussed in Chapters 4 and 5, race and ethnicity affect opinions on civil rights and civil liberties issues. Blacks and Hispanics, for example, are generally more supportive of affirmative action and less trusting of police and the judicial system than are non-Hispanic whites. Blacks and Hispanics also tend to differ from non-Hispanic whites on social welfare spending, although this difference largely reflects differences in their income levels.

HOW THE 50 STATES DIFFER

CRITICAL THINKING THROUGH COMPARISONS

Party Loyalties in the States

The states differ widely in the number of residents who identify with the Republican and Democratic Parties. In classifying states by party, the Gallup organization lists a state as solidly Republican or Democratic if a party has an advantage in party identifiers of five percentage points or more. States in which the advantage is less than five points are judged as competitive. By Gallup's indicator, Republican strength is concentrated in the Plains and Rocky Mountains, and Democratic strength is found in the Northeast and the West Coast. The six most heavily Republican states are, in order, Wyoming, Utah, North Dakota, Alaska, Alabama, and Idaho, whereas Massachusetts, Vermont, Hawaii, New York, Maryland, and California (in that order) are the six most heavily Democratic states.

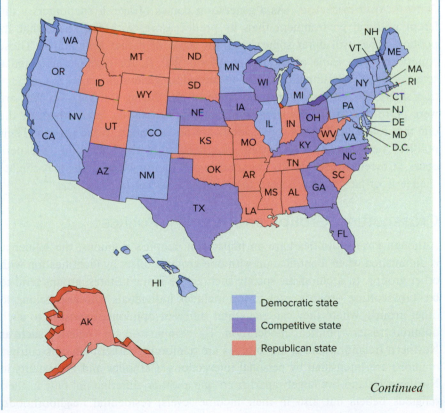

Continued

Q: Why might some states be classified as "competitive," even though they regularly tend to vote Republican or Democratic?

A: The Gallup indicator is based on people's party identification rather than on how they actually vote and whether they turn out to vote on Election Day. Turnout differences between Republicans and Democrats, as well as their level of party loyalty, largely explain why some "competitive" states regularly tend to vote Republican or Democratic.

Gender   Although men and women think alike on many issues, they diverge on others.[32] Polls have found, for example, that women have more liberal opinions than men on education and social welfare issues, reflecting their greater economic vulnerability and greater role in child care. Women also differ from men on issues of national defense. Polls indicate, for example, that women were less supportive than men of America's use of military force in Afghanistan and Iraq.[33]

Generations and Age   As a generation comes of age, it encounters a different political environment than its predecessors, with the result that its political views will differ somewhat from those of earlier generations. Those Americans who came of age during World War II, for example, acquired a sense of civic duty unmatched by the preceding generation or by any generation since. By contrast, those who came of age during the Vietnam War era were more distrustful of government than the generation before them or the one that followed. Today's young adults are no exception to the pattern. Their political views are, to some extent, a reflection of their generation's experiences. A recent Kaiser Family Foundation poll found, for example, that climate change is of far greater concern to young adults than to older ones.[34]

Crosscutting Groups and Identity Politics

Although group loyalties have an impact on people's opinions, the influence is diminished when identification with one group is offset by identification with other groups. In a pluralistic society such as the United States, groups tend to be "crosscutting"—that is, each group includes individuals who also belong to other groups, where they can encounter different opinions. Exposure to such opinions fosters political moderation. By comparison, in societies such as Northern Ireland, where group loyalties are reinforcing rather than crosscutting, opinions are intensified by personal interactions. Catholics and Protestants in Northern Ireland live largely apart from one another, differing not only in their religious beliefs but also in their income levels, residential neighborhoods,

Americans' crosscutting group attachments have long been a unifying force in the nation's politics, but this influence is weakening, Americans are increasingly divided by how they look and where they live, contributing to the rise of identity politics, which pits groups against each other politically. (dotshock/Shutterstock)

ethnic backgrounds, and loyalties to the government. The result has been widespread mistrust between Northern Ireland's Catholics and Protestants and a willingness on the part of some on each side to resort to violence.

The moderating influence of crosscutting group attachments in the United States is weakening. Although the situation is still far different than in a place like Northern Ireland, Americans today interact less with those of different backgrounds. Residential neighborhoods have become less diverse in recent decades. That's true also of the workplace. Many office workers and professionals, for example, spend their workday interacting almost entirely with others of similar background and occupation. Americans' "virtual" interaction has also narrowed. Before the 1980s, Americans were exposed through television to a version of news that included Republican and Democratic arguments in roughly equal amounts. Today, many Americans get their news from a cable outlet or an Internet site that plays up one side of the partisan debate while playing down the other side (see Chapter 10).

In addition, three of America's deepest divides—race, religion, and geography—are now more closely linked to partisanship.[35] White Americans, the religious-minded, and suburban and rural residents now lean strongly toward the Republican Party, while minorities, the secular-minded, and urban residents lean heavily Democratic. The party polarization that defines today's politics thus goes beyond conflict over issues. Republicans and Democrats are increasingly separated by how they look and where they live, making partisan conflict a question of identity as well as a question of issues.[36] **Identity politics** is the term used to describe the situation where people base their concerns on a group identity (such as race or religion) and align themselves politically with those who share that identity and against those who don't.[37]

THE INFLUENCE OF PUBLIC OPINION ON POLICY

Observers disagree on the impact public opinion *should* have on policy. One view holds that a representative should act as his or her constituents' **delegate** by responding to what constituents say they want. That view was embraced by George Gallup, a pioneer in the field of polling. Said Gallup, "The task of the leader is to decide how best to achieve the goals set by the people."[38] An opposing view was put forth by 18th-century English theorist Edmund Burke, who argued that representatives should act as their constituents' **trustees**. Burke argued that they should take constituents' interest into account but use their own judgment in deciding which policies will best serve that interest. That view was embraced by journalist and writer Walter Lippmann. "Effective government," Lippmann wrote, "cannot be conducted by legislators and officials who, when a question is presented, ask themselves first and last not what is . . . the right and necessary course, but 'What does the Gallup Poll say?'"[39]

Limits on the Public's Influence

Even if officials were intent on governing by public opinion, they would face obstacles, including contradictions in what citizens say they want. In the entire history of polling, there has never been a national survey in which a majority of respondents said their taxes should be raised significantly.[40] In a 2020 Gallup poll, for example, 45 percent of respondents claimed that taxes were too high, and only 7 percent said taxes were too low. At the same time, when respondents are asked in polls whether they would support steep cuts in Social Security, defense, and other costly spending programs in order to pay for a large tax cut, a majority says no.

The example points to a problem with basing policy on public opinion—people's opinions are often inconsistent, contradictory, or poorly informed. Poll after poll have shown that most citizens are not well informed about politics and some are badly misinformed.[41] That's true even for highly publicized issues. Early in the COVID-19 coronavirus pandemic, despite countless news reports and official announcements, roughly a third of American adults were convinced that the virus was no more dangerous than the seasonal flu.[42]

To become an American citizen, immigrants must pass a citizenship test that asks basic questions about the U.S. political system. Ironically, when the test is given to a cross section of Americans who are already citizens, many of them fail it. Citizens' lack of information limits the impact of public opinion on policy. (John Moore/Getty Images)

Of course, citizens do not have to be well informed to have a reasonable opinion on some issues.[43] Knowing only that the economy is performing poorly, a citizen could reasonably expect government to take action to fix it and judge officials by what happens.[44] It's also the case that information is not a prerequisite for judgment on some policy issues. Opinions on the abortion issue, for example, are largely a question of people's values and beliefs.

Nevertheless, the public's weak understanding of issues can make it difficult for policymakers to respond to public opinion, even when they're inclined to do so. The problem has become more acute with the rise in misinformation. When citizens lose touch with reality, lawmakers face an impossible task. Even if they wanted to respond to public opinion, it would make no sense for them to do so on issues where citizens' opinions bear no relationship to reality.

Another obstacle to using public opinion as a guide is that there are many issues on which most citizens have no opinion. These are issues that get so little attention from the

> **CITIZEN ACTION!**
> **TAKING RESPONSIBILITY**
>
> Studies indicate that most Americans are largely uninformed about politics. Citizenship entails responsibility, including taking time to inform yourself. As an informed citizen, you will be better able to make judgments about policy issues, to choose wisely when voting during elections, and to recognize situations that call for greater engagement.

media that most people aren't even aware of them.[45] Agricultural conservation programs, for example, are of keen interest to some farmers, hunters, and environmentalists but of little or no concern to most people.[46] In deciding such issues, policymakers tend to respond to those who are interested (see Chapter 9). A study by political scientists Martin Gilens and Benjamin Page examined nearly 1,800 policy issues and concluded that "economic elites and organized groups representing business interests" have far more influence on most policies than do "average citizens."[47]

The influence of public opinion is also limited by what's been called "manufactured consent."[48] Political scientists James Druckman and Lawrence Jacobs have shown, for example, that presidents typically pursue their own goals, using the power of their office to try to get the public to think their way.[49] When they succeed, policy and opinion will coincide, but it speaks more to the power of leaders than to the power of public opinion. A case in point is the period leading up to the U.S. invasion of Iraq in 2003. Although Americans had been hearing about Iraqi leader Saddam Hussein for years and had concluded that he was a tyrant, they were unsure whether an attack on Iraq made sense. Polls indicate that many Americans preferred to have UN inspectors investigate Iraq's weapons program before an invasion decision was made. Other Americans expressed support for an invasion only if the United States had the backing of its European allies. Still others thought that, if a war were launched, it should be conducted entirely through the air. However, over the course of a roughly six-month period, the Bush administration pressed the case for a ground invasion, which led to a gradual increase in public support for an invasion.[50] When the war began, polls showed that President Bush's decision to invade Iraq had the backing of 70 percent of Americans.

The way in which citizens often form their opinions also limits the influence of public opinion. Most citizens are far too busy to take the time to carefully assess every policy issue, relying instead on what scholars call heuristics, or shortcuts, as when they take their cue from what a trusted political leader or their political party is saying.[51] In 2015, for example, Republicans had a more favorable view of free-trade agreements than did Democrats. Nearly 60 percent of Republicans said that free trade was good for the country. Two years later, however, Republicans had switched sides on the issue. More than 60 percent now said that these agreements were bad for the country.[52] Free trade itself hadn't changed in any significant way during this period. What, then, would explain the shift? It was the rise of Donald Trump to leadership in the Republican Party. Before then, top Republican leaders had been proponents of free trade. Trump opposed it, arguing that it resulted in a loss of American jobs and the closing of American factories. Taking their cue from Trump, many Republicans lined up behind him on the issue.[53]

Public Opinion and the Boundaries of Action

Although there are limits to the influence of public opinion, it nevertheless affects the choices that officials make. For one thing, it limits their options. As political scientist V. O. Key noted, officials typically must operate within the boundary of what the public will accept.[54] Social Security is a prime example. During his second presidential term, George W. Bush attempted to privatize a part of Social Security, only to back down in the face of determined opposition from senior citizens. The founder of Social Security, Franklin D. Roosevelt, understood that public opinion would protect the program. Because Social Security benefits are funded by payroll taxes, workers feel that they have earned their retirement benefits and will fight to keep them. "No damn politician," Roosevelt said, "can ever scrap my social security program."[55]

Public opinion also puts boundaries on officials' actions in a second way. Sweeping changes in public opinion invariably lead to lasting and substantial changes in the direction of national policy. During the Great Depression of the 1930s, for example, a massive shift in popular support from the Republican Party to the Democratic Party ushered in a three-decade period of Democratic dominance of American politics, as well as a host of major policies, including Social Security, the minimum wage, and Medicare. Then, in the 1970s, the American public began to question the scope of federal power and spending, which led to a range of policy changes, including major tax cuts and a tightening of the eligibility rules for welfare assistance. Public opinion was also behind the tougher crime and sentencing laws enacted in the 1990s, which led to a sharp increase in the nation's prison population. As a congressman said at the time, "Voters were afraid of criminals, and politicians were afraid of voters."[56]

Abrupt shifts in opinion on a top issue can change the boundaries of acceptable action. As mentioned earlier, until Donald Trump came out strongly against free-trade agreements, Republican members of Congress were strong advocates of free trade. Over 90 percent of Senate and House Republicans had voted in 2011 to enact the most recent trade agreements—bilateral arrangements with Colombia, Panama, and South Korea. However, when Republican voters flipped from being pro–free trade to anti–free trade, most congressional Republicans stopped promoting free trade.

Nowhere is the impact of public opinion felt more clearly than in Congress. Members of Congress are career politicians who want to keep their jobs, which requires them to maintain the support of their home state or district. They tend to side with the opinion of the voters who hold the key to their reelection.[57] "Running scared" is how political scientist Anthony King described the strategy.[58] In 2014, Eric Cantor, the House majority leader and next in line to become Speaker, lost in his district's Republican primary to a

Public opinion places boundaries on what public officials will do. Republican lawmakers backed away from their support of free trade after Republican voters turned against it in response to Donald Trump's vow to "make America great again." (George Sheldon/Shutterstock)

right-wing political unknown. Cantor had said that Republicans should give legal status to "dreamers"—those who had come to the country illegally as children. For anti-immigration voters in his district, Cantor's stand amounted to treachery. The lesson of Cantor's defeat was not lost on House Republicans. "Immigration reform, any hope of it, just basically died," said a Republican insider.[59]

The immigration issue illustrates what is broadly true about the power of public opinion. When an issue is highly salient and people feel intensely about it, elected officials tend to follow public opinion. Numerous studies support the conclusion that the power of public opinion is greatest on issues of high salience that people care deeply about.[60]

SUMMARY

Public opinion can be defined as the opinions held by ordinary citizens that they openly express. Public officials have many ways of assessing public opinion, such as the outcomes of elections, but they have increasingly come to rely on public opinion polls. There are many possible sources of error in polls, and surveys sometimes present a misleading portrayal of the public's views. However, a properly conducted poll can be an accurate indication of what the public is thinking. Polls are typically used to measure three attributes of people's policy opinions: direction (whether they favor or oppose a particularly policy), intensity (how strongly they feel about their position on a policy), and salience (how important they think a policy issue is relative to other issues).

The process by which individuals acquire their political opinions is called political socialization. During childhood, the family, schools, and church are important sources of basic political attitudes, such as beliefs about the parties and the nature of the U.S. political and economic systems. Many of the basic orientations that Americans acquire during childhood remain with them in adulthood, but socialization is a continuing process. Adults' opinions are affected mostly by peers, the news media, and political leaders. Events themselves also have a significant short-term influence on opinions.

The frames of reference that guide Americans' opinions include political ideology, although most citizens do not have a strong and consistent ideological attachment. In addition, individuals develop opinions as a result of group orientations—notably, religion, economic class, region, race and ethnicity, gender, and generation and age. Partisanship is the main source of political opinions; Republicans and Democrats differ in their voting behavior and views on many policy issues.

Public opinion has a significant influence on government but seldom determines exactly what government will do in a particular instance. Public opinion constrains the policy choices of officials but also is subject to their efforts to influence what the public is thinking. Evidence indicates that officials are particularly attentive to public opinion on highly visible issues of public policy that are of great concern to a large number of people.

CRITICAL THINKING ZONE

KEY TERMS

agents of socialization (*p. 167*)

cultural (social) conservatives (*p. 173*)

cultural (social) liberals (*p. 173*)

delegate (*p. 180*)

direction (*p. 162*)

economic conservatives (*p. 173*)

economic liberals (*p. 173*)

identity politics (*p. 180*)

ideology (*p. 173*)

intensity (*p. 162*)

party identification (*p. 171*)

political socialization (*p. 166*)

population (*p. 161*)

public opinion (*p. 160*)

public opinion poll (*p. 161*)

salience (*p. 164*)

sample (*p. 161*)

sampling error (*p. 162*)

trustee (*p. 180*)

APPLYING THE ELEMENTS OF CRITICAL THINKING

Conceptualizing: *Population, sample,* and *sampling error* are terms associated with public opinion polling. Explain each term and how it relates to the others.

Synthesizing: Contrast the views of conservatives and liberals on how far government should go to help individuals who are economically disadvantaged, and then contrast their views on how far government should go to promote traditional social (cultural) values. Note that each group wants government to be active or inactive, depending on which approach serves its policy goals.

Analyzing: What factors limit the influence of public opinion on the policy choices of public officials?

EXTRA CREDIT

A Book Worth Reading: Amy Chua, *Political Tribes: Group Instinct and the Fate of Nations* (New York: Penguin Books, 2019). Written by a best-selling author and Yale Law School professor, this book argues that political identity has come to define both the American left and the right and threatens our national unity.

A Website Worth Visiting: **www.people-press.org** The Pew Research Center for the People and the Press is an independent, nonprofit institute. Its website includes recent and past poll results, including cross-national comparisons.

Design credit: (People, Flag, U.S., Globe, Vote Icons): McGraw-Hill Education; (Eagle): Feng Wei Photography/Moment/Getty Images; (Lincoln): Photographs in the Carol M. Highsmith Archive, Library of Congress, Prints and Photographs Division [LC-DIG-highsm-12542].

7
CHAPTER

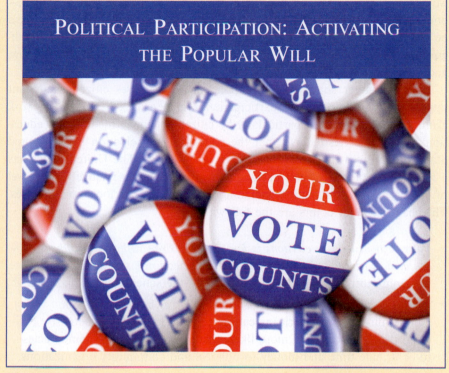

POLITICAL PARTICIPATION: ACTIVATING THE POPULAR WILL

Leigh Prather/Shutterstock

❝ We are concerned in public affairs, but immersed in our private ones. ❞

WALTER LIPPMANN[1]

At stake in the 2020 elections was control of the presidency, House, and Senate. Which political party would end up with the larger say on issues like gun control, health care, immigration, wage stagnation, foreign trade, and the war on terrorism? With so much at stake, it might be thought that Americans would have rushed to the polls to vote for the party of their choice. Many did so, but many did not. Tens of millions of vote-eligible Americans did not bother to cast a ballot on Election Day.

Political participation refers to involvement in activities intended to influence public policy and leadership. Besides voting, political participation includes activities such as joining political groups, writing to elected officials, demonstrating for political causes, and giving money to political candidates.

Democracies need citizen participation if they are to thrive. Self-government would be an empty promise if citizens did not participate in public affairs. It would also be an empty promise without *meaningful* opportunities to participate—ones that will make a difference in how the country is governed. It would also be empty if those opportunities were provided only to a select few. For self-government to be meaningful, the barriers to citizen participation must be low, and they must be low for all citizens.

As this chapter shows, the U.S. political system gives citizens abundant opportunities for meaningful participation while erecting barriers that work against full participation, particularly by citizens of lower income and education. The chapter also shows that the pattern of participation in the United States differs from that of most Western democracies. The United States has a relatively low level of voter participation while having a relatively high level of other types of participation, including volunteer work in local communities. The chapter's main points are the following:

- *Voter turnout in U.S. elections is low in comparison with that of other Western democracies.* The reasons include U.S. election laws, particularly those pertaining to registration requirements and the scheduling of elections.

- *Most citizens do not participate actively in politics in ways other than voting.* Only a minority of Americans can be classified as political activists. Nevertheless, Americans are more likely than citizens of other democracies to contribute time and money to political and community organizations.

- *Political movements are a way for citizens dissatisfied with government to express their opposition through protest rallies, marches, and the like.* Most political movements do not succeed, but a few of them, including the Black civil rights movements, have had a large and lasting impact on the nation's politics.

- *Most Americans distinguish between their personal lives and public lives.* This outlook reduces their incentive to participate and contributes to a pattern of participation that favors citizens of higher income and education.

VOTER PARTICIPATION

In its original form, the Constitution gave states control over **suffrage**—the right to vote. State legislatures were granted the power to decide the "Times, Place, and Manner of holding elections" for federal office.

The states at first chose to restrict voting to property-owning males, a practice that Benjamin Franklin ridiculed. Observing that a man whose only item of property was a jackass would lose his right to vote if the jackass died, Franklin asked, "Now tell me, which was the voter, the man or the jackass?" Fifty years elapsed before all of the states eliminated the property restriction on voting.

African Americans appeared to have gained suffrage after the Civil War with passage of the Fifteenth Amendment, which says that a state cannot

Alabama Literacy Test Questions (1940s)

- A United States Senator elected at the general election in November takes office the following year on what date?
- How many states were required to approve the original Constitution in order for it to be in effect?
- After the presidential electors have voted, to whom do they send the count of their votes?
- Of the original 13 states, the one with the largest representation in the first Congress was _____.
- Does enumeration affect the income tax levied on citizens in various states?
- On the impeachment of the Chief Justice of the Supreme Court, who tries the case?

Until literacy tests were banned in the 1960s, they were used in some states to keep Black citizens (and, in some cases, poor white citizens) from registering to vote. The tests often contained questions on obscure topics and were selectively graded to allow most whites to pass and to disqualify most Blacks. The questions shown here were taken from Alabama literacy tests of the 1940s, a time when less than 20 percent of the state's eligible Black voters were registered to vote.

abridge the right to vote "on account of race, color, or previous condition of servitude." Nevertheless, African Americans were disenfranchised throughout the South by intimidation and electoral trickery. One such trick was to require a literacy test as a precondition for eligibility to vote. The tests were selectively administered to exclude Black voters and contained questions so difficult that often the examiner had to look up the answers. If that was not enough of an obstacle, the names of those who took the test were sometimes published in the local newspaper so that employers, the local police, and even the KKK would know the names of the "troublemakers." The state of Mississippi was the extreme case in its disenfranchisement of Black Americans. Even as late as the 1950s, only about 1 in 25 of its Black citizens was registered to vote. Not until the 1960s did Congress and the courts sweep away the last legal barriers to equal suffrage for African Americans (see Chapter 5).

Women did not secure the right to vote until 1920, with ratification of the Nineteenth Amendment. Decades earlier, Susan B. Anthony had tried to vote in her hometown of Rochester, New York, claiming that as a U.S. citizen she had a right to vote. She was arrested for "illegal voting" and was told that her proper place was in the home. By 1920, men had run out of excuses for denying the vote to women. As social activist Wendell Phillips observed, "One of two things is true: either woman is like man—and if she is, then a ballot based

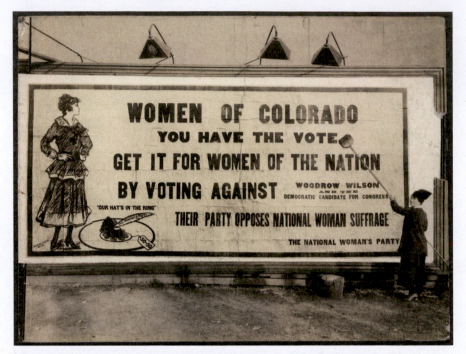

After a hard-fought, decades-long campaign, women across the nation finally won the right to vote in 1920. Fifteen states, most of them west of the Mississippi River, had earlier granted suffrage to women. Wyoming in 1869 was the first to do so. Colorado in 1893 was the second. (Library of Congress, Manuscript Division [159016])

on brains belongs to her as well as to him. Or she is different, and then man does not know how to vote for her as she herself does."[2]

The nation's youngest adults are the most recent beneficiaries of a suffrage amendment. Ratified during the Vietnam War—a time when the military draft was in full swing and the minimum voting age in nearly every state was 21 years—the Twenty-Sixth Amendment lowered the voting age to 18 years. "If you're old enough to die, you're old enough to vote" was the rallying cry of its proponents.

Factors in Voter Turnout: The United States in Comparative Perspective

Nearly all Americans embrace the symbolism of the vote, saying that they have a duty to vote in elections. Nevertheless, many Americans shirk their duty. Millions choose not to vote in national elections, a tendency that sets Americans apart from citizens of most other Western democracies. Turnout in U.S. presidential elections is typically lower than turnout in the national elections of many Western democracies (see "How the U.S. Differs").

HOW THE U.S. DIFFERS

CRITICAL THINKING THROUGH COMPARISONS

Voter Turnout

The United States ranks near the bottom among the world's democracies in the percentage of eligible citizens who vote in elections. One reason for the relatively low turnout is that Americans are individually responsible for registering to vote, whereas in most democracies the government takes responsibility for automatically registering citizens to vote. In addition, unlike most democracies, the United States holds elections on a weekday rather than during a weekend or on a holiday, when people have more free time. Shown here is the approximate average turnout rate in recent national elections for select democracies:

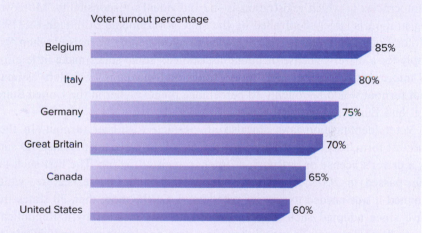

Voter turnout percentage

Belgium	85%
Italy	80%
Germany	75%
Great Britain	70%
Canada	65%
United States	60%

Q: By law, U.S. elections are held on a Tuesday in early November. Some observers have proposed moving the date to Veterans Day, a national holiday that takes place every November 11. What might be the consequence of such a change?

A: The idea behind the proposal is that Americans are less busy on a holiday and thus would find it easier to get to the polls, which could increase the level of voter turnout. Proponents of the idea also say it would be a fitting way to honor the nation's military veterans.

And turnout in U.S. midterm elections, which are the congressional elections that occur midway between presidential elections, is lower still.

Registration Requirements   America's relatively low turnout rate owes partly to its demanding registration requirement. Before Americans are allowed to vote, they must make the effort to register—that is, they need to get their names on the official list of eligible voters. **Registration** began around 1900 as a way of preventing voters from casting more than one ballot on Election Day. Multiple balloting had become a tactic of big-city party machines—"vote early and often" was their motto. Although registration reduced illegal voting, it also placed a burden on honest citizens. Because they were required to register beforehand, citizens who forgot or otherwise failed to register were unable to vote. Turnout in U.S. elections declined after registration began.

Although other democracies also require registration, most of them place the responsibility on government. When someone moves to a new address, for example, the postal service will notify registration officials of the change. In keeping with its culture of individualism, the United States is one of the few democracies in which registration is the individual's responsibility. Moreover, registration is largely controlled by the state governments. Although the 1993 Motor Voter Act requires state agencies to allow people to register when they apply for a driver's license or public assistance,[3] some states make little effort to inform citizens about registration times and locations.[4] Scholars estimate that turnout would be roughly 10 percentage points higher in the United States if it had European-style registration.[5]

Voter identification laws are also an obstacle to higher turnout. In their strictest form, such laws require a citizen to have a government-issued ID such as a driver's license or passport in order to register to vote. The first such law was passed in 2005 by Indiana's Republican-controlled legislature, which claimed it was needed to prevent voter fraud. Of the more than 30 states that have since adopted such a law, all but one was enacted by a Republican-controlled legislature. Young adults, minorities, and low-income individuals, all of whom tend to vote Democratic, are the Americans who are least likely to have a driver's license or passport.[6] In a 2008 case involving Indiana's law, the Supreme Court upheld such laws by a 6-3 vote, saying that states have a "valid interest" in deterring fraud. The Court acknowledged that Indiana's Republican legislators were seeking a partisan advantage in enacting the law but argued that the law "should not be disregarded simply because partisan interests may have provided one motivation for the votes of individual legislators."[7]

Some states make registration easy, and they have higher turnout than do other states. About 10 states, including Idaho, Maine, and Minnesota, allow people to register at their polling places on Election Day. The turnout rate in these states is more than 10 percentage points above the national average. States with the most restrictive registration laws—for example, those that make it difficult to cast an absentee ballot and require a government-issued ID to register—have turnout rates well below the national average. Indiana, Mississippi, and Alabama are among the states in this category.

Detecting Misinformation

Is Illegal Voting Widespread?

A poll conducted by researchers at Stanford University found that most Americans believe that a "meaningful amount" of illegal voting takes place in U.S. elections. The poll revealed that large numbers of Americans believe that many noncitizens vote illegally and that a significant number of people vote using the names of registered voters who have died.[8]

Guy J. Sagi/Shutterstock

Is that claim fact, or is it fake?

Studies indicate that illegal voting is extremely rare.[9] One study, for example, obtained the election fraud records of every state and found an "infinitesimal" amount of documented fraud, concluding that the odds of an individual being hit by lightning is 40 times greater than the likelihood that the individual will commit voter fraud.[10] In an attempt to show that voter fraud was widespread, Texas's attorney general launched an exhaustive investigation and found only two prosecutable instances of it—this in a state where 9 million voters go to the polls.[11] Kansas's secretary of state sought to prosecute illegal voters, searching the state's nearly 2 million registered voters, looking for violations. He ended up with only a few, which a judge concluded were "explained by administrative error, confusion or mistake."[12] There are reasons that voter fraud is rare. It's difficult enough to get eligible voters to the polls, much less to get those who are ineligible to knowingly take the risk. The penalty for illegal voting can be high—as much as a $10,000 fine and five years in prison in some states—and the incentive is low—the probability that a single vote will change the outcome of a national or state election is virtually zero.

Frequency of Elections   Just as America's registration system places a burden on voters, so does its election schedule. The United States holds elections more often than other nations. No other democracy has elections for the lower chamber of its national legislature (the equivalent of the U.S. House of Representatives) as often as every two years, and no democracy schedules the election of its chief executive more frequently than every four years.[13] In addition, most local elections in the United States are held in odd-numbered years, unlike the even-year schedule of federal elections and most state elections. Finally, the United States uses primary elections to select the party nominees. In other democracies, party leaders pick them. Americans are asked to vote two to three times as often as Europeans, which increases the likelihood that they will not vote every time.[14]

In an earlier period, most statewide elections coincided with the presidential election, when turnout is highest. This scheduling usually worked to the advantage of the party that won the presidential race—its candidates got a boost from the strong showing of its presidential nominee. In an effort to eliminate "presidential coattails" that could help the weaker party in its state, states began in the 1930s to hold gubernatorial elections in nonpresidential years. Over three-fourths of the states have adopted this schedule, and two states—Virginia and New Jersey—elect their governors in odd-numbered years, insulating them even further from the turnout effects of federal elections.

Why Some Americans Vote and Others Do Not

Even though turnout is lower in the United States than in other major Western democracies, some Americans vote regularly, while others seldom or never vote. Among the explanations for these individual differences are education and income, age, civic attitudes, and political interest.

Education and Income   College-educated and upper-income Americans have above-average voting rates. They have the financial resources and communication skills that encourage participation and make it personally rewarding. Nevertheless, the United States is unusual in the degree to which education and income are related to voter participation. Europeans with less education and income vote at only slightly lower rates than other citizens. By comparison, Americans with a high income or college degree turn out to vote at a much higher rate in presidential elections than do those with a low income or an education that did not extend beyond high school.

Why do income and education make a greater difference in the United States than they do in Europe? For one thing, Europeans with less income and education are prompted to participate by class-based organizations. Labor unions are stronger in Europe, and most European democracies have a major socialist or labor party that seeks to represent lower-income voters. The United States has never had a major socialist or labor party. In addition, Europeans do not have the imposing voter registration requirements that some U.S. states place on their residents. Americans with less income and education are the individuals most adversely affected by the coun-

CITIZEN ACTION!
GETTING READY

You must be a registered voter in order to vote in elections. If you're not registered, you can obtain a registration form from the election clerk in your community of residence. Several nonpartisan websites also provide state-by-state registration information and forms. One such site is http://turbovote.org.

try's registration system. Many of them do not own cars or homes and are thus less likely to be registered in advance of an election or have the documentation that some states require as a condition for registration. They are also less familiar with registration locations and times.[15]

Age Young adults are substantially less likely than middle-aged and older citizens to vote. For one thing, younger adults are more likely to change residence from one election to the next, which requires them to register again in order to retain their eligibility to vote. Even senior citizens, despite the infirmities of old age, have a much higher turnout rate than do voters under the age of 30.

Civic Attitudes and Political Interest People differ in their attitudes toward politics, which affects the likelihood they will exercise their right to vote.

Apathy—a lack of interest—in politics typifies some citizens. They rarely, if ever, vote. Just as some people would not attend the Super Bowl even if it were free and being played across the street, some Americans care so little about politics that they would not bother to vote even if a ballot were delivered to their door.

Still other Americans refrain from voting because of **alienation**—a feeling of powerlessness rooted in the belief that government ignores their interests. The Hispanic vote was expected to surge in the 2016 presidential election as a result of the prominence of immigration as a campaign issue. However, the surge did not materialize. Some Hispanics had concluded, after years of government inaction on immigration reform, that their votes don't make a difference.[16]

By contrast, some Americans have a keen sense of **civic duty**—a belief that they ought to participate in public affairs. Citizens who hold this belief tend to vote more regularly. Civic duty and apathy are attitudes that are usually acquired from one's parents. When parents vote regularly and take an active interest in politics, their children usually grow up thinking they have a duty to participate. When parents never vote and show no interest in public affairs, their children are likely to be politically apathetic as adults.

Finally, it's no surprise that citizens with an interest in politics are more likely to vote than are those with little or no interest.[17] What makes **political interest** noteworthy is that it stems largely from partisanship. Although "independents" are idealized in high school civics classes, they have lower voting rates than citizens who identify with a political party. Party loyalty is like people's other loyalties. It deepens their interest, which includes going to the polls to support their party's candidates (see "Party Polarization: Party Identification and Voter Turnout").

P A R T Y
POLARIZATION

Conflicting Ideas

Party Identification and Voter Turnout

American politics in recent decades has been marked by party polarization—a widening divide between Republicans and Democrats. The divide is exaggerated in elections because party identifiers are more likely than those who call themselves independents to turn out to vote. That's the case in all elections and particularly in primaries and midterm congressional elections. Following are the percentages of adults who say they voted in the 2018 midterm elections by whether they were Republican, independent but leaned Republican, independent, independent but leaned Democratic, or Democratic.

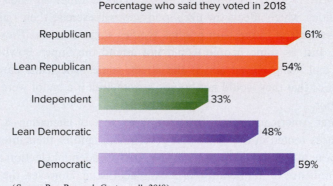

Percentage who said they voted in 2018

Republican	61%
Lean Republican	54%
Independent	33%
Lean Democratic	48%
Democratic	59%

(*Source:* Pew Research Center poll, 2018)

Q: How might higher voter turnout among Republican and Democratic identifiers affect what happens in Congress?

A: Higher turnout among party identifiers increases the likelihood that candidates with more strongly held partisan views will get elected to Congress. Their presence in Congress results in heightened partisan conflict over bills, which can lead to legislative deadlock.

CONVENTIONAL FORMS OF PARTICIPATION OTHER THAN VOTING

No form of political participation is as widespread as voting. Nevertheless, voting is a limited form of participation. Citizens have the opportunity to vote only at specific times and then only for the choices listed on the ballot. Fuller opportunities exist, however, including contributing to political and civic organizations.

Campaign and Lobbying Activities

Compared with voting, working for a candidate or political party is more time-consuming. Not surprisingly, only a small percentage of citizens engage in such activities. Nevertheless, the number is much higher in the United States than in Europe. A study found, for example, that Americans were five times more likely than Europeans to take an active part in political campaigns and twice as likely to talk with other people about their preferred candidate or party.[18]

Why the reversal? Why are Americans more likely than Europeans to take part in election activity even though they are less likely to vote? The explanation rests in part on differences in the American and European election systems. For one thing, American campaigns last for months, whereas those in Europe start and end within a few weeks. Unlike European democracies, the United States has primary elections, which prompt candidates to start their campaigns long before Election Day, offering citizens plenty of chances to join in. Then, too, the United States has a federal system. Each state elects its legislative and executive officials. Most European democracies are unitary systems (see Chapter 3) and thus do not have elected state officers.

Americans are also more likely than Europeans to be involved in groups that seek to influence public policy. This support typically takes the form of monetary contributions but can also take more active forms, such as contacting lawmakers or attending public rallies. Among the hundreds of groups that rely on citizen participation are Greenpeace, Common Cause, AARP (formerly known as the American Association of Retired Persons), the Christian Coalition of America, and the National Rifle Association. (Lobbying groups are discussed further in Chapter 9.)

Virtual Participation

The advent of the World Wide Web in the 1990s opened up an entirely new venue for political participation—the Internet. Although this participation is "virtual" rather than face-to-face, much of it involves contact with friends, acquaintances, and activists through Facebook, Twitter, Instagram, e-mail, and

Although Americans are less likely than Europeans to vote, they are more likely than Europeans to participate actively in political campaigns. Most Americans are not active participants, but many do get involved by working for a candidate or party, contributing to a favorite candidate, or, as in the case of those pictured here, encouraging people to register and vote. (Ariel Skelley/Blend Images)

other social media. Internet participation peaks during presidential campaigns and now easily outstrips conventional participation.

Internet fundraising is also flourishing. In the 2020 presidential race, for example, Donald Trump and Joe Biden each raised tens of millions of dollars for their campaigns through small, online donations. Many lobbying groups also rely on online contributions. MoveOn.org, for example, has a network of roughly 3 million "online activists," which it mobilizes in support of liberal candidates and issues. In 2020, MoveOn concentrated on congressional elections, raising $20 million and fielding 30,000 volunteers in support of Democratic House and Senate candidates.[19] Americans for Prosperity is another example. It has roughly 3 million members and has chapters in 35 states, each of which is dedicated to electing conservative candidates. (The Internet is discussed further in Chapter 10.)

Community Activities

Political participation extends beyond campaigns and elections to involvement in the community. Citizens can join community groups, work to accomplish community goals, and contact local officials. Such efforts generate what Harvard University's Robert Putnam has labeled **social capital**—face-to-face interactions between people. Research indicates that such contacts contribute to a sense of community and help foster civic cooperation.[20]

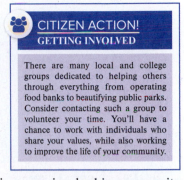

CITIZEN ACTION!
GETTING INVOLVED

There are many local and college groups dedicated to helping others through everything from operating food banks to beautifying public parks. Consider contacting such a group to volunteer your time. You'll have a chance to work with individuals who share your values, while also working to improve the life of your community.

The main obstacle to civic participation is motivation. Most people choose not to get involved, particularly when it requires a major commitment. Nevertheless, many Americans are involved in community affairs through local organizations, such as parent–teacher associations, neighborhood groups, business clubs, and church-affiliated groups (see "How the 50 States Differ"). Studies have found that participation in local organizations is twice as high in the United States as it is in Europe.[21] Religious practice is a reason. Americans are more than twice as likely as Europeans to attend church regularly, and many of them engage in church-related community work. As well, cities and towns in the United States have greater control over local policy than do those in Europe, which creates an incentive for residents to participate. The same is true of American schools; local control and parental involvement are a stronger tradition in the United States than in Europe. Americans' volunteer activity takes many forms, but more than 70 percent of this participation takes place through church-related groups, school-related groups, and civic organizations.[22]

HOW THE 50 STATES DIFFER

CRITICAL THINKING THROUGH COMPARISONS

Volunteer Activity

Although community volunteering is a tradition in every state, the rate varies greatly, as indicated by a recent study by the Corporation for National and Community Service. Utah, at 51 percent, and Minnesota, at 45 percent, have the highest volunteer rate in terms of the percentage of residents 16 years of age or older who are engaged yearly in community volunteer work. Mississippi, at 23 percent, and Florida, at 22 percent, rank lowest.

Continued

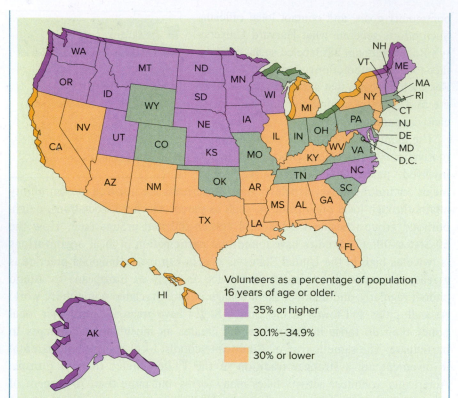

Volunteers as a percentage of population 16 years of age or older.

- 35% or higher
- 30.1%–34.9%
- 30% or lower

(*Source:* Corporation for National and Community Service, 2020)

Q: Why might the more northern states that lie west of the Mississippi River have higher-than-average volunteer rates?

A: Many residents of these states live in smaller communities with relatively stable populations. People in such communities are more likely to know each other and work together on community activities. In addition, these states were identified by political scientist Daniel Elazar as having participatory cultures as a result of their settlement by immigrants who came from European countries, such as Sweden and Norway, with a tradition of civic participation.

Unconventional Activism: Political Movements and Protests

During the pre-democratic era, people resorted to protest as a way of expressing displeasure with government. Tax and food riots were the typical forms of protest. When democratic governments came into existence, elections gave citizens a regular and less disruptive way to express themselves. Nevertheless, voting is double-edged. It gives citizens power over government while giving government power over citizens.[23] Election by the people grants legitimacy to those in power, and they can use it to justify policies of their choosing.

Political movements, or *social movements* as they are also called, are a way for citizens dissatisfied with government to openly express their opposition.[24] As political scientist Sidney Tarrow notes, political movements take place largely outside established institutions in the form of protest rallies, marches, and the like. Thus, participation in political movements differs from participation through a political party, which takes place through scheduled elections.[25]

Hundreds of political movements have arisen during the nation's history, including a number of highly successful ones. No modern protest movement has had a larger or more lasting impact than the Black civil rights movement. Beginning in the 1950s with boycotts of businesses that treated African Americans as second-class citizens, the movement grew to include mass demonstrations and marches. It succeeded on a level beyond what even its leaders might have imagined. The landmark 1964 Civil Rights Act and 1965 Voting Rights Act were a direct result of the pressure that the Black civil rights movement placed on lawmakers (see Chapter 5).

Recent Protest Movements

Recent years have witnessed a rise in protest activity. As Republicans and Democrats have moved apart, the issues that divide them have intensified and in some cases spilled over into protest activity. As well, because of partisan deadlock in Washington, many policy problems have been neglected, compounding the anxiety and frustration that result when problems worsen. In any case, Americans have increasingly looked outside established political channels to make their voices heard. The following discussion highlights several recent protest movements and their success in achieving their goals.

Tea Party Movement   The Tea Party came to the public's attention on April 15, 2009—the date that federal income taxes were due. The timing was not a coincidence, nor was the movement's name. Like the participants in the legendary Boston Tea Party, those who took to the streets in hundreds of cities and towns on that April day were expressing their opposition to taxes. Tea Party advocates called for sharp reductions in federal spending, saying in their "Contract for America," "Our moral, political, and economic liberties are inherent, not granted by our government. It is essential to the practice of these liberties that we be free from restriction over our peaceful political expression and free from excessive control over our economic choices."

Tea Party protestors stage a rally at the Capitol against federal spending and taxes. (Cheryl Casey/ Shutterstock)

Occupy Wall Street   When the Occupy Wall Street (OWS) movement emerged in 2011, it began small—a single encampment in New York City's Zuccotti Park, adjacent to Wall Street. Within a few weeks, however, it had spread to dozens of American cities. OWS was sparked by anger at the government's bailout of the financial industry and its failure to hold bankers accountable for their role in the financial crisis of 2008. Unlike the Tea Party, OWS's target was the widening income gap between the wealthiest 1 percent of Americans and the rest of society. "We are the 99%" was the movement's rallying cry.

Black Lives Matter   Sparked by the killing of unarmed young Black men by police officers in several cities, including Baltimore, Chicago, and Ferguson, Missouri, the Black Lives Matter movement sought to change not just local law enforcement but local governments generally, many of which provide inferior services in Black neighborhoods. Through public demonstrations, marches, and the reenactment of police killings, the movement has sought to highlight disparities in how white and Black citizens are treated by local officials. The movement gained force in 2020 after George Floyd, who was handcuffed and face down in the street, was killed by Minneapolis police officers. His death led to the largest protests yet of police violence directed at Black Americans.

The #MeToo Movement   In 2017, #MeToo spread virally as a social media hashtag to show the extent to which women are subjected to sexual assault and harassment. Popularized by actress Alyssa Milano, the hashtag was used 200,000 times the day that she proposed it and was subsequently posted millions of times, often accompanied by the sender's personal story. It contributed to the firing or resignation of a large number of powerful men, including Hollywood producer Harvey Weinstein, television host Charlie Rose, casino magnate Steve Wynn, and U.S. representative John Conyers. The movement's larger goal was to raise awareness of the level of sexual misconduct, show its devastating effect on victims, and pressure firms and organizations to take steps to stop it.

Movement Against Gun Violence   The movement against gun violence had a relatively low profile until the 2018 mass killing at Marjory Stoneman Douglas High School in Parkland, Florida. The school's students responded with impassioned pleas for an end to school shootings. Their pleas captured the nation's attention. It led to National School Walkout Day and March for

The #MeToo movement emerged rapidly in 2017 as thousands of women used social media to say that they, too, had been the victims of sexual assault or harassment. Within a relatively few weeks, powerful men in media, politics, and business who were credibly accused of sexual misconduct had been fired or resigned. The movement sought to raise public awareness of sexual misconduct and to get firms and organizations to take steps to prevent such abuses. (Tassii/E+/Getty Images)

Our Lives demonstrations in hundreds of cities and towns. The movement sought to pressure lawmakers at the national, state, and local levels to enact tougher gun control measures, including rigorous background checks on gun buyers and a ban on military-style assault rifles, which had been used in several recent mass killings, including the Parkland shooting.

Factors in the Success of Social Movements

Most political movements fail to achieve their goals. Some of the past movements, including anarchist and communist movements, had goals that were so at odds with American values that they failed to attract sizable followings. Others failed because they lacked the resources to sustain the effort. Typically, a lengthy period of intense and sustained action is required for a movement to succeed. Finally, movements can fail if they are unable to find ways to institutionalize their goals. If, for example, the Black civil rights movement had not succeeded in getting some of its goals institutionalized through the 1964 Civil Rights Act and the 1965 Voting Rights Act, its impact would have been far less substantial.

Recent political movements differ in their level of success. All of them have been able to draw attention to their core issue, but they have otherwise differed in one or more ways. To date at least, the Tea Party has been the most successful. It was able to transform itself from a movement to a permanent force within the Republican Party, which provided it with an institutional base from which to pursue cuts in taxes and government spending. At one point, nearly 150 congressional Republicans called themselves a Tea Party member or sympathizer. In contrast, Occupy Wall Street protesters rejected the idea of developing institutional links, which meant that, when their encampments were disbanded, they didn't have an organization through which to pursue their goals. OWS subsequently tried to resurrect itself through a website but failed to attract a large following (see Case Study: The Rise and Fall of Occupy Wall Street).

It is too early to say with certainty whether Black Lives Matter, the #MeToo movement, and the movement against gun violence will achieve lasting institutional and policy gains. Each movement has had an impact. Black Lives Matter has led to changes in police practices, a process that accelerated after widespread protests erupted in the wake of George Floyd's killing by Minneapolis police. The #MeToo movement has led some firms and organizations to establish policies aimed at curbing sexual misconduct. The movement against gun violence has led some states and localities to curb the sale and possession of particular types of firearms and accessories. But none of these movements, as of yet, has succeeded in bringing about wholesale policy change. The history of the Black civil rights movement suggests that any judgment on the success of these movements could come years from now.

CASE STUDY

Politics in Action

The Rise and Fall of Occupy Wall Street

The Occupy Wall Street (OWS) movement began as a single encampment near New York City's Wall Street but then spread rapidly to other American cities and even some foreign cities. OWS was a protest movement against the widening income divide. The income of the average American had been stagnant for three decades, whereas the incomes of top earners had increased sharply. OWS received heavy media attention, resulting in heightened awareness of the income gap and rising support for the movement. The momentum slowed when local offi-

(Erica Simone Leeds)

cials, citing safety and health concerns, began to disband OWS encampments. In some locations, the protesters clashed with police, which weakened OWS's support.

OWS's lack of resources also weakened it. OWS refused to take money from large donors, saying that doing so would violate its principles. OWS also rejected ties with the Democratic Party, even though polls indicated that support for OWS was much higher among Democrats than Republicans. The effect of these actions was to deny OWS an institutional base when its encampments were disbanded. It had no money and no formal ties with political organizations and leaders. Within a relatively short period, OWS faded nearly out of existence. It tried to resurrect itself on the Internet but, compared with the close ties between its followers that had been created during the encampments, the Internet ties proved to be too weak to sustain the movement.

Q: What are the lessons that political movements could derive from what happened with OWS?

ASK YOURSELF: How important are resources, such as adequate funding, to the success of a political movement? How important are ties to political leaders and institutions that can lend support to the movement and help it to achieve its policy goals?

It took several decades before the Black civil rights movement was able to get lawmakers to enact the landmark laws that are now its lasting legacy.

The Public's Response to Protest Activity

Protest politics has a long history in America. Indeed, the United States was founded on a protest movement that sparked a revolution against Britain. Despite this tradition, protest activity is less common today in the United States than in many Western democracies. Spain, France, Germany, Sweden, and Mexico are among the countries that have higher rates of protest participation.

Public support for protest activity depends on what's at issue. When the protesters' grievance is widely shared and seen as legitimate, the public is supportive. A Reuters poll found, for example, that Americans by a ratio of three to one believed that protests over the death of George Floyd by police were justified. By contrast, when U.S. military action has been the object of protest, public support has at times been weak. The Vietnam War protests were accompanied in some cases by the burning of American flags, and the protests struggled to gain widespread public support. When unarmed student protesters at Kent State University and Jackson State University were shot to death in May 1970 by members of the National Guard, most American polls faulted the students. In a *Newsweek* poll, 58 percent of respondents blamed the Kent State killings on the student demonstrators, while only 11 percent said the guard soldiers were at fault. The Iraq War protest in 2003 had a higher level of public support. Three in every five Americans said they saw the protests as "a sign of a healthy democracy." Nevertheless, almost two in five poll respondents said that "opponents of the war should not hold antiwar demonstrations," and half of them said that antiwar demonstrations should be outlawed.

In short, although most Americans recognize that protests are part of America's tradition of free expression, they do not embrace them as fully as they do voting. Many Americans would prefer that people voice their discontent at the ballot box rather than by taking to the streets. In this sense, most Americans see protest as something to be accepted, but not always something to be admired.

PARTICIPATION AND THE POTENTIAL FOR INFLUENCE

Most Americans are not highly active in politics. One reason is the emphasis that the American culture places on individualism. Most Americans under most conditions expect to solve their problems on their own rather than through political action. "In the United States, the country of individualism

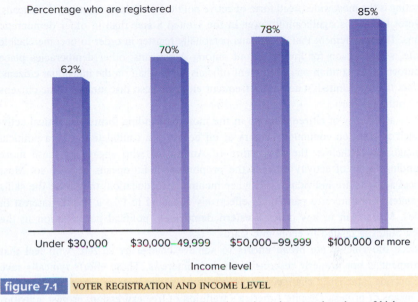

Percentage who are registered

62% 70% 78% 85%

Under $30,000 $30,000–49,999 $50,000–99,999 $100,000 or more

Income level

figure 7-1   VOTER REGISTRATION AND INCOME LEVEL

Americans of lower income are much less likely to be registered to vote than those of higher income. (*Source:* U.S. Census Bureau, 2020)

par excellence," William Watts and Lloyd Free write, "there is a sharp distinction in people's minds between their own personal lives and national life."[26]

Paradoxically, although they have more need for government help, lower-income Americans are the least likely to engage in collective action. Lower-income individuals tend to have less education, less access to transportation, less access to permanent housing, and less understanding of how to get involved in politics—all of which work to reduce their level of political participation.[27] Indeed, Americans at the low end of the income ladder are a third less likely to be registered to vote than those at the high end (see Figure 7-1). Not surprisingly, studies have found that elected officials are far less responsive to the concerns of poorer constituents than to the concerns of wealthier ones.[28]

Without question, Americans who have the least economic power also have the least political power. However, the issue of individual participation is only one piece of the larger puzzle of how power is distributed in America. Subsequent chapters will provide additional pieces.

SUMMARY

Political participation is involvement in activities designed to influence public policy and leadership. A main issue of democratic government is the question of who participates in politics and how fully they participate.

Voting is the most widespread form of active political participation among Americans, yet voter turnout is significantly lower in the United States than in other democratic nations. The requirement that Americans personally register in order to become eligible to vote is one reason for lower turnout among Americans; other democracies place the burden of registration on government officials rather than on the individual citizens. The fact that the United States holds frequent elections also discourages some citizens from voting regularly.

Only a minority of citizens engage in the more demanding forms of political activity, such as work on community affairs or on behalf of a candidate during a political campaign. Nevertheless, the proportion of Americans who engage in these more demanding forms of activity exceeds the proportion of Europeans who do so. Most political activists are individuals of higher income and education; they have the skills and material resources to participate effectively and tend to take a greater interest in politics. More than in any other Western democracy, political participation in the United States is related to economic status.

Social movements are broad efforts to achieve change by citizens who feel that government is not properly responsive to their interests. These efforts typically take place outside established channels; demonstrations, picket lines, and marches are common means of protest. Despite America's tradition of free expression, protest activities do not always have a high level of public support.

Overall, Americans are only moderately involved in politics. Although they are concerned with political affairs, they are mostly immersed in their private pursuits—a reflection, in part, of a cultural belief in individualism. The lower level of participation among low-income citizens has particular significance in that it works to reduce their influence on public policy and leadership.

CRITICAL THINKING ZONE

KEY TERMS

alienation (*p. 195*)
apathy (*p. 195*)
civic duty (*p. 195*)
political interest (*p. 196*)
political movements (*p. 201*)

political participation (*p. 187*)
registration (*p. 192*)
social capital (*p. 199*)
suffrage (*p. 188*)

APPLYING THE ELEMENTS OF CRITICAL THINKING

Conceptualizing: How do alienation, apathy, and civic duty differ?

Synthesizing: Why is voter turnout relatively low in the United States? Why are community participation rates relatively high in the United States?

Analyzing: Why does economic status—differences in Americans' education and income levels—make such a large difference in their level of political participation? Why does it make a larger difference in the United States than in Europe?

EXTRA CREDIT

A Book Worth Reading: Thomas Paine, *The American Crisis* (Scotts Valley, Calif.: CreateSpace, 2017). A compilation of Thomas Paine's pamphlets written between 1776 and 1783, including his famed *Common Sense*. The pamphlets have a message for citizens: Get involved in politics; there's a lot at stake.

A Website Worth Visiting: **www.votesmart.org** Project Vote Smart is a non-partisan, nonprofit organization. Its website includes helpful information for voters on the backgrounds and policy positions of Republican and Democratic candidates for office.

CHAPTER

POLITICAL PARTIES, CANDIDATES, AND CAMPAIGNS: DEFINING THE VOTERS' CHOICE

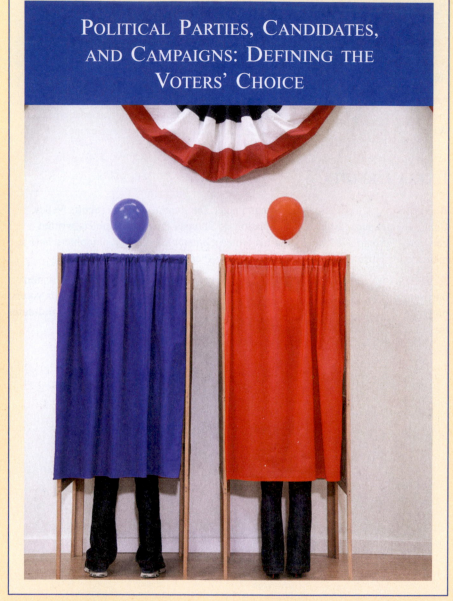

Hill Street Studios/Getty Images

"Political parties created democracy and . . . modern democracy is unthinkable save in terms of the parties."

E. E. SCHATTSCHNEIDER[1]

210

Toe-to-toe, they slugged it out in states and districts across the breadth of America, each side claiming it had the answers to America's problems. One side promised to raise the minimum wage, reduce student loan obligations, enhance the status of women, widen access to health care, promote racial progress, protect immigrants, and tighten gun controls. The other side pointed to tax cuts it had enacted into law, its tough action on illegal immigration, its buildup of the military, its efforts to improve the nation's trade imbalance, and its deregulation of business activity. The scene of this showdown was the 2020 election. The opposing sides were the Democratic Party and the Republican Party, each with a slate of candidates that carried carry its message to voters across America.

Political parties are in the business of offering voters a choice. A **political party** is an ongoing coalition of interests joined together under a common label in an effort to get its candidates elected to public office.[2] By offering a choice between policies and leaders, parties give voters a chance to influence the direction of government. "It is the competition of [parties] that provides the people with an opportunity to make a choice," political scientist E. E. Schatt-schneider wrote. "Without this opportunity popular sovereignty amounts to nothing."[3]

This chapter examines political parties and the candidates who run under their name. U.S. campaigns are **party-centered campaigns** in the sense that the Republican and Democratic Parties compete across the country, election after election. However, they are also **candidate-centered campaigns** in the sense that individual candidates devise their own strategies, choose their own issues, and form their own campaign organizations. The following points are emphasized in this chapter:

- *Political competition in the United States has centered on two parties, a pattern that is explained primarily by America's single-member district system of elections.* Minor parties exist in the United States but have been unable to attract enough votes to win legislative seats.

- *To win an electoral majority, candidates of the two major parties must appeal to a large number of voters.* This can lead them to advocate moderate policies, although in recent years they've increasingly positioned themselves away from the political center because of party polarization and a decline in the number of competitive states and districts.

- *U.S. party organizations play an important role in campaigns, although one that is less substantial than in their heyday.* The introduction of primary elections and the emergence of televised campaigning gradually shifted control of elections toward candidates and away from parties.

Nevertheless, party organizations at the local, state, and national levels are major players in election campaigns.

- *Presidential and congressional campaigns are largely candidate centered.* These campaigns are based on money and media and utilize the skills of professional consultants.

PARTY COMPETITION AND MAJORITY RULE

Because of their large number, citizens can exert influence but only if they are able to act together. Parties give them that ability. Parties are **linkage institutions**; they connect citizens with political leaders. When Americans go to the polls, they have a choice between candidates representing the Republican and Democratic Parties. This **party competition** narrows voters' options to two and, in the process, enables people with different backgrounds and opinions to act in unison. In casting a majority of its votes for one party, the electorate chooses that party's candidates, philosophy, and policies over those of the opposing party.

The history of democratic government is inseparable from the history of parties. When the people of Eastern Europe gained their freedom from the Soviet Union in the early 1990s, one of their first steps toward democracy was the formation of political parties. When the United States was founded over two centuries ago, the formation of parties was also a first step toward building its democracy. The reason is simple: It is the competition among parties that gives popular majorities a choice over how they will be governed.[4]

The First Parties

Many of America's early leaders mistrusted parties. George Washington, in his farewell address, warned the nation of the "baneful effects" of parties, and James Madison likened parties to special interests. However, Madison's misgivings about parties slowly gave way to grudging admiration. He came to realize that parties were the best way for like-minded leaders and citizens to act together to achieve common goals.

America's first parties originated in the rivalry between Alexander Hamilton and Thomas Jefferson. Hamilton envisioned a nation connected by commerce and a strong central government and organized his followers into the Federalist Party, taking the name from the faction that had championed ratification of the Constitution (see Figure 8-1). Siding with small farmers and states' rights advocates, Jefferson responded by creating the Democratic-Republican Party, a name that evoked the spirit of the Declaration of Independence. The Federalists' efforts to promote wealthy interests fueled Jefferson's claim that they were determined to create a government that favored the rich and wellborn.

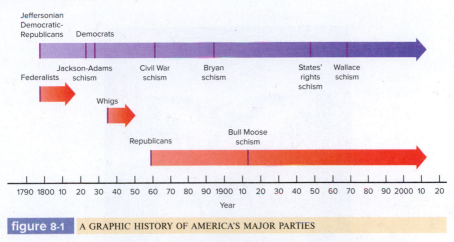

figure 8-1   A GRAPHIC HISTORY OF AMERICA'S MAJOR PARTIES

The U.S. party system has been remarkable for its continuity. Competition between two major parties has been a persistent feature of the system.

In the election of 1800, Jefferson defeated John Adams, who had succeeded Washington as president. Adams's presidency marked the end of the Federalist Party's reign. It would never again hold power and over the next two decades it all but disappeared.

During the so-called Era of Good Feeling, when James Monroe ran unopposed in 1820 for a second presidential term, it appeared as if the political system might operate without competing parties. However, by the end of Monroe's second term, policy differences had split the Democratic-Republicans. The larger faction, under the leadership of Andrew Jackson, embraced Jefferson's commitment to the common people and adopted the label "Democrats." Thus, the Democratic-Republican Party of Jefferson is the forerunner of today's Democratic Party rather than of today's Republican Party.

Andrew Jackson and Grassroots Parties

Jackson's goal was to take political power from entrenched elites. Each of the previous presidents had come from a prominent family, as had many of those in Congress and top executive positions. Jackson saw a reorganized Democratic Party as the vehicle for reform. Whereas Jefferson's party had operated largely at the leadership level, Jackson sought a **grassroots party**. As such, it was organized chiefly at the local level and was open to all citizens. During campaigns, the Democratic Party held parades, rallies, and barbecues in order to engage voters. Such efforts, along with the extension of voting rights to citizens without property, contributed to a nearly fourfold rise in election turnout during the 1830s.[5]

Although largely forgotten, the Whig Party was once one of America's two major parties. Four Whigs served as president—William Henry Harrison, John Tyler, Zachary Taylor, and Millard Fillmore. The party came into being in the early 1830s and lasted into the 1850s before being replaced by the newly created Republican Party. (Library of Congress, Prints and Photographs Division [LC-DIG-pga-09004])

During this period, a new opposition party—the Whig Party—emerged to challenge the Democrats. The Whigs were united less by a governing philosophy than by their opposition to Jackson and his followers. However, competition between the Whigs and the Democrats was relatively short-lived. During the 1850s, the slavery issue began to tear both parties apart. The Whig Party disintegrated, and a new, northern-based party, calling itself Republican, emerged as the Democrats' main challenger. In the 1860 presidential election, the Democratic Party's northern faction nominated Stephen A. Douglas, who held that the question of whether slavery would be allowed in a new state was for its voters to decide, while the southern faction nominated John C. Breckinridge, who called for legalized slavery in all states. The Democratic vote split along regional lines between the two nominees, enabling the Republican nominee,

Abraham Lincoln, who had called for the gradual elimination of slavery, to win the presidency with only 40 percent of the popular vote. Lincoln's election prompted southern states to secede from the Union.

The Civil War was the first and only time in the nation's history that the party system failed to peacefully settle Americans' political differences. The issue of slavery was simply too explosive to be settled through electoral competition.[6]

Republicans Versus Democrats: Realignments and the Enduring Party System

After the Civil War, the nation settled into the pattern of competition between the Republican and Democratic Parties that has lasted through today. The durability of the two parties is due not to their ideological consistency but to their ability to change during periods of crisis. By abandoning their old ways of doing things at these crucial times, the Republican and Democratic Parties have reorganized themselves—with new bases of support, new policies, and new public philosophies.

These periods of extraordinary party change are known as **party realignments**. A realignment typically involves three basic elements:

1. The emergence of unusually powerful and divisive issues

2. Election contests in which the voters shift their partisan support

3. An enduring change in the parties' policies and coalitions

Realignments are rare. They do not occur simply because one party takes control of government from the other in a single election. Realignments result in deep and lasting changes in the party system, which affect subsequent elections as well. By this standard, there have been four realignments since the 1850s.

The first was a result of the nation's Civil War and worked to the advantage of the Republicans. Called the "Union Party" by many, the Republicans dominated elections in the larger and more populous North, while the Democrats had a stronghold in what became known as "the Solid South." During the next three decades, the Republicans held the presidency, except for Grover Cleveland's two terms in office, and had a majority in Congress for all but four years.

The 1896 election also resulted in realignment. Three years earlier, a banking crisis had caused a severe depression. The Democrat Grover Cleveland was president when the crash happened, and people blamed him and his party. In the aftermath, the Republicans made additional gains in the Northeast and Midwest, solidifying their position as the nation's dominant party. During the four decades between the 1890s realignment and the next one in the 1930s,

In addition to triggering the Civil War, the election of 1860 reshaped America's party system. Republican Party presidential nominee Abraham Lincoln, whose vice presidential running mate was Maine's Hannibal Hamlin, won the 1860 election, which began a seven-decade period of Republican dominance. Note the motto at the top of the campaign poster. It underpinned Lincoln's decision to wage war on southern states after they seceded from the Union. When the war ended, southern states aligned with the Democratic Party and maintained that alignment for the next century. (W.H. Rease/The Library of Congress [LC-DIG-pga-07990])

the Republicans held the presidency, except for Woodrow Wilson's two terms, and had a majority in Congress for all but six years.

The Great Depression of the 1930s triggered a third realignment. The Republican Herbert Hoover was president when the stock market crashed in 1929, and many Americans blamed Hoover, his party, and its business allies for the crisis. When the Democratic Party won the presidency in 1932 and gained the confidence of the American people through its economic recovery programs, it set itself up to be the nation's dominant party for years to come. Franklin D. Roosevelt's election as president began a 36-year period of Democratic presidencies that was interrupted only by Dwight D. Eisenhower's two terms in the 1950s. In this period, the Democrats also dominated Congress, losing control only in 1947–1948 and 1953–1954.

Party realignments have a lasting effect because they are powered by changes in people's long-term party loyalties. Young voters, in particular, embrace the newly ascendant party, giving it a solid base of support for years to come.

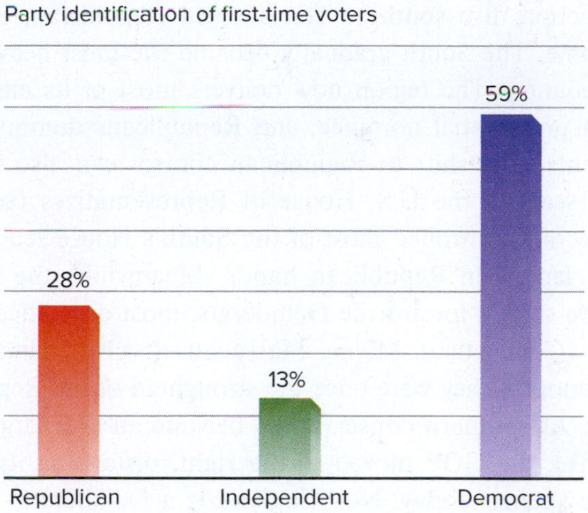

Party identification of first-time voters

28%	13%	59%
Republican	Independent	Democrat

figure 8-2   THE MAKING OF A DEMOCRATIC MAJORITY

During the Great Depression, first-time voters strongly backed the Democratic Party, positioning it to dominate national politics for the next three decades. (*Source:* Kristi Andersen, *The Creation of a Democratic Majority, 1928–1936* [Chicago: University of Chicago Press, 1979], 63. Based on first-time eligible voters in 1932, 1936, and 1940.)

First-time voters in the 1930s came to identify with the Democratic Party by a two-to-one margin (see Figure 8-2). They retained their loyalty to the Democratic Party, enabling it to dominate national politics into the 1960s.[7]

The Democratic Party that was built during the New Deal era was made up largely of low- and moderate-income groups, including blue-collar workers, inner-city dwellers, minority-group members, and small farmers. Democrats prided themselves on being "the party of the little man." In contrast, the Republican Party in this period was dominated by middle- and upper-income groups, including business people, merchants, well-to-do farmers, and professionals.

The Nature and Origins of Today's Party Alignment

The fourth and most recent party realignment began with the predictable decline of the Democrats' New Deal coalition. Party realignments don't last indefinitely. They gradually loses strength as the issues that gave rise to them decline in importance. By the late 1960s, with the Democratic Party divided over the Vietnam War and civil rights, it was apparent that the era of New Deal politics was coming to an end.[8]

The change was most dramatic in the South. The region had been solidly Democratic at all levels since the Civil War, but the Democratic Party's leadership on civil rights alienated the region's white conservatives. In the 1964 presidential election, five southern states voted Republican, an indicator of what was to come. The South gradually became the most heavily Republican region in the country. The region now delivers most of its electoral votes to the Republican presidential nominee, and Republicans dominate the South's state governments. The shift to Republican control can also be seen in the distribution of seats in the U.S. House of Representatives (see Figure 8-3). Whereas Democrats controlled most of the South's House seats in the 1960s, they are today largely in Republican hands. Meanwhile, the Northeast and West Coast have shifted toward the Democrats, most dramatically in the New England states (Connecticut. Maine, Massachusetts, New Hampshire, Rhode Island, and Vermont). They were once the stronghold of the Republican Party's moderate wing. As southern conservatives became an ever larger force within Republican ranks, the GOP moved to the right, distancing itself from many of its moderate voters.[9] Today, New England is a Democratic bastion. It is a reliable source of electoral votes for Democratic presidential candidates, and nearly all of the region's top elected officials are Democrats.

The net result of these and other regional changes has been a party realignment. Rather than occurring abruptly in response to a disruptive issue, as happened with the earlier realignments, the change took place gradually and is the product of several issues rather than an overriding one. Civil rights was the triggering issue, but it was soon followed by what analysts Richard Scammon and Ben Wattenberg called the "social issue"—a loose set of controversies including crime, abortion, drugs, school prayer, and changing sexual and family norms.[10]

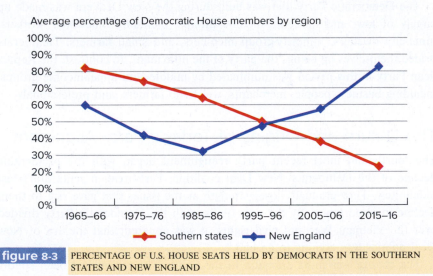

Average percentage of Democratic House members by region

Southern states ◆ New England

figure 8-3   PERCENTAGE OF U.S. HOUSE SEATS HELD BY DEMOCRATS IN THE SOUTHERN STATES AND NEW ENGLAND

In elections to the U.S. House of Representatives in recent decades, the southern states have increasingly elected Republicans, while the New England states have increasingly elected Democrats.

Conservative Christians were the ones most alarmed by the changes, solidifying Republican gains in the southern and border states, particularly among white evangelicals.[11] Ronald Reagan's presidency completed the transformation. President Lyndon Johnson's Great Society programs, which included programs such as Medicare and Medicaid, had expanded the federal government's social welfare role and increased federal spending. Conservatives felt the government was spending way too much and doing far too many things that were better left to the states. Reagan gave voice to their concerns, vowing to cut taxes, reduce the welfare rolls, trim the federal budget, and devolve power to the states.

Although America's parties had realigned themselves without going through the sudden shock of a single realigning election, the change has been dramatic, particularly for the Republican Party.[12] Although it began under Lincoln as the party of national power, it is now more clearly a states' rights party that seeks to shift power from Washington to the states (see Chapter 3). And the coalitions of both parties are now dramatically different than they were in the New Deal era. During that period, working-class whites were the backbone of the Democratic Party. Now they're aligned with the GOP. Meanwhile, college-educated voters, who were once heavily Republican, now lean slightly Democratic. Catholics and evangelical Protestants once voted Democratic but now side with the Republicans. White southerners were once reliably Democratic

White working-class Americans voted heavily Democratic during the period of the New Deal realignment. As a result of the party realignment that began in the 1960s, they now vote heavily Republican.
(Disability Images/Alamy Stock Photo)

PARTY POLARIZATION

Conflicting Ideas

Voting a Straight Ticket

A leading indicator of heightened party polarization has been a shift toward *straight-ticket voting*—the tendency of voters to support the same party's presidential and congressional candidates. As recently as the 1970s, a period when voters' party loyalties were in flux, there was a high level of *split-ticket voting*. More than a fourth of voters supported one party's presidential candidate and the other party's congressional candidate. However, as the gap between Republicans and Democrats has widened, and the choice between the two parties has become sharper, straight-ticket voting has increased, as can be seen in the following figure.

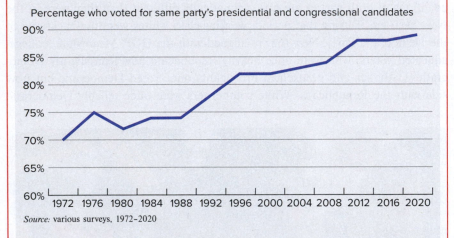

Percentage who voted for same party's presidential and congressional candidates

Source: various surveys, 1972-2020

Q: How might the rise in straight-ticket voting have contributed to the level of polarization in Congress?

A: When fewer voters split their ticket, candidates have less incentive to moderate their positions in order to appeal to voters of the other party. As a result, fewer moderates get elected to Congress. The decline in the number of congressional moderates is a reason that Republican and Democratic lawmakers have found it harder to compromise on legislative issues.

but are now reliably Republican. Minority groups were a small part of the electorate during the New Deal era; they now constitute nearly a third of all voters and have voted strongly Democratic ever since the Democratic Party took the lead on civil rights in the 1960s.[13]

The realignment of America's parties has been accompanied by a widening gap in the opinions of Republicans and Democrats. On the question of federal assistance for the economically disadvantaged, the gap in Republican and Democratic opinions has more than doubled since the 1980s and is now nearly 40 percentage points. In terms of a belief in traditional family and social values, the gap has widened from less than 5 percentage points to nearly 30 points. On the issue of programs aimed directly at helping minority groups, the gap has doubled.[14]

Parties and the Vote

The enduring power of partisanship is at no time clearer than when, election after election, Republican and Democratic candidates reap the vote of their party's identifiers. It is relatively rare—in congressional races as well as the presidential race—for a party nominee to get less than 80 percent of the partisan vote.

The power of partisanship can be seen in the tendency of most voters to cast a *straight ticket*—meaning that they uniformly support their party's candidates. Most voters who cast a ballot for the Republican or Democratic presidential candidate also vote for that party's congressional candidate. Less than 20 percent of today's voters cast a *split-ticket*—meaning that they voted for one party's presidential candidate and the other party's congressional candidate (see "Party Polarization: Voting a Straight Ticket").

ELECTORAL AND PARTY SYSTEMS

Throughout nearly all of its history, the United States has had a **two-party system**: Federalists versus Jeffersonian Democratic-Republicans, Whigs versus Democrats, Republicans versus Democrats. A two-party system, however, is the exception rather than the rule (see "How the U.S. Differs"). Most democracies have a **multiparty system**, in which three or more parties have the capacity to gain control of government, separately or in coalition. Why the difference? Why are there three or more major parties in most democracies but only two major parties in the United States?

The Single-Member System of Election

America's two-party system is largely the result of the nation's method of choosing its officials. They are elected by winning a plurality of the votes in **single-member districts**. Each constituency elects a single member to a particular office, such as U.S. senator or state representative; the candidate with the most votes (*the plurality*) in a district wins the office. The **single-member system** (sometimes called the *winner-take-all or plurality* system) discourages minor parties by reducing their chances of winning anything, even if they perform well by minor-party standards. Assume, for example, that a minor party receives exactly 20 percent of the vote in each of America's 435 congressional races. Even though one in five voters nationwide backed the minor party, it does not win a single seat in Congress because none of its candidates placed first in any

HOW THE U.S. DIFFERS
CRITICAL THINKING THROUGH COMPARISONS

Party and Electoral Systems

Since 1860, electoral competition in the United States has centered on the Republican and Democratic Parties. By comparison, most democracies have a multiparty system, in which three or more parties receive substantial support from voters.

Whether a country has a two-party or a multiparty system depends on several factors, but particularly its electoral system. The United States has a single-member system in which only the top candidate in a district is elected. This system is biased against smaller parties; they win nothing unless one of their candidates places first in an electoral district. By comparison, proportional representation systems enable smaller parties to compete. Parties acquire legislative seats in proportion to their share of the total vote, meaning that a party will receive seats even if it receives fewer votes than do the larger parties. Nearly every democracy with proportional representation, which includes most European countries, has at least three competitive parties, usually more than three.

Q: Like the United States, Canada and Great Britain have the single-member-district system of election. However, unlike the United States, they have more than two parties. Why?

A: Canada's third parties have stemmed from regional differences and resentments. French-speaking Quebec has a strong regional party, and strong regional parties have appeared from time to time in Canada's western provinces. Britain's strongest third party at the moment, the Scottish National Party, also derives strength from having a regional base.

of the 435 single-member-district races. The winning candidate in each race is the major-party candidate, with the larger share of the remaining 80 percent of the vote.

By comparison, most European democracies use a **proportional representation system** in which seats in the legislature are allocated according to a party's percentage of the popular vote. This type of electoral system enables smaller parties to compete for power. In Germany's 2017 election, for example, the Green Party received 9 percent of the national vote and thereby won roughly 9 percent of the seats in the German parliament. If the Greens had been competing under America's electoral rules, they would not have won any seats.

Politics and Coalitions in the Two-Party System

The overriding goal of a major American party is to gain power by getting its candidates elected to office. Because there are only two major parties, the Republicans and Democrats need to attract more votes than the other party in order to win. If either party confines its support to too narrow a slice of voters, it forfeits its chance of victory.

Seeking the Center Without Losing the Support of the Party Faithful   A two-party system typically requires the major parties to avoid positions that will carry them too far from the political center. The **median voter theorem** holds that, if there are two parties, the parties can maximize their vote only if they position themselves at the location of the median voter—the voter whose preferences are exactly in the middle.[15]

Although hypothetical, the median voter theorem helps explain the risk a party faces if it moves too far from the center, leaving it open to the other party. In 1964, the Republican nominee, Barry Goldwater, proposed the elimination of mandatory Social Security and suggested he might be open to the use of small nuclear weapons in the Vietnam conflict—extreme positions that cost him many votes. Eight years later, the Democratic nominee, George McGovern, took positions on Vietnam and income security that alarmed many voters. Like Goldwater, he was buried in one of the biggest landslides in presidential history.

Although voters in the political center can hold the balance of power in an election, they are less important in the parties' strategies than they once were. As a result of party polarization, most voters today are positioned to the right or left of center.[16] If candidates move too close to the center, they risk alienating their party's core voters, some of whom may choose not to vote on Election Day.

In addition, there are fewer competitive states and districts than in the past. The party realignment of recent decades occurred along geographic lines, with the effect that most states and congressional districts are now so lopsidedly

Republican or Democratic that the stronger party is virtually certain to win the general election.[17] In these cases, the critical election is the stronger party's primary election. Primaries have relatively low turnout, and the voters who do show up are disproportionately the party's most committed voters. These voters, rather than the moderates, are the key to victory in a primary. Thus, rather than positioning themselves toward the political center, candidates take positions away from the center in order to appeal to their party's hard-core voters. It's a reason that Congress has far fewer moderate members today than in the past.

Party Coalitions   The groups and interests that support a party are collectively referred to as the **party coalition**. The Republican and Democratic coalitions differ in their composition. In recent elections, for example, women have voted disproportionately for Democratic candidates, whereas men have voted disproportionately for Republican candidates, resulting in what's been labeled the **gender gap**.[18]

The Republican Party is made up largely of non-Hispanic white Americans. In the 2020 election, they cast roughly 9 of every 10 votes that Republicans received.[19] Not since Lyndon Johnson's landslide victory in the 1964 election has the Democratic presidential nominee won a majority of the white vote. White evangelical or born-again Christians are the largest Republican voting bloc, accounting for more than a third of the party's vote. They vote roughly three-to-one Republican.[20] By smaller margins, most older adults and higher-income Americans vote Republican.[21]

The Democratic Party coalition is more diverse. White voters make up the majority of Democratic voters, but roughly two-fifths of the party's vote comes from minority-group members. Black Americans vote roughly nine-to-one Democratic. Hispanics and Asian Americans vote roughly two-to-one Democratic. Younger voters and lower-income Americans also vote disproportionately Democratic.

CITIZEN ACTION!
GETTING READY

Political philosopher John Stuart Mill said that citizens who don't understand the opinion of others have no firm basis for trusting their own opinion. Consider examining a few of the opinion polls conducted by the nonpartisan Pew Research Center. Once on its site, you'll find the results of recent polls that reveal how Americans of various backgrounds differ in their opinions.

The parties' future prospects might depend on whether recent trends persist.[22] The Democratic Party has a significant edge with three groups—Hispanics, Asian Americans, and younger adults—who are becoming an ever larger part of the electorate. Meanwhile, the Republican Party's edge is with older white Americans, who are declining in number. The Hispanic vote is a key to the long-term prospects of both parties. With the exception of Cuban Americans, who are concentrated in southern Florida, Hispanics strongly back the

Democratic Party. Nevertheless, polls show that many Hispanics have conservative opinions on issues such as abortion and same-sex marriage, which Republicans see as an opportunity to attract Hispanic voters.[23]

Few developments have more implications for the parties' future chances than the voting pattern of young adults. Over the past five presidential elections, voters under 30 years of age have preferred the Democratic nominee by an average of roughly 20 percentage points (see Figure 8-4). It's the first time since the New Deal era that young voters have heavily backed the same party in a sequence of presidential elections. These voters now include everyone between the ages of 18 and 45, which is more than a third of the electorate. And they have remained loyal to the Democratic Party as they have aged. If they continue to support it, the Democratic Party at some point will come to dominate U.S. elections. No greater challenge faces the Republican Party than finding ways to make inroads among the nation's younger voters.[24]

Minor (Third) Parties

Although the U.S. electoral system discourages the formation of minor parties (or third parties, as they are sometimes called), the nation has always had minor parties—more than 1,000 over its history.[25] Even the more successful ones have usually been short-lived. If a minor party starts to gain a following,

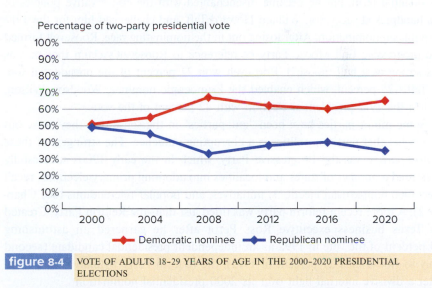

figure 8-4   VOTE OF ADULTS 18–29 YEARS OF AGE IN THE 2000–2020 PRESIDENTIAL ELECTIONS

Since the presidential election of 2004, young adults have voted heavily Democratic each time, marking the first time since the Great Depression era that they have voted overwhelmingly for the same party in a lengthy series of elections. (*Source:* Exit polls, 2000-2020. Votes for third-party candidates not included in percentages.)

one of the major parties is likely to pick up its issue, at which time it will begin to take support away from the minor party. Another problem for minor parties is that their candidates rarely win office. Most voters don't want to waste their ballot on what they know will be a losing cause. Only one minor party, the Republican Party, has achieved majority status.

Minor parties peaked in the 19th century, a time when the party system was still in flux.[26] Many of these parties were *single-issue parties* formed around an issue of overriding interest to their followers. Examples are the Free Soil Party, which fought the extension of slavery into new territories, and the Greenback Party, which sought a currency system based on paper money rather than gold and silver. The role that single-issue parties played in the 19th century is now played by single-issue interest groups (see Chapter 9).

The most important minor parties of the 20th century were *factional parties* that resulted from a split within one of the major parties. Although the Republican and Democratic Parties are usually successful at managing internal conflict, it has sometimes prompted a dissident faction to break away and form its own party. The States' Rights Party in 1948 and George Wallace's American Independent Party in 1968 are examples of these factional parties. They were formed by white southern Democrats angered by northern Democrats' support of Black civil rights. The most electorally successful factional party was the Bull Moose Party in 1912.[27] Four years earlier, Theodore Roosevelt had declined to seek another presidential term, but he became disenchanted with the conservative policies of his handpicked successor, William Howard Taft, and challenged him for the 1912 Republican nomination. After losing out in the nominating race, Roosevelt formed the progressive Bull Moose Party (a reference to Roosevelt's claim that he was "as strong as a bull moose"). Roosevelt won 27 percent of the presidential vote to Taft's 25 percent, which enabled the Democratic nominee, Woodrow Wilson, to win the 1912 presidential election with 42 percent of the vote.

Some minor parties have been "anti-parties" in the sense that they arose out of a belief that partisan politics is a corrupting influence. The strongest of these *reform parties* was the Progressive Party, which in the early 1900s successfully pressured a number of states and localities into adopting primary elections, recall elections, nonpartisan elections, initiatives, and popular referendums (see Chapter 2). A more recent reform party was titled just that—the Reform Party. Created by Texas business executive Ross Perot after he garnered an astonishing 19 percent of the vote in 1992 as an independent presidential candidate (second only to Roosevelt's 27 percent in 1912), the Reform Party virtually disappeared after a divisive internal fight over its 2000 presidential nomination.

Other minor parties have been characterized by an ideological commitment such as redistribution of wealth. The strongest *ideological party* was the Populists, whose 1892 presidential nominee, James B. Weaver, won 9 percent of the

PUCK

THE CROWD AS IT LOOKS TO THEODORE.

Although the United States has long had a two-party system, numerous minor parties have surfaced. The most electorally successful was the Bull Moose Party, a factional party that split from the Republican Party. Headed by former president Theodore Roosevelt, it garnered 27 percent of the popular vote. The Republican nominee, incumbent William Howard Taft, came in third with 25 percent of vote. The Democratic nominee, Woodrow Wilson, won the presidency with 42 percent of the vote. (Library of Congress Prints & Photographs Division [LC-DIG-ppmsca-38463])

national vote and carried six western states on a radical platform that included a call for government takeover of the railroads.[28] The strongest ideological parties today are the Libertarian Party, which calls for less government intervention in the marketplace and people's lives, and the Green Party, which promotes social equality and environmentalism. In the 2016 presidential election, the Libertarian Party's Gary Johnson and the Green Party's Jill Stein received a combined 4 percent of the popular vote. Polls indicated that, if they had not been in the race, most of their votes would have gone to Hillary Clinton, perhaps by a margin large enough to tip the election in her favor.[29]

PARTIES AND CANDIDATES IN THE CAMPAIGN

The Democratic and Republican Parties have organizational units at the national, state, and local levels. These **party organizations** concentrate on electing candidates to office. A century ago, party organizations enjoyed nearly complete control of elections. Two developments—the introduction of primary elections and changes in the media system—gradually shifted control to the candidates. Today, they have the lead role in presidential and congressional elections.[30]

Primary Elections and Candidate Control

Nomination is the selection of the individual who will run as the party's candidate in the general election. Until the early 20th century, the party organizations picked the nominees, who, if elected, were expected to share with it the spoils of office—government jobs and contracts. The party built its organization by giving the jobs to loyalists and by granting contracts to donors. Bribes and kickbacks were part of the process in some locations. New York City's legendary Boss Tweed once charged the city 20 times what a building had actually cost, amassing a personal fortune before winding up in prison. Reform-minded Progressives invented primary elections as a way to deprive party bosses of their power over nominations (see Chapter 2).

A **primary election** (or *direct primary*) gives control of nominations to the voters (see Chapters 2 and 12). The candidate with the most votes in a party's primary gets its nomination for the general election. In some states, the nominees are chosen in *closed primaries,* where participation is limited to voters registered with the party. Registered voters of the other party are not allowed to "cross over" to vote in the primary. The logic of a closed primary is that a party's voters should have the power to choose its general election candidate. In contrast, some states use *open primaries,* which allow independents and sometimes voters of the other party to vote in the party's primary (although they cannot vote simultaneously in both parties' primaries). The logic of the open primary is that it gives all voters a say in the choices they will have in the general election. California, Louisiana, Nebraska, and Washington conduct *top-two primaries.* Candidates are listed on the primary ballot without regard to party; the top two finishers become the general election candidates (see "How the 50 States Differ").

Primaries shift the control of campaigns from the parties to the candidates. In Europe, where there are no primary elections, the parties are stronger. They control their nominations, and their candidates are expected to support the party's national platform. A candidate or an officeholder who fails to do so is likely to be denied renomination by the party in the next election. In the United States, however, candidates can seek nomination on their own by entering the party's primary. Primary elections require candidates to organize and run their campaigns. They raise the funds, hire the staff, and pick the issues on which they'll run. Once in office, they are largely free to act as they please as long as they retain the support of the voters in their home district.

HOW THE 50 STATES DIFFER

CRITICAL THINKING THROUGH COMPARISONS

Primary Elections

All states hold primary elections, but they differ in the types of primaries they hold. Roughly a third of them have *open primaries,* which allow any registered voter to vote in the primary. Another third have *closed primaries,* which are limited to voters registered as members of the party holding the primary, or *partially closed primaries*, which give the parties the option of conducting a closed primary. Other states have *partially open primaries*, which allow independents but not registered voters of the other party to participate. Finally, four states—California, Louisiana, Nebraska, and Washington—have *top-two primaries*, in which candidates of both parties are on the same ballot and the top two finishers compete in the general election.

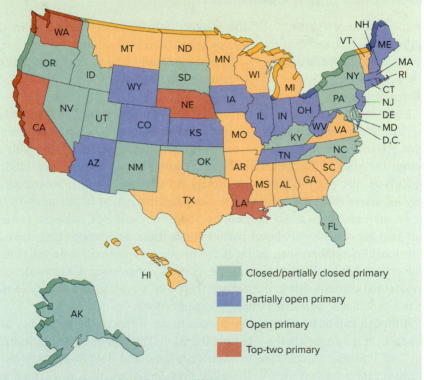

(Source: National Council of State Legislatures, 2014.)

Continued

Q: The top-two primary is relatively new. What do you think are the chief arguments for and against this type of primary?

A: Proponents argue that top-two primaries give independent voters a larger say in the selection of nominees and may result in the selection of more moderate nominees. Opponents say that this type of primary hurts the state's weaker party and can limit voters' choice in the general election to two candidates of the same party.

The Parties' Role in Campaigns

Although the parties have less control over campaigns than in their heyday, they retain a key role.[31] They provide a permanent organizational base for party activists and candidates. Moreover, certain activities, such as get-out-the-vote efforts on Election Day, affect all of a party's candidates and are done most efficiently through party organizations.

Local Political Parties   Of the roughly 500,000 elective offices in the United States, fewer than 500 are contested statewide and only 2—the presidency and vice presidency—are contested nationally. The rest are local offices; not surprisingly, at least 95 percent of party activists work within local organizations.

Local parties vary greatly in their activities. Only a few local parties, including the Democratic organizations in Philadelphia and Chicago, have even a faint resemblance to the fabled old-time party machines that were able to deliver the vote on Election Day. In many urban areas, and in most suburbs and towns, the party organizations today do not have enough volunteers to play an active role except during the campaign period, at which time—to the extent their resources allow—they conduct registration drives, hand out leaflets, and help get out the vote. Local parties concentrate on elections that coincide with local boundaries, such as races for mayor, city council, state legislature, and county offices. Local parties take part in congressional, statewide, and presidential contests, but in these cases their role is typically secondary to that of the candidates' personal campaign organizations.

Although candidates rely on the parties to get voters to the polls, they also conduct their own get-out-the-vote operations, making use of computer technology and information collected through telephone and door-to-door efforts to construct their contact lists. In the 2020 presidential election, the Trump and Biden campaigns spent millions of dollars to amass huge voter lists, which were used to raise funds as well as to get out the vote on Election Day.

Campaign signs on a lawn in Irving, Texas. Local party organizations help the party's candidates through get-out-the-vote efforts and other activities. (Trong Nguyen/Shutterstock)

State Party Organizations   At the state level, each party is headed by a central committee made up of members of local party organizations and local and state officeholders. State central committees do not meet regularly and provide only general guidance to the state party organization, which is directed by a chairperson, who is a full-time, paid employee. Most of the state party organizations are relatively small, having fewer than 20 full-time employees. The state party organizations engage in activities, such as fundraising and voter registration, that can improve their candidates' chances of success. State party organizations concentrate on statewide races, including those for governor and U.S. senator, as well as races for the state legislature. They play a smaller role in campaigns for national or local offices and, in most states, do not endorse candidates in statewide primaries.[32]

National Party Organizations   The parties also have organizational units at the national level, although there is no chain of command that connects the local, state, and national organizations. The national party organization cannot tell the state organizations what to do, and, in turn, the state organizations cannot tell the local organizations what to do. The Texas state Democratic Party, for example, does not take orders from the national Democratic Party and does not give orders to the state's local Democratic party organizations, whether in a large city such as Dallas or Houston or in a smaller one such as McAllen or Amarillo. Each party organization is free to act as it wants. Nevertheless, party organizations at all levels have a shared stake in their party's success and thus have an incentive to work together to get the party's candidates elected to office and to build up a loyal base of voters.[33]

The national Republican and Democratic party organizations, which are located in Washington, D.C., are structured much like those at the state level: They have a national committee and a national party chairperson. Neither the Democratic National Committee (DNC) nor the Republican National Committee (RNC) has great power. The RNC (with more than 150 members) and the DNC (with more than 300 members) are too large and meet too infrequently to actually run the national organization. Their power is largely confined to establishing organizational policy, such as determining the site of the party's presidential nominating convention and deciding the rules governing the selection of convention delegates. They have no power to pick nominees or to dictate the candidates' policy positions.

Each national party's day-to-day operations are directed by a national chair chosen by the national committee, although the committee defers to the president's choice when the party controls the White House. The national parties run training programs for candidates and their staffs, raise money, seek media coverage of party positions and activities, conduct issue and group research, and send field representatives to help state and local parties with their operations. In some cases, the national parties also try to recruit potentially strong candidates to run in House and Senate races.

CITIZEN ACTION!
GETTING INVOLVED

Consider becoming a campaign or political party volunteer. The opportunities are many. Parties and candidates at every level from national politics on down seek volunteers to help in organizing, canvassing, fundraising, and other activities. As a college student, you have communication and knowledge skills of use to a candidate or party organization.

The national parties' major role in campaigns is raising money. Although the RNC and the DNC spend most of the money they raise to fund their own operations, they give some of it to the party's House and Senate candidates, who also get funding from campaign committees that the parties have formed in the House and Senate. In any case, the amount of money that a party committee can give directly to a candidate is limited by law—$5,000 for House candidates and $49,600 for Senate candidates. However, the total amount of money raised and spent by national party organizations is substantial. It easily exceeded $1 billion in the 2020 elections.[34]

Media Changes and Candidate Control

Primaries are not the only reason for the shift in control of election campaigns from parties to candidates. Changes in the media also contributed. When primaries were introduced in the early 1900s, the party organizations remained strong enough to pick most of the nominees. Although it was possible for candidates to run and win on their own in primaries, it was difficult. They could buy newspaper ads to promote their candidacy, but newspaper advertising was not a good foundation on which to base a campaign.[35]

Rise of Television   The introduction of television in the 1950s provided candidates with the tool they needed to take greater control of their campaigns. Televised ads proved to be an effective way to promote their candidacies, and television quickly became the principal medium of election campaigning.

Candidates now spend heavily on televised political advertising, which enables them to communicate directly—and on their own terms—with voters. *Air wars* is the term that political scientist Darrell West applies to candidates' use of televised ads.[36] Modern production techniques enable well-funded candidates to get new ads on the air within a few hours' time, which allows them to rebut attacks and exploit fast-breaking developments, a tactic known as *rapid response*. The production and airing of televised political ads account for roughly half of all campaign spending.[37] Indeed, televised ads are a main reason for the high cost of U.S. campaigns. In most democracies, televised campaigning takes place through parties, which receive free air time to make their pitch. Many democracies, including France and Great Britain, prohibit the use of televised political ads.

Candidates also rely on the news media to get their message across, although the amount of coverage they get varies widely by location and office. Many candidates for the House of Representatives are almost completely ignored by local news media. The New York City media market, for example, includes more than 20 House districts in New York, New Jersey, Pennsylvania, and Connecticut, and House candidates in these districts get little or no coverage from the New York media. They also make little use of televised ads because it is too expensive to buy ads in a metropolitan area where the voters in a congressional district are only a small fraction of the audience. Such candidates conduct their campaigns the old-fashioned way, through leafleting, door-to-door canvassing, and the like. In contrast, presidential candidates get daily coverage from both national and local media. Between these extremes are Senate races, which always get some news coverage and can get heavy coverage if closely contested.[38]

The media campaign also includes candidate debates. In fact, they are the centerpiece of presidential and many Senate general election campaigns, although they are seldom decisive.[39] By the time of the debates, most voters have settled on their choice and find reason to stay with it even if their preferred candidate doesn't perform all that well.

Televised debates are a key moment in the presidential general election campaign, although they seldom influence enough voters to tip the balance in the election. Pictured here are Donald Trump and Joe Biden during the first general election debate of the 2020 presidential campaign. (Kevin Dietsch/ UPI/Bloomberg/Getty Images)

Rise of the Internet   New communication technology usually makes its way into campaign politics, and the Internet is no exception. Nearly all of the congressional candidates in the 2020 elections had websites dedicated to providing information, generating public support, attracting volunteers, and raising money.

Although television is still the principal medium of election politics, some analysts believe that the Internet will eventually overtake it. Internet messaging is much less expensive than television advertising and can more easily be targeted at particular types of voters. However, the Internet also has some disadvantages relative to television, especially in the greater control that individual users have over the message. With television, when a brief political ad appears during a favorite program, many viewers will sit through it. An unsolicited message on the Internet is more easily ignored or deleted. So far, the Internet has shown itself to be the better medium for fundraising and mobilizing supporters, whereas television has proven to be the better medium for building name recognition and reaching less interested voters.[40]

Rise of Campaign Money   The "election game" is how political consultant Joe Napolitan characterized television-based campaigning.[41] The game requires

Politics in Action

Donald Trump's Media Strategy

Donald Trump's 2016 presidential campaign began with a theatrical ride down the escalator in Trump Tower. Hired actors were at the bottom, cheering wildly as he arrived. Before long, news outlets were doing the cheering. He was a ratings hit. A Harvard University study found that, during

Official White House Photo by Joyce N. Boghosian

every month of his presidential campaign, Trump received by far the heaviest news coverage.[42] The media's fascination with Trump carried into his presidency. During his first 100 days in office, he received twice the media attention of other recent presidents during their first 100 days.[43] Trump's 2020 presidential campaign followed the same script. Even though he attacked the news media as "the lying media," there were times during the 2020 campaign where they gave him much heavier coverage than was given to Joe Biden, his Democratic rival.[44]

Trump's strategic insight about the media is that attention equals power. In an information system that overloads us with messages, there are few things more powerful than the ability, as Trump said, "to keep people interested." "And that gives you power," he said. "It's not the polls. It's the ratings."[45] From his years as a reality-TV host, Trump had come to understand that, if you can attract people's attention, the news media will shower you with free coverage. "If you get good ratings," he said, "you'll be on all the time. . . . It's a very simple business. Very simple."[46]

Q: Might future political candidates successfully follow Trump's strategy?

ASK YOURSELF: How important was Trump's experience as a reality-TV host to his understanding of how the media operate? Did his name recognition as a TV host affect audience interest in the early phase of his entry into politics? How unique were Trump's personality and agenda—might the typical candidate use the media strategy that Trump employed and expect the media to respond as fully as they responded to him?

money—lots of it. Campaigns for high office are expensive, and the costs keep rising. In 1980, about $250 million was spent by Senate and House candidates in the general election. By 1990, the figure had jumped to more than $400 million. In 2020, the figure exceeded $2 billion—eight times the 1980 level.[47] As might be expected, incumbents have a distinct advantage in fundraising. They have contributor lists from past campaigns and, because they are in office, have the policy influence that donors are seeking. House and Senate incumbents outraise their challengers by more than two to one.[48]

Because of the high cost of campaigns, candidates spend much of their time raising funds, which come primarily from individual contributors, political parties, and interest groups (discussed in Chapter 9). The **money chase** is relentless.[49] A U.S. senator must raise an average of $30,000 a week throughout the entire six-year term in order to raise the minimum of $10 million that it takes to compete in a close race, even in a small state. A Senate campaign in a larger state can easily cost far more than that amount. In the 2016 Texas Senate race, incumbent Ted Cruz and his Democratic challenger, Beto O'Rourke, combined to spend more than $100 million, making it one of the most expensive Senate races ever. House campaigns are less costly, but expenditures of $1 million or more are now commonplace.

The most expensive campaign, of course, is the presidential race. Several billion dollars were spent on the 2020 presidential campaign, including what was spent by candidates, party organizations, and independent groups.[50] There was a time when leading presidential candidates availed themselves of the option to fund their campaigns through public financing but that time has passed. The amount of funds available to candidates through public financing pales alongside what they need to raise in order to run a strong campaign.*

The money that candidates raise from political parties, individuals, and interest groups is subject to legal limits (for example, $2,800 from an individual contributor and $5,000 from a group per election). These contributions are termed **hard money**—the money is given directly to the candidate and can be spent as he or she chooses. Candidates are also the beneficiaries (and sometimes the casualties) of spending by super PACs, which are organizations

---

*Under the Federal Election Campaign Act of 1974 (as amended in 1979), a candidate qualifies for public financing of their primary election campaign by raising at least $5,000 in individual contributions in 20 or more states. In such cases, the government matches up to $250 per contributor, provided that the candidate agrees to limit campaign spending to a set amount in each state and overall (the overall limit for the 2020 election was roughly $50 million). For the general election, the major nominees have the option of conducting their campaigns on a specified amount of public funding (roughly $100 million for the 2020 campaign), provided that they limit their spending to that amount. The funds for public financing are obtained from an option available to taxpayers when they file their federal taxes. They have the choice of making a tax-fee contribution of $3 to the fund.

American political campaigns last longer and are more costly than campaigns in other democracies. The United States is almost alone in using primary elections as the means of selecting party nominees, which extends the campaign period. Pictured campaigning here is Senator Kamela Harris of California, the Democratic Party's 2020 vice-presidential nominee. (Erin Schaff/The New York Times/Redux Pictures)

that can raise and spend money freely on campaigns as long as they do not coordinate their efforts with those of the candidate they support. Super PACs spent more than $1 billion on the 2020 elections. (Super PACs are discussed at greater length in Chapter 9.)

Rise of Political Consultants   The key operatives in today's campaigns—congressional as well as presidential—are highly paid *political consultants*, including campaign strategists who help the candidate plot and execute a game plan. Over the years, some of these strategists, including James Carville and Roger Ailes, developed legendary reputations. Fundraising specialists are also part of the new politics. They are adept at tapping donors and interest groups that regularly contribute to election campaigns. Campaign consultants also include pollsters, whose surveys are used to identify issues and messages that will resonate with voters. Media consultants are another staple of the modern campaign. They are adept at producing televised political advertising, generating news coverage, and developing Internet-based strategies.

Campaign consultants are skilled at **packaging** a candidate—highlighting those aspects of the candidate's policy positions and personality that are thought to be most attractive to voters. Packaging is not new to politics; Andrew Jackson's self-portrayal in the 19th century as "the champion of the people" is an image that any modern candidate could appreciate. What is new is the need to fit the image to the requirements of a world of sound bites, 30-second ads, televised debates, and Internet messages. In the old days, it was sometimes enough for candidates to drive home the point that they were a Republican or a Democrat, playing on the tendency of voters to choose a candidate on that basis. Party appeals are still critical, but today's voters also expect to hear about a candidate's personal life and policy proposals.

Over the course of a campaign, voters usually hear more about the candidates' weaknesses than about their strengths.[51] Of course, negative campaigning is as old as American politics. Thomas Jefferson, Andrew Jackson, and Abraham Lincoln were the target of vicious attacks. Lincoln was portrayed as "a hick" and "a baboon" for his gangly looks and backwoods roots. But today's version of attack politics is unprecedented in its reach and scale. Negative television ads were once the exception, but they have increased to the point that they are now constitute a majority of candidate ads.[52] Many of the ads are "badly misleading," according to FactCheck.org, which monitors ads and assesses their accuracy.[53] Candidates' news coverage also tends to be negative. Journalists concentrate more on the candidates' weaknesses and missteps than they do on their strengths and achievements.[54]

Do Campaigns Make a Difference?   Because they consist of primary and general elections, American campaigns are lengthy affairs. Congressional campaigns go on for months, and a presidential campaign lasts longer than a year.

Given the amount of money and public attention they consume, it might be thought that campaigns determine who wins and who loses. But that's not the case in most races. Less than half the states are considered competitive in the sense that both parties have a reasonable chance of winning a statewide race. The other states are so heavily Republican or Democratic that only in unusual circumstances does the weaker party win. It can happen, but it's rare. In the 2017 special election to fill Alabama's vacant Senate seat, Republicans nominated Judge Roy Moore, who was accused of having sexually molested teenage girls when he was in his thirties. Moore was defeated in the general election, the first time in a generation that the Democratic nominee had won a Senate race in Alabama. In 2020, Alabama reverted to form. Republicans won back the Senate seat they had lost three years earlier.

House races are even less competitive than Senate races. Only about 75 of the 435 House seats could conceivably be won by either party. Realistically, the number is much smaller. About two dozen seats, on average, have switched from one party to the other in recent elections. Moreover, when parties do lose seats, it's often because of national conditions rather than what happens during the campaign. Nothing so tips the balance in close races as voters' satisfaction with the party that holds power. Although some voters are swayed by what candidates promise to do if elected (a form of voting known as *prospective voting*), a greater number respond to past performance (*retrospective voting*). National economic conditions are particularly important in voters' judgments. An analysis by political scientists John Sides and Lynn Vavreck found that the in-party nearly always loses votes when the economy is weak and nearly always gains votes when it's strong.[55]

Although the candidates' campaigns do not determine the outcome of most races, each political party has a stake in conducting a strong campaign. If a party can win enough seats to control the House or Senate, or get the votes needed to win the presidency, it gains political power. That's incentive enough for the parties and their candidates to mount large-scale campaign efforts.[56]

PARTIES, CANDIDATES, AND THE PUBLIC'S INFLUENCE

Candidate-centered campaigns have some distinct advantages. First, they can infuse new blood into electoral politics. Candidate recruitment is typically a slow process in party-centered systems. Would-be officeholders pay their dues by working in the party and, in the process, tend to adopt the outlook of those already there. By comparison, a candidate-centered system is more open and provides opportunities for newcomers to gain office quickly. Donald Trump is a case in point. He had never held, or even run for, political office before entering the race for the 2016 Republican presidential nomination. His public profile was based almost entirely on his real estate dealings and his role as host of a reality-TV show. Nevertheless, in a field of more than a dozen Republican candidates, most of whom had held high office, Trump easily prevailed. Trump's quick rise to political prominence would be almost unthinkable in a party-centered system.

Candidate-centered campaigns also encourage national officeholders to be responsive to local interests. In building personal followings among their state or district constituents, members of Congress respond to local needs. Nearly every significant domestic program enacted by Congress is adjusted to accommodate the interests of states and localities that otherwise would be hurt by the policy. Where strong national parties exist, national interests take precedence over local concerns. In both France and Britain, for example, the pleas of legislators from underdeveloped regions have often gone unheeded by their party's majority.

In other respects, candidate-centered campaigns have distinct disadvantages. They provide abundant opportunities for powerful interest groups to shower money on the candidates. The role of campaign money, and the

Detecting Misinformation

Do Republicans and Democrats Understand Each Other?

A recent YouGov/More in Common poll asked Americans what they personally believed and what they thought most people in the opposing party believed.[57] A substantial majority of the Republicans said, for example, that most Democrats would prefer an open border policy on immigration. As another example, most of the Democrats said that most Republicans believe that those of the Muslim religion cannot be good Americans. And Democrats and Republicans alike said that most people in the other party hold extreme views on political issues.

Lightwise/123RF

Is that claim fact, or is it fake?

These claims are untrue. The poll found that Americans' understanding of opposing partisans is highly distorted. Americans believe that nearly twice as many in the opposing party hold extreme views as the number who actually hold such views. As for open borders, only one in four Democrats prefers that policy to a policy of secure borders. For their part, most Republicans believe that Muslims are good citizens. The pollsters attribute the perception gap to a number of factors, including the news media's tendency to feed our misperceptions by playing up partisan conflict. Unless we start listening to the other side, we will continue to be less trusting of opposing partisans.

influence it buys, has long been an issue in American politics and has achieved new heights as a result of the Supreme Court's *Citizens United* decision (see Chapter 9). In no other Western democracy does money play as large a role as it does in American elections.

Candidate-centered campaigns also weaken accountability by making it easier for officeholders to deny personal responsibility for government's failings. An incumbent can always say that he or she represents only one vote out of many and that the real problem resides with "others" in Congress. The problem of accountability is apparent from surveys that have asked Americans about their confidence in Congress. Most citizens have a low opinion of Congress as a whole but say they have confidence in their local representative in Congress. This paradoxical attitude is so prevalent that the large majority of incumbents are reelected time and again (see Chapter 11).

Nevertheless, because of party polarization, America's parties are subject to greater voter accountability than previously. The parties are sharply divided on many issues, which has made it easier for voters to see the difference between them and to support or oppose candidates on the basis of what each party represents. Nevertheless, America's candidate-centered campaigns allow candidates to evade responsibility for government performance in ways that Europe's party-centered campaigns do not. In Europe, voters tend to hold the majority party responsible when things go badly and vote large numbers of its members out of office. When things go badly in the United States, the majority party nearly always loses congressional seats in the next election, but a far greater number of its incumbent candidates will escape unscathed. They survive in part as a result of the personal loyalties they've built among the voters in their state or district or because their state or district is so one-sided in its partisanship that they can win even if their level of support drops somewhat. (Congressional and presidential campaigns are discussed further in Chapters 11 and 12, respectively.)

SUMMARY

Political parties link the public with its elected leaders. In the United States, this linkage is provided by the two-party system. Only the Republican and Democratic Parties have a realistic chance of winning control of government. The fact that the United States has only two major parties is explained in large part by an electoral system (single-member districts) that favors large parties and makes it difficult for smaller parties (minor, or third, parties) to win legislative seats in an election.

For more than 150 years, competition in America's two-party system has centered on the Republican and Democratic Parties. The remarkable endurance of these two parties is due to their ability to adapt to change. They have undergone several realignments, emerging each time with somewhat different coalitions and philosophies. The most recent realignment began in the 1960s over the issue of civil rights and progressed further in response to social issues, such as abortion and the issue of the size of the federal government. The realignment led to party polarization—a widening divide between Republicans and Democrats, at the level of both elected officials and voters.

Because the United States has only two major parties, each of which seeks to gain majority support, their candidates traditionally have taken moderate positions in order to attract support from voters in the political center. However, as a result of party polarization and an increase in the number of states and districts that strongly favor the Republic or Democratic Party, candidates have increasingly appealed to their party's more ideologically extreme voters, who turn out more heavily than do moderate voters in primary elections.

At one time, America's party organizations largely controlled campaigns—picking the nominees, choosing the issues, and conducting the campaign. Candidates gradually came to the forefront in campaigns, largely because of primary elections, which allow them to gain nomination directly from the voters rather than going through the party organization, and changes in the media, which allow them to pitch their appeals directly to the voters. Nevertheless, party organizations continue to play a key role in elections. Local party organizations build support for the party's candidates and conduct get-out-the-vote efforts on Election Day. The state and national party organizations help the party's candidates through fundraising, issue research, media training, and other activities.

American political campaigns, particularly those for higher office, are candidate centered. Presidential and congressional candidates spend much of their time fundraising and creating personal campaign organizations built around pollsters, media producers, fundraisers, and campaign managers. Strategy and image making are key components of the modern campaign, as is televised political advertising, which accounts for half or more of all spending in presidential and congressional races.

The advantages of candidate-centered politics include heightened responsiveness to new leadership and local concerns. Yet this form of politics can result in campaigns that are personality-driven, depend on powerful interest groups, and blur responsibility for what government has done.

CRITICAL THINKING ZONE

KEY TERMS

candidate-centered campaigns (*p. 211*)

gender gap (*p. 224*)

grassroots party (*p. 213*)

hard money (*p. 236*)

linkage institutions (*p. 212*)

median voter theorem (*p. 223*)

money chase (*p. 236*)

multiparty system (*p. 221*)

nomination (*p. 228*)

packaging (*p. 237*)

party-centered campaigns (*p. 211*)

party coalition (*p. 224*)

party competition (*p. 212*)

party organizations (*p. 227*)

party realignments (*p. 215*)

political party (*p. 211*)

primary election (*p. 228*)

proportional representation
  system (*p. 223*)

single-member districts (*p. 221*)

single-member system (*p. 222*)

two-party system (*p. 221*)

APPLYING THE ELEMENTS OF CRITICAL THINKING

Conceptualizing: Explain the difference between proportional representation and single-member districts as methods of electing candidates to office. Why is the first method more likely than the second to foster a multiparty system?

Synthesizing: Contrast the pattern of earlier political party realignments (such as the realignment brought about by the Great Depression) with the pattern of the most recent party realignment.

Analyzing: Why are elections conducted so differently in the United States than in European democracies? Why are American campaigns more expensive and more candidate centered?

EXTRA CREDIT

A Book Worth Reading: Ezra Klein, *Why We're Polarized* (New York: Simon & Schuster, 2020). Written by one of America's most insightful journalists, this sophisticated but highly readable book examines the roots of party polarization.

A Website Worth Visiting: **www.gop.org** or **www.democrats.org** These are the websites of the Republican Party and the Democratic Party, respectively. Each site has information on the party's issue positions, as well as information on how to become a party volunteer.

9
CHAPTER

INTEREST GROUPS: ORGANIZING FOR INFLUENCE

James Crisp/AP Images

66 The flaw in the pluralist heaven is that the heavenly chorus sings with a strong upper-class bias. **99**

E. E. SCHATTSCHNEIDER[1]

As the 2017 Tax Cuts and Jobs Act was making its way through Congress, lobbyists were working feverishly. Public Citizen, a government watchdog group, found that 6,000 lobbyists were trying to influence the legislation—11 lobbyists for every member of Congress. Most of the lobbyists represented corporations and trade associations, which were seeking a steep cut in the corporate tax rate. The Chamber of Commerce alone had 100 lobbyists working on the tax issue, while 20 corporations and trade associations each had at least 50 lobbyists dedicated to the issue. "The mind-boggling number of lob-byists that corporate America has hired to reshape the tax code is of almost biblical proportions," said Lisa Gilbert, Public Citizen's vice president for leg-islative affairs.[2] When the bill passed, the corporate tax rate had indeed been slashed, reduced from 35 percent to 21 percent.

Corporate lobbyists' efforts to shape the 2017 tax cut bill suggest why inter-est groups are both necessary and unloved. Business firms have legitimate interests that are affected by public policy. It is perfectly appropriate for them to lobby on policy issues. The same can be said of farmers, consumers, minor-ities, college students—indeed, of virtually every interest in society. In fact, the *pluralist* theory of American politics (see Chapter 1) holds that society's interests are represented most effectively through groups.

However, groups can wield too much power, getting their way at an unrea-sonable cost to the rest of society. Did the 2017 tax bill make too many con-cessions to business firms? Or did it have the effect of protecting workers' jobs by making American products more competitive in world markets? Opinions differ on the answers to such questions, but there is no doubt that groups have considerable influence over public policy.

Group influence has increased significantly in recent decades, as has the amount of money spent on lobbying activities. The United States is often singled out for the high cost of its election campaigns, yet the amount of money spent on electioneering is less than the amount spent on lobbying (see Figure 9-1). And the official figures understate the difference. Loopholes in the reporting requirements allow many of the expenditures on lobbying to go unreported. It has been estimated that, when all spending is taken into account, lobbying spending is roughly twice the reported amount.[3]

The power of interest groups raises a perennial issue, one that James Madison addressed in his famous essay *Federalist* No. 10. Madison warned against "the dangers of faction"—the situation where factions (groups) become so powerful that their interests trump the interests of society as a whole. Madison

Billions of dollars

Campaign spending $6.1

Lobbying spending $13.6

figure 9-1   LOBBYING AND CAMPAIGN SPENDING

Although spending on lobbying gets less public attention than does election spending, far more money is spent on lobbying than on electioneering. (*Source:* Estimated by author from multiple sources based on campaign spending in the 2019-2020 election cycle and federal lobbying expenditures during the same two years.)

acknowledged that society has an obligation to protect the right of groups to freely organize but also said that society is harmed when groups are overly powerful.

An **interest group**—also called a "faction," "pressure group," "special interest," "organized interest," or "lobbying group"—can be defined as any organization that actively seeks to influence public policy.[4] Interest groups are similar to political parties in some respects but differ from them in important ways.[5] Like parties, groups are a linkage mechanism: They connect citizens with governing officials. However, unlike political parties, which address a range of issues in order to attract a coalition broad enough to win elections, groups focus narrowly on issues of direct concern. A group may get involved in elections, but its chief goal is to influence the policies that affect it.

This chapter examines the degree to which various interests in American society are represented by organized groups, the process by which interest groups exert influence, and the costs and benefits of group politics. The chapter makes the following main points:

- *Although nearly all interests in American society are organized to some degree, those associated with economic activity, particularly business activity, are by far the most thoroughly organized.* Their advantage rests on their superior financial resources and on the private goods (such as wages and jobs) they provide to those in the organization.

- *Groups that do not have economic activity as their primary function often have organizational difficulties.* These groups pursue public or collective goods (such as a safer environment) that are available even to individuals who are not group members, so individuals may free ride, choosing not to pay the costs of membership.

- *Lobbying and electioneering are the traditional means by which groups communicate with and influence political leaders.* Recent developments, including grassroots lobbying and political action committees, have heightened interest groups' influence.

- *The interest-group system overrepresents business interests and fosters policies that serve groups' interest more than society's broad interest.* Thus, although groups are an essential part of the policy process, they also distort that process.

THE INTEREST-GROUP SYSTEM

In the 1830s, Frenchman Alexis de Tocqueville wrote that the "principle of association" was nowhere clearer than in America.[6] His description still holds. No other nation has as many organized interest groups as does the United States. The country's tradition of free association makes it natural for Americans to join together for political purposes, and their diverse interests give them reason to pursue influence through group action (see "How the U.S. Differs").

The nation's political structure also contributes to group action. Because of federalism and the separation of powers, groups have multiple points of entry through which to influence policy. At the federal level, lobbying groups can

HOW THE U.S. DIFFERS

CRITICAL THINKING THROUGH COMPARISONS

Groups: "A Nation of Joiners"

"A nation of joiners" is how Frenchman Alexis de Tocqueville described the United States during his writing tour of this country in the 1830s. Tocqueville said that Europeans would find the level of group activity in America hard to believe. "The political activity that pervades the United States," said Tocqueville, "must be seen to be understood." Even today, Americans are more fully involved in groups than are Europeans, as the accompanying chart shows.

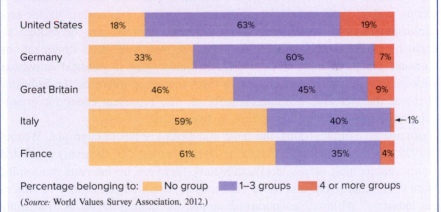

Percentage belonging to: ☐ No group ☐ 1–3 groups ☐ 4 or more groups

United States: 18% / 63% / 19%
Germany: 33% / 60% / 7%
Great Britain: 46% / 45% / 9%
Italy: 59% / 40% / ←1%
France: 61% / 35% / 4%

(*Source:* World Values Survey Association, 2012.)

Q: How do national tendencies contribute to Americans' greater tendency to participate in groups?

A: Compared with Europeans, Americans have a fuller commitment to individual enterprise and a deeper tradition of community involvement (see Chapter 7). Accordingly, Americans are more likely to organize as a means of promoting their economic interests and as a way to strengthen their local communities.

target the House, the Senate, the executive branch, and even the courts. Each of the 50 states is also a target. Few political systems offer as many paths for group influence as does the American system.

The extraordinary number of interest groups in the United States does not mean that the nation's various interests are equally well organized. Groups develop when people with a shared interest have the opportunity and incentive to join together. Some individuals or organizations have the skills, money, contacts, or time to participate in group politics; others do not. In addition, some groups are inherently more attractive to potential members than are others and thus find it easier to organize. Groups also differ in their financial resources and thus in their capacity for political action.

Accordingly, a first consideration about group politics is the issue of how thoroughly various interests are organized. Interests that are highly organized stand a good chance of having their views heard by policymakers. Those that are poorly organized run the risk of being ignored.

Economic Groups

No interests are more fully or effectively organized than those that have economic activity as their primary purpose. Corporations, labor unions, farm groups, and professional associations, among others, exist primarily for economic purposes—to make profits, provide jobs, improve pay, or protect an occupation. For the sake of discussion, we will call such organizations **economic groups**. Almost all such organizations engage in political activity as a means of promoting and protecting their economic interests. An indicator of this is the fact that Washington lobbyists who represent economic groups outnumber those of all other groups by two to one.

Among economic groups, the most numerous are business groups. Writing in 1929, political scientist E. Pendleton Herring noted, "Of the many organized groups maintaining offices in [Washington], there are no interests more fully, more comprehensively, and more efficiently represented than those of American industry."[7] Although corporations do not dominate lobbying as thoroughly as they once did, Herring's general conclusion still holds (see Figure 9-2). More than half of all groups formally registered to lobby Congress are business organizations. Virtually all large corporations and many smaller ones are politically active. Business firms are also represented through trade associations. Some of these "organizations of organizations" seek to advance the broad interests of business. One of the oldest associations is the National Association of Manufacturers, which was formed in 1894 and today represents 14,000 manufacturers. Another large business association is the U.S. Chamber of Commerce, which represents nearly 3 million businesses of all sizes. Other

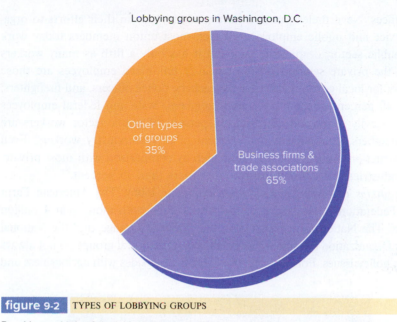

Lobbying groups in Washington, D.C.

Other types
of groups
35%

Business firms &
trade associations
65%

figure 9-2 TYPES OF LOBBYING GROUPS

Roughly two-thirds of the lobbying groups in Washington, D.C., are associated with business. Every large corporation has its lobbyists, as do business-related trade associations such as the National Association of Manufacturers. (*Source:* Compiled by author from multiple sources.)

business associations, such as the American Petroleum Institute and the National Association of Home Builders, are confined to a single trade or industry.

Economic groups also include those associated with organized labor. Labor groups seek to promote policies that benefit workers in general and union members in particular. Although there are some major independent unions, such as the United Mine Workers of America and the Teamsters, the dominant labor group is the AFL-CIO, which has its national headquarters in Washington, D.C. The AFL-CIO has roughly 12 million members in its 55 affiliated unions, which include the International Brotherhood of Electrical Workers and the American Federation of Teachers.

At an earlier time, about a third of the U.S. workforce was unionized. Today, only about 1 in 10 workers is a union member. Historically, skilled and unskilled laborers constituted the bulk of organized labor, but their numbers have decreased as the economy has changed, while the number of professionals, technicians, and service workers has increased. Professionals have shown little interest in union organization, perhaps because they identify with management or consider themselves economically secure. A mere 2 percent of professionals are union members. Service workers and technicians can also be difficult for unions to organize because they work closely with managers and, often, in small offices. Nevertheless, unions have made inroads in their efforts to organize service and public employees. In fact, most union members today work in the public sector, despite the fact that it has only a fifth as many workers as does the private sector. The most heavily unionized employees are those who work for local government, such as teachers, police officers, and firefighters; roughly 40 percent of them are union members. State and federal employees are also heavily unionized. All told, 34 percent of public-sector workers are union members, compared with 6 percent of private-industry workers. Even the construction industry, which ranks high by comparison with most private-sector industries, has a unionization rate of less than 15 percent.[8]

Farm groups represent another large economic lobby. The American Farm Bureau Federation is the largest of the farm groups, with more than 4 million members. The National Farmers Union, the National Grange, and the National Farmers Organization are smaller farm lobbies. Agricultural groups do not always agree on policy issues. For instance, the Farm Bureau sides with agribusiness and

This 1873 lithograph illustrates the benefits of membership in the National Grange, an agricultural interest group. Throughout their history, Americans have organized to influence government policy. (Library of Congress Prints and Photographs Division [LC-DIG-ppmsca-02956])

owners of large farms, while the Farmers Union promotes the interests of smaller "family" farms. There are also numerous specialty farm associations, including the National Association of Wheat Growers, the American Soybean Association, and the Associated Milk Producers. Each association acts as a separate lobby, seeking to obtain policies that will serve its members' particular interests.

Most professions also have lobbying associations. Among the most powerful of these *professional groups* is the American Medical Association (AMA), which includes roughly 200,000 physicians. Other professional groups include the American Bar Association (ABA) and the American Association of University Professors (AAUP).

Citizens' Groups

Economic groups do not have a monopoly on lobbying. There is another category of interest groups—**citizens' groups** (or *noneconomic groups*). Group members in this category are joined together not by a *material incentive*—such as jobs, higher wages, or profits—but by a *purposive incentive,* the desire to contribute to what they regard as a worthy cause.[9] Whether a group's purpose is to protect the environment, return prayer to the public schools, or feed the poor at home or abroad, there are citizens who are willing to participate simply because they believe the cause is a worthy one.

A simple but precise way to describe citizens' groups is that they are "groups anyone can join." This does not mean that everyone would want to join a particular group. A conservative would not choose to join a liberal group, just as a liberal would not join a conservative group. But there is no barrier to joining a citizens' group if one is willing to contribute the required time or money. In this way, citizens' groups are distinct from business firms, which are closed to all but their employees, as well as distinct from labor groups, farm groups, and professional associations, whose members have a particular type of training or occupation.[10]

Nearly every conceivable issue or problem has its citizens' group, often several of them. Some citizens' groups work to advance the interests of a particular social grouping; examples are the National Association for the Advancement of Colored People (NAACP), the National Organization for Women (NOW), and La Raza, which is the largest Hispanic American lobbying group. Other citizens' groups have a broad agenda that derives from an ideological or moral position. The American Conservative Union (ACU) is the largest conservative organization, and it lobbies on issues such as taxation

CITIZEN ACTION!
GETTING INVOLVED

Citizens' groups cover the political spectrum from right to left and depend on small donations to fund their activities. Consider contributing to such a group. You can easily locate a group that shares your values by searching the Internet. If you want to contribute time instead, some citizens' groups have college or local chapters.

and national defense. Americans for Democratic Action (ADA) is a liberal counterpart to the ACU. Another example is the Christian Coalition of America, which describes itself as "America's leading grassroots organization defending our godly heritage." The group addresses a wide range of issues, including school prayer, abortion, and television programming. Ideology is also a component of state-level Public Interest Research Groups (PIRGs), such as NYPIRG (New York), CALPIRG (California), and TexPIRG (Texas). Almost every state has a PIRG, which usually has chapters on college campuses. Drawing on their network of researchers, students, and advocates, they approach issues from a public interest perspective. Ideological groups on both the left and the right have increased substantially in number since the 1960s (see "Party Polarization: Ideological Interest Groups").

Most citizens' groups focus on a specific issue. *Single-issue groups* have risen sharply in number in the past half-century and now pressure government on almost every conceivable policy, from nuclear arms to drug abuse. Notable current examples are the National Rifle Association and the various right-to-life and pro-choice groups. Most environmental groups can also be seen as single-issue organizations in that they seek to influence public policy in a specific area, such as pollution reduction, wilderness preservation, or wildlife protection. The Sierra Club, one of the oldest environmental groups, was formed in the 1890s to promote the preservation of scenic areas. The Environmental Defense Fund, established in 1967, concentrates on environmental problems, such as air and water pollution. Since 1960, membership in environmental groups has more than tripled in response to increased public concern about the environment.[11]

The Organizational Edge: Economic Groups Versus Citizens' Groups

Although the number of citizens' groups has mushroomed in recent decades, they are outnumbered by economic groups. The predominance of economic interests was predicted in *Federalist* No. 10, in which James Madison declared that property is "the most common and durable source of factions." Stated differently, nothing seems to matter more to most people than their economic well-being. Several factors (summarized in Table 9-1) give economic groups an organizational advantage, including their resources and size.

Unequal Access to Resources   One reason for the abundance of economic groups is their ready access to financial resources. Political lobbying is not cheap. If a group is to make its views known, it typically must have a headquarters, an expert staff, and communication facilities. Economic groups pay for

PARTY POLARIZATION

Conflicting Ideas

Ideological Interest Groups

After the Watergate scandal in the early 1970s, Congress enacted campaign finance reforms that relaxed restrictions on group contributions to candidates. Most of the political action committees (PACs) that formed as a result were extensions of business groups, but citizen-based PACs also formed, many of which were ideological in nature. They have contributed to party polarization by favoring candidates who hold strongly conservative or liberal views. Examples of such groups are Emily's List, which promotes liberal Democratic candidates, and the Family Research Council, which supports conservative Republican candidates. The tendency of ideological groups to support one side of the partisan divide can also be seen in the figures shown here, which indicate how ideological PACs in a few areas divide their money between Republican and Democratic candidates.

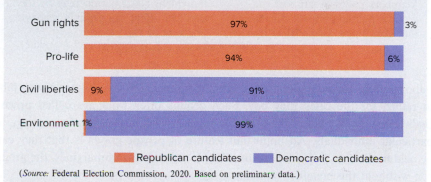

(*Source:* Federal Election Commission, 2020. Based on preliminary data.)

Q: Why do you think politically active citizens' groups are generally more ideological—whether conservative or liberal—than is the society as a whole? Are citizens with strong views more inclined to get involved in organized political activity than are those with moderate opinions?

these things with money generated by their economic activity. Corporations have the greatest built-in advantage. They do not have to charge membership dues or conduct fundraisers to support their lobbying. Their funds come from business profits.

Other economic groups rely on dues rather than profits to support their lobbying, but they have something of economic value to offer in exchange.

table 9-1	ADVANTAGES AND DISADVANTAGES HELD BY ECONOMIC AND CITIZENS' GROUPS
Economic Groups	**Citizens' Groups**
Advantages	*Advantages*
Economic activity provides the organization with the resources necessary for political action.	Members are likely to support leaders' political efforts because they joined the group in order to influence policy.
Individuals are encouraged to join the group because of economic benefits they individually receive (such as wages).	*Disadvantages*
	The group has to raise funds, especially for its political activities.
In the case of firms within an industry, their small number encourages organization because the contribution of each firm can make a difference.	Potential members may choose not to join the group because they get collective benefits even if they do not join.
Disadvantages	Potential members may choose not to join the group because their individual contribution may be too small to affect the group's success one way or the other.
Members may not support the group's political efforts because they didn't join for political reasons.	

Labor unions, for example, provide their members access to higher-paying jobs in return for the dues they pay. Such groups offer what are called **private (individual) goods**, which are benefits, such as jobs, that are given directly to particular individuals. An important feature of private goods is that they can be held back. If an individual is unwilling to pay organizational dues, the group can withhold the benefit.

Citizens' groups do not have these inherent advantages. They do not generate profits or fees as a result of economic activity. Moreover, the incentives they offer to members are available to others as well. As opposed to the private or individual goods provided by many economic groups, most noneconomic groups offer **collective (public) goods** as an incentive for membership. By definition, collective goods are goods that belong to all; they cannot be granted or withheld on an individual basis. The air that people breathe and the national forests they visit are examples of collective goods. These goods are available to one and all, those who do not pay dues to a clean-air group or a wilderness preservation group as well as those who do.

The shared characteristic of collective goods creates what is called the **free-rider problem**: Individuals can obtain the goods even if they do not contribute to the group's effort. National Public Radio (NPR) is an example. Although NPR's programs are funded primarily through listeners' donations, those who do not contribute are free to listen to its programs. They are free riders, getting the benefit of NPR's programs without helping to pay for them. A mere 1 in 10 listeners donate to NPR.[12]

As economist Mancur Olson noted, it's not rational for an individual to contribute to a group when its benefit can be obtained for free.[13] Moreover, the dues paid by any single member are too small to affect the group's success one way or another. Why pay dues to an environmental group when any improvements in the air, water, or wildlife from its lobbying efforts are available to everyone and when one's individual contribution is too small to make a difference? Although many people do join such groups, anyway, the free-rider problem is one reason citizens' groups are organized less fully than economic groups.

In recent decades, the free-rider problem has been reduced, but not eliminated, by changes in technology. Computer-assisted direct mail, e-mail, and social networks have made it easier for citizens' groups to reach out to prospective donors. For some individuals, a contribution of $25 to $50 annually represents no great sacrifice and offers the satisfaction of supporting a cause in which they believe. "Checkbook members" is how political scientist Theda Skocpol describes such contributors.[14]

Business interests dominate the lobbying sector. Their advantage stems largely from the fact that they can use their profits to fund their lobbying activities. Citizens' groups are in a weaker financial position. They depend on voluntary contributions to fund their lobbying efforts. (Sundry Photography/ Shutterstock)

The Advantages and Disadvantages of Size   Although the number of citizens' groups has multiplied in recent decades, the organizational muscle in American politics rests primarily with economic groups. Business interests, in particular, have an advantage that economist Mancur Olson calls "the size factor."[15] Although it might be thought that groups with large memberships typically prevail over smaller groups, the reverse is often true. Olson notes that small groups are ordinarily more united on policy issues and often have more resources, enabling them to win out against large groups. Business groups in a specific industry are usually few in number and have an incentive to work together to influence government on issues of joint interest. The U.S. automobile industry, for example, has its "Big Three"—General Motors, Ford, and Chrysler. Although they compete for car sales, they usually work together on policy issues. They have succeeded, for example, in persuading government to delay or reduce higher fuel efficiency and safety standards, which has meant billions in additional profits for them at an incalculable cost to car owners, who are many in number but are not an organized group.

Business associations exemplify the advantage of small size. The business sector is divided into numerous industries, most of which include only a small number of major firms. Virtually every one of these industries, everything from oil to cereals, has its own trade association. More than 1,000 trade associations, including the National Mining Association and PhRMA (Pharmaceutical Research and Manufacturers of America), are represented in Washington and collectively spend hundreds of millions of dollars annually on lobbying. Their situation is far different from that of, say, taxpayers, who number in the tens of millions. Although taxpayers would be enormously powerful if they all joined together in a single, cohesive group, most taxpayers have no interest in paying dues to a taxpayers' group that would lobby on their behalf.

The 2017 Tax Cut and Jobs Act revealed the power of business groups. At issue was the largest overhaul of the tax code since the 1980s. When the legislation was passed, individual taxpayers clearly benefited, receiving an average annual tax cut of nearly $1,300, increasing their after-tax income by 1.7 percent. Corporations got a significantly larger cut, having their income tax rate reduced from 35 percent to 21 percent. Moreover, whereas the corporate tax cut has no time limit, the individual tax cut will end in 10 years, at which time, unless the cut is extended, a fourth of taxpayers will be paying a higher rate than they would have under the previous tax law.[16] Getting millions of taxpayers to join together to influence policy is infinitely more difficult than getting top corporations to work together. "[T]he larger the group," Olson wrote, "the less it will further its common interests."[17]

Nevertheless, there can be strength in numbers. No group illustrates this better than AARP (formerly known as the American Association of Retired

Persons). Although not every retired person belongs to AARP, its annual dues are so low ($16) that it has nearly 40 million members. AARP has a staff of more than 1,000 and is a formidable lobby on Social Security, Medicare, and other issues affecting retirees. Congress receives more mail from members of AARP than from members of any other group. A *Fortune* magazine survey of 2,200 Washington insiders, including members of Congress and their staffs, ranked AARP as the nation's most powerful lobbying group.[18]

INSIDE LOBBYING: SEEKING INFLUENCE THROUGH OFFICIAL CONTACTS

Modern government is involved in so many issues—business regulation, income maintenance, urban renewal, cancer research, and energy development, to name only a few—that nearly every interest in society could benefit from having influence on federal policy. Moreover, officials are more inclined to solve problems than to ignore them. For example, when Hurricane Harvey flooded Houston, Beaumont, Port Arthur, and other communities along the Gulf Coast in 2017, the federal government provided grants and loans for the cleanup and rebuilding effort.

Groups seek government's support through **lobbying**—efforts by groups to influence public policy through contact with public officials.[19] Interest groups rely on two main lobbying strategies, which have been called *inside lobbying* and *outside lobbying.*[20] This section discusses **inside lobbying**, which is based on group efforts to develop and maintain direct ("inside") contact with policymakers. (Outside lobbying is described in the next section.)

Gaining Access to Officials

Lobbying once depended significantly on tangible payoffs, including bribes. Such incidents are rare today. Bribery is illegal, and lobbying behavior is regulated more closely than in the past. Lobbyists are required by law to register and to file detailed reports on their lobbying expenditures.

Modern lobbying rests primarily on the skillful use of information. Lobbyists concentrate on providing lawmakers with arguments and evidence that support their position. The goal is to persuade officials that what the group wants done is the best course of action.[21] "If I don't explain what we do . . . Congress

CITIZEN ACTION!
GETTING READY

To be an effective citizen advocate, it's important to recognize where to target your efforts. You could attend a meeting of the city council in your home or college committee to get a sense of the policy issues it handles. If you're close to the state capital, you could go to a session of the state legislature to better understand the issues that fall within in its policy domain.

will make uninformed decisions without understanding the consequences to the industry," said one lobbyist.[22]

Inside lobbying is typically directed at policymakers who are inclined to support the group rather than at those who have opposed it in the past. This tendency reflects both the difficulty of persuading opponents to change long-held views and the advantage of working through sympathetic officials. Thus, union lobbyists work mainly with pro-labor officeholders, just as corporate lobbyists work mainly with pro-business policymakers.

For lobbyists to be effective, they need to know how the policy process works. That knowledge is a reason for the "revolving door" between lobbying firms and government. Many lobbyists worked previously in government, and some top officials were once lobbyists. Upon retirement, many members of Congress join lobbying firms. Although prohibited by law from lobbying Congress for a set period of time after leaving office, they are free to do so thereafter and usually lobby in the policy areas that they worked on while in Congress.[23]

Money is a key ingredient of inside lobbying. Many groups have a Washington office and a professional staff of lobbyists and public relations specialists. Roughly 12,000 registered lobbyists work in Washington, along with a greater number who lobby informally or assist those who are registered.[24] Given the costs of maintaining a Washington lobby, the domination by corporations and trade associations is understandable. They have the money to retain high-priced lobbyists, while many other interests do not. The amount of money spent on lobbying is staggering. In a 2010 study, the Center for Responsive Politics divided the amount of money spent on lobbying by the number of hours Congress was in session to dramatize the extent of lobbying. The figure turned out to be more than $1 million per hour.[25] Currently, the biggest spender by far is the pharmaceutical and health products sector, which spends over $200 million annually on Washington lobbying. The insurance, electronics, energy, real estate, and health care sectors are also among the heavy spenders (see Figure 9-3).

Lobbying Congress   Officials of all three government branches are the targets of lobbying, but the benefit of a close relationship with members of Congress is the most obvious. With supporters in Congress, a group has a chance of getting favorable legislation enacted or of blocking harmful legislation. By the same token, members of Congress benefit from ties to lobbyists. The volume of legislation facing Congress is heavy, and members rely on trusted lobbyists to identify bills that deserve their attention. When Democratic lawmakers took control of the House of Representatives in 2019, they consulted closely with labor lobbyists on legislative issues affecting labor. Congressional Republicans complained, but Democrats said they were merely getting advice from those who best understood

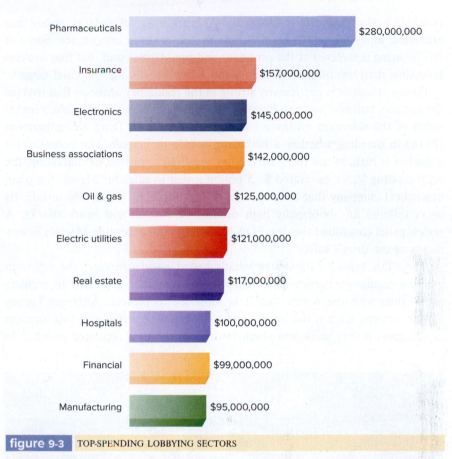

figure 9-3   TOP-SPENDING LOBBYING SECTORS

Lobbying is big business in two ways. First, huge sums of money are spent each year on lobbying. Second, most of the money is spent by business lobbies. (*Source:* Center for Responsive Politics, 2020. Data are 2018 spending amounts.)

labor's needs and noted that Republicans had worked closely with business lobbyists when they were in power.

Lobbyists' effectiveness depends in part on their reputation for playing it straight. Said one member of Congress, "If any [lobbyist] gives me false or misleading information, that's it—I'll never see him again."[26] Bullying is also frowned upon. During the debate over the North American Free Trade Agreement in 1993, the AFL-CIO threatened to campaign against congressional Democrats who supported the legislation. The backlash from Democrats on both sides of the issue was so intense that the union withdrew its threat. The safe lobbying strategy is the aboveboard approach: Provide information, rely on trusted allies in Congress, and push steadily but not aggressively for favorable legislation.

Lobbying the Executive Branch   As the range of federal policy has expanded, lobbying of the executive branch has grown in importance. Some of this lobbying is directed at the president and presidential staff, but they are less accessible than top officials in the federal agencies, who are the chief targets.

Group influence is particularly strong in the regulatory agencies that oversee the nation's business sectors. Pharmaceutical companies, for example, provide much of the scientific evidence used by the Food and Drug Administration (FDA) in deciding whether a new drug is safe to market. The potential for influence is high, as are the stakes. After the FDA approved its marketing, the arthritis drug Vioxx generated $2.5 billion a year in sales for Merck, the pharmaceutical company that developed it. As it turned out, Vioxx was unsafe. Its users suffered an abnormally high number of strokes and heart attacks. A review panel concluded that the FDA had been lax in accepting Merck's assessments of the drug's safety.[27]

The FDA example illustrates what's called *agency capture,* the situation where a regulatory agency sides with the industry it is supposed to regulate rather than with the public that it is supposed to protect. Although agency capture occurs, it's not the norm. Agencies realize that they can lose support in Congress if they show too much favoritism toward a regulated group.[28] In

Washington, D.C., is a lobbyist's dream. Congress has two chambers, and all of its 535 members have the power to introduce legislation. The executive branch has scores of agencies. Even the judiciary offers lobbyists a channel through which they can exert influence. (Carol M. Highsmith's America, Library of Congress, Prints and Photographs Division [LC-DIG-highsm-01901])

response to the Vioxx controversy, for example, Congress passed legislation that forced the FDA to tighten its safety tests.

Lobbying the Courts   Interest groups can sometimes achieve their policy goals through the courts.[29] Groups have several judicial lobbying options, including efforts to influence the selection of federal judges. Right-to-life groups have pressured Republican administrations to make opposition to abortion a prerequisite for nomination to the federal bench. Democratic administrations have, in turn, faced pressure from pro-choice groups in their judicial nominations.[30] Judicial lobbying also includes lawsuits. For some organizations, such as the American Civil Liberties Union (ACLU), legal action is the primary means of influencing policy. The ACLU often takes on unpopular causes, such as the free-speech rights of fringe groups. Such causes have little chance of success in legislative bodies but may prevail in a courtroom. Even when groups are not a direct party to a lawsuit, they sometimes get involved through amicus curiae ("friend of the court") briefs. An amicus brief is a written document in which an interested party explains to a court its position on a case under review.

As interest groups have increasingly resorted to legal action, they have often found themselves facing one another in court. Environmental litigation groups, such as the Environmental Defense Fund, have fought numerous court battles with oil, timber, and mining interests in recent decades.

Webs of Influence: Groups in the Policy Process

To get a fuller picture of how inside lobbying works, it is helpful to consider two policy processes—iron triangles and issue networks—of which many groups are a part.

Iron Triangles   An **iron triangle** consists of a small and informal but relatively stable set of bureaucrats, legislators, and lobbyists who seek to develop policies beneficial to a particular interest. The three "corners" of one such triangle are the Department of Agriculture (bureaucrats), the agriculture committees of Congress (legislators), and farm groups such as the Associated Milk Producers and the Association of Wheat Growers (lobbyists). Together, they determine many of the policies affecting farmers. Although the support of the president and a majority in Congress are needed to enact new policies, they often defer to the judgment of the agricultural triangle, whose members are intimately familiar with farmers' needs.

Groups embedded in iron triangles have an inside track to well-positioned legislators and bureaucrats. They can count on getting a full hearing on issues affecting them. Moreover, because they have something to offer in return, the triangular relationship tends to be solid and enduring, which is why they're called "iron" triangles. The groups provide lobbying support for agency programs and campaign contributions to members of Congress. Defense contractors, for instance, donate millions of dollars to congressional campaigns during each election cycle. In the 2020 elections, as is typically the case, defense contractors' donations went primarily to the campaigns of House and Senate incumbents on the armed services committees.[31] Figure 9-4 summarizes the benefits that flow to each member of an iron triangle.

Issue Networks   Iron triangles represent the pattern of influence in only certain policy areas and are less common now than in the past. A more frequent pattern of influence today is the **issue network**—an informal grouping of officials, lobbyists, and policy specialists (the "network") who come together *temporarily* around a policy problem (the "issue").

Issue networks are a result of the increasing complexity of policy problems. An issue network is built around specialized knowledge. Participants must understand the issue in question in order to engage it in a meaningful way. On any given issue, the participants might come from a variety of executive agencies, congressional committees, interest groups, and institutions such as universities or think tanks. Issue networks are less stable than iron triangles. As the issue develops, new participants may join the debate and old ones may drop out. Once the issue is resolved, the network disbands.[32]

An example of an issue network is the set of participants who would come together over the issue of whether a large tract of old forest should be opened to logging. A few decades ago, this issue would have been settled in an iron triangle consisting of the timber companies, the U.S. Forest Service, and relevant

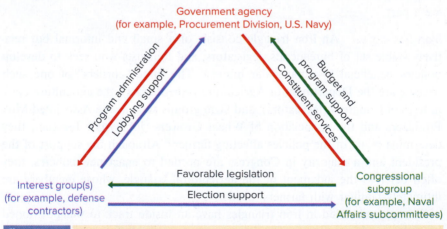

Government agency
(for example, Procurement Division, U.S. Navy)

Program administration

Lobbying support

Budget and program support

Constituent services

Favorable legislation

Election support

Interest group(s)
(for example, defense contractors)

Congressional subgroup
(for example, Naval Affairs subcommittees)

figure 9-4   HOW AN IRON TRIANGLE BENEFITS ITS PARTICIPANTS

An iron triangle works to the advantage of each of its participants—an interest group, a congressional subgroup, and a government agency.

members of the House and Senate agriculture committees. However, as forest lands have diminished and environmental concerns have grown, such issues can no longer be controlled by those who are linked through an iron triangle. Today, an issue network would form that included logging interests, the U.S. Forest Service, House and Senate agriculture committee members, research scientists, and representatives of environmental groups, the housing industry, and animal-rights groups. Unlike the old iron triangle, which was confined to like-minded interests, this issue network would include opposing interests (for example, the loggers and the environmentalists). And, unlike an iron triangle, the issue network would dissolve once the issue that brought the parties together was resolved.

In sum, issue networks differ substantially from iron triangles. In an iron triangle, a common interest brings the participants together in a long-lasting and mutually beneficial relationship. In an issue network, an immediate issue brings together the participants in a temporary network that is based on their ability to knowledgeably address the issue and where they voice their separate interests before disbanding once the issue is settled.

Despite these differences, iron triangles and issue networks have one thing in common: They are arenas in which organized groups exercise influence. The interests of the general public may be taken into account in these webs of power, but the interests of the participating groups are the primary focus.

OUTSIDE LOBBYING: SEEKING INFLUENCE THROUGH PUBLIC PRESSURE

Although an interest group may rely solely on inside lobbying, this approach is more likely to be successful when the group can demonstrate that it represents an important constituency. Accordingly, groups also engage in **outside lobbying**, which involves bringing public ("outside") pressure to bear on policymakers (see Table 9-2).[33]

table 9-2	TACTICS USED IN INSIDE AND OUTSIDE LOBBYING EFFORTS
Inside Lobbying	**Outside Lobbying**
Developing contacts with legislators and executives	Encouraging group members to contact their representatives
Providing information to key officials	Promoting their message through advertising and public relations
Forming coalitions with other groups	Supporting political candidates through money and endorsements

Constituency Advocacy: Grassroots Lobbying

Outside lobbying includes efforts, such as letter-writing campaigns or public demonstrations, aimed at convincing lawmakers that a group's policy position has popular support. Few groups have been better at outside lobbying than the National Rifle Association (NRA). Opposition from the NRA is a reason that the United States has lagged behind other Western societies in its gun control laws, despite opinion polls indicating that most Americans would like to see stricter controls on guns.[34] Influential groups usually have one of two resources: either a lot of money or a committed membership. The NRA has had both. It has spent heavily on election campaigns, although its spending dropped in the 2020 elections due to a decline in its fundraising. Its signature resource, however, is its more than 3 million members, many of whom can be counted on to support pro-gun candidates and oppose those who seek stricter gun laws.[35]

Electoral Action: Votes and Money

"Reward your friends and punish your enemies" is a political adage that loosely describes how interest groups approach elections. One lobbyist said it directly: "Talking to politicians is fine, but with a little money they hear you better."[36] The possibility of campaign opposition from a powerful group can restrain an officeholder. In 2017, for example, the AARP lobbied hard, and did so success-fully, against a bill that would have imposed additional health care costs on older Americans.[37]

Political Action Committees (PACs)   A group's contributions to candi-dates are funneled through its **political action committee (PAC)**. A group cannot give organizational funds (such as corporate profits or union dues) directly to candidates, but through its PAC a group can solicit voluntary contributions from members or employees and then donate this money to candidates. A PAC can back as many candidates as it wants but is legally limited in the amount it can contribute to a single candidate. The ceiling is $10,000 per candidate—$5,000 in the primary campaign and $5,000 in the general election campaign. (These financial limits apply only to candidates for federal office. State and local campaigns are regulated by state laws, and some states allow PACs to make unlimited contributions to individual candidates.)

There are roughly 4,000 PACs, and more than 60 percent of them are associated with business.[38] Most of these are corporate PACs, such as the Ford Motor Company Civic Action Fund, the Sun Oil Company Political Action Committee, and the Coca-Cola PAC. The others are tied to trade associations, such as the National Association of Realtors (RPAC). The next largest set of PACs consists of those linked to citizens' groups (that is, public-interest, single-issue, and ideological groups), such as the liberal People for the American Way and the conservative National Conservative Political Action Committee. Labor unions, once the major source of group contributions, constitute less than 10 percent of PACs.

PACs contribute roughly seven times as much money to incumbents as to their challengers (see Figure 9-5). PACs recognize that incumbents are likely to win and thus to remain in a position of power. Business PACs are more pragmatic than issue-based PACs and bestow roughly 95 percent of their contributions on incumbents.[39] "Anytime you go against an incumbent, you take a minute and think long and hard about what your rationale is," said Desiree Anderson, director of Realtors PAC.[40]

Super PACs   A decade ago, the term *super PAC* was not part of the political lexicon. That changed when the Supreme Court ruled, in *Citizens United v. Federal Election Commission* (2010), that federal laws restricting campaign spending by corporations and unions violated their right of free expression. The Court held that corporations and unions can spend an unlimited amount of their funds on elections, as long as the spending is not directly coordinated with that of the candidate or party they're supporting (see Chapter 8).[41] In a follow-up case, a lower federal court ruled that political activists can form independent campaign committees to solicit and spend unlimited corporate, union, and individual contributions.

These rulings spawned **super PACs**, or, as they are officially called, *independent-expenditure-only committees (IEOCs)*. Super PACs are not allowed to give money directly to candidates or parties, but they are otherwise more or less free to spend as much as they want. Super PACs have become major players in U.S. election campaigns. They spent more than a billion dollars to influence

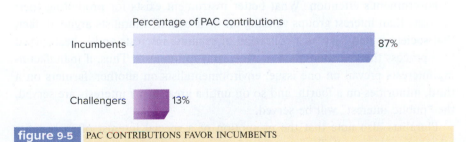

Percentage of PAC contributions

Incumbents — 87%

Challengers — 13%

figure 9-5   PAC CONTRIBUTIONS FAVOR INCUMBENTS

In allocating campaign contributions, PACs favor incumbent members of Congress over their challengers by a large margin. (*Source*: Center for Responsive Politics, 2020. Based on average PAC contribution in past five election cycles to incumbents and challengers only.)

the 2020 elections, more than 10 times the amount they spent in 2010, the first election after the *Citizens United* ruling.

Critics have assailed the fact that super PACs can spend unlimited amounts of money and, unlike regular PACs, can take advantage of loopholes in the law to delay or not report the sources of their money.[42] Vermont Democratic senator Bernie Sanders is critical of super PACs, saying that election outcomes should reflect the will of "all of the people, and not just those wealthy individuals and corporations who can put millions into political campaigns."[43] Advocates of super PACs say that they communicate messages that voters have a right to hear. Bradley Smith, a Republican who served as chair of the Federal Election Commission, said, "While people like to complain about political spending, research shows that increased spending improves voter knowledge of candidates and issues."[44]

THE GROUP SYSTEM: INDISPENSABLE BUT BIASED IN FAVOR OF ECONOMIC GROUPS

As was noted in the chapter's introduction, pluralist theory holds that Americans' interests are best represented through group activity. On one level, this claim is justified. Groups are a means of getting government to pay attention to people's particular needs and interests. Yet the issue of representation through groups is also a question of whether the various interests in society are each fairly represented, and here the pluralist argument is less persuasive.

The Contribution of Groups to Self-Government: Pluralism

The fact that most people are not retirees, union members, farmers, or college students does not mean that the interests of such "minorities" are unworthy of government's attention. What better instrument exists for promoting their interests than interest groups working on their behalf? Pluralists argue, in fact, that society is best seen as a collection of separate interests and is best served by a process that accommodates a wide array of interests. Thus, if manufacturing interests prevail on one issue, environmentalists on another, farmers on a third, minorities on a fourth, and so on until a great many interests are served, the "public interest" will be served.

Pluralists also note that the promotion of a special interest often benefits other interests as well. Tax incentives for corporations that encourage research and capital investment, for example, can result in job creation and improved goods and services.

HOW THE 50 STATES DIFFER

CRITICAL THINKING THROUGH COMPARISONS

Lobbyists

Although Washington, D.C., has the largest concentration of registered lobbyists, they are also found in significant numbers in state capitals, as the accompanying map indicates. States decide many of the policies in areas such as education, health, social welfare, business, policing, and transportation. States are also in charge of licensing everything from doctors to liquor stores. All these policy areas are lobbying targets.

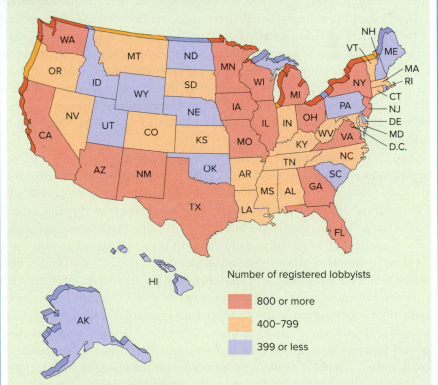

Number of registered lobbyists

- 800 or more
- 400–799
- 399 or less

(*Source:* Center for Public Integrity, 2014.)

Q: What do states with large numbers of lobbyists have in common?

A: Most of them have diverse economies and large populations, which result in high levels of policy activity. Most of them also have comparatively long legislative sessions, providing lobbyists with more opportunities to interact with lawmakers.

Finally, interest groups expand the range of issues that get lawmakers' attention. Political parties sometimes avoid controversial issues and, in any case, concentrate on the most prominent issues, which leaves hundreds of issues unaddressed through the party system. Interest groups advocate for and against many of these issues.[45]

Flaws in Pluralism: Interest-Group Liberalism and Economic Bias

If much of what pluralists say is valid, it's not the full story of group influence. Political scientist Theodore Lowi points out that there is no concept of the public interest in a system that gives special interests the ability to decide the policies affecting them.[46] Nor can it be assumed that what a lobbying group receives is what the majority would also want. Consider the case of the federal law that required auto dealers to list the known defects of used cars on window stickers. The law was repealed after the National Association of Automobile Dealers contributed more than $1 million to the reelection campaigns of members of Congress. Auto dealers won another victory when their loans to car buyers were exempted from regulation by the new consumer protection agency that was created as part of the Dodd-Frank Act of 2010 (see "Case Study: Dodd-Frank Act and the Auto Lobby").

Another weakness in the pluralist argument resides in its claim that the group system is broadly representative. Although pluralists acknowledge that well-funded interests have more clout, they say that the group process is relatively open and few interests are entirely left out. This claim contains an element of truth, but it is not the full story. As this chapter has shown, economic interests, particularly corporations, are the most highly organized and the most advantaged when it comes to exerting influence on policy.[47] Of course, economic groups do not dominate everything, nor do they operate unchecked. Most environmental groups, for example, work to shield the environment from threats posed by business activity. Activist government has also brought the group system into closer balance; the government's poverty programs have spawned groups that act to protect the programs. Nevertheless, the power of poverty-related groups is a pittance compared with the power of wealthy interests. Nearly two-thirds of all lobbying groups in Washington are business-related, and their political clout is enormous.

A Madisonian Dilemma

James Madison recognized the dilemma inherent in group activity. Although he worried that interest groups would have too much political influence, he

C A S E
S T U D Y

Politics in Action

Dodd-Frank Act and the Auto Lobby

In 2008, the U.S. economy went into a deep recession as a result of reckless lending by the financial industry. Banks had given out huge numbers of mortgages to unqualified home buyers. When home prices then dropped sharply, many of the mortgages were "under water," meaning that the houses were worth less than their mortgages. At that point, many homeowners stopped making their monthly payments. Banks were left with vacant houses and mortgage defaults. It put many of them in the red, sparking the financial crisis. Many banks survived only because they received bailout money from the federal government.

RainerPlendl/iStock/Getty Images

In 2010, Congress passed the Dodd-Frank Act in order to protect borrowers and end risky lending on everything from mortgages to credit cards to consumer loans. The legislation was named for its chief sponsors, Senator Christopher Dodd of Connecticut and Representative Barney Frank of Massachusetts.

As the Dodd-Frank bill was being drafted, more than 500 lobbyists from the auto industry—nearly one per member of Congress—went to Capitol Hill in an effort to get auto loans removed from the new regulations. They argued that auto loans do not pose the same risk as home mortgages. Failed mortgages, the lobbyists claimed, can bring down the economy but repossessed cars cannot. The auto industry succeeded in its effort. Members of Congress removed auto loans from the legislation. It was not the automobile lobby's first such victory. A few years earlier, it had persuaded Congress to repeal a law that required auto dealers to list on window stickers the known defects of the used cars they were selling.

Q: Why do you think the auto industry has so much influence in Congress?

ASK YOURSELF: How many jobs, directly and indirectly, does the auto industry generate? How prominent are auto dealers in their local communities? Are automobiles a commodity important to both labor and business and thus important to both Democratic and Republican lawmakers? What type of financial resources does the auto industry have to invest in lobbying and election campaigns?

argued in *Federalist* No. 10 that a free society must allow the pursuit of self-interest. Unless people can promote the separate opinions that stem from differences in their needs, values, and possessions, they are not a free people.

Ironically, Madison's constitutional solution to the problem of factions is now part of the problem. Madison thought that the American system of

F A K E
or
F A C T

Detecting Misinformation

Do "the People" Govern?

Democracy is a system of government by the people, although in practice the people govern through their elected representatives. By implication, the major influence on representatives' decisions should be the voters' policy preferences.

Steve Allen/Brand X Pictures/Getty Images

Is that claim fact, or is it fake?

Political scientists Martin Gilens and Benjamin Page conducted a massive study to address the question of policy influence. They examined nearly 1,800 policy decisions between 1981 and 2002 on which there was related polling data on Americans' policy preferences. They then tested lawmakers' policy decisions against four possible explanations: whether their decisions aligned with the preferences of the majority of citizens ("majoritarian electoral democracy"), with the preferences of wealthier citizens ("economic-elite domination), with the preferences of mass-based interest groups ("majoritarian pluralism"), or with the preferences of business/professional interest groups ("biased pluralism").

Their analysis found that the the preferences of wealthy citizens and business/professional interest groups had far more influence on policy than did those of the majority of citizens and those of mass-based interest groups. Gilens and Page concluded that "policymaking is dominated by powerful business organizations and a small number of affluent Americans."[48] Other studies have found stronger evidence of majority influence,[49] but nearly all studies of policy influence have concluded that interest groups, particularly those associated with business, exert a powerful influence on public policy.

checks and balances, with a separation of powers at its core, would prevent a majority faction from trampling on the interests of smaller groups. This system, however, makes it relatively easy for minority factions—or, as they are called today, special-interest groups—to gain government support. Because of the system's division of power, they have numerous points at which to gain access and exert influence. Often, they need only to find a single ally, whether it is a congressional committee, an executive agency, or a federal court, to get at least some of what they seek. And, once they obtain a government benefit, it is likely to last. Benefits are hard to eliminate because concerted action by the executive branch and both houses of Congress is usually required. If a group has strong support in even a single institution, it can usually fend off attempts to eliminate a policy or program that serves its interest. Such support can be easy to acquire if the group has resources—information, money, and votes—that officeholders want. (Chapters 11 and 13 discuss further the issue of interest-group power.)

SUMMARY

A political interest group is composed of a set of individuals organized to promote a shared concern. Most interest groups owe their existence to factors other than politics. These groups form for economic reasons, such as the pursuit of profit, and they maintain themselves by making profits (in the case of corporations) or by providing their members with private goods, such as jobs and wages. Economic groups include corporations, trade associations, labor unions, farm organizations, and professional associations. Collectively, economic groups are by far the largest set of organized interests. The group system tends to favor interests that are already economically and socially advantaged.

Citizens' groups do not have the same organizational advantages as economic groups. They depend on voluntary contributions from potential members, who may lack interest and resources or who recognize that they will get the collective good from a group's activity even if they do not participate (the free-rider problem). Citizens' groups include public-interest, single-issue, and ideological groups. Their numbers have increased dramatically since the 1960s despite their organizational problems.

Organized interests seek influence largely by lobbying public officials and contributing to election campaigns. Using an inside strategy, lobbyists develop direct contacts with legislators, government bureaucrats, and members of the judiciary in order to persuade them to accept the group's perspective on policy. Groups also use an outside strategy, seeking to mobilize public support for their goals. This strategy relies in part on grassroots lobbying—encouraging group members and the public to communicate their policy views to officials. Outside lobbying also includes efforts to elect officeholders who will support group aims. Through political action committees (PACs), organized groups now provide nearly a fourth of all contributions received by congressional candidates. A more recent development is the emergence of super PACs. They are independent campaign committees that can raise and spend nearly unrestricted amounts of money on elections as long as they do not coordinate their efforts with those of the candidate they are supporting.

The policies that emerge from the group system bring benefits to many of society's interests and often serve the collective interest as well. However, when groups can essentially dictate policy, the common good is rarely served. The majority's interest is subordinated to group (minority) interests. In most instances, the minority consists of business firms and individuals who already enjoy a substantial share of society's benefits.

CRITICAL THINKING ZONE

KEY TERMS

citizens' groups (*p. 251*)

collective (public) goods (*p. 254*)

economic groups (*p. 248*)

free-rider problem (*p. 254*)

inside lobbying (*p. 257*)

interest group (*p. 246*)

iron triangle (*p. 261*)

issue network (*p. 262*)

lobbying (*p. 257*)

outside lobbying (*p. 263*)

political action committee (PAC) (*p. 264*)

private (individual) goods (*p. 254*)

super PACs (*p. 265*)

APPLYING THE ELEMENTS OF CRITICAL THINKING

Conceptualizing: How do iron triangles and issue networks differ? How do they contribute to group influence?

Synthesizing: Contrast the methods of inside lobbying with those of outside lobbying.

Analyzing: Why are there so many more organized interest groups in the United States than in other Western democracies? Why are so many of these groups organized around economic interests, particularly business?

EXTRA CREDIT

A Book Worth Reading: Lee Drutman, *The Business of America Is Lobbying: How Corporations Became Politicized and Politics Became More Corporate* (New York: Oxford University Press, 2015). Written by an astute political analyst, this book details corporate lobbying and its influence on national policy.

A Website Worth Visiting: **www.opensecrets.org** The Center for Responsive Politics is a nonpartisan, nonprofit organization. Its website includes up-to-date analysis and data on lobbying, PAC spending, and other interest-group activity.

Design credit: (People, Flag, U.S., Globe, Vote Icons): McGraw-Hill Education; (Eagle): Feng Wei Photography/Moment/Getty Images; (Lincoln): Photographs in the Carol M. Highsmith Archive, Library of Congress, Prints and Photographs Division [LC-DIG-highsm-12542].

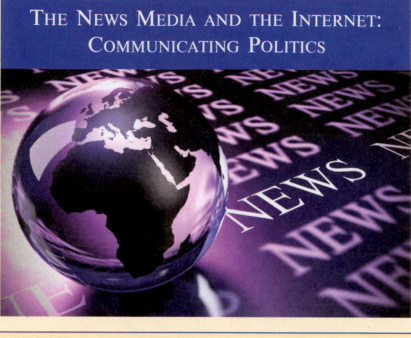

Le Moal Olivier/123RF

10
CHAPTER

THE NEWS MEDIA AND THE INTERNET: COMMUNICATING POLITICS

> **❝** The press in America . . . determines what people will think and talk about, an authority that in other nations is reserved for tyrants, priests, parties, and mandarins. **❞**
>
> THEODORE H. WHITE[1]

Speaking at a press conference in early 2020, President Donald Trump took credit for containing the risk posed by the COVID-19 coronavirus, which had surfaced in China and was now infecting people across the globe. "We've done a great job in keeping it down to a minimum," Trump said. The *Washington Post* told a different story, saying that Trump had ignored early warnings about the threat from the nation's intelligence agencies, resulting in a delay that put Americans' lives at risk. Fox News's Greg Gutfeld sided with Trump, asserting that "you cannot match the deeds that this administration is doing. They're doing amazing work." MSNBC's Rachel Maddow slammed Trump, saying, "If Trump is going to keep lying like he has been every day on stuff this important, we should, all of us, stop broadcasting it." The *Washington Times* praised Trump, quoting a public figure as saying, "You're taking charge & leading in a manner needed & wanted for this country."

The **news** is mainly an account of obtruding events, particularly those that are *timely* (new or unfolding developments rather than old or static ones), *dramatic* (striking developments rather than commonplace ones), and *compelling* (developments that arouse people's emotions).[2] The threat posed by the coronavirus fit that definition; it had far-reaching effects and was thus a dramatic and compelling development. At the same time, the news is not fixed in stone. News outlets differ in their reporting practices and thus in how they portray developments. Trump's handling of the health crisis was big news in every media outlet, but it was presented differently from one outlet to the next.

Media outlets are a key intermediary between American citizens and their leaders. For nearly everyone, politics is a secondhand experience, something they hear about through the media rather than observe directly. However, the media are a different kind of intermediary than are political parties or interest groups. Parties and groups seek influence in order to promote particular leaders or policies. Some media outlets have that as their goal, but other media outlets primarily seek to inform the public about current events, and still other media outlets present events in a way designed to attract as large an audience as possible. Most citizens are exposed, in varying degrees, to all of these types of media outlets.

This chapter describes the media's role in American politics, starting with the history of the media and proceeding to a discussion of the media's functions. The chapter concludes with a look at the media audience. These are the main ideas presented in the chapter:

- *The American news media were initially tied to the nation's political party system (the partisan press) but gradually developed an independent position (the objective press).* In the process, the news shifted from a political orientation, which emphasizes political values and ideas, to a journalistic orientation, which stresses newsworthy information and events.

- *In recent decades, new forms of media have emerged—cable television shows, partisan talk shows, and Internet outlets.* Their norms and standards differ from each other, as well as from those of the traditional news media.

- *Media outlets seek to attract an audience by meeting people's information needs, playing to their partisan bias, or feeding their desire to be entertained.* All media outlets engage in each of these activities to a degree, but most outlets have one of the three as their primary focus.

- *The audience for public affairs has been fragmenting, largely as a result of the expanded number of media outlets created by the advent of cable television and the Internet.* Citizens have more choices than ever before and have tailored their choices to their information interests and partisan leanings.

President Donald Trump speaking at a press conference about the COVID-19 coronavirus pandemic. His pronouncements were covered by every leading news outlet but, whereas some of them heaped praise on what he said, others were sharply critical of his remarks. (Official White House Photo by Tia Dufour)

MEDIA CHANGE: FROM THE NATION'S FOUNDING TO TODAY

The writers of the Constitution recognized a need to protect the press so as to ensure the free flow of information on which a self-governing nation depends.[3] The First Amendment provides for freedom of the press, a guarantee that the Supreme Court has strongly upheld (see Chapter 4). Press freedom has contributed to a robust American media system that has been shaped throughout its history by technological, political, and economic change.

Rise of the Partisan Press

America's early political leaders quickly recognized the value of newspapers in achieving their goals. Alexander Hamilton persuaded John Fenno to start a newspaper, the *Gazette of the United States,* as a means of publicizing the policies of George Washington's administration. Hamilton was secretary of the treasury and helped finance the paper by granting it the Treasury Department's printing contracts. Hamilton's political rival, Thomas Jefferson, dismissed the *Gazette*'s reporting as "pure Toryism" and convinced Philip Freneau to start the *National Gazette* as an opposition paper. Jefferson, as secretary of state, gave Freneau the authority to print State Department documents.

Early newspapers were printed a page at a time on flat presses, a process that limited production and kept the cost of the newspaper copy beyond the reach of most citizens. Leading papers, such as the *Gazette of the United States,* had fewer than 1,500 readers and needed party patronage to survive. Not surprisingly, the "news" they printed was laced with partisanship.[4] In this era of the **partisan press**, most newspapers openly backed one party or the other.

The partisan press persisted for more than a century, although it was gradually weakened by technological change. When the telegraph came into use in the middle of the 1800s, newspapers had easier access to news from outside the local area, which led them to replace partisan commentary with news reports. The subsequent invention of the power-driven printing press enabled publishers to print their newspapers more cheaply and quickly. As circulations rose, so did advertising revenues, reducing newspapers' dependence on government patronage.

By 1900, some American newspapers had daily circulations in excess of 100,000 copies. This period marked the height of newspapers' power and the low point in their civic responsibility. A new style of reporting—"yellow journalism"—emerged as a way of selling papers. It was "a shrieking, gaudy, sensation-loving, devil-may-care kind of journalism which lured the reader by any possible means."[5] A circulation battle between William Randolph Hearst's *New York Journal* and Joseph Pulitzer's *New York World* may have contributed to the outbreak of the Spanish-American War through sensational (and largely inaccurate) reports on the cruelty of Spanish rule in Cuba. Frederic Remington (who later became a noted painter and sculptor) was working in Cuba as a news artist for Hearst and planned to return to New York because Cuba appeared calm. Hearst allegedly cabled back "Please remain. You furnish the pictures and I'll furnish the war."[6]

Rise of Objective Journalism

The excesses of yellow journalism led some publishers to develop ways of reporting the news more responsibly. One step was to separate the newspaper's advertising department from its news department, thus reducing the influence of advertisers on news content. A second development was **objective journalism**, which is based on the reporting of "facts" rather than opinions and is "fair" in that it presents both sides of partisan debate. An architect of the new model was Adolph Ochs of *The New York Times.* Ochs bought the *Times* in 1896, when its daily circulation was 9,000. Four years later, its readership had grown to 82,000. Ochs told his reporters that he "wanted as little partisanship as possible . . . as few judgments as possible."[7] The *Times* gradually acquired a

Yellow journalism was built on sensationalism. William Randolph Hearst's *New York Journal* whipped up support for a war in Cuba against Spain through inflammatory reporting on the sinking of the U.S. battleship *Maine* in Havana Harbor in 1898. (Everett Historical/Shutterstock)

reputation as the country's best newspaper. Objective reporting was also promoted through newly formed journalism schools, such as those at Columbia University and the University of Missouri. Within a few decades, objective journalism had become the dominant reporting model.

Until the 20th century, the print media were the only form of mass communication. By the 1920s, however, hundreds of radio stations were broadcasting throughout the nation. At first, the government did not regulate radio broadcasting, and the result was chaos. Nearby stations often used the same or adjacent radio frequencies, interfering with each other's broadcasts. Finally, in 1934, Congress passed the Communications Act, which regulated broadcasting and created the Federal Communications Commission (FCC) to oversee the process. Broadcasters had to be licensed by the FCC, and, because broadcasting frequencies are limited in number, licensees were required to be impartial in their political coverage and were prohibited from selling or giving airtime to a political candidate without offering to sell or give an equal amount of airtime to other candidates for the same office.

Television followed radio, and, by the late 1950s, more than 90 percent of American homes had a TV set. In this period, the FCC imposed a second restriction on broadcasters, the Fairness Doctrine. It required radio and television broadcasters to "afford reasonable opportunity for the discussion of conflicting views of public importance." Broadcasters were prohibited from using their news coverage to promote one party or issue position at the expense of another. In effect, the objective-reporting model practiced voluntarily by the newspapers was imposed by law on broadcasters.

During the era of objective journalism, the news was not entirely devoid of partisanship. Although broadcasters were prohibited by law from editorializing, newspapers were not. Most of them backed one political party on their editorial and opinion (op-ed) pages. Nevertheless, it was difficult to tell from a paper's news pages which party it backed editorially. The objective model, with its emphasis on factual and balanced reporting, led journalists in different news outlets to cover political developments in similar ways. They did not always do so, but in their quest for balance they tended toward a common interpretation of political developments, as opposed to a Republican version or a Democratic version.

The result was what scholars call the *information commons*—a shared set of facts and ideas transmitted to citizens through the news media.[8] Not every American derived the same meaning from the news they were getting, and the reporting had its blind spots, including downplaying stories about ordinary Americans in favor of stories about the rich and powerful.[9] But it was a balanced rendition of the news that treated Republican and Democratic leaders in much the same way and fostered a shared understanding of the nation's politics. Research found that it had a depolarizing effect. Differences in Americans' opinions narrowed and respect for the opposing party increased.[10]

Rise of Cable TV and Partisan Talk Shows

The information commons began to break apart in the 1980s. A major development occurred in 1987, when the FCC rescinded the Fairness Doctrine, claiming that the emergence of cable television and the expansion of FM radio had alleviated the problem of scarce frequencies. Radio stations quickly responded to the change in policy. They had previously been required to air public affairs content, which meant that even radio stations that featured rock or country music carried brief newscasts each hour. When the Fairness Doctrine was rescinded, most of them dropped their newscasts.

The elimination of the Fairness Doctrine also spawned partisan radio talk shows. The doctrine had discouraged the airing of such shows by requiring stations to offer a balanced lineup of liberal and conservative content. When the doctrine was eliminated in 1987, station owners no longer had to worry

Broadcast news dominated television until the advent of cable. Today, the ABC, CBS, and NBC broadcast newscasts compete with cable-based Fox News, CNN, and MSNBC for viewers. Cable news includes partisan outlets. Fox News pursues a politically conservative news agenda, while MSNBC pursues a liberal one. (Scott J. Ferrell/Congressional Quarterly/Alamy Stock Photo)

about carrying programs that ran counter to their political beliefs. Hundreds of radio stations shifted to talk shows, most of which had a conservative slant.[11] Partisan talk shows offered a version of politics radically different—more opinionated and less devoted to factual accuracy—than that of traditional news outlets. Talk shows quickly found an audience. In less than a decade, the weekly audience for partisan talk shows jumped nearly 10-fold to almost 20 million listeners. It would grow to more than 40 million listeners.[12]

During this period, cable television came into existence. There were virtually no cable channels in the 1970s, but by 1990 half of American homes had cable access. Because cable television was transmitted by privately owned wire rather than through broadcasting, it was not subject to broadcasting regulations. Nevertheless, when media mogul Ted Turner in 1980 started CNN, the first of the cable news channels, he instructed his correspondents to use the objective model of reporting.

Turner's policy was not followed by Fox News, the second cable news channel. The success of conservative talk radio had convinced billionaire Rupert Murdoch to start Fox in 1996. Murdoch reasoned that conservatives, because of their distrust of the established networks, would embrace a channel that offered a conservative version of news. He hired Roger Ailes, a Republican political consultant, to run it. Ailes, in turn, hired a number of conservative talk show hosts. Within a few years, propelled by a largely Republican audience, Fox News had become the nation's most heavily watched cable news network.

In the early 2000s, the third major cable news network, MSNBC, recast itself as the liberal alternative to Fox. It followed the Fox model, placing less emphasis on news reporting than on talk shows, building its evening programming around its biggest attraction, Rachel Maddow.

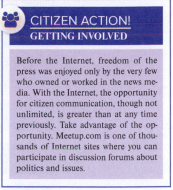

CITIZEN ACTION!
GETTING INVOLVED

Before the Internet, freedom of the press was enjoyed only by the very few who owned or worked in the news media. With the Internet, the opportunity for citizen communication, though not unlimited, is greater than at any time previously. Take advantage of the opportunity. Meetup.com is one of thousands of Internet sites where you can participate in discussion forums about politics and issues.

Partisanship also seeped into other cable programming, particularly comedy talk shows. Unlike partisan talk shows, where the top draws are conservative hosts, such as Rush Limbaugh, Sean Hannity, and Laura Ingraham, the top-rated partisan comedy talk shows have liberal hosts, such as Stephen Colbert, Bill Maher, John Oliver, and Samantha Bee.

Rise of the Internet

Cable television expanded Americans' media options. The Internet expanded them even further. Although the First Amendment protects each individual's right to press freedom, this right in practice has been confined to only a few. Journalist A. J. Liebling wrote that freedom of the press belonged to those with enough money to own a news outlet.[13] Today, because of the Internet, and its lower cost of entry, freedom of the press is actively enjoyed by a larger number of Americans than ever before.

Nevertheless, the Internet has not been the democratic instrument that some analysts expected. Although there are hundreds upon hundreds of websites where news is regularly displayed, news on the Internet is characterized by what analysts call "the long tail."[14] When news-based websites are arrayed by the number of visitors to each site, there are a few heavily visited sites on one end and thousands of lightly visited sites on the other end—the long tail.[15] Most of the heavily visited sites are those of the traditional media, including CNN.com and nytimes.com. Moreover, most of the other heavily visited sites, such as Yahoo News, carry news that was gathered and reported first by traditional media. Audience concentration has also occurred for search engines and social media. Two-thirds of online users rely on Google as their core search engine, and four-fifths of online users have a Facebook account.

figure 10-1   UNIQUE MONTHLY VISITORS TO MOST POPULAR POLITICAL WEBSITES

Although a few traditional outlets, like CNN and *The New York Times,* have larger online audiences, some Internet-based political websites have succeeded in attracting a substantial following. (*Source:* eBiz|MBA.com, "Top 15 Most Popular Political Websites, February 2020," http://www.ebizmba.com/articles/political-websites)

However, some Internet-based outlets have succeeded in attracting a large audience (see Figure 10-1). The largest such website is the *Huffington Post,* which was started by liberal activist Arianna Huffington. Second is the conservative *Breitbart News,* which was founded over a decade ago and is backed by conservative donor Robert Mercer. *Breitbart* attracts about 75 million visitors a month to its site.[16] Until his firing in 2017, one of *Breitbart*'s key figures was Steve Bannon, who served for a time as President Trump's top political adviser. In addition to websites, the Internet has spawned thousands of bloggers, many of whom rely on YouTube to carry their messages. Those with the largest audiences are concentrated on the extreme right and have 100,000 or more followers.[17]

Most of the partisan messaging on the Internet is done by Americans, but foreign actors are also involved. Just as it did during the 2016 election, Russia used social media in the 2020 election to spread false information in an effort to divide Americans and undermine confidence in the election process (see "How the U.S. Differs").[18]

THE MEDIA: CONTENT AND FUNCTIONS

Media outlets act as *gatekeepers.* Among the countless message possibilities each day, they determine which ones will be transmitted to the public. In turn, their messages affect what citizens will see and hear, and thus what they will think and talk about.

HOW THE U.S. DIFFERS

CRITICAL THINKING THROUGH COMPARISONS

Russian Interference in Western Elections

Americans have become aware of Russia's attempts to influence the outcome of their elections. What many Americans might not know is that Russia's activities are part of a larger pattern. Russia has used Internet messaging to disrupt elections in a dozen Western countries, including Germany, France, Great Britain, Norway, the Netherlands, and Austria.

Q: Is there a pattern to Russia's efforts?

A: A common element of Russia's disinformation efforts is to pit citizens against each other. A widely circulated fake story during the 2016 U.S. election, for instance, tried to stir up anger against Muslims. It falsely claimed that Muslim men in Michigan with multiple wives were collecting welfare checks for each of them.[19] Such messages seek to undermine the trust between citizens that is essential in a democracy. Russia has also tried to stir up resentments that could weaken Western alliances. In referendums in Britain and the Netherlands, for example, Russia's disinformation efforts were aimed at undermining support for the European Union. Russia has also tried to tilt popular support toward right-wing parties on the assumption that such parties are more likely to take ultra-nationalist foreign policy positions rather than positions that would contest Russia's efforts to expand its sphere of influence. Russia used that strategy during the French, Austrian, and Bulgarian elections. What is different about Russia's involvement in U.S. elections is the scale of the effort. Russian interference has been more substantial in U.S. elections than in those of other Western democracies.

What determines these selections? For one thing, messages are shaped by the need of media outlets to attract an audience.[20] Without advertising or other revenue sources, a media outlet would quickly go out of business. Media outlets typically attract attention by providing content that meets people's information needs, plays to their partisan bias, or feeds their desire to be entertained.

Information-Centered Communication

Media outlets, whether broadcast, print, cable, or Internet, that are in the business of creating and reporting original news stories are called the **news media (press)**. They traditionally have performed three functions—the signaling, common-carrier, and watchdog functions—that contribute to the public's information needs. We'll look first at the signaling function.

The Signaling Function   The news media's responsibilities include a **signaling (signaler) function**—alerting the public to important developments as soon as possible after they happen. Occasionally, an event enters the news stream through social media, usually when someone captures a newsworthy scene on his or her cell phone camera. Nevertheless, hundreds of news stories enter the news stream daily, the great majority of which are generated by journalists working for regular news outlets.

In the media's capacity as signalers, they have the power to focus the public's attention. **Agenda setting** is the media's ability to influence what is on people's minds.[21] By covering the same events, problems, issues, and leaders—simply by giving them space or time in the news—the media place them on the public agenda. The press, as Bernard Cohen notes, "may not be successful much of the time in telling people what to think, but it is stunningly successful in telling them what to think about."[22]

A striking example was the coverage of the spread of the COVID-19 coronavirus. For months, it dominated the news coverage. Americans were told of

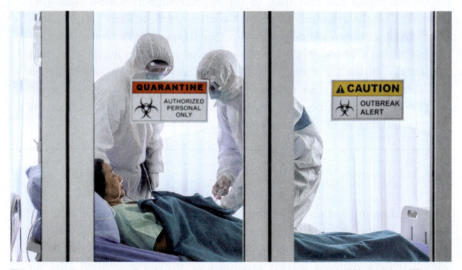

The news media act as signalers, bringing important developments to the public's attention. When the deadly COVID-19 coronavirus swept through the United States in 2020, it dominated news coverage. (Mongkolchon Akesin/Shutterstock)

its spread, how to protect themselves, what governments and health care workers were doing to save lives, and the damage it was doing to the economy. Not since the terrorist attacks of September 11, 2001, had a single story so dominated the news. In its monthly poll in February 2020, the Gallup organization found that fewer than 1 percent of adult Americans thought the coronavirus was the nation's most important problem. By April, it was at the top of the list.

The Common-Carrier Function   The press also exercises a **common-carrier function**, serving as a conduit through which political leaders communicate with the public. The justification for this role is straightforward. Leaders need news coverage to get the public's attention and support, and citizens need to know what government is doing. The COVID-19 coronavirus outbreak is again a prime example. Leaders at all levels of government relied on the media to get their messages out.

The American leader with greatest access to the media is the president (see Chapter 12). More than 200 reporters are assigned to cover the White House, where they receive daily briefings. The presidency gets more coverage in the national press than does Congress and its 535 members combined.[23] That pattern has never been clearer than during Donald Trump's presidency.[24] His frequent tweets prompted journalists to drop what they were covering and report the latest one. An estimated 99 percent of Americans' exposure to Trump's tweets was not from seeing them directly but from learning of them through the news media.[25]

Although officials sometimes succeed in getting favorable coverage, two things blunt their efforts to control the news. Reporters depend heavily on official sources, but they often present the positions of leaders of both parties—the "he said, she said" style of reporting. If the president, secretary of defense, Senate majority leader, or other high-ranking official says something newsworthy, the news report often includes a contrary statement by another individual, usually of the opposite party.

Second, although news typically originates in the words and actions of political leaders, they do not monopolize the news, particularly on television.[26] In an effort to keep viewers tuned in, television newscasts use a fast-paced format in which each story has multiple pieces woven together in story form, with the journalist acting as the storyteller. One indicator of this format is the "shrinking sound bite." In the 1960s, a newsmaker's sound bite (the length of time within a television story that a newsmaker speaks without interruption) was more than 40 seconds, on average.[27] Today, the average sound bite is less than 10 seconds, barely enough time for the newsmaker to utter a long sentence. Journalists rather than newsmakers do most of the talking on television news.[28]

The fact that journalists are able to shape the content of their news stories is a major source of their power. **Framing** is the process by which journalists select a particular aspect of a situation and build their story around it.[29] Consider a presidential candidate's campaign speech on dealing with unemployment. A journalist could frame the story in the context of the policy actions that the candidate proposes to take, which would highlight the policy issue. Or a journalist could frame the story in the context of whether the candidate is seeking to use the jobless issue to gain voter support. As it happens, journalists usually frame their stories in the second way.[30] They portray politics largely as the competition between political leaders for power. That's true when journalists are covering campaigns, Congress, the presidency, and most other aspects of politics.

The way that journalists frame their stories has what scholars call a priming effect.[31] **Priming** is the way in which the framing of a message affects how people will interpret it.[32] When the press frames a politician as seeking to win at all costs, people are "primed" to see that politician as self-serving.[33] In contrast, when the press frames a politician as involved in a worthy effort, as in the case of helping victims of a natural disaster, people are "primed" to see that politician as acting in the public interest. Of course, other influences will also affect how individuals respond to news stories. People are more inclined, for instance, to attribute good intentions to politicians they trust than to those they don't.

The Watchdog Function   Through its **watchdog function**, the American press takes responsibility for exposing incompetent, hypocritical, and corrupt officials. The news media have been called the fourth branch of government—part of the political system's checks on abuses by those in power.

Journalists tend to be skeptical of politicians' motives and actions. A turning point was the Watergate scandal. Led by investigative reporters at *The Washington Post,* the press uncovered evidence that high-ranking officials in the Nixon administration had lied about their role in the 1972 burglary of the Democratic National Committee's headquarters and the subsequent cover-up. President Richard Nixon was forced to resign, as was his attorney general, John Mitchell.

Ever since then, the press has been quick to pounce on any sign of public wrongdoing. After it became known that Donald Trump, in a phone call with Ukraine's president, had linked military assistance to Ukraine to its willingness to announce a corruption investigation into Joe and Hunter Biden, major news outlets put dozens of reporters on the story. *The Washington Post* and *New York Times* were among the news outlets that uncovered additional information, including the Office of Management and Budget's role in withholding the military assistance and the part played by Trump's personal attorney, Rudy Giuliani, in pressuring the Ukrainian government to announce an investigation of the Bidens. The media's discoveries worked their way into the House hearings, resulting in the impeachment of President Trump on grounds of abuse of power.

Although the importance of the press's watchdog role is widely acknowledged, critics have questioned whether the press is overly zealous, turning even minor transgressions or gaffes into major stories. "Scandals" were once a relatively small part of the news. They are now often the lead story, which heightens public distrust of political leaders and institutions.[34]

Partisan-Centered Communication

Partisanship was present in the media even after newspapers transitioned to objective journalism. They kept their editorial and opinion pages, and most of them retained the tradition of endorsing candidates for public office. Nevertheless, news outlets saw themselves as being in the business of informing the voters rather than trying to influence their decisions. The **partisan function**—serving as an advocate for a particular viewpoint or interest—was seen as the business of political leaders and organizations. That has changed for some media outlets. They act as partisan advocates.

Radio and television partisan talk shows are the clearest form of this type of media. When talk shows emerged in the late 1980s, their hosts discovered through trial and error what listeners wanted to hear. Thoughtful give and take

MSNBC's Rachel Maddow is one of the best known partisan talk show hosts. Maddow offers a liberal slant on news developments. Like other high-profile talk show hosts, Maddow is one of the highest paid individuals in media today—an indication of the popularity and profitability of talk shows. (Newsies Media/Alamy Stock Photo)

between guests turned out to be a ratings bust. What listeners liked best were rants about the opposing party, a discovery that, as Tufts University's Sarah Sobieraj and Jeffrey Berry found in their landmark study, has made partisan "outrage" the basis for their programming.[35]

Outrage is the selling card of conservative and liberal talk shows alike. They differ in their ideology but not in how in how they speak, the images they invoke, or the devices they use. Name calling, misrepresentation, mockery, character assassination, belittling, and imagined catastrophe are but a few of their tools. The goal is to make the target look stupid, inept, or dangerous. Democratic senator Charles Schumer is "Up-Chuck," and Republican president Donald Trump is "a clown." As for the ordinary citizens who side with the other party, they're "fools" or "morons."[36] The partisan divide is the main point of attack for talk show hosts, but the cultural divide is a close second. Issues are played less as policy questions than as questions of cultural identity. On conservative talk shows, for example, gun control isn't about trigger locks or background checks but instead about guns as cultural identity. Attempts to control guns are portrayed as a liberal plot to destroy a way of life that's been around since frontier days.[37]

Outrage is also the approach of most partisan Internet sites. They seek to inflame the partisan divide by nearly every conceivable means, including, in some cases, outright lies and distortions. The clearest example is *fake news*— entirely fictional stories that originate on the Internet and aim to undermine a political opponent. Early in the coronavirus outbreak in 2020, stories circulated that the disease was "a hoax" devised by Democrats in order to damage President Trump's chances of winning the 2020 election.

Not all partisan programs fit the outrage model. In their newscasts, Fox and MSNBC, for example, stick largely to the objective-journalism model, with its emphasis on factual accuracy. The newscasts on Fox and MSNBC differ primarily in what they choose to highlight, each playing up developments that it thinks will work to the advantage of its side of the political divide. During the Trump impeachment committee hearings in the House of Representatives, for example, conservative-leaning Fox played up the statements of Republican committee members while playing down those of Democratic members, whereas liberal-leaning MSNBC did just the opposite.[38]

Entertainment-Centered Communication

News has long included a dose of entertainment as a means of attracting a larger audience. Legendary publisher William Randolph Hearst, who helped pioneer yellow journalism, said that an "editor has no objection to facts if they are also novel. But he would prefer a novelty that is not a fact to a fact that is not a novelty."[39]

The onset of cable increased the entertainment content in traditional news outlets. As cable spread into American homes in the 1980s and 1990s, the audience for traditional outlets began to shrink. Americans now had additional choices, everything from HBO's movies to ESPN's sporting events. Soon thereafter, a theatrical style of news emerged that was designed to compete with cable entertainment. It was aimed at marginal news consumers—those with a weak interest in news who might stay tuned in if the news was made more entertaining. Celebrity gossip, hard-luck stories, good-luck tales, sensational crimes, scandals in high places, and other human interest stories became a larger part of the news mix. Such stories were labeled *soft news* to distinguish them from traditional *hard news* stories (breaking events involving public figures, major issues, or significant disruptions to daily routines).[40] A few news outlets, including *The New York Times*, *The Wall Street Journal*, and *The Washington Post*, stuck to the old way of doing things, but most outlets softened their news in an effort to attract a broader audience.[41]

Of the cable news networks, CNN has been the one that most fully treats news as a form of entertainment. CNN has pumped up any number of "trials of the decade"—the Menendez brothers, O.J. Simpson (three times, two criminal and one civil), Scott Peterson, Phil Spector, Clark Rockefeller, Jodi Arias, Casey Anthony, and so on. When Anthony went on trial for her daughter's murder, CNN and its sister station, HLN, devoted more than 500 stories to it. CNN even constructed a temporary, two-story, air-conditioned structure across from the Florida courthouse where the Anthony trial was being held so that its crews could work in comfort.[42]

The heightened competition for audience resulting from the advent of cable and the Internet has led media outlets to search for ways to gain a competitive advantage. A service called CrowdTangle, for example, is used by hundreds of local newsrooms. It alerts them to topics that are trending on social media, a signal to begin producing stories on that topic until the traffic slows down.[43] Many of the newer digital publishers have embraced the entertainment strategy, doing little in the way of serious original reporting while letting readers' tastes drive what they display.[44] In posting its stories, Upworthy puts out a large sampling using a dozen or more versions of the headline. Whichever headline attracts the most attention—usually a variation of "You Won't Believe What Just Happened"—is then slapped onto the rest of the feed.[45]

Nevertheless, the idea that news can be entertaining is clearest on the humor programs that focus on current affairs. One of the first was *The Daily Show*, hosted by Jon Stewart. Its format had the look of a conventional newscast, but its content aimed to entertain—its headlines were slanted, its news reports poked fun at those in power, and its editorials blended satire with serious commentary.

CASE STUDY

Politics in Action

The Ebola Scare

The news media are a civic institution, charged with informing the public, but they're also business organizations that depend on advertising for revenue. Even serious subjects can get distorted by the media's desire to attract a large audience. In 2014, an Ebola epidemic broke out in West Africa. When the first Ebola patient in the United States was diagnosed, some news reports went so far as to speculate what would happen if Ebola, which is transmitted by direct contact with bodily fluids, went airborne and could be caught in the same way as the common cold. "Ebola in the Air? A Nightmare That Could Happen" is how CNN headlined one of its stories, which also warned that most people who get Ebola die. In fact, according to the World Health Organization, there is *no* recorded case in human history in which a fluid-transmitted disease, like Ebola, has transformed itself into an airborne-transmitted disease.

No one who contracted Ebola while in the United States died from it. But the sensationalized news coverage frightened millions of Americans, even those hundreds of miles from the nearest Ebola patient. Two in five Americans worried that they or a family member would catch the disease, as a Pew Research Center poll found.

Q: As a result of the special protections provided to the news media by the First Amendment, do they have an obligation to report the news in a responsible way, even if that results in smaller audiences?

ASK YOURSELF: Is the First Amendment intended to force individuals or organizations to act in a responsible way? Or is hyped-up news a price that society must pay in order to receive the benefits that come from having a free press?

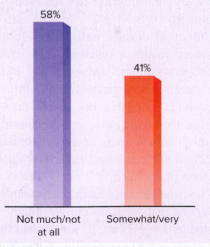

"How worried are you that someone in your family will be exposed to the Ebola virus?"

58%   Not much/not at all

41%   Somewhat/very

It was a ratings hit and helped spawn similar programs, many of which are carried on Comedy Central and other, nontraditional news channels. The most frequent target of their jokes is whoever happens to be president at the moment. According to research by the Center for Media and Public Affairs, President Trump holds the record, having bumped Bill Clinton from the top. The research found that Trump was the object of nearly half the jokes in the opening monologues of shows hosted by Stephen Colbert, Jimmy Fallon, Jimmy Kimmel, and Trevor Noah. In 2017 alone, Trump was the butt of 3,128 jokes.[46]

MEDIA AUDIENCES AND EFFECTS

Today's media system is far different from the one of only a few decades ago. America's earlier system was a **low-choice media system**. Most locations had a single daily newspaper and three television networks—ABC, CBS, and NBC. Each outlet featured nearly the same lineup of stories told in much the same way. In contrast, Americans today have access to a **high-choice media system**, one in which they have a wide variety of alternatives.[47] As a result, people have greater control over what they see and hear, as well as what they choose not to see and hear. A consequence is that the United States today has essentially three public affairs audiences—the traditional audience, the partisan audience, and, for lack of a better term, the inattentive audience.

The Traditional Audience

In the 1970s, news was the only available dinner-hour television programming, and most viewers tuned in. More than 50 million viewers watched the network news each evening.[48] Newspaper circulation was also high. The combined daily circulation of morning and evening daily papers was roughly 60 million.[49] The introduction of cable television in the 1980s precipitated a decline in the audience of traditional news outlets. Today, the network evening newscasts draw roughly 25 million viewers each evening, while daily newspaper circulation is less than 30 million copies.[50]

The decline has not been as sharp as it might appear. Some newspaper readers now get their daily news online, and some television viewers rely on cable newscasts as their regular source of news. Nevertheless, the audience for traditional news outlets is significantly smaller than it was at peak. Although it's still the largest audience, it's shrinking. So has the amount of time that people devote to traditional news. In the 1970s, the average reader devoted more than 30 minutes to reading the printed newspaper. It's now down to 16 minutes.[51] When people read a paper online, they spend even fewer minutes.[52]

Older Americans make up the largest share of the traditional news audience. They came of age during the broadcast era and developed a habit of reading the print newspaper and watching newscasts at a scheduled time. In 1980, the viewers of ABC, CBS, and NBC evening news were, on average, roughly 40 years of age. Today, the average is roughly 60. Even the audience for cable news is aging—the average now exceeds 50 years of age.[53]

As a whole, heavy consumers of traditional news are the best informed Americans. Newspaper reading, in particular, has been found to be correlated with a higher level of political knowledge.[54] Compared with other Americans, heavy consumers of traditional news also tend to hold relatively moderate political views as a result of their exposure to news that highlights the actions of both parties.[55]

Nonetheless, most traditional news consumers are not highly informed about politics. One reason is that citizens don't "study" the news; they "follow" it. Most of what people see and hear in the news is quickly forgotten. Moreover, issues do not figure all that prominently in the news. Issues are rooted in conditions that don't change much from week to week and thus don't yield the type of stories that journalists prize. That's true even of journalists in the top news outlets. During the closing weeks of the 2016 presidential election campaign, for example, only 5 of 150 front-page *New York Times* articles compared Trump's and Clinton's policy stands, and fewer than a dozen discussed their policy positions in detail.[56] Instead of issues, journalists focus on political conflict and strategy, which provide a constant source of fresh material.[57] Barely a day passes during an election when journalists don't cite a new opinion poll as proof that one side is getting the better of the other.[58]

In addition, the marketing strategy of blending soft news with hard news to broaden the appeal of news has diluted the coverage of public affairs. A study of broadcast evening news found, for example, that stories about government and politics have declined from about 70 percent of the newscast to roughly 50 percent.[59] Noting the shift in news content, New York University's Neil Postman warned about the consequences of treating news as a form of entertainment. "I am saying something far more serious than that we are being deprived of authentic information," Postman wrote. "I am saying we are losing our sense of what it means to be well informed. Ignorance is always correctable. But what shall we do if we take ignorance to be knowledge?"[60]

The Partisan Audience

In the era of the information commons, partisan media outlets were few in number. Several weekly partisan magazines, such as *The Nation* and *The National Review*, were available. However, when it came to daily news, there

Attention to news has been declining. Americans have replaced some of the time formerly spent on news with exposure to the alternative content available through cable TV and the Internet. Accompanying the decline in attention to news has been a decline in Americans' factual knowledge of public affairs. (Jupiterimages/Goodshoot/Alamy Stock Photo)

was no partisan option in most locations. Today is different. On television, radio, the Internet, and social media, partisan outlets are readily available.

Some Americans rely on partisan outlets as their primary information source.[61] They're outnumbered by those who prefer the traditional news media, but their numbers are growing.[62] And their choices are clear. They prefer sources that cater to what they already believe. Republicans are 13 times more likely than Democrats to say that Fox is their main source of news. Democrats are 5 times more likely than Republicans to cite MSNBC as their main news source.[63] The audience for *Breitbart News*'s website is 10-to-1 Republican over Democratic, while the audience for *Huffington Post*'s website is 3-to-1 Democratic over Republican.[64] The same pattern holds for talk shows. The audience of every conservative talk show is made up mostly of Republicans, while Democrats make up a majority of the audience of every liberal talk show.[65]

Most citizens who rely on partisan outlets also get news from traditional outlets, but an increasing number pay no attention to such outlets. Those who hold the most intense views, right or left, are the people most likely to do so. They reside in *echo chambers*—the information they receive aligns with their partisan loyalty. "We're increasingly able to choose our information sources based on their tendency to back up what we already believe," notes *Vox*'s Ezra Klein. "We don't even have to hear the arguments from the other side."[66]

Social media also act as an echo chamber for some people. Because social media are used mainly for staying in touch with friends and associates, the messages that people encounter on social media are not as one-sided as those on partisan blogs or talk shows. But Republicans are more likely to associate with other Republicans, while Democrats are more likely to associate with other Democrats.[67] As a result, when politics is discussed on social media, most people are hearing from those who share their point of view.

Exposure to partisan outlets leads people to be more politically interested and engaged.[68] Evidence also suggests that such exposure can improve partisans' understanding of their own party's philosophy and policy positions.[69] At the same time, this type of exposure diminishes people's understanding of the opposing party and generates hostility toward those who identify with it.[70] Exposure to partisan outlets is also associated with more extreme political opinions, although scholars differ on whether the correlation is a result of exposure or a result of individuals seeking messages that reinforce their views (see "Party Polarization: Living in Different Worlds").[71] Studies have also found that heavy exposure to partisan outlets fosters distrust of the traditional media and of political institutions generally.

The Inattentive Audience

In the period before cable TV, when the only viewing choice at the dinner hour was news, many of the viewers were "inadvertent viewers." They watched less out of a keen interest in news than because they were addicted to watching television. Even young adults, who generally pay less attention to news than older adults, were affected, as the research of political scientist Martin Wattenberg revealed. "There was little variation in news viewing habits by age," Wattenberg wrote. "TV news producers could hardly write off young adults, given that two out of three said they had watched such broadcasts every night."[72]

Inadvertent viewers are now few in number. Cable TV and the Internet have expanded the choices available at any hour. Movies, sports, and nearly everything else imaginable are available on demand. Those with a keen interest in news can access it around the clock. Those without much interest have no difficulty finding other programs. The result has been a decline in news consumption among all age groups, but particularly among young adults.[73] Compared with adults over 50, those under 30 are only a third as likely to follow public affairs closely through a newspaper, only half as likely to watch television news regularly, and less likely even to consume news on the Internet.[74]

PARTY POLARIZATION

Conflicting Ideas

Living in Different Worlds

In the 1970s, Americans' choice of TV news programs was limited to the three broadcast networks—ABC, CBS, and NBC. Each headlined the same stories and interpreted them in much the same way while giving more or less equal coverage to the two major parties. The emergence of cable TV changed the pattern. Today, Americans have a range of choices, including outlets that heap praise on one party while attacking the other.

Americans who prefer partisan news rely on news outlets aligned with their beliefs, which can be seen from a 2019 Pew Research Center poll. As the figure below indicates, Republicans are far more likely than Democrats to say they get "most" of their news from conservative leaning Fox News, whereas Democrats are far more likely than Republicans to say they get "most" of their news from liberal leaning MSNBC. Research indicates that exposure to partisan news contributes to party polarization by reinforcing partisans' faith in their party's positions while convincing them that the other party's positions are flawed.[75]

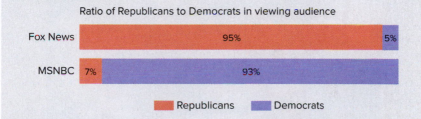

Ratio of Republicans to Democrats in viewing audience

Fox News: Republicans 95%, Democrats 5%

MSNBC: Republicans 7%, Democrats 93%

Republicans | Democrats

Q: Do you find it troubling that partisan media outlets contribute to party polarization, or do you think they help clarify the differences between the two parties? Do you personally rely more heavily on traditional news outlets or on partisan outlets?

Many Americans pay only sporadic attention to news. They tune in when something momentous occurs, such as the spread of the COVID-19 coronavirus in 2020. Otherwise, their news exposure is hit or miss. They constitute what can be called "the inattentive audience."

Such citizens typically know very little about politics.[76] And much of what they think they know about politics is inaccurate, based on what they've heard

Detecting Misinformation

Are Our Attention Spans Shrinking?

Democracy affords citizens a chance to participate in politics. But participation by itself is not the standard of good citizenship. That standard is informed participation, whereby citizens, when forming an opinion or casting a vote, understand what is actually at stake. Studies indicate that Americans' understanding of politics is declining. On average, citizens know less about politics than they did a few decades ago and are more likely to have bizarre notions of reality. Analysts have suggested that the change is attributable to a decline in attention to traditional news sources and an increase in attention to less reliable sources, such as talk show hosts and bloggers. Some analysts have also suggested that the digital age, with its onslaught of short messages, has shortened our attention spans, which makes learning harder.

DGLimages/Shutterstock

Is that claim fact, or is it fake?

A 2015 Microsoft study used surveys and electroencephalograms (EEGs) to study the length of people's attention spans, finding that individuals lose their concentration after 8 seconds, on average. When the study was conducted in 2000, the average was 12 seconds, leading the research team to conclude that today's fast-paced digital environment is reducing our ability to concentrate. And just how short is an 8-second attention span? Before the 2015 study was conducted, the baseline for comparisons was the attention span of a goldfish, which is 9 seconds.[77]

from unreliable sources or inferred from fragments of information. They are also more susceptible to disinformation and unfounded conspiracy theories than are other citizens. The best protection against being misled by false claims is having the facts. Accurate information outweighs false information, but only if people have it.[78]

There is another element to today's media system that works against an informed public, and it affects even those who pay attention to news. It's the distraction that results from the accelerated pace of media messages. As the media have become an ever larger part of Americans' lives—the typical citizen now devotes about 10 hours a day to media—the number of messages to which people are exposed has multiplied (see "How

> ### CITIZEN ACTION!
> #### GETTING INVOLVED
>
> Although it's more passive than other forms of involvement, attention to daily news allows you to keep up with events and can inform your judgment about the issues of the moment. If you're not now a daily consumer of news, consider becoming one. Rely on several outlets so that you get a range of viewpoints, not just one.

the 50 States Differ").[79] The typical American is exposed to hundreds of discrete messages every day, everything from the ads they see on television to the social media messages they receive to the images and statements they encounter in news stories. Message abundance might be thought to be a good thing. However, as Nobel Laureate Herbert Simon noted, message abundance tends to create information overload, reducing people's ability to concentrate on any particular message.[80] Our digital tools magnify the effect. Cognitive psychologist David Meyer calls digital media a modern-day "Skinner box," a reference to psychologist B. F. Skinner's famed stimulus–response studies of the 1930s.[81] Cell phones, TV remotes, and other devices offer instant gratification, conditioning us to seek more of it. The typical American sends more than 30 texts a day, up sharply from just a few years ago and rising by the year.[82]

The onslaught of messages has diminished our capacity to concentrate and, thus, to learn about public affairs. During the era of the information commons, citizens got a degree of protection from information overload by the fact that the messages were mutually reinforcing. What citizens were seeing and hearing from media outlets was consistent. That's not the situation today. Our news sources offer different and conflicting messages, increasing the likelihood that confusion and misunderstanding will result from what we see and hear.

SUMMARY

In the nation's first century, the press was allied closely with the political parties and helped the parties mobilize public opinion. Gradually, the press freed itself from this partisan relationship and developed a form of reporting known as objective journalism,

HOW THE 50 STATES DIFFER

CRITICAL THINKING THROUGH COMPARISONS

Internet Access

The Internet has greatly expanded Americans' exposure to news and information. Most Americans have regular access to the Internet in their homes or through their work, but the percentage varies by state. Nearly 9 of every 10 residents in Washington and New Hampshire—the states with the highest levels of Internet penetration—have regular access. In contrast, fewer than 8 of every 10 residents of West Virginia and Montana—the states with the lowest levels of Internet penetration—have regular access.

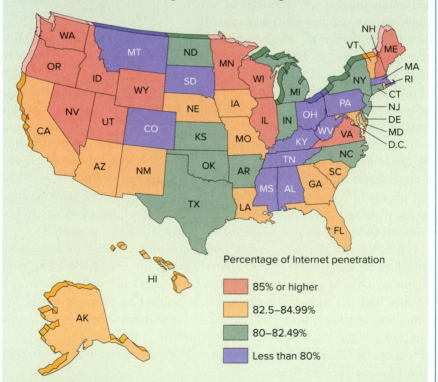

Percentage of Internet penetration

- 85% or higher
- 82.5–84.99%
- 80–82.49%
- Less than 80%

(*Source:* Statista, 2020.)

Q: What might account for state-to-state differences in Internet penetration?

A: States that have more low-income and rural residents tend to have lower rates of Internet access. Less affluent citizens are less able to afford the Internet, and Internet companies are less likely to offer it in rural areas because of higher installation costs.

which emphasizes fair and accurate accounts of newsworthy developments. That model still governs the news reporting of the traditional media—daily newspapers and broadcasters—but does not hold for the newer media—radio talk shows, cable TV talk shows, and Internet outlets. Although some of them cover politics in the traditional way, many of them transmit news through a partisan lens. They slant information to favor their preferred party.

The traditional press performs three basic functions. First, in their signaling function, journalists communicate information to the public about breaking events and new developments. This information makes citizens aware of developments that affect their lives. However, because of the media's need to attract an audience, breaking news stories often focus on developments, such as celebrity scandals, that have little to do with issues of politics and government. Second, the press functions as a common carrier in that it provides political leaders with a channel for addressing the public. Increasingly, however, the news has centered nearly as much on the journalists themselves as on the newsmakers they cover. In a third function, that of watchdog, the press acts to protect the public by exposing deceitful, careless, or corrupt officials.

The news audience has changed substantially in the past few decades. Daily newspapers and broadcast news have lost audience to cable television and the Internet. Although most Americans continue to rely on traditional news outlets, an increasing number prefer partisan outlets, where they find support for what they already believe. And a larger number of Americans today pay little or no attention to news, preferring instead to use the media almost solely as a source of entertainment.

CRITICAL THINKING ZONE

KEY TERMS

agenda setting (*p. 284*)

common-carrier function (*p. 285*)

framing (*p. 285*)

high-choice media system (*p. 291*)

low-choice media system (*p. 291*)

news (*p. 275*)

news media (press) (*p. 284*)

objective journalism (*p. 277*)

partisan function (*p. 287*)

partisan press (*p. 277*)

priming (*p. 286*)

signaling (signaler) function (*p. 284*)

watchdog function (*p. 286*)

APPLYING THE ELEMENTS OF CRITICAL THINKING

Conceptualizing: Define *high-choice media system*. How does it contribute to a less informed public? To a more partisan public?

Synthesizing: Contrast the media's watchdog role with their common-carrier role. Is there a tension between these roles—does carrying out one of them work against carrying out the other?

Analyzing: What are the consequences of the fact that the press is charged with informing the public but at the same time needs to attract an audience in order to make a profit and fund its news-gathering operations?

EXTRA CREDIT

A Book Worth Reading: Diana Mutz, *In-Your-Face Politics: The Consequences of Uncivil Media* (Princeton, N.J.: Princeton University Press, 2015). This award-winning book explores the impact of the increasingly heated and partisan messaging in today's media.

A Website Worth Visiting: www.mediatenor.com Media Tenor is a nonpartisan organization that analyzes U.S. and overseas news coverage on a daily basis. The site has information of interest to anyone curious about tendencies in news coverage, such as how various news outlets portray the president.

CONGRESS: BALANCING NATIONAL GOALS AND LOCAL INTERESTS

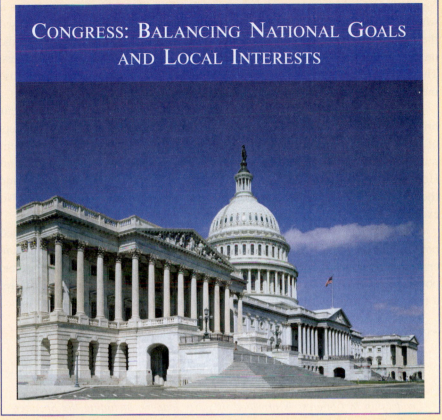

Carol M. Highsmith Archive, Library of Congress [LC-DIG-highsm-12945]

> 66 There are two Congresses. . . . The tight-knit complex world of Capitol Hill is a long way from [the member's district], in perspective and outlook as well as in miles. 99
>
> ROGER DAVIDSON AND WALTER OLESZEK[1]

It was a bill the likes of which Washington had rarely seen in recent years. Partisan animosity had given way to bipartisanship. And it wasn't a small bill. At issue was one of the largest spending bills in the nation's history. It authorized $2 trillion to cushion the economic impact of the COVID-19 coronavirus outbreak. Included in the bill was money for small and large businesses, unemployed workers, hospitals, and individuals and families. Indeed, money had been set aside for nearly everyone affected. When the bill came up for a vote, no senator and only a handful of House members voted against it.

The spending bill illustrates the dual nature of Congress. It is both a lawmaking institution for the country and a representative assembly for states and districts.[2]

Members of Congress have a duty to serve both the interests of the nation as a whole and the interests of their individual constituencies. The spending bill addressed the need to keep the national economy afloat while addressing local economic needs, including support for medical facilities, small business owners, and workers. The nation's needs are of concern to lawmakers, but so, too, are local needs because members' reelection depends on the support of the voters back home.[3]

The framers of the Constitution regarded Congress as the preeminent branch of the federal government and granted it the greatest of all the powers of government, the power to make the laws: "All legislative powers herein granted shall be invested in a Congress, which shall consist of a Senate and House of Representatives." Congress is granted the authority even to decide the form and function of the executive departments and the lower courts. No executive agency or lower court can exist unless authorized by Congress.

The positioning of Congress as the first among equals in a system of divided powers reflected the framers' faith in representative institutions. However, the framers' vision of a preeminent Congress has not fully stood the test of time. Over time, power has shifted from Congress to the presidency, and today both institutions have a central role in lawmaking. This chapter emphasizes the following points:

- *Congressional elections usually result in the reelection of the incumbent.* Congressional office provides incumbents with substantial resources (free publicity, staff, and legislative influence) that give them (particularly House members) a major advantage in election campaigns.

- *Leadership in Congress is provided by party leaders, including the Speaker of the House and the Senate majority leader.* Party leaders are in a stronger position today than a few decades ago because the party caucuses in Congress are more ideologically cohesive than in the past.

- *Much of the work of Congress is done through its committees, each of which has its own leadership and its designated policy jurisdiction.*

- *Because of its fragmented structure, Congress is not well suited to take the lead on major national policies, which has allowed the president to assume this role. At the same time, Congress is well organized to handle policies of narrower scope.*

- *In recent decades, congressional Republicans have become more uniformly conservative and congressional Democrats have become more uniformly liberal. This has made it easier for each party's members to band together but harder for them to reach agreement with the other party's members, which has increased the frequency of legislative deadlock.*

- *Congress's policymaking role is based on three major functions: lawmaking, representation, and oversight.*

CONGRESS AS A CAREER: ELECTION TO CONGRESS

"Single-minded seekers of reelection" is how political scientist David Mayhew described members of Congress.[4] They are professional politicians, and a seat in the House or Senate is about as high on the political ladder as they can expect to rise. The pay is attractive (about $175,000 a year), as is the prestige of their office. It's not surprising that members of Congress make the effort to stay in office, a goal that most of them achieve (see Figure 11-1). **Incumbents** (as office-holders are called) have about a 90 percent probability of winning reelection.

Although Congress is an institution that operates by established rules and norms, members' preoccupation with reelection is a key to understanding what happens in Congress. Members seldom act in ways that will put their reelection at risk. The priority attached to reelection can be seen in Congress's work schedule. It's typically in session from Tuesday through Thursday only, which enables its members to spend a considerable amount of time in their home state or district.

Using Incumbency to Stay in Congress

A reason incumbents have high reelection rates is that most congressional districts and some states are so lopsidedly Democratic or Republican that candidates of the stronger party seldom lose. No more than 75 of the 435 House seats—about 1 in 6—are competitive enough that each party has a realistic

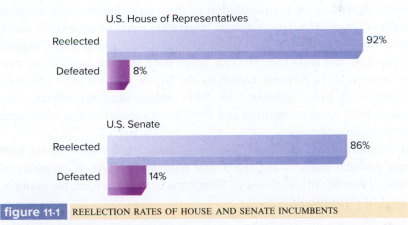

figure 11-1   REELECTION RATES OF HOUSE AND SENATE INCUMBENTS

Congressional incumbents have a very good chance of winning another term, as indicated by the reelection rates of U.S. representatives and senators who sought reelection during the last six congressional elections. The actual chances of reelection are somewhat less than the rates indicate. Faced with a reelection campaign that they might lose, some incumbents chose not to seek reelection.

chance of victory. In any case, whether their constituency is lopsided or competitive, incumbents have substantial advantages over their challengers, as will now be explained.

The Service Strategy: Taking Care of Constituents Incumbents promote their reelection prospects by catering to their **constituency**: the people residing in their state or district. Members of Congress pay attention to constituency opinions when taking positions on legislation, and they work hard to get their share of federal spending projects. Such projects are often derided as **pork** (or *pork-barrel spending*) by outsiders but are welcomed by those who live in the state or district that gets a federally funded project, such as a new hospital, research center, or highway. Incumbents also respond to their constituents' individual requests, a practice known as the **service strategy**. Whether a constituent is seeking information about a government program or looking for help in obtaining a federal benefit, the representative's staff is ready to assist.

Congressional staffs spend most of their time not on legislative matters but on constituency service and public relations—efforts that can pay off on Election Day.[5] Each House member receives an annual office allowance of roughly $1 million with which to hire up to 18 permanent staff members.[6] Senators receive annual office allowances that range between $3 million and $5 million, depending on the population of their state. Smaller-state senators have staffs of about 30 people, whereas larger-state senators have staffs closer in number to 50 people.[7] Although subject to limits, each member of Congress is also provided free trips back to their home state and free mailings to constituent households (a privilege known as the "frank"). These trips and mailings, along with press releases and other public relations efforts, help incumbents build name recognition and constituent support—major advantages in their reelection campaigns.

It is noteworthy that legislators in other Western democracies do not have the large personal staffs or the travel and publicity budgets of members of Congress. A member of the House of Commons in Great Britain, for example, has a staff of three people.[8]

Campaign Fundraising: Raking in the Money Incumbents also have a clear edge in campaign fundraising. The cost of running a successful House campaign in a competitive district exceeds a million dollars (see Figure 11-2).

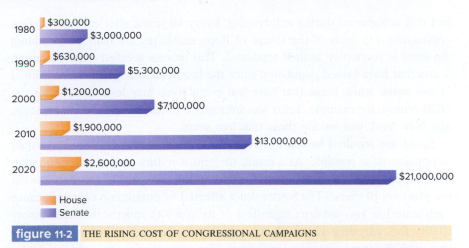

figure 11-2   THE RISING COST OF CONGRESSIONAL CAMPAIGNS

Each decade, the cost of running for congressional office has risen sharply as campaign techniques—TV advertising, opinion polling, and so on—have become more elaborate and sophisticated. The increase in spending can be seen from a comparison of the approximate median spending by both candidates per House or Senate seat at 10-year intervals, beginning in 1980. The figures for 2020 are based on preliminary data. (*Source:* Federal Election Commission.)

Rarely do House incumbents have trouble raising enough money to conduct an effective campaign, whereas their challengers usually fall far short of their fundraising needs.[9] House incumbents outspend their challengers by roughly five to one on average.[10] Senate races are more expensive than House races, often costing more than $20 million. Senate incumbents also have a fundraising advantage, although less so than House incumbents. Senate races often get national attention and attract high-profile challengers who are also adept at fundraising.

Individual contributions, most of which are $200 or less, account for the single largest share of all funds received by congressional candidates and are obtained mainly through fundraising events, websites, and direct-mail solicitation.[11] Incumbents' past campaigns and constituent service provide them a ready list of potential contributors, which gives them an edge over their challengers. Incumbents also have an edge with political action committees (PACs), which are the fundraising units of interest groups (see Chapter 9). Most PACs are reluctant to oppose an incumbent unless the candidate appears beatable. More than 85 percent of PAC contributions in recent elections have gone to incumbents.[*,12]

Redistricting: Favorable Boundaries for House Incumbents   House members, but not senators, have a final electoral advantage. Because House incumbents are hard to unseat, they are always a force to be reckoned with, a

---

*A race without an incumbent—called an open-seat election—typically brings out a strong, well-funded candidate from each party when the parties are closely matched in a state or district.

fact that is apparent during redistricting. Every 10 years, after each population census, the 435 seats in the House of Representatives are reallocated among the states in proportion to their population. This process is called **reapportionment**. States that have gained population since the last census may acquire additional House seats, while those that have lost population may lose seats. After the 2020 census, for example, Texas was among the states that gained House seats, and New York was among those that lost seats.

States are required by law to have House districts that are as nearly equal in population as possible. As a result, they must redraw their district boundaries after each census to account for population shifts within the state during the previous 10 years. (The Senate is not affected by population change because each state has two senators regardless of its size.) In most states, the responsibility for redrawing House election districts—a process called **redistricting**—rests with the respective state legislatures. The party that controls the legislature typically redraws the boundaries in a way that favors candidates of its party—a process called **gerrymandering**. (Among the few exceptions to this practice are Arizona, California, and Iowa, which entrust redistricting to an independent commission.)

Incumbents typically benefit from gerrymandering. When redistricting, the majority party in the state legislature places enough of its party's voters in its incumbents' districts to ensure their reelection. Many of the minority party's incumbents are also awarded a safe district. If opposing incumbents have a strong base of support and would be difficult to defeat, the optimal strategy is to pack their district with as many voters of their party as possible so that, in effect, the party "wastes" votes, reducing its competitiveness elsewhere in the state. Gerrymandering can have the effect of taking the choice of a representative out of the hands of the voters and giving it to the state legislature, but the Supreme Court has refused to limit the practice.[13]

Although gerrymandering is widely thought to be the reason so many House seats are not competitive, a more important reason is the increased geographic concentration of Republican and Democratic voters, a development that writer Bill Bishop calls "The Big Sort."[14] In recent decades, most states have become more heavily Republican or Democratic. And, within states, urban areas have become more heavily Democratic, while rural areas have become more heavily Republican, which has made their elections less competitive.[15]

Pitfalls of Incumbency

Incumbency is not without its risks. Senate and House incumbents can fall victim to disruptive issues, personal misconduct, turnout swings, strong challengers, and campaign money.

Although incumbents have a high reelection rate, they can be vulnerable if they represent a competitive district at a time when voters are looking for change and seeking it from the opposing party, as was the case in the 2018 congressional elections. Republican representative Brian Fitzpatrick narrowly escaped defeat in 2018, winning 51–49 percent over his Democratic rival. He had won in 2016 by 8 percentage points. (Tom Williams/CQ Roll Call/Newscom)

Disruptive Issues   Most elections are not waged in the context of disruptive issues, but, when they are, incumbents are at greater risk. When voters are angry about existing political conditions, they are more likely to believe that those in power should be tossed from office. The 2018 congressional election, which was waged in the context of contentious issues such as immigration, gun control, and income inequality, saw the retirement or defeat of an unusually large number of incumbents. The majority of them were Republicans, which was the party in power at the time of the election.

Personal Misconduct   Life in Washington can be fast paced, glamorous, and expensive, and some members of Congress get caught up in influence peddling, sex scandals, and other forms of misconduct. "The first thing to being reelected is to stay away from scandal, even minor scandal," says political scientist John Hibbing.[16] More than a few members of Congress have lost their bid for reelection or resigned as a result of personal scandal. California representative Duncan Hunter, for example, resigned his seat in 2020 after pleading guilty to diverting campaign funds for personal use, including school tuition, vacations, and flying his pet rabbit across the country.

Turnout Variation: The Midterm Election Problem   In 21 of the last 25 **midterm elections**—those that occur midway through a president's term—the president's party has lost House seats. The 2018 midterm elections, when the Republican Party lost seats, fit that pattern. The tendency is partly attributable to the drop-off in turnout that accompanies a midterm election. Turnout in presidential elections is much higher than it is in the midterm elections. People who vote only in the presidential election tend to have weaker party ties and are more responsive to the issues of the moment. These issues typically favor one party, which contributes to the success not only of its presidential candidate but also of its congressional candidates. Two years later in the midterm elections, many of these voters stay home, and those who do go to the polls vote largely along party lines. Accordingly, congressional candidates of the president's party do not get the boost of extra votes that they enjoyed in the previous election, and House seats are lost as a result.[17] Moreover, some voters treat the midterm elections as a referendum on the president's performance. Presidents usually lose popularity during their term of office as a result of the policy decisions they make. As the president's support declines, so does voters' support of congressional candidates of the president's party.[18] Polls indicated that disapproval of President Donald Trump's handling of the presidency contributed to the Democrats' strong showing in the 2018 midterm elections that gave them control of the U.S. House of Representatives.[19]

Primary Election Challengers   Primary elections can also be a time of risk for incumbents, especially those who hold politically moderate views. If they are confronted with a strong challenger from the extreme wing of their party, they stand a chance of losing because strong partisans are more likely than party moderates to vote in primary elections.[20] Some moderate incumbents have responded by shifting their position on legislation toward the extreme wing of their party.[21] Others have risked the possibility of a primary challenger and have not always survived. A leading example is Eric Cantor, a House majority leader who was next in line to become Speaker. He lost in a 2014 Republican primary to a Tea Party–backed political unknown after saying that Republicans should grant legal status to undocumented aliens ("Dreamers") brought to the United States as children.[22]

General Election Challengers: A Problem for Senators   Incumbents, particularly those in the Senate, are also vulnerable to strong challengers. Senators often find themselves running against a high-ranking politician, such as the state's governor or attorney general. Such opponents have the voter base, campaign organization, fundraising ability, public recognition, and credentials to mount a strong campaign.

House incumbents are less likely to face strong challengers. A House seat is often not attractive enough to induce a leading local politician, such as a mayor or state legislator, to risk losing to an incumbent.[23] As a result, most House incumbents face opponents who struggle to raise enough money to run a strong campaign. The situation changes somewhat when election conditions strongly favor one party. In that case, the advantaged party finds it easier to convince strong challengers to enter the race. Polls in advance of the 2018 election, for example, indicated that voters were trending toward the Democratic Party, which enabled it to field an unusually strong lineup of House candidates.[24] And, in fact, the Democrats picked up 41 seats, their largest gain in four decades and enough to give them control of the House of Representatives.

A New Threat: Super PACs   Although incumbents ordinarily have a funding advantage over their challengers, the situation can change when they appear vulnerable. Donors from outside the state or district may target the race. Although this threat has existed for years, it has increased with the emergence of super PACs, which have the capacity to pour millions of dollars into a race (see Chapters 8 and 9). This scenario played itself out in the 2018 Senate race in Missouri, which pitted the Democratic incumbent Claire McCaskill against Republican Josh Hawley. Their race turned out to be one of the most expensive campaigns in Senate history, with much of the money coming from outside donors. McCaskill lost her reelection bid, running against not only Hawley but also the $40 million that outside groups spent to defeat her.[25]

Who Are the Winners in Congressional Elections?

The Constitution places only a few restrictions on who can be elected to Congress. House members must be at least 25 years of age and have been a citizen for at least 7 years. For senators, the age and citizenship requirements are 30 years and 9 years, respectively. Senators and representatives alike must be residents of the state from which they are elected.

However, if the formal restrictions are minimal, the informal limits are substantial. Congress is not a microcosm of the population. Although lawyers constitute less than 1 percent of the population, they make up a fourth of the House and more than half of the Senate. Attorneys enter politics in large numbers in part because knowledge of the law is an asset in Congress and because campaign publicity—even if a candidate loses—is a good way to build up a law practice. Along with lawyers, professionals such as business executives, educators, bankers, and journalists account for roughly 90 percent of congressional membership.[26] Blue-collar workers, clerical employees, and homemakers are seldom elected to Congress. Farmers and ranchers fare better; a number of House members from rural districts have an agricultural background.

Women and minorities are also underrepresented in Congress. Although the number of women in Congress is 10 times that of a half century ago, they account for only a fourth of the membership (see Chapter 5). Minorities account for roughly a fifth of the membership.

PARTIES AND PARTY LEADERSHIP

The U.S. Congress is a **bicameral legislature**, meaning it has two chambers, the House and the Senate. Both chambers are organized largely along party lines. At the start of each two-year congressional term, party members in each chamber meet to elect their **party leaders**, the individuals who will lead their party's efforts in the chamber. Party members also meet periodically in closed session, which is called a **party caucus**, to plan strategy, develop issues, and resolve policy differences. (Table 11-1 shows the party composition in Congress during the past decade.)

Party Unity in Congress

Political parties are the strongest force within Congress. Parties are the primary source of unity among members of Congress, as well as the primary source of division.

The partisan divide in Congress is wider than in the past. Earlier, Republicans had both a conservative wing and a progressive wing, while Democrats had a liberal northern wing and a conservative southern wing. Since then, the Republican progressive wing and the Democratic southern wing have withered.

table 11-1 THE NUMBER OF DEMOCRATS AND REPUBLICANS IN THE HOUSE OF REPRESENTATIVES AND THE SENATE, 2013–2022					
	2013–2014	2015–2016	2017–2018	2019–2020	2021–2022
House					
Democrats	197	184	194	236*	222
Republicans	238*	251*	241	199	213
Senate					
Democrats	55	46	48	47	48
Republicans	45	54*	52	53	50

*Chamber not controlled by the president's party. Independents are included in total for party with which they caucused. Figures based on election results. Subsequent changes due to resignation or death are not included. 2021–2022 Senate totals exclude two Georgia seats that were scheduled for runoff election at time of text's publication.

In a recent study, political scientists Keith Poole and Howard Rosenthal found, for both the House and the Senate, that the least conservative Republican was more conservative than the most conservative Democrat.[27] As a result, each congressional party has attained a high level of **party unity**—the situation where members of a party band together on legislation and stand against the opposite party.[28]

The trend can be seen by looking at *roll-call votes*, which are votes on which each member's vote is officially recorded, as opposed to voice votes where the members simply call out an unrecorded "aye" or "nay" on a bill. Since the mid-1980s, party-line voting on roll calls has risen sharply (see "Party Polarization: Partisan Conflict in Congress"). The Tax Cuts and Jobs Act of 2017, for example, was enacted along party lines. Whereas 98 percent of Republican senators and 95 percent of House Republicans voted for it, 100 percent of Senate and House Democrats voted against it.

As the partisan divide in Congress has widened, there has been a decline in the number of lawmakers in the political center. At an earlier time, congressional moderates were the key players. They were large enough in number to force other lawmakers to join them in the middle if they wanted a voice in shaping legislation. Today, there are too few moderates in Congress to force other members to come to the center.[29] Legislative deadlock has often resulted. Republicans and Democrats have taken opposite positions on a bill, with neither side being willing to make the concessions that would produce the bipartisan support necessary to pass it. (The effects of heightened partisanship on the congressional process are discussed further in later sections of the chapter.)

Party Leadership in Congress

Each party has House and Senate leaders who are expected to promote the party's legislative agenda. However, unlike the party leaders of most national legislatures, those in Congress cannot count on the backing of their party's members. Members elsewhere can be denied nomination in the next election if they fail to support their party leaders' position on a bill. In the United States, however, incumbents largely win election through their own efforts, which gives them the freedom to decide for themselves how they will vote on a bill. Party leaders in Congress can't assume that party members will automatically follow their lead. The challenge for congressional leaders is to craft legislative proposals that will gain their members' support.

House Leaders   The Constitution specifies that the House of Representatives will be presided over by a Speaker, elected by the vote of its members.

PARTY POLARIZATION

Conflicting Ideas

Partisan Conflict in Congress

Until the 1990s, most roll-call votes in Congress did not pit a majority of Republicans on one side of the bill against a majority of Democrats on the other side. Since then, as the graph indicates, roll-call votes have usually divided along party lines. Underlying these developments is the eclipse of the Democratic Party's conservative southern wing and the Republican Party's progressive northern wing. As congressional Democrats have become more uniformly liberal and congressional Republicans more uniformly conservative, the overlap between the congressional parties has diminished, resulting in increased party-line voting on legislation.

Percentage of roll-call votes in the House and Senate in which a majority of Democrats voted against a majority of Republicans

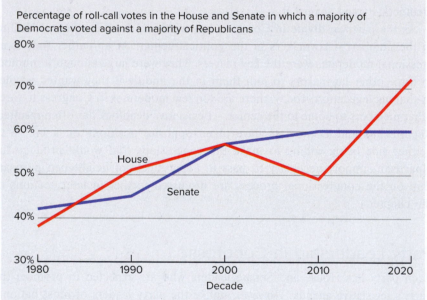

Source: Brookings Institution's Vital Statistics on Congress. The numbers are the average for the previous decade. The 2020 numbers, for example, are the House and Senate averages for the 2011–2020 period.

Q: Some observers claim that heightened partisanship in Congress is crippling the institution as a legislative body. Party disputes on everything from health care to immigration policy have produced legislative deadlock and delay. Do you share the view that excessive partisanship is undermining the legislative process, or do you think members of Congress should stick to their partisan principles, whatever the consequences?

HOW THE 50 STATES DIFFER

CRITICAL THINKING THROUGH COMPARISONS

Women in the State Legislatures

Women have had more success in gaining election to state legislatures than to Congress, partly because there is more turnover and less incumbency advantage at the state level, which creates more opportunities for newcomers to run and win. Three in 10 state legislators are women, a sixfold increase since 1970. Nevada (52 percent) and Colorado (44 percent) have the highest percentage. West Virginia (14 percent) and Tennessee (15 percent) have the lowest.

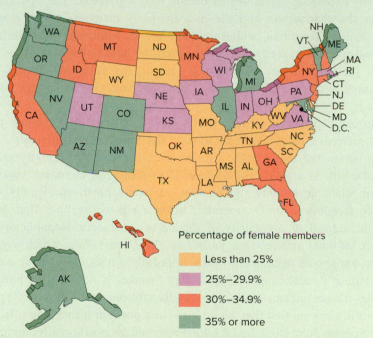

Percentage of female members

- Less than 25%
- 25%–29.9%
- 30%–34.9%
- 35% or more

Source: Created from data gathered by the Center for the American Woman and Politics (CAWP); National Information Bank on Women in Public Office; and Eagleton Institute of Politics, Rutgers University, 2018.

Q: What do states with the fewest women legislators have in common?

A: With the exception of Delaware, these states tend to vote Republican in state legislative races. Although the Republican Party has increased its effort to recruit women to run for public office, it has been less successful at doing so than the Democratic Party. Two-thirds of the women serving in state legislatures today are Democrats; a third are Republicans.

Since the majority party has the largest number of members, it also has the most votes, and the Speaker has always been a member of the majority party.

The Speaker of the House has been called the nation's most powerful elected national official aside from the president. The Speaker's power owes primarily to the large size of the House. With 435 members, it requires strict rules to operate effectively, and the Speaker is in charge of many of the rules. The Speaker's formal powers include the right to speak first during House debate on legislation and the power to recognize members—that is, to grant them permission to speak from the floor. Because the House places a time limit on floor debate, only a relatively few members will get the chance to speak on a given bill, and the Speaker can sometimes influence legislation simply by exercising the power to decide who will speak. The Speaker also chooses the chairperson and the majority-party members of the powerful House Rules Committee, which controls the scheduling of bills. Bills that the Speaker wants passed are likely to reach the floor under conditions favorable to their enactment. The Speaker might, for example, ask the Rules Committee to delay sending a bill to the floor until there's enough support to pass it.

Although a powerful official, the Speaker is ultimately beholden to the party's members. Party members look to the Speaker for leadership on legislative issues, but the Speaker cannot force them to vote for or against a particular bill. As a result, the Speaker must take party members' views into account when developing the party's legislative positions. Rarely will a Speaker, Republican or Democratic, bring a bill to the floor that doesn't have the support of a majority of the party's members. Republicans even have an informal arrangement known as the *Hastert Rule,* which says that the Speaker should bring a bill to the floor only if it's supported by a majority of House Republicans. A Republican Speaker is not literally bound by the rule—it's an informal directive—but Republican speakers have typically honored it, knowing that they could lose their position if they don't. In 2015, House Speaker John Boehner (R-Ohio) resigned his position after he ignored the rule on a few key bills and lost the support of his party's most conservative members. He was replaced by Paul Ryan (R-Wisc.), who promised to abide by the rule.[30]

The Speaker is assisted by the House majority leader and the House majority whip, who are chosen by the majority party's members. The majority leader acts as the party's floor leader, organizing the debate on bills and lining up legislative support. The whip has the job of informing party members when key votes are scheduled. As voting is getting under way on the House floor, the whip will sometimes stand at a location that is easily seen by party members and let them know where the leadership stands on the bill by giving them a thumbs-up or thumbs-down signal.

The minority party also has its House leaders. The House minority leader heads the party's caucus and plays the leading role in developing the party's legislative positions. The minority leader is assisted by a minority whip.

Senate Leaders   In the Senate, the most important party leadership position is that of the majority leader. This role resembles that of the Speaker of the House in that the Senate majority leader develops the majority party's legislative agenda. Like the Speaker, the Senate majority leader chairs the party's policy committee and acts as the party's voice in the chamber. The majority leader is assisted by the majority whip, who sees to it that members know when important votes are scheduled. The minority party in the Senate also has its leaders. The minority leader and minority whip have roles comparable to those of their House counterparts.

The House of Representatives, with its 435 members, is a very large legislative body that could not operate effectively without strict rules, such as a limit on the number of House members who are allowed to speak on a bill and for how long. Control over many of these rules rests with the Speaker of the House. (Office of Photography, U.S. House of Representatives.)

The Senate majority leader's position is less powerful than that of the House Speaker. Unlike the House, where the Speaker directs the floor debate, the Senate has a tradition of unlimited debate. Ordinarily, any senator who wishes to speak on a bill can do so and for any length of time.*

Moreover, unlike the Speaker, the Senate majority leader does not strictly control the rules of debate on a bill. Through the House Rules Committee, the Speaker can introduce a bill under what's called a *closed rule*. This rule prohibits amendments to the bill. In contrast, the Senate allows its members to propose amendments to any bill. Such amendments do not have to relate to the bill's content—for example, a senator could propose an anti-abortion amendment to a bill dealing with defense expenditures. Such amendments are called *riders*. The House does not permit riders. Only amendments that relate

Because the Senate has only 100 members, it operates differently than the much larger House. Senators are allowed to speak on any bill, which increases their power individually while diminishing the power of party leaders. The Senate majority leader has less control over Senate business than the House Speaker does over House business. (United States Senate)

---

*Unlike the Speaker of the House, the Senate majority leader is not the chamber's presiding officer. The Constitution assigns this position to the vice president of the United States. But because the vice president is allowed to vote only in case of a tie, the vice president rarely attends Senate sessions. In the absence of the vice president, the president pro tempore (temporary president) has the right to preside over the Senate. By tradition, the president pro tempore is the majority party's most senior member, but the position is largely honorary. The Senate's presiding officer has no real power because any senator who wants to speak on a bill has the right to do so.

directly to a bill's content are allowed in the House, and, as noted, some House bills are debated under a closed rule, which prohibits amendments of any kind.

Finally, the Senate majority leader's power is limited by the fact that individual senators have more stature than do individual House members. The Senate is smaller in size—100 members versus 435 House members—which leads senators to act as coequals in a way that House members cannot. As well, senators serve six-year terms and do not face the unrelenting reelection pressures faced by House members, who serve two-year terms. Bob Dole of Kansas, who served as Republican Senate leader, remarked,"There's a lot of free spirits in the Senate. About 100 of them."[31]

Party Leaders and Their Members

Viewed from afar, party leaders can look very powerful. They're often in the news, and the high level of party unity on roll-call votes—Republicans lined up against Democrats—suggests that they're able to keep their fellow partisans in line. There's no question that party leaders have power or that their leadership at times is decisive in forging a bill that can make its way through Congress. However, they're less powerful than they might appear. It's not loyalty to the party leadership that holds party lawmakers together, but instead the fact that they have far more in common with each other than they do with lawmakers of the other party.

In addition, members of Congress are more indebted to the hardcore partisan voters in their state or district, as well as to the wealthy donors who fund their campaigns, than they are to their party leaders. It can be uncomfortable for them to go against their party leaders on legislation, but it can be fatal to their reelection chances if they take positions that alienate their voters and donors. There's not much a party leader can do to offset that reality. "Trying to be a leader where you have no sticks and very few carrots is dang near impossible," said former Senate Republican leader Trent Lott.[32]

COMMITTEES AND COMMITTEE LEADERSHIP

Most of the work in Congress is conducted through **standing committees**, which are permanent committees with responsibility for particular areas of public policy. At present, there are 20 standing committees in the House and 16 in the Senate (see Table 11-2). Each chamber has, for example, a standing committee that handles foreign policy issues. Other important standing committees are those that deal with agriculture, commerce, the interior (natural resources and public lands), defense, government spending, labor, the judiciary, and taxation. House committees, which average about 35 to 40 members each, are about twice the size of Senate committees.

table 11-2	THE STANDING COMMITTEES OF CONGRESS	
House of Representatives	**Senate**
Agriculture	Agriculture, Nutrition, and Forestry
Appropriations	Appropriations
Armed Services	Armed Services
Budget	Banking, Housing, and Urban Affairs
Education and Labor	Budget
Energy and Commerce	Commerce, Science, and Transportation
Ethics	Energy and Natural Resources
Financial Services	Environment and Public Works
Foreign Affairs	Finance
Homeland Security	Foreign Relations
House Administration	Health, Education, Labor, and Pensions
Judiciary	Homeland Security and Governmental Affairs
Natural Resources	Judiciary
Oversight and Reform	Rules and Administration
Rules	Small Business and Entrepreneurship
Science, Space, and Technology	Veterans' Affairs
Small Business	
Transportation and Infrastructure	
Veterans' Affairs	
Ways and Means	

Each standing committee has legislative authority in that it can draft and rewrite proposed legislation and can recommend to the full chamber the passage or defeat of the bills it handles. Legislative committees in some democracies don't have this power. They simply act as advisory bodies to party leaders.

Most of the standing committees have subcommittees, each of which has a defined jurisdiction. The Senate Committee on Health, Education, Labor, and Pensions, for instance, has three subcommittees: Primary Health and Retirement Security, Children and Families, and Employment and Workplace Safety. Each House and Senate subcommittee has about a dozen members. These few individuals do most of the work and have a leading voice in the fate of most bills in their policy area.

Congress could not manage its workload without the help of its committee system. About 10,000 bills are introduced during each two-year session of Congress. Even though a large majority of these bills do not get serious consideration, Congress would grind to a halt if its work were not divided among its standing committees, each of which has its own staff. Unlike the members' personal staffs, which concentrate on constituency relations, the committee staffs perform an almost entirely legislative function. They help draft legislation, gather information, and organize hearings.

In addition to its permanent standing committees, Congress also has a few *select committees* that have a designated responsibility but, unlike the standing committees, do not produce legislation. An example is the Senate Select Committee on Intelligence, which receives periodic classified briefings from the intelligence agencies. Congress also has *joint committees,* composed of members of both houses, which perform advisory functions. The Joint Committee on the Library, for example, oversees the Library of Congress, the largest library in the world. Finally, Congress has *conference committees*—joint committees formed temporarily to work out differences in House and Senate versions of a particular bill. The role of conference committees is discussed more fully later in the chapter.

Committee Jurisdiction

The 1946 Legislative Reorganization Act requires that each bill introduced in Congress be referred to the proper committee. An agricultural bill introduced in the Senate must be assigned to the Senate Agriculture Committee, a bill dealing with foreign affairs must be sent to the Senate Foreign Relations Committee, and so on. This requirement is a source of each committee's power. Even if a committee's members are known to oppose certain types of legislation, bills clearly within its **jurisdiction**—the policy area in which it is authorized to act—must be assigned to it.

Jurisdiction is not always clear-cut, however. Which House committee, for example, should handle a bill addressing the role of financial institutions in global commercial trade? The Financial Services Committee? The Energy and Commerce Committee? The Foreign Affairs Committee? All committees seek legislative influence, and each is jealous of its jurisdiction, so a bill that overlaps committee boundaries can provoke a "turf war" over which committee will handle it.[33] Party leaders can take advantage of these situations by assigning the bill to the committee that is most likely to handle it in the way they would like. However, because party leaders depend on the committees for support, they cannot regularly ignore a committee that has a strong claim to a bill. At times, party leaders have responded by dividing up a bill, handing over some of its provisions to one committee and other provisions to a second committee.

Committee Membership

Each committee has a fixed number of seats, with the majority party holding most of the seats. The ratio of Democrats to Republicans on each committee is approximately the same as the ratio in the full House or Senate, but there is no fixed rule on this matter, and the majority party determines the ratio (mindful that at the next election it could become the chamber's minority party). Members of the House typically serve on only two committees. Senators often serve on four, although they can sit on only two major committees, such as the Finance Committee or the Foreign Relations Committee. Once appointed to a committee, a member can usually choose to stay on it indefinitely.

Because each committee has a fixed number of seats, a committee must have a vacancy before a new member can be appointed. Most vacancies occur after an election as a result of the retirement or defeat of committee members. Each party has a special committee in each chamber that decides who will fill the vacancies. A variety of factors influence these decisions, including members' preferences. Most newly elected members of Congress ask for and receive assignment to a committee on which they can serve their constituents' interests and at the same time improve their reelection chances. For example, when

Most of the work in Congress is done through its standing committees, each of which has a policy jurisdiction and the authority to rewrite legislation and hold hearings. Typically, bills reach the floor of the House or Senate after first being shaped and voted on in committee. Pictured here is a hearing of the House Ways and Means Committee, which handles tax bills. (Ways and Means Committee/ U.S. House of Representatives)

Rick Scott was elected to the Senate from Florida in 2018, he was appointed to the Committee on Commerce, Science, and Technology, where he serves on the Subcommittee on Science, Oceans, Fisheries and Weather, which are areas important to Florida's economy.

Some members of Congress prefer a seat on the most prestigious committees, such as the Senate Foreign Relations Committee or the House Ways and Means (taxation) Committee.[34] Although these committees do not align closely with constituency interests, they handle leading policy issues. Factors such as party loyalty, level of knowledge, work ethic, and length of congressional service determine whether a member is granted a seat on a prestigious committee.*

Committee Chairs

Each committee (as well as each subcommittee) is headed by a chairperson. The position of committee chair is a powerful one. The chair schedules committee meetings, determines the order in which committee bills are considered, presides over committee discussions, directs the committee's majority staff, and can choose to lead the debate when a committee bill goes to the floor of the chamber for a vote.

Committee chairs are always members of the majority party and usually are the party member with the most **seniority** (consecutive years of service) on the committee. Seniority is based strictly on time served on a committee, not on time spent in Congress. Thus, if a member switches committees, the years spent on the first committee do not count toward seniority on the new one. The seniority system has advantages: It reduces the number of power struggles that would occur if the chairs were decided each time by open competition, it places committee leadership in the hands of experienced members, and it enables members to look forward to the reward of a position as chair after years of service on the same committee. The seniority system is not absolute, however, and is applied less uniformly than in the past, as the next section will explain.

Committee or Party: Which Is in Control?

In a sense, committees are an instrument of the majority party in that it controls a majority of each committee's seats and appoints its chair. In another sense, each committee is powerful in its own right. Committees have been described as "little legislatures," each secure in its jurisdiction and membership, and each wielding considerable influence over the legislation it handles.

---

*Subcommittee assignments are handled differently. The members of each party on a committee decide who among them will serve on each of its subcommittees. The member' preferences and seniority, as well as the interests of their constituencies, are key factors in subcommittee assignments.

Committees decentralize power in Congress and serve individual members' power and reelection needs. Less than a dozen members hold a party leadership position, but several hundred serve as committee or subcommittee chairs or are *ranking members,* the term for the minority party's committee and subcommittee leaders. In these positions, they can pursue local or personal policy agendas that may or may not coincide with the party leadership's goals.

Nevertheless, as a result of party polarization, the power of committees has been reduced somewhat. An effect of polarization has been to increase the number of issues on which Republicans and Democrats compete nationally. This development has led party leaders in Congress to seek greater control over the legislative agenda, including the bills in committee. The consolidation of control has been more pronounced among Republicans, who, for example, have placed a six-year limit on how long a member can chair a particular committee, which limits the chair's ability to accumulate power.

Although the parties have more influence in Congress than they did a few decades ago, the balance between party power and committee power is an ongoing issue. Congress is at once a place where the parties pursue their national policy agendas and where the members pursue the policy interests of their local constituencies through their committee work. The balance of power has at times tipped toward the committees and at other times toward the party leaders. At all times, there has been an effort to strike a workable balance between the two. The distinguishing feature of congressional power is its division among the membership, with provision for added power—sometimes more and sometimes less—in the hands of the top party leaders.

How a Bill Becomes Law

Parties, party leaders, and committees are critical actors in the legislative process. Their roles and influence, however, vary with the nature of the legislation under consideration. The formal process by which bills become law is shown in Figure 11-3. A **bill** is a proposed legislative act. Many bills are prepared by executive agencies, interest groups, or other outside parties, but members of Congress also draft bills, and they alone can formally submit a bill for consideration by their chamber.

Committee Hearings and Decisions

When a bill is introduced in the House or the Senate, it receives a bill number and is sent to the relevant committee, which assigns it to one of its subcommittees. Less than 10 percent of the bills referred to committee will get to the floor for a vote; the others are "killed" when committees decide they lack merit.

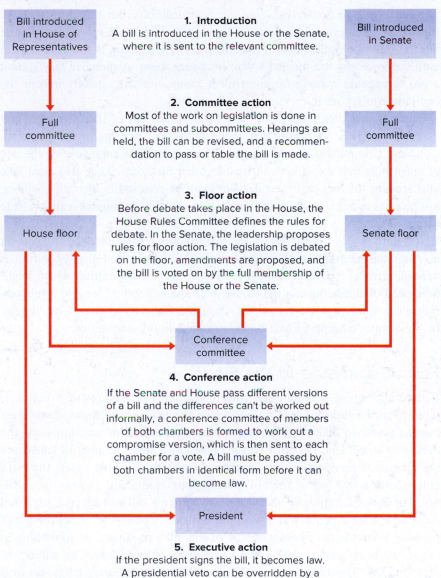

1. Introduction
A bill is introduced in the House or the Senate,
where it is sent to the relevant committee.

Bill introduced in House of Representatives

Bill introduced in Senate

2. Committee action
Most of the work on legislation is done in
committees and subcommittees. Hearings are
held, the bill can be revised, and a recommen-
dation to pass or table the bill is made.

Full committee

Full committee

3. Floor action
Before debate takes place in the House, the
House Rules Committee defines the rules for
debate. In the Senate, the leadership proposes
rules for floor action. The legislation is debated
on the floor, amendments are proposed, and
the bill is voted on by the full membership of
the House or the Senate.

House floor

Senate floor

Conference committee

4. Conference action
If the Senate and House pass different versions
of a bill and the differences can't be worked out
informally, a conference committee of members
of both chambers is formed to work out a
compromise version, which is then sent to each
chamber for a vote. A bill must be passed by
both chambers in identical form before it can
become law.

President

5. Executive action
If the president signs the bill, it becomes law.
A presidential veto can be overridden by a
two-thirds majority in each chamber.

figure 11-3   HOW A BILL BECOMES LAW

Although the legislative process can be short-circuited in many ways, this simplified diagram shows the major steps through which a bill becomes law. A key difference between the House and Senate that's not shown in the diagram is the role of the House Rules Committee, which has no equivalent in the Senate. The House Rules Committee controls the scheduling of House bills and the conditions under which they will be debated, including whether amendments will be allowed.

The full House or Senate can overrule such decisions, but this rarely occurs. Most bills die in committee because they are poorly conceived or are of little interest to anyone other than a few members of Congress. Some bills are not even supported by the members who introduce them. A member may submit a bill to appease a powerful constituent group and then quietly inform the committee to ignore it.

The fact that committees kill more than 90 percent of the bills submitted in Congress does not mean that they exercise 90 percent of the power in Congress. Committees do not operate in a vacuum. They rarely decide the fate of major bills that are of keen interest to other members. They also must take into account the fact that their decisions can be reversed by the full chamber, just as subcommittees must recognize that the full committee can override their decisions.[35]

If a bill appears to have merit, the subcommittee will schedule hearings on it. After the hearings, if the subcommittee still feels that the legislation is needed, members will recommend the bill to the full committee, which might hold additional hearings. In the House, both the full committee and a subcommittee can *mark up* a bill—that is, they have the authority to change its content. In the Senate, markup usually is reserved for the full committee.

From Committee to the Floor

If the majority on a committee vote to recommend passage of a bill, it is referred to the full chamber for action. In the House, the Rules Committee has the power to determine when the bill will be voted on and how long the debate on it will last. On most House bills, only a small number of legislators are granted the opportunity to speak on the floor; in most cases, the bill's chief sponsor and one of the bill's leading opponents will choose the speakers. The Rules Committee also decides whether a bill will receive a "closed rule" (no amendments will be permitted), an "open rule" (members can propose amendments relevant to any of the bill's sections), or something in between (for example, only certain sections of the bill will be subject to amendment). The rules are a means by which the majority party controls legislation. When Democrats had a majority in the House in the period before 1995, they used closed rules to prevent Republicans from proposing amendments to major bills, a tactic House Republicans said they would forgo when they took control in 1995. Once in control, however, the Republicans applied closed rules to a number of major bills. The tactic is too effective for either party to ignore.

In the Senate, the majority leader, often in consultation with the minority leader, schedules bills. Although the Senate has a rules committee, it doesn't

Shown here is Senator Rand Paul (R-Ky.). Paul is a critic of federal spending and frequently filibusters spending bills. The filibuster affords senators an opportunity to delay or defeat a bill that they oppose. A three-fifths majority vote in the Senate is required to end a filibuster. (Senate TV/AP Images)

set the terms of debate. All Senate bills are subject to unlimited debate unless a three-fifths majority (60 of the 100 senators) vote for **cloture**, which limits debate to 30 hours. Cloture is a way of defeating a Senate **filibuster**, which is a procedural tactic whereby a minority of senators can block a bill by talking until other senators give in and the bill is withdrawn from consideration or is altered to fit opponents' demands. (In 2013, the filibuster was eliminated for Senate votes on presidential nominees, although it was retained for legislation and the confirmation of Supreme Court justices. In 2017, it was eliminated for Supreme Court justices as well.)

Leadership and Floor Action

A bill that emerges from committee with the support of all or nearly all of its members is usually passed by an overwhelming majority of the full chamber. By contrast, when the committee vote is closely divided, other members may conclude that they need to give the bill a close look before deciding whether to support it. Other members are also less deferential to committee action on major bills and those that affect their constituents.

On major bills, the majority party's leaders have increasingly assumed the lead.[36] They shape the bill's broad content and work closely with the relevant committee during the committee phase. Once the bill clears the committee, they often direct the floor debate. In these efforts, they depend on the ongoing support of their party's members. To obtain it, they consult their members informally and through the party caucus. (The role of parties in Congress is discussed further in the section "The Representation Function of Congress.")

Conference Committees and the President

For a bill to pass, it must have the support of a simple majority (50 percent plus one) of the House or Senate members voting on it. To become law, however, a bill must first be passed in identical form by both the House and the Senate. About 10 percent of the bills that pass both chambers differ in important respects in their House and Senate versions. Unless the differences can be worked out informally, these bills are referred to conference committees to resolve the differences. Each **conference committee** is formed temporarily for the sole purpose of handling a particular bill. Its members are usually appointed from the House and Senate standing committees that drafted the bill. The conference committee's job is to develop a compromise version, which then goes back to the House and Senate floors for a final vote.

A bill passed in identical form by the House and the Senate is not yet a law. The president also has a say. If the president signs the bill, it becomes a **law**. If the president rejects the bill through use of the **veto**, the bill is sent back to Congress with the president's reasons for not signing it. Congress can override a veto by a two-thirds vote of each chamber; the bill then becomes law without the president's signature.*

CONGRESS'S POLICYMAKING ROLE

The framers of the Constitution expected Congress as the embodiment of representative government to be the institution that the people would look to for policy leadership. During most of the 19th century, Congress had that stature. Aside from a few strong leaders, such as Andrew Jackson and Abraham Lincoln, presidents did not play a major legislative role (see Chapter 12). However, as national and international forces combined to place greater policy demands on the federal government, the president assumed a central role in the legislative process. Today, Congress and the president share the legislative effort, although their roles differ.[37]

Congress's policymaking role revolves around its three major functions: lawmaking, representation, and oversight (see Table 11-3). In practice, the three functions overlap, but they are conceptually distinct.

---

*Although the large majority of bills are signed or vetoed by the president, a bill can also become law if the president fails to take action within 10 days (Sundays excepted). In that instance, the bill becomes law if Congress is still in session. However, if Congress has concluded its term and the president fails to sign a bill within 10 days, the bill does not become law. This last situation, called a pocket veto, forces Congress, in its next term, to start over from the beginning: The bill again must pass both chambers and again is subject to presidential veto.

table 11-3	THE MAJOR FUNCTIONS OF CONGRESS
Function	**Basis and Activity**
Lawmaking	Through its constitutional grant to enact law, Congress makes the laws authorizing federal programs and appropriating the funds necessary to carry them out.
Representation	Through its elected constitutional officers—U.S. senators and representatives—Congress represents the interests of constituents and the nation in its deliberations and its lawmaking.
Oversight	Through its constitutional responsibility to see that the executive branch carries out the laws faithfully and spends appropriations properly, Congress oversees and sometimes investigates executive action.

The Lawmaking Function of Congress

Under the Constitution, Congress is granted the **lawmaking function**: the authority to make the laws necessary to carry out the powers granted to the national government. The constitutional powers of Congress are substantial; they include the powers to tax, to spend, to regulate commerce, and to declare war. However, whether Congress takes the lead in the making of laws usually depends on the type of policy at issue.

Broad Issues: Fragmentation as a Limit on Congress's Role   Although Congress sometimes takes the lead on major national policy issues,[38] it often looks to the president to take the lead. One reason is that the structure of Congress is not well suited to tackling large, complex issues. Congress is not one house but two, each with its own authority and constituency base. Neither the House nor the Senate can enact legislation without the other's approval, and the two chambers are hardly identical. California and North Dakota have exactly the same representation in the Senate (two senators each), but, in the House, which is apportioned by population, California has 53 seats compared to North Dakota's 1. Moreover, the House and the Senate are sometimes controlled by opposite parties, making agreement between the two chambers even harder to achieve.

Congress also includes a lot of lawmakers: 100 members of the Senate and 435 members of the House. They come from different constituencies and represent different and sometimes opposing interests, which can lead to disagreement even among members of the same party. Most members of Congress, for example, say they are in favor of global free trade. However, when it comes to specific trade issues, they may take the opposite position. Foreign competition means different things to manufacturers who produce automobiles, computer chips, or underwear; and it means different things to farmers who produce corn, sugar, or grapes. Because free trade means different things to different people in different parts of the country, members of Congress who represent those different areas can have opposing views on when it is advantageous.

As an institution, the presidency is better suited to the task of providing leadership on major national issues. First, whereas Congress's authority is divided, executive power is vested constitutionally in the hands of a single individual—the president. The president, unlike congressional leaders, doesn't have to bargain with other officeholders in staking out a policy position. Second, whereas members of Congress often see issues from the perspective of their state or constituency, presidents have a national constituency and tend to look at policy from that perspective.

The president has another noteworthy advantage over Congress when it comes to major legislative initiatives, especially those involving complex problems. The president, as will be explained in Chapter 12, is assisted by hundreds of policy specialists, both directly and through the executive agencies, such as the Departments of Treasury and Defense. These specialists have the expertise required for crafting intricate legislative initiatives. Congress does not have anywhere near the same level of access to policy experts.*

Presidential leadership on major policy issues means that Congress will listen to White House proposals, not that Congress will back them. It may reject a proposal outright, particularly when the president is from the opposing party. After Democrats took control of the House in 2019, most of President Trump's legislative proposals were pronounced "dead on arrival" when they reached the House. House Democrats had the votes to block action on his proposals. By contrast, if a presidential proposal has enough congressional support, it becomes the starting point for negotiations, saving Congress the

---

*Congress's expertise is concentrated largely in its committee system, where members acquire policy knowledge in the policy area handled by the committees on which they serve. Each committee also has a staff, some of whose members are hired for their expertise in the committee's policy area. Congress also has three agencies of its own, although they function as nonpartisan bodies rather than as policy bodies. One of these agencies is the Congressional Budget Office (CBO), which has a staff of 250 employees and provides Congress with estimates of government expenditures and revenues, which Congress uses in determining fiscal policy. A second congressional agency is the Government Accountability Office (GAO), with 3,000 employees. Its job is to determine whether executive agencies are complying with laws passed by Congress. The third agency is the Congressional Research Service (CRS) with 1,000 employees. The CRS functions as a research and information service for congressional members and committees. By law, it is prohibited from making policy recommendations.

Democrat Tammy Baldwin was first elected to the U.S. Senate in 2012, becoming the first woman from Wisconsin to do so and the first openly gay person, male or female, to serve in the Senate. Baldwin is among the growing number of women who sit in the U.S. Congress. She won reelection to a second term in 2018. (Alex Wroblewski/Getty Images)

time and trouble of developing the legislation from scratch. (The legislative roles of Congress and the president are discussed further in Chapter 12.)

Congress in the Lead: Fragmentation as a Policymaking Strength

Congress's strength as a legislative body is its ability to handle scores of small issues simultaneously. The great majority of the hundreds of bills that Congress considers each session deal with narrow issues, such as providing grants-in-aid to cities for their mass transit systems or authorizing a new weapons system for the navy. Such bills are handled largely through Congress's standing committees, each of which has policy expertise resulting from the fact that it concentrates on a particular policy area, such as taxation, agriculture, or military affairs. And, because the standing committees operate separately, the committee system as a whole can work simultaneously on a large number of bills. As political scientist James Sundquist noted, "Congress [is] organized to deal with narrow problems but not with broad ones."[39]

Many narrow policy issues serve the reelection interests of members of Congress. The resulting legislation tends to be "distributive"—that is, it confers a benefit on a particular group while spreading the cost across the taxpaying public.

Politics in Action

Leadership Style of Women in Congress

The 2018 elections marked the first time ever that more than 100 women were elected to the House of Representatives. On the Senate side, 25 members were women, the highest number ever. Although women are still greatly underrepresented, their growing presence is said by some analysts to foreshadow a change in how Congress operates. They see female legislators as being more collaborative, more focused on problem solving, and more responsive to the policy needs of families than their male counterparts.

Joe Ferrer/Shutterstock

Evidence supports the claim. A 2017 study by Rutgers's Center for Women and Politics found that women bring new issues and perspectives to congressional deliberations and have distinctive work styles that can foster bipartisanship.[40] Another study found that women sponsor and co-sponsor more bills than do men while introducing more bills relating to education, health, and poverty.[41] That study's findings coincide with those of another that examined more than 150,000 bills introduced in the House over a 40-year period. It identified health, education, and civil rights bills as ones that female members disproportionately introduced.[42]

At the same time, the distinctive contribution of women may be declining as a result of the polarization that has reshaped Congress in recent years. A study of House roll-call votes found that the votes of male and female members of the same party have been converging to the point that they are almost indistinguishable, a pattern that analysts have attributed to the election of fewer female moderates.[43] Increasingly, female members of Congress—Republican Senator Cindy Hyde-Smith and Democratic Representative Alexandria Ocasio-Cortez being examples—have taken positions that reflect their party's ideology more than they reflect their gender. Jennifer Lawless, who directs American University's Women & Politics Institute, notes that polarization has reduced the "incentive for anyone, male or female, to reach across the aisle."[44]

> **Q:** Blacks, Hispanics, and Asian Americans are, like women, underrepresented in Congress relative to their population percentage. What issues might get more attention in Congress if they were more fully represented?
>
> **ASK YOURSELF:** What problems do most Black Americans face that are more severe or different from those faced by most white Americans? What distinctive problems do Hispanics face? Asian Americans?

An example is the 2011 Veterans Jobs Act that provided tax credits to businesses that hire veterans and funding for job training for veterans. Distributive policies have a clear political advantage. The benefit is large enough that members of the recipient group will recognize and appreciate getting it, while the cost to each taxpayer is barely noticeable. Such policies are also the type that Congress, through its committee system, is organizationally best suited to handle. Most committees parallel a major constituent interest, such as agriculture, commerce, labor, or veterans.

The Representation Function of Congress

In the process of making laws, the members of Congress represent various interests within American society, giving them a voice in the national legislature. How they should carry out their **representation function** has been debated since the nation's founding. Should representatives be guided by the interests of the nation as a whole? Or should they be guided by the narrower interests of their constituents? These interests overlap but do not coincide exactly. Policies that benefit the nation are not necessarily advantageous to a particular locality. Free trade in steel is an example. Although U.S. manufacturers as a whole benefit from access to low-priced steel from abroad, domestic steel producers and the communities where they're located are hurt by it.

Representation of States and Districts   The choice between national and local interests is not a simple one, even for legislators who are inclined toward one or the other orientation. To be fully effective, members of Congress must be reelected time and again, which compels them to pay attention to local demands, yet they serve in the nation's legislative body and cannot ignore national needs. In making the choice, most members of Congress, on narrow issues at least, vote in a way that will not antagonize local interests.[45] Opposition to gun control legislation, for example, is stronger among members of Congress representing rural areas where hunting is prevalent than it is among those from urban areas where guns tend to be seen as a threat to public safety.

Local representation occurs, in part, through the committee system. Although studies indicate that the policy positions of most committees are not radically different from those of the full House or Senate,[46] committee memberships roughly coincide with constituency interests. For example, farm-state legislators dominate the membership of the House and Senate Agriculture Committees. Committees are also the site of most *logrolling*—the practice of trading one's vote with another member's so that both get what they want, as in the case of agricultural committee members from corn-producing northern states trading votes with members from cotton-producing southern states.

Local representation also shapes how Congress distributes funds for federal programs. Members of Congress will often withhold their support unless their locality gets a share of the money, even if it makes the program less efficient and effective. An example is the bill that Congress passed in 2020 to help states deal with the COVID-19 pandemic. Even though the threat was much worse in more populous states, the legislation automatically granted each state a minimum of $1.25 billion in aid.

CITIZEN ACTION!
GETTING INVOLVED

Consider e-mailing or writing to your congressional representative to express your opinion on a current issue. You can inform yourself about the member's position on the issue through his or her website, which will also have the contact information you need.

Nevertheless, representation of constituency interests has its limits. Constituents have little awareness of most issues that come before Congress. Whether Congress appropriates a few million dollars in foreign aid to Bolivia is not the sort of issue that local residents will hear or care about. Moreover, members of Congress often have no choice but to go against the wishes of a significant portion of their constituency. In such cases, members of Congress typically side with the interest that aligns with their party. When local business and labor groups take opposing sides on issues before Congress, for example, Republican members tend to back business's position, whereas Democratic members tend to line up with labor.

Representation of the Nation Through Parties

When a vital national interest is at stake, members of Congress can be expected to respond to it. For example, when the economy went into a tailspin in the face of the outbreak of the COVID-19 coronavirus in 2020, Congress enacted legislation that gave most taxpayers a payout of more than a thousand dollars in the hope that they would spend it, thereby giving the economy a boost. The Senate voted unanimously in favor of the bill containing the payout, while the House passed it with a nearly unanimous voice vote.

In most cases, however, members of Congress, although agreeing on a need for national action, disagree on the best course of action. Most lawmakers believe, for example, that the nation's immigration system needs to be overhauled. The nation has a need for immigrant labor yet has roughly 11 million undocumented immigrants already here. The situation creates pressure for political action. But what action is necessary and desirable? Should undocumented immigrants already here be given a path to citizenship? Should the immigration system favor immigrants with high skill levels or those with family members in the United States? What should be done to prevent additional individuals from unlawfully entering the United States?

There is no general agreement in Congress on such issues. Republican and Democratic lawmakers have different perspectives on national issues because their parties differ philosophically and politically. Differences in the parties' approaches to immigration policy, for example, have played out whenever an immigration bill has been debated, with Republicans pushing for more control over the nation's borders and Democrats pushing to accommodate the undocumented immigrants already in the country.

Congressional discord has increased as a result of party polarization. The increase in the number of liberal Democrats and conservative Republicans in Congress has made it harder for the two sides to bridge their differences. Party polarization has also fostered a *nationalization* of congressional politics. Although constituency influences still have a powerful effect on Congress's members, party ideology has risen in importance. On small and large issues alike, party ideology has increasingly separated Republicans from Democrats, even those who come from the same state or region.

A positive aspect of this development is that party differences are increasingly apparent to voters. At times in the past, political scientists have argued that the overlap between the parties was a barrier to accountability. They argued that America's voters deserved to have a choice between parties that took clear-cut and opposing policy positions.[47] That argument has lost favor as the costs of polarization have mounted. The argument failed to account for the structure of U.S. institutions. In a European parliamentary system, the majority party has full control of legislative and executive power and can enact its policies. At the next election, the voters can hold it to account by approving or rejecting its agenda. In the American system, however, executive and legislative powers are divided, and legislative power is further divided between the House and the Senate (see "How the U.S. Differs"). The separation of powers can result in policy deadlock when the two parties are closely divided in strength and far apart on the issues, as is the case today.[48]

The fact that the parties are currently so closely matched has intensified the conflict between them. Each party sees the next election as a critical showdown that will determine whether it will control the House and the Senate. As a result, each party has an incentive to deny the other party any claim to legislative success.

HOW THE U.S. DIFFERS

CRITICAL THINKING THROUGH COMPARISONS

Legislative Structure

The U.S. House and Senate are equal in their legislative powers; without their joint agreement, no law can be enacted. This arrangement is unusual. Although most democracies have a bicameral (two-chamber) legislature, one chamber is usually more powerful than the other. In the Canadian parliament, for example, nearly all bills originate in the House of Commons, with the Senate functioning more as a check on its actions than as a co-equal body. Moreover, some democracies, including Sweden and Israel, have unicameral (one-chamber) legislatures. If the United States had an equivalent legislature, it would consist only of the House of Representatives.

Power in the U.S. Congress is divided in other ways as well: Congress has elected leaders with limited formal powers, a network of committees, and members who are free to follow or ignore other members of their party. It is not uncommon for a legislator to vote against the party's position on legislative issues. In contrast, European legislatures have a centralized power structure. Top leaders have substantial authority, the committees are weak, and the parties are unified. European legislators are expected to support their party unless granted permission to vote otherwise on a particular bill. If they defy the party leadership, they might be denied renomination in the next election.

Q: In terms of enacting legislation, what is the relative advantage and disadvantage of the way in which Congress is structured, compared with a national legislature with a dominant chamber in which the majority party can count on its members to support its policy agenda?

A: A relative advantage of Congress is that it is structured in a way that slows the passage of legislation, which can be a safeguard against ill-conceived or weakly supported bills. A relative disadvantage of Congress's structure is that it can result in legislative deadlock even on pressing national issues. A Senate filibuster can enable a determined minority to block legislation even if it has majority support within and outside Congress. And, if one party controls the House and the other party controls the Senate, each party has the power to block the other from acting.

The minority party in Congress tries to block the policy initiatives of the party in power. In turn, the majority party does everything possible to marginalize the weaker party in order to undermine its credibility. Each party portrays the other in stark terms—too extreme and too beholden to special interests to govern in the interests of ordinary Americans. As Frances Lee notes in *Insecure Majorities*, members of Congress are engaged in "messaging" rather than "governing."[49] In positioning themselves on bills, they are sometimes less concerned with whether their position will prevail in Congress than whether it will attract votes in the next election. Reflecting on the partisan fights and policy deadlock, a longtime congressional veteran said that Congress is a "campaign stage" rather than a place to debate legislation.[50]

As congressional partisanship has intensified, the public's image of Congress has plummeted (see Figure 11-4). In the 1980s, before partisan deadlock gripped Congress, roughly 6 in 10 Americans approved of how Congress was doing its job. Today, barely more than 2 in 10 approve.

The Oversight Function of Congress

In addition to enacting the laws, Congress has responsibility for seeing that its laws are carried out properly by the executive branch. This responsibility is known as Congress's **oversight function**.[51]

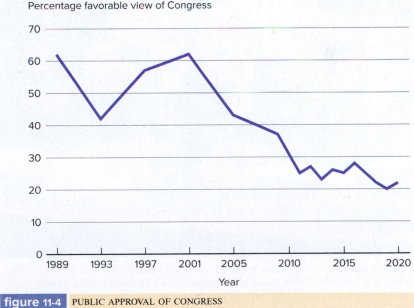

figure 11-4   PUBLIC APPROVAL OF CONGRESS

Partisan polarization in Congress has been accompanied by declining public approval of Congress. (*Source:* Pew Research Center for the People and the Press surveys.)

Oversight is carried out largely through the committee system of Congress, with each standing committee overseeing part of the executive branch. The House and Senate Agriculture Committees, for example, monitor the Department of Agriculture. The Legislative Reorganization Act of 1970 spells out each committee's responsibility for overseeing its parallel agency: "Each standing committee shall review and study, on a continuing basis, the application, administration, and execution of those laws, or parts of laws, the subject matter of which is within the jurisdiction of that committee."

Oversight is a demanding task. The bureaucracy has hundreds of agencies and thousands of programs. Congress gets some leverage from the fact that federal agencies have their funding renewed each year, which provides an opportunity for congressional committees to review agency activities.[52] Nevertheless, because the task is so large, oversight is not pursued vigorously unless members of Congress are annoyed with an agency, have discovered that a legislative authorization is being abused, or are intending to modify an agency program.

Special Counsel Robert Mueller testifying in 2019 at a House Judiciary Committee hearing on links between Russia and the 2016 Trump presidential campaign. The high-profile hearings became a source of controversy, with Republican members accusing Democratic members of conducting "a witch hunt" aimed at harming President Trump, while the Democrats accused the Republicans of trying to "cover up" the evidence. Mueller headed a months-long Justice Department investigation of Russian meddling and Trump's attempts to impede the investigation. (Chip Somodevilla/Getty Images)

When an agency is alleged to have acted improperly, committee hearings into the allegations can occur. Congress's investigative power is not listed in the Constitution, but the Supreme Court has upheld this power as a reasonable extension of Congress's power to make the laws. Except in cases involving *executive privilege* (the right of the executive branch to withhold confidential information), executive branch officials are ordinarily required to testify when called by Congress to do so. If they refuse, they can be cited for contempt of Congress, which is a criminal offense if a court upholds the contempt charge. On the other hand, an executive official's refusal to testify requires Congress to go to court to compel the testimony, which would delay the inquiry. In such cases, Congress will sometimes forego the testimony, as House committees did during their impeachment inquiry of President Trump (see Chapter 12).

Congress's interest in oversight diminishes when the White House is the target and the president is from the same party as the congressional majority. During the House Intelligence Committee's initial investigation of Russian meddling in the 2016 presidential election, for example, the committee's Republican majority refused to call key witnesses or subpoena those who refused to answer questions. It then issued a report claiming that Russian meddling was inconsequential—a claim at odds with the conclusion of the CIA, FBI, National Security Agency, and director of national intelligence.[53]

CONGRESS: AN INSTITUTION DIVIDED

Congress is not an institution in which majorities rule easily. Agreement within each chamber, and between the two chambers, is required to pass legislation. That can typically be achieved only if lawmakers are willing to act in a spirit of compromise. Such was the intention of the framers of the Constitution. They designed the institution to foster compromise, for the purpose of having the resulting legislation reflect the interests of the many rather than that of a powerful faction.

SUMMARY

Members of Congress, once elected, are likely to be reelected. Members of Congress can use their office to publicize themselves, to pursue a service strategy of responding to the needs of individual constituents, and to secure pork-barrel projects for their states or districts. The fact that they hold a position in Congress also helps them attract campaign contributions from individual donors and PACs. Incumbency carries some risks. Members of Congress must take positions on controversial issues, may blunder into political scandal or indiscretion, must deal with changes in the electorate, or may face strong challengers. By and large, however, the advantages of incumbency far outweigh the disadvantages.

Detecting Misinformation

Are Policy Problems Easy to Fix?

A recent poll found that most people think "ordinary Americans" would do a better job than "elected officials" of "solving the country's problems."[54] That finding coincides with what political scientists John Hibbing and Elizabeth Theiss-Morse discovered in *Stealth Democracy*: Millions of Americans believe that the nation's elaborate legislative process is a waste of time.[55] If, as these Americans think, policy problems are simple and easy to fix, there is no reason for debate and deliberation. All that's required is for politicians to get out of the way and turn the job of lawmaking over to no-nonsense leaders.

adempercem/Shutterstock

Is that claim fact, or is it fake?

It's understandable that Americans would be frustrated by the failure of elected leaders to resolve pressing national problems. Petty partisan feuds have frequently blocked congressional action in recent years. At the same time, although policy issues may look simple, they seldom are. Foreign trade, for example, affects thousands of American businesses, some of which benefit from free trade and some of which don't. Moreover, foreign trade is not simply an economic issue. It's also a means of strengthening ties between nations, which has implications for national security. As a result, the notion that America's trade problem, or other major problems, has an easy fix is mistaken. Legislating requires the weighing of many considerations, some of which are complex and interrelated. Moreover, policy making in a democratic system includes a wide range of competing interests; accommodating such interests requires time-consuming negotiation and compromise.

Congress is a fragmented institution. It has no single leader; rather, the House and the Senate have separate leaders, neither of whom can presume to speak for the other chamber. The chief party leaders in Congress are the Speaker of the House and the Senate majority leader. They share leadership power with committee and subcommittee chairpersons, who have influence on the policy decisions of their respective committees or subcommittees.

Congress's fragmentation is offset partially by partisanship, which serves as a common bond between members of the same party. In the past few decades, that bond has strengthened to the point that congressional Republicans and Democrats have regularly found themselves on the opposite sides of legislative issues. In some cases, the partisan gap has been so wide that compromise has failed, resulting in legislative delay and deadlock.

Committees are the locus of most of the day-to-day work of Congress. Each House and Senate standing committee has jurisdiction over bills in a particular area (such as agriculture or foreign relations), as does each of its subcommittees. In most cases, the full House and Senate accept committee recommendations about the passage of bills, although amendments to bills are not uncommon and committees are careful to take other members of Congress into account when making legislative decisions. On major bills, committees work closely with the party leaders, knowing that a bill will not win the necessary support if it is at odds with what party leaders and the party caucus are expecting.

The major function of Congress is to enact legislation, yet the role it plays in developing legislation depends on the type of policy involved. Because of its divided chambers and committee structure, as well as the concern of its members with state and district interests, Congress, through its party leaders and caucuses, only occasionally takes the lead on broad national issues. Congress instead typically looks to the president for this leadership. Nevertheless, presidential initiatives are passed by Congress only if they meet its members' expectations and usually only after a lengthy process of compromise and negotiation. Congress is more adept at handling legislation that deals with problems of narrow interest. Legislation of this sort is decided mainly in congressional committees, where interested legislators, bureaucrats, and groups concentrate their efforts on issues of mutual concern.

A second function of Congress is the representation of various interests. Members of Congress are highly sensitive to the state or district on which they depend for reelection. They do respond to overriding national interests, but local concerns usually take priority. National or local representation often operates through party representation, particularly on issues that divide the Democratic and Republican Parties and their constituent groups, which is increasingly the case.

Congress's third function is oversight—the supervision and investigation of the way the bureaucracy is implementing legislatively mandated programs. Although oversight is a difficult and time-consuming process, it is one of the major ways that Congress exercises control over the executive branch.

CRITICAL THINKING ZONE

KEY TERMS

bicameral legislature (*p. 310*)

bill (*p. 322*)

cloture (*p. 325*)

conference committee (*p. 326*)

constituency (*p. 304*)

filibuster (*p. 325*)

gerrymandering (*p. 306*)

incumbent (*p. 303*)

jurisdiction (*p. 319*)

law (*p. 326*)

lawmaking function (*p. 327*)

midterm election (*p. 308*)

oversight function (*p. 335*)

party caucus (*p. 310*)

party leaders (*p. 310*)

party unity (*p. 311*)

pork (*p. 304*)

reapportionment (*p. 306*)

redistricting (*p. 306*)

representation function (*p. 331*)

seniority (*p. 321*)

service strategy (*p. 304*)

standing committees (*p. 317*)

veto (*p. 326*)

APPLYING THE ELEMENTS OF CRITICAL THINKING

Conceptualizing: Explain the lawmaking, representation, and oversight functions of Congress.

Synthesizing: Contrast the advantages that incumbents have in seeking reelection with the disadvantages they have. Which of these advantages and disadvantages apply only to House members? Which apply only to senators?

Analyzing:

1. How does the structure of Congress—for example, its two chambers and its committee system—affect its role in the making of policy on broad national issues, as compared with its role on narrower, group-centered issues?

2. Compared with past times, there are now fewer conservative Democrats and fewer progressive Republicans in Congress. How has this development increased the importance of party and party leaders in Congress? How has it increased the chances of partisan deadlock on key legislative issues?

EXTRA CREDIT

A Book Worth Reading: Frances E. Lee, *Insecure Majorities: Congress and the Perpetual Campaign* (Chicago: University of Chicago Press, 2016). An insightful book by a leading political scientist that examines the destructive interplay of election pressures and the work of Congress.

A Website Worth Visiting: **www.house.gov** and **www.senate.gov** The websites of the U.S. House of Representatives and the U.S. Senate, respectively. Each site has information on the chamber's party leaders, pending legislation, and committee hearings, as well as links to each member's office and website.

THE PRESIDENCY: LEADING THE NATION

Steve Allen/Getty Images

❝ The presidency has made every man who occupied it, no matter how small, bigger than he was; and no matter how big, not big enough for its demands. ❞

LYNDON JOHNSON

Donald Trump's presidency was expected to be different, but few predicted just how different it would be. Presidents traditionally have sought to unite the country. Trump relished conflict. Asked about it, he said, "I like conflict. . . . I like watching it, I like seeing it, and I think it's the best way to go." When nationwide protests erupted after George Floyd, an unarmed and handcuffed Black man, was killed in the custody of Minneapolis police in 2020, Trump said that the states should use force to quell the demonstrators. Claiming that many of the governors and mayors were "weak," Trump sent federal officers into several cities to disrupt the demonstrations. Former Marine General James Mattis, who had served as secretary of Defense earlier in the Trump administration, said, "Donald Trump is the first president in my lifetime who does not try to unite the American people—does not even pretend to try. Instead, he tries to divide us."[1]

The presidency is America's least predictable institution. Lyndon Johnson's and Richard Nixon's pursuit of the Vietnam War led to talk of "the imperial presidency," an office so powerful that constitutional checks and balances were no longer an effective constraint. Within a few years, because of the Watergate scandal and disruptive events during the Ford and Carter presidencies, the watchword became "the imperiled presidency," an office too weak to meet the nation's needs. The foreign policy successes of Ronald Reagan and George H. W. Bush hearkened to earlier claims of "a heroic presidency" that disappeared as the economy weakened. Bill Clinton overcame a fitful start to his presidency to win a second term but then got mired in a scandal that led to his impeachment and weakened his claim to national leadership. After the terrorist attacks of September 11, 2001, George W. Bush's job approval rating soared to a record high. By the time he left office, Americans had turned against his economic

The presidency is the most visible of America's political institutions but also the least predictable, not only from one president to the next but also during a president's term of office. (Official White House Photo by David Lienemann)

and war policies and only a third of the public had a positive view of his leadership. Barack Obama, in his first two years of office, had a level of legislative success higher than any president since Johnson. In his last six years, his legislative success rate was the lowest of any president in six decades.

No other political institution has been subject to such varying characterization as the modern presidency. One reason is that the presidency, unlike Congress or the courts, is in the hands of a single individual, whose personal style and ambitions shape its direction. Moreover, the formal powers of the office are relatively modest, so presidential power changes with political conditions and the personal capacity of the office's occupant. The American presidency is always a central office in that its occupant is a focus of national attention, yet the presidency operates in a system of divided powers, which means that presidential power is conditional. It depends on the president's own abilities but even more on circumstances—on whether the situation demands strong leadership and whether there is public and congressional support for that leadership. When circumstances are favorable, the president exercises considerable power. When circumstances are unfavorable, the president struggles to exercise power effectively.

This chapter examines the roots of presidential power, the presidential selection process, the staffing of the presidency, and the factors associated with the success and failure of presidential leadership. The chapter covers the following main ideas:

- *Over time, the presidency has become a more powerful office.* This development owes largely to the legacy of strong presidents and to domestic and international developments that have increased the need for executive leadership.

- *The formal authority of the president is not substantial enough to meet the broad array of domestic and foreign policy issues the president is expected to address.* Presidents can seek to bridge the gap through their agenda-setting and support-building capacity but, unless they gain the backing of other Washington officials, they are unlikely to fulfill their goals.

- *The president could not control the executive branch without a large number of presidential appointees—advisers, experts, and skilled managers—but the sheer number of these appointees is itself a challenge to presidential control.*

- *The president's election by national vote and position as sole chief executive make the presidency the focal point of national politics.* Nevertheless, whether presidents are able to accomplish their goals depends on their personal capacity for leadership, national and international conditions, the stage of their presidency, the partisan composition of Congress, and whether an issue is foreign or domestic.

ORIGINS OF THE MODERN PRESIDENCY

The Constitution states that the president must be at least 35 years old and must have been a U.S. resident for at least 14 years. It also requires the president to be a natural-born U.S. citizen, a provision that was added to the Constitution in the final draft and reflected the belief of some of the framers that an individual born elsewhere might have divided loyalties. Ratification of the 22nd Amendment placed another limitation on the occupant. It limits a president to two terms of office.*

The informal barriers to becoming president are greater (see Table 12-1). Until Donald Trump won the presidency in 2016, no one had been elected

table 12-1	THE PATH TO THE WHITE HOUSE (SINCE 1901)	
President	**Years in Office**	**Highest Previous Office**
Theodore Roosevelt	1901–1908	Vice president*
William Howard Taft	1909–1912	Secretary of war
Woodrow Wilson	1913–1920	Governor
Warren G. Harding	1921–1924	U.S. senator
Calvin Coolidge	1925–1928	Vice president*
Herbert Hoover	1929–1932	Secretary of commerce
Franklin D. Roosevelt	1933–1945	Governor
Harry S Truman	1945–1952	Vice president*
Dwight D. Eisenhower	1953–1960	U.S. Army general
John F. Kennedy	1961–1963	U.S. senator
Lyndon Johnson	1963–1968	Vice president*
Richard Nixon	1969–1974	Vice president
Gerald Ford	1974–1976	Vice president*
Jimmy Carter	1977–1980	Governor
Ronald Reagan	1981–1988	Governor
George H. W. Bush	1989–1992	Vice president
Bill Clinton	1993–2000	Governor
George W. Bush	2001–2008	Governor
Barack Obama	2009–2016	U.S. senator
Donald Trump	2017–2020	None
Joe Biden	2021–	Vice president

*Became president on death or resignation of incumbent.

---

*The 25th Amendment might also be considered a limit on who can hold the office of president. It provides that, if the president is physically or mentally unfit to serve, the vice president becomes acting president. A determination that a president is unfit requires agreement of the the vice president and a majority of the president's cabinet.

without having first served in high public office or a top military rank. Until Barack Obama's election in 2008, all presidents had been white. In 2016, Hillary Clinton came the closest that a woman has come to becoming president. Historians have devised rankings of the presidents, and their rankings reveal that there is no template for a successful presidency. Of the four army generals, for example, two of them (George Washington and Dwight D. Eisenhower) are ranked high, while the other two (Ulysses S. Grant and Zachary Taylor) are ranked low.

From the Founding to Today

The framers expected the president to provide leadership in national affairs, take command in time of war, provide direction in foreign affairs, and properly execute the laws, but they didn't have a clear sense of how the office would work in practice. Accordingly, they described the powers of the president in general terms. By comparison with the precise listing of Congress's powers in Article I of the Constitution, the provisions in Article II that define the president's authority are briefly stated.[2] The clause that establishes the president as **chief executive** says simply, "He shall take care that the laws be faithfully executed, and shall commission all the officers of the United States." The clause that establishes the president's role as **commander in chief** says simply, "The President shall be commander in chief . . . ." The role of **chief diplomat** rests largely on provisions granting the president the power to "appoint" and "receive" ambassadors. These provisions also establish the president as **head of state**, which refers to the president's ceremonial role as representative of the government. The president's role as **chief legislator** is found largely in the provision that says the president can "recommend" measures to Congress and inform it on the "state of the Union."

Over the course of American history, each of the president's constitutional roles has been expanded in practice beyond the framers' intent. For example, the Constitution grants the president command of the nation's military, but only Congress can declare war. In *Federalist* No. 69, Alexander Hamilton wrote that insurrections and surprise attacks on the United States were the only situations that would justify a president's use of military force without congressional authorization. And presidents have at times sought congressional authorization for such action. The Korean, Vietnam, Persian Gulf, Afghanistan, and Iraq Wars, for example, were waged with the backing of Congress. Nevertheless, more than 80 percent of U.S. military engagements since World War II have been waged solely on presidential authority (see Figure 12-1)[3]. That was the case, for instance, when President Donald Trump launched a cruise missile attack on Syria, President Barack Obama ordered a bombing campaign against

Percentage of military engagements

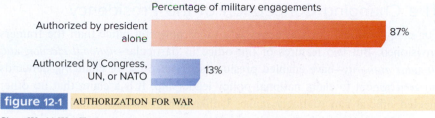

figure 12-1 AUTHORIZATION FOR WAR

Since World War II, the great majority of U.S. military engagements have been fought solely on the basis of the president's authority as commander in chief of the armed forces. (*Source:* Compiled by author from U.S, Department of Defense documents)

Libya, President Bill Clinton ordered an air attack on Serbia, and President George H. W. Bush ordered an invasion of Panama.

The Constitution also empowers the president to act as diplomatic leader with the authority to appoint ambassadors and to negotiate treaties with other countries, subject to approval by a two-thirds vote of the Senate. The framers anticipated that Congress would define the nation's foreign policy objectives, while the president would oversee their implementation. However, presidents gradually took charge of U.S. foreign policy, and today nearly every foreign policy initiative originates with the president.

The Constitution also vests "executive power" in the president. This power includes the responsibility to execute the laws faithfully and to appoint the heads of federal agencies. In *Federalist* No. 76, Hamilton indicated that the president's real authority as chief executive was to be found in this appointive capacity. Presidents have, indeed, exercised power through their appointments, but they have also found their administrative authority—the power to execute the laws—to be significant because it enables them to decide how laws will be implemented. President Barack Obama used his executive power to *permit* the use of federal funds by family-planning clinics that offered abortion counseling. President Donald Trump exerted the same power to *prohibit* the use of federal funds for this purpose. The same act of Congress was the basis for each of these decisions. The act authorizes the use of federal funds for family-planning services, but it neither requires nor prohibits their use for abortion counseling, enabling the president to decide the issue.

Finally, the Constitution provides the president with legislative authority, including use of the veto and the ability to propose legislation to Congress. The framers expected this authority to be used in a limited way. George Washington acted as the framers anticipated: He proposed only three legislative measures and vetoed only two acts of Congress. Modern presidents have assumed a more active legislative role. They regularly submit proposals to Congress and do not hesitate to veto legislation they find objectionable.

The Changing Conception of the Presidency

For many reasons, the presidency is a more powerful office than the framers envisioned. But two features of the office in particular—*national election* and *singular authority*—have enabled presidents to make use of changing demands on government to claim national policy leadership. It is a claim that no other elected official can routinely make. Unlike the president, who is elected by nationwide vote and is the sole chief executive, members of Congress are elected from separate states or districts and operate in an institution where they share power with the other members.

The first president to forcefully assert a broad claim to national policy leadership was Andrew Jackson, who was elected in 1828 on a tide of popular support that broke the upper class's hold on the presidency (see Chapter 2). Jackson used his popular backing to challenge Congress's claim to national policy leadership, contending that he represented "the people's voice." Jackson's view, however, was not shared by his immediate successors. The nation's major issues were of a sectional nature (especially the North–South split over slavery) and were suited to action by Congress, which represented state interests. In fact, throughout most of the 19th century (the Civil War presidency of Abraham Lincoln was an exception), Congress jealously guarded its constitutional authority over national policy. James Bryce wrote in the 1880s that Congress normally paid no more attention to the president's policy statements than it did to the editorials of leading newspaper publishers.[4]

The 19th-century conception of the presidency was expressed in the **limited presidency theory** (also called the *Whig theory*), which holds that the presidency is a constrained office. According to this theory, the president has important duties, but they are largely administrative. The president is not a policy leader, but instead is a chief executive whose primary job is to carry out the will of Congress. President James Buchanan, who held this view of the office, said, "My duty is to execute the laws . . . and not my individual opinions."[5]

On taking office in 1901, Theodore Roosevelt cast aside the limited presidency tradition.[6] He embraced what he called the **stewardship theory**, which calls for a "strong presidency" that is limited, not by what the Constitution allows but by what it prohibits. The stewardship theory holds that presidents are free to act as they choose, as long as they do not violate the law. In his autobiography, Roosevelt wrote, "My belief was that it was not only [the president's] right but his duty to do anything that the needs of the nation demanded unless such action was forbidden by the Constitution or by the laws."[7] Acting on his belief, Roosevelt took on the job of breaking up the business monopolies that had surfaced during the nation's Industrial Revolution (see Chapter 3). He also opened world markets to American goods, using the navy and marines to

Theodore Roosevelt is widely regarded as the first of the "modern" presidents. Roosevelt ignored the nation's isolationist tradition and extended America's influence into Latin America and the Pacific. On the domestic front, he battled the business trusts, believing that unregulated capitalism was incompatible with social justice. Roosevelt held the presidency as a Republican from 1901 to 1908 and was defeated when he tried to recapture it as a third-party candidate in 1912. (*Source:* Library of Congress, Prints and Photographs Division [LC-DIG-pga-08163])

project U.S. influence southward into the Caribbean and Latin America and westward toward Hawaii, the Philippines, and China (the "Open Door" policy). When congressional leaders objected, he forced a showdown, knowing that the American people would support the troops. Roosevelt said, "I have the money to send [the navy's ships] halfway around the world—let Congress bring them back."

Theodore Roosevelt's notion of a strong presidency was not shared by his successor, William Howard Taft. He said, "The President can exercise no power which cannot be fairly and reasonably traced to some specific grant of power." Nor did most of those who followed Taft embrace the idea of an inherently powerful presidency.[8] Herbert Hoover was slow to respond to hardships caused by the Great Depression, claiming that he lacked the constitutional authority to take strong action. His successor, Franklin D. Roosevelt (a distant cousin of Theodore

CITIZEN ACTION!
GETTING READY

Citizens can empower themselves by expanding their understanding of politics. One of the most enjoyable ways of doing so is an online or personal visit to a presidential library. Every president since Calvin Coolidge has been honored by one. Go online to discover where the presidential libraries are located and what they offer.

Roosevelt), believed differently. His New Deal policies included unprecedented public works projects, social welfare programs, and economic regulatory actions (see Chapter 3). The New Deal effectively marked the end of the notion of a limited presidency. FDR's successor, Harry S Truman, wrote in his memoirs "The power of the President should be used in the interest of the people and in order to do that the President must use whatever power the Constitution does not expressly deny him."[9]

The Need for a Strong Presidency

Today, the presidency is an inherently strong office, made so by the federal government's increased policy responsibilities. Although individual presidents differ in their capacity for leadership, the office they hold is one that requires active involvement in a broad range of policy areas.

Modern government consists of thousands of programs and hundreds of agencies. Congress is ill suited to directing and coordinating them. Congress is a fragmented institution that acts through negotiation, bargaining, and compromise. It is simply not structured in a way that would enable it to easily and regularly oversee government activity and develop comprehensive approaches to policy. The presidency is structured in a way that enables it to do so. Final authority rests with an individual, the president, who is thereby able to direct the actions of others and to undertake large-scale planning.[10] As a result, major domestic policy initiatives since the New Deal era have usually come from the White House. When President Dwight D. Eisenhower took office in 1953 and didn't immediately put forth legislative initiatives, a House committee chair told him, "That's not the way we do things here—you draft the bills, and we work them over."[11]

The presidency has also been strengthened by the expanded scope of foreign policy. World War II fundamentally changed the nation's international role and the president's role in foreign policy. The United States emerged from the war as a global superpower, a giant in world trade, and the recognized leader of the noncommunist world—a development that had a one-sided effect on America's institutions.[12] Because of the president's constitutional authority as chief diplomat and military commander and the special demands of foreign policy leadership, the president, not Congress, assumed the dominant role.[13] Foreign policy requires singleness of purpose and, at times, fast action. The president, as sole head of the executive branch, can act quickly and speak authoritatively for the nation as a whole in its relations with other nations. Congress—a large, divided, and often unwieldy institution—is poorly suited to such a response. Congress's weakness was reluctantly admitted by Senator William Fulbright, a leading critic of the Vietnam War. Said Fulbright, "It has been circumstance rather than design which has given the executive its great predominance in foreign policy. The circumstance has been crisis, an entire era of crisis in which urgent decisions have been required again and again, decisions of a kind Congress is ill-equipped to make. . . . The President has the means at his disposal for prompt action; the Congress does not."[14]

The presidency has also been strengthened by changes in how the president is chosen. In the nation's earliest years, the voters had no direct voice in the selection process (see Chapter 2). The decision resided with electors chosen by the state legislatures. In the 1830s, voters were brought into the process when states decided to allocate their electoral votes to the winner of the state's popular vote. Voters gained additional power in the early 1900s when some states adopted primary elections as the means of choosing their delegates to the national conventions where the presidential nominees are chosen. In the 1970s, a reform of the nominating process required all states to choose their delegates through popular voting (see "Case Study: Presidential Nominating Campaigns"). The effect was to give control over presidential nominations to the voters. These changes in the presidential selection process have strengthened the presidency by providing the office with the added authority that the vote of the people confers while strengthening the president's claim to national leadership.[15]

C A S E
S T U D Y

Politics in Action

Presidential Nominating Campaigns

To win their party's presidential nomination, candidates enter state primaries and open caucuses. The goal is to run strongly enough to accumulate a majority of the delegates to the party's national party convention where the nominee is formally chosen. The competition can be stiff. A dozen and a half candidates entered the 2016 Republican nominating race, which was won by Donald Trump. The 2020 Democratic race, won by Joe Biden, also attracted a large field of contenders.

Candidates for nomination have no choice but to start early and run hard. The year before the first contest in Iowa is a critical period, one that has been called the *invisible primary*.

Matt Smith/Shutterstock

Continued

It is the time when candidates demonstrate through their fundraising ability, poll standing, and debate performance that they are serious contenders. A candidate who falls short in these areas is quickly dismissed as an also-ran. Once the state caucuses and primaries get under way, a key to success is *momentum*— a strong showing in the early contests that contributes to voter support in subsequent ones. Nobody—not the press, not donors, not the voters—has an interest in candidates who are far back in the pack.

The race starts with stand-alone single contests in Iowa, New Hampshire, Nevada, and South Carolina but then broadens to include days on which multiple states hold their contests. Money is a key factor at this point. Candidates need money to buy the televised ads and hire the staff to run a multi-state campaign. In 2020, Biden and his main Democratic rival, Senator Bernie Sanders, each spent more than $200 million on their nominating campaigns. But money is not everything, as billionaire and former New York mayor Michael Bloomberg discovered in his quest for the 2020 Democratic nomination. Bloomberg spent nearly $500 million of his own money and ended up with little to show for it. Biden and Sanders had a huge edge over Bloomberg in the amount of news coverage (so-called free media) that they received, and it gave their campaigns a level of credibility that paid advertising alone cannot buy.[16]

In theory, a presidential nominating race could unfold in a way in which no candidate is able to secure a majority of delegates by the time of the national convention. In that case, bargaining and negotiation at the convention would determine which contender received the party's nomination. In practice, nominating races have had a winnowing effect whereby the strongest candidate gradually accumulated a majority of the delegates before the convention began. The last time that a nominee wasn't picked in advance was 1952, when, as it happened, both the Republican nominee (Dwight D. Eisenhower) and the Democratic nominee (Adlai Stevenson) were chosen in brokered conventions.

Q: Every election process has features that favor certain types of candidates over others. Which types of candidates benefit from the way presidential nominees are chosen?

ASK YOURSELF: How much does name recognition in advance of the race affect a candidate's chances? How about the ability to raise campaign funds? Support from party leaders? A candidate's qualifications to hold the nation's highest office? Whether a candidate has the backing of a particular group of voters, such as Hispanics, white evangelical Christians, or young adults?

STAFFING THE PRESIDENCY

As the policy responsibilities of the presidency have expanded and as the executive bureaucracy has grown in size in response to heightened demands on the federal government (see Chapter 13), the staffing of the presidency has increased greatly. When Theodore Roosevelt was president, he had a personal secretary and a handful of assistants. There was no White House Communication Office available to Roosevelt, or even a presidential press secretary.

All of that has changed. Today's presidents are assisted by a huge staff, one that is so large, in fact, that it challenges presidents' ability to control what's done in their name.

The Executive Office of the President (EOP)

The key staff organization is the **Executive Office of the President (EOP)**, created by Congress in 1939 to provide the president with the staff necessary to coordinate the activities of the executive branch.[17] The EOP has since become the command center of the presidency. The EOP includes a number of units, including the White House Office (WHO), which consists of the president's closest personal advisers; the Office of Management and Budget (OMB), which consists of experts who formulate and administer the federal budget (see Chapter 13); the National Security Council (NSC), which advises the president on foreign and military affairs; and the National Economic Council (NEC), which assists the president on economic policy.

Most EOP units are staffed by specialists, including economists, legal analysts, and policy experts. The National Security Council illustrates the policy support that a president gets from units within the EOP. Headed by the national security advisor, who is appointed by and has an office near the president, the NSC has a staff of roughly 400 people, many of whom are foreign or defense policy experts. The NSC gathers information and receives guidance from the State, Defense, and Intelligence Agencies in order to provide the president with precise assessments of national security threats and with plausible options when the need for policy action exists.

A central EOP unit is the White House Office (WHO). It includes the Communications Office, the Office of the Press Secretary, and the Office of Legislative Affairs. As these labels suggest, the WHO consists of the president's personal assistants, including top political advisers and press agents. These individuals tend to be skilled at developing political strategy and communicating with the public, the media, and other officials. Because of their close relationship with the president, they are among the most influential individuals in Washington.

The Vice President

The vice president holds a separate elective office from the president but, in practice, is part of the presidential team. Indeed, presidents handpick the vice president. At the national conventions that nominate the parties' presidential candidates, the delegates defer to the nominee's choice of a vice presidential candidate. In the 2020 election, Donald Trump stayed with Mike Pence, whom he had picked to run with him in 2016. Joe Biden selected California senator Kamala Harris as his running mate. Of black and South Asian descent, Harris was the first person of either descent to be nominated for the vice presidency by a major party.

Because the Constitution assigns no executive authority to the office, the vice president's duties within the administration are determined by the president. At an earlier time, presidents largely ignored their vice presidents, who did not even have an office in the White House. A number of leading politicians, including Daniel Webster and Henry Clay, declined the chance to become vice president. Said Webster, "I do not propose to be buried until I am really dead."[18]

The vice presidency is a separately elected office. However, because the Constitution assigns it no authority other than to serve as president of the Senate and to cast a Senate vote only in case of a tie, the duties of the vice president are determined by the president. Recent presidents have assigned significant responsibilities to their vice presidents. Pictured here is Kamala Harris who is expected to be a close political and policy advisor to President Joe Biden, a role that he played as Barack Obama's vice president. (Paul Kitagaki Jr./ZUMA Wire/Alamy Stock Photo.)

When Jimmy Carter assumed the presidency in 1977, he redefined the office by assigning important duties to his vice president and relocating him to an office in the White House, a practice followed by every president since then. Trump assigned Vice President Mike Pence the job of strengthening the administration's international ties, which included numerous trips abroad. Then, in 2020, Pence was placed in charge of the largest challenge that the Trump administration had faced. He headed the task force responsible for coordinating the federal government's response to the COVID-19 pandemic. That position placed him at times in the uncomfortable position of promoting practices such as the use of face masks that conflicted with what President Trump was saying.

The Cabinet and Agency Appointees

The heads of the 15 executive departments, such as the Department of Defense and the Department of Agriculture, constitute the president's **cabinet**. They are appointed by the president, subject to confirmation by the Senate. Although the cabinet once served as the president's major advisory group, it has not played this role in nearly a century. As issues have grown in complexity, presidents have increasingly relied on presidential advisers for advice rather than seeking it from the cabinet as a whole. Nevertheless, cabinet members, as heads of major departments, are important figures in any administration. The president selects them for their prominence in politics, business, government, or the professions.[19] In every administration, a few of them, usually the attorney general or the secretary of state, defense, or treasury, become trusted advisers.

The responsibilities of the secretary of state provide an example of the key role played by cabinet officers. As head of the State Department, the secretary's duties include advising the president on foreign policy, overseeing the work of U.S. ambassadors, representing the United States in meetings with foreign leaders, participating as the U.S. representative in international conferences, and protecting U.S. citizens living abroad. During their tenure, recent secretaries of state have visited about 100 countries and traveled roughly a million miles in doing so.[20]

Although presidents rely on all of the cabinet departments, they work particularly closely with the departments of State and Defense (as well as the intelligence agencies). Other departments are sometimes more responsive to Congress than to the president. The Department of Agriculture, for example, relies more heavily on the support of farm-state senators and representatives than on the president's backing. The defense, diplomatic, and intelligence agencies are different. Their missions closely parallel the president's constitutional roles as commander in chief and chief diplomat.

In addition to cabinet secretaries, the president appoints the heads and top deputies of federal agencies and commissions, as well as the nearly 200 ambassadors. There are more than 2,000 full-time presidential appointees, a much larger number than are appointed by the chief executive of any other democracy.[21] About a third of these appointees (including ambassadors and agency heads, but not the president's personal advisers) are subject to Senate confirmation.

The Problem of Control

Although the president's appointees are a major asset, their large number poses a control problem for the president. President Truman kept a wall chart in the Oval Office that listed the more than 100 officials who reported directly to him. He often told visitors, "I cannot even see all of these men, let alone actually study what they are doing."[22] Since Truman's time, the number of bureaucratic agencies has more than doubled, compounding the problem of presidential control over subordinates.[23]

The president's problem is most severe in the case of appointees who work in the departments and agencies. Their offices are located outside the White House, and their loyalty is sometimes split between their commitment to the president and their commitment to the agency they head. In 2018, President Trump fired Attorney General Jeff Sessions, who had recused himself from overseeing the Justice Department's investigation into links between Russia and Trump's 2016 presidential campaign. When Trump pressured Sessions to unrecuse himself and halt the investigation, Sessions refused, citing Justice Department rules. Calling Sessions "disgraceful" and "very weak," Trump replaced him with a critic of the investigation.[24]

Lower-level appointees within the departments and agencies pose a different type of control problem. The president rarely, if ever, sees them, and many are political novices (most have less than two years of government or policy experience). They sometimes come to side with the agency in which they work because they depend on the agency's career bureaucrats for advice and information.

In short, the modern presidential office is a mixed benefit. Although presidential appointees enable presidents to extend their influence into every executive agency, these appointees do not always act in ways that serve the president's interest. (The subject of presidential control of the executive branch is discussed further in Chapter 13.)

Presidents' control of the executive branch takes place largely through the people that they appoint to head the executive agencies. Most appointees act as the president expects, but some do not. In 2018, President Trump fired Jeff Sessions, his attorney general, after Sessions refused to halt the Justice Department's investigation into links between Russia and Trump's 2016 presidential campaign. (Mark Reinstein/Shutterstock)

BRIDGING THE POWER GAP

Presidents operate in a system of divided powers, and their formal authority is not substantial enough to meet the broad range of domestic and foreign policy challenges that they're expected to address.[25] A president can propose a legislative initiative, but any such proposal is little more than words on paper if Congress, which has lawmaking authority, fails to agree. Most executive actions, such as the carrying out of the president's foreign policy, also depend on the cooperation of others. Presidents can threaten and plead, but, in the end, they need the cooperation of others to achieve their goals. As one analyst observed, the powers of the president "fall well short of the tasks expected to be performed and the challenges to be faced."[26]

Nevertheless, presidents have ways to bridge some of the gap between the formal authority of their office and what's expected of them. The same two features of the presidency—a national constituency and singular authority—that have enabled them to claim national leadership also can enable them to build the support they need.

Agenda Setter: The Bully Pulpit

President Theodore Roosevelt described the presidency as a **bully pulpit**, by which he meant it offered a platform from which to shape the nation's agenda. Presidents are the center of national attention, giving them an unrivaled opportunity to define what is at issue at any given moment. The president, in fact, gets more news coverage than all of the members of Congress combined.[27]

Every communication breakthrough of the past half century has enlarged the bully pulpit. Franklin Roosevelt used the new medium of radio for "fireside chats," in which he calmed Americans' fears of the Great Depression and told them what he was doing to put them back to work. Telegenic John F. Kennedy popularized the televised press conference as a way to speak directly to Americans about issues of the moment. Donald Trump turned social media into an instrument of everyday governing. In his first year in office alone, he sent out several thousand tweets on everything from his admiration for Vladimir Putin to his disdain for Hillary Clinton. And most of his tweets, in one way or another, made their way into the news. Trump remarked that, within "two seconds" of sending a tweet, it's "breaking news."[28]

Presidents' agenda-setting capacity is a source of power. Dozens of policy problems exist at any given time, and only those that catch Congress's attention have a chance of making it into law. For weeks in 2019, Trump demanded that Congress allocate the funds needed to build a wall the length of the nation's southern border. It dominated the news and consumed debate in Congress. In the end, Trump failed to convince Congress to appropriate the money, which illustrates a limit on the bully pulpit. Presidents' ability to focus attention on issues is no guarantee that others will do what's being asked of them.[29]

It is also the case that presidents don't fully control their message. The journalists who cover the White House are adept at putting their own spin on what is said, and they tend to play up the negative aspects. Every president since Ronald Reagan, Republican and Democratic, has received more negative than positive news coverage.[30] Even President Trump's tweets didn't arrive unfiltered. A study found that about 1 percent of those who saw a Trump tweet saw it through his Twitter feed; the rest of them heard about it through a news report.[31]

The Permanent Campaign

Except for their constitutional authority, few things are more important to presidents' success than their public support. President Woodrow Wilson said it clearly: "Let [the president] win the admiration and confidence of the people

F A K E
or
F A C T

Detecting Misinformation

Are the News Media Politically Biased?

The traditional news media—the nation's daily papers and broadcast television networks—claim that they report the news in a fair and unbiased way. Some analysts and many Americans don't believe it, claiming instead that they have a liberal bias.[32] President Trump was among the critics, having labeled the traditional press as the "liberal media," "Democratic media," and "left-wing media."

Official White House Joyce N. Boghosian

Is that claim fact, or is it fake?

Scholars have found evidence of a liberal slant, although on a much smaller scale than claimed.[33] Nor is it true that liberals routinely get better coverage. In the 2016 presidential campaign, for example, Hillary Clinton's coverage was 62 to 38 percent negative to positive, while Donald Trump's was 56 percent negative to 44 percent positive.[34] And, until Trump became president, the president with the worst coverage had been a Democrat. Bill Clinton's coverage was negative during every quarter of his eight-year presidency.[35]

As the examples suggest, the real bias of the traditional press is a negative one.[36] The news turned sour at the time of Watergate and has stayed that way. Congressional coverage, for example, has been steadily negative since the 1970s, regardless of which party has controlled Congress or how much or little was accomplished.[37] The traditional media's negativity helps explain why they are perceived as biased. Research indicates that partisans tend to see negative news stories about the other party as accurate and negative stories about their party as biased.[38] It is not surprising, then, that Democrats during Bill Clinton's presidency thought that the television networks favored the Republicans, while Republicans during George W. Bush's presidency thought that the networks favored the Democrats. Such findings do not mean that the traditional media are unbiased, but they do indicate that some of the perceived bias is in the eye of the beholder.[39]

and no other single voice will easily overpower him." During his first two years in office, when President George W. Bush was buoyed by public support resulting from his handling of the September 11th terrorist attacks, Congress enacted 17 of his major initiatives, the second highest total in such a short period among post World War II presidents.[40] But congressional opposition mounted as Bush's popularity fell in response to a deteriorating economy and a worsening of the Iraq conflict. He had few legislative successes in subsequent years and several notable failures, including the rejection by Congress of his efforts to reform Social Security and immigration.

Presidents' efforts to maintain public support have blurred the line between campaigning and governing, resulting in what has come to be known as the **permanent campaign**.[41] The emergence of an advertising style of governing occurred when, in response to changes in the presidential nominating process, presidential hopefuls began to build their campaigns around rallies, the media, and polling.[42] That approach carried over into the presidency. When Jimmy Carter was elected in 1976, his pollster, Patrick Caddell, advised him that "governing with public approval requires a continuing political campaign."[43]

It has been estimated that presidents now spend nearly half of their time preparing for and pitching their messages, a process that political scientist Samuel Kernell calls "going public."[44] Bill Clinton went so far as to have his pollster ask respondents where he should vacation. During his first three years in office, George W. Bush took more than 400 trips within the United States, predominantly to states that were a key to his reelection.[45] Donald Trump took the permanent campaign to its highest level yet with his daily tweets, campaign-style rallies, and a social media advertising campaign that began during his first year in office.[46]

There is a risk in presidents' relentless pursuit of public support. It can lead them to seek options that provide immediate advantage, as opposed to what might work best for them in the long run. As one observer put it, the danger is that a president will "never stop campaigning long enough to govern."[47] It's also the case that there is a limit to the ability of presidents to control their image. Difficult policy problems and adverse developments at home or abroad invariably cut away at a president's popularity. More than half of post–World War II presidents have left office with a **presidential approval rating** of less than 50 percent (see Table 12-2). Bill Clinton is the only one who finished above 50 percent and had a higher rating at the end than during his first year.

Chief Legislator and Party Leader

As the center of national attention, presidents can start to believe that their ideas should prevail over those of Congress. This belief invariably gets a

HOW THE 50 STATES DIFFER

CRITICAL THINKING THROUGH COMPARISONS

The Permanent Campaign

The line between electioneering and governing has blurred, so much so that presidents devote a large amount of their time to activities once associated with election campaigns. An indicator is the frequency with which presidents travel to electorally competitive states. As the map shows, in Donald Trump's first three years as president, he was a more frequent visitor (five or more visits) to states where the margin of victory in the 2016 presidential election was 10 percentage points or less than he was to states where the victory margin was larger. He was a frequent visitor to nearly 60 percent of the more competitive states but only about 25 percent of the less competitive ones. And several of the less competitive states that he did visit frequently were ones where he had a personal reason for doing so, including his home state, New York, and Vice President Mike Pence's home state, Indiana.

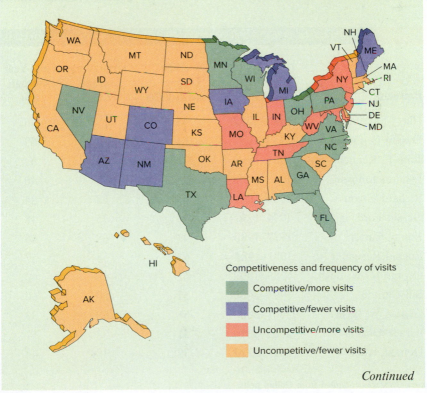

Competitiveness and frequency of visits

- ■ Competitive/more visits
- ■ Competitive/fewer visits
- ■ Uncompetitive/more visits
- ■ Uncompetitive/fewer visits

Continued

Q: The importance of the competitive states in a presidential election rests on the fact that the states, with the exception of Maine and Nebraska, give all of their electoral votes (the unit rule) to the state's popular vote winner. What would be the result if states instead allocated their electoral votes in proportion to each candidate's share of the state's popular vote?

A: The change would affect which states got the most attention. Particularly important would be populous states, like California, Texas, New York, Illinois, and Florida. A large number of electoral votes are at stake in these states, and a shift in the percentage of the vote toward one side would affect the allocation of the states' electoral votes.

president into trouble. Jimmy Carter had not held national office before he was elected president in 1976 and lacked a sense of how Washington operates.[48] Soon after taking office, Carter cut from his budget a large number of public works projects that he regarded as a waste of taxpayers' money, ignoring the interest of members of Congress in getting federally funded

table 12-2 | PERCENTAGE OF PUBLIC EXPRESSING APPROVAL OF PRESIDENT'S PERFORMANCE

President	Years in Office	Average During Presidency (%)	First-Year Average (%)	Final-Year Average (%)
Harry S Truman	1945–1952	41	63	35
Dwight D. Eisenhower	1953–1960	64	74	62
John F. Kennedy	1961–1963	70	76	62
Lyndon Johnson	1963–1968	55	78	40
Richard Nixon	1969–1974	49	63	24
Gerald Ford	1974–1976	46	75	48
Jimmy Carter	1977–1980	47	68	46
Ronald Reagan	1981–1988	53	58	57
George H. W. Bush	1989–1992	61	65	40
Bill Clinton	1993–2000	57	50	60
George W. Bush	2001–2008	51	68	33
Barack Obama	2009–2016	51	58	51
Donald Trump	2017–2020	39	38	44

Source: Averages compiled from Gallup polls.

projects for their states and districts. Carter's action set the tone for a conflict-ridden relationship with Congress.

Congress is a constituency that presidents must court if they expect to get its support. Political scientist Richard Neustadt concluded that presidential power, at base, is "the power to persuade."[49] Like any singular notion of presidential power, Neustadt's view has limits. Presidents at times can appeal directly to the American people as a means of pressuring Congress. They can also pressure Congress with the threat to veto legislation. Congress can seldom muster the two-thirds majority in each chamber required to override a **presidential veto**, so the threat can make Congress bend to the president's demands. However, as Neustadt noted, the veto is as much a sign of presidential weakness as it is a sign of strength because it arises when Congress refuses to accept the president's ideas.[50] President Trump's failed effort to get Congress to fully fund his request for a wall along the length of the U.S.–Mexico border is a case in point. When Congress was debating a comprehensive spending bill, Trump threatened a veto if it didn't include funding for the wall. When the Republican-controlled Congress defied the president and passed the bill without full funding, Trump begrudgingly signed it, saying that it included other things that he wanted. But he didn't hide his displeasure. "There are a lot of things that I'm unhappy about in this bill," he said.[51]

The reality is that every president needs Congress's support to get policies enacted into law.[52] Although the president gets most of the attention, Congress has lawmaking authority, and presidents need its help. Presidents can cajole members of Congress but have no way to force them to act. President Truman expressed the dilemma in colorful terms: "The people can never understand why the President does not use his supposedly great power to make 'em behave. Well, all the President is, is a glorified public relations man who spends his time flattering, kissing and kicking people to do what they are supposed to do anyway."[53]

Presidents acquire leverage with Congress from their role as **party leader**. As their party's highest elected official, presidents are their party's chief policy advocate. Members of Congress from the president's party expect policy leadership from the president and have a stake in helping the president succeed. Their careers are at risk if the president fails. Since World War II, the largest midterm congressional election losses for the president's party have come when the president's approval rating has been low.

The interdependence of the president and congressional members of the same party has increased as a result of party polarization. In the bipartisan era that existed after World War II, a president could expect to attract a reasonable amount of support from members of the opposing party on most

The State of the Union address, delivered annually in January by the president to the full Congress, symbolizes the president's dependence on Congress. As in the State of the Union, the president can propose legislation, but, in the end, Congress alone has the power to make laws and thereby decides whether the policies that the president wants take effect. Shown here is President John F. Kennedy delivering his 1963 State of the Union address. Behind him to the left in the photo is Vice President Lyndon Johnson, who would become president when Kennedy was assassinated on November 22, 1963. (*Source:* Cecil Stoughton. White House Photographs. John F. Kennedy Presidential Library and Museum, Boston)

legislative issues. That's not true today, making it difficult for presidents to lead when the opposing party controls one or both houses of Congress. There is often little that they can offer that would get Congress to embrace their initiatives.[54] When Republicans took control of the House in Obama's third year in office, his legislative agenda came to a virtual standstill. Republican House Speaker John Boehner said of Obama's agenda "We're going to do everything—and I mean everything we can do—to kill it, stop it, slow it down, whatever we can." Democrats reciprocated when they took control of the House at the start of Trump's third year in office.

Going It Alone

When rebuffed by Congress, presidents sometimes try to go it alone, pushing the limits of their formal authority to achieve what they can. They have important

P A R T Y
POLARIZATION

Conflicting Ideas

President of All the People, or Only Those from the Same Party?

Americans have been increasingly divided in their opinion of the president's performance. As would be expected, Democrats are more likely to approve of the performance of a Democratic president and disapprove of that of a Republican president, while the reverse is true of Republicans. However, as indicated by Gallup polls, the gap in Democrats' and Republicans' opinions has widened in recent years. During the three-decade period from Harry Truman's presidency in the late 1940s to Jimmy Carter's in the late 1970s, the difference between the presidential approval levels of Republicans and Democrats averaged roughly 35 percent. The difference now exceeds 80 percent, as can be seen in the accompanying figure. As two *Washington Post* reporters said, "We are simply living in an era in which Democrats dislike a Republican president (and Republicans dislike a Democratic one) even before he has taken a single official action."

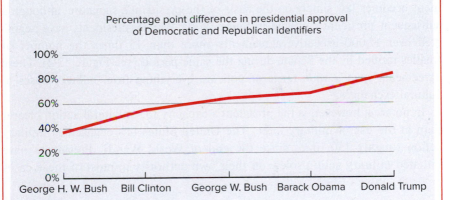

Percentage point difference in presidential approval
of Democratic and Republican identifiers

Q: Why has the partisan approval gap widened?

A: The reasons are many, but one of them is that Democrats and Republicans are now further apart in their opinions on controversial policy issues. When it comes to these issues, presidents typically take positions that are in line with the prevailing view in their party. As a result, their positions please most of their party's followers while displeasing, even angering, most of those in the other party.

powers that they can invoke unilaterally, all of which have a valid purpose. It's only when they stretch them to the limit that they run into trouble with Congress or the courts.

Executive Action   One way presidents can act on their own is through the use of an **executive order**, which is a presidential directive that implements or interprets a law passed by Congress. Such orders must occur within the context of a law and cannot violate its provisions. During the 2020 COVID-19 outbreak, for example, Trump issued an executive order based on the Defense Production Act that directed the production of ventilators and other medical supplies. Presidents have issued about 75 such orders on average each year.[55]

Presidents have even broader authority to act on their own when it comes to foreign policy. They have, for example, the power to make treaty-like arrangements with other countries. In 1937, the Supreme Court ruled that **executive agreements**—which are formal agreements that presidents make on their own with foreign nations—are legally binding as long as they do not conflict with the Constitution or laws enacted by Congress.[56] A treaty requires Senate approval and cannot normally be voided by the president. In contrast, an executive agreement becomes law simply on the basis of the president's signature, although a subsequent president can void it. Since World War II, presidents have negotiated over 17,000 executive agreements—more than 15 times the number of treaties ratified by the Senate during the same period (see Figure 12-2). These agreements span a wide range of policies, everything from military bases to cultural exchanges.[57]

In no area, however, is the president's capacity for unilateral action clearer than in the use of military force. The United States has engaged in military action roughly 150 times since the end of World War II. Presidents have initiated military action solely on their own authority in most of these cases

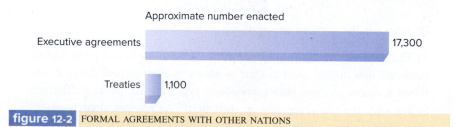

Approximate number enacted

Executive agreements   17,300

Treaties   1,100

figure 12-2   FORMAL AGREEMENTS WITH OTHER NATIONS

In the past eight decades, presidents have signed over 17,000 executive agreements with other countries—more than 15 times the number of treaties ratified by the Senate during the same period. Treaties require a two-thirds vote of the Senate for ratification. Executive agreements require only the signature of the president. (*Source:* U.S. Department of State. Figure based on the 1939–2013 period.)

and, in some of them, have hidden their plans from Congress until they were operational. When President Ronald Reagan ordered the invasion of Grenada in 1983, he waited until after the troops were on their way to inform congressional leaders. Speaker of the House Tip O'Neill was among those briefed by Reagan. "We weren't asked for advice," O'Neill said, "we were informed what was taking place."[58] Other members of Congress learned of the invasion when they woke in the morning to news reports saying that U.S. marines had landed in Grenada and were engaged in heavy fighting with Cuban troops stationed there.

Impeachment   Unilateral action can enable presidents to achieve their goals, but it comes at a cost if widely seen as an abuse of presidential power. On rare occasions, presidents have pursued their goals so zealously that Congress has taken steps to curb their use of power.

Congress's ultimate sanction is its constitutional authority to impeach and remove the president from office. The House of Representatives decides by majority vote whether the president should be impeached (placed on trial),

Pictured here is a House committee hearing into whether President Donald Trump abused the power of his office in pressuring Ukraine to announce an investigation of his political rival Joe Biden. The House approved two articles of impeachment, one for abuse of power and the other for obstruction of Congress for refusing to make documents and witnesses available to House investigators. Trump was acquitted of both impeachment articles in the ensuing trial in the Senate. (Samuel Corum/ Pool/Getty Images)

and the Senate conducts the trial and then votes on the president's case, with a two-thirds vote required for removal from office. In 1868, Andrew Johnson came within one Senate vote of being removed from office for his opposition to Congress's Reconstruction policies after the Civil War. In 1974, Richard Nixon's resignation halted congressional proceedings on the Watergate affair that almost certainly would have ended in his impeachment and removal from office. In 1998, the House of Representatives impeached President Clinton on grounds he had lied under oath about a sexual relationship with intern Monica Lewinsky. The Senate acquitted Clinton by a 55–45 vote. Most senators concluded that Clinton's behavior, while wrong, did not rise to the the level of "treason, bribery, or other high crimes and misdemeanors," which is what the Constitution defines as the grounds for removing a president from office.

By votes of 52–48 and 53–47, the Senate in 2020 reached the same conclusion in the impeachment trial of Donald Trump. The House had passed two articles of impeachment, one for abuse of power and one for obstruction of Congress in conjunction with Trump's withholding of military assistance to Ukraine in return for Ukraine initiating a corruption investigation against Joe Biden, Trump's political rival. The Senate votes split along party lines, with all of the Democratic senators voting for both articles of impeachment and all of the Republican senators voting against them, except for Utah's Mitt Romney, who voted to convict Trump on the charge of abuse of power.

Curbing Presidential Power   The gravity of impeachment action makes it an unsuitable basis for curbing presidential action except in rare instances. More often, Congress has responded with legislation aimed at limiting the president's discretion. An example is the Budget and Impoundment Control Act of 1974, which prohibits a president from indefinitely withholding funds that have been appropriated by Congress. The legislation grew out of President Nixon's practice of withholding funds from programs he disliked.

Congress's most ambitious effort to curb presidential discretion is the War Powers Act. During the Vietnam War, Presidents Johnson and Nixon misled Congress, supplying it with intelligence estimates that painted a falsely optimistic picture of the military situation. Having been told the war was being won, Congress regularly voted to provide the money to keep it going. However, congressional support changed abruptly in 1971 with publication in *The New York Times* of classified documents (the so-called Pentagon Papers) that revealed the White House had not been truthful about the war's progress.

In an effort to prevent future presidential wars, Congress in 1973 passed the War Powers Act. Nixon vetoed the measure, but Congress overrode his veto. The act does not prohibit the president from sending troops into combat but does require the president to consult with Congress, whenever feasible, before doing so and requires the president to inform Congress within 48 hours of the reasons for the military action. Unless Congress approves an extension, the War Powers Act requires hostilities to end within 60 days, although the president has an additional 30 days to safely withdraw the troops.

Presidents have claimed that the War Powers Act infringes on their constitutional power as commander in chief, but the Supreme Court has not ruled on the issue, leaving open the question of whether it constrains the president's war-making powers. Nevertheless, Congress has made it clear that it wants more say in America's use of military force. After President Trump ordered the targeted assassination of Iran's top military general in early 2020, the House and Senate passed separate nonbinding resolutions that opposed a war with Iran unless Congress authorized it.

Presidents also invite trouble when they push executive orders to the limits of the law or beyond. When Congress blocked one after another of his legislative initiatives, President Obama shifted to executive orders. "We can't wait for an increasingly dysfunctional Congress to do its job," Obama said. "Whenever they won't act, I will."[59] Obama proceeded to sign an executive order granting temporary deportation relief to roughly 4 million undocumented immigrants who had been in the United States for a substantial period of time and were leading productive lives. Obama's executive order had no clear basis in law and was invalidated by federal courts. President Trump suffered the same fate with an executive order that banned entry by foreign nationals from seven Muslim countries. The ban contravened laws that prohibit discrimination based on national origin or religion, including the Immigration and Nationality Act. The ban was later upheld by the Supreme Court after Trump modified it to bring it into compliance with the law.

If they act too aggressively, presidents can weaken their claim to national leadership when they go it alone. Presidents operate in a system of divided powers. Congress and the courts are co-equal branches of government and, however inconvenient presidents may find that to be, it's a reality they cannot avoid (see "How the U.S. Differs"). Dwight D. Eisenhower, whose personal integrity made him perhaps the most trusted president of the 20th century, had a keen awareness of a president's need to work with others. "I'll tell you what leadership is," he said. "It's persuasion, and conciliation, and education, and patience. It's long, slow, tough work."[60]

HOW THE U.S. DIFFERS

CRITICAL THINKING THROUGH COMPARISONS

Systems of Executive Leadership

The United States instituted a presidential system in 1789 as part of its constitutional checks and balances. This form of executive leadership was not copied in Europe. European democracies adopted parliamentary systems, in which the prime minister is both chief executive and head of the legislative branch.

The policy leadership of a president differs from that of a prime minister. As the head of a separate branch of government, presidents do not share executive authority but depend on Congress to get their legislative proposals enacted. Congress cannot always be counted on to act and, if controlled by members of the opposing party, will not act unless the legislation is something that they also want. In contrast, prime ministers share executive leadership with a cabinet, but, once agreement within the cabinet is reached, they typically have the support that is required to enact legislation.

Q: Which executive leadership do you think is preferable—a presidential system, in which the chief executive heads only the executive branch, or a parliamentary system, in which the chief executive heads both the executive and the legislative branches? Why?

FACTORS IN PRESIDENTIAL SUCCESS

All presidents are expected to provide national leadership, but not all presidents are equally skilled at it.[61] Strong presidents have typically had a clear sense of where they want to lead the country and an ability to communicate that vision effectively.[62] Ronald Reagan had it, which helped him alter the direction of domestic and foreign policy. Jimmy Carter lacked it. In what was arguably the most important speech of his presidency, Carter said that Americans were having "a crisis of confidence" and needed to be more positive. At a time when Americans were struggling with rising inflation and unemployment and wanted strong leadership, Carter chastised them for being pessimistic.

Presidents' success in achieving their policy goals depends on several factors, including whether circumstances are such that bold action is needed, the stage of the president's term, the nature of the issue, and the makeup of Congress.

The Force of Circumstance

During his first months in office and in the midst of the Great Depression, Franklin D. Roosevelt accomplished the most sweeping changes in domestic policy in the nation's history. Congress moved quickly to pass nearly every New Deal initiative he proposed. In 1964 and 1965, Lyndon Johnson pushed landmark civil rights and social welfare legislation through Congress on the strength of the civil rights movement, the legacy of the assassinated President Kennedy, and large Democratic majorities in the House and Senate. When Ronald Reagan assumed the presidency in 1981, inflation and high unemployment had greatly weakened the national economy and created a mood for change, enabling Reagan to persuade Congress to enact some of the largest taxing and spending changes in history.

From presidencies such as these has come the popular impression that presidents unilaterally decide national policy. However, each of these presidencies was marked by a special set of circumstances—a decisive election victory that gave added force to the president's leadership, a compelling national problem that convinced Congress and the public that bold presidential action was needed, and a president who was mindful of what was expected and pursued policies consistent with that expectation.[63]

When conditions are favorable, the power of the presidency is remarkable. The problem for most presidents is that they serve at a time when conditions are not conducive to ambitious policies. Political scientist Erwin Hargrove suggests that presidential influence depends largely on circumstance.[64] Some presidents serve in periods when resources are scarce or when important problems are surfacing in American society but have not yet reached a critical stage. Such situations work against the president's efforts to accomplish significant policy changes. In 1994, reflecting on budget deficits and other constraints beyond his control, President Bill Clinton said he had no choice but "to play the hand that history had dealt."

Every president has to deal with developments that they can only partially control, if at all. The economy is among them. Over the years, economic conditions have had the most impact on the president's popularity. When the economy is strong and growing, presidents' approval ratings are much higher on average than when the economy is weak or trending downward.[65] The importance of the economy to a president's standing is also apparent in the fact that, when the economy is strong, incumbent presidents nearly always win reelection. When the economy is weak, incumbents do not fare nearly as well. Gerald Ford, Jimmy Carter, and the first President Bush all lost their reelection bids as their popularity plummeted during a dip in the economy.

The irony, of course, is that presidents do not have all that much control over the economy. If they did, they would make sure the economy was strong when the time came to run for reelection. That fact says a lot about the American presidency. It's a powerful office, but much of what happens during a president's watch is beyond the president's control. All presidents seek greatness. Only a few achieve it.

The Stage of the President's Term

If conditions conducive to great accomplishments occur irregularly, every president has favorable moments. Most newly elected presidents enjoy a **honeymoon period** during which Congress, the press, and the public anticipate initiatives from the Oval Office and are particularly predisposed to support them. Even a few months can make a difference. Political scientist Paul Light found that presidents are twice as likely to get bills through Congress in the first half of their first year in office than in the second half.[66]

Most presidents propose more new programs in their first year in office than in any subsequent year.[67] Later in their terms, the momentum of their election is gone, and sources of opposition will have emerged. Even successful presidents, like Johnson and Reagan, have had weak records in their final years. Franklin D. Roosevelt began his presidency with a remarkable period of achievement—the celebrated "Hundred Days"—that he didn't duplicate at any time later during his four terms as president.

An irony of the presidency, then, is that presidents are often most powerful when they are least experienced—during their first months in office. As a result, these months can be times of risk as well as times of opportunity. The slow start to Donald Trump's presidency owed in part to his inexperience in government. He didn't understand, for instance, the full importance of America's traditional military alliances. He wavered on the nation's commitment to NATO and, though he eventually announced his support of NATO, his remarks infuriated European leaders. Even with a Republican majority in the House and Senate, Trump did not get a major legislative initiative enacted until the tail end of his first year in office, when Congress passed the 2017 Tax Cut and Jobs Act.

The Nature of the Issue: Foreign or Domestic

In the 1960s, political scientist Aaron Wildavsky wrote that the nation has only one president but two presidencies: one domestic and one foreign.[68] Wildavsky noted that, after World War II, Congress had enacted almost twice as many presidential proposals in the foreign policy area as in the domestic policy area. Wildavsky's finding is now regarded as a product of the postwar era, a time when Republican and Democratic leaders were agreed on the need to contain Soviet communism and strengthen America's global diplomatic, military, and economic position (see Chapter 17). Today, presidents' legislative success in the foreign policy area is affected by many of the same factors that affect their success in the domestic policy area, such as the partisan makeup of Congress and the strength of opposing lobby groups. As well, Congress in recent decades has passed legislation to place some restrictions on, for example, the executive branch's intelligence gathering activities and use of foreign aid.

Nevertheless, although the level of deference is not as high as during the post-war era, presidents still have an edge with foreign policy as compared to domestic policy. Upholding America's credibility abroad can lead Congress, however reluctantly, to back an agreement that a president has made with another country or countries.[69] And presidents have greater leverage over foreign policy resulting from their natural advantages in the area, including their superior access to relevant information. As a noted legal scholar observed, "The verdict of history, in short, is that the substantive content of American foreign policy is a divided power, with the lion's share falling usually, though by no means always, to the president."[70]

In some foreign policy areas, Congress has essentially ceded decision-making power to the president. Although the Constitution gives Congress the power to "regulate commerce with foreign nations," it has handed much of that power to the president. Through the 1962 Trade Expansion Act, the 1974 Trade Act, and the 1977 International Emergency Economic Powers Act, for example, the president has the power to impose tariffs and economic sanctions on other countries. Every president since then has found reason to make use of these authorizations. President Trump, for instance, used them to start a trade war with China, putting tariffs on everything from Chinese-made steel to Chinese-made television sets. Some members of Congress spoke out against the tariffs, but Congress took no formal action and federal courts upheld the tariffs as a valid application of authority granted to the president by Congress.[71]

The Makeup of Congress

Presidents have the power to focus the nation's attention on policy problems, but it's Congress that has the power to pass laws that address the problem. That's the reality of America's separation of powers, which at one time or another has frustrated every occupant of the White House. Theodore Roosevelt expressed the wish that he could "be the president and Congress too for just ten minutes." Roosevelt would then have had the power to enact as well as to propose legislation.

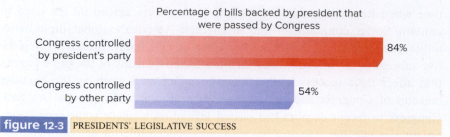

Percentage of bills backed by president that were passed by Congress

Congress controlled by president's party — 84%

Congress controlled by other party — 54%

figure 12-3 PRESIDENTS' LEGISLATIVE SUCCESS

Presidents can endorse legislation, but it takes Congress to enact it. Although presidents have had considerable success in getting congressional support for bills they have backed, they have fared much better when their party controlled Congress than when the other party controlled one or both chambers. (*Source:* Calculated by author from Congressional Quarterly reports from 1952-2020.)

For most presidents, the next best thing to being "Congress too" is having a Congress loaded with members of their own party. The sources of division within Congress are many. Legislators from urban and rural areas, wealthier and poorer constituencies, and different regions of the country often have conflicting policy views. To obtain majority support in Congress, the president must find ways to overcome these divisions.

No source of support is more important to presidential success than whether the president's party controls Congress. Because the president, Senate, and House are elected separately, presidents are not guaranteed to have a Congress controlled by their party. When it is, a situation known as *unified government,* presidents usually enjoy considerable legislative success (see Figure 12-3). When the other party controls one or both houses, a situation known as *divided government,* presidents have greater difficulty convincing Congress to follow their lead. During Trump's first two years in office, when Republicans controlled both the House and the Senate, 95 percent of the bills that he supported were enacted into law.[72] In 2019, with Democrats in control of the House, it dropped to 27 percent.[73] Clearly, presidential power depends significantly on which party has a numerical majority in Congress. As historian Arthur Schlesinger put it, "In the end, arithmetic is decisive."[74]

THE ILLUSION OF PRESIDENTIAL GOVERNMENT

Presidents strive to be the center of national attention. It's a key to their policy influence and ability to win the support of other leaders and the American people. However, by thrusting themselves into the limelight, presidents contribute to the public's belief that they are in charge of the national government, a perception that political scientist Hugh Heclo calls "the illusion of presidential government."[75] If presidents are as powerful as they project themselves to be, they will be held responsible for policy failures as well as policy successes.

Because the public's expectations are high, presidents tend to get too much credit when things go well and too much blame when things go badly. Therein rests an irony of the presidential office. More than from any constitutional grant, statute, or crisis,

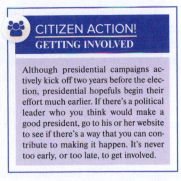

CITIZEN ACTION!
GETTING INVOLVED

Although presidential campaigns actively kick off two years before the election, presidential hopefuls begin their effort much earlier. If there's a political leader who you think would make a good president, go to his or her website to see if there's a way that you can contribute to making it happen. It's never too early, or too late, to get involved.

presidential power derives from the president's position as the sole official who can claim to represent the entire American public. However, because presidential power rests on a popular base, it erodes when public support declines. The irony is that the presidential office typically grows weaker as problems mount, which is the time when strong presidential leadership is most needed.[76]

SUMMARY

The presidency has become a much stronger office than the framers envisioned. The Constitution grants the president substantial military, diplomatic, legislative, and executive powers, and in each case the president's authority has increased measurably over the nation's history. Underlying this change is the president's position as the one leader chosen by the whole nation and as the sole head of the executive branch. These features of the office have enabled presidents to claim broad authority in response to the increased demands placed on the federal government by changing global and national conditions.

The responsibilities of the modern presidency require large numbers of advisers, policy experts, and managers. These staff members enable the president to extend control over the executive branch while providing the information necessary for policymaking. All recent presidents have discovered, however, that their control of staff resources is incomplete and that some things that others do on their behalf can work against what they are trying to accomplish.

Presidents operate in a system of divided powers, and their formal authority is not substantial enough to meet the demands placed on them. Nevertheless, they have ways to bridge the power gap. As the center of national attention, they have a "bully pulpit" from which to influence the nation's agenda. Their office also provides the basis for an ongoing effort (the permanent campaign) to generate public support for their initiatives. Then, too, members of Congress from the president's party look to the president for leadership, recognizing that the president's success can affect their reelection chances. Presidents also have some capacity "to go it alone." On their own authority, they can issue executive orders, forge executive agreements with other nations, and send troops into combat.

As sole chief executive and the nation's top elected leader, a president can always expect that his or her policy and leadership efforts will receive attention. However, other institutions, particularly Congress, have the authority to make presidential leadership effective. No president has come close to winning approval of all the programs he has placed before Congress, and presidents' records of success have varied considerably. The factors in a president's success include whether national conditions that require strong leadership from the White House are present, the stage of the president's term, and whether the president's party has a majority in Congress.

Presidential success ultimately rests on the backing of the American people. Recent presidents have made extensive use of the media to build public support for their programs, yet they have had difficulty maintaining that support throughout their terms of office. A major reason is that the public expects far more from its presidents than they can deliver.

CRITICAL THINKING ZONE

KEY TERMS

bully pulpit (*p. 358*)
cabinet (*p. 355*)
chief diplomat (*p. 346*)
chief executive (*p. 346*)
chief legislator (*p. 346*)
commander in chief (*p. 346*)
executive agreements (*p. 366*)
Executive Office of the President
 (EOP) (*p. 353*)

executive order (*p. 366*)
head of state (*p. 346*)
honeymoon period (*p. 372*)
limited presidency theory (*p. 348*)
party leader (*p. 363*)
permanent campaign (*p. 360*)
presidential approval rating (*p. 360*)
presidential veto (*p. 363*)
stewardship theory (*p. 348*)

APPLYING THE ELEMENTS OF CRITICAL THINKING

Conceptualizing: Define the *Whig theory* of the presidency and the *stewardship theory*. How did the increase in the federal government's policy responsibilities and the expanded role of the United States in world affairs contribute to the emergence of the powerful presidency suggested by the stewardship theory?

Synthesizing: Contrast the pre-1972 methods of selecting presidential nominees with the post-1972 method, noting particularly the public's increased role in the selection process.

Analyzing: Why is presidential power "conditional"—that is, why is it affected so substantially by circumstance, the nature of the issue, the makeup of Congress, and popular support? (The separation of powers should be part of your answer.)

EXTRA CREDIT

A Book Worth Reading: Richard E. Neustadt, *Presidential Power and the Modern Presidents* (New York: Free Press, 1990). A winner of multiple awards, this book is the classic analysis of presidential power. Although now somewhat dated in its arguments, it has had, as one leading political scientist put it, "a greater effect than any other book about a political institution."

A Website Worth Visiting: **www.ipl.org/div/potus** A site that profiles the nation's presidents, their cabinet officers, and key events during their time in office.

Design credit: (People, Flag, U.S., Globe, Vote Icons): McGraw-Hill Education; (Eagle): Feng Wei Photography/Moment/Getty Images; (Lincoln): Photographs in the Carol M. Highsmith Archive, Library of Congress, Prints and Photographs Division [LC-DIG-highsm-12542].

THE FEDERAL BUREAUCRACY: ADMINISTERING THE GOVERNMENT

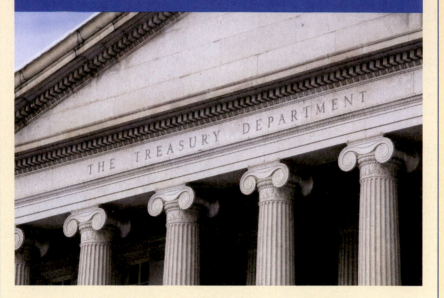

Ryan Rodrick Beiler/Shutterstock

> From a purely technical point of view, a bureaucracy is capable of attaining the highest degree of efficiency, and is in this sense formally the most rational known means of exercising authority over human beings.
>
> MAX WEBER[1]

Seeking to extend the success of its popular 737 jet airliner, Boeing produced the 737 MAX. It had a new software system, the Maneuvering Characteristics Augmentation System (MCAS), which was intended to stabilize the aircraft while in flight. Barely a year after the jet entered service in 2017, 189 people died when a 737 MAX crashed after taking off in Indonesia. Five months later, a second 737 MAX went down after taking off in Ethiopia, killing all 157 people on board. The U.S. government blamed the crashes on Boeing, ordering the grounding of MAX 737s until the faulty new software system could be fixed. The system had repeatedly pushed down the nose of the fated aircraft even as the pilots tried desperately to bring it up.

The government itself had an indirect hand in the crashes. Oversight of commercial aircraft is entrusted to the Federal Aeronautics Administration (FAA), which had given Boeing wide latitude in determining whether the 737 MAX met minimum FAA standards before certifying that it was safe to fly. The FAA pursued the policy even though an internal watchdog warned that it could lead Boeing to cut corners on safety tests. The FAA was also slow in following up on the cause of the first crash, even though the MCAS software was among the possibilities cited by Indonesian investigators.[2]

As with the FAA, government agencies are seldom in the headlines unless something goes wrong. Nor do federal agencies rank high in public esteem. Even though most Americans respond favorably to personal encounters with the federal bureaucracy (as, for example, when a senior citizen applies for Social Security), they have a low opinion of the bureaucracy as a whole. One poll found, for example, that roughly two-thirds of Americans see the bureaucracy as "inefficient and wasteful."[3]

Studies have found that the U.S. federal bureaucracy compares favorably to government bureaucracies elsewhere. "Some international bureaucracies," Charles Goodsell writes, "may be roughly the same [as the U.S. bureaucracy]

A 737 MAX sits at the Bangkok, Thailand, airport after 737 MAXs were grounded for safety reasons. It was a Lion Airways 737 MAX that crashed in Indonesia in 2018, the first fatal accident involving Boeing's newest airliner. Contributing to the disaster was the Federal Aeronautics Administration's lax oversight in certifying the safety of the 737 MAX. (Pataporn Kuanui/Shutterstock)

in quality of performance, but they are few in number."[4] The U.S. Postal Service, for example, has an on-time and low-cost record that few national postal services can match. On the other hand, high-level bureaucratic failures appear to be on the increase. Political scientist Paul Light documented a series of recent failures, including government's failure to properly assess intelligence relating to the terrorist attacks of September 11, 2001 and its failure to react in ways that would have saved lives when Hurricane Katrina devastated New Orleans in 2005.[5] More recently, the government was slow to respond after the COVID-19 coronavirus surfaced in China. If it had acted sooner, thousands of lives would have been saved.[6]

Whatever its performance level, the federal bureaucracy is essential. Ambitious programs such as space exploration, Social Security, interstate highways, and the postal service would be impossible without the federal bureaucracy. In fact, the bureaucratic form of organization is found wherever there is a need to manage large numbers of people and tasks. Its usefulness is clear from the fact that virtually every large private organization is also a bureaucracy, although such organizations typically operate by a different standard than do most public organizations. Efficiency is the chief goal of private bureaucracies but is only sometimes the goal of public bureaucracies. The most efficient way to administer government loans to college students, for instance, would be to give money to the first students who applied and then shut down the program when the money ran out. However, college loan programs, like many other government programs, operate on principles of fairness and need, which require that each application be judged on its merits.

In formal terms, **bureaucracy** is a system of organization and control that is based on three principles: hierarchical authority, job specialization, and formalized rules. These features are the reason bureaucracy, as a form of organization, is the most efficient means of getting people to work together on tasks of large magnitude. **Hierarchical authority** is a chain of command in which the officials and units at the top of a bureaucracy have authority over those in the middle, who in turn control those at the bottom. Hierarchy speeds action by reducing conflict over the power to make decisions. **Job specialization** refers to explicitly defined duties for each job position and a precise division of labor within the organization. Specialization yields efficiency because each individual concentrates on a particular job and becomes proficient at it. **Formalized rules** are the established procedures and regulations by which a bureaucracy conducts its operations. Formalized rules enable workers to make quick and consistent judgments because decisions are based on preset rules rather than on a case-by-case basis.

Noted German sociologist Max Weber (1864–1920) was the first scholar to systematically analyze the bureaucratic form of organization. Weber admired the bureaucratic form of organization for its efficiency but recognized that it carried a price. Bureaucrats' actions are dictated by position, specialty, and rule. In the process, they can become insensitive to circumstance. They often stick to the rules even when it's clear that bending them would produce better outcomes. "Specialists without spirit" was Weber's unflattering description of the bureaucratic mindset.[7]

This chapter examines both the need for bureaucracy and the problems associated with it. The chapter describes the bureaucracy's responsibilities, organizational structure, and management practices. The chapter also explains the "politics" of the bureaucracy. Although the three constitutional branches of government impose a degree of accountability on the bureaucracy, its sheer size confounds their efforts to control it fully. The chapter presents the following main points:

- *Bureaucracy is an inevitable consequence of complexity and scale.* Modern government could not function without a large bureaucracy. Through authority, specialization, and rules, bureaucracy provides a means of managing thousands of tasks and employees.

- *Bureaucrats naturally take an "agency point of view," seeking to promote their agency's programs and power.* They do this through their expert knowledge, support from clientele groups (those that benefit from the agency's programs), and backing by Congress or the president.

- *Although agencies are subject to oversight by the president, Congress, and the judiciary, bureaucrats exercise considerable power in their own right.*

ORIGIN AND STRUCTURE OF THE FEDERAL BUREAUCRACY

The federal bureaucracy was initially small (3,000 employees in 1800, for instance). The federal government's role was confined largely to defense and foreign affairs, currency and interstate commerce, and delivery of the mail. In the latter part of the 1800s, the bureaucracy began to grow rapidly in size, largely because economic growth was creating new demands on government. Farmers were among the groups clamoring for help, and in 1889 Congress created the Department of Agriculture. Business and labor interests also pressed their claims, and in 1903 Congress established the Department of Commerce and Labor. (A decade later, the department was split into separate commerce and labor departments.) The

NUMBER OF FULL-TIME FEDERAL EMPLOYEES

Despite the widespread view that the federal bureaucracy grows ever larger, the number of federal employees has been relatively stable since an expansion in the 1960s. One reason for the stability is improved technology. Many clerical tasks, for example, are now done with the help of computers. (*Source:* U.S. Bureau of the Census. Figure excludes federal grant and contract workers.)

biggest spurt in the bureaucracy's growth, however, took place in the 1930s. Franklin D. Roosevelt's New Deal included creation of the Securities and Exchange Commission (SEC), the Social Security Administration (SSA), the Federal Deposit Insurance Corporation (FDIC), the Tennessee Valley Authority (TVA), and numerous other federal agencies. Three decades later, Lyndon Johnson's Great Society initiatives, which thrust the federal government into policy areas traditionally dominated by the states, resulted in the creation of additional federal agencies, including the Department of Transportation and the Department of Housing and Urban Development.

Although the federal bureaucracy is sometimes portrayed as an entity that grows larger by the year, the facts say otherwise. Federal employment today is at roughly the same level that it was 40 years ago (see Figure 13-1), despite the fact that the U.S. population has increased greatly in size since then. Nevertheless, it is a large bureaucracy by any standard, particularly when the employment numbers include the several million workers who are hired through temporary federal grants and contracts, such as research scientists and highway construction workers.[8]

Types of Federal Agencies

At present, the U.S. federal bureaucracy has roughly 2.8 million full-time employees, who have responsibility for administering thousands of programs. The president and Congress get far more attention in the news, but the federal bureaucracy has a more direct impact on Americans' daily lives. It performs a wide range of functions; for example, it delivers the mail, oversees the national forests, administers Social Security, enforces environmental protection laws, maintains the country's defense systems, provides foodstuffs for school lunch programs, and regulates the stock markets.

The U.S. federal bureaucracy is organized along policy lines. One agency handles veterans' affairs, another specializes in education, a third is responsible for agriculture, and so on. No two units are exactly alike. Nevertheless, most of them take one of five forms: cabinet department, independent agency, regulatory agency, government corporation, or presidential commission.

The leading administrative units are the 15 **cabinet (executive) departments** (see Figure 13-2). Except for the Department of Justice, which is led by the attorney general, the head of each department is its secretary (for example,

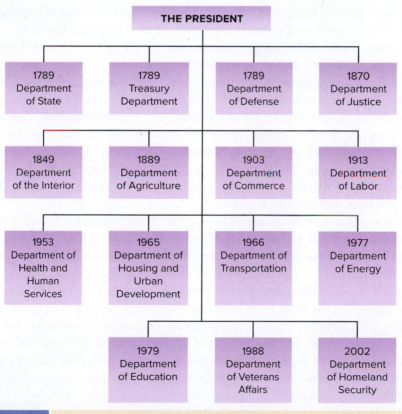

THE PRESIDENT

| 1789 Department of State | 1789 Treasury Department | 1789 Department of Defense | 1870 Department of Justice |

| 1849 Department of the Interior | 1889 Department of Agriculture | 1903 Department of Commerce | 1913 Department of Labor |

| 1953 Department of Health and Human Services | 1965 Department of Housing and Urban Development | 1966 Department of Transportation | 1977 Department of Energy |

| 1979 Department of Education | 1988 Department of Veterans Affairs | 2002 Department of Homeland Security |

figure 13-2   CABINET (EXECUTIVE) DEPARTMENTS

Each cabinet department is responsible for a general policy area and is headed by a secretary or, in the case of Justice, the attorney general, who serves as a member of the president's cabinet. Shown is each department's year of origin.

the secretary of defense), who also serves as a member of the president's cabinet. Cabinet departments vary greatly in their size and budgets. The smallest, with a mere 4,000 employees, is the Department of Education. The Department of Defense has the largest budget and workforce, with more than 700,000 civilian employees (apart from the nearly 1.4 million uniformed active service members). The Department of Health and Human Services has the second largest budget, most of which goes for Medicaid and Medicare payments (but not Social Security payments, which are handled by the Social Security Administration, an independent agency).

The newest cabinet-level agency is the Department of Homeland Security (DHS), which was created in 2002 in response to the terrorist attacks on New York and Washington on September 11, 2001. DHS has responsibility for coordinating domestic antiterrorism efforts, including securing the nation's borders, enhancing defenses against biological attacks, preparing emergency personnel (police, firefighters, and rescue workers) for their roles in responding to terrorist attacks, and coordinating efforts to stop domestic terrorism.[9] The U.S. Immigration and Customs Enforcement (ICE) agency is located within DHS and is charged with stopping illegal immigration.

Each cabinet department has responsibility for a general policy area, such as defense or law enforcement. This responsibility is carried out within each department by operating units that typically carry the label "bureau," "agency," "division," or "service." Indeed, the cabinet departments are themselves bureaucracies in that most of the work is done by their units. The Department of Justice, for example, has 13 operating units, including the Federal Bureau of Investigation (FBI), the Civil Rights Division, the Tax Division, and the Drug Enforcement Administration (DEA).

Independent agencies resemble the cabinet departments but typically have a narrower area of responsibility. They include organizations such as the Central Intelligence Agency (CIA) and the National Aeronautics and Space Administration (NASA). The heads of these agencies are appointed by and report to the president but are not members of the cabinet. Some independent agencies exist apart from cabinet departments because their placement within a department would pose symbolic or practical problems. NASA, for example, could be located in the Department of Defense, but such positioning would suggest that the space program exists for military purposes and not also for civilian purposes, such as space exploration and satellite communication.

The largest independent agency is the U.S. Postal Service. It has more than half a million career employees, which makes it larger than all of the cabinet departments except the Department of Defense. Established at the nation's

Fake or Fact?: Detecting Misinformation

Is There a "Deep State"?

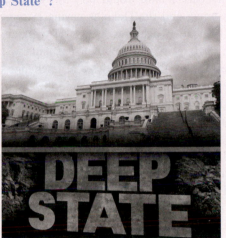

In recent years, the claim that the United States is run by a "deep state" has gained wide acceptance. The claim holds that high-ranking people in government agencies are able to control much of what government does, separate from the influence of the voters and elected officials. In a recent ABC News/*Washington Post* poll, respondents were asked whether they agreed that "military, intelligence, and government officials . . . secretly

Lightspring/Shutterstock

manipulate government policy." Half of the respondents agreed, while a third called the claim a "conspiracy theory," with the rest saying they were unsure. Republicans and Democrats were equally likely to believe in the deep state's existence, whereas young adults (ages 18–29) were the most likely (59 percent) to say the deep state is real, while senior citizens were the least likely (37 percent) to accept the claim.

Is that claim fact, or is it fake?

Investigations by journalists and others have failed to uncover any evidence of the deep state's existence. The origins of the claim would also lead one to question its validity. The idea of a deep state was initially pushed on the Internet by conspiracy theorists. Although the deep state claim is unfounded, it is accurate to say that the interests of career government officials are sometimes at odds with those of elected officials and the voters. Career bureaucrats are committed to their agencies' programs, funding, and mission, and they try to protect them even when such action runs counter to what the people's representatives are seeking to do.

founding, the postal service delivers a first-class letter for the same low price to any postal address in the United States, a policy made possible by its status as a government agency. If the postal service were a private firm, the price of a first-class stamp would vary by location, with remote areas of states such as Wyoming and the Dakotas paying extremely high rates.

Regulatory agencies have been created when Congress recognized a need for ongoing regulation of a particular economic activity. Examples of such agencies are the Securities and Exchange Commission (SEC), which oversees the stock and bond markets, and the Environmental Protection Agency (EPA), which regulates industrial pollution. In addition to their administrative function, regulatory agencies have a legislative function. They develop law-like regulations that regulated entities are required to follow. They also have a judicial function. They assess whether regulated entities are complying with legal requirements. They can impose fines and other penalties on entities that fail to comply. In 2017, for example, Volkswagen paid a $2.8 billion fine for use of illegal software to cheat on emissions tests in an effort to avoid compliance with the Clean Air Act.

Government corporations are similar to private corporations in that they charge for their services and are governed by a board of directors. However, government corporations receive federal funding to pay for some of their operating expenses, and their directors are appointed by the president with Senate approval. Government corporations include the Federal Deposit Insurance Corporation (FDIC), which insures personal savings accounts against bank failures, and the National Railroad Passenger Corporation (Amtrak), which provides passenger rail service.

Presidential commissions provide advice to the president. Some of them are permanent bodies; examples include the Commission on Civil Rights and the Commission on Fine Arts. Other presidential commissions are temporary. An example is the Presidential Commission on Law Enforcement and the Administration of Justice, which was created by President Trump in 2020 to study ways to build community trust in law enforcement officers.

Federal Employment

The nearly 3 million full-time civilian employees of the federal government include professionals who bring their expertise to the problems involved in governing a large and complex society, service workers who perform such tasks as delivering the mail, and middle and top managers who supervise the work of the federal agencies. Most civil servants are hired through the government's **merit system**, whereby they have to score high on a competitive exam (as in the case of postal service, civil service, and foreign service

HOW THE 50 STATES DIFFER

CRITICAL THINKING THROUGH COMPARISONS

The Size of State Bureaucracies

Although the federal bureaucracy is criticized as being "too big," it is smaller on a per-capita basis than every state bureaucracy. There is less than 1 federal employee for every 100 Americans. Illinois and Indiana, with roughly 1 state employee per 100 residents, have the smallest state bureaucracies. Hawaii, with more than 4 state employees per 100 residents, has the largest.

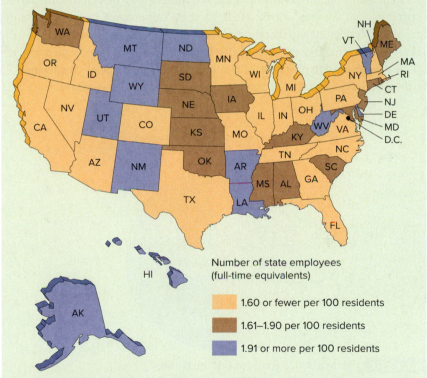

Number of state employees (full-time equivalents)

- 1.60 or fewer per 100 residents
- 1.61–1.90 per 100 residents
- 1.91 or more per 100 residents

Source: U.S. Bureau of Labor Statistics, 2020

Q: What typifies the states with larger per-capita bureaucracies?

A: In general, the less populous states, especially those that cover a large geographic area, have larger bureaucracies on a per-capita basis. This pattern reflects the fact that a state, whatever its population or area, must provide basic services such as highway maintenance and policing.

employees) or have specialized training (as in the case of lawyers, engineers, and scientists).*

The merit system is an alternative to the **patronage system**, which governed federal employment during much of the 19th century. Patronage was the post-election practice of filling administrative offices with people who had supported the winning party. Critics labeled it a **spoils system**—a device for awarding government jobs to friends and party hacks. However, as the federal government grew in size and complexity, the need for a more skilled workforce emerged. In 1883, Congress passed the Pendleton Act, which established a merit system for certain positions. By 1885, roughly 10 percent of federal positions were being filled on a merit basis. The proportion increased sharply when the Progressives championed the merit system as a way of eliminating partisan corruption (see Chapter 2). By 1920, as the Progressive Era was concluding, more than 70 percent of federal employees were merit appointees. Today, they make up more than 95 percent of the federal workforce (see Figure 13-3).[10]

The administrative objective of the merit system is **neutral competence**.[11] A merit-based bureaucracy is "competent" in the sense that employees are hired

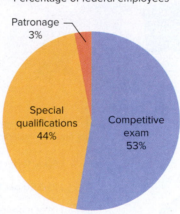

Percentage of federal employees

Patronage
3%

Special
qualifications
44%

Competitive
exam
53%

figure 13-3   HOW FEDERAL EMPLOYEES GOT THEIR JOBS

In the 19th century, most federal workers were patronage appointees. Today, only a small percentage get their jobs through that route. The great majority are merit appointees, having obtained federal employment either by placing high on a competitive civil service exam or by having specialized training, such as a medical or engineering degree. (*Source:* Estimated by author from Office of Personnel Management data.)

---

*The merit system is overseen by two independent agencies. The Office of Personnel Management supervises the hiring and job classification of federal employees. The Merit Service Protection Board hears appeals from career civil servants who have been fired or face other disciplinary action.

and retained on the basis of their ability, and it is "neutral" in the sense that employees are not partisan appointees and are expected to be of service to everyone, not just those who support the incumbent president. Although the merit system contributes to impartial and proficient administration, it has its own biases and inefficiencies. Career bureaucrats tend to place their agency's interests ahead of those of other agencies and typically oppose efforts to trim their agency's programs. They are not partisans in a Democratic or Republican sense, but they are partisans in terms of protecting their own agencies, as will be explained more fully later in the chapter.

The large majority of federal employees have a Graded Service (GS) job ranking. The regular civil service rankings range from GS-1 (the lowest rank) to GS-15 (the highest). College graduates who enter the federal service usually start at the GS-5 level, which provides an annual salary of roughly $28,000 for a beginning employee. With a master's degree, employees begin at level GS-9 with a salary of roughly $42,000 a year. Federal employees' salaries increase with rank and length of service, reaching the $100,000 to 150,000 range for those who attain the highest level (GS-15). Although higher-level federal employees are underpaid in comparison with their counterparts in the private sector, while those in some lower-level jobs are comparatively overpaid, federal workers receive better fringe benefits—including full health insurance, secure retirement plans, and substantial vacation time and sick leave—than do most private-sector employees.

Federal employees can form labor unions, but by law their unions have limited scope; the government has full control of job assignments, compensation, and promotion. Moreover, the Taft-Hartley Act of 1947 prohibits strikes by federal employees and permits the firing of striking workers. When federal air traffic controllers went on strike anyway in 1981, President Reagan fired them. There are also limits on the partisan activities of civil servants. The Hatch Act of 1939 prohibited them from holding key jobs in election campaigns. Congress relaxed this prohibition in 1993, although some high-ranking administrators are still barred from holding such positions.

THE BUDGETARY PROCESS

Of special importance to executive agencies is the **budgetary process**—the process through which annual federal spending and revenue decisions are made. It is no exaggeration to

CITIZEN ACTION!
GETTING INVOLVED

If you are considering a semester or summer internship, you might want to look into working for a federal, state, or local agency. Compared with legislative interns, executive interns are more likely to get paid and to be given significant duties. (Many legislative interns spend the bulk of their time answering phones or responding to mail.) Internship information can often be obtained through an agency's website. You should apply as early as possible; some agencies have application deadlines.

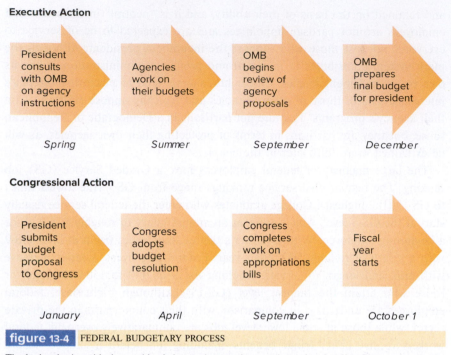

Executive Action

President consults with OMB on agency instructions → Agencies work on their budgets → OMB begins review of agency proposals → OMB prepares final budget for president

Spring — *Summer* — *September* — *December*

Congressional Action

President submits budget proposal to Congress → Congress adopts budget resolution → Congress completes work on appropriations bills → Fiscal year starts

January — *April* — *September* — *October 1*

figure 13-4   FEDERAL BUDGETARY PROCESS

The budget begins with the president's instructions to the agencies and ends when Congress enacts the budget. The entire process spans about 18 months. (*Source:* See Schick, Allen, *The Federal Budget: Politics, Policy, Process,* 3d ed., Washington, D.C.: Brookings Institution, 2007.)

say that agencies live and die by their budgets. No agency or program can exist without funding.

Agencies play an active role in the budgetary process, but the elected branches have final authority. The Constitution assigns Congress the power to tax and spend, but the president, as chief executive, also has a major role in determining the budget (see Chapter 12). The budgetary process involves give-and-take between Congress and the president as each tries to influence how federal funding will be distributed among various agencies and programs.[12] From beginning to end, the budgetary process lasts a year and a half (see Figure 13-4).

The President and Agency Budgets

The budgetary process begins in the executive branch when the president, in consultation with the Office of Management and Budget (OMB), establishes general budget guidelines. OMB is part of the Executive Office of the President (see Chapter 12) and takes its directives from the president. Hundreds of agencies are covered by the budget, and OMB uses the president's directives to issue guidelines for each agency's budget preparations. Each agency, for example, is assigned a budget ceiling that it cannot exceed in developing its budget proposal.

The agencies receive their guidelines in the spring and then work through the summer to create a detailed agency budget, taking into account their existing programs and new proposals. Agency budgets are then submitted to OMB in September for a full review, which invariably includes further consultation with each agency and the White House. OMB then finalizes the agency budgets and combines them into the president's budget proposal.

The agencies naturally seek additional funding for their programs, whereas OMB has the job of matching the budget to the president's priorities. However, the president does not have any real say over most of the budget, about two-thirds of which involves mandatory spending. This spending is required by law, as in the case of Social Security payments to retirees. The president has no authority to suspend or reduce such payments. Accordingly, OMB focuses on the one-third of the budget that involves discretionary spending, which includes spending in areas such as defense, foreign aid, education, national parks, space exploration, and highways. In reality, even a large part of this spending is not truly discretionary. No president would slash defense spending to almost nothing or cut off funding for the national parks. The president, then, works on the margins of the budget. In most policy areas, the president will propose a modest spending increase or decrease over the previous year.

Presidents occasionally take bolder action. In his first budget proposal, President Trump called for cutting funding for the State Department and the U.S. Agency for International Development by roughly 25 percent, a reflection of his belief that diplomacy was not the most effective way to advance America's global interests.

Congress and Agency Budgets

In January, the president's budget is submitted to Congress. During its work on the budget, the president's recommendations undergo varying degrees of change. Congress has constitutional authority over government spending, and its priorities are never exactly the same as the president's, even when the congressional majority is of the same political party. When it is of the opposite party, its priorities differ substantially from those of the president.

On reaching Congress, the president's budget proposal goes to the House and Senate budget committees. Their job is to recommend overall spending and revenue levels. Once approved by the full House and Senate, the levels are a constraint on the rest of Congress's work on the budget.

The House and Senate appropriations committees take over at this point. As with the executive branch, these committees focus on discretionary spending programs, which are basically the only budget items subject to change. The House Appropriations Committee, through its 12 subcommittees, reviews the budget, which includes hearings with officials from each federal agency. Each subcommittee has responsibility for a particular substantive area, such as defense or agriculture. A subcommittee may cut an agency's budget if it concludes that the agency is overfunded or may increase the budget if it concludes that the agency is underfunded. The subcommittees' recommendations are then reviewed by the House Appropriations Committee as a whole. The budget is also reviewed by the Senate Appropriations Committee and its subcommittees. However, the Senate is a smaller body, and its review of agency requests is less exacting than that of the House. To a degree, the Senate Appropriations Committee serves as a "court of last resort" for agencies that have had their funding requests cut by OMB or by the House Appropriations Committee. The Senate, for example, restored most of the cuts to the State Department budget that President Trump had proposed. Senator Lindsey Graham (R-S.C.) had declared Trump's proposal "dead on arrival" when it was announced, and, indeed, Congress overrode Trump's plan during its budget negotiations.[13]

Congress has final authority over the budget, subject to a presidential veto. Shown here is a session of the House Appropriations Committee, which, through its 12 subcommittees, does most of Congress's work on budget details. (Chine Nouvelle/SIPA/Newscom)

Throughout the budgetary process, members of the House and the Senate rely on the Congressional Budget Office (CBO), which is the congressional equivalent of OMB. If CBO believes that OMB or an agency has miscalculated the amount of money needed to carry out its mandated programs, it will alert Congress to the discrepancy.

After the House and Senate appropriations committees have completed their work, they submit their recommendations to the full chambers for a vote. If approved by a majority in the House and in the Senate, differences in the Senate and House versions are then reconciled in conference committee (see Chapter 11). The reconciled version of the budget is then voted upon in the House and Senate and, if approved, is sent to the president to sign or veto. The threat of a presidential veto can be enough to persuade Congress to accept many of the president's recommendations. In the end, the budget inevitably reflects both presidential and congressional priorities. Neither branch gets everything it wants, but each branch always gets some of what it seeks.

After the budget has been signed by the president, it takes effect on October 1, the starting date of the federal government's fiscal year. If agreement on the budget has not been reached by October 1, which has happened regularly in recent years, temporary funding legislation is required in order to maintain government operations until the final budget is enacted.

POLICY AND POWER IN THE BUREAUCRACY

The Constitution mentions executive agencies but does not grant them authority. Their authority derives from grants of power to the three constitutional branches: Congress, the president, and the courts. Administrative agencies' main task is **policy implementation**—that is, the carrying out of decisions made by Congress, the president, and the courts. When a directive is issued by Congress, the president, or the courts, the bureaucracy is charged with executing it. In implementing these decisions, the bureaucracy is constrained by the budget. It cannot spend money on an activity unless Congress has appropriated the necessary funds.

Some of what the bureaucracy does is fairly straightforward, as in the case of delivering the mail, processing government loan applications, and imprisoning those convicted of crime. Yet the bureaucracy sometimes has considerable discretion in implementing policy. Consider the example of the Consumer Financial Protection Bureau (CFPB), which Congress created in 2010 to protect consumers from financial institutions that exploit consumers in the granting of home mortgages, credit cards, and the like. The legislation that created the CFPB instructed the agency to do the following:

- Conduct rule-making, supervision, and enforcement for federal consumer financial protection laws

- Restrict unfair, deceptive, or abusive acts or practices
- Take consumer complaints
- Promote financial education
- Research consumer behavior
- Monitor financial markets for new risks to consumers

However, the legislation did not spell out in detail how the CFPB was to implement these tasks. What type of enforcement would it conduct? Which unfair practices would it restrict, and how would this be done? What action would be taken on consumer complaints? How would financial education occur? What consumer behaviors would be studied? How would financial markets be monitored and new risks identified? It was left to CFPB bureaucrats to formulate these policies. Such **rule-making**—determining how a law will work in practice—is the chief way administrative agencies exercise control over policy.[14]

The rule-making process is subject to checks. After an agency develops the initial rules for an activity, they are published in the *Federal Register* and are then subject to comments and objections by interested parties. When the agency then publishes the final rules, it cannot implement them for 60 days, during which time Congress can change them, although it seldom does so.

In the course of their work, administrators also develop policy ideas, which they then propose to the White House or Congress. In 2019, for example, for the first time in more than two decades, Congress appropriated funds for gun violence research. Pressure to do so came from organizations that argued the funding was needed to study a problem that results in the death of more than 30,000 Americans annually. But pressure also came from agencies such as the National Institutes of Health, which are charged with protecting public health and which recognize that gun violence is more than a criminal justice problem. It's also a public health problem.

In sum, administrators initiate policy, develop it, evaluate it, apply it, and decide whether others are complying with it. The bureaucracy does not simply administer policy. It also *makes* policy.

The Agency Point of View

A key issue of bureaucratic policymaking is the perspective that bureaucrats bring to their decisions. Do they operate from the perspective of the president, or do they operate from the perspective of Congress? The answer is that, although bureaucrats are responsive to both of them, they are even more responsive to the needs of the agency in which they work, a perspective called

Some government agencies are noteworthy for their performance. One of them is the U.S. Postal Service, which is regarded by many as the best entity of its kind anywhere. It delivers more mail to more addresses than any other postal service in the world, and it does so inexpensively and without undue delay. (Photodisc/PunchStock)

the **agency point of view**. This outlook comes naturally to most high-ranking civil servants. More than 80 percent of top bureaucrats reach their high-level positions by rising through the ranks of the same agency.[15] As one top administrator said when testifying before the House Appropriations Committee, "Mr. Chairman, you would not think it proper for me to be in charge of this work and not be enthusiastic about it . . . would you? I have been in it for thirty years, and I believe in it."[16] One study found, for example, that social welfare administrators were twice as likely as other civil servants to believe that social welfare spending should be increased (see Figure 13-5).[17]

Professionalism also cements agency loyalties. High-level administrative positions have increasingly been filled by scientists, engineers, lawyers, educators, physicians, and other professionals. Most of them take a job in an agency whose mission they support, as in the case of the aeronautical engineers who work for NASA or the doctors who work for the National Institutes of Health (NIH).

Although the agency point of view distorts government priorities, bureaucrats have little choice but to look out for their agency's interests. The president

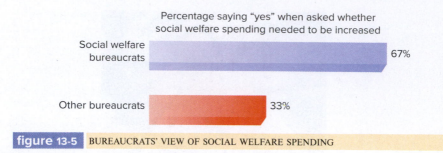

figure 13-5   BUREAUCRATS' VIEW OF SOCIAL WELFARE SPENDING

Bureaucrats in social welfare agencies are far more likely than bureaucrats in other agencies to think increased spending on social welfare is necessary. An "agency point of view" is prevalent in the federal bureaucracy. (*Source:* Adapted from Aberbach, Joel D., and Rockman, Bert A., "Clashing Beliefs within the Executive Branch," *American Political Science Review,* vol. 70, 1970, 461.)

and members of Congress differ in their constituencies and thus in the agencies to which they are most responsive. Republican and Democratic officials also differ in their priorities, a reality that is never more apparent than when party control of the presidency or Congress changes. Some agencies rise or fall in their level of political support for that reason alone. In sum, if an agency is to operate successfully in America's partisan system of divided power, it must seek support wherever it can find it. If the agency is a low priority for the president, it needs to find backing in Congress. If Republican lawmakers want to cut the agency's programs, it must turn to Democratic lawmakers for help. In other words, agencies are forced to play politics if they want to protect their programs.[18] An agency that sits on the sidelines while other agencies seek support from the White House and Congress is likely to lose out in budget negotiations.

CITIZEN ACTION!
GETTING INVOLVED

President John F. Kennedy called government service "the highest calling." A study by Harvard's Kennedy School of Government found that public-sector managers get more intrinsic satisfaction from their work, which focuses on improving public life, than do private-sector managers. If you are thinking of a career in government, consider first obtaining a master's degree in public administration or public policy. The entry-level salary is much higher than for those with a bachelor's degree, and the responsibilities are greater, as are the prospects for promotion to a top position.

Sources of Bureaucratic Power

In promoting their agency's interests, bureaucrats rely on their specialized knowledge, the support of interests that benefit from their programs, and the backing of the president and Congress.

The Power of Expertise   Most of the policy problems confronting the federal government are extraordinarily complex. Whether the problem relates to space travel or hunger in America, a solution requires deep knowledge of the problem. Much of this expertise is provided by bureaucrats. They spend their careers working in a particular policy area, and many of them have had scientific, technical, or other specialized training (see "How the U.S. Differs").[19] For their part, elected officials are generalists, none more so than the president, who must deal with dozens of issues. Members of Congress acquire some expertise through their committee work, but most of them lack the time, training, or inclination to become deeply knowledgeable of the issues they handle. It's not surprising that Congress and the president rely heavily on career administrators for policy advice.

All agencies acquire some influence over policy through their careerists' expertise. No matter how simple a policy issue may appear at first, it nearly always has layers of complexity. The recognition that the United States has a trade deficit with China, for example, can be the premise for policy change, but this recognition does not begin to address basic issues such as the form the new policy might take, its probable cost and effectiveness, and its links to other issues, such as America's standing in Asia. Among the officials most likely to understand these issues are the career bureaucrats in the Treasury Department, the State Department, the Commerce Department, and the Federal Trade Commission.

The Power of Clientele Groups   Most federal agencies were created for the purpose of promoting, protecting, or regulating an economic interest. Indeed, nearly every major interest in society—commerce, labor, agriculture, banking, and so on—has a corresponding federal agency. In most cases, these interests are **clientele groups** in the sense that they benefit directly from the agency's programs. As a result, clientele groups can be counted on to lobby Congress and the president on behalf of their agency when its programs and funding are being reviewed.[20] When President Trump, in his fiscal year 2021 budget, proposed to make deep cuts in affordable housing funds, food stamps, and Medicaid, the affected groups lobbied Congress to protect the programs, arguing that the federal government's safety net was what kept the economically vulnerable from succumbing to abject poverty and ill health.[21]

The relationship between an agency and its clientele group is a reciprocal one. Just as a clientele group can be expected to protect its agency, the agency will work to protect the group.[22] The Department of Agriculture, for instance, is a dependable ally of farm interests year after year. The same cannot be said of the president or Congress as a whole, which must balance farmers' demands against those of other groups.

The Power of Friends in High Places   Although the goals of the president or Congress can conflict with those of the bureaucracy, they need it as much as it needs them. An agency's resources—its programs, expertise, and group

HOW THE U.S. DIFFERS

CRITICAL THINKING THROUGH COMPARISONS

Educational Backgrounds of Bureaucrats

In staffing its bureaucracy, the U.S. government tends to hire persons with specialized education to hold specialized jobs. In contrast, Great Britain tends to recruit its top bureaucrats from the arts and humanities, on the assumption that a broad education is the best preparation. Germany takes a different approach, believing that a legal education is advantageous because of the part played by high-ranking bureaucrats in determining how laws will be implemented. These tendencies (see figure) were documented by political scientist Guy Peters in his comparative study of the college majors of senior civil servants.[23]

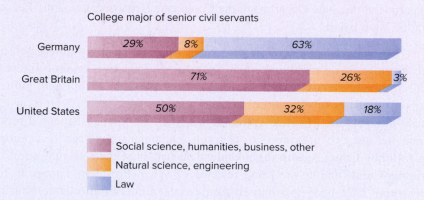

College major of senior civil servants

Q: Why might the hiring pattern for the U.S. bureaucracy make it more likely that civil servants in the United States will take an agency point of view than will civil servants in some other democracies?

A: The U.S. bureaucracy has a high proportion of employees with a specialized education. They tend to take jobs in agencies where their specialty is particularly desirable, as in the case of the aeronautical engineers who work at NASA. Accordingly, their training would incline them to support their agency's mission—the agency point of view. European civil servants are more likely to have a type of education, as in the case of law or the humanities, that is less specific to the work of a particular agency, which presumably makes them less likely to deeply embrace their agency's mission.

support—can help elected officials achieve their policy goals. When Barack Obama announced early in his presidency the goal of making the United States less dependent on foreign oil, he needed the help of the Department of Energy's experts to develop programs that would further that objective. At a time when other agencies were feeling the pinch of a tight federal budget, the Department of Energy's budget nearly doubled.

Agencies also have allies in Congress. Agencies with programs that benefit important key voting blocs are particularly likely to have congressional support. A prime example is the Department of Agriculture. Although the agricultural sector is just one of the president's many concerns, it is a primary concern of farm-state senators and representatives. They can typically be counted on to support Department of Agriculture funding and programs.

DEMOCRACY AND BUREAUCRATIC ACCOUNTABILITY

The federal bureaucracy's policy influence is at odds with democratic principles. The bureaucratic form of governing is the antithesis of the democratic form. Bureaucracy entails hierarchy, command, permanence of office, appointment to office, and fixed rules, whereas self-government involves equality, consent, rotation of office, election to office, and open decision making. The president and members of Congress are accountable to the people through elections. Bureaucrats are not elected and yet exercise a significant degree of independent power.

Their influence raises the question of **bureaucratic accountability**—the degree to which bureaucrats are held accountable for the power they exercise. To a small degree, they are accountable directly to the public. In some instances, for example, agencies are required to hold public hearings before issuing new regulations. For the most part, however, bureaucratic accountability occurs largely through the president, Congress, and the courts.[24]

Accountability Through the Presidency

Periodically, presidents have launched broad initiatives aimed at making the bureaucracy more responsive. The most recent was the National Performance Review, which Bill Clinton began when he assumed the presidency in 1993. He had campaigned on the issue of "reinventing government" and assembled "reinventing teams," which produced 384 specific recommendations grouped into four broad imperatives: reducing red tape, putting customers first, empowering administrators, and eliminating wasteful spending.[25] Although different

Politics in Action

Control of Bureaucratic Agencies

B Christopher/Alamy Stock Photo

Every president has sought to tighten White House control over executive agencies, sometimes against the wishes of Congress. In 2010, Congress authorized creation of the Consumer Financial Protection Bureau (CFPB), charging it with protecting consumers from unfair and deceptive practices by banks, credit card companies, and other financial entities. To protect its independence from presidential influence, Congress specified that the bureau would be headed by a single director, serving a five-year term, who could be removed from office by the President only for "inefficiency, neglect of duty or malfeasance." After coming into office, President Trump pressured the seated director into resigning, expressing disagreement with the director's policies, which did not meet the congressional criteria for the director's removal.

In 2020, the Supreme Court ruled on a challenge to the Bureau's structure, holding in a 5-4 decision that it was unconstitutional for Congress to have placed conditions on the President's ability to remove an agency's director. Noting that the CFPB's director has "vast rulemaking, enforcement, and adjudicatory authority over a significant portion of the US economy," Chief Justice John Roberts wrote that the CFPB's removal clause was "incompatible with the structure of the Constitution, which—with the sole exception of the Presidency—scrupulously avoids concentrating power in the hands of any single individual."[26]

Q: Where do you stand on the question of a president's authority to remove an agency head for any reason, at any time?

ASK YOURSELF: How much power should the president have over executive agencies relative to Congress? Would you apply the Supreme Court's reasoning to older regulatory agencies, like the Federal Communications Commission? Those agencies are governed by a board of commissioners who serve fixed terms and cannot be removed by the president except for cause. Does it make a difference that power in those agencies is shared by several individuals, whereas it was vested in a single individual in the case of the CFPB?

in its particulars, the National Performance Review was like earlier reform panels, including the Brownlow, Hoover, and Volcker Commissions,[27] which sought with some success to improve the bureaucracy's efficiency, responsiveness, and accountability.

Presidents can also intervene more directly through *executive orders* to force agencies to pursue particular administrative actions. In the closing days of his presidency, for example, Bill Clinton ordered federal agencies to take the steps necessary to ensure that eligible individuals with limited English proficiency obtained full access to federal assistance programs.

Nevertheless, presidents do not have the time or knowledge to exercise personal oversight of the federal bureaucracy. It is far too big and diverse. Presidents rely instead on management tools that include reorganization, presidential appointees, and the executive budget.[28]

Reorganization   The bureaucracy's size—its hundreds of separate agencies—makes it difficult for presidents to coordinate its activities. Agencies pursue independent and even conflicting paths. For example, the United States spends more than $50 billion annually to gather intelligence on threats to the nation's security and does so through several agencies. Each of them has its own priorities and a desire to retain control of the intelligence information it has gathered. A lack of communication between the CIA and the FBI may have contributed to the failure to prevent the terrorist attacks on the World Trade Center and the Pentagon on September 11, 2001. Each agency had information that might have disrupted the attack if the information had been shared.

Presidents have sought to streamline the bureaucracy in an attempt to make it more accountable. After the intelligence breakdown in 2001, for example, President George W. Bush commissioned a study of the intelligence agencies, which resulted in creation of the Office of the Director of National Intelligence in 2004. Fifteen intelligence agencies, including the CIA and the FBI, now report directly to the director of national intelligence, who has responsibility for coordinating their activities. Like most reorganizations, this one improved agency performance, but not dramatically. Although the various intelligence agencies now share more information than previously, they have continued to operate somewhat independently of each other—an indication of the tendency of agencies to protect their sphere of operation.

Presidents have had more success in controlling the bureaucracy by moving activities out of the agencies and into the Executive Office of the President (EOP). As explained in Chapter 12, the EOP is directly under White House control and functions to a degree as the president's personal bureaucracy. The EOP now makes some policy decisions that, at an earlier time, would have been made in the agencies. For example, the National Security Council staff, which is part of the EOP, has assumed some of the policy responsibility that once belonged to State and Defense Department staffs.

Presidential Appointments   For day-to-day oversight of the bureaucracy, presidents rely on their political appointees. The president has roughly 2,000 full-time partisan appointees, 20 times the number appointed, for example, by the British prime minister.

The top positions in every agency are held by presidential appointees (see "Party Polarization: The Politicization of the Bureaucracy"). They are appointed by the president and can be removed from office at the president's discretion. Their influence is greatest in agencies that have broad authority. Some agencies, like the Social Security Administration (SSA), operate within guidelines that limit what agency heads can do. Although the SSA has a huge budget and makes monthly payments to more than 40 million Americans, recipient eligibility is determined by fixed rules. The head of the SSA does not have the option, say, of granting a retiree an extra $100 a month because the retiree is facing financial hardship. At the other extreme are the regulatory agencies, which have considerable latitude in their decisions. For example, in the first year of the Trump administration, the Environmental Protection Agency (EPA)

Some observers believe that, if the nation's various intelligence agencies had been more willing to share information, the terrorist attacks on U.S. soil on September 11, 2001, might have been prevented. Although they now share their information more fully, they still operate somewhat independently—a tendency that reflects agencies' determination to protect their turf. (Source: Central Intelligence Agency)

initiated 40 percent fewer cases for violation of pollution laws and imposed 65 percent fewer monetary penalties than the EPA did in the Obama administration's first year.[29]

Nevertheless, there are limits to what presidents can accomplish through their appointees. Many appointees lack detailed knowledge of the agencies they head, making them dependent on agency careerists. By the time they come to understand the agency's programs, they often leave. The typical presidential appointee stays on the job for only two years before moving on to other employment.[30]

PARTY POLARIZATION

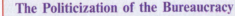

Conflicting Ideas

The Politicization of the Bureaucracy

The top-level positions in the federal bureaucracy—the positions occupied by presidential appointees—have become increasingly partisan. Although presidents normally seek to appoint well-qualified individuals, they increasingly want them to be loyal to the president's policy agenda. More than any other recent president, President Trump used that standard in selecting his top administrators. Many of his cabinet-level appointments, for example, were individuals with little or no experience with the programs and policies that their department was charged with administering. Several of them had an antagonistic view of the agency they headed. Secretary of Energy Rick Perry, for example, had said before his appointment that the Department of Energy should be abolished.

The politicization of top administrators has been both praised and criticized. Some analysts say that the overriding principle of the bureaucracy should be neutral competence—impartial and expert administration. Other observers dismiss this claim, arguing that the bureaucracy needs to be responsive to partisan politics—that the will of the voters should be reflected in administrative staffing. They do not deny the need for competent administrators but argue that strong political leadership at the top—even if highly partisan—is the key to a more accountable and responsive bureaucracy.

Q: What's your view of the increased politicization of the bureaucracy? On balance, do you regard it as a favorable development? Would you have the same opinion if control of the presidency were to change to the other party?

OMB: Budgets and Rule-Making   Of the management tools available to the president, few are more direct than the Office of Management and Budget. Funding is the foundation of every agency, and OMB has substantial control over agency budgets.

OMB also reviews agency regulations before they go into effect. As noted earlier, rule-making is the chief way that bureaucratic agencies create policy. Rules established by the agencies affect everything from how business will be regulated to how student loans will be administered. In practice, OMB lacks the resources to review all such rules and closely examines fewer than a thousand out of the tens of thousands of rules proposed each year. One study found that OMB's rule-making oversight tends to be reactive—triggered in most cases when an affected firm or group complains about a proposed rule. "Reactive oversight," notes scholar William West, "allows the White House to focus its limited resources on agency initiatives that are problematic while ignoring the majority that are not."[31]

Accountability Through Congress

A common misconception is that the president, as the chief executive, has sole authority over executive agencies. In fact, Congress also claims ownership because it is the source of each agency's programs and funding. One presidential appointee asked a congressional committee whether it had a problem with his plans to reduce an agency's programs. The committee chair replied, "No, you have the problem, because if you touch that bureau I'll cut your job out of the budget."[32]

The most substantial control that Congress exerts over the bureaucracy is through its "power of the purse." Congress has constitutional authority over spending; it decides how much money will be appropriated for agency programs. Without funding, a program simply does not exist, regardless of how important the agency believes it is. Congress can also void an administrative decision through legislation that instructs the agency to follow a different course of action. In addition, Congress can exert control by taking authority away from the bureaucracy. In 1978, as a first step in what would become a decades-long wave of deregulation, Congress passed the Airline Deregulation Act, which took away the Civil Aeronautics Board's authority to set airfares and gave it to the airlines.

Congress also has control through its oversight function, which involves monitoring the bureaucracy's work to ensure its compliance with legislative intent.[33] If an agency steps out of line, Congress can call hearings to ask tough questions and, if necessary, take legislative action to correct the problem.

Bureaucrats are required by law to appear before Congress when asked to do so, and the mere possibility of being grilled by a congressional panel can lead administrators to stay in line. The effect is not altogether positive. Bureaucrats are sometimes reluctant to try innovative approaches out of a fear that some members of Congress will disapprove.[34]

Nevertheless, Congress lacks the time and expertise to define in detail how programs should be run.[35] Accordingly, Congress has delegated much of its oversight responsibility to the Government Accountability Office (GAO). At an earlier time, the GAO's role was limited largely to keeping track of agency spending. The GAO now also monitors whether agencies are implementing policies in the way that Congress intended. When the GAO finds a problem with an agency's handling of a program, it notifies the appropriate congressional committees, which can then take corrective action.

Oversight cannot correct mistakes or abuses that have already occurred. Recognizing this limit, Congress has devised ways to constrain the bureaucracy *before* it acts. The simplest method is to draft laws that contain specific instructions on how the bureaucracy is to implement them. In doing so, Congress limits administrators' options. *Sunset provisions* are another restrictive device. These provisions establish specific dates when all or part of a law will expire unless extended by Congress. Sunset provisions are a method of countering the bureaucracy's reluctance to give up outdated programs. However, because members of Congress usually want the programs they create to last, most bills do not include a sunset provision.

Accountability Through the Courts

The bureaucracy is also overseen by the judiciary. Legally, the bureaucracy derives its authority from acts of Congress, and an injured party can bring suit against an agency on the grounds that it has failed to carry out a law properly. If the court agrees, the agency must change its policy.[36] In 1999, for example, a federal court approved a settlement in favor of African American farmers who had demonstrated that the Department of Agriculture had systematically favored white farmers in granting federal farm loans.[37]

Nevertheless, the courts tend to support administrators if their actions are at least somewhat consistent with the law they are administering. The Supreme Court has held that agencies can apply any reasonable interpretation of statutes unless Congress has stipulated something to the contrary.[38] This position reflects the Court's recognition that administrators must have discretionary authority if they are to operate effectively and that the federal courts would be overloaded with cases if petitioners could challenge every administrative rule they disliked.

Accountability within the Bureaucracy Itself

Recognition of the difficulty of ensuring adequate accountability of the bureaucracy through the presidency, Congress, and the courts has led to the development of mechanisms of accountability within the bureaucracy itself. Four of these mechanisms—the Senior Executive Service, administrative law judges, whistleblowing, and demographic representativeness—are particularly noteworthy.

Senior Executive Service   The agency point of view within the bureaucracy is partly a result of career patterns. Most civil servants work in the same agency throughout their time in government service. As they acquire the skills and knowledge associated with a particular agency, they rise through its ranks and derive job satisfaction and security from supporting its mission.

Recognizing that the bureaucracy's employment system encourages an agency point of view, in 1978 Congress established the **Senior Executive Service (SES)**. The SES represents a compromise between a president-led bureaucracy and an expert one.[39] The SES consists of roughly 7,000 top-level career civil servants who qualify through a competitive process to receive a higher salary than their peers but, in return, can be assigned by the president to any position within the bureaucracy. Unlike the president's regular appointees, SES bureaucrats cannot be fired; if the president relieves them of their job, they have "fallback rights" to their former rank in the regular civil service.

The SES has been less successful in practice than its proponents anticipated. A study found that SES employees are usually assigned to agencies that match their policy expertise, which is typically the same agency in which they have spent their career. Their value rests in significant part on their knowledge of its programs, and to locate them elsewhere would diminish that value. Said a former senior executive, "I got promoted because I became an expert in the policies in that area, not because I'm such a great executive who can go anywhere and do anything."[40]

Administrative Law Judges   Individuals will sometimes believe that they have been unfairly disadvantaged by a bureaucrat's decision and will contest it. Such disputes are usually handled by an **administrative law judge**. Administrative law judges are charged with protecting individuals from arbitrary, prejudicial, or incorrect decisions by an agency. These judges are empowered to administer oaths, seek evidence, take testimony, make factual and legal determinations, and render decisions. However, they operate through a less formal process than do regular federal judges. Administrative law hearings usually take place in an office or a meeting room rather than a courtroom, and administrative law judges do not wear a robe or sit on a high bench. The system is designed to provide a less formal, less expensive, and faster method of resolving administrative disputes than would be the case if they were handled through the regular federal courts. Under some circumstances, the decision of an administrative law judge can be appealed to such a court, although this seldom occurs.

Whistleblowing   Although the bureaucratic corruption that is commonplace in some countries is rare in the United States, a certain amount of fraud and abuse is inevitable in any large bureaucracy. One way to limit such practices is **whistleblowing**—encouraging employees to report misconduct by their superiors. The Whistleblower Protection Act protects them from retaliation by their superiors and gives them a financial reward when their information results in substantial savings to government.

Nevertheless, whistleblowing is not for the fainthearted. Many federal employees are reluctant to report instances of misbehavior because they fear retaliation. Their superiors might claim that they are malcontents or liars and seek ways to ruin their careers. A case in point is the whistleblower who alerted Congress that President Trump appeared to be withholding military assistance to Ukraine in an effort to solicit its investigation into Democratic presidential candidate Joe Biden. Trump tweeted that the whistleblower was "a liar" and said, "I want to know who's the [whistleblower], who's the person who gave the whistleblower the information? Because that's close to a spy." Although the Whistleblower

Employees who report misconduct by their superiors are known as whistleblowers. Although they're protected by law, they can become the target of reprisals by the superiors whose misconduct they report. (Lightspring/Shutterstock)

Protection Act prohibits officials from publicly revealing the identity of a whistle-blower, Trump continued to press for the information. Senator Rand Paul (R-Ky.) subsequently released the alleged whistleblower's name on the Senate floor.[41]

Demographic Representation   Although the bureaucracy is an unrepresentative institution in the sense that its officials are not elected, it can be representative in the demographic sense. This concept was endorsed in 1961 by the President's Commission on Equal Employment Opportunity, which was created by President John F. Kennedy. The commission concluded that, if civil servants were more demographically representative of the general public, they would treat the various groups and interests in society more fairly.[42]

The federal government has made progress in improving the employment status of women and, to a lesser extent, minorities. If all employees are taken into account, the federal bureaucracy comes reasonably close to being representative of the nation's population. Moreover, women and minorities are better represented among the top ranks of administrators than they are in Congress or the judiciary. Nevertheless, the bureaucracy is not demographically representative at the top level. The highest-ranking federal employees are those in the Senior Executive Service (SES). About 2 in every 3 such employees are male, and about 4 in every 5 are white (see Figure 13-6). However, the SES is far more representative today than four decades ago, when white males accounted for roughly 9 in 10 SES employees.

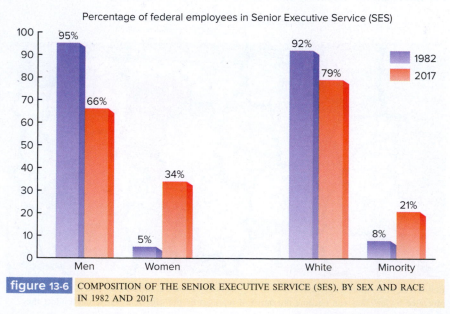

figure 13-6   COMPOSITION OF THE SENIOR EXECUTIVE SERVICE (SES), BY SEX AND RACE IN 1982 AND 2017

(*Source:* Office of Personnel Management, 2020.)

In any case, **demographic representativeness** is only a partial answer to the problem of bureaucratic accountability. Careerists in the defense and welfare agencies, for example, have similar demographic backgrounds but differ markedly in their policy views. Each group believes that the goals of its agency should be a top priority. In this sense, agency loyalty trumps demographics. Once in an agency, civil servants—regardless of demographic background—tend to become advocates for its programs.

SUMMARY

Bureaucracy is a method of organizing people and work, based on the principles of hierarchical authority, job specialization, and formalized rules. As a form of organization, bureaucracy is the most efficient means of getting people to work together on tasks of great magnitude and complexity. It is also a form of organization that is prone to waste and rigidity, which is why efforts are always being made to reform it.

The United States could not be governed without a large federal bureaucracy. The day-to-day work of the federal government, from mail delivery to provision of Social Security to international diplomacy, is done by federal agencies. Federal employees work in roughly 400 major agencies, including cabinet departments, independent agencies, regulatory agencies, government corporations, and presidential commissions, yet the bureaucracy is more than simply an administrative giant. Administrators have discretion when making policy decisions. In the process of implementing policy, they make important policy and political choices.

Administrative agencies operate within budgets established by the president and Congress, and they participate in the budgetary process. The process begins with the president's budget instructions, conveyed through OMB, to the agencies. They then develop their budgets, which are consolidated and sent by the president to Congress, where the House and Senate budget and appropriations committees do the bulk of the work, including holding hearings involving agency heads. Throughout, Congress, the president, and the agencies seek to promote their respective budgetary goals.

Administrators are actively engaged in politics and policymaking. The fragmentation of power and the pluralism of the American political system result in a contentious policy process, which leads government agencies to compete for power and resources. Accordingly, civil servants tend to have an agency point of view: They seek to advance their agency's programs and to repel attempts by others to weaken them. In promoting their agencies, civil servants rely on their policy expertise, the backing of their clientele groups, and the support of the president and Congress.

Administrators are not elected by the people they serve, yet they wield substantial independent power. Because of this, the bureaucracy's accountability is a central issue. The major checks on the bureaucracy occur through the president, Congress, and the courts. The president has some power to reorganize the bureaucracy and the authority to appoint the political head of each agency. The president also has management tools (such as the executive budget), which can be used to limit administrators' discretion.

Congress has influence on bureaucratic agencies through its authorization and funding powers and through various devices (including enabling provisions, sunset provisions, and oversight hearings) that can increase administrators' accountability. The judiciary's role in ensuring the bureaucracy's accountability is smaller than that of the elected branches, but the courts have the authority to force agencies to act in accordance with legislative intent, established procedures, and constitutionally guaranteed rights. Internal checks on the bureaucracy—the Senior Executive Service, administrative law judges, whistleblowing, and demographic representativeness—are also mechanisms for holding the bureaucracy accountable.

CRITICAL THINKING ZONE

KEY TERMS

administrative law judge (*p. 406*)
agency point of view (*p. 395*)
budgetary process (*p. 389*)
bureaucracy (*p. 380*)
bureaucratic accountability (*p. 399*)
cabinet (executive) departments
 (*p. 383*)
clientele groups (*p. 397*)
demographic representativeness
 (*p. 409*)
formalized rules (*p. 380*)
government corporations (*p. 386*)
hierarchical authority (*p. 380*)

independent agencies (*p. 384*)
job specialization (*p. 380*)
merit system (*p. 386*)
neutral competence (*p. 388*)
patronage system (*p. 388*)
policy implementation (*p. 393*)
presidential commissions (*p. 386*)
regulatory agencies (*p. 386*)
rule-making (*p. 394*)
Senior Executive Service (SES) (*p. 406*)
spoils system (*p. 388*)
whistleblowing (*p. 407*)

APPLYING THE ELEMENTS OF CRITICAL THINKING

Conceptualizing: Explain what is meant by *agency point of view*. Why do bureaucrats tend to have an agency point of view?

Synthesizing: Contrast the patronage system and the merit system as methods of hiring government employees.

Analyzing: What are the major sources of bureaucrats' power? What mechanisms for controlling that power are available to the president and Congress?

EXTRA CREDIT

A Book Worth Reading: Charles T. Goodsell, *The New Case for Bureaucracy* (Washington, D.C.: CQ Press, 2014). A well-written book by an eminent scholar that documents the importance and effectiveness of the U.S. federal bureaucracy.

A Website Worth Visiting: **www.whistleblower.org** The Government Accountability Project is a nonpartisan organization devoted to protecting and encouraging whistleblowers in the private sector as well as the public sector.

Design credit: (People, Flag, U.S., Globe, Vote Icons): McGraw-Hill Education; (Eagle): Feng Wei Photography/Moment/Getty Images; (Lincoln): Photographs in the Carol M. Highsmith Archive, Library of Congress, Prints and Photographs Division [LC-DIG-highsm-12542].

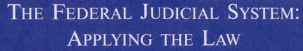

THE FEDERAL JUDICIAL SYSTEM: APPLYING THE LAW

Cass Gilbert /Pixtal/age fotostock

❝ It is emphatically the province and duty of the judicial department to say what the law is. Those who apply the rule to particular cases, must of necessity expound and interpret that rule. If two laws conflict with each other, the courts must decide on the operation of each. ❞

JOHN MARSHALL[1]

Through its ruling in *Obergefell v. Hodges* (2015), the Supreme Court by a 5–4 vote legalized same-sex marriage in all states. At issue in the case was whether the Fourteenth Amendment's due process and equal-protection clauses prevent states from banning marriages between individuals of the same sex. The Supreme Court's majority concluded that a ban on same-sex marriage violated the Fourteenth Amendment. The Court said, "The Constitution promises liberty to all within its reach, a liberty that includes certain specific rights that allow persons, within a lawful realm, to define and express their identity. . . . [Same-sex couples] ask for equal dignity in the eyes of the law. The Constitution grants them that right." Regarding the issue of whether state legislatures have the power to ban such marriages, the Court held that "fundamental rights may not be submitted to a vote. . . ."[2]

The Court's same-sex marriage ruling illustrates three key points about court decisions. First, the judiciary is an important policymaking body. Some of its rulings are as consequential as a law of Congress or an executive order of the president. Second, the judiciary has considerable discretion in its rulings. The *Obergefell* decision was not based on a straightforward reading of the law, or else the justices would not have divided 5–4 on the ruling. Third, the judiciary is a political as well as a legal institution. The same-sex marriage ruling was decided by political appointees. Four of the five justices who voted to allow same-sex marriage were appointed to the Court by a Democratic president. Of the four justices who dissented, all were Republican appointees.

This chapter describes the federal judiciary. Like the executive and legislative branches, the judiciary is an independent branch of the U.S. government, but, unlike the other two branches, its top officials are not elected by the people. The judiciary is not a democratic institution, and its role is different from and sometimes more controversial than those of the executive and legislative branches. This chapter explores this issue in the process of discussing the following main points:

- *The federal judiciary includes the Supreme Court of the United States, which functions mainly as an appellate court; courts of appeals, which hear appeals; and the district courts, which hold trials.* Each state has a court system of its own, which for the most part is independent of supervision by the federal courts.

- *Judicial decisions are constrained by applicable constitutional law, statutory and administrative law, and precedent.* Nevertheless, political factors have a major influence on judicial appointments and decisions; judges are political officials as well as legal ones.

- *The judiciary has become an increasingly powerful policymaking body in recent decades, raising the question of the judiciary's proper role in a democracy.* The philosophies of judicial restraint and judicial activism provide different answers to this question.

THE FEDERAL JUDICIAL SYSTEM

The Constitution establishes the judiciary as a separate and independent branch of the federal government. The Constitution provides for the Supreme Court of the United States but gives Congress the power to determine the number and types of lower federal courts.

All federal judges are nominated and appointed to office by the president, subject to confirmation by majority vote in the Senate. The Constitution places no age, residency, or citizenship requirements on the office of federal judge, unlike the office of president, senator, or representative. Nor does the Constitution require judges to have legal training, although by tradition they do. Once seated on the bench, as specified in the Constitution, they "hold their offices during good behavior." This has meant, in effect, that federal judges serve until they die or retire voluntarily. No Supreme Court justice and only a handful of lower-court judges have been removed through impeachment and conviction by Congress, the method of early removal specified by the Constitution.

Alexander Hamilton argued forcefully for life tenure for federal judges in *Federalist* No. 78. Responding to arguments by Anti-Federalists that life-appointed judges would be a threat to the republic, Hamilton argued that the judicial branch would be the weakest of the three branches. Whereas congressional power rests on spending authority ("the power of the purse") and presidential power rests on control of military force ("the power of the sword"), judicial power rests on what Hamilton called "judgment"—the reasonableness and fairness of its decisions. The best way to ensure that judicial decisions meet this standard, Hamilton argued, is to grant life tenure to federal judges so that they are free of all allegiances except to the rule of law (see "How the U.S. Differs").

The Supreme Court of the United States

The Supreme Court of the United States is the nation's highest court. It has nine members—the chief justice and eight associate justices. The chief justice presides over the Court but has the same voting power as each of the other justices.

Article III of the Constitution grants the Supreme Court both original and appellate jurisdiction. A court's **jurisdiction** is its authority to hear cases of a particular type. **Original jurisdiction** is the authority to be the first court to hear a case. The Supreme Court's original jurisdiction includes legal disputes involving foreign diplomats and cases in which the opposing parties are state governments. The Court has convened as a court of original jurisdiction only a few hundred times in its history and has seldom done in recent decades. One of the rarities was *South Carolina v. North Carolina* (2010), which involved a dispute between the two states over the distribution of water in the Catawba River, which flows through both states.[3]

The Supreme Court does its most important work as an appellate court. **Appellate jurisdiction** is the authority to review cases that have already been heard in lower courts and are appealed to a higher court by the losing party. These higher courts are called *appeals courts* or *appellate courts.* Appellate courts do not retry cases; rather, they determine whether a trial court, in hearing a case, has

HOW THE U.S. DIFFERS

CRITICAL THINKING THROUGH COMPARISONS

Supreme Court Justices' Term of Office

Once appointed to office, Supreme Court justices effectively have lifetime tenure, which distinguishes them from the president, senators, and House members, each of which serves a limited fixed term. Lifetime tenure also distinguishes Supreme Court justices from the judges in the high courts of other Western democracies. There, they serve for a fixed term or until a specified retirement age, or both.[4] In Germany, for example, federal judges serve a 12-year term and face mandatory retirement at age 68. It's common now for Supreme Court justices to serve past 75 years of age and to spend more than 20 years on the Court.

Q: What are the advantages and disadvantages of a system of lifetime tenure for Supreme Court justices versus a system where they would serve for a fixed term with a mandatory retirement age?

A: The main advantage of lifetime tenure, which Alexander Hamilton identified at the writing of the Constitution, is that it frees justices from political interference. It might also be argued, although the claim would be difficult to prove, that justices make better decisions during their later years on the bench than during their earlier years. The advantages of a fixed term with a mandatory retirement age include lowering the risk of having on the Supreme Court a justice with severe physical or mental health problems. Another advantage is that it would reduce the incentive, which occurs with lifetime tenure, to appoint young individuals to the Supreme Court on the expectation that they will serve for decades. Presumably with a fixed term, a nominee's qualifications would weigh more heavily than age in the selection process. Finally, a fixed term would reduce the random nature of Supreme Court vacancies, which can unfairly advantage or disadvantage a political party. The extreme examples from the past half century are the presidency of Richard Nixon, during which five vacancies occurred, and the presidency of Jimmy Carter, when no vacancy occurred.

applied the law properly. The Supreme Court's appellate jurisdiction extends to cases arising under the Constitution, federal law and regulations, and treaties. The Court also hears appeals involving legal controversies that cross state or national boundaries. Article III of the Constitution gives Congress the power to create "exceptions" to the Supreme Court's appellate jurisdiction, whereas the Constitution prohibits Congress from altering its original jurisdiction.

Selecting and Deciding Cases

Nearly all cases that reach the Supreme Court do so after the losing party in a lower court asks the Court to hear its case. At this point, the **rule of four** comes into play. For a case to be accepted, at least four of the justices must agree to hear it. When that occurs, the Court issues a **writ of certiorari**, which is a request to the lower court to submit to the Court a record of the case. Each year, roughly 8,000 parties apply for certiorari, but the Court grants it in fewer than 100 cases (see Figure 14-1).[5] When the Supreme Court does accept a case, chances are that most of the justices disagree with the lower court's ruling. About three-fourths of Supreme Court decisions reverse the lower court's judgment.[6]

The Supreme Court seldom accepts a routine case, even if the justices believe that a lower court made a mistake. The Court's job is not to correct every error made by lower courts but to resolve major legal issues. The Court's own guidelines say that there must be "compelling reasons" for accepting a case, which include resolving issues that are being decided inconsistently by the lower courts, correcting serious departures from accepted standards of justice, settling key questions of federal law, and reviewing lower-court rulings that conflict with a previous Supreme Court decision.

The Court also weighs the specific features of a case in deciding whether to accept it. One feature is *ripeness*, which refers to whether the legal claim in a case is real and significant rather than speculative or based on future conditions that might not materialize. Another is *mootness*, which asks whether the

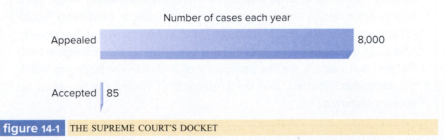

Number of cases each year

Appealed   8,000

Accepted   85

figure 14-1   THE SUPREME COURT'S DOCKET

The Supreme Court accepts only a small fraction of the roughly 8,000 cases appealed to it each year. The Court normally agrees to hear only those cases that have broad legal significance.
(*Source:* Supreme Court of the United States. Figures based on yearly average for 1990–2020 period)

Shown here are the Supreme Court justices during the 2019–2020 term. Left to right in front are Stephen Breyer, Clarence Thomas, John Roberts, Ruth Bader Ginsburg, and Samuel Alito. Left to right in back are Neil Gorsuch, Sonia Sotomayor, Elena Kagan, and Brett Kavanaugh. Ginsburg died shortly before the Court's 2020–2021 term began. (Chip Somodevilla/Getty Images)

circumstances that gave rise to the case still exist or have changed to such a degree that a decision is no longer relevant. A final is *standing*, which asks whether the party bringing the case is actually harmed by the action in question or is only marginally affected by it, if at all.[7]

During a Supreme Court hearing, the attorney for each side presents its oral argument, which typically is limited to 30 minutes.[8] Each side also provides the Court a written *brief,* which contains its fuller argument. The oral session is followed by the *judicial conference,* which is attended only by the nine justices and in which they discuss and vote on the case. The conference's proceedings are secret, which allows the justices to speak freely about a case and to change their minds as the discussion progresses.[9]

Issuing Decisions and Opinions

After a case has been decided, the Court issues its ruling, which consists of a decision and one or more opinions. The **decision** indicates which party won the case. The most important part of the ruling, however, is the **opinion**, which explains the legal basis for the decision. In the landmark *Brown v. Board of Education* opinion, for instance, the Court held that government-sponsored school segregation is unconstitutional because it violates the Fourteenth Amendment guarantee of equal protection under the law to all citizens (see the discussion in Chapter 5). This opinion became the legal basis on which public schools throughout the South were ordered by lower courts to end their policy of racial segregation.

When a majority of the justices agree on the legal basis of a decision, the result is a **majority opinion**. In some cases, there is no majority opinion because, although a majority of the justices agree on the decision, they disagree on the legal basis for it. The result in such cases is a **plurality opinion**, which presents the view held by most of the justices who vote with the winning side. Another type of opinion is a **concurring opinion**, a separate view written by a justice who votes with the majority but disagrees with all or part of its reasoning. Another type is a **dissenting opinion**; in it, a justice (or justices) on the losing side explains the reasons for disagreeing with the majority position. A final type is a **per curiam opinion**, which is an unsigned decision written for the Court as a whole. However, a justice who disagrees with a per curiam decision may choose to write a dissent and, if so, must sign it.

The Chief Justice, if among the justices in the majority, decides which justice will be tasked with writing the majority opinion. Otherwise, the senior justice in the majority picks the author. The justice who writes the Court's majority opinion has the responsibility to express accurately the majority's reasoning. The vote on a case is not considered final until the opinion is written and agreed upon, so give-and-take can occur during the writing stage. In rare instances, the writing stage has produced a change in the Court's decision. In *Lee v. Weisman* (1992), a case involving prayer at a public school graduation, Justice Anthony Kennedy originally sided with the four justices who said the prayer was permissible. While writing the 5–4 majority opinion, Kennedy found that he could not make a persuasive case for allowing it. He switched sides, resulting in a 5–4 majority the other way.

Other Federal Courts*

The Supreme Court's position at the top of the judicial system gives it unrivaled importance. Nevertheless, the Supreme Court is not the only court that

---

*In addition to the Supreme Court, the courts of appeals, and the district courts, the federal judiciary includes a few specialty courts. Among them are the U.S. Claims Court, which hears cases in which the U.S. government is being sued for damages; the U.S. Court of International Trade, which handles cases involving appeals of U.S. Customs Office rulings; and the U.S. Court of Military Appeals, which hears appeals of military courts-martial. Some federal agencies and commissions also have judicial powers (for example, the issuing of fines), and their decisions can be appealed to a federal court of appeals.

matters. Judge Jerome Frank once wrote of the "upper-court myth," which is the view that lower courts dutifully follow the rulings handed down by the courts above them.[10] The reality is different, as the following discussion explains.

U.S. District Courts   The lowest federal courts are the district courts (see Figure 14-2). There are 94 federal district courts altogether—at least 1 in every state and as many as 4 in the most populous states. Each district includes several judges, who number roughly 800 in all. The federal district courts are the chief trial courts of the federal system. Virtually all criminal and civil cases arising under federal law are argued first in the district courts. They are the only courts in the federal system where the two sides present their case to a jury for a verdict. Nearly all cases at this level are presided over by a single judge.

Lower federal courts rely on and follow Supreme Court decisions in their own rulings. The Supreme Court reiterated this requirement in a 1982 case, *Hutto v. Davis*: "Unless we wish anarchy to prevail within the federal judicial system, a precedent of this Court must be followed by the lower federal courts no matter how misguided the judges of those courts may think it to be."[11] However, the idea that lower courts are rigidly bound to Supreme Court rulings is part of the upper-court myth. The facts of a case before a district court

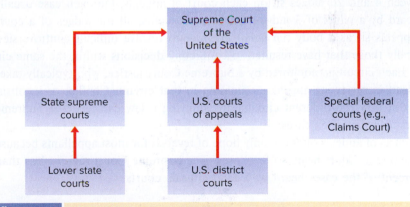

figure 14-2   THE FEDERAL JUDICIAL SYSTEM

This simplified diagram shows the relationships among the various levels of federal courts and between state and federal courts. The losing party in a case can appeal a lower-court decision to the court at the next highest level, as the arrows indicate. Decisions normally cannot be moved from state courts to federal courts unless they raise a U.S. constitutional issue, such as whether a defendant's right to a fair trial has been violated.

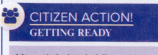

CITIZEN ACTION!
GETTING READY

Most criminal and civil cases involve state law, not federal law. Yet, state judiciaries are among the least visible of the nations' political institutions, even in states where judges are elected by voters. To gain an understanding of your state's judiciary, go online to see how it's structured, including how it divides responsibilities between different types of courts.

are seldom identical to those of a case settled by the Supreme Court. The lower-court judge must decide whether a different legal judgment is appropriate. As well, ambiguities or unaddressed issues in Supreme Court rulings give lower courts some flexibility in deciding cases. Most federal cases end with the district judge's decision. Typically, the losing party decides not to appeal the decision to a higher court.

U.S. Courts of Appeals Cases appealed from district courts go to federal courts of appeals, which are the second level of the federal court system. Courts of appeals do not use juries. Ordinarily, no new evidence is submitted in an appealed case. Instead, appellate courts base their decision on a review of the lower court's records. Appellate judges act as overseers, reviewing trial court decisions and correcting what they consider to be legal errors.

The United States has 13 courts of appeals. Eleven of them have jurisdiction over a "circuit" made up of the district courts in anywhere from three to nine states (see Figure 14-3). Of the other 2 appeals courts, 1 has jurisdiction over the District of Columbia (the D.C. "circuit"), and the other (the U.S. Court of Appeals for the Federal Circuit) has jurisdiction over appeals involving patents and international trade, regardless of the circuit in which they arise. Between 4 and 26 judges sit on each court of appeals, but each case usually is heard by a panel of 3 judges. On rare occasions, all the judges of a court of appeals sit as a body (*en banc*) in order to resolve difficult controversies, typically those that have resulted in conflicting decisions within the same circuit. Each circuit is monitored by a Supreme Court justice, who typically takes the lead in reviewing appeals originating in that circuit. Conflict or inconsistency in how the different circuits are applying a law can lead the Supreme Court to review such cases.

Courts of appeals offer the only hope of reversal for most appellants because the Supreme Court hears so few cases. The Supreme Court reviews less than 1 percent of the cases heard by federal appeals courts.

The State Courts

The American states are separate governments within the U.S. political system. The Tenth Amendment protects each state in its sovereignty, and each state has its own court system. Like the federal courts, state court systems have trial courts at the bottom level and appellate courts at the top.

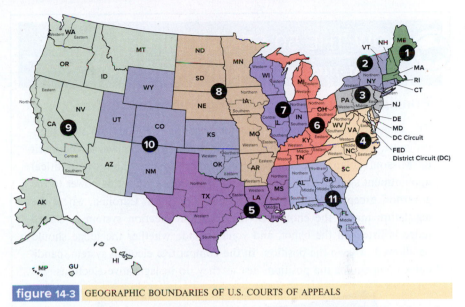

figure 14-3 GEOGRAPHIC BOUNDARIES OF U.S. COURTS OF APPEALS

The United States has 13 courts of appeals, each of which serves a "circuit." Eleven of these circuit courts serve anywhere from three to nine states, as the map shows. The other 2 are located in the District of Columbia: the Court of Appeals for the District of Columbia and the Court of Appeals for the Federal Circuit, which specializes in appeals involving patents and international trade. Within each circuit are federal trial courts, most of which are district courts. Each state has at least one district court within its boundaries. Larger states, such as California (which has four district courts, as can be seen on the map), have more than one. (*Source:* Administrative Office of the U.S. Courts.)

Each state decides for itself the structure of its courts and the method of selecting judges. In some states, the governor appoints judges, but in most states judges are elected to office. The most common form involves competitive elections of either a partisan or a nonpartisan nature. Other states use a mixed system called the *retention election plan* (also called the *merit plan* or the *Missouri Plan* because Missouri was the first state to use it). In this system, the governor appoints a judge from a short list of acceptable candidates provided by a judicial selection commission. At the first scheduled election after the judge has served for a year, the voters, by a simple "yes" or "no" vote, decide whether the judge should be retained in office (see "How the 50 States Differ").

Besides the upper-court myth, there exists a "federal court myth," which holds that the federal judiciary is the most significant part of the judicial system and that state courts play a subordinate role. This view is also inaccurate. More than 95 percent of the nation's legal cases are decided by state

HOW THE 50 STATES DIFFER

CRITICAL THINKING THROUGH COMPARISONS

Principal Methods of Selecting State Judges

The states use a variety of methods for selecting the judges on their highest court, including the retention election system (also known as the merit or Missouri Plan), the competitive election system, and the political appointment system. The states that appoint judges grant this power to the governor, except in Virginia, Connecticut, and South Carolina, where the legislature makes the choice. In the retention election system, a seated judge is listed on the ballot, and voters decide whether the judge should be allowed to keep the position. In the competitive election system, candidates compete for the position, just as they do in legislative elections.

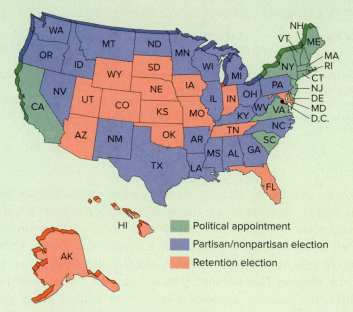

■ Political appointment
■ Partisan/nonpartisan election
■ Retention election

Source: The Council of State Governments.

Q: What might explain why several states in the middle of the nation use the retention election plan for selecting judges?

A: The retention election plan originated in the state of Missouri. Innovations in one state sometimes spread to adjacent states with similar political cultures.

or local courts. Most cases arising under *criminal law* (from shoplifting to murder) and most cases arising under *civil law* (such as divorces and business disputes) are defined by state laws or by local ordinances, which are derived from state laws.*

Moreover, nearly all cases that originate in state or local courts also end there. The federal courts do not come into the picture because the case does not involve a federal issue. The losing party in a divorce suit, for example, cannot appeal the decision to federal court because no federal law is involved. In most state criminal cases, there is also no federal issue, unless state authorities are alleged to have violated a right protected by the U.S. Constitution, such as the right of the accused to remain silent (see Chapter 4). In such instances, an individual convicted in a state court, after exhausting the avenues of appeal in the state system, can appeal to a federal court. If the federal court accepts the appeal, it ordinarily confines itself to the federal aspects of the case, such as whether the defendant's constitutional rights were, in fact, violated.

Issues traditionally within the jurisdiction of the states sometimes become federal issues. Before the Supreme Court's *Obergefell* (2015) ruling, for example, states had the authority to deny a marriage license to same-sex couples. In deciding that the right to marry is protected by the due process and equal-protection clauses of the Fourteenth Amendment, the Supreme Court made it a federal issue.

---

*Laws fall into three broad categories—procedural, civil, and criminal. *Procedural law* refers to rules that govern the legal process. In some cases, these rules apply to government, as in the example of the obligation of police to inform suspects of their right to an attorney. In other cases, the rules apply to private parties. For example, in some states, a homeowner cannot take an insurance company to court over a policy claim without first having that claim heard, and possibly resolved, by an arbitration board. *Civil law* governs relations with and between private parties, as when a person injured in an accident sues the other party for monetary damages. Marriage, divorce, business contracts, and property ownership are examples of relations covered by civil law. The losing party in a civil suit might be ordered to pay or otherwise compensate the other party but would not face jail unless he or she refused to comply with a court order, which can be a punishable offense. Government can also be a party to a civil suit, as when the IRS sues a taxpayer in a dispute over how much the taxpayer owes the government. *Criminal law* deals with acts that government defines as illegal, which can result in a fine, imprisonment, or other punishment. Murder, assault, and drunk driving are examples of acts covered by criminal law. The government is always a party to a criminal law case; the other party is the individual alleged to have broken the law. (Legal relationships between government and private parties, whether criminal or civil, are defined as *public law*. The term *private law* is used to refer to the legal rights and relationships between private parties.)

FEDERAL COURT APPOINTEES

Appointments to the federal courts are controlled by the president, who selects the nominees, and by the Senate, which confirms or rejects them. The quiet dignity of the courtroom gives the impression that the judiciary is as far removed from the world of politics as a governmental institution can be. In reality, federal judges and justices bring their political views with them to the courtroom and have opportunities to promote their beliefs through the cases they decide. Not surprisingly, the process by which federal judges are appointed is a partisan one.

Supreme Court Nominees

A Supreme Court appointment is a significant opportunity for a president.[12] Most justices retain their positions for many years, enabling presidents to influence judicial policy through their appointments long after they have left office. The careers of some Supreme Court justices provide dramatic testimony to the enduring nature of judicial appointments. For example, Franklin D. Roosevelt appointed William O. Douglas to the Supreme Court in 1939, and, for 30 years after Roosevelt's death in 1945, Douglas remained a strong liberal influence on the Court.

Presidents usually appoint jurists who have a compatible political philosophy. Although Supreme Court justices are free to make their own decisions, their legal positions can usually be predicted from their background. A study by judicial scholar Robert Scigliano found that about three of every four appointees have behaved on the Supreme Court approximately as presidents could have expected.[13] Of course, a president has no guarantee that a nominee will actually do so. Justices Earl Warren and William Brennan, for example, proved to be more liberal than President Dwight D. Eisenhower had anticipated. Asked whether he had made any mistakes as president, Eisenhower replied, "Yes, two, and they are both sitting on the Supreme Court."[14]

The importance of Supreme Court appointments has not been lost on the justices. They have sometimes timed their departure from the Court so that their replacement will be nominated by a like-minded president. Thurgood Marshall, the first Black justice, failed in his effort to do so. Marshall's health was in decline while Ronald Reagan was president, and he hated the idea of being replaced by a conservative justice. Marshall told his law clerk, "If I die when that man's president, I want you to just prop me up and keep me voting."[15] As it happened, Marshall outlived the Reagan presidency but resigned due to illness when Reagan's successor, George H. W. Bush, also a Republican, was in office. Bush chose Clarence Thomas, the second Black justice, to replace Marshall. Marshall was one of the most liberal justices ever to serve on the Court, while Thomas has been one of the Court's most conservative justices ever.

When a president picks a nominee to fill a vacancy on the Supreme Court, the nominee is appointed to the Court only if confirmed by majority vote in the Senate. In 2016, following the death of Justice Antonin Scalia, the Senate's Republican majority refused to hold a vote on Democratic president Barack Obama's nominee, Merrick Garland. It was the first time in history such action had been taken. It enabled Donald Trump to fill the seat with Neil Gorsuch when he became president in early 2017. However, in 2020, after the death of Justice Ruth Bader Ginsburg, Republicans were worried that they would lose the seat if Trump lost the upcoming election and rushed to confirm Amy Comey Barrett to fill it. Democrats denounced the move, noting that Republicans in 2016 had claimed that the only fair way to fill a vacancy in an election year was to let the winner of the presidential election make the choice.

Nearly 20 percent of presidential nominees to the Supreme Court have been rejected by the Senate on grounds of judicial qualification, legal views, personal

Shown here is Brett Kavanaugh testifying before the Senate Judiciary Committee during a hearing on his nomination to a seat on the Supreme Court. The Senate proceedings were the most heated in memory and included allegations of sexual misconduct when Kavanaugh was in high school and college. He was confirmed on a 50–48 Senate vote. (Win McNamee/Getty Images)

ethics, or partisanship. Most of these rejections occurred before 1900, and partisan politics was the usual reason. Today, a nominee with strong professional and ethical credentials is less likely to be blocked for partisan reasons alone. Garland was the first nominee to be blocked since Robert Bork in 1987. His nomination by President Reagan was rejected because Senate Democrats objected to his statements on abortion rights and civil rights. In 2017, Senate Republicans abolished the use of the filibuster to block Supreme Court nominees, which has decreased the likelihood that future nominees will be rejected by the Senate. None of the three most recent appointees would have been seated without the change. Each nominee was confirmed by a Senate vote of less than the 60–40 vote margin that would have been required if the filibuster had remained in place. Each nomination was bitterly contested with the vote dividing sharply along party lines.

Lower-Court Nominees

The president typically delegates to the deputy attorney general the task of identifying nominees for lower-court positions, a process that includes seeking recommendations from U.S. senators of the president's party, and sometimes House members as well.

More than 90 percent of recent district and appeals court nominees have come from the president's party.[16] A constraint on these appointments is the fact that nominees must be confirmed by the Senate. Senators from the opposing party will try to derail any nominee whom they perceive as holding extreme judicial views. They sometimes succeed, although their ability to do so has diminished. In 2014, Senate Democrats abolished the filibuster for lower-court nominations, a move that presaged its elimination for Supreme Court nominees in 2017 by Senate Republicans.

Although presidents are not as personally involved in selecting lower-court nominees as in naming potential Supreme Court justices, lower-court appointments are collectively significant. A president who serves two terms can shape the federal judiciary for years to come. By the time he left office, Democrat Barack Obama had appointed about a third of the seated federal judges. Republican George W. Bush appointed a similar number during his eight years in office.

Judges' partisan backgrounds have an effect on their decisions. A study of the voting records of appellate court judges found, for example, that Democratic appointees were more likely than Republican appointees to side with defendants who claimed the government violated their civil liberties.[17] Such tendencies should not be interpreted to mean that federal judges engage in blatant partisanship on the bench. Most lower-court cases are clear-cut enough that judges have limited leeway in how they interpret the law. In addition, judges prize their judicial independence. They are officers of a separate branch of government and secure in their tenure, factors that allow them to apply the law in impartial ways. Nevertheless, analysts worry that the judiciary is changing. Some recent judicial nominees have been chosen more on the basis of partisan ideology than on their legal qualifications, raising the question of whether they will act impartially in deciding cases.[18]

Personal Backgrounds of Judicial Appointees

Women and minorities are underrepresented on the federal bench, just as they are underrepresented in Congress and at the top levels of the executive branch. Roughly 25 percent of federal judges are women and 20 percent are minorities. Women and minorities are key Democratic constituencies, and most of the female and minority-group judges were appointed by a Democratic president (see Figure 14-4).

In recent decades, the Supreme Court has become more demographrepresentative. Until Sandra Day O'Connor was appointed in 1981, no woman had served on the Supreme Court. Since then, four more women have been appointed. For more than 200 years, the Court always had a Protestant majority. Prior to the 20th century, only one Catholic (Roger Taney) had served on the Court. Until the appointment of Louis D. Brandies in 2016, no Jewish justices had ever served. Today, two of the justices are Jewish and a majority are Catholic. Thurgood Marshall in 1967 was the first Black justice. Antonin Scalia in 1986 was the Supreme Court's first justice of Italian descent. Sonia Sotomayor, who was appointed in 2009, is the first Hispanic justice.

In one respect, however, the Supreme Court is less diverse than in the past. Elective office (particularly a seat in the U.S. Senate) was once a common route to the Supreme Court, but recent appointees have come from the appellate courts (see Table 14-1). The assumption is that such individuals have the type of experience best suited to the duties of a Supreme Court justice. Not

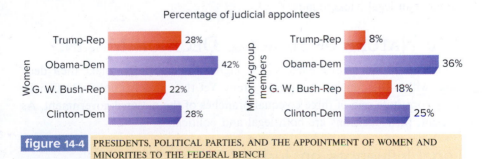

Percentage of judicial appointees

Women
- Trump-Rep: 28%
- Obama-Dem: 42%
- G. W. Bush-Rep: 22%
- Clinton-Dem: 28%

Minority-group members
- Trump-Rep: 8%
- Obama-Dem: 36%
- G. W. Bush-Rep: 18%
- Clinton-Dem: 25%

figure 14-4 PRESIDENTS, POLITICAL PARTIES, AND THE APPOINTMENT OF WOMEN AND MINORITIES TO THE FEDERAL BENCH

Reflecting differences in their parties' coalitions, recent Republican and Democratic presidents differed in the percentage of women and minority-group members that they appointed to the federal bench. (*Source:* Pew Research Center, 2019. Figures for past presidents are based on all confirmed nominees. Figures for Trump based on judicial appointees during first two years in office.)

table 14-1	JUSTICES OF THE SUPREME COURT		
Justice	Year of Appointment	Nominating President	Position Before Appointment
Clarence Thomas	1991	G. H. W. Bush	Judge, D.C. Circuit Court of Appeals
Stephen Breyer	1994	Clinton	Judge, 1st Circuit Court of Appeals
John Roberts Jr.	2005	G. W. Bush	Judge, D.C. Circuit Court of Appeals
Samuel Alito Jr.	2006	G. W. Bush	Judge, 3rd Circuit Court of Appeals
Sonia Sotomayor	2009	Obama	Judge, 2nd Circuit Court of Appeals
Elena Kagan	2010	Obama	Solicitor general of the United States
Neil Gorsuch	2017	Trump	Judge, 10th Circuit Court of Appeals
Brett Kavanaugh	2018	Trump	Judge, D.C. Circuit Court of Appeals
Amy Comey Barrett	2020	Trump	Judge, 7th Circuit Court of Appeals

all observers agree. They contend that, because Supreme Court decisions have political as well as legal consequences, the Court would be better served if some of the justices had high-level political experience. Many of the leading justices of the past, including John Marshall and Earl Warren, had political rather than legal backgrounds.

THE NATURE OF JUDICIAL DECISION MAKING

Unlike the president or members of Congress, federal judges make their decisions within the context of a legal system. Yet they are also political officials: They constitute one of three co-equal branches of the national government. As a result, their decisions are both legal and political.

Legal Influences on Judicial Decisions

Article III of the Constitution bars a federal court from issuing a decision except in response to a case presented to it. This restriction is a substantial one. For one thing, it limits judges to issues that arise from actual legal disputes.

As federal judge David Bazelon noted, a judge "can't wake up one morning and simply decide to give a helpful little push to a school system, a mental hospital, or the local housing agency."[19]

The facts of a particular case also limit judicial action. The **facts** of a case are the relevant circumstances of a legal dispute or offense. In the case of a person accused of murder, for example, the key facts would include evidence about the crime and whether the rights of the accused had been upheld by police. A judge must handle a murder case as a murder case, applying to it the laws that define murder and the penalties for it. A murder case cannot be used as an occasion for a judge to pronounce judgment on free-speech rights or campaign finance laws.

The law is also a major constraint on the courts. Although a president or Congress can make almost any decision that is politically acceptable, the judiciary must work within the limits of the law. When asked by a friend to "do justice," Justice Oliver Wendell Holmes Jr. said that he was bound to follow the law rather than his personal sense of right and wrong.[20]

The judiciary works within the context of three main sources of law: the Constitution, legislative statutes, and legal precedents (see Table 14-2). The Constitution of the United States is the nation's highest law, and judges and justices are sworn to uphold it. When a case raises a constitutional issue, a court has the duty to apply relevant provisions of the Constitution to the case. For example, the Constitution prohibits the states from printing their own currency. If a state decided that it would do so, anyway, a federal judge would be obligated to rule against the practice.

The large majority of cases that arise in courts involve issues of statutory law rather than constitutional law. *Statutory law* is legislative (statute) law.

table 14-2	SOURCES OF LAW THAT CONSTRAIN THE DECISIONS OF THE FEDERAL JUDICIARY

U.S. Constitution: The federal courts are bound by the provisions of the U.S. Constitution. The sparseness of its wording, however, requires the Constitution to be applied in the light of present circumstances. Thus, judges are accorded some degree of discretion in their constitutional judgments.

Statutory law: The federal courts are constrained by statutes and by administrative regulations derived from the provisions of statutes. Many laws, however, are somewhat vague in their provisions and often have unanticipated applications. As a result, judges have some freedom in deciding cases based on statutes.

Precedent: Federal courts tend to follow precedent (or *stare decisis*), which is a legal principle developed through earlier court decisions. Because times change and not all cases have a clear precedent, judges have some discretion in their evaluation of the way earlier cases apply to a current case.

Congress has enacted tens of thousands of laws in its history, many of which sooner or later became the subject of court action. In such cases, courts must apply the statute in question. A company that is charged with violating an air pollution law, for example, will be judged within the context of that statute—what it permits and what it prohibits, as well as what penalties apply if the company is found to have broken the law. In most cases involving statutory law, the law is clear enough that, when the facts of the case are determined, the decision is fairly straightforward. Statutory law also comes into play in judges' decisions in cases involving *administrative law,* which consists of the rules, regulations, and judgments that government agencies make in the process of implementing and enforcing statutory law.

The U.S. legal system developed from the English common-law tradition, which includes the principle that a court's decision on a case should be consistent with **precedent** (or *stare decisis*), a term that refers to previous court rulings on similar cases. Deference to precedent gives predictability to the application of law. Government has an obligation to make clear what its laws are and how they are being applied. If courts routinely ignored how similar cases had been decided in the past, they would create confusion and uncertainty about what is lawful and what is not. A business firm that is seeking to comply with environmental protection laws, for example, can develop company policies that will keep the company safely within the law if court decisions in this area are consistent. If courts routinely ignored precedent, a firm could unintentionally engage in an activity that a court might conclude was unlawful.

Although judges are required to follow the Constitution, statutes, administrative laws, and precedent, the law is not always a precise guide, with the result that judges can have leeway in their rulings.[21] The Constitution, for example, is a sparsely worded document and must be adapted to new and changing situations. The judiciary also has no choice at times but to impose meaning on statutory law. Statutes are typically more detailed in their provisions than is the Constitution, but Congress cannot always anticipate the specific applications of a legislative act and often expresses statutory provisions in general terms. The judiciary is then required to determine what the language means in the context of a specific case. Precedent is an even less precise guide in that precedent is specific to particular cases. A new case may differ in important ways from its closest precedent or rest at the intersection of conflicting precedents. In such instances, a judge must determine which precedent, if any, applies to the case at hand.

When hearing a case involving statutory law or administrative regulation, judges often try to determine whether the meaning of the statute or regulation can be determined by common sense (the "plain meaning rule"). The question for the judge is the intent of the law or regulation. Sometimes, the courts study the legislative record to determine what Congress had in mind when enacting a law. An example is a case that involved the question of whether employment protection for those with disabilities should be extended to include nearsighted people. In this instance, it was ruled that they were not protected by the legislation. If nearsighted people were to be classified as "disabled," then half of the American public would be considered disabled, which clearly was not what Congress had in mind.

The Supreme Court's ruling in *Bostock v. Clayton County* (2020), involving LGBT discrimination in the workplace, illustrates the ambiguity that sometimes exists in the law. The Court developed its ruling in the context of the 1964 Civil Rights Act. The act prohibits workplace discrimination but makes no mention of discrimination on the basis of sexual orientation. The Court concluded that this type of discrimination is among the types of job-related discrimination prohibited by the Civil Rights Act.[22] In this instance, the Court was "making" law. It was deciding how legislation enacted by Congress applied to behavior that Congress had not specifically addressed when it wrote the legislation.

Political Influences on Judicial Decisions

When judges have leeway in deciding a case, political influences can affect their decisions. These influences come from both inside and outside the judicial system.

Inside the Court: Judges' Political Beliefs   Although the judiciary symbolizes John Adams's description of the U.S. political system as "a government of laws, and not of men," court rulings are not simply an extension of the laws. They are also influenced by the political beliefs of the men and women who sit on the federal bench.[23] Changes in the Supreme Court's membership, for example, can bring about a change in its position (see "Party Polarization: Has Polarization Reached into the Supreme Court?"). Samuel Alito's appointment to the Court in 2006 produced that kind of change. Although the justice he replaced, Sandra Day O'Connor, usually voted with the Court's four most conservative justices, she sometimes switched sides. Voting with the Court's four most liberal justices, she cast the deciding vote, for example, in a 2003 case that upheld limits on campaign spending by corporations.[24] In contrast, Alito cast the deciding vote in the 2010 *Citizens United* case, which struck down the limits.[25]

Studies by political scientists Jeffrey Segal and Harold Spaeth show that justices tend to vote in line with their political background. Segal and Spaeth examined thousands of nonunanimous Court decisions, looking at the extent to which each justice voted on the same side or the opposite side from each of the other justices. Clear patterns emerged. Compared with Democratic

Detecting Misinformation

Are Federal Judges Biased?

Angered by a court ruling, President Donald Trump said that the judge was biased, blasting him as an "Obama judge." It prompted a rare public rebuke from John Roberts, the Chief Justice of the Supreme Court. Roberts said, "We do not have Obama judges or Trump judges, Bush judges or Clinton judges. What we have is an extraordinary group of dedicated judges doing their level best to do equal right to those appearing before them."

moodboard/Getty Images

Is that claim fact, or is it fake?

Studies of judicial decisions don't provide a simple answer to the question. Federal judges work within the limits of the law, and, in the great majority of cases, the law predicts their decision, whether they were appointed to the federal bench by a Republican or Democratic president. However, studies also show that Republican and Democratic appointees differ somewhat in their decisions. For example, Republican appointees, on average, impose slightly longer sentences on those convicted of crime than do Democratic appointees.[26] The relationship between judges' partisan background and their decisions is most pronounced in Supreme Court cases. Many recent Supreme Court cases have been decided by a vote of 5-4 or 6-3; and typically the lineup has had Republican appointees on one side of the issue and Democratic appointees on the other side. Cases heard by the Supreme Court tend to be those for which the law is conflicting or ambiguous, allowing justices' partisan beliefs to influence their decisions.[27]

appointees to the Court, Republican appointees were more likely to side with employers rather than with employees, with law enforcement officials rather than with the criminally accused, with corporations rather than with unions, and with government rather than with those claiming discrimination. Segal and Spaeth conclude that the "[policy] preferences of the justices go a long way toward explaining their decisions."[28]

PARTY POLARIZATION

Conflicting Ideas

Has Polarization Reached into the Supreme Court?

University of Chicago law professor William Landes and federal appellate judge Richard Posner, who was appointed to the bench in the 1980s by President Reagan, examined the voting records of the 43 Supreme Court justices who had sat on the Court between 1937 and 2008. For each case heard by the Court during this period, Landes and Posner assessed whether a vote could be said to favor the liberal or the conservative side. For example, in cases alleging that the government had violated a criminal defendant's constitutional rights, a vote in favor of the government would be considered conservative and a vote in favor of the defendant would be considered liberal. Landes and Posner then ranked the 43 justices from the justice who voted most consistently in the conservative direction to the justice who voted most consistently in the liberal direction. Following are the 5 most conservative and 5 most liberal Supreme Court justices since 1937 (with the president who appointed the justice in parentheses):

Five Most Conservative	Five Most Liberal
1. Clarence Thomas (G. H. W. Bush)	1. Thurgood Marshall (Johnson)
2. William Rehnquist (Nixon)	2. William O. Douglas (Roosevelt)
3. Antonin Scalia (Reagan)	3. Frank Murphy (Roosevelt)
4. John Roberts (G. W. Bush)	4. Wiley Blount Rutledge (Roosevelt)
5. Samuel Alito (G. W. Bush)	5. Arthur Goldberg (Johnson)

Q: Is there anything in the rankings that would suggest today's party polarization has reached into the Supreme Court?

A: Three of the most conservative justices of the past 80 years are currently on the Court (Thomas, Roberts, and Alito). They tend to vote together on cases, forming what Court observers have labeled the institution's "conservative bloc."

It is true, of course, that disputes that reach the Supreme Court are anything but clear-cut. If they were, they would have been settled in the lower federal courts. It is also true that Supreme Court justices have less leeway in making their decisions than elected officials have in making their choices. Justices operate within the confines of established laws and legal principles, which constrain their choices. The fact that Republican appointees to the Supreme Court are more likely than Democratic appointees to side with law enforcement officials than with the criminally accused does not mean that they invariably do so or that they are unmindful of legal restraints on law enforcement officials. In *United States v. Jones* (2012), for example, the Supreme Court unanimously held that law enforcement officials had exceeded their authority under the law by placing a GPS tracking device on a suspect's car without first obtaining a search warrant from a judge (see Chapter 4). Nevertheless, when viewed as a whole, Supreme Court decisions are unquestionably a mix of law and politics.[29]

Outside the Court: The Public, Interest Groups, and Elected Officials   The courts can and do make unpopular decisions. In the long run, however, judicial decisions must be seen as fair if they are to be obeyed. In other words, the judiciary cannot routinely ignore the expectations of the general public, interest groups, and elected officials.

Judges are less responsive than elected officials to public opinion as a result of the fact that, once appointed to office, they hold the position indefinitely. Early in his tenure as chief justice, John Roberts said, "I think the most important thing for the public to understand is that we are not a political branch of government. They don't elect us. If they don't like what we're doing, it's more or less just too bad."[30] Nevertheless, the Supreme Court usually stays close enough to public opinion to reduce the likelihood of outright defiance of its decisions.[31] It has sometimes tempered its rulings in an effort to get public support or reduce public resistance. In the 1954 *Brown v. Board of Education* case, for example, the justices, recognizing that school desegregation would be an explosive issue in the South, required only that desegregation take place "with all deliberate speed" rather than immediately or on a fixed timetable.

Interest groups also have an influence on the judiciary. Groups petition the White House and Congress to appoint judges and justices who share their outlook on legal disputes. More directly, they submit *amicus curiae* ("friend of the court") briefs to make their positions known on court cases (see Chapter 9), and they file

CITIZEN ACTION!
GETTING READY

An understanding of the governing system will help you develop informed opinions. Supreme Court rulings are one of the least understood of key policy decisions. Consider going online and reading an actual Supreme Court case, such as *Citizens United* or *Obergefell*, including the majority and dissenting opinions. You'll come away with a clearer understanding of the nature of judicial decision making.

Even though the Supreme Court tried to temper the public response to its 1954 *Brown v. Board of Education* decision by ruling that desegregation of public schools should proceed with "all deliberate speed" rather than immediately or on a fixed timetable, the delay in implementation did little to quell the anger of many white southerners. Shown here is one of the many billboards in the South that called for the impeachment of Chief Justice Earl Warren. (AP Images)

lawsuits to advance their policy goals. Groups that rely on a judicial strategy pick their cases carefully, choosing those that offer the greatest chance of success. They also carefully pick the courts in which they file their lawsuits, knowing that some judges will be more sympathetic than others to their argument. In fact, some groups rely almost entirely on legal action, knowing they have a better chance of success in the courts than in Congress or the White House. The American Civil Liberties Union (ACLU), for example, has filed hundreds of lawsuits over the years on issues of individual rights, including suits aimed at protecting the privacy of information stored on cell phones and computers.

Groups and individuals can also try to influence the judiciary through so-called test cases, which are cases designed to set precedent on an issue not previously ruled on by the courts. An example is the lawsuit that challenged the District of Columbia's restriction on handguns. In *District of Columbia v. Heller* (2008), the Supreme Court issued its first-ever ruling on the meaning of the Second Amendment, holding that it protects an individual's right to keep and bear arms and that the District of Columbia's prohibition on handguns violated this guarantee.[32]

Elected officials also have ways of influencing the courts. Congress can rewrite legislation that it feels the judiciary has misinterpreted. Meanwhile, the president has some influence over the cases that come before the courts. During President Trump's first year in office, for example, the Justice Department pursued only a third as many civil rights lawsuits as the Justice Department averaged each year during the Obama administration.[33] The president through the Justice Department is also responsible for enforcing court decisions. Courts make decisions but depend on executive officials to carry them out. In *Gonzales v. Raich* (2005), for example, the Supreme Court ruled that the production and use of homegrown marijuana even in states that allow its use for medical purposes is a federal offense.[34] The Justice Department rarely pursues or prosecutes such cases.

Judicial appointments offer the president and Congress their biggest opportunity to influence the courts. As a result of the party polarization that has worked its way into the nation's politics, the judicial appointment process has become increasingly contentious. Democratic and Republican lawmakers alike recognize the power of the courts to determine policy in areas such as affirmative action and environmental protection, and each party's lawmakers have been determined to confirm judicial appointees whose policy views align with their own. They have been joined in these efforts by interest groups on both sides of the partisan divide. In the case of Supreme Court appointments, there have even been televised advertising campaigns supporting or opposing nominees. In *Electing Justices,* political scientist Richard Davis shows that the Supreme Court appointments are now conducted more like political campaigns than like the dignified process the writers of the Constitution envisioned.[35]

JUDICIAL POWER AND DEMOCRATIC GOVERNMENT

Federal judges are unelected officials with lifetime appointments, which places them beyond the reach of the voters. A basic question is how far judges should go in substituting their judgments for those of elected officials. This question is most compelling when courts apply their power of **judicial review** to declare that an executive or legislation action is unconstitutional. In such instances, they are placing their judgment above that of the people's representatives and in a way that is nearly always final. The difficulty of amending the Constitution, which requires approval by two-thirds majorities in the House and Senate and three-fourths of the state legislatures, makes it an impracticable means of reversing a constitutional law ruling.

Judicial review applies only in cases where a provision of the Constitution is at issue. Most cases that involve executive or congressional actions arise under ordinary law. In these cases, if a court determines that officials have acted unlawfully, they can respond by changing the law or acting within it. When it was discovered, for example, that the National Security Agency (NSA) was collecting information about Americans' cell phone calls, a federal appeals court blocked the program, ruling that it was not authorized by law.[36] Congress responded by passing a law authorizing the program, which was subsequently upheld by the courts.

Nevertheless, judicial review is a major source of the courts' power, and one that is particularly formidable in the American case. Few democracies divide power as thoroughly as does the United States, which splits it among three branches as well as between the national and state levels. Also, the U.S. system grants individuals a broad range of rights that are protected from infringement by government. Each of these features of the American system is a source of constitutional dispute. What's the dividing line between legislative and executive power? Between national and state power? Between individual rights and the power of government? U.S. federal courts typically have the final say on these questions. As Chief Justice Charles Evans Hughes noted in 1907, "We live under a constitution, but the Constitution is what the judges say it is."

What is the proper role of an unelected judiciary in a system rooted in the principle of majority rule? How far should judges go in substituting their judgment for that of the people's elected representatives? There are competing schools of thought on this issue, none of which is definitive. The Constitution is silent on the question of how it should be interpreted, which has left the judiciary's proper role open to dispute. Nevertheless, it's instructive to briefly review two leading competing theories, judicial restraint and judicial activism. They differ over the degree to which judges should defer to precedent and the policy decisions of elected officials.

Judicial Restraint Versus Judicial Activism

The doctrine of **judicial restraint** holds that policy decisions in nearly every instance should be decided by elected lawmakers and not by appointed judges. The role of the judge is to apply the law rather than create it. Advocates of judicial restraint say that, when judges substitute their views for those of elected representatives, they undermine the fundamental principle of self-government—the right of the majority, through its elected representatives, to determine how it will be governed.[37] Underlying this argument is the idea that policy is the result of conflicts between contending interests and that elected representatives, because they have to deal directly with these interests, are better positioned than judges to determine how these conflicts should be resolved.

In contrast, the doctrine of **judicial activism** holds that judges should actively interpret the Constitution, statutes, and precedents in light of fundamental principles and should intervene when elected representatives fail to protect these principles. Although advocates of judicial activism acknowledge the need for deference to majority rule, they claim that the courts should not blindly uphold the decisions of elected officials when core principles—such as liberty, equality, and self-government—are at issue. They also contend that precedent should be respected only if based on legal reasoning that is as sound today as it was when the precedent was established.[38]

Over its history, the Supreme Court has had strong proponents of each doctrine. Chief Justice John Marshall was an avowed activist who used the Court to enlarge the judiciary's power and to promote the national government (see Chapters 2 and 3). Judicial review—the most substantial form of judicial power—is not granted explicitly by the Constitution but was claimed through Marshall's opinion in *Marbury v. Madison.*

Associate Justice Oliver Wendell Holmes Jr. was Marshall's philosophical opposite. One of the nation's most influential jurists, Holmes argued that the judiciary should defer to the elected branches unless they blatantly overstep their authority.[39] An example of judicial restraint is the Supreme Court's 2012

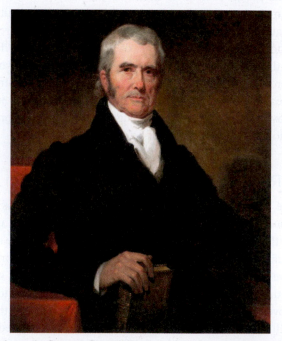

John Marshall presided over the Supreme Court during the nation's formative years. A judicial activist, he worked through court rulings to strengthen the power of the national government and bolster the Court as an independent and co-equal branch of government. Marshall is the longest-serving chief justice in the nation's history. He was on the Court from 1801 to 1835, which spanned the administrations of six presidents. (Art Reserve/Alamy Stock Photo)

ruling upholding the individual mandate provision of the health care reform bill enacted by Congress in 2010. The Court's majority creatively invoked Congress's taxing power in order to uphold the provision (see Chapter 3). "Because the Constitution permits such a tax, it is not our role to forbid it, or to pass upon its wisdom or fairness," said the Court's majority.[40]

Although judicial activism is sometimes associated with liberal justices, history indicates that conservative justices also engage in it. During the period between the Civil War and the Great Depression, the Supreme Court was dominated by conservatives and had an activist agenda, striking down most state and congressional legislation aimed at economic regulation (see Chapter 3). In the period after World War II, the Court was again in an activist mode, but this time in a different direction. Dominated by liberal justices, the Court struck down numerous state statutes in the course of expanding fair-trial rights and civil rights (see Chapters 4 and 5).

In recent years, the conservative-dominated Supreme Court has been an activist court. In the past two decades, the Supreme Court has struck down more acts of Congress than were invalidated during the previous half century.[41] An example is the Court's 2010 *Citizens United* ruling (see "Case Study: *Citizens United v. Federal Election Commission (2010)*"). It was an activist decision in regard to both precedent and deference to elected officials. In deciding that corporations and unions could spend freely on election campaigns, the Court overturned a law of Congress, thus substituting its judgment for that of elected officials. The ruling also overturned precedent—in earlier cases, the Court had held that Congress could regulate election spending by corporations and unions.

What Is the Judiciary's Proper Role?

The debate between advocates of judicial restraint and advocates of activism is a normative one. There is no conclusive way of settling the issue because the Constitution does not define the method by which judges should arrive at their decisions.

Nevertheless, the debate is important because it addresses the fundamental question of the role of judges in a governing system based on the conflicting concepts of majority rule and individual rights. The United States is a constitutional democracy that recognizes both the power of the majority to rule and the claim of the minority to protection of its rights and interests. The judiciary was not established as the nation's final authority on all things relating to the use of political power. Yet the judiciary was established as a co-equal branch of government charged with responsibility for protecting individual rights and limiting political authority. The question of how far the courts should go in asserting their authority is one that every student of government should ponder.

CASE STUDY

Politics in Action

Citizens United v. Federal Election Commission (2010)

In *Citizens United*, the Supreme Court concluded that Congress had overstepped its constitutional authority, ruling that spending restrictions infringed on the free-speech rights of corporations and unions. Writing for the majority, Justice Anthony Kennedy said, "If the First Amendment has any force, it prohibits Congress from fining or jailing citizens, or associations of citizens, for simply engaging in political speech." The Court's minority dissented, arguing that corporations and unions are not what the framers had in mind in when referring to "the people" in the First Amendment.

Sean Locke Photography/Shutterstock

In deciding *Citizens United*, the Supreme Court's nine justices split 5–4. All five justices (Roberts, Alito, Kennedy, Scalia, and Thomas) who claimed that the First Amendment allowed for unlimited campaign spending by corporations and unions were appointed to the Court by Republican presidents. The four justices (Breyer, Ginsburg, Sotomayor, and Stevens) who claimed Congress had the power to regulate spending were Democratic appointees, with the exception of Stevens, who had been appointed to the Court three decades earlier by President Gerald Ford, a moderate Republican.

Q: If you had been on the Supreme Court, how would you have voted in the *Citizens United* case?

ASK YOURSELF: Does the First Amendment's guarantee of "freedom of speech" protect corporations as well as individuals? Is the spending of money a form of speech protected by the First Amendment? Even if money is considered a form of protected speech, does the First Amendment prevent Congress from placing a reasonable limit on how much an individual or corporation could spend on a campaign?

SUMMARY

At the lowest level of the federal judicial system are the district courts, where most federal cases begin. Above them are the federal courts of appeals, which review cases appealed from the lower courts. The U.S. Supreme Court is the nation's highest court. Each state has its own court system, consisting of trial courts at the bottom and one or two appellate levels at the top. Cases originating in state courts ordinarily cannot be appealed to the federal courts unless a federal issue is involved, and then the federal courts can choose to rule only on the federal aspects of the case. Federal judges at all levels are nominated by the president, and, if confirmed by the Senate, they are appointed by the president to the office. Once on the federal bench, they serve until they die, retire, or are removed by impeachment and conviction.

The Supreme Court is unquestionably the most important court in the country. The legal principles it establishes are binding on lower courts, and its capacity to define the law is enhanced by the control it exercises over the cases it hears. However, it is inaccurate to assume that lower courts are inconsequential (the upper-court myth). Lower courts have considerable discretion, and the great majority of their decisions are not reviewed by a higher court. It is also inaccurate to assume that federal courts are far more significant than state courts (the federal court myth).

The courts have less discretionary authority than elected institutions do. The judiciary's positions are constrained by the facts of a case and by the laws as defined through the Constitution, legal precedent, and statutes (and government regulations derived from statutes). However, existing legal guidelines are seldom so precise that judges have no choice in their decisions. As a result, political influences have a strong impact on the judiciary. It responds to national conditions, public opinion, interest groups, and elected officials, particularly the president and members of Congress. Another political influence on the judiciary is the personal beliefs of judges, who have individual preferences that affect how they decide issues that come before the courts. It's not surprising that partisan politics plays a significant role in judicial appointments.

In recent decades, as the Supreme Court has crossed into areas traditionally left to lawmaking majorities, the issue of judicial power has become more pressing, which has prompted claims and counterclaims about the judiciary's proper role. Advocates of judicial restraint claim that the justices' personal values are inadequate justification for exceeding the proper judicial role; they argue that the Constitution entrusts broad issues of the public good to elected institutions and that the courts should be exceptionally deferential to their judgment. Judicial activists counter that the courts were established as an independent branch and should seek to protect and advance fundamental constitutional principles even when such action conflicts with the policies adopted by elected institutions.

CRITICAL THINKING ZONE

KEY TERMS

appellate jurisdiction (*p. 414*)

concurring opinion (*p. 418*)

decision (*p. 417*)

dissenting opinion (*p. 418*)

facts (*p. 429*)

judicial activism (*p. 437*)

judicial restraint (*p. 437*)

judicial review (*p. 436*)

jurisdiction (*p. 414*)

majority opinion (*p. 418*)

opinion (*p. 417*)

original jurisdiction (*p. 414*)

plurality opinion (*p. 418*)

per curiam opinion (*p. 418*)

precedent (*p. 430*)

rule of four (*p. 416*)

writ of certiorari (*p. 416*)

APPLYING THE ELEMENTS OF CRITICAL THINKING

Conceptualizing: Define *majority opinion, concurring opinion,* and *dissenting opinion* in the context of Supreme Court decision making. What role is the majority opinion expected to play in decisions made by lower-court judges?

Synthesizing: Contrast the doctrines of judicial restraint and judicial activism.

Analyzing: Explain the influence of politics on the selection of Supreme Court justices and on the decisions the justices make. In comparison with lower-court judges, why would Supreme Court justices be expected to let their political beliefs play a greater role in their decisions? (Consider the nature of the cases heard by the Supreme Court.)

EXTRA CREDIT

A Book Worth Reading: Jeffrey Toobin, *The Nine: Inside the Secret World of the Supreme Court* (New York: Anchor, 2008). Winner of the J. Anthony Lewis Book Prize, this book by a noted journalist provides a riveting look at the inside workings of the Supreme Court.

A Website Worth Visiting: www.oyez.org/ An easy-to-use website that includes the full versions of historic and recent Supreme Court decisions and information on cases currently being heard by the Court.

ECONOMIC AND ENVIRONMENTAL POLICY: CONTRIBUTING TO PROSPERITY

moodboard/Getty Images

> 66 We the People of the United States, in Order to . . . insure domestic Tranquility. 99
>
> PREAMBLE, U.S. CONSTITUTION

The economy was in turmoil in 2020. Restaurants, theaters, and small businesses by the tens of thousands were shuttered. Weekly unemployment applications were the highest on record. The stock market was tanking; it lost 10 percent of its value on one day alone, the biggest one-day drop ever. Streets in many of the country's cities were largely empty of traffic. Americans were sheltering in their homes, trying to avoid the threat of the COVID-19 coronavirus. Was the United States headed for an economic meltdown that would rival the Great Depression of the 1930s?

Few economists predicted as much, and for good reason. When the Great Depression struck in 1929, there were no government programs in place to stabilize and stimulate the economy. Back then, panic had swept society, accelerating the downturn. Businesses cut back on production, investors fled the stock market, depositors withdrew their bank savings, and consumers slowed

The COVID-19 coronavirus pandemic brought normal life to a standstill. It was a health crisis but also an economic crisis that the government fought with loans, monetary transfers, and other programs aimed at protecting the financial well-being of businesses, workers, and families. (StockMediaSeller/Shutterstock)

their spending—all of which fueled the downward spiral. In 2020, however, government stepped in to steady the economy through adjustments in interest rates and government spending. A key initiative was a $2 trillion stimulus bill, which included direct cash payments to individuals and families, increased unemployment benefits, financial assistance to hospitals, aid to small businesses, and loans to financially strapped companies.

This chapter examines economic and environmental policy. As was discussed in Chapter 1, public policy is a decision by government to follow a course of action designed to produce a particular result. In this vein, economic policy aims to promote and regulate economic interests and, through fiscal and monetary actions, to foster economic growth and stability. This chapter presents the following main ideas:

- *Through regulation, the U.S. government imposes restraints on business activity for the purpose of promoting economic efficiency and equity.* Regulatory action includes protecting the environment from the harmful effects of business and consumer activity.

- *Through promotion, the U.S. government helps private interests achieve their economic goals.* Business, in particular, benefits from the government's promotional efforts, including tax breaks and loans.

- *Through its taxing and spending decisions (fiscal policy), the U.S. government seeks to generate a level of economic supply and demand that will maintain economic prosperity.* Fiscal policy can be conducted through the use of either demand-side or supply-side tools.

- *Through its money supply decisions (monetary policy), the U.S. government—through the Federal Reserve System ("the Fed")—seeks to stimulate economic growth at a level that's not inflationary.*

GOVERNMENT AS REGULATOR OF THE ECONOMY

An **economy** is a system of production and consumption of goods and services that are allocated through exchange. When a shopper selects an item at a store, and pays for it with cash or a credit card, the transaction is one of the millions of exchanges that make up the economy.

In *The Wealth of Nations* (1776), Adam Smith advanced the doctrine of **laissez-faire economics**, which holds that private firms should be free to make their own production decisions. Smith reasoned that firms will produce a good when there is a demand for it (that is, when people are willing and able to buy it). Smith argued that the profit motive is the "invisible hand" that guides supply decisions in a capitalist system. He also acknowledged that laissez-faire capitalism has limits. Certain areas of the economy, such as roadways, are natural monopolies and are better handled by government than by private firms. Government is also needed to impose order on private transactions by regulating banking, currency, and contracts. Otherwise, Smith argued, the economy should be left largely in private hands.

Although laissez-faire economics prevailed in the United States during the 19th century, government was not sidelined completely. Through the Pacific Railways Act of 1862, for example, Congress authorized the issuance of government bonds and the use of public lands to build the transcontinental railroad, which, although operated by private firms, was subject to government regulation. Nevertheless, it was not until the 1930s Great Depression that government assumed a broad economic role. Today, the United States has what is called a *mixed economy.* Although the economy operates mainly through private transactions, government plays a significant role. New prescription drugs, for example, cannot be marketed until they've been tested and the Food and Drug Administration (FDA) has certified them as safe and effective. The U.S. government even owns some industries (for example, the Tennessee Valley Authority, which produces electricity). Nevertheless, in comparison, say, with the Scandinavian countries, where government provides health care to all citizens and controls several major industries, including the airlines, the United States relies more heavily on free-market mechanisms.

One way the U.S. government participates in the economy is through the **regulation** of business activity.[1] U.S. firms are not free to act as they please, but instead operate within the limit of government regulation, which is designed to promote economic *efficiency* and *equity* (see Table 15-1).

table 15-1	THE MAIN OBJECTIVES OF REGULATORY POLICY	
Objective	Definition	Representative Actions by Government
Efficiency	Fulfillment of society's needs with as few of its resources as possible; the greater the output for a given input, the greater the efficiency	Preventing restraint of trade; requiring producers to pay the costs of environmental damage; regulating business only when justified on a cost–benefit basis
Equity	Ensuring that the outcome of an economic transaction is fair to each party	Requiring firms to treat workers and consumers fairly

Efficiency Through Government Intervention

Economic efficiency results when the output of goods and services is the highest possible, given the amount of input (such as labor and material) used to produce it.[2] *Efficiency* means that society is getting as many goods and services as possible from the resources used to produce them.

Promoting Competition   Adam Smith and other classical economists argued that the free market is the optimal means of achieving efficiency. In producing goods and services, firms will try to use as few resources as possible in order to keep their prices low, which will make their products more attractive to consumers. To compete, less efficient producers will have to cut their production costs or face the loss of customers to lower-priced competitors.

Markets are not always competitive, however. If a producer can acquire a monopoly on a particular product or conspires with other producers to fix the price of the product at an artificially high level, the producer does not have to be concerned with efficiency. Consumers who need a product will have no choice but to pay the seller's price. Price fixing was prevalent in the United States in the late 19th century, when large trusts came to dominate many areas of the economy, including the oil, railroad, and sugar industries. Railroad companies, for example, had no competition on short routes and charged such high rates that many farmers went broke because of the cost of shipping their crops to markets. In 1887, Congress enacted the Interstate Commerce Act, which created the Interstate Commerce Commission (ICC) and assigned it responsibility for regulating railroad practices, including shipping rates.

This 1914 cartoon shows railroad companies petitioning the Interstate Commerce Commission (depicted as Uncle Sam) for permission to raise their rates. The first federal regulatory agency, the ICC was created by Congress in 1887 to regulate the railroads to stop them from gouging their customers on routes where they had a monopoly. The ghost in the background is that of William Henry Vanderbilt, the wealthiest of the railroad tycoons. (*Source:* Library of Congress Prints & Photographs Division [LC-DIG-ppmsca-28030])

The goal of such regulatory activity is to improve efficiency by restoring market competition or by placing a limit on what monopolies can charge for goods and services. Business competition today is overseen by a wide range of federal agencies, including the Federal Trade Commission (FTC). In 2016, the FTC blocked, for a second time, an attempted merger of Office Depot and Staples, saying "it would lead to higher prices" for office supplies. On the other hand, the FTC has allowed concentrated ownership in industries such as oil and automobiles, where the capital costs are so high that small firms cannot hope to compete.[3] Government acceptance of corporate giants also reflects the fact that market competition is no longer simply an issue of domestic firms. For example, the major U.S. automakers—Chrysler, Ford, and General Motors—compete for customers not only with each other but also with Asian and European auto manufacturers, such as Honda and BMW.

Deregulation and Underregulation   Although government regulation is intended to increase economic efficiency, it can have the opposite effect if it unnecessarily increases the cost of doing business.[4] Firms have to devote work hours to monitor and implement government regulations. These costs are efficient to the degree that they produce corresponding benefits. However, if government places excessive regulatory burdens on firms, they waste resources in the process of complying. The result of overregulation is higher-priced goods that are more expensive for consumers and less competitive in the domestic and global markets.

To curb overregulation, Congress in 1995 enacted legislation that prohibits administrators in some instances from issuing a regulation unless they can show that its benefits outweigh its costs. A more concerted response is **deregulation**—the rescinding of regulations already in force for the purpose of improving efficiency. This process began in 1977 with passage of the Airline Deregulation Act, which eliminated the requirement that airlines provide service to smaller cities and gave the airlines the authority to set ticket prices (before then, the prices were set by a government agency). The change worked as intended. Competition between airlines increased on routes between larger cities, resulting in cheaper airfares on these routes. Congress followed airline deregulation with partial deregulation of, among others, the trucking, banking, energy, and communications industries.

Deregulation, however, can be carried too far.[5] Freed of regulatory restrictions, firms can engage in reckless or unethical practices. Such was the case with the subprime mortgage crisis that struck in 2008 (see "Case Study: The Subprime Mortgage Crisis"). In 1999, Congress had repealed the Great Depression–era Glass-Steagall Act, which had restricted retail banks from using depositors' funds to make risky investments. Banks jumped at the opportunity, luring marginally qualified home buyers by offering low interest rates and small down payments. When the economy weakened, many homeowners defaulted on their mortgages, precipitating the 2008 financial crisis. In 2010, Congress responded by enacting the most substantial regulation of financial institutions since the New Deal era. Designed to curb the abuses that contributed to the financial crisis, the Dodd-Frank Wall Street Reform and Consumer Protection Act empowers government to oversee financial activities more closely. It also created a new federal agency, the Consumer Financial Protection Bureau, to protect consumers from exploitation by credit card companies, lending institutions, and other creditors.

CASE STUDY

Politics in Action

The Subprime Mortgage Crisis

"Moral hazard" is a justification for government regulation. Economist Paul Krugman describes moral hazard as the situation in which "one person makes the decision about how much risk to take, while someone else bears the cost if things go badly."

Few developments illustrate the problem more clearly than the subprime home mortgage crisis that triggered the near collapse of America's financial sector in 2008. Several years earlier, financial regulations on mortgage lending had been relaxed. By 2006, a third of mortgages were being given to people with weak or unconfirmed credit

Ryan McVay/Photodisc/Getty Images

records. Banks had leveraged their assets at roughly 30 to 1—up from the previous level of 12 to 1—in an effort to make ever larger profits. This put the entire housing industry at risk if the economy turned bad and homeowners were unable to keep up with their mortgages, which is what happened in 2007-2008. Banks found themselves in possession of millions of houses that had been abandoned or were in default.

America's taxpayers were the ones who saved the banks from collapsing. Congress appropriated hundreds of billions of dollars in loans to keep Bank of America, Citibank, and other major banks from going bankrupt. They were considered "too big to fail." If they went down, the entire economy could have gone down with them, yet it was their risky investments that had imperiled them. Another party—the taxpayers—bore the cost, which is the precise definition of a "moral hazard."

Q: Are there circumstances in which "too big to fail" is sensible public policy? What's the best way to prevent the problem from happening in the first place?

ASK YOURSELF: Would you bail out the banks if their collapse would have a domino effect, taking down other businesses with them? If you would bail out the banks in that situation, then they're "too big to fail." In terms of preventing the problem, do you trust banks to regulate themselves? Or is strict government regulation necessary?

The crisis in America's financial system demonstrates that the issue of business regulation is not a simple question of whether or not to regulate. Too much regulation can burden firms with excessive implementation costs, whereas too little regulation can give firms the leeway to engage in risky or unethical practices. Either too little or too much regulation can result in economic inefficiency.

Equity Through Government Intervention

The government intervenes in the economy to bring equity as well as efficiency to the marketplace. **Economic equity** occurs when an economic transaction is fair to each party.[6] A transaction can be considered fair if each party enters into it freely and ethically. For example, if a seller knows that a product is defective, equity requires that the buyer also know of the defect.

The first wave of equity regulation came during the Progressive Era of the early 1900s, when reformers sought to stop corrupt business practices. One such reform was creation of the Food and Drug Administration (FDA) in 1907. Unsafe foods and drugs were being sold to unsuspecting customers, and the FDA was charged with keeping them off the market.

The second wave of equity regulation came during the 1930s Great Depression, when New Deal reformers sought to restrict unfair business practices. The Securities and Exchange Act of 1934, for example, aimed to protect investors from dishonest or imprudent stock and bond brokers. The New Deal also provided greater equity for organized labor. The Fair Labor Standards Act of 1938, for example, required employers to pay workers a minimum wage.

The third wave of regulatory reforms came in the 1960s and 1970s and sought to promote environmental protection, consumer protection, and worker safety. Ten federal agencies, including the Consumer Product Safety Commission and the Environmental Protection Agency, were established to curtail harmful business activity. Among the products declared to be unsafe in the 1960s and 1970s were cigarettes, leaded paint, and leaded gasoline.

This regulatory activity has had a remarkable effect. Consider cigarettes, for example. Beginning in the 1960s, the federal government required cigarette manufacturers to put warning labels about the dangers of smoking on cigarette packs. At the time, more than 40 percent of American adults were cigarette smokers. Today, that figure is 20 percent. As the number of smokers has declined, so has the incidence of lung cancer, emphysema, and other smoking-related ailments. A Yale University study estimated that 8 million lives have been saved in the United States through antitobacco regulation.[7] How many lives is that? That's twice the number of all the people currently living in Boston, San Francisco, Seattle, Dallas, Atlanta, and Minneapolis combined.

SURGEON GENERAL'S WARNING:
Smoking Causes Lung Cancer,
Heart Disease, Emphysema, And
May Complicate Pregnancy.

In the 1960s, the federal government began requiring tobacco companies to put health warnings on cigarette packs. The warning labels and other efforts to get Americans to stop smoking have saved millions of lives. (DanBrandenburg/E+/Getty Images)

The FDA recently started to regulate e-cigarettes, banning their free distribution on grounds that the practice was designed to lure young people into using them. Manufacturers challenged the ban, but a federal appeals court sided with the FDA, finding that the products are "indisputably highly addictive and pose health risks, especially to youth, that are not well understood."[8]

The Politics of Regulatory Policy

Although business firms fought the Progressive Era and New Deal reforms, their opposition diminished when they came to realize that they could influence the new regulatory agencies. Because the agencies were charged with overseeing particular industries, such as banking or pharmaceuticals, a regulated industry could develop a close relationship with its associated agency. Pharmaceutical firms, for example, cultivated a relationship with the FDA that, at times, has served their interest. In the 1990s, for instance, drug companies convinced the FDA to streamline its drug-safety reviews in order to speed the marketing of new drugs.[9] One fast-tracked drug, Vioxx, had to be taken off the market in 2004 after it was found to cause strokes and heart attacks.

The third wave of regulatory reforms of the 1960s and 1970s differed from the Progressive and New Deal reforms in their structure. Most of the regulatory agencies established in the third wave were granted a broader mandate than those created earlier. They have responsibility not for a single industry but for firms of all types, and their responsibilities cover a wide range of activities. The Environmental Protection Agency (EPA), for example, is charged with regulating environmental pollution of almost any kind by almost any firm. Because newer agencies such as the EPA deal with so many industries, no single industry can easily influence their decisions.

Most of the older agencies, including the Federal Communications Commission (FCC) and the Securities and Exchange Commission (SEC), are run by a commission whose members are nominated by the president and serve fixed terms but cannot be removed by the president during their term of office, which is a reason they sometimes get too friendly with the industries they regulate. Most of the newer agencies, including the EPA, are headed by a single director who can be removed from office at the president's discretion. As a result, the newer agencies tend to be more responsive to the president than to the firms they oversee.

As in other policy areas, Republican and Democratic lawmakers often disagree on regulatory issues. Although lawmakers of both parties see a need to regulate business, Republican lawmakers have closer ties to business and lean toward less regulation. When the Dodd-Frank Act came up for a vote in 2010, for example, nearly every congressional Democrat voted for it and nearly every congressional Republican voted against it. In 2017, with the Republicans in control of the presidency and Congress, Republican lawmakers weakened the Dodd-Frank Act by reducing restrictions on the lending practices of small banks.

GOVERNMENT AS PROTECTOR OF THE ENVIRONMENT

The full costs of business activity are not always borne by producers and consumers. Consider, for example, a company whose industrial wastes seep into a nearby lake. The price that consumers pay for the company's products does not reflect the cost to society of the polluted water. **Externalities** is the term that economists use to describe such unpaid costs.

Before the 1960s, the federal government did not require firms to pay to reduce externalities. The publication in 1962 of Rachel Carson's *Silent Spring* helped launch the environmental movement.[10] Written at a time when the author was dying of breast cancer, *Silent Spring* exposed the threat to birds and animals of pesticides such as DDT. Carson's appearance at a Senate hearing contributed to legislative action that produced the 1963 Clean Air Act and the 1965 Water Quality Act—the first major federal laws aimed at protecting the environment from human pollution. Firms would be required to install antipollution devices in order to reduce their harmful air and water emissions.

Environmental Protection

The Environmental Protection Agency was created in 1970. Proposed by Republican president Richard Nixon and enacted by the Democratic-controlled Congress, the EPA was given responsibility for enforcing the nation's environmental laws, including the levying of fines and sanctions on firms that violate them.

Environmental laws and regulations have led to greatly reduced levels of air and water pollution. Shown on the left is a photo of Los Angeles from the time when yellowish-gray polluted air ("smog") regularly hung over the city. On the right is a photo of today's Los Angeles. (smog: Daniel Stein/E+/ Getty Images; clear: ekash/E+/Getty Images)

Environmental regulation has led to dramatic improvements in air and water quality. Pollution levels today are far below their levels of the 1960s, when yellowish-gray fog ("smog") hung over cities such as Los Angeles and New York and when some bodies of water, like the Potomac River and Lake Erie, were open sewers. In 1969, the Cuyahoga River, which flows through Cleveland, burned for a half hour after sparks from a passing train ignited oil-slickened debris floating on it. Over the past five decades, as a result of regulatory policies, toxic waste emissions have been halved, hundreds of polluted lakes and rivers have been revitalized, energy efficiency has increased, food supplies have been made safer, and urban air pollution has declined by 60 percent.[11]

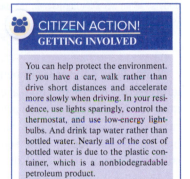

CITIZEN ACTION!
GETTING INVOLVED

You can help protect the environment. If you have a car, walk rather than drive short distances and accelerate more slowly when driving. In your residence, use lights sparingly, control the thermostat, and use low-energy light-bulbs. And drink tap water rather than bottled water. Nearly all of the cost of bottled water is due to the plastic container, which is a nonbiodegradable petroleum product.

Climate Change and Energy Policy

No environmental issue receives more attention today than global warming. The earth's temperature level has been rising, and the rate of increase has accelerated since the mid-1970s (see Figure 15-1). The National Oceanic and Atmospheric Administration has been measuring annual temperatures for nearly 150 years. Seven of the globe's warmest years on record have occurred since 2010.[12] Scientists theorize that the temperature rise is attributable to emissions from oil, coal, and other carbon-based fuels, and they say that dire consequences—including water shortages, rising sea levels, and extreme heat waves—will result unless carbon emissions are curbed.

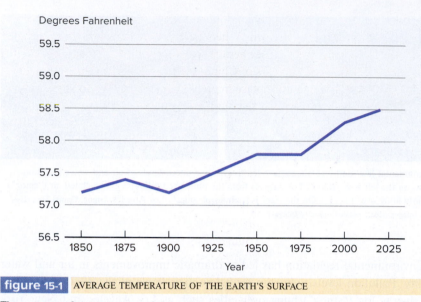

Degrees Fahrenheit

figure 15-1   AVERAGE TEMPERATURE OF THE EARTH'S SURFACE

The average surface temperature of the earth has risen substantially in the past century and has done so at an accelerating pace in the past four decades. (*Source:* National Aeronautics and Space Administration, 2020)

Some U.S. policymakers believe that climate change needs to be urgently addressed. Others say that a concerted effort should wait until the consequences of climate change are better understood. Still others say that the remedies for climate change, such as requiring companies to reduce their carbon emissions, would slow economic growth to an unacceptable level. And still others have challenged the scientific consensus, saying that the evidence for the climate change thesis is faulty or inconclusive.

The United States has lagged behind most Western countries, including Germany, France, and Great Britain, in reducing its greenhouse gas emissions. The reasons are several, including policy disagreement and the structure of the U.S. political system. The division of power among the president, the House, and the Senate makes it difficult to garner the support necessary to implement costly regulatory policies. In 2015, at the United Nations Climate Change Conference in Paris, the participating countries, including the United States, unanimously agreed to voluntarily "reduce their carbon emissions as soon as possible." On becoming president in 2017, Donald Trump, a skeptic of climate change, withdrew the United States from the Paris accord, placing it among the handful of countries not in the agreement. After his election in 2020, Joe Biden, a proponent of action on climate change, promised to reverse Trump's decision upon taking office.

The issue of climate change is confounded by the fact that no single nation can solve the problem on its own. When carbon emissions get into the atmosphere, they affect conditions elsewhere. The problem is also confounded by the rapid expansion of the economies of China, India, and other developing nations, which has contributed to the increase in carbon emissions. Developing countries say they should not bear most of the burden of curbing global warming, arguing

F A K E
or
F A C T

Detecting Misinformation

Is Weather an Indicator of Climate Change?

After the usually warm winter of 2020, polls found an increase in the number of Americans who believed that climate change was occurring. Polls conducted during the winter of 2019, when a polar vortex settled in over a large part of the central United States, found an increase in the number of people who denied climate change. Clearly, many Americans equate climate change and the weather.

Is that claim fact, or is it fake?

Stacey Bramhall/Getty Images

Climate change and weather are not the same thing. Weather is what's happening today. Climate change is what's been happening over a lengthy period of time. Seven of the warmest years on record have occurred in the past decade, which is a sign of climate change. However, on any given day or period during the past decade, it might have been unusually warm or cold—that's the weather. It's not shocking that many people conflate the two. We tend to rely on personal experience for many of our opinions, and a string of cold winter days can persuade us that global warming is a fiction. During a severe ice storm, Donald Trump said climate change is a "total, and very expensive, hoax." Climate scientists draw their conclusions in a different way. They examine decades of temperature and other data from hundreds of locations across the globe, looking for patterns over time. A conclusion based on the weather we're experiencing today is one data point. Climate scientists deduce what's happening from millions of data points stretching back more than a century.

that the problem stems from decades of carbon emissions by the industrialized nations, including the United States. In turn, fully industrialized countries have argued that recent increases in carbon emissions are coming largely from developing countries and that the problem cannot be solved unless they rein in their emissions (see "How the U.S. Differs").

HOW THE U.S. DIFFERS

CRITICAL THINKING THROUGH COMPARISONS

Carbon-Fuel Emissions and Global Warming

The United States is topped only by China as the world's largest source of carbon-fuel emissions. In fact, as European Commission data indicate, the five leading countries account for two-thirds of the world's total. Developing nations say the global warming problem was caused largely by decades of pollution by the United States and other fully industrialized nations. Industrialized nations say that China and other developing nations are today the biggest source of the problem.

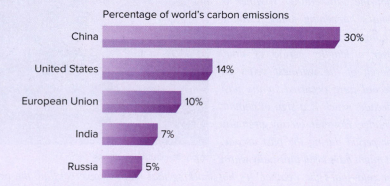

Percentage of world's carbon emissions

China — 30%
United States — 14%
European Union — 10%
India — 7%
Russia — 5%

Q: Why might it make sense to place most of the burden for reducing carbon-fuel emissions on nations with developing economies, such as China and India?

A: Carbon emissions in developing countries are increasing at the fastest rate. Advanced industrialized nations, such as the United States and Germany, could assist them by providing the financial subsidies and technology needed to create clean-energy economies.

GOVERNMENT AS PROMOTER OF ECONOMIC INTERESTS

Congress in 1789 gave a boost to the nation's shipping industry by imposing a tariff on goods brought into the United States on foreign ships, which prompted importers to make greater use of American ships. Since that first favor, the U.S. government has provided thousands of direct and indirect benefits to economic interests. The following sections describe some of these benefits.

Promoting Business

Business firms are not opposed to government regulation as such. They object only to regulatory policies that harm their interests. At various times and in different ways, as in the case of the FDA and pharmaceutical firms, some regulatory agencies have sided with the very industries they are supposed to regulate in the public interest.

Loans and tax breaks are other ways that government promotes business interests. Firms receive loan guarantees, direct loans, tax credits for capital investments, and tax deductions for capital depreciation. The $2 trillion stimulus bill that Congress enacted in early 2020 in response to the COVID-19 coronavirus pandemic included $500 billion for financially strapped firms. For its part, the Federal Reserve set aside hundreds of billions for loans to banks.

Nevertheless, the most significant contribution that government makes to business is in the traditional services it provides, such as education, transportation, and defense. Colleges and universities, which receive substantial funding from federal and state governments, furnish business with most of its professional and technical workforce and with much of the basic research that goes into product development. The nation's roadways, waterways, and airports are other public-sector contributions without which business could not function. The U.S. Navy patrols ocean shipping lanes in order to keep them safe for commercial traffic. In short, America's business has no bigger booster than government.

Promoting Labor

Laissez-faire thinking dominated government's approach to labor well into the 20th century. Union activity was held by the courts to be illegal because it interfered with the rights of business. Government hostility toward labor included the use of police and soldiers to break up strikes. In 1914 in Ludlow, Colorado, state militia attacked a tent colony of striking miners and their families, killing 19, including 11 children.

A major contribution that government makes to economic interests—particularly business but also labor and agriculture—is through public colleges and universities. Supported in significant part by taxpayer dollars, they provide research and workforce training of benefit to economic interests, which otherwise would have to pay the costs themselves. Shown here is a campus scene of the University of Texas at San Antonio. (Courtesy of The University of Texas at San Antonio)

The 1930s Great Depression brought about a change in labor's position. The National Labor Relations Act of 1935, for example, gave workers the right to bargain collectively and prohibited business from disrupting union activities or discriminating against union employees. Government support for labor now also includes minimum-wage and maximum-work-hour guarantees, unemployment benefits, safer and more healthful working conditions, and nondiscriminatory hiring practices. Although the federal government's support of labor extends beyond these examples, its support is much less extensive than its support of business.

Labor has been the target of policies that have weakened its position. Slightly more than half of the states, for example, have right-to-work laws that give workers in a unionized workplace the option of not joining the union. They get the benefit of union-negotiated contracts but don't contribute dues to the union.

In a major 2018 decision, the U.S. Supreme Court, in a 5–4 vote, dealt unions a sharp blow by ruling that public-sector unions can no longer collect mandatory dues. Most union members today work in the public sector. The 2018 ruling reversed a 1977 ruling that held public-sector workers could be required to pay union dues because they benefit from the collective bargaining agreements negotiated by their unions. In overturning precedent, the Court held that the mandatory requirement violates members' First Amendment rights because the dues could be used by their union to support policy positions that the member finds objectionable.[13]

Promoting Agriculture

Government support for agriculture has a long history. The Homestead Act of 1862, for example, opened government-owned lands to settlement. The federal government provided 160 acres of land free to any family that staked a claim, built a house, and farmed the land for five years.

Government programs today provide billions of dollars of assistance annually to farmers, small and large. Federal payments account for more than a fifth of net agricultural income, making America's farmers among the most heavily subsidized in the world. This assistance is intended, in part, to reduce the market risks associated with farming. Weather, global conditions, and other factors can radically affect crop and livestock prices from one year to the next, and federal subsidies lend a degree of stability to farmers' income.

FISCAL POLICY AS AN ECONOMIC TOOL

Before the 1930s, prevailing economic theory held that the economy was self-regulating, that it would correct itself after a downturn. The greatest economic collapse in the nation's history—the Great Depression of the 1930s—shattered that idea. The economy did not recover on its own, but instead continued to decline. President Franklin D. Roosevelt's spending and job programs, which stimulated the economy and helped put Americans back to work, ushered in the modern era.[14] Today, government is expected to intervene when the economy dips.

The government's efforts to maintain a thriving economy occur in part through its taxing and spending decisions, which together are referred to as its **fiscal policy**. Through changes in its level of spending and taxation, government can stimulate or slow the economy.

Demand-Side Policy

Fiscal policy has its origins in the early-20th-century economic theories of John Maynard Keynes. Noting that employers tend to cut their production and workforce when the economy begins to weaken, Keynes challenged the traditional idea that government should also cut back on its spending. Keynes argued that a downturn can be shortened only if government compensates for the slowdown in private spending by increasing its spending level. In doing so, the government pumps money into the economy, which stimulates consumer spending, which in turn stimulates business production and creates jobs, thereby hastening the economic recovery.[15]

HOW THE 50 STATES DIFFER

CRITICAL THINKING THROUGH COMPARISONS

Federal Taxes and Benefits: Winners and Losers

Fiscal policy (the federal government's taxing and spending policies) varies in its impact on the states. Businessinsider.com calculated how much firms and residents in each state send to the federal government in tax and other payments, and then how much firms and residents in each state receive from the federal government as a result of Social Security payments, contracts, facility costs, and so on. The biggest loser is New Jersey, which sends $2,784 more per capita to Washington than it gets back. Massachusetts ($1,532) and Connecticut ($1,242) are the next two biggest losers. The biggest winner is New Mexico, which gains $9,624 per capita from federal spending and taxing. West Virginia ($7,981) and Mississippi ($7,902) are the next biggest winners.

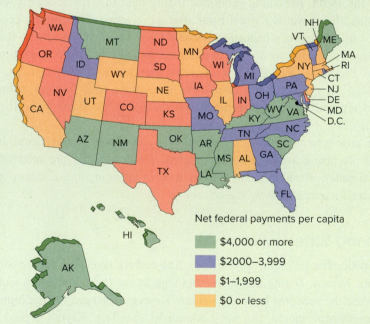

Net federal payments per capita

- $4,000 or more
- $2000–3,999
- $1–1,999
- $0 or less

Q: Why are many of the "winners" in the southeastern part of the U.S.?

A: States in the southeastern area are not as wealthy as most states. Because of this, they pay fewer federal taxes while getting more federal assistance for programs designed to help low-income individuals. As well, a large number of the nation's military installations and defense contractors—a large source of federal money—are located in the southeastern area of the country.

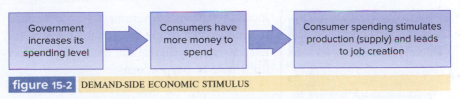

| Government increases its spending level | → | Consumers have more money to spend | → | Consumer spending stimulates production (supply) and leads to job creation |

figure 15-2 DEMAND-SIDE ECONOMIC STIMULUS

When the economy is sluggish, demand-side economics holds that government should increase its spending in order to boost consumer spending (demand), which will create jobs and stimulate production (supply).

Keynesian theory holds that the level of the government's response should be commensurate with the severity of the downturn. During an **economic depression**—an exceptionally steep and sustained decline in the economy—the government should engage in massive new spending programs to speed the recovery. During an **economic recession**, which is a more common but less severe downturn, government spending should also be increased but by a lesser amount.

Keynes's theory is based on **demand-side economics**. It emphasizes the consumer "demand" component of the supply–demand relationship (see Figure 15-2). When the economy is sluggish, the government, by increasing its spending, places additional money in consumers' hands. With more money in their pockets, consumers spend more, which boosts demand for products, prompting firms to retain or hire workers to produce the goods and services. This line of reasoning affected the $2 trillion economic stimulus bill that Congress passed in 2020 in response to the coronavirus pandemic. It included cash payments directly to individuals and families, with the expectation that the resulting spending would create jobs and spark production.

Although demand-side policy is typically applied during an economic downturn, it can also be used to slow down the economy during an inflationary period—when prices are rising rapidly. By cutting back on its spending, government places less money into consumers' hands, helping slow the rise in prices.

Demand-side stimulation has been the preferred policy of Democratic lawmakers. Lower-income Americans are a core Democratic constituency and are usually the most deeply affected by rising unemployment. Accordingly, Democratic leaders have typically responded to a sluggish economy with increased government spending (demand-side fiscal policy), which offers direct help to the unemployed and stimulates consumption.

Supply-Side Policy

Republican Party leaders are more likely to see an economic downturn through the lens of business firms. Republicans have typically resisted large spending

CITIZEN ACTION!
GETTING READY

"To decide, you first have to know." That maxim applies when it comes to holding an informed opinion about the choice between demand-side fiscal policy and supply-side fiscal policy. Consider doing extra reading to better understand their relative strengths and weaknesses, as well as who benefits most from their application.

increases because government has to borrow the money, which creates upward pressure on interest rates, including the rates that business firms have to pay for loans.

A fiscal policy alternative to demand-side stimulation, preferred by Republicans, is **supply-side economics**, which emphasizes the production side of the supply–demand equation. Supply-side policies were a cornerstone of the Reagan and Bush administrations' response to slowing economic growth.[16] Rather than relying on government spending programs to boost consumer spending, Republican presidents Reagan and Bush turned to large tax cuts for companies and upper-income taxpayers as a means of stimulating business activity. In the case of the Bush tax cuts, the tax savings to Americans in the top 1 percent of income were $54,493 per year, compared with an average of $67 for those in the bottom 20 percent and $611 for those in the middle 20 percent.[17] The assumption of supply-side theory is that, if firms and wealthier individuals have more money to spend, they will invest it in production (supply), which will boost employment and consumer spending (see Figure 15-3). Supply-side policy has been called *trickle-down economics*–the notion that wealth at the top will trickle down to the benefit of those lower on the economic ladder.

Fiscal Policy: Practical and Political Limits

Both demand-side policy and supply-side policy have risks as well as rewards. Although they can stimulate the economy, they come at a cost–large budget deficits and a rising level of national debt.

High levels of government spending or deep cuts in taxes result in a **budget deficit**–in which the federal government spends more in a year than it receives

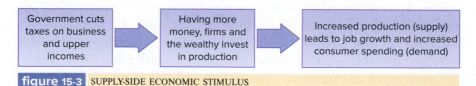

| Government cuts taxes on business and upper incomes | → | Having more money, firms and the wealthy invest in production | → | Increased production (supply) leads to job growth and increased consumer spending (demand) |

figure 15-3 SUPPLY-SIDE ECONOMIC STIMULUS

When the economy is sluggish, supply-side economics holds that government should cut taxes on business and wealthy taxpayers in order to boost investment in production (supply), which will create jobs and increase consumer spending (demand).

in tax and other revenues. The shortfall increases the **national debt**, which is the total cumulative amount the federal government owes to its creditors (see Figure 15-4). In recent years, the government has spent far more than it has received in taxes, forcing it to borrow funds to cover the shortfall. The U.S. government has not had a **balanced budget** (in which revenues are equal to government expenditures) since the late 1990s. Projections indicate that high deficits will continue far into the future, adding to the national debt, which already exceeds $25 trillion. The U.S. government spends more than $400 billion each year just to pay the interest on the debt. That amount exceeds the combined annual federal spending on the Departments of Education, Labor, Transportation, and Housing and Urban Development.[18]

Each political party blames the other party for the nation's fiscal problems, but, in fact, both parties have contributed. When the Democrats have been in power, they've sponsored increases in domestic spending. When the Republicans have been in power, they've adopted tax reductions and military spending increases. Republicans and Democrats have each been in power several times in the past four decades. The national debt has risen every year during that period.

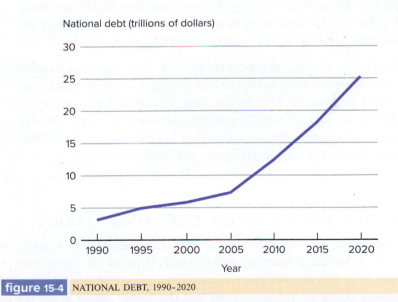

National debt (trillions of dollars)

figure 15-4 NATIONAL DEBT, 1990–2020

The national debt, which is the total cumulative amount the federal government owes to its creditors, has risen sharply since 1990 owing to overly steep tax cuts, wars in the Middle East, and severe economic downturns that began in 2008 and 2020. (*Source:* Federal Reserve)

PARTY POLARIZATION

Conflicting Ideas

Taxes

There is barely an economic issue on which Republican and Democratic lawmakers now agree. It was not always that way. In the period after World War II, Republicans and Democrats often worked together on economic issues. An example is the Federal-Aid Highway Act of 1956, which led to the building of the nation's interstate highway system. Proposed by Republican president Dwight D. Eisenhower, it was backed by an overwhelming bipartisan majority in Congress.

Bipartisanship began to wane in the 1980s, when Republican president Ronald Reagan, despite Democratic opposition, got Congress to cut taxes on upper incomes. The divide over tax policy has persisted, with Republicans pushing for lower taxes overall and on higher-income taxpayers particularly, whereas Democrats have pushed for higher taxes on the wealthy and reduced taxes on lower-income individuals.

The difference between the parties was evident in the Tax Cuts and Jobs Act, which the Republican-controlled Congress enacted in 2017. The bill featured large tax cuts for corporations and upper-income taxpayers. The Senate vote divided strictly along party lines, with every Republican voting for it and every Democrat voting against it. In the House, nearly all of the Republicans supported it, while every Democrat opposed it.

Q: What's your view on tax policy? Do you side with supply-side Republicans who argue that taxes on high-income taxpayers should be kept low so that they will invest the extra income, thereby contributing to economic growth? Or do you side with Democratic lawmakers who argue that tax cuts should be targeted for the less well off because they are more likely to spend the extra dollars, thereby giving the economy a boost?

MONETARY POLICY AS AN ECONOMIC TOOL

Fiscal policy is not the only instrument of economic management available to government. A second is **monetary policy**, which is based on adjustments in the amount of money in circulation. Monetarists, as economists who emphasize monetary policy are called, contend that the money supply is the key to sustaining a healthy economy. Their leading theorist, economist Milton Friedman, held that supply and demand are best controlled by manipulating the money supply.[19] Too much money in circulation contributes to inflation because too many dollars are chasing too few goods, which drives up prices. Too little

Pictured here are the two most influential economists of the 20th century. On the left is Milton Friedman, who pioneered the theory of monetary policy. On the right is John Maynard Keynes, who devised fiscal policy theory. (left: Financial Times/ullstein bild /Getty Images; right: Keystone-France/ Gamma-Keystone/Getty Images)

money in circulation results in a slowing economy and rising unemployment because consumers lack the ready cash and easy credit required to maintain spending levels. Monetarists believe in increasing the money supply when the economy needs a boost and decreasing the supply when it needs to be slowed down.

The Fed

Control over the money supply rests not with the president or Congress but with the Federal Reserve System ("the Fed"). Created by the Federal Reserve Act of 1913, the Fed is directed by a board of governors whose seven members serve for 14 years, except for the chair and vice chair, who serve 4-year terms. All members are appointed by the president with the approval of the Senate. The Fed is a "bankers' bank." It does not have "customers" as do other banks. Instead, it assists and regulates all national banks and those state banks that chose to become members of the Federal Reserve System—about 6,000 banks in all.

The Fed has several tools by which to add or subtract money from the economy, seeking a balance that will permit steady growth without causing an unacceptable level of inflation (see Table 15-2). One method the Fed uses is to raise or lower the percentage of funds that member banks are required to hold in reserve—meaning that they cannot loan or invest the funds. When the Fed raises the reserve rate, member banks are required to keep more of their money out of circulation, thereby reducing the money supply. When it lowers

table 15-2	MONETARY POLICY: A SUMMARY OF THE FED'S POLICY TOOLS
Reserve Rate	Amount of their assets that member banks must keep on hand: The rate can be lowered to increase the money supply or raised to decrease it.
Interest Rate	Interest rate charged to member banks when they borrow from the Fed: The rate can be lowered to increase the money supply or raised to decrease it.
Buying of Securities	By buying securities, the Fed gives money to the seller, which increases the money supply. By selling securities, the Fed receives money from the buyer, which decreases the money supply.

the reserve rate, the Fed allows banks to release more of their money for loans to consumers and firms. During the 2008 subprime mortgage crisis, the Fed reduced the reserve rate several times so that member banks would have more money available to deal with the shortfall resulting from failed mortgages.

A second and more publicly visible way in which the Fed affects the money supply is by lowering or raising the interest rate that member banks pay when they borrow money from the Federal Reserve. When the Fed raises the interest rate for banks, they in turn raise the rate they charge their customers for new loans, which discourages borrowing, thereby reducing the amount of money entering the economy. Conversely, when the Fed lowers the interest rate on its loans to member banks, they are able to lower the rate they charge customers for their loans, which leads to additional borrowing by firms and consumers, resulting in an increase in the money supply. As the economy slowed in 2020, for example, the Fed dropped the interest rate nearly to zero, enabling member banks to lower their rates, making loans more affordable.

There is also a third mechanism that the Fed routinely uses—the buying and selling of government securities. When it sells government securities in exchange for cash, the Fed is taking that money out of circulation, thereby reducing the money supply. By contrast, when it buys government securities, the Fed is putting the money used to purchase the securities into private hands to be spent or invested, thus stimulating the economy.

The severity of the 2008 economic downturn, which has been labeled the Great Recession, prompted the Fed to unleash a controversial fourth mechanism. Known as *quantitative easing (QE)*, it came into use after the Fed had lowered interest rates almost to the point of zero and therefore could not lower them further as a means of injecting money into the economy. So it turned to quantitative easing, It began to purchase the assets of member banks, such as their mortgage-backed securities. The goal was to take risky securities off the banks' hands in return for money that they could loan out to firms and consumers at historically low rates. Eventually, the Fed spent more than $3 trillion on quantitative easing, which is more money than is generated in a full year by the economy of every country on earth except the United States, China, Japan, and Germany.

Where did the Fed come up with this vast amount of money? For all practical purposes, it created the money out of paper. The Fed is the nation's central bank and essentially has the power to print money, and keep printing it. And that's what it did from 2009 until it stopped in 2014. The spending had the effect of strengthening financial institutions by relieving them of questionable assets while giving them cash that they could lend out, thereby increasing the money supply.

Quantitative easing is considered a tool of "last resort," to be used only when other tools have reached the point that they are no longer effective.[20] If too much money is pumped into the economy, it can eventually trigger an inflationary rise in the prices of goods and services.

The Fed and Control of Inflation

Although the meltdown of financial markets in 2008 placed the Fed in the role of trying to stimulate the economy, a sluggish economy is not the only problem the Fed is expected to address. Another is **inflation**—an increase in the prices of goods and services. Before the late 1960s, inflation was a minor problem, rising by less than 4 percent annually. However, inflation jumped during the last years of the Vietnam War and remained high throughout the 1970s, reaching a postwar high of 13 percent in 1979. The impact was substantial. Prices were rising but personal income was stagnant. Many Americans were forced to cut back on basics, such as food purchases and medical care. Borrowing rates skyrocketed. The interest rate on business loans and home mortgages topped 15 percent—up from 5 percent a few years earlier.

To fight inflation, the Fed applies policies exactly the opposite of those used to fight an economic downturn. By increasing interest and reserve rates and by selling government securities, the Fed takes money out of the economy, which has the effect of reducing economic demand. As demand weakens, the prices of goods and services drop, thereby easing inflationary pressure.

The Politics of the Fed

Compared with fiscal policy, monetary policy can be implemented more quickly. The Fed can adjust interest and reserve rates on short notice, thus providing the economy with a psychological boost to go along with the actual

Jerome "Jay" Powell was appointed by President Donald Trump to chair the Federal Reserve in 2018. Unlike other recent chairs, who were trained economists, Powell previously worked as an attorney and investment banker. The chair of the Fed has been called the second most powerful official in Washington. (Michael Reynolds/EPA-EFE/Shutterstock)

effect of a change in the money supply. In contrast, changes in fiscal policy usually take months to implement. Congressional action is relatively slow, and new taxing and spending programs ordinarily require a preparation period before they can be put into effect. The greater flexibility of monetary policy is a reason the Fed has emerged as the institution with the primary responsibility for keeping the U.S. economy on a steady course.[21]

When the Fed was created in 1913, no one imagined that it would have such a large policy role. Economists had not yet "invented" the theory of monetary policy. All of that has changed, which raises a basic issue of democratic governing. Should the Fed, which is not an elected institution, have so much power over Americans' lives? Although appointed by the president, members of the Federal Reserve Board are not subject to removal. They serve for fixed terms and are relatively insulated from popular control. And whose interests should the Fed represent—those of the public as a whole or those of the banking sector? The Fed is not a wholly impartial body. Although it makes decisions in the context of economic theories and projections, it is a "bankers' bank" and tends to be protective of banks, as in 2020 when it stepped in to make cash loans available to banks in the face of the economic threat posed by the coronavirus pandemic. If banks had struggled to operate, Americans, too, would have been harmed. In that sense, the Fed was serving the public's interest as well as that of the banks. But did the Fed give banks too much leeway in their use of the money? Rather than recommending that banks use some of the money to make small loans to consumers at sharply reduced rates, should it have required banks to do so as a condition of receiving the loans? As it happened, most of the loans made available to consumers carried relatively high interest rates.[22]

Regardless, the Fed is part of the new way of thinking about the federal government's role in the economy that emerged during the Great Depression of the 1930s. Roosevelt's New Deal permanently changed how policymakers thought about the government and the economy. Through its economic management and regulatory activities, the government has assumed an ongoing role in managing the economy, and the overall result has been impressive. Although the American economy has suffered from economic downturns during the roughly three-quarters of a century in which the U.S. government has played a significant policy role, none of them has matched the severity of earlier depressions. The more recent downturns have been made shorter and less severe through government intervention. (The economic policies of the federal government in the areas of social welfare and national security are discussed in Chapters 16 and 17.)

SUMMARY

Although private enterprise is the main force in the American economic system, the federal government plays a significant role through its policies to regulate, promote, and stimulate the economy.

Regulatory policy is designed to achieve efficiency and equity, which require the government to intervene, for example, to maintain competitive trade practices (an efficiency goal) and to protect vulnerable parties in economic transactions (an equity goal). Many of the regulatory decisions of the federal government, particularly those of older agencies (such as the Food and Drug Administration), are made largely in the context of group politics. Business lobbies have an especially strong influence on the regulatory policies that affect them. In general, newer regulatory agencies (such as the Environmental Protection Agency) have policy responsibilities that are broader in scope and apply to a larger number of firms than those of the older agencies. As a result, the policy decisions of the newer agencies are more often made in the context of party politics. Republican administrations are less vigorous in their regulation of business than are Democratic administrations.

Business is the major beneficiary of the federal government's efforts to promote economic interests. A large number of these programs, including those that provide loans and research grants, are designed to assist business firms, which are also protected from failure through measures such as tariffs and favorable tax laws. Labor, for its part, obtains government assistance through laws covering areas such as worker safety, the minimum wage, and collective bargaining. Yet America's individualistic culture tends to put labor at a disadvantage, keeping it less powerful than business in its dealings with the government. Agriculture is another economic sector that depends substantially on government's help, particularly in the form of income stabilization programs such as crop insurance subsidies.

The U.S. government pursues policies that are designed to protect and conserve the environment. Today, there are many environmental programs, including those aimed at preventing air and water pollution. The continuing challenge, exemplified by climate change, is to find a proper balance among the nation's natural environment, its economic growth, and its energy needs.

Through its fiscal and monetary policies, Washington attempts to maintain a strong and stable economy—one characterized by high productivity, high employment, and low inflation. Fiscal policy is based on government decisions in regard to spending and taxing, which are aimed at either stimulating a weak economy or dampening an overheated (inflationary) economy. Fiscal policy is worked out through Congress and the president and consequently is responsive to political influences. Democratic lawmakers typically prefer demand-side fiscal policy, which relies on increased government spending as a way to put more money in consumers' pockets. When they spend the money, it stimulates business production and job growth. Republican lawmakers typically prefer supply-side fiscal policy, which relies on tax cuts for business and high-income taxpayers. They are expected to invest much of their extra income in business activity, resulting in an increase in jobs and consumer spending.

Monetary policy is based on the money supply and works through the Federal Reserve System, which is headed by a board whose members hold office for fixed terms. The Fed, as the Federal Reserve is commonly called, has become the primary instrument for managing the economy. It can affect the amount of money circulating in the economy by raising or lowering the interest rate that banks are charged for borrowing from the Fed, by raising or lowering the percentage of the funds (reserve rate) that member banks are required to keep on hand, and by buying and selling securities.

CRITICAL THINKING ZONE

KEY TERMS

balanced budget (*p. 463*)
budget deficit (*p. 462*)
demand-side economics (*p. 461*)
deregulation (*p. 448*)
economic depression (*p. 461*)

economic efficiency (*p. 446*)
economic equity (*p. 450*)
economic recession (*p. 461*)
economy (*p. 445*)
externalities (*p. 452*)

fiscal policy (*p. 459*)
inflation (*p. 467*)
laissez-faire economics (*p. 445*)
monetary policy (*p. 464*)

national debt (*p. 463*)
regulation (*p. 445*)
supply-side economics (*p. 462*)

APPLYING THE ELEMENTS OF CRITICAL THINKING

Conceptualizing: Define *economic efficiency* and *economic equity.* Provide an example of a regulatory policy aimed at achieving economic efficiency. Also provide one that has economic equity as its goal.

Synthesizing: Contrast demand-side economics and supply-side economics in terms of theory, government policy, and partisan politics.

Analyzing: What are the tools of monetary policy? How are they applied to deal with an economic recession? How are they applied to deal with high inflation?

EXTRA CREDIT

A Book Worth Reading: Milton Friedman, *Capitalism and Freedom* (Chicago: University of Chicago Press, 2002). First published in 1962, this classic by the Nobel Prize–winning economist provides a defense of free markets that argues against Keynesian economics, which at the time was the prevailing approach to managing the economy.

A Website Worth Visiting: www.ftc.gov The website of the Federal Trade Commission, one of the older regulatory agencies, has information on pending disputes. The site gives the reader a sense of how the regulatory process works in practice.

CHAPTER

INCOME, WELFARE, AND EDUCATION POLICY: PROVIDING FOR PERSONAL SECURITY

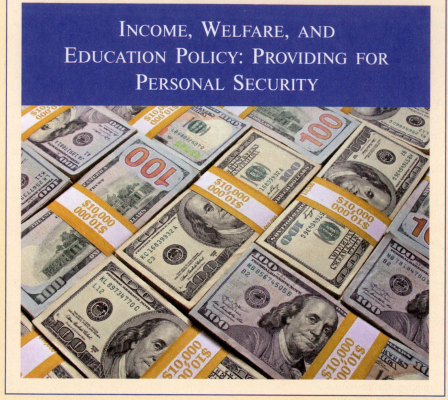

CashGuy/Shutterstock

❝ We the People of the United States, in Order to . . . promote the general Welfare. ❞

PREAMBLE, U.S. CONSTITUTION

At issue was the 2017 Tax Cuts and Jobs Act, the first major tax overhaul in nearly two decades. Republican Mitch McConnell, the Senate majority leader, said the legislation "tells middle class Americans 'we heard you.'" Republican senator Tim Scott of South Carolina exclaimed, "This is a monumental moment that marks a clear win for the American people." Republican congressman John Curtis of Utah said that the legislation would help "families by simplifying the tax code, making American businesses more competitive, and by generating hundreds of thousands of American jobs and producing real economic growth."

Congressional Democrats had a sharply different view. House minority whip Steny Hoyer of Texas said, "Today, 227 Republicans voted to raise taxes on 36 million middle-class households and to add at least \$1.7 trillion to our national debt, all in order to provide massive tax breaks to the top one percent. This is not tax reform; it doesn't even merit being called a tax cut." Vermont senator Bernie Sanders called it a "farce." Oregon senator Ron Wyden called it "an unpopular, deficit exploding corporate giveaway . . . . This is the ultimate betrayal of the middle class."

At the writing of the Constitution, James Madison noted that no issue is more likely to provoke conflict than the question of how society's resources are distributed.[1] And, indeed, a host of government policies, including taxes, touch directly or indirectly on the distribution of resources and have rarely been resolved without a partisan fight. This chapter examines three such policy areas: income policy, which centers on the question of how taxes are distributed; welfare policy, which addresses how those who are economically disadvantaged are helped; and education policy, which includes the issue of how to prepare individuals for economically productive lives. The chapter covers the following main points:

- *Tax policy and market changes have contributed to America's widening income gap.* Democrats and Republicans differ sharply in their tax policies and philosophies.

- *Welfare policy has been a partisan issue, with Democrats taking the lead on government programs to alleviate economic insecurity and Republicans acting to slow down or limit these initiatives.* Social welfare programs are designed to reward and foster self-reliance or, when this is not possible, to provide benefits only to those individuals who are truly in need.

- *A prevailing principle in the United States is equality of opportunity, which in terms of policy is most evident in the area of public education.* The United States invests heavily in its public schools and colleges.

INCOME POLITICS AND POLICIES

America's middle class was once the envy of the world. The nation's economic boom after World War II had launched an unprecedented era of shared prosperity—good-paying jobs, rising levels of home ownership, growing numbers of college graduates.

The situation today is different. The American middle class has shrunk, numerically and financially (see Figure 16-1). In 1970, 62 percent of Americans lived in a middle-class household, defined as a household earning between two-thirds and two times the nation's median income. Americans in that category earned 61 percent of the nation's income. By 2015, however, middle-class Americans had declined to 50 percent of the nation's population and their

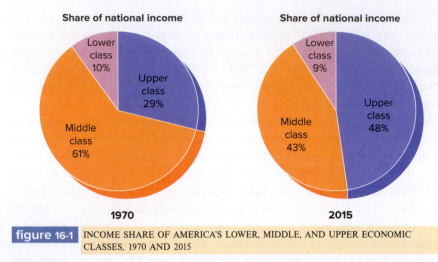

1970   **2015**

figure 16-1	INCOME SHARE OF AMERICA'S LOWER, MIDDLE, AND UPPER ECONOMIC CLASSES, 1970 AND 2015

Between 1970 and 2015, the nation's income shifted to the upper class, such that it now gets nearly half of all income that Americans receive each year. (*Source:* Pew Research Center, 2015. Middle-income households are those whose annual household income is two-thirds to double the U.S. median household income after incomes have been adjusted for household size. In terms of 2014 U.S. dollars, this amounts to $42,000 to $126,000 annually for a household of three. Lower-income households have adjusted incomes below $42,000 while upper-income households have adjusted incomes above $126,000)

share of the nation's income had slipped even more, falling to 43 percent. The plight of lower-class Americans was worse. Even though they made up more of the population than in 1970, their share of the nation's income was smaller. The winners in Americans' shifting income fortunes were those of higher income, who accounted for about a fifth of Americans and received half the nation's income, up from less than a third in 1970.

The Shifting Income Distribution

Until the 1930s Great Depression, the federal government openly sided with business and the wealthy. Efforts to organize unions and improve wages were repeatedly blocked by government action. That approach changed with Franklin D. Roosevelt's New Deal. Congress enacted pro-labor legislation that included a minimum-wage law, collective bargaining rights, and social security for retirees. Congress also imposed a steeply **progressive income tax**, which is a tax where the marginal tax rate increases as income rises. The top rate was set at 79 percent on incomes above $5 million, more than three times the 24 percent rate in place before the Depression.

Business claimed that these policies would wreck the nation's economy, but it grew rapidly after World War II. As it boomed, so did workers' wages, spawning

The years after World War II were marked by a boom in American manufacturing. The war had devastated the factories of Europe and Japan, and the United States was producing more than half of the world's manufactured goods. Factory jobs were plentiful. Most of them paid well, and many of them included health and retirement benefits, contributing to an expanding middle class. (Nara Archives/Shutterstock)

an ever larger middle class. The boom was fueled by the strength of America's manufacturing sector. The United States had emerged from the war with its factories intact, whereas factories elsewhere were damaged by the war. The United States was far and away the world's leading manufacturer, which was a boon for America's factory workers.

The best-paying factory jobs were those held by union workers. Armed with collective bargaining rights, they had achieved high wages and, in some cases, employer-paid health insurance and pensions. At peak in the 1950s, a third of America's workers were unionized, and in some occupations their income was a third higher than those of their nonunion counterparts. The minimum wage also contributed to the rising standard of living, particularly for unskilled workers. It put a floor on their income and helped push up the hourly pay of those just above them on the wage scale. Social Security was also making a difference. It provided retired workers a guaranteed source of monthly income.

Equally dramatic was the impact of the GI Bill, which Congress enacted near the end of World War II. It gave military veterans cash payments for college and vocational training and provided nearly interest-free loans for home purchases and small business ventures. Before the GI Bill, college and home ownership were out of the reach of most families. By the time the original GI Bill expired, nearly 8 million veterans had participated in its education benefits, 2.5 million had acquired a home loan, and hundreds of thousands had received small business and farm loans.

Income nearly doubled in every income category during the post-war boom and, in the case of poorer families, more than doubled.[2] But the gain then came to an abrupt halt. During the past four decades, the income of most American households has been nearly stagnant (see Figure 16-2). In terms of real income, which is the amount of income adjusted for inflation, households in the bottom 60 percent of income make close to the same amount today as they did in 1980. On the other hand, the top two-fifths of American households have seen a rise in their income. Income in real dollars for the next-to-top fifth rose on average from about $82,000 in 1980 to roughly $105,000 today. The top fifth have done even better—their income rose over the four decades from about $148,000 a year on average to more than $240,000 today. The major winners by far, however, have been the top 1 percent. Their average income increased more than three-fold, going from more than $400,000 in 1980 to more than $1.3 million today.[3] Their share of national income is at the level of the 1920s, a time when income inequality was as its peak.

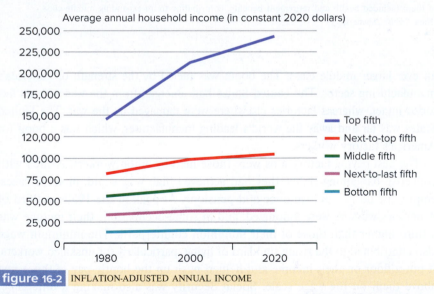

Average annual household income (in constant 2020 dollars)

- Top fifth
- Next-to-top fifth
- Middle fifth
- Next-to-last fifth
- Bottom fifth

figure 16-2 INFLATION-ADJUSTED ANNUAL INCOME

Over the past four decades, the real income of the bottom 60 percent of households has not changed significantly, whereas those in the top 40 percent, and particularly those in the top 20 percent, have seen substantial increases in their real income. (*Source:* U.S. Census Bureau figures. Dollar amounts are expressed in 2020 dollars to control for the effect of inflation.)

Policy and Economic Change

Politicians and pundits regularly link income gains among top earners with wage stagnation among middle earners, as if the first explained the second. In fact, the two developments are only somewhat related. The explanation for why top earners have done so well in recent decades owes substantially to changes in tax policy, whereas wage stagnation owes chiefly to changes in the nation's economy.

Tax Policy Change and Income Inequality   In the period after World War II, income inequality was kept in check by tax policy. The estate tax and a high marginal tax rate on upper incomes—through 1963, the top rate never dropped below 70 percent—worked against the accumulation of large fortunes.[4] Tax policy, as economist Paul Krugman has noted, had a "compression effect."[5] The downward pressure it put on high incomes kept the gap between high earners and other Americans from growing.

The gap widened when Republican Ronald Reagan became president in 1981 and pursued supply-side economics, which is rooted in the assumption that cuts in taxes for business and high-income earners will stimulate economic growth (see Chapter 15). Under Reagan, the highest marginal tax rate dropped from 70 percent to 50 percent, and then to 28 percent. The rate was subsequently increased to 38.5 percent when Democrat Bill Clinton was president. However, when Republican George W. Bush became president in 2001, he, like Reagan, pursued a supply-side economic policy that brought the rate down to 35 percent. All tax brackets got a tax cut under Bush, but the big winners were those with high incomes. The middle fifth, on average, paid about $1,000 less in taxes a year as a result of the Bush-era tax cuts, whereas the average was about $6,000 for those in the top fifth. But the biggest tax savings went to those in the top 1 percent. Their average tax cut—nearly $55,000 a year—was more than 50 times that of middle-income taxpayers. During the nine years the Bush-era tax cuts were in effect, the top 1 percent of taxpayers had roughly $500,000 in tax savings, compared with roughly $10,000 for middle-income taxpayers.

Even more advantageous for high earners was a cut in the **capital gains tax** (the tax individuals pay on gains in capital investments such as stocks and property) that was part of the Bush tax package. It dropped from 28 percent to 15 percent, far below the tax that Americans pay on their regular income. Although most Americans do not buy and sell stocks, a large majority of high earners do so.[6] For those in the top 1 percent, capital gains account for about a third of their pretax income.[7] That situation reflects the fact that *wealth* (the value of a person's assets, such as the property and stocks they own) is highly concentrated in the United States. The top 1 percent of households own 40 percent of all the nation's wealth, averaging more than $10 million per household. The bottom 80 percent of Americans have a mere 7 percent of the nation's wealth.[8]

The cut in the capital gains tax during the Bush era was a windfall for the top 1 percent. They received about 75 percent of the total tax savings from the cut.[9] In fact, even more than the income tax cut, the cut in the capital gains tax disproportionately helped the wealthy. A Congressional Research Service study concluded that "changes in capital gains and dividends were the largest contributor to the increase in the overall income inequality."[10]

It is important to note, however, that the income gains of America's top earners from the Reagan and Bush tax cuts did not come at the direct expense of other taxpayers. Instead, their income gains were financed through government borrowing, which means the cost was shifted to future generations. The Congressional Budget Office (CBO) estimated that the Bush tax cuts added more than $1.5 trillion to the national debt, not including interest on the borrowed money.

The 2017 Tax Cuts and Jobs Act had the same features as the Reagan and Bush tax cuts. All income categories received tax reductions, which are being funded through government borrowing. The CBO estimates that the bill will add roughly $1.7 trillion to the budget deficit over the following 10 years. Like the earlier tax cuts, the 2017 cuts were tilted in favor of higher-income tax payers. According to the nonpartisan Tax Policy Center, middle-income households will see an average annual tax cut of $930, while those in the top 1 percent will get an average of $51,140 (see Figure 16-3).

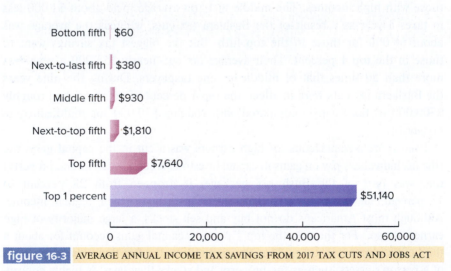

Bottom fifth	$60
Next-to-last fifth	$380
Middle fifth	$930
Next-to-top fifth	$1,810
Top fifth	$7,640
Top 1 percent	$51,140

figure 16-3 AVERAGE ANNUAL INCOME TAX SAVINGS FROM 2017 TAX CUTS AND JOBS ACT

The tax cuts resulted in tax savings for all income groups, but high-income households had by far the biggest tax savings. (*Source:* Tax Policy Center, 2020.)

Economic Change and Wage Stagnation   Wage stagnation has different roots than does the widening income gap. Changes in the American economy are the main reason that lower- and middle-income workers have not realized a gain in their real income since 1970.

American goods and services after World War II accounted for roughly half of all goods being produced worldwide, which created millions of well-paying factory jobs (see Chapter 17). That situation gradually gave way to a competitive global market in which U.S. manufacturers had to compete with those of Japan, Germany, Korea, and other countries. Beginning in the 1970s, the United States became a net importer. It was buying more goods from abroad than it was selling overseas. Factory jobs were lost in the process. That loss was accompanied by a sharp decline in union membership. Today, only about one in eight workers is a union member, and most of them work not in the private sector but in the public sector, such as teachers, police, and civil servants. Economist Lawrence Mishel estimates that as much as a third of the wage erosion among some categories of workers owes to the decline in private-sector unions.[11]

U.S. job growth since the 1970s has been in the service sector—areas such as banking, rental services, health care, entertainment, fast food, and housekeeping. Some service-sector employees are well paid, particularly those who work for large corporations. But there's a much larger number of service-sector

In the 1970s, manufacturing-sector jobs began to disappear as Americans increasingly purchased goods made abroad. Most of the newer American jobs are in the service sector. Many of these jobs pay lower wages and provide fewer benefits than do factory jobs. (Photodisc/Getty Images)

workers—such as food servers, store clerks, hotel staff, artists, lower-level administrators, and taxi drivers—who make less money than their factory counterparts.[12] In addition, service-sector jobs generate less economic activity than do factory jobs. A basic axiom of economics is that jobs generate jobs. Those who work in stores, for example, generate jobs for workers in firms that provide supplies to stores. However, manufacturing jobs generate three times as much economic activity as do retail trade jobs.[13] Auto workers are a prime example. When new cars leave the factory, they generate a wide range of economic activity—they support car dealerships, gas stations, repair shops, auto parts makers, tire makers, and more. Such jobs have been disappearing, at great cost to the financial well-being of America's workers.

In his 2016 presidential campaign, Donald Trump promised to deal with wage stagnation and low-paying jobs. On taking office, his efforts centered on revitalizing the nation's manufacturing sector, largely through tax incentives, reduced regulation, and trade policy. Trump withdrew the United States from the Trans-Pacific Partnership (TPP) free-trade agreement, which would have reduced tariffs on trade between the United States and 11 nations bordering on the Pacific Ocean. Trump argued that TPP would result in the loss of factory jobs to the TPP's lower-wage countries. He also imposed tariffs on some products, including imported steel and aluminum, in an effort to protect U.S. manufacturers from lower-priced foreign competitors, particularly those in China (see Chapter 17). Some U.S. lawmakers criticized these actions on grounds that they would raise the prices that U.S. companies and consumers pay for products. But the policies, which were a sharp break from past policies, also had significant support. What's uncertain is the long-term picture. America's manufacturing sector has been shrinking for decades and for numerous reasons. Whether the nation's manufacturing section can be substantially resurrected in an era of globalized trade is an open question.

The Partisan Divide

The political parties are far apart on income policy. In Congress, Democrats have pressed for increased taxes on the wealthy, opposed at each step by Republican lawmakers. Democrats have framed their argument in terms of fairness, while Republicans have framed their argument in terms of economic growth. Their positions mirror those of their party's voters. A Pew Research Center poll found that 75 percent of Democrats, compared with only 29 percent of Republicans, would support a tax increase on the wealthy and corporations to expand aid to the poor.

If the parties are split on the issue, business groups are not. They dominate Washington lobbying (see Chapter 9) and are attentive to tax issues. As the tax cut bill was being negotiated in Congress in late 2017, business groups lobbied aggressively for its passage.[14] The U.S. Chamber of Commerce alone spent $17 million lobbying Congress during the last three months of 2017.[15] The lobbying effort by business groups paid off. They gained a large tax cut. The legislation reduced the corporate tax rate from 35 percent to 21 percent,

WELFARE POLITICS AND POLICIES

Most Americans are able to meet their housing, food, clothing, and transportation needs. But some cannot. They are the nation's poor.

The U.S. government defines the **poverty line** as the annual cost of a thrifty food budget, multiplied by three to include the cost of housing, clothes, and other necessities. Families whose income falls below that line are officially considered poor. In 2020, the poverty line for a family of four was set at an annual income of roughly $26,000. That works out to $18 per person per day to cover all of a family's needs. By the government's formula, roughly one in seven American families lives in poverty.[16] If they could somehow join hands and form a line, it would stretch all the way from New York City to Los Angeles, then back again.

The United States has more poverty than other Western democracies. Its poverty level is twice that of France and Germany and significantly higher than that of neighboring Canada. Compared with the United States, most Western democracies have more programs aimed at keeping families from falling into poverty, including universal government-provided health care, family and children cash allowances, and subsidized child care.[17]

America's poor include individuals of all ages, races, and regions, but they are concentrated among certain groups. Urban and rural dwellers have much higher poverty rates than do suburbanites. Minority-group members have a poverty rate twice that of whites. Women have a poverty rate exceeding that of men. Children are one of America's most impoverished groups. One in every five American children—more than 10 million in total—lives in poverty (see "How the 50 States Differ"). Most poor children live in families with a single parent, usually the mother. Single-parent, female-headed families are roughly five times as likely as two-income families to fall below the poverty line, a situation referred to as "the feminization of poverty."[18]

Public Assistance Programs

Until the 1930s Great Depression, state governments had responsibility for the poor. Welfare was among the policy areas deemed reserved to the states by the Tenth Amendment and to be adequately addressed by them, even though they offered few welfare services. Individuals were expected to fend for themselves, and those unable to do so were usually supported by relatives and friends.

HOW THE 50 STATES DIFFER

CRITICAL THINKING THROUGH COMPARISONS

Child Poverty Rates

Based on the government-defined poverty line, about one in five American children lives in poverty. However, poverty is spread unevenly among the states. At one extreme are New Mexico, Louisiana, and Mississippi, each of which has a child poverty rate above 25 percent. At the other extreme are Utah and North Dakota, where less than 10 percent of children live in poverty.

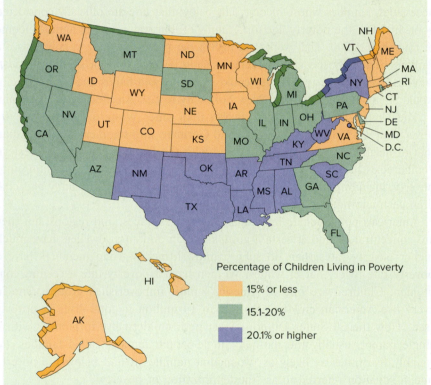

Percentage of Children Living in Poverty

- 15% or less
- 15.1-20%
- 20.1% or higher

Source: U.S. Census Bureau, 2020.

Q: What might explain the difference in child poverty levels between the states?

A: States differ considerably in their natural wealth, level and type of economic activity, level of education, number of newer immigrants, and percentage of minority-group members. Each of these factors is correlated with level of child poverty.

That approach changed as a result of the Depression—a period when one in four workers couldn't find a job and another one in four had only part-time work. Income fell sharply and, as it did, so did state tax revenues. Most states were too broke to help the poor. Federal tax revenues had also declined but, unlike the states, the federal government has unlimited power to print and borrow money.

Expanding the Federal Role   During the Depression, the federal government was in the hands of officials—President Franklin D. Roosevelt and a Democratic congressional majority—who were willing to use the federal government's spending power to help the poor.[19] Republican leaders opposed their initiatives but gradually accepted the idea that the federal government had a welfare role, while arguing it should be kept as small as practicable.[20]

Most Depression-era poverty programs were meant to be temporary, such as the Works Progress Administration, which put millions of Americans to work constructing roads, public hospitals, and the like. But a few programs were designed to last. One was Supplemental Security Income (SSI), which provides federal assistance to low-income elderly people and individuals with disabilities. Another was the Aid for Dependent Children program, later renamed the Aid for Families with Dependent Children (AFDC) program, which provided financial assistance to poor single mothers—those who had little or no income by reason of the father's death or desertion.

A second wave of antipoverty programs came in the 1960s, when the federal government was again in the hands of a Democratic president, Lyndon Johnson, and a Democratic-controlled Congress. They enacted the largest set of antipoverty programs in the nation's history, including the Food Stamps program, subsidized housing, and Medicaid, which is government-paid health insurance for those of low income. These programs had broad public support. A Gallup poll at the time found that two-thirds of Americans believed that government had "a responsibility to try to do away with poverty in this country." Nevertheless, there was a clear partisan divide on the issue. When the Medicaid program came up for a vote, for example, more than 70 percent of congressional Republicans voted against it, claiming that the federal government had no business getting involved in health care.

The 1960s were the high water mark of the government's antipoverty efforts. Since then, only a few major programs have been created. The largest of the newer programs is the 2010 Affordable Care Act, which, among its provisions, expanded Medicaid eligibility to those who are slightly above the poverty line and provides subsidies to enable other lower-income families to buy

Scholar and activist Michael Harrington called the poor "the other America." One in seven American adults and one in five American children live in poverty. Homelessness among America's poor has increased. Shown here is a homeless teenager sleeping near a bridge. (Roman Bodnarchuk/Shutterstock)

health insurance.* The legislation was enacted solely on Democratic votes. No Senate or House Republican voted for the bill.

There have also been cutbacks in welfare programs, most notably through the 1996 Welfare Reform Act (see Chapter 3). The 1996 legislation eliminated the AFDC program, which had placed no limit on how long a family could receive benefits, replacing it with the Temporary Assistance to Needy Families (TANF) program, which limits eligibility for most families to five years (see "Case Study: Welfare Reform Act of 1996"). In addition, TANF provides states with a block grant to be used to conduct training programs to teach job skills to able-bodied adults. Developed by Republican lawmakers as a way to cut welfare rolls and costs, the 1996 act had the overwhelming support of congressional Republicans, whereas a majority of congressional Democrats voted against it.

---

*The Affordable Care Act was not strictly an antipoverty program, though it had provisions aimed at helping low-income people. The legislation's larger goal was to increase health insurance coverage primarily through mandates on companies and individuals. Most companies with more than 200 employees are now required to provide their employees with health insurance, and most companies with 50 to 200 employees must provide insurance or pay a tax penalty. Individual Americans initially faced a tax penalty if they didn't have health insurance. In 2017, the Republican-controlled Congress eliminated that requirement.

The 1996 legislation dramatically reduced the size of the welfare rolls. Within five years of its enactment, the number of people on welfare had dropped by 50 percent. The decline was not simply the result of TANF.

C A S E   S T U D Y

Politics in Action

Welfare Reform Act of 1996

In his 1992 presidential campaign, Bill Clinton promised "to end welfare as we know it." Democratic and Republican lawmakers alike shared his view that the welfare system—which gave people government assistance indefinitely without demanding something in return—had the perverse effect of allowing people to go on welfare and stay there.

Clinton was unable to get his fellow Democrats to agree on a fix to the welfare system and, when Republicans took control of Congress in 1995, they quickly proposed one.

Source: Photographs in the Carol M. Highsmith Archive, Library of Congress, Prints and Photographs Division [LC-DIG-highsm-15970]

The bill's provisions troubled Clinton, who feared it put too many children and young mothers at risk, but he was in a weak political position. He vetoed the first version passed by congressional Republicans, demanding that it include more protections for children. He also vetoed a second version, insisting on more concessions. Republicans responded with a few modifications, including increased funding for child care for poor working mothers. When Republicans passed a third welfare bill, and made it clear there would be no more changes, Clinton was on the spot. In the end, he signed the Republican bill. Clinton had run out of room. Republicans controlled the House and Senate and he didn't have the option of taking his case to the people—on this issue, their opinions aligned with those of Republican lawmakers.

The 1996 Welfare Reform Act placed a five-year limit on welfare eligibility and requires able-bodied recipients to take job training and apply for work. The legislation has had a dramatic impact on the welfare rolls, as the accompanying figure indicates.

Continued

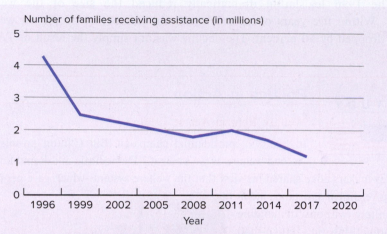

Number of families receiving assistance (in millions)

Source: U.S. Department of Health and Human Services, 2020.

Q: The 1996 legislation placed a five-year limit on eligibility for welfare assistance, although states are permitted to exempt a proportion of recipients to accommodate those who are unemployable for reasons such as health. What do you see as the advantages and disadvantages of the five-year limit?

ASK YOURSELF: What incentive to get a job or training is provided by a time-limited benefit? What are the circumstances, either personal in nature or due to the nature of the local economy, in which a time limit might hurt rather than help individuals?

The American economy was expanding at a rapid rate in the late 1990s, which created millions of new jobs.[21] Nevertheless, even as the economy weakened in 2000, the number of welfare recipients continued to decline. Although the downward trend was reversed somewhat during the economic recession that began in 2008, the number of American families receiving assistance payments has dropped sharply since TANF replaced AFDC.

Eligibility for Public Assistance   Programs such as TANF, Medicaid, and food stamps are **public assistance** programs. They are labeled as such because they're funded with general tax revenues and are available only to individuals in financial need. These programs are often referred to as "welfare" and the recipients as "welfare cases." Eligibility for these programs is established by a **means test**; that is, applicants must prove that they are poor enough to qualify for the benefit. Means-tested programs are typically based on an income threshold. Those with incomes above a specified level of income are ineligible for the benefit, whereas those below the level are eligible for it.

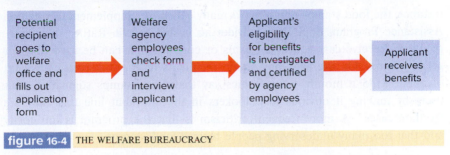

| Potential recipient goes to welfare office and fills out application form | Welfare agency employees check form and interview applicant | Applicant's eligibility for benefits is investigated and certified by agency employees | Applicant receives benefits |

figure 16-4 THE WELFARE BUREAUCRACY

Because U.S. social welfare benefits are distributed on the basis of demonstrated need, a large bureaucracy is required to ascertain applicants' eligibility and to monitor whether changes in recipients' circumstances render them ineligible for further assistance.

The requirement that individuals must prove that they're poor in order to receive a benefit adds to the expense of public assistance programs. In addition to payments to recipients, the programs require local caseworkers and supervisors to determine whether applicants' incomes are below the designated amount and then to monitor recipients' income levels in case there's a change that would render them ineligible for the benefit (see Figure 16-4). Administrative costs account for about 10 percent of federal spending on food stamps and about 5 percent of spending on Medicaid.

Means testing is consistent with America's culture of individualism—the belief that people should be self-reliant. That belief supports the notion that public assistance should be available only to those who are able to prove they can't make it on their own. The distinctiveness of the American approach can be seen by comparing the U.S. health care system with that of European countries. They provide government-paid medical care to their citizens. If people become ill, they simply go to a clinic or hospital for treatment at government expense, no questions asked. In contrast, Americans receive government-paid health care only if they meet the eligibility criteria. Even then, to be eligible, they must apply beforehand for insurance and prove they are too poor to buy it on their own.[22]

Because of America's federal system, most public assistance programs, although funded primarily by the federal government, are administered by the states, which have a degree of control over benefits and eligibility. There is considerable variation, for example, in the amount of family assistance that states provide. Some states provide more than $600 a month, while others provide less than $400.

Not all forms of public assistance involve direct cash payments to recipients. For

CITIZEN ACTION!
GETTING INVOLVED

Local religious, civic, social, and economic groups run programs to help the poor, such as food kitchens and clothing drives. Also, many national organizations work locally to assist the poor, including Habitat for Humanity, which builds modest houses with volunteer labor and makes them available to low-income families. Consider volunteering time to help those in need.

instance, the food stamps program (formally called the Supplemental Nutrition Assistance Program, or SNAP) provides an **in-kind benefit**. Rather than cash, recipients receive cash-equivalent cards or coupons that can be used only for grocery items. On average, food stamp recipients receive the cash equivalent of about $135 a month. Some critics say that food stamps stigmatize their users by making it obvious to onlookers in the checkout line that they are "welfare cases." A more frequent criticism is that the program is too costly and that too many undeserving people receive food stamps.

Social Insurance Programs

Public assistance programs are not America's only social welfare policies. It also has **social insurance** programs, which are based on the same pay-to-be-eligible principle as insurance. Only those individuals who pay special payroll taxes while working are eligible for the benefit. Social Security is the prime example. Established in the 1930s as part of Franklin D. Roosevelt's New Deal, it provides monthly Social Security benefits to retirees who paid Social Security taxes on their income during their working years. The current payroll tax rate on employees is 6.2 percent, with employers also required to pay a 6.2 percent tax.

When Medicaid—health care for the poor—was enacted in 1965, Congress also enacted Medicare, which is health care for retirees. Unlike Medicaid, which is a public assistance program, Medicare is a social insurance program. As is the case with Social Security, it is financed by a special tax—currently 1.45 percent—on workers' wages, with employers also paying 1.45 percent.

Social Security and Medicare are **entitlement programs**, meaning that individuals who meet the eligibility criteria are entitled to the benefit. Government cannot decide one day to cancel an entitlement program or to deny the benefit to some eligible recipients while granting it to others. In contrast, public assistance programs are not entitlement programs. The poor do not have an unqualified claim to benefits. Government can choose at will to cancel a public assistance program or change its eligibility criteria, as in the case of TANF, which reduced the length of time a family can receive assistance.

Social Security and Medicare are federal programs in their entirety. States do not administer them or have a say in eligibility or benefits. Accordingly, recipients get the same level of benefits regardless of where they live.

Social Security and Medicare are highly efficient programs in that they do not require a large bureaucracy to check and recheck recipients' eligibility. When workers reach the prescribed age and conditions of eligibility, they automatically qualify for the benefits. Less than 1 percent of Social Security spending is taken up by administrative costs. Medicare is more administratively complex in that it involves payments to doctors and hospitals. Even so, according to a Kaiser Family Foundation study, only about 2 percent of Medicare spending is for expenses other than patient care. In contrast, some private insurance companies—which seek to make a profit and heavily advertise their products—spend up to 20 percent of their revenue on non-patient care.[23]

Social Security and Medicare are not poverty programs in a literal sense. Recipients come from all income groups. In fact, the higher one's income while working, the larger the Social Security payment on retirement. Such individuals pay more in Social Security taxes during their working years and accordingly get a larger benefit on retirement. The average monthly benefit is about $1,200, but some recipients get less than $1,000, whereas others get

---

F A K E or F A C T — Detecting Misinformation

Does Welfare Create Dependency?

Many Americans believe that public assistance programs, commonly known as welfare programs, create dependency, reducing recipients' interest in finding work. A recent Cato Institute poll found, for example, that nearly half of the respondents believed that welfare programs "make poor people dependent and encourage them to stay poor."[24]

Is that claim fact, or is it fake?

Jonathan Weiss/Shutterstock

There are people who make no effort to hold a job and for whom public assistance is nearly a way of life.[25] However, most poor Americans are on welfare as a result of circumstance rather than by personal choice. In an exhaustive poverty study, economists Signe-Mary McKernan and Caroline Ratcliffe found that most recipients are on welfare only for a while, and for reasons largely beyond their control, such as a job layoff or desertion by the father.[26] When the COVID-19 coronavirus outbreak in early 2020 led to business closures, more than 10 million Americans lost their jobs in the first two weeks alone. Many of them received some form of public assistance before returning to work when businesses reopened.

more than $2,000. Nevertheless, Social Security helps keep millions of Americans out of poverty. About one-fourth of America's seniors have no significant monthly income aside from what they receive from Social Security.

The Politics of Welfare Policy

Public assistance and social insurance programs differ markedly in their level of public support. Americans are more than twice as likely to oppose cuts in Social Security—a social insurance program—than to oppose cuts in antipoverty programs.The difference reflects America's cultural values. Social insurance programs are funded by special payroll taxes on workers and, in that sense, are widely seen as something that recipients have "earned." In contrast, public assistance programs are funded by the taxpayers as a whole and are widely seen as "handouts"—not earned and, in the minds of many, not deserved by some of the recipients.

Support for public assistance is weakened by the perception that people on welfare prefer it to working and gradually become dependent on it, even though the evidence says otherwise.[27] Support is also weakened by the widespread belief that the government spends far more on such programs than on social insurance programs. The opposite is true. Spending on Social Security and Medicare, which assist retirees regardless of their other income, is nearly double the amount spent on public assistance programs, which help only those in financial need. In fact, families in the top fifth of the income population receive more in Social Security and Medicare benefits than the government spends in total on TANF, SSI, food stamps, and housing subsidies for the poor.[28]

Because they don't have strong public support, public assistance programs are a political target (see "Party Polarization: Government's Social Welfare Role"). In 2014, for instance, congressional Republicans sought a $40 billion reduction in the food stamp program, settling for an $8 billion cut after a threatened veto by Democratic president Barack Obama. Social Security, by contrast, has withstood partisan challenges. In 2005, President George W. Bush proposed to partially privatize Social Security—workers would have had the option of putting a portion of their Social Security tax payments into a personal retirement account. Bush was forced to back down in the face of strong resistance from senior citizens, spearheaded by AARP—a seniors' group that is one of Washington's most powerful lobbies. In contrast, groups that lobby Congress on behalf of the poor are relatively weak. Spending on Social Security has risen substantially in recent years, while spending on TANF assistance to poor families has declined.[29]

Polls over the past 50 years have repeatedly found that Americans, consistent with their cultural values, see jobs rather than public assistance as the

Social Security has arguably been the most successful federal program in history, giving tens of millions of older Americans a level of economic security they would otherwise not have. The fact that Social Security is funded through a special payroll tax on employees during their working years has protected it from political criticism and budget cuts. Social Security is a benefit that is perceived as having been "earned," and therefore deserved, by its recipients. (Scott Olson/Getty Images)

answer to poverty. That outlook is the basis for the Earned Income Tax Credit (EITC), which was enacted in 1975 under President Gerald Ford and expanded during the presidencies of Ronald Reagan and Bill Clinton. EITC provides a refundable tax credit to low-income wage earners. Workers with sufficiently low income receive an EITC payment on filing their taxes, with the amount varying with income level and number of dependents. The maximum yearly payment for a family with two children, for instance, is roughly $5,600. EITC is now the federal government's largest means-tested cash assistance program. According to U.S. Census Bureau calculations, the EITC lifts about a third of low-income Americans above the poverty line. EITC is a reward for working— a program that's in line with America's cultural values.

EDUCATION POLITICS AND POLICIES

Nearly all Americans endorse the principle of **equality of opportunity**—the idea that people should have a reasonable chance to succeed if they make the effort. It is a form of equality shaped by personal freedom because personal success or failure depends on what people do with their opportunities. It has been said that equality of opportunity gives individuals an equal chance to become unequal.

The Supreme Court has held that American children are entitled to an "adequate" education but do not have a right to an "equal" education. America's public schools differ greatly in quality primarily as a result of differences in the wealth of the communities they serve. Some public schools are over-crowded and have few facilities and little equipment. Others are very well equipped, have spacious facilities, and offer small class sizes. (FatCamera/E+/Getty Images)

Equality of opportunity is an ideal. Americans do not start life on an equal footing. It was said of one successful American politician, whose father was rich and successful in politics, that "he was born on third base and thought he hit a triple."[30] Some Americans are born into privilege, and others start life in such abject poverty that few of them escape it. Nonetheless, equality of opportunity is more than a catchphrase. It is the philosophical basis for a number of government programs, none more so than public education.

Public Education: Leveling Through the Schools

During the nation's first century, the question of a free education for all children was a contentious issue. Wealthy interests feared that an educated public would challenge their political and economic power. For their part, egalitarians saw free public education as a means of helping ordinary people succeed. The egalitarians won out. Public schools quickly sprang up in nearly every community.[31]

Equality continues to be a guiding principle of American public education. Unlike countries that divide children, even at the grade school level, into different tracks that lead ultimately to different occupations, the curriculum in U.S. schools is relatively standardized. Of course, public education has never been a uniform experience for American children. During the first half of the

20th century, public schools for Black children in the South were designed to keep them down, not lift them up. Today, many children in poorer neighborhoods attend overcrowded, understaffed, and underfunded public schools. The quality of education depends significantly on the wealth of the community in which the child resides. The Supreme Court has upheld disparities in school funding, saying that the states are obliged to give all children an "adequate" education as opposed to one that is "equal" across communities.[32]

The uneven quality of America's public schools is a reason its students rank below Canadian and European students on standardized reading, math, and science tests (see "How the U.S. Differs"). Because U.S. neighborhoods are more segregated by income than are European neighborhoods, America's poor children are more likely to go to schools where most of the other students are also poor. Moreover, because the wealth of a community affects the level of school funding, schools with a high proportion of poor students tend to have fewer resources, even though their need is greater. In fact, the best predictor of students' performance on standardized tests is the wealth of the community in which their school is located.[33] A Stanford University study found that children from low-income families are five years behind children from high-income families in average literacy skills by the time they reach high school.[34]

Nevertheless, through its public schools, the United States seeks to broadly educate its children. Public education was labeled "the great leveler" when it began in the early 19th century, and the tradition continues. Few countries make an equivalent spending effort. Per-pupil spending on public schools is substantially higher in the United States than it is in Europe. America's commitment to broad-based education extends to college. The United States has the world's largest system of higher education—it has roughly 4,000 two- and four-year colleges.[35] The nation's extensive education system preserves both the myth and the reality of an equal-opportunity society. The belief that success is within the reach of anyone who works for it could not be sustained if the public education system were open only to the privileged few.

The Federal Government's Role in Education Policy

Education is largely the responsibility of state and local governments, and they continue to provide roughly 90 percent of school funding, They also decide most school policies, everything from the length of the academic year to teachers' qualifications.

Historically, the federal government played little part in education policy. The situation began to change after World War II, when economic and social change made the public more aware of deficiencies in the nation's education

HOW THE U.S. DIFFERS

CRITICAL THINKING THROUGH COMPARISONS

Education Performance

Research indicates that U.S. students score comparatively low on standardized tests. In the most recent Organization for Economic Cooperation and Development (OECD) assessment, based on 15-year-old student performance in math, the United States trailed nearly every Asian and Western European country. The accompanying chart shows the average math test scores for selected countries.

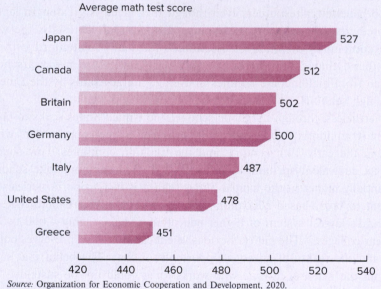

Average math test score

Japan	527
Canada	512
Britain	502
Germany	500
Italy	487
United States	478
Greece	451

Source: Organization for Economic Cooperation and Development, 2020.

Q: Why might the United States lag behind other advanced, industrialized democracies in student performance even though it spends more heavily on public education?

A: Compared with most democracies, the United States has a relatively high proportion of non-native-speaking children, who on average do less well in school than other students. The United States also has a high level of residential segregation. Children residing in poor neighborhoods tend to perform less well in school than do their peers.

system. Since the 1960s, the federal government has played a larger, although still secondary, role in education policy. Federal
education programs are administered through
the Department of Education, a cabinet-level
agency that was created in 1979. The size of
the Department of Education is an indicator
of the degree to which education remains
largely a state and local policy responsibility.
The Department of Education is by far the

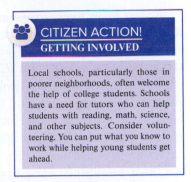

CITIZEN ACTION!
GETTING INVOLVED

Local schools, particularly those in poorer neighborhoods, often welcome the help of college students. Schools have a need for tutors who can help students with reading, math, science, and other subjects. Consider volunteering. You can put what you know to work while helping young students get ahead.

smallest of the executive departments, with only 4,000 employees. The next
smallest is the Department of Labor, which is four times the size.

Federal Grants-in-Aid for Education   As part of President Johnson's War
on Poverty, the federal government began in the 1960s to provide financial
assistance in the education area. The 1965 Elementary and Secondary Education Act became the cornerstone of the federal government's efforts to assist
public schools. The legislation authorizes funds for items such as school construction, textbooks, special education, and teacher training. Although Johnson's goal was to help schools in poorer areas, members of Congress insisted
that all states and districts be eligible for some funding. As a result, the for-
mulas for allocating the grants favor poorer school districts, but not totally.

Johnson's War on Poverty also included a targeted education program—
Head Start. Aimed at helping poor children at an early age, Head Start provides free preschool education to low-income children in order to help them
succeed when they reach kindergarten age. However, Head Start has never
been funded at a level that would allow all eligible children to participate.
Today, only about a third of eligible children are enrolled.[36]

The 1965 Higher Education Act, which President Johnson signed into law
at his alma mater, Texas State University, is the basis for federal assistance
to institutions of higher education. Among its components are Pell Grants,
federal loans to college students, and federally subsidized college work-study
programs. Pell Grants account for the largest share of federal spending.
Millions of college students over the years have received Pell Grants, which
are reserved for students from modest- and low-income families. The federal
student loan program has also helped millions of students, although it is a
relatively small spending item in that most of the money is returned through
loan repayment. In 2010, as a cost-saving measure, the federal government
took control of the loan program. Before then, some student loans were issued
by banks, which had the safety of government-insured loans while receiving
a fee for handling them.

Student loans have become increasingly burdensome. According to Federal Reserve Bank data, state governments in the 1970s provided nearly 75 percent of the funding for public colleges, which had the effect of holding down college costs. But states in the 1980s started to cut their funding and continued to do so, such that the states now provide less than 25 percent of college funding. As a result, college costs have been shifted to students, most of whom have no choice but to rely heavily on student loans. In fact, student loan debt now exceeds credit card debt (see Figure 16-5).

The scale of the student debt problem has made it a political issue. During the 2020 presidential campaign, Democratic nominee Joe Biden proposed tying student loan repayment to an individual's income, with those making less than $25,000 being allowed to defer their payments interest free, while those making more than $25,000 would be required to pay 5 percent of their discretionary income toward repaying the loan. After 20 years, any remaining debt would be canceled. Opponents of such proposals argue that the costs would be prohibitive. They also say that former students are getting the salary boost that comes with a college education and that it would be unfair for taxpayers, many of whom don't have a college degree, to pay part of the cost of student loans. Given the size of the student loan debt problem, the issue is unlikely to go away anytime soon.

Partisan Conflict over Education Policy   Many of the partisan and philosophical differences that affect federal welfare policy also affect federal education policy. Democrats are more inclined to find the answer to how to improve schools in increased federal spending on education, particularly in poorer communities, whereas Republicans are more inclined to look to market-like mechanisms such as achievement tests.

Partisan conflict has spilled even into policy areas largely outside the scope of federal authority. School choice is one example. Charter schools, which are publicly funded but have wider latitude than other public schools in designing

Billions of dollars

Credit card debt $1,080

Student loan debt $1,480

figure 16-5   STUDENT LOAN AND CREDIT CARD DEBT

In recent decades, state and local governments have reduced their spending on public colleges and universities, which has shifted a larger share of the cost to students. Student loan debt in the United States now exceeds what Americans owe on their credit cards. (*Source:* Federal Reserve Bank of New York, 2020.)

curricula and picking students, are strongly championed by many Republican lawmakers. Many Democratic lawmakers have criticized charter schools on the grounds they weaken the regular public schools by siphoning away funding and top students.

Federal involvement in public school education is inherently partisan and controversial, given America's tradition of state and local control over schools. Yet lawmakers at all levels have shown from time to time that they can come together. In 2015, with majority support from Democrats and Republicans, Congress passed the Every Student Succeeds Act (ESSA). It replaced the controversial 2001 No Child Left Behind Act (NCLB), which had mandated standardized national testing and tied schools' federal funding to student test performance. ESSA also includes mandatory testing and sanctions on schools that underachieve but eliminates NCLB's "one size fits all" approach, giving states flexibility in determining the form of student testing and what constitutes underachievement. ESSA is funded through $25 billion in federal assistance each year to the states.

THE AMERICAN WAY OF PROMOTING ECONOMIC SECURITY

All democratic societies promote economic security, but they do so in different ways and to different degrees. Economic security has a higher priority in European democracies than in the United States. European democracies have instituted programs such as government-paid health care for all citizens, compensation for all unemployed workers, and retirement benefits for all elderly citizens. As this chapter shows, the United States provides these benefits only to some citizens in each category. By contrast, the American system of higher education dwarfs those in Europe.

The differences between the European and American approaches to welfare stem from historical and cultural differences. Democracy in Europe developed in reaction to centuries of aristocratic rule, which brought the issue of economic privilege to the forefront. European democracies initiated sweeping social welfare programs and high taxes on the wealthy as ways to create greater economic equality. Social inequality was harder to root out because it was thoroughly embedded in European society, shaping everything from social manners to education. Private schools and university training were the preserve of the elite, a tradition that, although now in the past, has had a lingering effect on how Europeans think about educational opportunity.

The American experience was a different one. Democracy in America grew out of a tradition of limited government that emphasized personal liberty, which included a belief in self-reliance. This belief contributed to Americans' strong support for public education, their weak support for public assistance, and their preference for low tax rates. Unlike political equality, the idea of economic equality has never captured Americans' imagination. Political scientists Stanley Feldman and John Zaller found that Americans' support for public assistance programs rests more on feelings of compassion for the poor than on an ideological commitment to economic sharing.[37] Or, as political scientist

P A R T Y
POLARIZATION

Conflicting Ideas

Government's Social Welfare Role

The two major ways that economic benefits are distributed in America is through the economic marketplace in the form of jobs, wages, dividends, and the like and through the government in the form of programs such as Social Security, Medicaid, and food stamps. In few areas have the differences between the Republican and Democratic parties been more consistent over the years than their positions on the use of government as an instrument of economic security. Although both parties see a need for some sort of safety net for the economically vulnerable, the Democratic Party has taken the lead on extending it. Nearly every major U.S. social insurance and public assistance program was put into place by Democratic lawmakers, usually in the face of opposition from their Republican counterparts. The policy differences among lawmakers are in line with the opinions of Republican and Democratic voters, as the figure indicates.

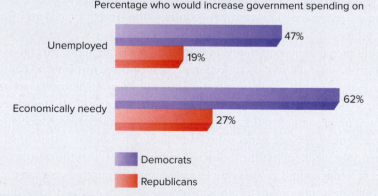

Percentage who would increase government spending on

Unemployed — Democrats 47%, Republicans 19%

Economically needy — Democrats 62%, Republicans 27%

■ Democrats
■ Republicans

Source: Pew Research Center for the People & the Press survey, 2019.

Q: What's your opinion on how far government should go in providing economic assistance to those who are less well off?

Robert Lane expressed it, Americans have a preference for market justice, meaning that they prefer that society's material benefits be allocated largely through the economic marketplace rather than through government policies.[38] It is thus not surprising that the United States has a higher level of income inequality and poverty than do other Western democracies.

SUMMARY

The United States has several areas of policy that affect Americans' economic well-being. Tax policy is one of these policy areas. In recent decades, taxes on higher incomes and capital gains have been lowered substantially, which has contributed to a dramatic increase in income inequality. At an earlier time, a range of government policies, everything from a high tax rate on upper incomes to the GI Bill, had the opposite effect, reducing the gap between the wealthy and the rest of America.

Wage stagnation has been a persistent problem for a half century. In terms of real income, America's lower- and middle-income workers are getting roughly the same pay today as they did in 1970. Although government policy has played a part in this development, it is mainly a consequence of changes in the U.S. economy. In the period after World War II, the U.S. manufacturing sector was booming, providing millions of well-paying jobs, particularly for union workers. Since 1970, the manufacturing sector has shrunk dramatically, giving way to the service sector, where jobs on average pay less.

The United States has a complex social welfare system of multiple programs addressing specific welfare needs. Many social welfare problems are targeted for the poor. Roughly one in seven Americans falls below the government-defined poverty line, including a disproportionate number of children, female-headed families, minority-group members, and rural and inner-city dwellers. Public assistance programs, as anti-poverty programs are called, are available only to individuals who qualify for benefits by meeting the specific eligibility criteria.

Not all welfare programs are in the public assistance category. There are also social insurance programs, including Social Security and Medicare, which are funded by payroll taxes paid by potential recipients, who, in this sense, earn the benefits they later receive. Because of this arrangement, social insurance programs have broad public support. In contrast, public assistance programs are funded with general tax revenues and are targeted at individuals and families in financial need. Because of a widespread belief that many welfare recipients could get along without assistance if they tried, these programs do not have broad public support, receive only modest funding, and sharply divide the two parties. Democrats have taken the lead on government programs to alleviate economic insecurity, while Republicans have sought to cut back or decentralize these initiatives.

Compared to other democracies, the United States spends more heavily on public education, a policy consistent with its cultural emphasis on equality of opportunity. That policy is evident, for example, in standardized school curricula and the nation's extensive system of public colleges and universities. Like social welfare, however, education is a partisan issue involving disputes over such issues as charter schools and spending levels.

CRITICAL THINKING ZONE

KEY TERMS

capital gains tax (*p. 477*)
entitlement programs (*p. 488*)
equality of opportunity (*p. 491*)
in-kind benefit (*p. 488*)
means test (*p. 486*)

poverty line (*p. 481*)
progressive income tax (*p. 474*)
public assistance (*p. 486*)
social insurance (*p. 488*)

APPLYING THE ELEMENTS OF CRITICAL THINKING

Conceptualizing: The Supreme Court has held that American children are entitled to an "adequate education" but not an "equal education." Explain the difference.

Synthesizing: Contrast social insurance benefits and public assistance benefits. How do they differ in terms of how individuals qualify to get a benefit? How do they differ in terms of the level of public support they have?

Analyzing: How has U.S. social welfare policy been influenced by America's federal system of government and by Americans' belief in individualism?

EXTRA CREDIT

A Book Worth Reading: Thomas Piketty, *Capital in the Twenty First Century* (Cambridge, Mass.: Belknap Press, 2014). This award-winning bestseller explores the history of income inequality and its reemergence in extreme form in recent decades.

A Website Worth Visiting: www.journalistsresource.org Journalist's Resource, located at Harvard University's Kennedy School of Government, is dedicated to identifying the top policy-relevant research and connecting it to current issues. Many of its postings are in the areas of income, social welfare, and education policy.

17
CHAPTER

FOREIGN POLICY: PROTECTING THE AMERICAN WAY

amagnawa1092/Shutterstock

&& We the People of the United States, in Order to . . . provide for the common defence. **&&**

PREAMBLE, U.S. CONSTITUTION

President Donald Trump fired the first shot, imposing tariffs on Chinese steel and aluminum imports, saying that they were being subsidized by the Chinese government to keep the price low, enabling them to undercut American-made steel and aluminum. Said Trump, "We cannot let this continue." He then quickly followed with tariffs on more than a thousand Chinese-made goods, including flat-panel TV sets and medical devices. Within a month, China retaliated by placing tariffs on more than a hundred American goods, including cars, pork, and soybeans. And so it went for nearly two years, with each side upping the stakes. Meanwhile, the economic costs kept rising. Agricultural exports to China fell by more than half. The resulting drop in farm income prompted the Trump administration to provide farmers a $16 billion emergency subsidy. As it became apparent that neither side would benefit from an escalating trade war, China and the United States sat down at the bargaining

501

table, The first major sign that tensions were easing came in early 2020. In return for a reduction of tariffs on some of its products, China agreed to buy an additional $200 billion in U.S. goods within the next year.

As the U.S.-China trade dispute illustrates, foreign policy is an issue of economic vitality as well as one of military strength. The motivation behind every nation's foreign policy is its *national interest*—what's best for the nation in terms of protecting its physical security and promoting economic prosperity. National leaders do not always agree on the best way to protect the national interest, but it's the central goal of foreign policy.[1]

Unlike other policy areas, foreign policy rests on relations with actors outside rather than within the country. As a result, the chief instruments of national security policy differ from those of domestic policy. One of these instruments is *diplomacy*—the process of negotiation between countries. The lead agency in U.S. diplomatic efforts is the Department of State, which is headed by the secretary of state and coordinates the efforts of U.S. embassies abroad, each of which is directed by a U.S. ambassador. American diplomacy also takes place through international organizations—such as the United Nations—to which the United States belongs. A second instrument of foreign policy is *military power*. The lead agency in military affairs is the Department of Defense, which is headed by the secretary of defense and oversees the

The United States is the world's leader in the production of livestock and grain, much of which is shipped to overseas markets. When China imposed tariffs on U.S. farm products in its trade war with the United States, farm income dropped sharply. (Orientaly/Shutterstock)

military services—the army, air force, navy, and marine corps. Here, too, the United States sometimes works through alliances, the most important of which is the North Atlantic Treaty Organization (NATO). NATO has nearly 30 member nations, including the United States, Canada, and most European countries. A third instrument of world politics is *intelligence gathering*—the process of monitoring other countries' activities. For many reasons, but primarily because all countries pursue their self-interest, each nation keeps a watchful eye on other nations. In the United States, the task of intelligence gathering falls to specialized federal agencies, including the Central Intelligence Agency (CIA) and the National Security Agency (NSA). *Economic exchange,* the fourth instrument of foreign affairs, involves both international trade and foreign aid. U.S. interests in this area are promoted by a range of U.S. agencies, such as the Agriculture, Commerce, Labor, and Treasury Departments, as well as specialty agencies such as the Federal Trade Commission. The United States also pursues its economic goals through international organizations of which it is a member, including the World Trade Organization, the World Bank, and the International Monetary Fund.

The national security policies of the United States include an extraordinary array of activities—so many, in fact, that they could not be addressed adequately in an entire book, much less a single chapter. There are roughly 200 countries in the world, and the United States has relations of one kind or another—military, diplomatic, economic—with all of them. This chapter narrows the subject by concentrating on a few main ideas:

- *Since World War II, the United States has acted in the role of world leader, which has substantially affected its military, diplomatic, and economic policies.*

- *The United States maintains a high degree of defense preparedness, which requires a substantial level of defense spending and a worldwide deployment of U.S. conventional and strategic forces.*

- *Changes in the international marketplace have led to increases in trade and greater economic interdependence among nations, which has had a marked influence on the U.S. economy and on America's security planning.*

U.S. FOREIGN AND DEFENSE POLICY SINCE WORLD WAR II

Before World War II, except within its own hemisphere, the United States was a mostly **isolationist** country. It was preoccupied with its internal development and intent on avoiding European entanglements. A different America emerged after World War II. It had more land, sea, and air power than any other country and more than a hundred overseas military installations. The United States had become a fully **internationalist** country—a nation deeply involved in world affairs.[2]

The Cold War and Its Lessons

Although the United States was victorious in its fight against Germany and Japan in World War II, it was not fully at peace. The global power structure was **bipolar**—the United States versus the Soviet Union. After World War II, backed by the power of the Soviet army, communists seized power in Poland, Hungary, Czechoslovakia, and other Eastern European nations.

The United States was suddenly embroiled in the **Cold War** with the Soviet Union. The two nations were not directly at war, but the United States pursued a doctrine of **containment**—the notion that Soviet aggression could be stopped only by the determined use of American power.[3] This doctrine had roots in the failed efforts to appease Germany's Adolf Hitler in the years leading up to World War II. At the 1938 Munich conference, Germany was allowed to annex Czechoslovakia's Sudetenland, but it served only to whet Hitler's appetite for conquest. The *lesson of Munich* was that totalitarian leaders could not be appeased; they had to be confronted.

Containment policy led the United States to base troops in Europe and Asia and then into costly wars. When the Soviet-backed North Koreans invaded South Korea in 1950, President Truman sent U.S. forces into the conflict. Nearly 35,000 U.S. troops lost their lives in the Korean War, which ended in stalemate. A decade later, the United States was again at war. Communists were making inroads in South Vietnam, and U.S. policymakers believed that, if it fell to the communists, so would Laos, Cambodia, and the rest of Southeast Asia—the *domino theory*. Although U.S. forces had military superiority, Vietnam was a guerrilla war, with no front lines and few set battles.[4] U.S. public opinion, most visibly among the young, gradually turned against the war. U.S. combat troops left Vietnam in 1973, and two years later North Vietnamese forces completed their takeover of the country. Vietnam was the costliest and most painful application of containment doctrine: 58,000 Americans lost their lives in the fighting.

America's failure in Vietnam led U.S. policymakers to reconsider the country's international role. The *lesson of Vietnam* was that there were limits to the country's power. President Richard Nixon proclaimed that the United States could no longer act as the free world's "Lone Ranger" and needed to reduce tensions with communist countries. Nixon sought to normalize relations with China's communist government and initiated the Strategic Arms Limitation Talks (SALT), which resulted in reductions in the nuclear arsenals of the United States and the Soviet Union. This spirit of cooperation lasted until the

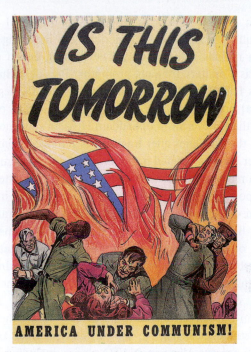

IS THIS TOMORROW

AMERICA UNDER COMMUNISM!

Cold War propaganda, like this poster warning of the danger of communism, contributed to a climate of opinion in the United States that led to public support for efforts to contain Soviet power. (©The Michael Barson Collection)

Soviet invasion of Afghanistan in 1979, which convinced U.S. leaders that the Soviet Union had not changed its ways. When Ronald Reagan was elected president in 1980, he called for a renewed hard line toward the Soviet Union.

Although U.S. policymakers did not realize it, the Soviet Union was collapsing under the weight of its heavy defense expenditures, its isolation from Western technology, and its inefficient centralized economy. In 1989, the Soviet Union withdrew its troops from Eastern Europe. Two years later, the Soviet Union was dissolved. The bipolar power structure of the Cold War era was over. The new structure was **unipolar**—the United States was now the world's unrivaled superpower.

Multilateralism and Its Lessons

The end of the Cold War prompted the first President Bush in 1990 to call for a "new world order." George H. W. Bush advocated **multilateralism**—the idea that major nations should act together in response to problems and crises. Included in Bush's plan was a stronger role for multinational organizations such as the United Nations and NATO.

Multilateralism defined America's response to the 1990 Iraqi invasion of Kuwait. A half-million troops, mostly American but including contingents from nearly two dozen nations, attacked Iraq. The fighting ended in four days. The Gulf operation was a military triumph, prompting President Bush to declare that the United States had "kicked the Vietnam syndrome [the legacy of America's defeat in Vietnam] once and for all." But the Gulf War was otherwise less successful. Believing that an overthrow of Saddam Hussein's regime would destabilize Iraq, Bush halted the hostilities after Iraqi forces retreated from Kuwait. Hussein remained in power but was ordered by a UN resolution to dismantle his weapons program. Hussein repeatedly interfered with UN inspectors' attempts to verify the status of his weapons programs, raising suspicions about his intentions.

Multilateralism carried over into Bill Clinton's administration. Confronting Serb atrocities in Bosnia—where tens of thousands of Muslims and Croats were murdered, raped, or driven from their homes—the United States and its NATO allies attacked Serb forces with air power in 1995, which culminated in a U.S.-negotiated peace agreement (the Dayton Accords), which included the deployment to Bosnia of nearly 60,000 peacekeeping troops, including 20,000 Americans. War in the Balkans flared again in 1999 when the Serbs undertook a campaign of "ethnic cleansing" in the Serbian province of Kosovo, whose population was 90 percent Albanian. NATO planes, including U.S. aircraft, then attacked Serbia.[5] After nearly three months of intensive bombing, Serb president Slobodan Milošević (who died in 2006 while on trial for war crimes) pulled his troops out of Kosovo. (In 2008, Kosovo became an independent state.)

As the examples indicate, multilateralism was not a wholly successful strategy for resolving international conflicts. Military intervention offered no guarantee of long-term success. Regional and internal conflicts typically stem from enduring ethnic, religious, factional, or national hatreds or from chronic problems such as famine, overcrowding, or government corruption. Even if these hatreds or problems can be suppressed momentarily, they are often too deep-seated to be settled permanently.

CITIZEN ACTION!
GETTING READY

History can inform your political judgment. Consider studying a post–World War II development. Particularly instructive is America's deepening involvement in Vietnam, which led eventually to the deployment of a half-million U.S. troops. The difficulties that ensued after the U.S. invasions of Afghanistan and Iraq are also instructive.

War on Terrorism

On becoming president in 2001, George W. Bush rejected his father's multilateral approach to foreign policy. He announced plans to reduce America's military presence abroad, a position that changed abruptly when terrorists attacked the World Trade Center and the Pentagon on September 11, 2001. In a televised address, Bush urged other nations to join the United States in a multilateral "war on terrorism."

The Afghanistan War   The first U.S. military response was an attack on Afghanistan, which commenced barely a month after the September 11 attacks. Afghanistan's Taliban-led government had granted sanctuary and training sites to the al Qaeda terrorists who carried out the attacks. Supported by troops from other NATO countries, U.S. forces quickly toppled the Taliban government but failed to destroy the Taliban's fighting capacity. The Taliban regrouped, slowly reasserting control over large parts of the country. In 2011, U.S. forces succeeded in locating and killing al Qaeda's leader Osama bin Laden, but the Afghan conflict otherwise dragged on. In 2020, President Trump signed a peace agreement with the Taliban in which the United States would slowly withdraw all of its forces from Afghanistan, while the Taliban would refrain from harboring or cooperating with terrorist organizations. If the Taliban were to do so, and U.S. troops were to totally leave Afghanistan, it would mark the end of the longest war in American history.

The Iraq War   In 2002, President George W. Bush labeled Iraq, Iran, and North Korea "the axis of evil." A few months later, he announced a new national security doctrine: the **preemptive war doctrine**.[6] Speaking at West Point, Bush asserted that the United States would not wait until it was attacked by hostile nations. Instead, America would take "preemptive action."[7] The concept

Terrorist attacks on New York City and Washington, D.C., led the United States into wars in Afghanistan and Iraq. Initial projections that the military engagements would be relatively brief proved inaccurate, forcing policymakers to deal with the human and financial costs of wars that had no clear ending or outcome. (Przemek Tokar/Shutterstock)

was not entirely new—U.S. officials had long maintained a right to strike first if faced with an imminent attack. What was new in the Bush Doctrine was its embrace of a first-strike option before a threat was imminent.

The target of the new doctrine was the regime of Iraq's Saddam Hussein. Claiming that Iraq was stockpiling weapons of mass destruction (WMDs)—chemical and biological weapons, and possibly nuclear weapons—for use against U.S. interests, Bush obtained authorization from Congress to use military force if Iraq did not disarm voluntarily (see "Case Study: Invasion of Iraq). Despite opposition from France, Germany, and Russia, Bush ordered U.S. forces to invade Iraq in early 2003. British troops were also involved, but the attack was essentially an act of **unilateralism**—a situation in which one nation takes action against another state or states.[8] The Iraqi regime collapsed quickly, but the post-invasion phase was far more difficult than the Bush administration had anticipated. Age-old animosities among Sunni, Shiite, and Kurdish groups within Iraq blocked political compromise and fueled internal violence. Moreover, weapons inspectors did not find the WMDs that the Bush administration had claimed were in Iraq's possession, which undermined public support for the war.[9] In 2011, by order of President Obama, the last of the U.S. combat units were withdrawn from Iraq, although U.S. military advisers remained. Nearly nine years of war there had resulted in the deaths of more than 4,500 American troops and had cost nearly a trillion dollars.

C A S E
STUDY

Politics in Action

Invasion of Iraq

Although the U.S. system is based on checks and balances, there is an area where one branch has the upper hand. Since World War II, the United States has engaged in military hostilities roughly 150 times, usually at the instigation of the president. A case in point is the 2003 invasion of Iraq. The signal that President George W. Bush was targeting Iraq came in his 2002 State of the Union address, when he grouped Iraq with Iran and North Korea in what he called an "axis of evil." Later, Bush asked Congress for authorization to attack Iraq if it refused to turn over its weapons of mass destruction (WMDs). Bush claimed Iraq had WMDs and was preparing to use them. Citing intelligence reports, Bush said, "The evidence indicates that Iraq is reconstituting its nuclear weapons program."

During the congressional debate, Senator Robert Byrd (D-W. Va.) repeatedly asked the administration to reveal its intelligence reports, but few were forthcoming. The vote in Congress, which occurred a year after the 9/11 terrorist attacks—a time when Americans were still worried about the possibility of another such attack—was one-sided. The House vote was 297-133 in Bush's favor, while the Senate vote was 77-23.

When Bush first indicated the possibility of an invasion, opinion polls indicated that less than half the public thought it was a good idea. But Bush, as the accompanying figure indicates, was able to use the news media to carry his message. Reporters were focused so intently on the White House that Bush administration sources were quoted roughly 10 times as often as were the war's congressional opponents. By the time of the invasion, 76 percent of respondents in a Gallup poll expressed approval—with four of every five of them expressing "strong approval."

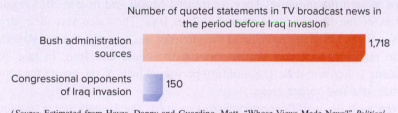

Number of quoted statements in TV broadcast news in the period before Iraq invasion

Bush administration sources   1,718

Congressional opponents of Iraq invasion   150

(*Source:* Estimated from Hayes, Danny and Guardino, Matt, "Whose Views Made News?" *Political Communication, vol.* 27, 2010, 73. Based on ABC, CBS, and NBC coverage, August 1, 2002–March 19, 2003.)

As it turned out, the Bush administration's claim that Iraq had weapons of mass destruction was faulty. Although U.S. weapons inspectors searched high and low in Iraq for such weapons, they found none of consequence. However, having started a war, the United States was caught up in it and, more than a decade later, was still engaged in hostilities in the region.

Q: What checks are there on a president who is determined to take the nation to war? What are the conditions, if any, in which those checks might be powerful enough to dissuade the president from doing so?

ASK YOURSELF: What actions are available to Congress? When is Congress likely to invoke them? If the president were to order U.S. forces into combat in the face of congressional opposition, would Congress have any recourse? What about a situation in which most Americans were opposed to the prospect of war? What costs would that impose on a president and the president's party? Are these costs significant enough to dissuade a president from acting?

The Islamic State and Syria   America's withdrawal of combat units from Iraq, in combination with a deadly civil war in Syria, created a power vacuum that spawned a radical Islamic group—the Islamic State (also known as ISIS and ISIL). From its initial base in Syria, it swept across the border into Iraq, seizing a large swath of territory that included Iraq's second-largest city, Mosul. Comprised of Sunni Muslims, ISIS brutally murdered as heretics the Shiite Muslims and Christians it captured and declared its intention to establish a Caliphate—an Islamic state headed by a supreme religious and political leader. As the threat mounted, President Obama ordered targeted air strikes on Islamic State forces in an effort to bolster Iraq's government, which was too weak and divided to counter ISIS on its own. Obama subsequently stepped up the air attacks and deployed several hundred military advisers and special operations troops to assist Iraqi government forces.

On taking office, President Trump continued that policy, which helped Iraqi troops to gain the initiative. They recaptured Mosul and in late 2017 regained the last of the Islamic State strongholds in Iraq. They also lost their strongholds in Syria, although in that case the territory was taken by the anti-American Syrian regime, which had aligned itself with Russia and Iran. In late 2019, President Trump withdrew U.S. military personnel from Syria, except for a small number in a few border areas.

Even with the world's most powerful military, the United States has found it difficult to achieve success in the war against terrorism. Wars of this type do not lend themselves to quick and tidy battlefield solutions. It is one thing to defeat a conventional army in open warfare but quite another to prevail in a conflict in which the fight is not so much a battle for territory as it is a struggle for people's loyalties, especially when they harbor age-old distrust of each other, as in the case of the competing religious and ethnic groups in Afghanistan, Iraq, and Syria.

Such wars also have few boundaries. In late 2015, for example, terrorists aligned with the Islamic State murdered more than one hundred people in Paris and then nearly three dozen people in Brussels four months later. The Islamic State had developed a sophisticated, Internet-based recruiting strategy to lure disaffected Muslim youth outside the Middle East into its ranks. With ISIS's battlefield defeat in Iraq and Syria, the fear now is that some of its soldiers will slip into Europe and engage in terrorist attacks there. Moreover, al Qaeda and the Islamic State have both established a military presence in other Muslim countries, including Yemen and Libya. Brian Michael Jenkins, who served as an adviser to the National Commission on Terrorism, concluded that the United States will be at war with radical Islamic terrorists "for years to come."[10]

Although terrorism and turmoil in the Middle East have dominated national attention for the past two decades, it is only one of America's foreign policy challenges. Containing the spread of nuclear weapons is another. The United States and other countries have worked together to block or retard nuclear weapon development by North Korea and Iran but have been only partially successful. Pakistan's nuclear arsenal is also a concern. Pakistan is a predominantly Muslim country and has a large number of extremists who identify with al Qaeda and other terrorist groups. If they should somehow gain control of nuclear material, much less nuclear weapons, the threat to U.S. interests would increase sharply.

Russia and China

Russia's actions are also of concern. In 2014, Russia forcefully annexed the Crimean Peninsula, which was part of Ukraine. It then armed and encouraged Russian separatists to take over parts of eastern Ukraine, a strategy it had previously pursued in Georgia and Moldova. As mentioned previously, Russia also interceded in the Syrian civil war, providing air power and advisers in support of Syrian president Bashar Hafez al-Assad, which tipped the war in his favor. These and other actions, including efforts to disrupt elections in the United States and Europe, are part of Russia's increasingly aggressive foreign policy. Russian president Vladimir Putin seeks to reestablish Russia as a world power, believing that "the collapse of the Soviet Union was the greatest catastrophe of the 20th century."[11]

China, too, is pursuing an increasingly assertive foreign policy. It has enlarged its navy, which had been structured to protect China's territorial waters but is now being configured to operate throughout the Pacific. China launched its first aircraft carrier in 2012 and is in the process of building attack submarines and missile ships. China has also claimed huge coastal areas in the South China Sea as being within its territorial boundaries, even though by international law the areas belong to other countries, including Vietnam and the Philippines. When these countries have contested China's claims, the Chinese navy has responded with force.

Concern with China's military buildup has been magnified by its embrace of Russia after the annexation of Crimea. China was the only country to side with Russia when the UN Security Council voted to censure Russia for the Crimean takeover. The two countries subsequently signed a $400 billion deal to build a natural gas pipeline from Russia to China and then conducted joint naval exercises near disputed islands held by Japan. "We have powerful enemies but we don't have powerful friends, that's why we need the support of such a giant as China," said a top Russian official. In turn, China has embraced Russia, which historically has been more of an adversary than a friend. In 2018, China's foreign minister declared that his country's relationship with Russia is at "the best level in history."[12]

PARTY POLARIZATION

Conflicting Ideas

Hard Power or Soft Power?

Until the Vietnam War, there was little partisan difference in Americans' views on national security. A bipartisan consensus prevailed, with Republicans and Democrats alike convinced of the need to contain the spread of communism. America's defeat in Vietnam disrupted the consensus. Since then, nearly every American conflict has been supported more strongly by Republicans than by Democrats, who have placed more emphasis on diplomacy, economic sanctions, and foreign aid as the means of protecting U.S. interests. Harvard's Joseph Nye, who served in national security positions in the Carter and Clinton administrations, coined the term **soft power** to describe this approach, contrasting it with the use of military force, which he characterized as **hard power**.

The difference between Republicans and Democrats is one of degree rather than of kind. Democrats and Republicans alike recognize that military action, diplomacy, economic sanctions, and foreign aid all have a part to play in protecting the United States. Nevertheless, there are partisan differences when it comes to national security policy, as indicated by the spending priorities of Republicans and Democrats.

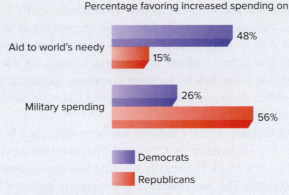

Percentage favoring increased spending on

Aid to world's needy — Democrats 48%, Republicans 15%

Military spending — Democrats 26%, Republicans 56%

Democrats
Republicans

Source: Pew Research Center survey, 2019.

Q: Where do you stand on the question of the relative use of hard power and soft power as instruments of national security policy? Why might Republicans and Democrats differ in their opinions on foreign aid and military spending?

The optimism created by the collapse of the Soviet Union in 1989 is gone. Former ambassador Nicholas Burns, one of America's most experienced diplomats, described today's world as "the most challenging . . . for the United States since World War II."[13]

THE MILITARY DIMENSION OF NATIONAL SECURITY POLICY

Defense spending by the United States is far higher than that of any other nation. In fact, the United States accounts for roughly 35 percent of all military spending worldwide (see "How the U.S. Differs"). The U.S. defense budget is nearly 3 times that of China and 10 times that of Russia.[14]

Military Power, Uses, and Capabilities

U.S. military forces are trained for different types of military action, ranging from nuclear conflict to terrorism.

Nuclear War   Although the possibility of all-out nuclear war declined dramatically with the collapse of the Soviet Union, the United States retains a nuclear arsenal designed to prevent such a war. Deterrence policy is based on the concept of **mutually assured destruction (MAD)**. The assumption is that any nation will be deterred from launching a full-scale nuclear attack on the United States by the knowledge that, even if it destroyed the United States, it, too, would be destroyed.

America's nuclear weapons are deployed in what is called the "nuclear triad." This term refers to the three ways—by land-based missiles, submarine-based missiles, and bombers—that nuclear weapons can be launched. The triad provides a second-strike capability—that is, the ability to absorb a first-strike nuclear attack and survive with enough nuclear capacity for a massive retaliation (second strike). Since the end of the Cold War, the United States and Russia have negotiated substantial reductions in their nuclear arsenals.

A greater fear today than nuclear war with Russia is the possibility that a terrorist group or rogue nation will smuggle a nuclear device into the United States and detonate it. The technology and materials necessary to build a nuclear weapon (or to buy one clandestinely) are more readily available than ever before. Accordingly, the United States, Russia, and other nations are cooperating to halt the spread of nuclear weapons, although, as the nuclear weapons program of North Korea illustrates, the effort has not been fully successful.

HOW THE U.S. DIFFERS

CRITICAL THINKING THROUGH COMPARISONS

Worldwide Military Spending

According to the Stockholm International Peace Research Institute's annual report, the United States accounts for roughly a third of worldwide military spending. China is second in military spending, but its expenditures are only about a third of those of the United States. Russia spends about a tenth as much.

The United States has had limited success in pressuring its European allies to spend more on defense, although Britain, France, and Germany spend more per capita on defense than any country except for the United States and Saudi Arabia.

Military spending (billions of dollars)

S. Korea	Japan	Germany	Britain	Russia	France	India	Saudi Arabia	China	U.S.
$43	$47	$49	$50	$61	$66	$67	$68	$250	$649

Q: What do you make of the disparity in military spending between the United States and its military allies? Do you think the allies spend too little on defense, relying too heavily on the United States for their security? Or do you think the United States spends too much on defense, placing too much emphasis on military force as an instrument of foreign policy?

Conventional War   Not since World War II has the United States fought an all-out conventional war, nor at present does it have the capacity to do so. The United States today relies on an all-volunteer military force (see "How the 50 States Differ"). All-out war would require reinstatement of the military draft and the full mobilization of the nation's industrial capacity.

HOW THE 50 STATES DIFFER

CRITICAL THINKING THROUGH COMPARISONS

The All-Volunteer Military's Recruits

The United States had an active military draft until 1973, during which time each state, on a per-capita basis, contributed nearly the same number of U.S. military personnel. Today's military is an all-volunteer force, and the states' contributions on a per-capita basis vary widely, as the accompanying map indicates. Hawaii and Alaska have the largest number of military volunteers relative to population, whereas Minnesota and Iowa have the lowest.

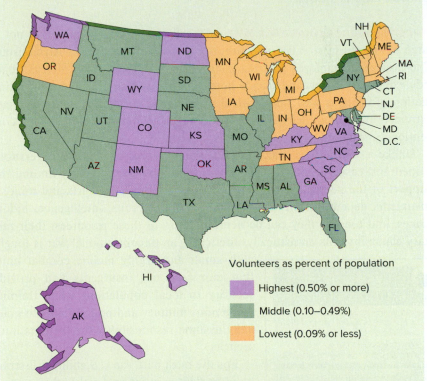

Volunteers as percent of population

- Highest (0.50% or more)
- Middle (0.10–0.49%)
- Lowest (0.09% or less)

Source: Calculated from Department of Defense and U.S. Census Bureau data, 2020

Q: What might explain why military recruits come disproportionately from states such as Alaska, Wyoming, and Oklahoma?

A: According to Department of Defense data, military recruits are more likely to come from rural areas, particularly those where hunting is prevalent and where there are fewer well-paying jobs for young adults.

Instead, the U.S. armed forces are structured to be capable of fighting two medium-sized wars simultaneously, although they are currently undergoing a restructuring in response to changing military tactics.[15]

The U.S. military is second to none in its destructive power. The U.S. Navy has 11 aircraft carriers, scores of attack submarines, and hundreds of fighting and supply ships. The U.S. Air Force has thousands of high-performance aircraft, ranging from fighter jets to jumbo transport planes. The U.S. Army has roughly 500,000 regular troops and more than 300,000 Reserve and National Guard soldiers, who are supplied with tanks, artillery pieces, armored personnel carriers, and attack helicopters. This armament is doubly lethal because it is linked to sophisticated surveillance, targeting, and communication systems. No other nation has anywhere near the advanced weapons systems that the United States possesses.

Unconventional (Guerrilla) War   America's military firepower is not a large advantage in so-called unconventional wars of the type in Afghanistan. The insurgents employed guerrilla tactics, including hit-and-run attacks, roadside explosive devices, and suicide bombings, as well as the killing and intimidation of civilians who sided with the Afghan government. Such tactics are extremely difficult to defend against and virtually impossible to stop by conventional means.

Unlike a conventional war, in which the measures of success are territory gained and casualties inflicted, an unconventional war requires winning the support of the people or, as it is labeled, "winning their hearts and minds." Insurgents depend on the local population for recruits, intelligence, hiding places, and food. If they can be denied access to these resources, their military capability falls dramatically. Tactically, an unconventional war is fought with small and highly mobile combat units that can seek out insurgents and provide security to local populations while training indigenous military and police forces to gradually assume responsibility for their nation's security.[16]

For the most part, the U.S. military is structured to fight conventional rather than unconventional wars, although most of the recent conflicts have been of the second type. In response, the U.S. military has been building its capacity in unconventional warfare. It has increased the number of special operations units (such as the Army Special Forces and

> **CITIZEN ACTION!**
> **GETTING INVOLVED**
>
> In his 1961 inaugural address, President John F. Kennedy said, "Ask not what your country can do for you. Ask what you can do for your country." His call was not just a call to military service. The Peace Corps provides Americans the opportunity to work for two years in a developing country. AmeriCorps is a network of public service programs, including Teach for America, where college grads teach for two years in high-need U.S. schools. In addition to salary, many of these programs include forgiveness of a portion of student loan debt.

the Navy SEALs) and is providing its regular units with additional training in counterinsurgency warfare.

Transnational Terrorism   The terrorist attacks of September 11, 2001, thrust the U.S. military into a new kind of war. The United States was not prepared to conduct a war on terrorism. Its military units were not trained for that kind of warfare and lacked even linguists who spoke the terrorists' languages. Moreover, as the United States was to discover, the war on terrorism could not be waged solely through military force. Law enforcement officials would also have to play a key role, charged with locating potential terrorists and providing security at airports, major events, and other "soft" targets.

Terrorism is not a new form of warfare. It has been used in many places over the centuries, but it has become a wider threat in recent years. Historically, terrorism was a domestic problem, employed by disgruntled groups against their own government. Terrorism today has an international dimension. **Transnational terrorism** is terrorism that transcends national borders and includes attacks on nonmilitary targets.[17] When terrorists attacked the United States in 2001, or Paris in 2015, they were not seeking to take over a country. They were seeking to alter the balance of power in the Middle East by forcing Western nations to rethink their presence in the region.

America's war on terrorism is aimed at groups such as al Qaeda and the Islamic State rather than at nations. The Islamic State is a nonstate actor without clearly defined borders, which complicates the task of isolating and destroying it. Moreover, transnational terrorists have become adept at waging "asymmetric war," so called because they lack the strength to directly engage opposing military forces. In fighting their wars, terrorists target civilians and use improvised weapons, including suicide bombers.

The Politics of National Defense

Policy elites, defense policy experts, the public, and special interests all play a role in national defense policy. Policy elites and experts have the largest say in that few citizens are interested in and informed about most defense policy issues. Even when citizens are attentive, they tend to defer to the judgment of political leaders on the use of military force. If a war begins to seem endless, however, public support inevitably erodes.[18] A swing in public opinion against the Vietnam War forced U.S. policymakers to withdraw American troops in 1973. Public opinion on the Iraq war soured even more quickly, partly because the stated reason for the war—the threat of Iraq's WMDs—proved faulty.

The defense industry has a large say in national security policy. In his 1961 farewell address, President Dwight D. Eisenhower, who commanded U.S.

In 2015, Islamic militants armed with assault weapons entered a concert hall in Paris, killing 89 people. Transnational terrorism is a new kind of warfare that transcends national boundaries and includes nonmilitary targets. (Thierry Chesnot/Getty Images)

forces in Europe during World War II, warned Americans against "the unwarranted influence" and "misplaced power" of what he termed "the military-industrial complex." Eisenhower was referring to the fact that national defense is big business, involving the annual expenditure of hundreds of billions of dollars.[19] As Eisenhower described it, the **military–industrial complex** has three main components: the military establishment, the arms industry, and the members of Congress from states and districts that depend heavily on the arms industry. All three benefit from a continuously high level of defense spending. And, as noted, roughly a third of all military spending worldwide is spent by the United States.

Although analysts disagree on whether defense spending is excessive, there is widespread agreement that the spending is not properly aligned. Much of what is spent is merely a continuation of the past spending pattern, as opposed to allocating the money to counter today's defense threats.[20]

THE ECONOMIC DIMENSION OF NATIONAL SECURITY POLICY

National security is more than an issue of military might. It is also a question of maintaining a strong position in the global economy. Geographically, the world has three major economic centers. One is the United States, which produces roughly a fifth of the world's goods and services. Another center, accounting for about a fourth of the world's economy, is the European Union (EU), which contains most European countries, including Germany and France. The third center is the Pacific Rim, anchored by the economies of Japan and China, which together account for more than a fifth of the world's economy.

On at least one dimension, the United States is the weakest of the three economic centers. Its trade deficit is easily the world's largest. The United States imports substantially more goods and services than it exports. In fact, the United States has not had a trade surplus since 1975, and its annual deficit has exceeded $300 billion every year in the past decade.

In other ways, however, the United States is easily the strongest of the three centers. According to the Switzerland-based World Economic Forum, the United States is economically more competitive than its major rivals. The United States owes this position to several factors, including its technological innovation, financial institutions, and extensive higher education system.[21] The U.S. economy is also the most diversified of the three. In addition to its industrial base, the United States has a strong agricultural sector and abundant natural resources. Its vast, fertile plains and advanced farming methods have made it the world's leading agricultural producer. The United States ranks among the top three countries worldwide in the production of wheat, corn, soybeans, peanuts, cotton, eggs, cattle, and pigs. As for natural resources, the United States ranks among the top five nations in, among other minerals, deposits of copper, zinc, coal, gold, iron ore, and magnesium.[22]

In recent years, as a result of changes in technology, the United States has also surged to the top in terms of oil and natural gas production. Although the United States continues to import about a fourth of its oil, mainly from Canada and Latin America, it is the only one of the three economic centers that has the capacity to be "energy independent" in the sense that, if necessary, it could meet its energy needs from domestic resources alone.

Nevertheless, the United States does not have the option of "going it alone" economically. To meet Americans' production and consumption needs, the country depends on other countries' raw materials, finished goods, markets, and capital. This imperative requires the United States to exert global economic influence. The efforts of the United States in the world economy include foreign trade, foreign assistance, and global economic security, each of which will now be discussed.

Foreign Trade

After World War II, the United States helped enact a global trading system with itself at the center. The U.S. dollar had become the leading currency of international trade, replacing the English pound, and the United States quickly asserted its economic dominance. A key initiative was the European Recovery Plan, better known as the Marshall Plan. It included an unprecedented amount of aid (more than $100 billion in today's dollars) for the postwar rebuilding of Europe. Apart from enabling the countries of Western Europe to better confront the perceived Soviet threat, the Marshall Plan served America's economic needs. Wartime production had lifted the United States out of the Great Depression, but the immediate postwar period was marked by a recession and renewed fears of hard times. A rebuilt Western Europe would become a much needed market for American products. In the early 1950s, the United States was producing nearly as many goods and services as the entire rest of the world and was by far the world's biggest exporter.[23]

That advantage was unsustainable. As the European and Japanese economies strengthened, they increasingly looked to sell their goods in foreign markets. America's trading partners had become its trading rivals. By the 1970s, the U.S. balance of trade had leveled out. Each year since then, the United States has had a negative balance of trade, consuming more goods from abroad than it has shipped overseas (see Figure 17-1).

By the 1980s, the American and world economies had changed fundamentally from what they were in the years immediately after World War II. **Economic globalization**—the increased interdependence of nations' economies—was under way. There was vastly more market competition between countries, and business

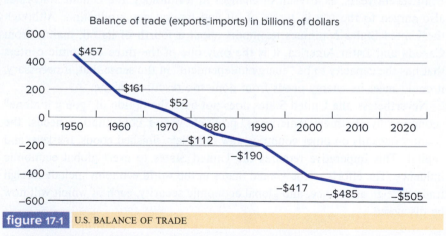

Balance of trade (exports-imports) in billions of dollars

figure 17-1   U.S. BALANCE OF TRADE

After World War II, the United States had a trade surplus. In recent years, as in every year since 1975, the United States has had a trade deficit, meaning that its imports have exceeded its exports. (*Source:* U.S. Bureau of Economic Analysis, 2020. Figures are constant 2010 U.S. dollars. Figure for 2020 based on projections.)

practices had evolved. Large U.S. firms had become *multinational corporations* (or *transnational corporations*), with operations in several countries. A firm could be headquartered in New York with its factories in Thailand, giving it the best of both worlds: access to management skills and finance in New York and access to low-wage workers in Thailand.

Free Trade Versus Protectionism   Although global trade was expanding, it was limited by **tariffs**—the taxes that countries levy on goods shipped in from another country. Even if a firm could manufacture a product more cheaply in one country, it would be prohibitively expensive in another country if that country levied a hefty tariff on the product. To deal with the problem, firms began lobbying Congress for agreements with other countries based on the principle of **free trade**—trade based on greatly reduced or no tariffs. They quickly gained the backing of a traditional ally, Republican leaders in Washington. "The freer the flow of world trade," said President Ronald Reagan, "the stronger the tides of human progress."

Developments elsewhere added to the momentum behind free trade. European nations were on a path to economic integration—a passport-free Europe with few tariffs. Trade between European countries would increase, with American products losing out unless tariff reductions could be achieved. Economists contributed to the free-trade momentum. Their economic models indicated that free trade would result in a net gain to the U.S. economy.[24] Free trade would lead to a loss of jobs, but that cost would be more than offset by the availability to American consumers of lower-priced goods, everything from clothing to television sets.

In 1993, Congress enacted the first major free-trade agreement, NAFTA (North American Free Trade Agreement), which established a largely free market between the United States, Canada, and Mexico. It passed with the support of more than 70 percent of Senate and House Republicans, whereas fewer than half of the Democrats in each chamber voted for it.* The political divide on NAFTA surfaced again the next time Congress voted on free trade. At issue in 2011 were bilateral free-trade agreements with Panama, Colombia, and

---

*The formal international institution that oversees trade agreements and international trade rules is the World Trade Organization (WTO), which was created in 1995 and of which the United States is a founding member. The WTO today includes more than 160 nations. The WTO's mission is to promote global free trade through reductions in tariffs, protections for intellectual property (copyrights and patents), and other policies. Trade disputes among WTO members are settled by arbitration panels, which consist of representatives from the member nations. Under WTO rules, an arbitration panel's ruling, once approved by the WTO's full membership, is binding on the countries involved in the dispute.

Korea. Each was voted on separately, and, on average, they won the support of 96 percent of congressional Republicans and only 32 percent of congressional Democrats.

To a member of Congress, free trade is often a question of its impact on his or her constituency. Although most members of Congress support free trade in principle, they don't always do so when confronted with an actual trade agreement. If it will harm a major interest in their district or state, they sometimes opt for **protectionism**—the use of tariffs or other trade barriers to protect domestic producers from foreign competitors. With their ties to labor, Democratic lawmakers tend to be more protectionist because of the threat that free trade poses to jobs.

Donald Trump's "America First" Policy   Donald Trump's five immediate predecessors, starting with Ronald Reagan and running through Barack Obama, were advocates of free trade, in part out of their belief that it was a net benefit and contributed to economic growth. Trump felt differently. In his inaugural address, he said, "From this moment on, it's going to be America First. Every decision on trade . . . will be made to benefit American workers and American

Nations' economies are increasingly interdependent. Not surprisingly, given that some interests benefit from global trade, whereas others are harmed by it, trade is a contentious political issue that pits advocates of free trade against those who would use tariffs as a means of protecting domestic producers from their foreign competitors. (EvrenKalinbacak/iStockphoto/Getty Images)

families. We must protect our borders from the ravages of other countries making our products, stealing our companies, and destroying our jobs. Protection will lead to great prosperity and strength."

On taking office, Trump withdrew the United States from the 12-nation Trans-Pacific Partnership (TPP) trade agreement that Obama had negotiated and was pending congressional approval. Trump then renegotiated NAFTA, unveiling the new agreement in 2018 under a new name, the United States–Mexico–Canada Agreement (USMCA). Trump also targeted China, claiming that it was stealing intellectual property, subsidizing its industries, and manipulating its currency, all for the purpose of gaining a trade advantage. He imposed tariffs on steel, aluminum and other goods imported from China, which reciprocated by erecting barriers to U.S. goods. In 2020, an escalating trade war with China eased somewhat, with a contingent agreement that requires China to purchase a specified amount of American goods and to take steps to eliminate intellectual property theft.[25]

Protectionism did not fully define Trump's "America First" policy. He negotiated a limited trade agreement with Japan in 2019 while seeking trade agreements with Great Britain and the European Union (EU). But he altered the path toward free trade forged by his presidential predecessors.[26]

Assisting Developing Nations

Since World War II, foreign assistance has been a cornerstone of U.S. foreign policy. Contributions include direct foreign aid as well as indirect assistance through international organizations, such as the International Monetary Fund (IMF) and the World Bank, which were created by the United States and Great Britain at the Bretton Woods Conference near the end of World War II. The IMF makes short-term loans to protect economically struggling countries from destructive practices, such as the unlimited printing of paper money. For its part, the World Bank makes long-term development loans to poor countries for capital investment projects, such as dams, highways, and factories.

No country comes even close to matching the United States in terms of total foreign aid spending since World II. Over the past couple of decades, however, Canada and several European countries have spent more per capita than has the United States. America's fiscal problems, and its costly wars in Iraq and Afghanistan, have weakened its ability to use aid as a tool of foreign policy. Public opinion is also an obstacle to increased foreign aid spending. Most Americans believe that the United States spends too heavily on foreign aid (see "Fake or Fact? Detecting Misinformation").

F A K E
or
F A C T

Detecting Misinformation

Would Eliminating Foreign Aid Balance the Budget?

A recent poll asked Americans for their "best guess" of the percentage of the federal budget spent on foreign aid. On average, respondents estimated it at 26 percent of the total budget. One in five who ventured a guess estimated it at 40 percent or higher. A large number said that eliminating foreign aid would produce enough savings to balance the federal budget.[27]

Is that claim fact, or is it fake?   POP-THAILAND/Shutterstock

The actual level of spending on foreign aid is less than 1 percent of the federal budget. And much of this spending is not actual dollars, but instead is in the form of foodstuffs and military hardware produced by American firms and sent overseas. If lawmakers were to seek ways to balance the budget, cutting foreign aid wouldn't have much effect. The only realistic way to balance the budget would be through a combination of tax increases and spending cuts in areas where the federal government spends heavily.

As the United States has cut back on foreign aid spending, China has stepped up its spending. China recently passed the United States in terms of total foreign aid spending.[28] Through loans and grants, China is spending heavily on infrastructure and commercial projects in scores of countries in Africa, South America, and Asia. It is also pursuing mining and drilling projects in many of these countries, seeking to secure the raw materials needed to sustain its economic growth. In a sense, China is following the path laid out by the United States after World War II, when it pursued an economic strategy as a means of expanding its global influence.

Protecting International Commerce

Although many Americans believe the nation's armed forces have a strictly military purpose, there is also an economic purpose: protecting international commerce. Trade depends on the free flow of goods, which requires open sea, air, and land routes. After World War II, the United States took the lead in this area and has maintained it, most visibly through its naval presence. The U.S. Navy patrols every major shipping lane, including the Persian Gulf, through which much of the world's oil flows, and the South China Sea, which is the shortest shipping route from Europe, the Middle East, and Africa to Pacific nations. An indicator of America's sea power is its fleet of aircraft carriers. The United States has 11 carriers, 1 in reserve, and 1 under construction. No other country has more than 2.

As these examples illustrate, the new global economy poses risks as well as benefits to the United States. After World War II, the U.S. economy accounted for nearly half of the world's economic output, and the United States was in a position to nearly define the terms of its economic relations with other countries. Today, it operates in a global economy marked by mutual dependence. The United States depends on the economic health of other nations, just as they depend on the health of the American economy. Thus, as the United States today faces a set of nearly unprecedented military challenges around the globe, so, too, is it confronting a set of nearly unprecedented economic ones. In the end, its national security will rest on its ability to respond effectively to both challenges.

The economic role of naval power has come into prominence in the past few years as China has flexed its power by laying claim to islands in the South China Sea off the coasts of Vietnam and the Philippines. The area surrounding the islands has untapped oil reserves, which China has claimed while also claiming the right to keep foreign shipping out of the islands' territorial waters. The United States has refused to recognize the claims and has sent ships through the disputed waters and conducted joint naval exercises. In 2019, for example, it held a naval exercise with Southeast Asian countries, one of whom was its former adversary, Vietnam.

The U.S. role in protecting international commerce goes far beyond the projection of military power, most notably in its efforts to strengthen global financial markets. The importance of this effort became apparent in the global economic downturn of 2008, when financial institutions worldwide teetered on the edge of failure.[29] In response, U.S. policymakers subjected America's leading banks to a "stress test" to determine their ability to withstand defaults on the debt they are owed. Banks that failed the test were provided government loans to protect them from such defaults. U.S. policymakers encouraged and helped other nations to do the same, recognizing that major financial institutions operate around the globe and that the collapse of even one of them could send the world economy into a downward spiral.

SUMMARY

The chief instruments of national security policy are diplomacy, military force, economic exchange, and intelligence gathering. These are exercised through specialized agencies of the U.S. government, which are largely responsive to presidential leadership, such as the Departments of State and Defense. National security policy has also relied on international organizations, such as the United Nations and the World Trade Organization, which are responsive to the global concerns of major nations.

From 1945 to 1990, U.S. foreign and defense policies were dominated by a concern with the Soviet Union. During most of this period, the United States pursued a policy of containment based on the premise that the Soviet Union was an aggressor nation bent on global conquest. Containment policy led the United States to enter into wars in Korea and Vietnam and to maintain a large defense establishment.

A first response to the end of the Cold War period was multilateralism—the idea that major nations could achieve common goals by working together, including the use of force to restrain regional conflicts. The interventions in the Persian Gulf and the Balkans during the 1990s are examples. They demonstrated that major nations can intervene with some success in global hot spots but also showed that the ethnic, religious, and national conflicts that fuel these conflicts are not easily resolved.

The terrorist attacks on the World Trade Center and the Pentagon in 2001 led to broad changes in national security organization and strategy. Increased defense and homeland security spending has been coupled with a partial reorganization of U.S. intelligence, law enforcement, and immigration agencies, as well as new laws affecting the scope of their activities. However, the defining moment of the post–September 11 period was America's invasion of Iraq in 2003, which was rooted in President George W. Bush's preemptive war doctrine and his willingness to commit the United States to unilateral action. America's inability to create a stable regime in Iraq, in conjunction with Syria's civil war, gave rise to the Islamic State, which became a primary target of U.S. military action.

In recent decades, the United States has increasingly taken economic factors into account in its national security policies. This has meant, for example, that trade has played a larger part in defining relationships between the United States and other countries. The trading system that the United States helped erect after World War II has given way to one that is global in scale and more competitive. Changes in communication, transportation, and computing have altered the way large corporations operate, and, as businesses have changed their practices, nations have had to adapt. The changes include the emergence of regional and international economic structures, such as the European Union and the United States-Mexico-Canada Trade Agreement. Nevertheless, nations naturally compete for economic advantage, including access to natural resources; accordingly, trade is a source of conflict as well as a source of cooperation.

CRITICAL THINKING ZONE

KEY TERMS

bipolar (*p. 504*)
Cold War (*p. 504*)
containment (*p. 504*)
economic globalization (*p. 520*)
free trade (*p. 521*)
hard power (*p. 512*)
internationalist (*p. 504*)
isolationist (*p. 503*)
military–industrial complex (*p. 518*)
multilateralism (*p. 505*)

mutually assured destruction
  (MAD) (*p. 513*)
preemptive war doctrine (*p. 507*)
protectionism (*p. 522*)
soft power (*p. 512*)
tariffs (*p. 521*)
transnational terrorism (*p. 517*)
unilateralism (*p. 508*)
unipolar (*p. 505*)

APPLYING THE ELEMENTS OF CRITICAL THINKING

Conceptualizing: Explain the difference between a bipolar international power structure and a unipolar one. With which one is containment doctrine associated?

Synthesizing: Contrast free trade and protectionism as approaches to global trade and competition. Identify policies associated with each approach.

Analyzing: Two objectives of U.S. foreign policy are defense security and economic security. What are the mechanisms for pursuing each of these objectives?

EXTRA CREDIT

A Book Worth Reading: Joseph Nye, *Presidential Leadership and the Creation of the American Era* (Princeton, N.J.: Princeton University Press, 2013). An insightful look at the role various U.S. presidents have played in shaping the nation's place in the world. The author's earlier award-winning book, *Soft Power,* helped change the way policymakers think about foreign policy.

A Website Worth Visiting: **www.cfr.org** The Council on Foreign Relations brings together foreign policy leaders, analysts, scholars, and others in order to promote a better understanding of international issues. Its website includes foreign policy reports, assessments, speeches, and other information.

The Declaration of Independence
IN CONGRESS, JULY 4, 1776

The Unanimous Declaration of the Thirteen United States of America

When, in the course of human events, it becomes necessary for one people to dissolve the political bands which have connected them with another, and to assume, among the powers of the earth, the separate and equal station to which the laws of nature and of natures God entitle them, a decent respect to the opinions of mankind requires that they should declare the causes which impel them to the separation.

We hold these truths to be self-evident, that all men are created equal; that they are endowed by their Creator with certain unalienable rights; that among these are life, liberty, and the pursuit of happiness. That, to secure these rights, governments are instituted among men, deriving their just powers from the consent of the governed; that, whenever any form of government becomes destructive of these ends, it is the right of the people to alter or to abolish it, and to institute a new government, laying its foundation on such principles, and organizing its powers in such form, as to them shall seem most likely to effect their safety and happiness. Prudence, indeed, will dictate that governments long established, should not be changed for light and transient causes; and, accordingly, all experience hath shown, that mankind are more disposed to suffer, while evils are sufferable, than to right themselves by abolishing the forms to which they are accustomed. But, when a long train of abuses and usurpations, pursuing invariably the same object, evinces a design to reduce them under absolute despotism, it is their right, it is their duty, to throw off such government and to provide new guards for their future security. Such has been the patient sufferance of these colonies, and such is now the necessity which constrains them to alter their former systems of government. The history of the present King of Great Britain is a history of repeated injuries and usurpations, all having, in direct object, the establishment of an absolute tyranny over these States. To prove this, let facts be submitted to a candid world:

He has refused his assent to laws the most wholesome and necessary for the public good.

He has forbidden his governors to pass laws of immediate and pressing importance, unless suspended in their operation till his assent should be obtained; and, when so suspended, he has utterly neglected to attend to them.

He has refused to pass other laws for the accommodation of large districts of people, unless those people would relinquish the right of representation in the legislature; a right inestimable to them, and formidable to tyrants only.

He has called together legislative bodies at places unusual, uncomfortable, and distant from the depository of their public records, for the sole purpose of fatiguing them into compliance with his measures.

He has dissolved representative houses repeatedly for opposing, with manly firmness, his invasions on the rights of the people.

He has refused, for a long time after such dissolutions, to cause others to be elected; whereby the legislative powers, incapable of annihilation, have returned to the people at large for their exercise; the state remaining, in the meantime, exposed to all the danger of invasion from without, and convulsions within.

He has endeavored to prevent the population of these States; for that purpose, obstructing the laws for naturalization of foreigners, refusing to pass others to encourage their migration hither, and raising the conditions of new appropriations of lands.

He has obstructed the administration of justice, by refusing his assent to laws for establishing judiciary powers.

He has made judges dependent on his will alone, for the tenure of their offices, and the amount and payment of their salaries.

He has erected a multitude of new offices, and sent hither swarms of officers to harass our people, and eat out their substance.

He has kept among us, in time of peace, standing armies, without the consent of our legislatures.

He has affected to render the military independent of, and superior to, the civil power.

He has combined, with others, to subject us to a jurisdiction foreign to our Constitution, and unacknowledged by our laws; giving his assent to their acts of pretended legislation:

For quartering large bodies of armed troops among us:

For protecting them by a mock trial, from punishment, for any murders which they should commit on the inhabitants of these States:

For cutting off our trade with all parts of the world:

For imposing taxes on us without our consent:

For depriving us, in many cases, of the benefit of trial by jury:

For transporting us beyond seas to be tried for pretended offences:

For abolishing the free system of English laws in a neighboring province, establishing therein an arbitrary government, and enlarging its boundaries, so as to render it at once an example and fit instrument for introducing the same absolute rule into these colonies:

For taking away our charters, abolishing our most valuable laws, and altering, fundamentally, the powers of our governments:

For suspending our own legislatures, and declaring themselves invested with power to legislate for us in all cases whatsoever.

He has abdicated government here, by declaring us out of his protection, and waging war against us.

He has plundered our seas, ravaged our coasts, burnt our towns, and destroyed the lives of our people.

He is, at this time, transporting large armies of foreign mercenaries to complete the works of death, desolation, and tyranny, already begun, with circumstances of cruelty and perfidy scarcely paralleled in the most barbarous ages, and totally unworthy of the head of a civilized nation.

He has constrained our fellow citizens, taken captive on the high seas, to bear arms against their country, to become the executioners of their friends, and brethren, or to fall themselves by their hands.

He has excited domestic insurrections amongst us, and has endeavored to bring on the inhabitants of our frontiers, the merciless Indian savages, whose known rule of warfare is an undistinguished destruction of all ages, sexes, and conditions.

In every stage of these oppressions, we have petitioned for redress, in the most humble terms; our repeated petitions have been answered only by repeated injury. A prince, whose character is thus marked by every act which may define a tyrant, is unfit to be the ruler of a free people.

Nor have we been wanting in attention to our British brethren. We have warned them, from time to time, of attempts made by their legislature to extend an unwarrantable jurisdiction over us. We have reminded them of the circumstances of our emigration and settlement here. We have appealed to their native justice and magnanimity, and we have conjured them, by the ties of our common kindred, to disavow these usurpations, which would inevitably interrupt our connections and correspondence. They, too, have been deaf to the voice of justice and of consanguinity. We must, therefore, acquiesce in the necessity which denounces our separation, and hold them as we hold the rest of mankind, enemies in war, in peace, friends.

We, therefore, the representatives of the United States of America, in general Congress assembled, appealing to the Supreme Judge of the world for the rectitude of our intentions, do, in the name, and by the authority of the good people of these colonies, solemnly publish and declare, that these united colonies are, and of right ought to be, free and independent states: that they are absolved from all allegiance to the British Crown, and that all political connection between them and the state of Great Britain is, and ought to be, totally dissolved; and that, as free and independent states, they have full power to levy war, conclude peace, contract alliances, establish commerce, and to do all other acts and things which independent states may of right do. And, for the support of this declaration, with a firm reliance on the protection of Divine Providence, we mutually pledge to each other our lives, our fortunes, and our sacred honor.

The foregoing Declaration was, by order of Congress, engrossed, and signed by the following members:

JOHN HANCOCK

New Hampshire
Josiah Bartlett
William Whipple
Matthew Thornton

Massachusetts Bay
Samuel Adams
John Adams
Robert Treat Paine
Elbridge Gerry

Rhode Island
Stephen Hopkins
William Ellery

Connecticut
Roger Sherman

Samuel Huntington
William Williams
Oliver Wolcott

New York
William Floyd
Philip Livingston
Francis Lewis
Lewis Morris

New Jersey
Richard Stockton
John Witherspoon
Francis Hopkinson
John Hart
Abraham Clark

Pennsylvania
Robert Morris
Benjamin Rush
Benjamin Franklin
John Morton
George Clymer
James Smith
George Taylor
James Wilson
George Ross

Delaware
Caesar Rodney
George Reed
Thomas McKean

Maryland
Samuel Chase
William Paca
Thomas Stone
Charles Carroll,
of Carrollton

Virginia
George Wythe
Richard Henry Lee

Thomas Jefferson
Benjamin Harrison
Thomas Nelson, Jr.
Francis Lightfoot Lee
Carter Braxton

North Carolina
William Hooper
Joseph Hewes
John Penn

South Carolina
Edward Rutledge
Thomas Heyward, Jr.
Thomas Lynch, Jr.
Arthur Middleton

Georgia
Button Gwinnett
Lyman Hall
George Walton

Resolved, That copies of the Declaration be sent to the several assemblies, conventions, and committees, or councils of safety, and to the several commanding officers of the continental troops; that it be proclaimed in each of the United States, at the head of the army.

The Constitution of the United States of America[1]

We the People of the United States, in Order to form a more perfect Union, establish Justice, insure domestic Tranquility, provide for the common defence, promote the general Welfare, and secure the Blessings of Liberty to ourselves and our Posterity, do ordain and establish this CONSTITUTION for the United States of America.

ARTICLE I

Section 1

All legislative Powers herein granted shall be vested in a Congress of the United States, which shall consist of a Senate and House of Representatives.

Section 2

The House of Representatives shall be composed of Members chosen every second Year by the People of the several States, and the Electors in each State shall have the Qualifications requisite for Electors of the most numerous Branch of the State Legislature.

No Person shall be a Representative who shall not have attained to the Age of twenty-five Years, and been seven Years a Citizen of the United States, and who shall not, when elected, be an Inhabitant of that State in which he shall be chosen.

[Representatives and direct Taxes[2] shall be apportioned among the several States which may be included within this Union, according to their respective Numbers, which shall be determined by adding to the whole Number of free Persons, including those bound to Service for a Term of Years, and excluding Indians not taxed, three fifths of all other Persons.][3] The actual Enumeration shall be made within three Years after the first Meeting of the Congress of the United States, and within every subsequent Term of ten Years, in such Manner as they shall by Law direct. The Number of Representatives shall not exceed one for every thirty Thousand, but each State shall have at Least one Representative; and until such enumeration shall be made, the State of New Hampshire shall be entitled to chuse three, Massachusetts eight, Rhode-Island and Providence Plantations one, Connecticut five, New York six, New Jersey four, Pennsylvania eight, Delaware one, Maryland six, Virginia ten, North Carolina five, South Carolina five, and Georgia three.

When vacancies happen in the Representation from any State, the Executive Authority thereof shall issue Writs of Election to fill such Vacancies.

The House of Representatives shall chuse their Speaker and other Officers; and shall have the sole Power of Impeachment.

---

[1]This version, which follows the original Constitution in capitalization and spelling, was published by the United States Department of the Interior, Office of Education, in 1935.
[2]Altered by the Sixteenth Amendment.
[3]Negated by the Fourteenth Amendment.

Section 3

The Senate of the United States shall be composed of two Senators from each State, chosen by the Legislature thereof, for six Years; and each Senator shall have one Vote.

Immediately after they shall be assembled in Consequence of the first Election, they shall be divided as equally as may be into three Classes. The Seats of the Senators of the first Class shall be vacated at the Expiration of the second Year, of the second Class at the Expiration of the fourth Year, and of the third Class at the Expiration of the sixth Year, so that one-third may be chosen every second Year; and if Vacancies happen by Resignation, or otherwise, during the Recess of the Legislature of any State, the Executive thereof may make temporary Appointments until the next Meeting of the Legislature, which shall then fill such Vacancies.

No Person shall be a Senator who shall not have attained to the Age of thirty Years, and been nine Years a Citizen of the United States, and who shall not, when elected, be an Inhabitant of that State for which he shall be chosen.

The Vice President of the United States shall be President of the Senate, but shall have no vote, unless they be equally divided.

The Senate shall chuse their other Officers, and also a President pro tempore, in the absence of the Vice President, or when he shall exercise the Office of President of the United States.

The Senate shall have the sole Power to try all Impeachments. When sitting for that purpose they shall be on Oath or Affirmation. When the President of the United States is tried, the Chief Justice shall preside: And no person shall be convicted without the Concurrence of two thirds of the Members present.

Judgment in Cases of Impeachment shall not extend further than to removal from Office, and disqualification to hold and enjoy any Office of honor, Trust, or Profit under the United States: but the Party convicted shall nevertheless be liable and subject to Indictment, Trial, Judgment and Punishment, according to Law.

Section 4

The Times, Place and Manner of holding Elections for Senators and Representatives, shall be prescribed in each State by the Legislature thereof; but the Congress may at any time by Law make or alter such Regulations, except as to the Places of Chusing Senators.

The Congress shall assemble at least once in every Year, and such Meeting shall be on the first Monday in December, unless they shall by Law appoint a different Day.

Section 5

Each House shall be the Judge of the Elections, Returns and Qualifications of its own Members, and a Majority of each shall constitute a Quorum to do Business; but a smaller number may adjourn from day to day, and may be authorized to compel the Attendance of absent Members, in such Manner, and under such Penalties, as each House may provide.

Each House may determine the Rules of its Proceedings, punish its Members for disorderly Behaviour, and, with the Concurrence of two thirds, expel a Member.

Each House shall keep a Journal of its Proceedings, and from time to time publish the same, excepting such Parts as may in their Judgment require Secrecy; and the Yeas and Nays of the Members of either House on any question shall, at the Desire of one fifth of those Present, be entered on the Journal.

Neither House, during the Session of Congress, shall, without the Consent of the other, adjourn for more than three days, nor to any other Place than that in which the two Houses shall be sitting.

Section 6

The Senators and Representatives shall receive a Compensation for their Services, to be ascertained by Law, and paid out of the Treasury of the United States. They shall in all Cases, except Treason, Felony, and Breach of the Peace, be privileged from Arrest during their Attendance at the Session of their respective Houses, and in going to and returning from the same; and for any Speech or Debate in either House, they shall not be questioned in any other Place.

No Senator or Representative shall, during the Time for which he was elected, be appointed to any civil Office under the Authority of the United States, which shall have been created, or the Emoluments whereof shall have been increased, during such time; and no Person holding any Office under the United States shall be a Member of either House during his continuance in Office.

Section 7

All Bills for raising Revenue shall originate in the House of Representatives; but the Senate may propose or concur with Amendments as on other bills.

Every Bill which shall have passed the House of Representatives and the Senate, shall, before it becomes a Law, be presented to the President of the United States; if he approve he shall sign it, but if not he shall return it, with his Objections, to that House in which it shall have originated, who shall enter the Objections at large on their Journal, and proceed to reconsider it. If after such Reconsideration two thirds of that House shall agree to pass the bill, it shall be sent, together with the objections, to the other House, by which it shall likewise be reconsidered, and if approved by two thirds of that House, it shall become a Law. But in all such Cases the Votes of both Houses shall be determined by Yeas and Nays, and the Names of the Persons voting for and against the Bill shall be entered on the Journal of each House respectively. If any Bill shall not be returned by the President within ten Days (Sundays excepted) after it shall have been presented to him, the Same shall be a Law, in like Manner as if he had signed it, unless the Congress by their Adjournment prevent its Return, in which Case it shall not be a Law.

Every Order, Resolution, or Vote to which the Concurrence of the Senate and House of Representatives may be necessary (except on a question of Adjournment) shall be presented to the President of the United States; and before the Same shall take Effect, shall be approved by him, or being disapproved by him, shall be repassed by two thirds of the Senate and House of Representatives, according to the Rules and Limitations prescribed in the Case of a Bill.

Section 8

The Congress shall have Power To lay and collect Taxes, Duties, Imposts and Excises, to pay the Debts and provide for the common Defence and general Welfare of the United States; but all Duties, Imposts and Excises shall be uniform throughout the United States;

To borrow money on the credit of the United States;

To regulate Commerce with foreign Nations, and among the several States, and with the Indian Tribes;

To establish a uniform rule of Naturalization, and uniform Laws on the subject of Bankruptcies throughout the United States;

To coin Money, regulate the Value thereof, and of foreign Coin, and fix the Standard of Weights and Measures;

To provide for the Punishment of counterfeiting the Securities and current Coin of the United States;

To establish Post Offices and post Roads;

To promote the Progress of Science and useful Arts, by securing for limited Times to Authors and Inventors the exclusive Right to their respective Writings and Discoveries;

To constitute Tribunals inferior to the Supreme Court;

To define and punish Piracies and Felonies committed on the high Seas, and Offenses against the Law of Nations;

To declare War, grant Letters of Marque and Reprisal, and make Rules concerning Captures on Land and Water;

To raise and support Armies, but no Appropriation of Money to that Use shall be for a longer Term than two Years;

To provide and maintain a Navy;

To make Rules for the Government and Regulation of the land and naval forces;

To provide for calling forth the Militia to execute the Laws of the Union, suppress Insurrections and repel Invasions;

To provide for organizing, arming, and disciplining the Militia, and for governing such Part of them as may be employed in the Service of the United States, reserving to the States respectively, the Appointment of the Officers, and the Authority of training the Militia according to the discipline prescribed by Congress;

To exercise exclusive Legislation in all Cases whatsoever, over such District (not exceeding ten Miles square) as may, by Cession of particular States, and the acceptance of Congress, become the Seat of the Government of the United States, and to exercise like Authority over all Places purchased by the Consent of the Legislature of the State in which the Same shall be, for the Erection of Forts, Magazines, Arsenals, Dock-yards, and other needful Buildings;—And

To make all Laws which shall be necessary and proper for carrying into Execution the foregoing Powers, and all other Powers vested by this Constitution in the Government of the United States, or in any Department or Officer thereof.

Section 9

The Migration or Importation of such Persons as any of the States now existing shall think proper to admit, shall not be prohibited by the Congress prior to the Year one thousand eight hundred and eight, but a tax or duty may be imposed on such Importation, not exceeding ten dollars for each Person.

The privilege of the Writ of Habeas Corpus shall not be suspended, unless when in Cases of Rebellion or Invasion the public Safety may require it.

No bill of Attainder or ex post facto Law shall be passed.

No capitation, or other direct, Tax shall be laid unless in Proportion to the Census or Enumeration herein before directed to be taken.

No Tax or Duty shall be laid on Articles exported from any State.

No Preference shall be given by any Regulation of Commerce or Revenue to the Ports of one State over those of another: nor shall Vessels bound to, or from, one State, be obliged to enter, clear, or pay Duties in another.

No Money shall be drawn from the Treasury, but in Consequence of Appropriations made by Law; and a regular Statement and Account of the Receipts and Expenditures of all public Money shall be published from time to time.

No Title of Nobility shall be granted by the United States: And no Person holding any Office of Profit or Trust under them, shall, without the Consent of the Congress, accept of any present, Emolument, Office, or Title, of any kind whatever, from any King, Prince, or foreign State.

Section 10

No State shall enter into any Treaty, Alliance, or Confederation; grant Letters of Marque and Reprisal; coin Money; emit Bills of Credit; make any Thing but gold and silver Coin a Tender in Payment of Debts; pass any Bill of Attainder, ex post facto Law, or Law impairing the Obligation of Contracts, or grant any Title of Nobility.

No State shall, without the Consent of the Congress, lay any Imposts or Duties on Imports or Exports, except what may be absolutely necessary for executing its inspection Laws; and the net Produce of all Duties and Imposts, laid by any State on Imports or Exports, shall be for the use of the Treasury of the United States; and all such Laws shall be subject to the Revision and Control of the Congress.

No state shall, without the Consent of Congress, lay any duty of Tonnage, keep Troops, or Ships of War in time of Peace, enter into any Agreement or Compact with another State, or with a foreign Power, or engage in War, unless actually invaded, or in such imminent Danger as will not admit of delay.

ARTICLE II

Section 1

The executive Power shall be vested in a President of the United States of America. He shall hold his Office during the Term of four years, and, together with the Vice President, chosen for the same Term, be elected, as follows:

Each State shall appoint, in such Manner as the Legislature thereof may direct, a Number of Electors, equal to the whole Number of Senators and Representatives to which the State may be entitled in the Congress: but no Senator or Representative, or Person holding an Office of Trust or Profit under the United States, shall be appointed an Elector.

[The Electors shall meet in their respective States, and vote by Ballot for two persons, of whom one at least shall not be an Inhabitant of the same State with themselves. And they shall make a List of all the Persons voted for, and of the Number of Votes for each; which List they shall sign and certify, and transmit sealed to the Seat of the Government of the United States, directed to the President of the Senate. The President of the Senate shall, in the Presence of the Senate and House of Representatives, open all the Certificates, and the Votes shall then be counted. The Person having the greatest Number of Votes shall be the President, if such Number be a Majority of the whole Number of Electors appointed; and if there be more than one who have such Majority, and have an equal Number of Votes, then the House of Representatives shall immediately chuse by Ballot one of them for President; and if no Person have a Majority, then from the five highest on the List the said House shall in like Manner chuse the President. But in chusing the President, the Votes shall be taken by States, the Representation from each State having one Vote; a quorum for this Purpose shall consist of a Member or Members from two-thirds of the States, and a Majority of all the States shall be necessary to a Choice. In every Case, after the Choice of the President, the Person having the greatest Number of Votes of the Electors shall be the Vice President. But if there should remain two or more who have equal votes, the Senate shall chuse from them by Ballot the Vice President.][4]

The Congress may determine the Time of chusing the Electors, and the Day on which they shall give their Votes; which Day shall be the same throughout the United States.

No person except a natural-born Citizen, or a Citizen of the United States, at the time of the Adoption of this Constitution, shall be eligible to the Office of President; neither shall any Person be eligible to that Office who shall not have attained to the Age of thirty-five years, and been fourteen Years a Resident within the United States.

In Case of the Removal of the President from Office, or of his Death, Resignation, or Inability to discharge the Powers and Duties of the said Office, the same shall devolve on the Vice President, and the Congress may by Law provide for the Case of Removal, Death, Resignation, or Inability, both of the President and Vice President, declaring what Officer shall then act as President, and such Officer shall act accordingly, until the disability be removed, or a President shall be elected.

The President shall, at stated Times, receive for his Services a Compensation, which shall neither be increased nor diminished during the Period for which he shall have been elected, and he shall not receive within that Period any other Emolument from the United States, or any of them.

Before he enter on the execution of his Office, he shall take the following Oath or Affirmation:—"I do solemnly swear (or affirm) that I will faithfully execute the Office of President of the United States, and will, to the best of my Ability, preserve, protect, and defend the Constitution of the United States."

Section 2

The President shall be Commander in Chief of the Army and Navy of the United States, and of the Militia of the several States, when called into the actual Service of the United States; he may require the Opinion, in writing, of the principal Officer in each of the executive Departments, upon any subject relating to the Duties of their respective Offices, and he shall have Power to Grant Reprieves and Pardons for Offenses against the United States, except in Cases of Impeachment.

He shall have Power, by and with the Advice and Consent of the Senate, to make Treaties, provided two-thirds of the Senators present concur; and he shall nominate, and by and with the Advice and Consent of the Senate, shall appoint Ambassadors, other public Ministers and Consuls, Judges of the supreme Court, and all other Officers of the United States, whose Appointments are not herein otherwise provided for, and which shall be established by Law: but the Congress may by Law vest the Appointment of such inferior Officers, as they think proper, in the President alone, in the Courts of Law, or in the Heads of Departments.

---

[4]Revised by the Twelfth Amendment.

The President shall have Power to fill up all Vacancies that may happen during the Recess of the Senate, by granting Commissions which shall expire at the End of their next Session.

Section 3

He shall from time to time give to the Congress Information of the State of the Union, and recommend to their Consideration such Measures as he shall judge necessary and expedient; he may, on extraordinary occasions, convene both Houses, or either of them, and in Case of Disagreement between them, with respect to the Time of Adjournment, he may adjourn them to such Time as he shall think proper; he shall receive Ambassadors and other public Ministers; he shall take care that the Laws be faithfully executed, and shall Commission all the Officers of the United States.

Section 4

The President, Vice President and all civil Officers of the United States, shall be removed from Office on Impeachment for, and Conviction of, Treason, Bribery, or other high Crimes and Misdemeanors.

ARTICLE III

Section 1

The judicial Power of the United States, shall be vested in one supreme Court, and in such inferior Courts as the Congress may from time to time ordain and establish. The Judges, both of the supreme and inferior Courts, shall hold their Offices during good Behaviour, and shall, at stated Times, receive for their Services, a Compensation, which shall not be diminished during their Continuance in Office.

Section 2

The judicial Power shall extend to all Cases, in Law and Equity, arising under this Constitution, the Laws of the United States, and Treaties made, or which shall be made, under their Authority;—to all Cases affecting ambassadors, other public ministers and consuls;—to all cases of admiralty and maritime Jurisdiction;—to Controversies to which the United States shall be a Party;—to Controversies between two or more states;—between a State and Citizens of another State;[5]—between Citizens of different States—between Citizens of the same State claiming Lands under Grants of different States, and between a State, or the Citizens thereof, and foreign States, Citizens, or Subjects.

In all Cases affecting Ambassadors, other public Ministers and Consuls, and those in which a State shall be Party, the supreme Court shall have original Jurisdiction. In all the other Cases before mentioned, the supreme Court shall have appellate Jurisdiction, both as to Law and Fact, with such Exceptions, and under such Regulations as the Congress shall make.

---

[5]Qualified by the Eleventh Amendment.

The trial of all Crimes, except in Cases of Impeachment, shall be by Jury; and such Trial shall be held in the State where the said Crimes shall have been committed; but when not committed within any State, the Trial shall be at such Place or Places as the Congress may by Law have directed.

Section 3

Treason against the United States, shall consist only in levying War against them, or in adhering to their Enemies, giving them Aid and Comfort. No Person shall be convicted of Treason unless on the Testimony of two Witnesses to the same overt Act, or on Confession in open Court.

The Congress shall have power to declare the Punishment of Treason, but no Attainder of Treason shall work Corruption of Blood, or Forfeiture except during the Life of the Person attainted.

ARTICLE IV

Section 1

Full Faith and Credit shall be given in each State to the public Acts, Records, and judicial Proceedings of every other State. And the Congress may by general Laws prescribe the Manner in which such Acts, Records and Proceedings shall be proved, and the Effect thereof.

Section 2

The Citizens of each State shall be entitled to all Privileges and Immunities of Citizens in the several States.

A Person charged in any State with Treason, Felony, or other Crime, who shall flee from Justice, and be found in another State, shall on demand of the executive Authority of the State from which he fled, be delivered up, to be removed to the State having Jurisdiction of the crime.

No Person held to Service or Labour in one State, under the Laws thereof, escaping into another, shall, in Consequence of any Law or Regulation therein, be discharged from such Service or Labour, but shall be delivered up on Claim of the Party to whom such Service or Labour may be due.

Section 3

New States may be admitted by the Congress into this Union; but no new State shall be formed or erected within the Jurisdiction of any other State; nor any State be formed by the Junction of two or more States, or parts of States, without the Consent of the Legislatures of the States concerned as well as of the Congress.

The Congress shall have Power to dispose of and make all needful Rules and Regulations respecting the Territory or other Property belonging to the United States; and nothing in this Constitution shall be so construed as to Prejudice any Claims of the United States, or of any particular State.

Section 4

The United States shall guarantee to every State in this Union a Republican Form of Government, and shall protect each of them against Invasion; and on Application of the Legislature, or of the Executive (when the Legislature cannot be convened) against domestic Violence.

ARTICLE V

The Congress, whenever two-thirds of both Houses shall deem it necessary, shall propose Amendments to this Constitution, or, on the Application of the Legislatures of two-thirds of the several States, shall call a Convention for proposing Amendments, which, in either Case, shall be valid to all Intents and Purposes, as part of this Constitution, when ratified by the Legislatures of three-fourths of the several States, or by Conventions in three-fourths thereof, as the one or the other Mode of Ratification may be proposed by the Congress; Provided that no Amendment which may be made prior to the Year One thousand eight hundred and eight shall in any Manner affect the first and fourth Clauses in the Ninth Section of the first Article; and that no State, without its Consent, shall be deprived of its equal Suffrage in the Senate.

ARTICLE VI

All Debts contracted and Engagements entered into, before the Adoption of this Constitution, shall be as valid against the United States under this Constitution, as under the Confederation.

This Constitution, and the Laws of the United States which shall be made in Pursuance thereof; and all Treaties made, or which shall be made, under the Authority of the United States, shall be the supreme Law of the Land; and the Judges in every State shall be bound thereby, any Thing in the Constitution or Laws of any State to the Contrary notwithstanding.

The Senators and Representatives before mentioned, and the Members of the several State Legislatures, and all executive and judicial Officers, both of the United States and of the several States, shall be bound by Oath or Affirmation to support this Constitution; but no religious Tests shall ever be required as a qualification to any Office or public Trust under the United States.

ARTICLE VII

The Ratification of the Conventions of nine States shall be sufficient for the Establishment of this Constitution between the States so ratifying the same.

Done in Convention by the Unanimous Consent of the States present the Seventeenth Day of September in the Year of our Lord one thousand seven hundred and Eighty seven, and of the Independence of the United States of America the Twelfth. In Witness whereof We have hereunto subscribed our Names.[6]

---

[6]These are the full names of the signers, which in some cases are not the signatures on the document.

George Washington
President and deputy from
  Virginia

New Hampshire
John Langdon
Nicholas Gilman

Massachusetts
Nathaniel Gorham
Rufus King

Connecticut
William Samuel Johnson
Roger Sherman

New York
Alexander Hamilton

New Jersey
William Livingston
David Brearley
William Paterson
Jonathan Dayton

Pennsylvania
Benjamin Franklin
Thomas Mifflin
Robert Morris
George Clymer
Thomas FitzSimmons
Jared Ingersoll
James Wilson
Gouverneur Morris

Delaware
George Read
Gunning Bedford, Jr.
John Dickinson
Richard Bassett
Jacob Broom

Maryland
James McHenry
Daniel of St. Thomas
  Jenifer
Daniel Carroll

Virginia
John Blair
James Madison, Jr.

North Carolina
William Blount
Richard Dobbs Spaight
Hugh Williamson

South Carolina
John Rutledge
Charles Cotesworth
  Pinckney
Charles Pinckney
Pierce Butler

Georgia
William Few
Abraham Baldwin

Articles in Addition to, and Amendment of, the Constitution of the United States of America, Proposed by Congress, and Ratified by the Legislatures of the Several States, Pursuant to the Fifth Article of the Original Constitution[7].

AMENDMENT I

Congress shall make no law respecting an establishment of religion, or prohibiting the free exercise thereof; or abridging the freedom of speech, or of the press; or the right of the people peaceably to assemble, and to petition the Government for a redress of grievances.

AMENDMENT II

A well regulated Militia, being necessary to the security of a free State, the right of the people to keep and bear Arms shall not be infringed.

AMENDMENT III

No Soldier shall, in time of peace, be quartered in any house, without the consent of the Owner, nor in time of war, but in a manner to be prescribed by law.

---

[7]This heading appears only in the joint resolution submitting the first ten amendments, which are collectively known as the Bill of Rights. They were ratified on December 15, 1791.

Amendment IV

The right of the people to be secure in their persons, houses, papers, and effects, against unreasonable searches and seizures, shall not be violated, and no Warrants shall issue, but upon probable cause, supported by Oath or affirmation, and particularly describing the place to be searched, and the persons or things to be seized.

Amendment V

No person shall be held to answer for a capital or otherwise infamous crime, unless on a presentment or indictment of a Grand Jury, except in cases arising in the land or naval forces, or in the Militia, when in actual service in time of War or public danger; nor shall any person be subject for the same offence to be twice put in jeopardy of life or limb; nor shall be compelled in any criminal case to be a witness against himself, nor be deprived of life, liberty, or property, without due process of law; nor shall private property be taken for public use, without just compensation.

Amendment VI

In all criminal prosecutions, the accused shall enjoy the right to a speedy and public trial, by an impartial jury of the State and district wherein the crime shall have been committed, which district shall have been previously ascertained by law, and to be informed of the nature and cause of the accusation; to be confronted with the witnesses against him; to have compulsory process for obtaining witnesses in his favour, and to have the Assistance of Counsel for his defence.

Amendment VII

In suits at common law, where the value in controversy shall exceed twenty dollars, the right of trial by jury shall be preserved, and no fact tried by a jury, shall be otherwise reexamined in any Court of the United States, than according to the rules of the common law.

Amendment VIII

Excessive bail shall not be required, nor excessive fines imposed, nor cruel and unusual punishments inflicted.

Amendment IX

The enumeration of the Constitution, of certain rights, shall not be construed to deny or disparage others retained by the people.

Amendment X

The powers not delegated to the United States by the Constitution, nor prohibited by it to the States, are reserved to the States respectively, or to the people.

AMENDMENT XI [1795]

The Judicial power of the United States shall not be construed to extend to any suit in law or equity, commenced or prosecuted against one of the United States by Citizens of another State, or by Citizens or Subjects of any Foreign State.

AMENDMENT XII [1804]

The Electors shall meet in their respective States and vote by ballot for President and Vice-President, one of whom, at least, shall not be an inhabitant of the same State with themselves; they shall name in their ballots the person voted for as President, and in distinct ballots the person voted for as Vice-President, and they shall make distinct lists of all persons voted for as President, and of all persons voted for as Vice-President, and of the number of votes for each, which lists they shall sign and certify, and transmit sealed to the seat of the government of the United States, directed to the President of the Senate;—The President of the Senate shall, in the presence of the Senate and House of Representatives, open all the certificates and the votes shall then be counted;—The person having the greatest number of votes for President, shall be the President, if such number be a majority of the whole number of Electors appointed; and if no person have such majority, then from the persons having the highest numbers not exceeding three on the list of those voted for as President, the House of Representatives shall choose immediately, by ballot, the President. But in choosing the President, the votes shall be taken by states, the representation from each state having one vote; a quorum for this purpose shall consist of a member or members from two-thirds of the states, and a majority of all the states shall be necessary to a choice. And if the House of Representatives shall not choose a President whenever the right of choice shall devolve upon them, before the fourth day of March next following, then the Vice-President shall act as President, as in the case of the death or other constitutional disability of the President.—The person having the greatest number of votes as Vice-President, shall be the Vice-President, if such number be a majority of the whole number of Electors appointed, and if no person have a majority, then from the two highest numbers on the list, the Senate shall choose the Vice-President; a quorum for the purpose shall consist of two-thirds of the whole number of Senators, and majority of the whole number shall be necessary to a choice. But no person constitutionally ineligible to the office of President shall be eligible to that of Vice-President of the United States.

AMENDMENT XIII [1865]

Section 1

Neither slavery nor involuntary servitude, except as a punishment for crime whereof the party shall have been duly convicted, shall exist within the United States, or any place subject to their jurisdiction.

Section 2

Congress shall have power to enforce this article by appropriate legislation.

Amendment XIV [1868]

Section 1

All persons born or naturalized in the United States, and subject to the jurisdiction thereof, are citizens of the United States and of the State wherein they reside. No State shall abridge the privileges or immunities of citizens of the United States; nor shall any State deprive any person of life, liberty, or property, without due process of law; nor deny to any person within its jurisdiction the equal protection of the laws.

Section 2

Representatives shall be apportioned among the several States according to their respective numbers, counting the whole number of persons in each State, excluding Indians not taxed. But when the right to vote at any election for the choice of electors for President and Vice-President of the United States, Representatives in Congress, the Executive and Judicial officers of a State, or the members of the Legislature thereof, is denied to any of the male inhabitants of such State, being twenty-one years of age, and citizens of the United States, or in any way abridged, except for participation in rebellion, or other crime, the basis of representation therein shall be reduced in the proportion which the number of such male citizens shall bear to the whole number of male citizens twenty-one years of age in such State.

Section 3

No person shall be a Senator or Representative in Congress, or elector of President and Vice-President, or hold any office, civil or military, under the United States, or under any State, who, having previously taken an oath, as a member of Congress, or as an officer of the United States, or as a member of any State legislature, or as an executive or judicial officer of any State, to support the Constitution of the United States, shall have engaged in insurrection or rebellion against the same, or given aid or comfort to the enemies thereof. But Congress may by a vote of two-thirds of each House, remove such disability.

Section 4

The validity of the public debt of the United States, authorized by law, including debts incurred for payment of pensions and bounties for services in suppressing insurrection or rebellion, shall not be questioned. But neither the United States nor any State shall assume or pay any debts or obligation incurred in aid of insurrection or rebellion against the United States, or any claim for the loss or emancipation of any slave; but all such debts, obligations, and claims shall be held illegal and void.

Section 5

The Congress shall have the power to enforce, by appropriate legislation, the provisions of this article.

AMENDMENT XV [1870]

Section 1

The right of citizens of the United States to vote shall not be denied or abridged by the United States or by any State on account of race, color, or previous condition of servitude.

Section 2

The Congress shall have power to enforce this article by appropriate legislation.

AMENDMENT XVI [1913]

The Congress shall have power to lay and collect taxes on incomes, from whatever source derived, without apportionment among the several States, and without regard to any census or enumeration.

AMENDMENT XVII [1913]

The Senate of the United States shall be composed of two Senators from each State, elected by the people thereof, for six years; and each Senator shall have one vote. The electors in each State shall have the qualifications requisite for electors of the most numerous branch of the State legislatures.

When vacancies happen in the representation of any State in the Senate, the executive authority of such State shall issue writs of election to fill such vacancies: Provided, That the legislature of any State may empower the executive thereof to make temporary appointments until the people fill the vacancies by election as the legislature may direct.

This Amendment shall not be so construed as to affect the election or term of any Senator chosen before it becomes valid as part of the Constitution.

AMENDMENT XVIII [1919]

Section 1

After one year from the ratification of this article the manufacture, sale, or transportation of intoxicating liquors within, the importation thereof into, or the exportation thereof from the United States and all territory subject to the jurisdiction thereof for beverage purposes is hereby prohibited.

Section 2

The Congress and the several States shall have concurrent power to enforce this article by appropriate legislation.

Section 3

This article shall be inoperative unless it shall have been ratified as an Amendment to the Constitution by the legislatures of the several States, as provided in the Constitution, within seven years from the date of the submission hereof to the States by the Congress.

AMENDMENT XIX [1920]

The right of citizens of the United States to vote shall not be denied or abridged by the United States or by any State on account of sex.

Congress shall have power to enforce this article by appropriate legislation.

AMENDMENT XX [1933]

Section 1

The terms of the President and Vice-President shall end at noon on the 20th day of January, and the terms of Senators and Representatives at noon on the 3d day of January, of the years in which such terms would have ended if this article had not been ratified; and the terms of their successors shall then begin.

Section 2

The Congress shall assemble at least once in every year, and such meeting shall begin at noon on the 3d day of January, unless they shall by law appoint a different day.

Section 3

If, at the time fixed for the beginning of the term of the President, the President elect shall have died, the Vice-President elect shall become President. If a President shall not have been chosen before the time fixed for the beginning of his term or if the President elect shall have failed to qualify, then the Vice-President elect shall act as President until a President shall have qualified; and the Congress may by law provide for the case wherein neither a President elect nor a Vice-President elect shall have qualified, declaring who shall then act as President, or the manner in which one who is to act shall be selected, and such person shall act accordingly until a President or Vice-President shall have qualified.

Section 4

The Congress may by law provide for the case of the death of any of the persons from whom the House of Representatives may choose a President whenever the right of choice shall have devolved upon them, and for the case of the death of any of the persons from whom the Senate may choose a Vice-President whenever the right of choice shall have devolved upon them.

Section 5

Sections 1 and 2 shall take effect on the 15th day of October following the ratification of this article.

Section 6

This article shall be inoperative unless it shall have been ratified as an amendment to the Constitution by the legislatures of three-fourths of the several States within seven years from the date of its submission.

AMENDMENT XXI [1933]

Section 1

The eighteenth article of amendment to the Constitution of the United States is hereby repealed.

Section 2

The transportation or importation into any State, Territory, or possession of the United States for delivery or use therein of intoxicating liquors, in violation of the laws thereof, is hereby prohibited.

Section 3

This article shall be inoperative unless it shall have been ratified as an amendment to the Constitution by conventions in the several States, as provided in the Constitution, within seven years from the date of the submission hereof to the States by the Congress.

AMENDMENT XXII [1951]

No person shall be elected to the office of the President more than twice, and no person who has held the office of President, or acted as President, for more than two years of a term to which some other person was elected President shall be elected to the office of the President more than once.

But this Article shall not apply to any person holding the office of President when this Article was proposed by the Congress, and shall not prevent any person who may be holding the office of President, or acting as President, during the term within which this Article becomes operative from holding the office of President or acting as President during the remainder of such term.

This article shall be inoperative unless it shall have been ratified as an amendment to the Constitution by the legislatures of three-fourths of the several states within seven years from the date of its submission to the states by the Congress.

AMENDMENT XXIII [1961]

Section 1

The District constituting the seat of Government of the United States shall appoint in such manner as the Congress may direct:

A number of electors of President and Vice-President equal to the whole number of Senators and Representatives in Congress to which the District would be entitled if it were a State, but in no event more than the least populous State; they shall be in addition to those appointed by the States, but they shall be considered, for the purposes of the election of President and Vice-President, to be electors appointed by a State; and they shall meet in the District and perform such duties as provided by the twelfth article of Amendment.

Section 2

The Congress shall have power to enforce this article by appropriate legislation.

Amendment XXIV [1964]

Section 1

The right of citizens of the United States to vote in any primary or other election for President or Vice President, for electors for President or Vice President, or for Senator or Representative in Congress, shall not be denied or abridged by the United States or any state by reason of failure to pay any poll tax or other tax.

Section 2

The Congress shall have the power to enforce this article by appropriate legislation.

Amendment XXV [1967]

Section 1

In case of the removal of the President from office or of his death or resignation, the Vice President shall become President.

Section 2

Whenever there is a vacancy in the office of the Vice President, the President shall nominate a Vice President who shall take office upon confirmation by a majority vote of both Houses of Congress.

Section 3

Whenever the President transmits to the President Pro Tempore of the Senate and the Speaker of the House of Representatives his written declaration that he is unable to discharge the powers and duties of his office, and until he transmits to them a written declaration to the contrary, such powers and duties shall be discharged by the Vice President as Acting President.

Section 4

Whenever the Vice President and a majority of either the principal officers of the executive departments or of such other body as Congress may by law provide, transmit to the President Pro Tempore of the Senate and the Speaker of the House of Representatives their written declaration that the President is unable to discharge the powers and duties of his office, the Vice President shall immediately assume the powers and duties of the office as Acting President.

Thereafter, when the President transmits to the President Pro Tempore of the Senate and the Speaker of the House of Representatives his written declaration that no inability exists, he shall resume the powers and duties of his office unless the Vice President and a majority of either the principal officers of the executive departments or of such other body as Congress may by law provide, transmit within four days to the President Pro Tempore of the Senate and the Speaker of the House of Representatives their written declaration that the President is unable to discharge the powers and duties of his office. Thereupon Congress shall decide the issue, assembling within forty-eight hours for that purpose if not in session. If the Congress, within twenty-one days after receipt of the latter written declaration, or, if Congress is not in session, within twenty-one days after Congress is required to assemble, determines by two-thirds vote of both Houses that the President is unable to discharge the powers and duties of his office, the Vice President shall continue to discharge the same as Acting President; otherwise, the President shall resume the powers and duties of his office.

Amendment XXVI [1971]

Section 1

The right of citizens of the United States, who are eighteen years of age or older, to vote shall not be denied or abridged by the United States or by any State on account of age.

Section 2

The Congress shall have the power to enforce this article by appropriate legislation.

Amendment XXVII [1992]

No law varying the compensation for the service of Senators and Representatives shall take effect until an election of Representatives shall have intervened.

GLOSSARY

administrative law judge An official who presides at a trial-like administrative hearing to settle a dispute between an agency and someone adversely affected by a decision of that agency.

affirmative action Programs designed to ensure that women, minorities, and other traditionally disadvantaged groups have full and equal opportunities in employment, education, and other areas of life.

agency point of view The tendency of bureaucrats to place the interests of their agency ahead of other interests and ahead of the priorities sought by the president or Congress.

agenda setting The power of the media through news coverage to focus the public's attention and concern on particular events, problems, issues, personalities, and so on.

agents of socialization Agents, such as the family and the media, that have significant impact on citizens' political socialization.

alienation A feeling of personal powerlessness that includes the notion that government does not care about the opinions of people like oneself.

Anti-Federalists Opponents of the Constitution during the debate over ratification.

apathy A feeling of personal disinterest in or lack of concern.

appellate jurisdiction The authority of a given court to review cases that have already been tried in lower courts and are appealed to it by the losing party; such a court is called an appeals court or appellate court. (See also **original jurisdiction.**)

authoritarian government A form of government in which those in power openly repress their opponents in order to stay in power.

authority The recognized right of officials to exercise power as a result of the positions they hold. (See also **power.**)

balanced budget The situation in which the government's tax and other revenues for the year are roughly equal to its expenditures.

bicameral legislature A legislature that has two chambers (the House and the Senate, in the case of the United States).

bill A proposed law (legislative act) within Congress or another legislature. (See also **law.**)

Bill of Rights The first 10 amendments to the Constitution. They include rights such as freedom of speech and religion and due process protections (for example, the right to a jury trial) for persons accused of crimes.

bipolar A power structure dominated by two powers only, as in the case of the United States and the Soviet Union during the Cold War.

block grants Federal grants-in-aid that permit state and local officials to decide how the money will be spent within a general area, such as education or health. (See also **categorical grants.**)

budget deficit The situation in which the government's expenditures exceed its tax and other revenues.

budgetary process The process through which annual federal spending and revenue determinations are made.

bully pulpit A term referring to the communication platform provided the president as a result of being the center of national attention.

bureaucracy A system of organization and control based on the principles of hierarchical authority, job specialization, and formalized rules. (See also **formalized rules; hierarchical authority; job specialization.**)

bureaucratic accountability The degree to which bureaucrats are held accountable for the power they exercise.

cabinet A group consisting of the heads of the (cabinet) executive departments, who are appointed by the president, subject to confirmation by the Senate. The cabinet was once the main advisory body to the president but no longer plays this role.

cabinet (executive) departments The major administrative organizations within the federal executive bureaucracy, each of which is headed by a secretary or, in the case of Justice, the attorney general. Each department has responsibility for a major function of the federal government, such as defense, agriculture, or justice. (See also **independent agencies.**)

candidate-centered campaigns Election campaigns and other political processes in which candidates, not political parties, have most of the initiative and influence. (See also **party-centered campaigns.**)

capital gains tax The tax that individuals pay on money gained from the sale of a capital asset, such as property or stocks.

categorical grants Federal grants-in-aid to states and localities that can be used only for designated projects. (See also **block grants.**)

checks and balances The elaborate system of divided spheres of authority provided by the U.S. Constitution as a means of controlling the power of government. The separation of powers among the branches of the national government, federalism, and the different methods of selecting national officers is part of this system.

chief diplomat The constitutional role that assigns the president responsibility for relations with other countries.

chief executive The constitution role that assigns the president responsible for executing the laws and administering the executive branch.

chief legislator The constitutional role that give the president authority to recommend legislative measures to Congress and to assess the state of the Union.

citizens' groups Also called noneconomic groups, organized interests formed by individuals drawn together by opportunities to promote a cause in which they believe but that does not provide them significant individual economic benefits. (See also **economic groups; interest group.**)

civic duty The belief of an individual that civic and political participation is a responsibility of citizenship.

civil liberties The fundamental individual rights of a free society, such as freedom of speech and the right to a jury trial, which in the United States are protected by the Bill of Rights.

clear-and-present-danger test A test devised by the Supreme Court in 1919 to define the limits of free speech in the context of national security. According to the test, government cannot abridge political expression unless it presents a clear and present danger to the nation's security.

clientele groups Special interest groups that benefit directly from the activities of a particular bureaucratic agency and therefore are strong advocates of the agency.

cloture A parliamentary maneuver that, if a three-fifths majority votes for it, limits Senate debate to 30 hours and has the effect of defeating a filibuster. (See also **filibuster.**)

Cold War The lengthy period after World War II when the United States and the USSR were not engaged in actual combat (a "hot war") but were nonetheless locked in a state of deep-seated hostility.

collective (public) goods Benefits that are offered by groups (usually citizens' groups) as an incentive for membership but that are nondivisible (such as a clean environment) and therefore are available to nonmembers as well as members of the particular group. (See also **free-rider problem; private [individual] goods.**)

commander in chief The constitutional role that places the president in charge of the nation's armed services.

commerce clause The authority granted Congress in Article I, Section 8, of the Constitution "to regulate commerce" among the states.

common-carrier function The media's function as an open channel through which political leaders can communicate with the public. (See also **partisan function; signaling [signaler] function; watchdog function.**)

concurring opinion A separate opinion written by a Supreme Court justice who votes with the majority in the decision on a case but who disagrees with the reasoning. (See also **dissenting opinion; majority opinion; plurality opinion.**)

confederacy A governmental system in which sovereignty is vested entirely in subnational (state) governments. (See also **federalism; unitary system.**)

conference committee A temporary committee that is formed to bargain over the differences in the House and Senate versions of a bill. A conference committee's members are usually appointed from the House and Senate standing committees that originally worked on the bill.

constituency The people residing within the geographic area represented by an elected official.

constitution The fundamental law that defines how a government will legitimately operate.

constitutional democratic republic A government that is constitutional in its provisions for minority rights and rule by law; democratic in its provisions for majority influence through elections; and a republic in its mix of deliberative institutions, which check and balance each other.

constitutionalism The idea that there are lawful limits on the power of government.

containment A doctrine, developed after World War II, based on the assumptions that the Soviet Union was an aggressor nation and that only a determined United States could block Soviet territorial ambitions.

cooperative federalism The situation in which the national, state, and local levels work together to solve problems.

corporate power The power that corporations exercise in their effort to influence government and maintain control of the workplace.

cultural (social) conservatives Those who believe government power should be used to uphold traditional values. (See also **economic liberals; economic conservatives; cultural [social] liberals.**)

cultural (social) liberals Those who believe it is not government's role to buttress traditional values at the expense of unconventional or new values. (See also **economic liberals; economic conservatives; cultural [social] conservatives.**)

de facto discrimination Discrimination on the basis of race, sex, religion, ethnicity, and the like that results from social, economic, and cultural biases and conditions. (See also **de jure discrimination.**)

de jure discrimination Discrimination on the basis of race, sex, religion, ethnicity, and the like that results from a law. (See also **de facto discrimination.**)

decision A vote of the Supreme Court in a particular case that indicates which party the justices side with and by how large a margin.

delegate An elected representative whose obligation is to act in accordance with the expressed wishes of the people he or she represents. (See also **trustee.**)

demand-side economics A form of fiscal policy that emphasizes "demand" (consumer spending). Government can use increased spending or tax cuts to place more money in consumers' hands and thereby increase demand. (See also **fiscal policy; supply-side economics.**)

democracy A form of government in which the people govern, either directly or through elected representatives.

demographic representativeness The idea that the bureaucracy will be more responsive to the public if its employees at all levels are demographically representative of the population as a whole.

denials of power A constitutional means of limiting governmental action by listing those powers that government is expressly prohibited from using.

deregulation The rescinding of excessive government regulations for the purpose of improving economic efficiency.

devolution The passing down of authority from the national government to the state and local governments.

direction An opinion dimension; whether people have a pro or con opinion on an issue.

dissenting opinion The opinion of a justice in a Supreme Court case that explains his or her reasons for disagreeing with the majority's decision. (See also **concurring opinion; majority opinion; plurality opinion.**)

dual federalism A doctrine based on the idea that a precise separation of national power and state power is both possible and desirable.

due process clause The clause of the Constitution (included in the Fourteenth Amendment) that has been used by the judiciary to apply Bill of Rights protections to the actions of state governments.

economic conservatives Those who believe government tries to do too many things that should be left to private interests and economic markets. (See also **economic liberals; cultural [social] liberals; cultural [social] conservatives.**)

economic depression A very severe and sustained economic downturn. Depressions are rare in the United States; the last one was in the 1930s.

economic efficiency An economic principle holding that firms should fulfill as many of society's needs as possible while using as few of its resources as possible. The greater the output (production) for a given input (for example, an hour of labor), the more efficient the process.

economic equity The situation in which the outcome of an economic transaction is fair to each party. An outcome can usually be considered fair if each party enters into a transaction freely and is not unknowingly at a disadvantage.

economic globalization The increased interdependence of nations' economies. The change is a result of technological, transportation, and communication advances that have enabled firms to deploy their resources across the globe.

economic groups Interest groups that are organized primarily for economic reasons but that engage in political activity in order to seek favorable policies from government. (See also **citizens' groups; interest group.**)

economic liberals Those who believe government should do more to assist people who have difficulty meeting their economic needs on their own. (See also **economic conservatives; cultural [social] liberals; cultural [social] conservatives.**)

economic recession A moderate but sustained downturn in the economy. Recessions are part of the economy's normal cycle of ups and downs.

economy A system for the exchange of goods and services between the producers of those goods and services and the consumers of them.

Electoral College An unofficial term that refers to the electors who cast the states' electoral votes.

electoral votes The method of voting used to choose the U.S. president. Each state has the same number of electoral votes as it has members in Congress (House and Senate combined). By tradition, electoral voting is tied to a state's popular voting. The candidate with the most popular votes in a state (or, in a few states, the most votes in a congressional district) receives its electoral votes.

elitism The notion that wealthy and well-connected individuals exercise power over certain areas of public policy.

entitlement program An individual benefit program, such as Social Security, that requires government to provide a designated benefit to any person who meets the legally defined criteria for eligibility.

enumerated (expressed) powers The 17 powers granted to the national government under Article I, Section 8, of the Constitution. These powers include taxation and the regulation of commerce, as well as the authority to provide for the national defense.

equal rights (civil rights) The right of every person to equal protection under the laws and equal access to society's opportunities and public facilities.

equal-protection clause A clause of the Fourteenth Amendment that forbids any state to deny equal protection of the laws to any individual within its jurisdiction.

equality The notion that all individuals are equal in their moral worth and are thereby entitled to equal treatment under the law.

equality of opportunity The idea that all individuals should be given an equal chance to succeed on their own.

establishment clause The First Amendment provision stating that government may not favor one religion over another or favor religion over no religion and prohibiting Congress from passing laws respecting the establishment of religion.

exclusionary rule The legal principle that government is prohibited from using in trials evidence that was obtained by unconstitutional means (for example, illegal search and seizure).

executive agreement A formal agreement with a foreign nation made by a president on his or her own authority.

Executive Office of the President (EOP) The EOP includes a number of units, including the White House Office (WHO), Office of Management and Budget (OMB), National Security Council (NSC), National Economic Council (NEC), which are staffed by political and policy experts to assist the president on policy issues and management of the executive branch.

executive order A presidential directive on how a law is to interpreted or administered. An executive order must be based on an existing law and cannot violate any provision of the law.

externalities Burdens that society incurs when firms fail to pay the full costs of production. An example of an externality is the pollution that results when corporations dump industrial wastes into lakes and rivers.

facts The relevant circumstances of a legal dispute or offense as determined by a trial court. The facts of a case are crucial because they help determine which law or laws are applicable in the case.

federalism A governmental system in which authority is divided between two sovereign levels of government: national and regional. (See also **confederacy; unitary system.**)

Federalists Supporters of the Constitution during the debate over ratification.

filibuster A procedural tactic in the U.S. Senate whereby a minority of legislators prevents a bill from coming to a vote by holding the floor and talking until the majority gives in and the bill is withdrawn from consideration. (See also **cloture.**)

fiscal federalism The expenditure of federal funds on programs run, in part, through states and localities.

fiscal policy A tool of economic management by which government can attempt to maintain a stable economy through its taxing and spending policies. (See also **demand-side economics; monetary policy; supply-side economics.**)

formalized rules A basic principle of bureaucracy; the standardized procedures and established regulations by which a bureaucracy conducts its operations. (See also **bureaucracy.**)

framing The process by which the media play up certain aspects of a situation while downplaying other aspects, thereby providing a particular interpretation of the situation.

free trade The condition in which tariffs and other barriers to trade between nations are kept to a minimum.

free-exercise clause A First Amendment provision that prohibits the government from interfering with the practice of religion.

free-market system An economic system based on the idea that government should interfere with economic transactions as little as possible. Free enterprise and self-reliance are the collective and individual principles that underpin free markets.

free-rider problem The situation in which the benefits offered by a group to its members are also available to nonmembers. The incentive to join the group and to promote its cause is reduced because nonmembers (free riders) receive the benefits (for example, a cleaner environment) without having to pay any of the group's costs. (See also **collective [public] goods.**)

freedom of expression Americans' freedom to communicate their views, the foundation of which is the First Amendment rights of freedom of conscience, speech, press, assembly, and petition.

gender gap The tendency of women and men to differ in their political attitudes and voting preferences.

gerrymandering The process by which the party in power draws election district boundaries in a way that enhances the reelection prospects of its candidates.

government corporations Government bodies, such as the U.S. Postal Service and Amtrak, that are similar to private corporations in that they charge for their services but differ in that they receive federal funding to help defray expenses. Their directors are appointed by the president with Senate approval.

grants of power The method of limiting the U.S. government by confining its scope of authority to those powers expressly granted in the Constitution.

grants-in-aid Federal cash payments to states and localities for programs they administer.

grassroots party A political party organized at the level of the voters and dependent on their support for its strength.

Great Compromise The agreement of the constitutional convention to create a two-chamber Congress with the House apportioned by population and the Senate apportioned equally by state.

hard money Campaign funds given directly to candidates to spend as they choose.

hard power The use of coercive force, military power in particular, as an instrument of foreign policy.

head of state The largely ceremonial role whereby the president serves as representative of the country (a role that in Great Britain, for example, is exercised by the monarch).

hierarchical authority A basic principle of bureaucracy; the chain of command within an organization whereby officials and units have control over those below them. (See also **bureaucracy.**)

high-choice media system A media system in which audiences have such a wide range of choices that they can largely control the type of information to which they are exposed.

honeymoon period The president's first months in office, a time when Congress, the press, and the public are more inclined than usual to support presidential initiatives.

identity politics The situation where people base their concerns on a group identity (such as race or religion) and align themselves with those who share that identity to the exclusion of other groups.

ideology A general belief about the role and purpose of government.

imminent lawless action A legal test that says government cannot lawfully suppress advocacy that promotes lawless action unless such advocacy is aimed at producing, and is likely to produce, imminent lawless action.

implied powers The federal government's constitutional authority (through the "necessary and proper" clause) to take action that is not expressly authorized by the Constitution but that supports actions that are so authorized. (See also **"necessary and proper" clause**.)

in-kind benefit A government benefit that is a cash equivalent, such as food stamps or rent vouchers. This form of benefit ensures that recipients will use public assistance in a specified way.

inalienable (natural) rights Those rights that persons theoretically possessed in the state of nature, prior to the formation of governments. These rights, including those of life, liberty, and property, are considered inherent and as such are inalienable. Since government is established by people, government has the responsibility to preserve these rights.

incumbent The current holder of a particular public office.

independent agencies Bureaucratic agencies that are similar to cabinet departments but usually have a narrower area of responsibility. Each such agency is headed by a presidential appointee who is not a cabinet member. An example is the National Aeronautics and Space Administration.

individualism The idea that people should take the initiative, be self-sufficient, and accumulate the material advantages necessary for their well-being.

inflation A general increase in the average level of prices of goods and services.

inside lobbying Direct communication between organized interests and policymakers, which is based on the assumed value of close ("inside") contacts with policymakers.

intensity An opinion dimension; how strongly people feel about an issue.

interest group Any organization that actively seeks to influence public policy. (See also **citizens' [noneconomic] groups; economic groups**.)

internationalist The view that the country should involve itself deeply in world affairs (See also **isolationist**.)

iron triangle A small and informal but relatively stable group of well-positioned legislators, executives, and lobbyists who seek to promote policies beneficial to a particular interest. (See also **issue network**.)

isolationist The view that the country should deliberately avoid a large role in world affairs and instead concentrate on domestic concerns (See also **internationalist**.)

issue network An informal and relatively open network of public officials and lobbyists who come together in response to a proposed policy in an area of interest to each of them. Unlike an iron triangle, an issue network disbands after the issue is resolved. (See also **iron triangle**.)

job specialization A basic principle of bureaucracy holding that the responsibilities of each job position should be defined explicitly and that a precise division of labor within the organization should be maintained. (See also **bureaucracy**.)

judicial activism The doctrine that the courts should develop new legal principles when judges see a compelling need, even if this action places them in conflict with precedent or the policy decisions of elected officials. (See also **judicial restraint**.)

judicial restraint The doctrine that the judiciary should broadly defer to precedent and the judgment of legislatures. The doctrine claims that the job of judges is to work within the confines of laws set down by tradition and lawmaking majorities. (See also **judicial activism**.)

judicial review The power of courts to decide whether a governmental institution has acted within its constitutional powers and, if not, to declare its action null and void.

jurisdiction The policy area in which a particular congressional committee is authorized to act.

jurisdiction A given court's authority to hear cases of a particular kind. Jurisdiction may be original or appellate. (See also **appellate jurisdiction; original jurisdiction.**)

laissez-faire economics A classic economic philosophy holding that owners of business should be allowed to make their own production and distribution decisions without government regulation or control.

law A legislative proposal, or bill, that is passed by both the House and the Senate and is not vetoed by the president. (See also **bill.**)

lawmaking function The authority (of a legislature) to make the laws necessary to carry out the government's powers. (See also **oversight function; representation function.**)

legal action The use of courts of law as a means by which individuals protect their rights and settle their conflicts.

***Lemon* test** A three-part test to determine whether a law relating to religion is valid under the religious establishment clause. To be valid, a law must have a secure purpose, serve neither to advance nor inhibit religion, and avoid excessive government entanglement with religion.

libel The publication of false material that damages a person's reputation.

liberty The principle that individuals should be free to act and think as they choose, provided they do not infringe unreasonably on the rights and freedoms of others.

limited government A government that is subject to strict limits on its lawful uses of power and, hence, on its ability to deprive people of their liberty.

linkage institutions Institutions that connect citizens with government. Linkage institutions include elections, political parties, interest groups, and the media.

lobbying The process by which interest-group members and lobbyists attempt to influence public policy through contacts with public officials.

low-choice media system A media system in which people have a small number of news

outlets available to them, which limits their choices.

majoritarianism The idea that the majority prevails not only in elections but also in determining policy.

majority opinion A court opinion that results when a majority of the justices are in agreement on the legal basis of the decision. (See also **concurring opinion; dissenting opinion; plurality opinion.**)

means test The requirement that applicants for public assistance must demonstrate they are poor in order to be eligible for the assistance. (See also **public assistance.**)

median voter theorem The theory that parties in a two-party system can maximize their vote by locating themselves at the position of the median voter—the voter whose preferences are exactly in the middle.

merit system An approach to managing the bureaucracy whereby people are appointed to government positions on the basis of either competitive examinations or special qualifications, such as professional training. (See also **patronage system.**)

midterm election The congressional election that occurs midway through the president's term of office.

military-industrial complex The three components (the military establishment, the industries that manufacture weapons, and the members of Congress from states and districts that depend heavily on the arms industry) that mutually benefit from a high level of defense spending.

monetary policy A tool of economic management based on manipulation of the amount of money in circulation. (See also **fiscal policy.**)

money chase The fact that U.S. campaigns are very expensive and candidates must spend a great amount of time raising funds in order to compete successfully.

multilateralism The situation in which nations act together in response to problems and crises.

multiparty system A system in which three or more political parties have the capacity to gain control of government, separately or in coalition.

mutually assured destruction (MAD) The assumption that any nation will be deterred from launching a full-scale nuclear attack on the United States by the knowledge that, even if it destroyed the United States, it, too, would be destroyed.

national debt The total cumulative amount that the U.S. government owes to creditors.

nationalization The process by which authority in the American federal system has shifted gradually from the states to the national government.

"necessary and proper" clause The authority granted Congress in Article I, Section 8, of the Constitution "to make all laws which shall be necessary and proper" for the implementation of its enumerated powers. (See also **implied powers.**)

neutral competence The administrative objective of a merit-based bureaucracy. Such a bureaucracy should be "competent" in the sense that its employees are hired and retained on the basis of their expertise and "neutral" in the sense that it operates by objective standards rather than partisan ones.

New Jersey (small-state) Plan A constitutional proposal for a strengthened Congress but one in which each state would have a single vote, thus granting a small state the same legislative power as a larger state.

news The news media's version of reality, usually with an emphasis on timely, dramatic, and compelling events and developments.

news media (press) Print, broadcast, cable, and Internet organizations that are in the news reporting business.

nomination The selection of a particular individual to run as a political party's candidate (its "nominee") in the general election.

objective journalism A model of news reporting that is based on the communication of "facts" rather than opinions and that is "fair" in that it presents all sides of partisan debate. (See also **partisan press.**)

open party caucuses Meetings at which a party's candidates for nomination are voted on and that are open to all the party's rank-and-file voters who want to attend.

opinion A court's written explanation of its decision, which informs others of the legal basis for the decision. Supreme Court opinions are expected to guide the decisions of lower courts. (See also **concurring opinion; dissenting opinion; majority opinion; plurality opinion.**)

original jurisdiction The authority of a given court to be the first court to hear a case. (See also **appellate jurisdiction.**)

outside lobbying A form of lobbying in which an interest group seeks to use public pressure as a means of influencing officials.

oversight function A supervisory activity of Congress that centers on its constitutional responsibility to see that the executive branch carries out the laws faithfully. (See also **lawmaking function; representation function.**)

packaging In modern campaigning, the process of recasting a candidate's record into an appealing image.

partisan function Efforts by media actors to influence public response to a particular party, leader, issue, or viewpoint.

partisan press Newspapers and other communication media that openly support a political party and whose news tends to follow the party line. (See also **objective journalism.**)

party (partisan) polarization The condition in which opinions and actions in response to political issues and situations divide substantially along political party lines.

party caucus A group that consists of a party's members in the House or Senate and that serves to elect the party's leadership, set policy goals, and plan party strategy.

party coalition The groups and interests that support a political party.

party competition A process in which conflict over society's goals is transformed by political parties into electoral competition in which the winner gains the power to govern.

party identification The personal sense of loyalty that an individual may feel toward a particular political party. (See also **party realignment.**)

party leaders The members of the House and Senate who are chosen by the Democratic or Republican caucus in each chamber to represent the party's interests in that chamber and who give some central direction to the chamber's work.

party organizations The party organizational units at national, state, and local levels; their influence has decreased over time because of many factors. (See also **candidate-centered campaigns; party-centered campaigns; primary election.**)

party realignments Elections or sets of elections in which the electorate responds strongly to an extraordinarily powerful issue that has disrupted the established political order. A realignment has a lasting impact on public policy, popular support for the parties, and the composition of the party coalitions. (See also **party identification.**)

party unity The degree to which a party's House or Senate members act as a unified group to exert collective control over legislative action.

party-centered campaigns Election campaigns and other political processes in which political parties, not individual candidates, hold most of the initiative and influence. (See also **candidate-centered campaigns.**)

patronage system An approach to managing the bureaucracy whereby people are appointed to important government positions as a reward for political services they have rendered and because of their partisan loyalty. (See also **merit system; spoils system.**)

per curiam opinion An unsigned decision written for the court as a whole.

permanent campaign The use by recent presidents of campaign-style methods, such as polls and mass rallies, on an ongoing basis in an effort to bolster their public support.

pluralism A theory of American politics that holds that society's interests are substantially represented through the activities of groups.

plurality opinion A court opinion that results when a majority of justices agree on a decision in a case but do not agree on the legal basis for the decision. In this instance, the legal position held by most of the justices on the winning side is called a plurality opinion. (See also **concurring opinion; dissenting opinion; majority opinion.**)

policy implementation The primary function of the bureaucracy; the process of carrying out the authoritative decisions of Congress, the president, and the courts.

political action committee (PAC) The organization through which an interest group raises and distributes funds for election purposes. By law, the funds must be raised through voluntary contributions.

political culture The characteristic and deep-seated beliefs of a particular people.

political interest The level of interest that a citizen has in politics; political interest is a prime determinant of whether a citizen will pay attention to politics and participate through voting.

political movements Also called social movements, active and sustained efforts to achieve social and political change by groups of people who feel that government has not been properly responsive to their concerns.

political participation Involvement in activities intended to influence public policy and leadership, such as voting, joining political groups, contacting elected officials, demonstrating for political causes, and giving money to political candidates.

political party An ongoing coalition of interests joined together to try to get their candidates for public office elected under a common label.

political science The systematic study of government and politics.

political socialization The learning process by which people acquire their political opinions, beliefs, and values.

politics The process through which a society settles its conflicts.

population In a public opinion poll, the people (for example, the citizens of a nation) whose opinions are being estimated through interviews with a sample of these people.

pork Also called pork-barrel spending; spending whose tangible benefits are targeted at a particular legislator's constituency.

poverty line As defined by the federal government, the annual cost of a thrifty food budget for an urban family of four, multiplied by three to allow also for the cost of housing, clothes, and other expenses. Families below the poverty line are considered poor and are eligible for certain forms of public assistance.

power The ability of persons or institutions to control policy. (See also **authority.**)

precedent A judicial decision that serves as a rule for settling subsequent cases of a similar nature.

preemptive war doctrine The idea, espoused by President George W. Bush, that the United States could attack a potentially threatening nation even if the threat had not yet reached a serious and immediate level.

presidential approval rating A measure of the degree to which the public approves or disapproves of the president's performance in office.

presidential commissions Organizations within the bureaucracy that are headed by commissioners appointed by the president. An example is the Commission on Civil Rights.

presidential veto The power of the president to veto an act of Congress. A veto can only be overridden by a two-thirds vote of the House and Senate.

primary election Also called a direct primary, a form of election in which voters choose a party's nominees for public office. In most states, eligibility to vote in a primary election is limited to voters who designated themselves as party members when they registered to vote.

priming The process in which the media highlight certain aspects of an issue or event and not other aspects, thereby affecting how people respond to the issue or event.

prior restraint Government prohibition of speech or publication before the fact, which is presumed by the courts to be unconstitutional unless the justification for it is overwhelming.

private (individual) goods Benefits that a group (most often an economic group) can grant directly and exclusively to individual members of the group. (See also **collective [public] goods.**)

procedural due process The constitutional requirement that government must follow proper legal procedures before a person can be legitimately punished for an alleged offense.

progressive income tax A tax on personal income in which the tax rate increases as income increases; in other words, the tax rate is higher for higher income levels.

proportional representation system A form of representation in which seats in the legislature are allocated proportionally according to each political party's share of the popular vote. This system enables smaller parties to compete successfully for seats. (See also **single-member districts.**)

protectionism The placing of the immediate interests of domestic producers (through, for example, protective tariffs) above that of free trade between nations.

public assistance Social welfare programs funded through general tax revenues and available only to those in financial need. Eligibility for such a program is established by a means test. (See also **means test; social insurance.**)

public opinion The politically relevant opinions held by ordinary citizens that they express openly.

public opinion poll A device for measuring public opinion whereby a relatively small number of individuals (the sample) are interviewed for the purpose of estimating the opinions of a whole community (the population). (See also **sample.**)

public policies Decisions by government to pursue particular courses of action.

reapportionment The reallocation of House seats among states after each census as a result of population changes.

reasonable-basis test A test applied by courts to laws that treat individuals unequally. Such a law may be deemed constitutional if its purpose is held to be "reasonably" related to a legitimate government interest.

redistricting The process of altering election districts in order to make them as nearly equal in population as possible. Redistricting takes place every 10 years, after each population census.

registration The practice of placing citizens' names on an official list of voters before they are eligible to exercise their right to vote.

regulation Government restrictions on the economic practices of private firms.

regulatory agencies Administrative units, such as the Securities and Exchange Commission (SEC) and the Environmental Protection Agency (EPA), that have responsibility for monitoring and regulating ongoing economic activities and regulating industrial pollution, respectively.

representation function The responsibility of a legislature to represent various interests in society. (See also **lawmaking function; oversight function.**)

representative government A government in which the people govern through the selection of their representatives.

republic A form of government in which the people's representatives decide policy through institutions structured in ways that foster deliberation, slow the progress of decision making, and operate within restraints that protect individual liberty. To the framers, the Constitution's separation of powers and other limits on power were defining features of a republican form of government, as opposed to a democratic form, which places no limits on the majority.

reserved powers The powers granted to the states under the Tenth Amendment to the Constitution.

right of privacy A right implied by the freedoms in the Bill of Rights that grants individuals a degree of personal privacy upon which government cannot lawfully intrude. The right gives individuals a level of free choice in areas such as reproduction and intimate relations.

rule of four A Supreme Court rule whereby, when a losing party appeals a lower-court ruling, the case is accepted by the Supreme only if at least four justices agree to hear it.

rule-making The process by which bureaucratic agencies develop and make known the details on how legislation will be implemented. Rule-making is a main source of bureaucratic power.

salience An opinion dimension; how highly people rank an issue relative to other issues.

sample In a public opinion poll, the relatively small number of individuals who are interviewed for the purpose of estimating the opinions of an entire population. (See also **public opinion poll.**)

sampling error A measure of the accuracy of a public opinion poll, mainly a function of sample size and usually expressed in percentage terms.

selective incorporation The process by which certain of the rights (for example, freedom of speech) contained in the Bill of Rights become applicable through the Fourteenth Amendment to actions by the state governments.

self-government The principle that the people are the ultimate source and proper beneficiary of governing authority; in practice, a government based on majority rule.

Senior Executive Service (SES) Top-level career civil servants who qualify through a competitive process to receive higher salaries than their peers but who can be assigned or transferred by order of the president.

seniority A member of Congress's consecutive years of service on a particular committee.

separated institutions sharing power The principle that, as a way to limit government, its powers should be divided among separate branches, each of which also shares in the power of the others as a means of checking and balancing them. The result is that no one branch can exercise power decisively without the support or acquiescence of the others.

separation of powers The division of the powers of government among separate institutions or branches.

service strategy The use of personal staff by members of Congress to perform services for constituents in order to gain their support in future elections.

signaling (signaler) function The responsibility of the media to alert the public to important developments as soon as possible after they happen or are discovered. (See also **common-carrier function; partisan function; watchdog function.**)

single-member districts The form of representation in which only the candidate who gets the most votes in a district wins office. (See also **proportional representation system.**)

single-member system Also called a winner-take-all system or a plurality, an electoral system in which the candidate who gets the most votes (the plurality) in an election district is elected to office from that district.

slander Spoken falsehoods that damage a person's reputation.

social capital The sum of the face-to-face interactions among citizens in a society.

social contract A voluntary agreement by individuals to form a government that is then obligated to work within the confines of that agreement.

social insurance Social welfare programs are based on the "insurance" concept, requiring that individuals pay into the program in order to be eligible to receive funds from it. An example is Social Security for retired people. (See also **public assistance.**)

soft power An approach that places emphasis on diplomacy, economic sanctions, and foreign aid as the means of protecting U.S. interests, in contrast with the use of military force, or *hard power*.

sovereignty The supreme (or ultimate) authority to govern within a certain geographic area.

spoils system The practice of granting public office to individuals in return for political favors they have rendered. (See also **patronage system.**)

standing committees Permanent congressional committees with responsibility for a particular area of public policy. An example is the Senate Foreign Relations Committee.

stewardship theory A theory that argues for a strong, assertive presidential role, with presidential authority limited only at points specifically prohibited by law. (See also **Whig theory.**)

strict-scrutiny test A test applied by courts to laws that attempt a racial or ethnic classification. In effect, the strict-scrutiny test eliminates race or ethnicity as legal classification when it places minority-group members at a disadvantage. (See also **suspect classifications.**)

suffrage The right to vote.

super PACs Election committees that are unrestricted in their fundraising and spending as long as they do not coordinate their campaign efforts with that of a candidate.

supply-side economics A form of fiscal policy that emphasizes "supply" (production). An example of supply-side economics is a tax cut for business. (See also **demand-side economics; fiscal policy.**)

supremacy clause Article VI of the Constitution, which makes national law supreme over state law when the national government is acting within its constitutional limits.

suspect classifications Legal classifications, such as race and national origin, that have invidious discrimination as their purpose and therefore are unconstitutional. (See also **strict-scrutiny test.**)

symbolic speech Action (for example, the waving or burning of a flag) for the purpose of expressing a political opinion.

tariffs The taxes that a country levies on goods shipped into it from other countries.

Three-Fifths Compromise A compromise worked out at the 1787 convention between northern states and southern states. Each slave was to be counted as three-fifths of a person for purposes of federal taxation and congressional apportionment (number of seats in the House of Representatives).

transnational terrorism Terrorism that transcends national borders and often targets people and locations other than the ones directly at issue.

trustee An elected representative whose obligation is to act in accordance with his or her own conscience as to what policies are in the best interests of the public. (See also **delegate.**)

two-party system A system in which only two political parties have a chance of acquiring control of the government.

tyranny of the majority The potential of a majority to monopolize power for its own gain and to the detriment of minority rights and interests.

unilateralism The situation in which one nation takes action against another state or states.

unipolar A power structure dominated by a single powerful actor, as in the case of the United States after the collapse of the Soviet Union.

unit rule The rule that grants all of a state's electoral votes to the candidate who receives most of the popular votes in the state.

unitary system A governmental system in which the national government alone has sovereign (or ultimate) authority. (See also **confederacy; federalism.**)

veto The president's rejection of a bill, thereby keeping it from becoming law unless Congress overrides the veto.

Virginia (large-state) Plan A constitutional proposal for a strong Congress with two chambers, both of which would be based on numerical representation, thus granting more power to the larger states.

watchdog function The accepted responsibility of the media to protect the public from incompetent or corrupt officials by standing ready to expose any official who violates accepted legal, ethical, or performance standards. (See also **common-carrier function; partisan function; signaling [signaler] function.**)

Whig theory A theory that prevailed in the nineteenth century and held that the presidency was a limited or restrained office whose occupant was confined to expressly granted constitutional authority. (See also **stewardship theory.**)

whistleblowing An internal check on the bureaucracy whereby employees report instances of mismanagement that they observe.

writ of certiorari Permission granted by a higher court to allow a losing party in a legal case to bring the case before it for a ruling; when such a writ is requested of the U.S. Supreme Court, four of the Court's nine justices must agree to accept the case before it is granted certiorari.

NOTES

CHAPTER ONE

[1]John Stuart Mill, *On Liberty,* ed. Michael B. Mathias and Daniel Kolak (New York: Longman, 2006), 43.

[2]Zacc Ritter, "Amid Pandemic, News Attention Spikes; Media Favorability Flat," *Gallup News,* April 9, 2020, https://news.gallup.com/opinion/gallup/307934/amid-pandemic-news-attention-spikes-media-favorability-flat.aspx.

[3]Thomas E. Patterson, *How America Lost Its Mind* (Norman: University of Oklahoma Press, 2019), 5.

[4]Economist/YouGov poll, December 2019, https://today.yougov.com/topics/politics/articles-reports/2019/12/05/america-ukraine-russia-poll.

[5]James D. Agresti, "National Poll Shows Voters Are Widely Misinformed About Key Issues," *Just Facts,* November 15, 2017, https://www.justfacts.com/news_2017_poll_voter_knowledge.asp.

[6]Wendy Gross, Tobias H. Stark, Jon Krosnick, Josh Pasek, Gaurav Soods, Trevor Tompson, Jennifer Agiesta, and Dennis Junius, "Americans' Attitudes Toward the Affordable Care Act," Stanford University, 2012, p. 9. https://pprg.stanford.edu/wp-content/uploads/Health-Care-2012-Knowledge-and-Favorability.pdf.

[7]American Council of Trustees and Alumni, "A Crisis in Civic Education," 2016, https://www.goacta.org/images/download/A_Crisis_in_Civic_Education.pdf.

[8]Theodore Sorsensen when he was a Institute of Politics Fellow at Harvard Kennedy School in 2002.

[9]Mark Bauerlein, *The Dumbest Generation* (New York: Penguin, 2008), 28.

[10]Bianca DiJulio, Jamie Firth, and Mollyann Brodie, "Data Note: Americans' Views On The U.S. Role In Global Health," *Kaiser Family Foundation,* Jan 23, 2015. http://www.kff.org/global-health-policy/poll-finding/data-note-americans-views-on-the-u-s-role-in-global-health/; "As Sequester Deadline Looms, Little Support for Cutting Most Programs," Pew Research Center, February 22, 2013, http://www.people-press.org/2013/02/22/as-sequester-deadline-looms-little-support-for-cutting-most-programs/.

[11]Scott Althaus, "Free Falls, High Dives, and the Future of Democratic Accountability." In *The Politics of News/The News of Politics,* 2nd ed. Doris Graber, Denis McQuail, and Pippa Norris, eds. (Washington, D.C.: Congressional Quarterly Press, 2007), 185.

[12]Steven Kull, Clay Ramsay, and Evan Lewis, "Misperceptions, the Media, and the Iraq War," *Political Science Quarterly,* 118 (Winter 2003-2004): 569–98.

[13]See, for example, Allyson Chiu, "Rush Limbaugh on coronavirus: 'The common cold' that's being 'weaponized' against Trump," *Washington Post,* February 25, 2020, https://www.washingtonpost.com/nation/2020/02/25/limbaugh-coronavirus-trump/; Aaron Rupar, "Hannity claims he's 'never called the virus a hoax' 9 days after decrying Democrats' 'new hoax,'" *Vox,* March 20, 2020, https://www.vox.com/2020/3/20/21186727/hannity-coronavirus-coverage-fox-news.

[14]See, for example, Norbert Schwarz, "Metacognitive Experiences in Consumer Judgment and Decision Making," *Journal of Consumer Psychology,* 14 (2004): 332–48, cited in Adam J. Berinsky, "Rumors and Health Care Reform: Experiments in Political Information," *British Journal of Political Science,* 47 (2017): 241–62.

[15]Derek Thompson, "Where Did All the Workers Go? 60 Years of Economic Change in 1 Graph," *The Atlantic,* January 26, 2012, https://www.theatlantic.com/business/archive/2012/01/where-did-all-the-workers-go-60-years-of-economic-change-in-1-graph/252018/.

[16]Daniel Kahneman, *Thinking Fast and Slow* (New York: Farrar, Straus and Giroux, 2011), 201.

[17]Gordon Pennycook and David G. Rand, "Lazy, Not Biased," *Cognition,* 188 (2018): 39–50.

[18]See Michael Foley, *American Credo: The Place of Ideas in American Politics* (New York: Oxford University Press, 2007).

[19]James Bryce, *The American Commonwealth,* vol. 2 (New York: Macmillan, 1960), 247–54. First published in 1900.

[20]Bryce, *The American Commonwealth,* 132.

[21]Louis Hartz, *The Liberal Tradition in America* (New York: Harcourt, Brace, 1952), 12.

[22]Alexis de Tocqueville, *Democracy in America,* vol. 2 (New York: Vintage Classics, 1990), 89.

[23]Bryce, *The American Commonwealth,* 182.

[24]T. J. Mathews and Anne K. Driscoll, "Trends in Infant Mortality in the United States, 2005–2014," Centers for Disease Control and Prevention, March 2017, https://www.cdc.gov/nchs/products/databriefs/db279.htm.

[25]Quoted in Ralph Volney Harlow, *The Growth of the United States,* vol. 2 (New York: Henry Holt, 1943), 497.

[26]Pew Research Center poll, April 2015.

[27]Michelangelo Landgrave and Alex Nowrasteh, "Criminal Immigrants: Their Numbers, Demographics, and Countries of Origin," Cato Institute, March 15, 2017. https://www.cato.org/publications/immigration-reform-bulletin/criminal-immigrants-their-numbers-demographics-countries.

[28]*Tinker v. Colwell,* 193 U.S. 473 (1904).

[29]Martin Luther King Jr., speech at civil rights march on Washington, August 28, 1963.

[30]William Watts and Lloyd A. Free, eds., *The State of the Nation* (New York: University Books, Potomac Associates, 1967), 131.

[31]Harold D. Lasswell, *Politics: Who Gets What, When, How* (New York: McGraw-Hill, 1936).

[32]Russell Hardin, *Liberalism, Constitutionalism, and Democracy* (New York: Oxford University Press, 1999).

[33]Foucault's phrasing was a deliberate inversion of von Clausewitz's famous line "War is politics by other means." Foucault is not the only writer who has applied this inversion.

[34]Bin Liang and Hong Lu, "Internet Development, Censorship, and Cyber Crimes in China," *Journal of Contemporary Criminal Justice,* 26 (2010): 103–20.

[35]Adam Przworski and José María Maravall, eds., *Democracy and the Rule of Law* (New York: Cambridge University Press, 2003).

[36]See Robert Dahl, *On Democracy* (New Haven, Conn.: Yale University Press, 2000).

[37]Washington Post-ABC News poll, June 2–4, 2017.

[38]Seymour Martin Lipset, *American Exceptionalism: A Double-Edged Sword* (New York: Norton, 1996), 37.

[39]*Gideon v. Wainwright,* 372 U.S. 335 (1963).

[40]Figures are based on a 40-hour work week for 52 weeks using 2020 national minimum-wage amounts, which were $7.25 for the United States, $10.09 for Germany, and $10.82 for France.

[41]See William G. Domhoff, *Who Rules America? Challenges to Corporate and Class Dominance,* 7th ed. (New York: McGraw-Hill, 2013).

[42]C. Wright Mills, *The Power Elite* (New York: Oxford University Press, 1965).

[43]See Joseph A. Schumpeter, *Capitalism, Socialism and Democracy* (New York: Harper, 1975).

[44]E. E. Schattschneider, *Two Hundred Million Americans in Search of a Government* (New York: Holt, Reinhart and Winston, 1969), 42.

CHAPTER TWO

[1]Quoted in Charles S. Hyneman, "Republican Government in America," in George J. Graham Jr. and Scarlett G. Graham, eds., *Founding Principles of American Government,* rev. ed. (Chatham, N.J.: Chatham House, 1984), 19.

[2]See John Harmon McElroy, *American Beliefs: What Keeps a Big Country and a Diverse People United* (Chicago: I. R. Dee, 1999).

[3]See Russell Hardin, *Liberalism, Constitutionalism, and Democracy* (New York: Oxford University Press, 1999); A. John Simmons, *The Lockean Theory of Rights* (Princeton, N.J.: Princeton University Press, 1994).

[4]Thomas Hobbes, *Leviathan* (1651).

[5]John Locke, *Second Treatise on Civil Government* (1690).

[6]Quoted in "The Constitution and Slavery," Digital History website, December 1, 2003.

[7]Speech of Melancton Smith at the New York Constitutional Ratifying Convention, June 20, 1788. http://teachingamericanhistory.org/library/document/melancton-smith-new-york-ratifying-convention/.

[8]Gaillard Hunt, ed., *The Writings of James Madison* (New York: Putnam, 1904), 274.

[9]See Vincent Ostrom, *The Political Theory of a Compound Republic: Designing the American Experiment* (Lanham, Md.: Lexington Books, 2007).

[10]See *Federalist* Nos. 47 and 48.

[11]Richard Neustadt, *Presidential Power* (New York: Macmillan, 1986), 33.

[12]Henry J. Abraham, *The Judicial Process,* 6th ed. (New York: Oxford University Press, 1993), 320–22.

[13]*Marbury v. Madison,* 1 Cranch 137 (1803).

[14]*United States v. Nixon,* 418 US 683 (1974); *Trump v. Vance,* No. 19-635 (2020); *Trump v. Mazers,* No. 19-715 (2020).

[15]Martin Diamond, *The Founding of the Democratic Republic* (Itasca, Ill.: Peacock, 1981), 62–71.

[16]Leslie F. Goldstein, "Judicial Review and Democratic Theory: Guardian Democracy vs. Representative Democracy," *Western Political Quarterly,* 40 (1987): 391–412.

[17]See Douglas Bradburn, *The Citizenship Revolution: Politics and the Creation of the American Union 1774-1804* (Charlottesville: University of Virginia Press, 2009).

[18]Benjamin Ginsberg, *The Consequences of Consent* (New York: Random House, 1982), 22.

[19]Robert Dahl, *Pluralist Democracy in the United States* (Chicago: Rand McNally, 1967), 92.

[20]This interpretation is taken from Walter Lippmann, *Public Opinion* (New York: Free Press, 1965), 178–79.

[21]Michael McGeer, *A Fierce Discontent: The Rise and Fall of the Progressive Movement in America, 1870-1920* (New York: Free Press, 2005).

[22]Charles S. Beard, *An Economic Interpretation of the Constitution* (New York: Macmillan, 1941). First published in 1913.

[23]John M. Scheb and John M. Scheb II, *Introduction to the American Legal System* (Clifton Park, N.Y.: Delmar Cengage Learning System, 2001), 6.

[24]See Randall G. Holcombe, *From Liberty to Democracy* (Ann Arbor: University of Michigan Press, 2002).

CHAPTER THREE

[1]Woodrow Wilson, *Constitutional Government in the United States* (New York: Columbia University Press, 1908), 173.

[2]*Printz v. United States,* 521 U.S. 898 (1997).

[3]*National Federation of Independent Business v. Sebelius,* 567 U.S. 510 (2012); see also *South Dakota v. Dole,* 483 U.S. 203 (1987).

[4]See Samuel Beer, *To Make a Nation* (Cambridge, Mass.: The Belknap Press of Harvard, 1984).

[5]Antifederalist No. 9. This essay appeared in the *Independent Gazetteer* on October 17, 1787, under the pen name "Montezuma."

[6]Alison L. LaCroix, *The Ideological Origins of American Federalism* (Cambridge, Mass.: Harvard University Press, 2010).

[7]William M. Lunch, *The Nationalization Of American Politics* (Berkeley, CA: University of California Press, 1987).

[8]*McCulloch v. Maryland,* 4 Wheaton 316 (1819).

[9]*Gibbons v. Ogden,* 22 Wheaton 1 (1824). [22 U.S. 1 (1824)].

[10]Oliver Wendell Holmes Jr., *Collected Legal Papers* (New York: Harcourt, Brace, 1920), 295–96.

[11]See John C. Calhoun, *The Works of John C. Calhoun* (New York: Russell & Russell, 1968).

[12]*Dred Scott v. Sanford,* 19 Howard 393 (1857).

[13]*U.S. v. Cruikshank,* 92 U.S. 452 (1876).

[14]*Slaughter-House Cases,* 16 Wallace 36 (1873); *Civil Rights Cases,* 109 U.S. 3 (1883).

[15]*Plessy v. Ferguson,* 163 U.S. 537 (1896).

[16]See, for example, Douglas A. Blackmon, *Slavery by Another Name: The Re-Enslavement of Black America from the Civil War to World War II* (New York: Anchor Books, 2009).

[17]*Santa Clara County v. Southern Pacific Railroad Co.,* 118 U.S. 394 (1886).

[18]*U.S. v. E. C. Knight Co.,* 156 U.S. 1 (1895).

[19]*Hammer v. Dagenhart,* 247 U.S. 251 (1918).

[20]*Lochner v. New York,* 198 U.S. 25 (1905).

[21]Alfred H. Kelly, Winifred A. Harbison, and Herman Belz, *The American Constitution,* 7th ed. (New York: Norton, 1991), 529; but also see Kimberley Johnson, *Governing the American State: Congress and the New Federalism, 1877-1929* (Princeton, N.J.: Princeton University Press, 2006).

[22]James E. Anderson, *The Emergence of the Modern Regulatory State* (Washington, D.C.: Public Affairs Press, 1962), 2–3.

[23]*Schechter Poultry Corp. v. United States,* 295 U.S. 495 (1935).

[24]*NLRB v. Jones and Laughlin Steel,* 301 U.S. 1 (1937).

[25]*American Power and Light v. Securities and Exchange Commission,* 329 U.S. 90 (1946).

[26]Louis Fisher, *American Constitutional Law,* 6th ed. (Durham, N.C.: Carolina Academic Press, 2005), 390.

[27]*United States v. Butler,* 297 U.S. 1 (1936).

[28] As will be discussed in Chapter 5, the Supreme Court also altered the constitutional doctrine of federalism in the area of civil rights. The two-race system upheld in the *Plessy* decision was struck down in 1954 as a violation of the Fourteenth Amendment's equal protection clause.

[29] See Thomas Anton, *American Federalism and Public Policy* (Philadelphia: Temple University Press, 1989).

[30] Morton Grodzins, *The American System: A New View of Government in the United States* (Chicago: Rand McNally, 1966).

[31] John D. Nugent, *Safeguarding Federalism: How States Protect Their Interests in National Policymaking* (Norman: University of Oklahoma Press, 2009).

[32] David Lazer, Matthew A. Baum, Katherine Ognyanova, and John Della Volpe, "A 50-State COVID-19 Survey, April 2020," http://www.kateto.net/COVID19%20CONSORTIUM%20REPORT%20April%202020.pdf.

[33] Rosella Levaggi, *Fiscal Federalism and Grants-in-Aid* (Brookfield, Vt.: Avebury, 1991).

[34] Beth Fouhy, "GOP Governors Press Congress to Pass Stimulus Bill," *Associated Press wire story,* January 31, 2009.

[35] Timothy J. Conlan, *From New Federalism to Devolution* (Washington, D.C.: Brookings Institution, 1998).

[36] Andrew W. Dobelstein, *Politics, Economics, and Public Welfare* (Englewood Cliffs, N.J.: Prentice-Hall, 1980), 5.

[37] Lloyd A. Free and Hadley Cantril, *The Political Beliefs of Americans* (New York: Simon & Schuster, 1968), 21.

[38] Survey for the Times Mirror Center for the People and the Press by Princeton Survey Research Associates, July 12–27, 1994.

Chapter Four

[1] Julian P. Boyd, ed., *The Papers of Thomas Jefferson,* vol. 12 (Princeton, N.J.: Princeton University Press, 1955), 440.

[2] *United States v. Jones,* No. 10-1250 (2012).

[3] *Barron v. Baltimore,* 32 U.S. (7 Pet.) 243 (1833).

[4] *Gitlow v. New York,* 268 U.S. 652, 1925.

[5] *Fiske v. Kansas,* 274 U.S. 30 (1927); *Near v. Minnesota,* 283 U.S. 697 (1931); *Hamilton v. Regents, U. of California,* 293 U.S. 245 (1934); *DeJonge v. Oregon,* 299 U.S. 253 (1937).

[6] *Near v. Minnesota,* 283 U.S. 697 (1931).

[7] *Mapp v. Ohio,* 367 U.S. 643 (1961).

[8] *Gideon v. Wainright,* 372 U.S. 335 (1963).

[9] *Malloy v. Hogan,* 378 U.S. 1 (1964).

[10] *Miranda v. Arizona,* 384 U.S. 436 (1966); see also *Escobedo v. Illinois,* 378 U.S. 478 (1964).

[11] *Pointer v. Texas,* 380 U.S. 400 (1965).

[12] *Klopfer v. North Carolina,* 386 U.S. 213 (1967).

[13] *Duncan v. Louisiana,* 391 U.S. 145 (1968).

[14] *Benton v. Maryland,* 395 U.S. 784 (1969).

[15] *Schenck v. United States,* 249 U.S. 47 (1919).

[16] *Dennis v. United States,* 341 U.S. 494, 1951.

[17] See, for example, *Yates v. United States,* 354 U.S. 298 (1957); *Noto v. United States,* 367 U.S. 290 (1961); *Scales v. United States,* 367 U.S. 203 (1961).

[18] *Brandenburg v. Ohio,* 395 U.S. 444 (1969).

[19] *R.A.V. v. St. Paul,* No. 90-7675 (1992).

[20] *Wisconsin v. Mitchell,* No. 92-515 (1993).

[21] *Snyder v. Phelps,* No. 09-7571 (2011).

[22] *Texas v. Johnson,* 109 S. Ct. 2544, (1989).

[23] *National Socialist Party v. Skokie,* 432 U.S. 43 (1977).

[24] *Forsyth County v. Nationalist Movement,* No. 91-538 (1992).

[25] *New York Times Co. v. United States,* 403 U.S. 713 (1971).

[26] *Nebraska Press Assn. v. Stuart,* 427 U.S. 539 (1976).

[27] *Milkovich v. Lorain Journal,* 497 U.S. 1 (1990); see also *Masson v. The New Yorker,* No. 89-1799 (1991).

[28] *New York Times Co. v. Sullivan,* 376 U.S. 254 (1964).

[29] *Engel v. Vitale,* 370 U.S. 421 (1962).

[30] *Abington School District v. Schempp,* 374 U.S. 203 (1963).

[31] *Wallace v. Jaffree,* 472 U.S. 38 (1985).

[32] *Van Orden v. Perry,* No. 03-1500 (2005).

[33] Ibid.

[34] *Lemon v. Kurtzman,* 403 U.S. 602 (1971).

[35] *Board of Regents v. Allen,* 392 U.S. 236 (1968).

[36] *Espinoza v. Montana Department of Revenue,* No. 18-1195 (2020); see also, *Zelman v. Simmons-Harris,* No. 00-1751 (2002); *Locke v. Davey,* No. 02-1315 (2004).

[37] *Burwell v. Hobby Lobby Stores,* No. 13-354 (2014); *Little Sisters of the Poor Saints Peter and Paul Home v. Pennsylvania,* No. 19-431 (2020).

[38] *Masterpiece Cakeshop v. Colorado Civil Rights Commission,* No. 16-111 (2018).

[39] *Edwards v. Aguillard,* 487 U.S. 578 (1987).

[40]*District of Columbia v. Heller,* 554 U.S. 570 (2008).

[41]*McDonald v. Chicago,* 561 U.S. 3025 (2010).

[42]*Griswold v. Connecticut,* 381 U.S. 479 (1965).

[43]*Roe v. Wade,* 401 U.S. 113 (1973).

[44]*Webster v. Reproductive Health Services,* 492 U.S. 490 (1989); see also *Rust v. Sullivan,* No. 89-1391 (1991).

[45]*Planned Parenthood v. Casey,* No. 91-744 (1992).

[46]*Gonzales v. Carhart,* 550 U.S. 124 (2007).

[47]*June Medical Services v. Russo,* No. 18-1323 (2020); see also *Whole Woman's Health v. Hellerstedt,* No. 15-274 (2016).

[48]*Bowers v. Hardwick,* 478 U.S. 186 (1986).

[49]*Lawrence v. Texas,* 539 U.S. 558 (2003).

[50]*McNabb v. United States,* 318 U.S. 332 (1943).

[51]The structure and content of the discussion that follows on arrest, search, interrogation, formal charge, trial, appeal, and punishment are informed by Walter F. Murphy and Michael N. Danielson, *Robert K. Carr and Marver H. Bernstein's American Democracy* (Hinsdale, Ill.: Dryden Press, 1977), 465–74.

[52]David Fellman, *The Defendant's Rights Today* (Madison: University of Wisconsin Press, 1979), 256.

[53]*Kyllo v. United States,* No. 99-8508 (2001), 533 U.S. 27 (2010).

[54]*Riley v. California,* No. 13-132 (2014); see also, *Carpenter v. United States,* No. 16-402 (2018).

[55]*Board of Education of Independent School District No. 92 of Pottawatomie County v. Earls,* No. 01-332 (2002).

[56]*Michigan v. Sitz,* No. 88-1897 (1990).

[57]*Indianapolis v. Edmund,* No. 99-1030 (2001).

[58]*Missouri v. Siebert,* 542 U.S. 600 (2004).

[59]*Miranda v. Arizona,* 384 U.S. 436 (1966).

[60]*Johnson v. Zerbst,* 304 U.S. 458 (1938).

[61]*Gideon v. Wainwright,* 372 U.S. 335 (1963).

[62]*Witherspoon v. Illinois,* 391 U.S. 510 (1968).

[63]*Flowers v. Mississippi,* No. 17-9572 (2019); the precedent was set in *Batson v. Kentucky,* 476 U.S. 79 (1986).

[64]*Ramos v. Louisiana,* 139 S. Ct. 1647 (2020).

[65]*Weeks v. United States,* 232 U.S. 383 (1914).

[66]*United States v. Leon,* 468 U.S. 897 (1984).

[67]*Nix v. Williams,* 467 U.S. 431 (1984).

[68]*Horton v. California,* 496 U.S. 128 (1990).

[69]*Lockyer v. Andrade,* No. 01-1127 (2003); see also *Ewing v. California,* No. 01-6978 (2003).

[70]*Atkins v. Virginia,* No. 01-8452 (2002); see also *Montgomery v. Louisiana,* No. 14-280 (2016).

[71]*Pennsylvania v. Finley,* 481 U.S. 551 (1987).

[72]*Townsend v. Sain,* 372 U.S. 293 (1963).

[73]*Williams v. Taylor,* No. 99-6615 (2000).

[74]See, for example, National Institute of Justice, "Racial Profiling and Traffic Stops," January 10, 2013, www.nij.gov/topics/law-enforcement/legitimacy/pages/traffic-stops.aspx.

[75]Charles Lane, "In Terror War, 2nd Track for Suspects," *The Washington Post,* December 1, 2001, A1.

[76]*Korematsu v. United States,* 323 U.S. 214 (1944).

[77]*Rasul v. Bush,* No. 03-334 (2004); *al-Odah v. United States,* No. 03-343 (2004).

[78]*Hamdi v. Rumsfeld,* No. 03-6696 (2004).

[79]*Hamdan v. Rumsfeld,* No. 05-184 (2006).

[80]See Alpheus T. Mason, *The Supreme Court: Palladium of Freedom* (Ann Arbor: University of Michigan Press, 1962); see also Jeffrey Rosen, *The Most Democratic Branch: How the Courts Serve America* (New York: Oxford University Press, 2006).

CHAPTER FIVE

[1]Abraham Lincoln, "Speech on the Dred Scott Decision," Springfield, Illinois, June 26, 1857.

[2]*The Washington Post* wire story, May 14, 1991.

[3]Robert Nisbet, "Public Opinion versus Popular Opinion," *Public Interest* 41 (1975): 171.

[4]*Plessy v. Ferguson,* 163 U.S. 537 (1896).

[5]Ada Lois Sipuel Fisher, Danney Gable, and Robert Henry, *A Matter of Black and White: The Autobiography of Ada Lois Sipuel Fisher* (Norman: University of Oklahoma Press, 1996).

[6]*Brown v. Board of Education* of Topeka, 347 U.S. 483 (1954).

[7]*Swann v. Charlotte-Mecklenburg County Board of Education,* 402 U.S. 1 (1971).

[8]Christopher Jencks and Meredith Phillips, eds., *The Black-White Test Score Gap* (Washington, D.C.: Brookings Institution, 1998).

[9]*Milliken v. Bradley,* 418 U.S. 717 (1974).

[10]*Parents Involved in Community Schools v. Seattle,* No. 05-908551 U.S. 701 (2007); *Meredith, Custodial Parent and Next Friend of McDonald v. Jefferson County Board of Education,* No. 05-915548 U.S. 938 (2007).

[11]Grover J. "Russ" Whitehurst, Richard V. Reeves, and Edward Rodrigues, "Segregation, Race, and Charter Schools," Center on Children and Families, Brookings Institution, October 2016, pp. 23–26.

[12]*Loving v. Virginia,* 388 U.S. 1 (1967).

[13]*Craig v. Boren,* 429 U.S. 190 (1976).

[14]*Rostker v. Goldberg,* 453 U.S. 57 (1980).

[15]*United States v. Virginia,* 518 U.S. 515 (1996), No. 94-1941 (1996).

[16]NBC/Marist poll, December 2014.

[17]"Findings," Stanford Open Policing Project, 2018. https://openpolicing.stanford.edu/findings/.

[18]National Office of Drug Control Policy, U.S. Department of Justice, 1997; see also, "Criminal Justice Facts," Sentencing Project, 2018. https://www.sentencingproject.org/criminal-justice-facts/.

[19] Sarah DeGue, Katherine A. Fowler, and Cynthia Calkins, "Deaths Due to Use of Lethal Force by Law Enforcement," *American Journal of Preventive Medicine* 51(2016): S173–S187.

[20]Michael J. Klarman, *From Jim Crow to Civil Rights: The Supreme Court and the Struggle for Racial Equality* (New York: Oxford University Press, 2004), 236.

[21]*Smith v. Allwright,* 321 U.S. 649 (1944).

[22]*Oregon v. Mitchell,* 400 U.S. 112 (1970).

[23]*Shelby County v. Holder,* No. 12-96 (2013).

[24]*Cooper v. Harris,* 136 S. Ct. 2512 (2017).

[25]See Manny Fernandez, "Study Finds Disparities in Mortgages by Race," *The New York Times,* October 15, 2007; see also U.S. Conference of Mayors report, 1998; Survey by Federal Financial Institutions Examination Council, 1998.

[26]"Public Backs Affirmative Action, but Not Minority Preferences," Pew Research Center report, June 2, 2009, web release.

[27]*University of California Regents v. Bakke,* 438 U.S. 265 (1978).

[28]*Adarand v. Peña,* 515 U.S. 200 (1995). This decision reversed an earlier ruling, *Fullilove v. Klutnick,* 448 U.S. 448 (1980).

[29]*Grutter v. Bollinger,* 539 U.S. 306 (2003).

[30]*Fisher v. University of Texas,* No. 14-981 (2016).

[31]See, for example, Gloria J. Browne-Marshall, *Race, Law, and American Society: 1607 to Present* (New York: Routledge, 2007).

[32]Douglas A. Blackmon, *Slavery by Another Name: The Re-enslavement of Black America from the Civil War to World War II* (New York: Anchor Books, 2009).

[33]Eric J. Sundquist, *King's Dream: The Legacy of Martin Luther King's "I Have a Dream" Speech* (New Haven, Conn.: Yale University Press, 2009).

[34]See, for example, Alejandro Del Carmen, *Racial Profiling in America* (Upper Saddle River, N.J.: Prentice-Hall, 2007).

[35]Sentencing Project, "Report of The Sentencing Project to the United Nations Human Rights Committee Regarding Racial Disparities in the United States Criminal Justice System," August 2013. http://sentencingproject.org/wp-content/uploads/2015/12/Race-and-Justice-Shadow-Report-ICCPR.pdf.

[36]See Keith Reeves, *Voting Hopes or Fears?* (New York: Oxford University Press, 1997); Tali Mendelberg, *The Race Card* (Princeton, N.J.: Princeton University Press, 2001); Juliet Eilperin, "What's Changed for African Americans since 1963, by the Numbers," *The Washington Post,* August 22, 2013.

[37]See Kathleen S. Sullivan, *Women and Rights Discourse in Nineteenth-Century America* (Baltimore, Md.: Johns Hopkins University Press, 2007).

[38]*Tinker v. Colwell,* 193 U.S. 473 (1904).

[39]See Jane Mansbridge, *Why We Lost the ERA* (Chicago: University of Chicago Press, 1986).

[40]U.S. Department of Education, National Center for Education Statistics, 2017.

[41]See Sara M. Evans and Barbara Nelson, *Wage Justice* (Chicago: University of Chicago Press, 1989).

[42]Jennifer L. Lawless and Richard L. Fox, *It Takes a Candidate: Why Women Don't Run for Office* (New York: Cambridge University Press, 2005).

[43]Marshall Ganz, *Why David Sometimes Wins: Leadership, Organization and Strategy in the California Farm Worker Movement* (New York: Oxford University Press, 2009).

[44]Fox News poll, September 2017.

[45]*Department of Homeland Security v. Regents of the University of California,* No. 18-1587 (2020).

[46]See David E. Wilkins, *American Indian Politics and the American Political System* (Lanham, Md.: Rowman & Littlefield, 2006); Eric C. Henson et al., *The State of the Native Nations: Conditions under U.S. Policies of Self-Determination* (New York: Oxford University Press, 2007).

[47]William Evans and Julie Topoleski, *The Social and Economic Impact of Native American Casinos,* NBER Working Paper No. 9198 (Cambridge, Mass.: National Bureau of Economic Research, September 2002).

[48]W. Dale Mason, "Tribes and States: A New Era in Intergovernmental Affairs," *Publius,* 28 (1998): 129.

[49]Data from U.S. Census Bureau, 2018, and Office of Minority Health, U.S. Department of Health and Human Services, 2018.

[50]*Lau v. Nichols,* 414 U.S. 563 (1974).

[51]See Timothy P. Fong, *Contemporary Asian American Experience: Beyond the Model Minority* (Upper Saddle River, N.J.: Prentice- Hall, 2009).

[52]Scott Jaschik, "The Numbers and the Arguments on Asian Admissions," *Inside Higher Ed,* August 7, 2017. https://www.insidehighered.com/admissions/article/2017/08/07/look-data-and-arguments-about-asian-americans-and-admissions-elite.

[53]Stefanie K. Johnson and Thomas Sy, "Why Aren't There More Asian Americans in Leadership Positions?," *Harvard Business Review,* December 19, 2016. https://hbr.org/2016/12/why-arent-there-more-asian-americans-in-leadership-positions.

[54]See Gordon Chang, ed., *Asian Americans and Politics* (Stanford, Calif.: Stanford University Press, 2001).

[55]*Kimel v. Florida Board of Regents,* No. 98-791528 U.S. 62 (2000); but see *CBOCS West, Inc. v. Humphries,* No. 06-1431553 U.S. 442 (2008).

[56]*Board of Trustees of the University of Alabama v. Garrett,* No. 99-1240 (2002); *Tennessee v. Lane,* No. 02-1667541 U.S. 509 (2004).

[57]*Obergefell v. Hodges,* 576 U.S. No. 14-556 (2015).

[58]*Bostock v. Clayton County,* No. 17-1618 (2020).

[59]Gunnar Myrdal, *An American Dilemma: The Negro Problem and Modern Democracy* (New York: Harper, 1944).

[60]Clyde W, Yancy, "COVID-19 and African Americans," Journal of the American Medical Association (JAMA) Network, April 15, 2020, https://jamanetwork.com/journals/jama/fullarticle/2764789.

CHAPTER SIX

[1]James Bryce, *The American Commonwealth,* vol. 2 (Indianapolis, Ind.: Liberty Fund, 1995), 225. First published in 1888.

[2]Quinnipiac University poll, February 2018.

[3]Elisabeth Noelle-Neumann, *The Spiral of Silence,* 2nd ed., ch. 1 (Chicago: University of Chicago Press, 1993).

[4]See, for example, Dean R. Hoge and Teresa L. Ankney, "Occupations and Attitudes of Student Activists Ten Years Later," *Journal of Youth and Adolescence,* 11 (1982): 365.

[5]See Herbert Asher, *Polling and the Public,* 7th ed. (Washington, D.C.: CQ Press, 2007).

[6]Data for Progress poll, February. 2020, https://norml.org/library/national-legalization-polls.

[7]See, for example, Benjamin G. Bishin, *Tyranny of the Minority* (Philadelphia: Temple University Press, 2009).

[8]"If Polls Say People Want Gun Control, Why Doesn't Congress Just Pass It?" *Associated Press,* March 7, 2018, https://wtop.com/national/2018/03/if-polls-say-people-want-gun-control-why-doesnt-congress-just-pass-it/.

[9]Seth Stevens-Davidowitz, *Everybody Lies: Big Data, New Data, and What the Internet Can Tell Us About Who We Really Are* (New York: Dey St., 2017), 7-9.

[10]Morning Consult/Politico poll, August 2017.

[11]Thomas E. Patterson, *How America Lost Its Mind* (Norman: University of Oklahoma Press, 2019), 33.

[12]Herbert Hyman, *Political Socialization* (Glencoe, Ill.: Free Press, 1959), 51.

[13]M. Kent Jennings and Richard G. Niemi, *Generations and Politics* (Princeton, N.J.: Princeton University Press, 1981).

[14]See Orit Ichilov, *Political Socialization, Citizenship Education, and Democracy* (New York: Teachers College Press, 1990).

[15]See, however, Dietram A. Scheufele, Matthew C. Nisbet, and Dominique Brossard, "Pathways to Political Participation: Religion, Communication Contexts, and Mass Media," *International Journal of Public Opinion Research,* 15 (Autumn 2003): 300-24; Michele F. Margolis, *From Politics to the Pews* (Chicago: University of Chicago Press, 2018).

[16]Noelle-Neumann, *Spiral of Silence.*

[17]Walter Lippmann, *Public Opinion* (New York: Free Press, 1965), p. 3.

[18]Thomas E. Patterson, *The Vanishing Voter* (New York: Knopf, 2003), 89-90.

[19]Brad Plumer and Nadja Popovich, "Traffic and Pollution Plummet as U.S. Cities Shut Down for Coronavirus," *New York Times,* March 22, 2020, https://www.nytimes.com/interactive/2020/03/22/climate/coronavirus-usa-traffic.html.

[20]See, for example, Kristi Andersen, *The Creation of a Democratic Majority, 1928-1936* (Chicago: University of Chicago Press, 1979).

[21]Ronald J. Inglehart, "How Much Should We Worry?" *Journal of Democracy,* 27 (2016): 18,

http://pscourses.ucsd.edu/ps200b/Inglehart%20
How%20Much%20SHould%20we%20Worry.
pdf.

[22]*Washington Post* poll, 2002.

[23]*Washington Post*–University of Maryland poll, October 2017.

[24]See Angus Campbell, Philip Converse, Warren Miller, and Donald Stokes, *The American Voter* (New York: Wiley, 1960), chs. 3 and 4.

[25]Martin P. Wattenberg, *Where Have All the Voters Gone?* (Cambridge, Mass.: Harvard University Press, 2002).

[26]Donald Green, Bradley Palmquist, and Eric Schickler, *Partisan Hearts and Minds* (New Haven, Conn.: Yale University Press, 2002).

[27]"Ku Klux Klan," *History,* undated. Downloaded January 2, 2018, http://www.history.com/topics/ku-klux-klan.

[28]Kenneth D. Wald, *Religion and Politics in the United States* (Lanham, Md.: Rowman & Littlefield, 2003); Robert D. Putnam and David E. Campbell, *American Grace: How Religion Divides and Unites Us* (New York: Simon & Schuster, 2012).

[29]Elana Schor and Emily Swanson, "Poll: White Evangelicals Distinct on Abortion, LGBT Policy," *Associated Press,* January 2, 2020, https://apnews.com/8d3eb99934accc2ad795aca0183290a7.

[30]Arlie Russell Hochschild, *Strangers in Their Own Land* (New York: The New Press, 2016).

[31]Ibid.

[32]Lois Duke Whitaker, ed., *Voting the Gender Gap* (Urbana: University of Illinois Press, 2008).

[33]Yuval Feinstein, "The Rise and Decline of 'Gender Gaps' in Support for Military Action: United States, 1986–2011," *Gender & Society* 13 (2017): 618-655.

[34]Liz Hamel, Lunna Lopes, Cailey Munana, and Mollyann Brodie, "The Kaiser Family Foundation/Washington Post Climate Change Survey," *KFF,* November 27, 2019, https://www.kff.org/report-section/the-kaiser-family-foundation-washington-post-climate-change-survey-main-findings/.

[35]Andrew Sullivan, "America Wasn't Built for Humans," *New York Magazine*, September 19, 2017, http://nymag.com/daily/intelligencer/2017/09/can-democracy-survive-tribalism.html.

[36]Christopher Achen and Larry Bartels, *Democracy for Realists: Why Elections Do Not Produce Responsive Government* (Princeton, N.J.: Princeton University Press, 2016).

[37]See, for example, Amy Chua, *Political Tribes: Group Instincts and the Fate of Nations* (New York: Penguin Press, 2018). American politics has been trending in that direction, which has deepened the divide between America's groups and has contributed to political polarization (see "Party Polarization" boxes throughout the book).

[38]George Gallup, "Polls and the Political Process—Past, Present, and Future," *Public Opinion Quarterly,* 40 (1965): 547-48.

[39]Clinton Rossiter and James Lare, *The Essential Lippmann: A Political Philosophy for Liberal Democracy* (Cambridge, Mass.: Harvard University Press, 1982), 99.

[40]Robert J. Samuelson, "What If We're to Blame? Public Opinion and Muddled Policies," *The Washington Post,* November 1, 2006.

[41]See Bruce Ackerman and James Fishkin, *Deliberation Day* (New Haven, Conn.: Yale University Press, 2004), 5; Christopher Achen and Larry Bartels, *Democracy for Realists: Why Elections Do Not Produce Responsive Government* (Princeton, N.J.: Princeton University Press, 2016).

[42]Zacc Ritter, "Amid Pandemic, News Attention Spikes; Media Favorability Flat," *Gallup News,* April 9, 2020, https://news.gallup.com/opinion/gallup/307934/amid-pandemic-news-attention-spikes-media-favorability-flat.aspx.

[43]See R. Michael Alvarez and John Brehm, *Hard Choices, Easy Answers* (Princeton, N.J.: Princeton University Press, 2002); see also Samuel L. Popkin, *The Reasoning Voter* (Chicago: University of Chicago Press, 1991).

[44]Robert S. Erikson, Michael B. MacKuen, and James A. Stimson, *The Macro Polity* (New York: Cambridge University Press, 2008), xxi.

[45]Vincent Hutchings, *Public Opinion and Democratic Accountability: How Citizens Learn About Politics* (Princeton, N.J.: Princeton University Press, 2005).

[46]See, for example, Sidney Verba and Norman H. Nie, *Participation in America: Political Democracy and Social Equality* (New York: Harper & Row, 1972), 332.

[47]Martin Gilens and Benjamin I. Page, "Testing Theories of American Politics: Elites, Interest Groups, and Average Citizens," *Perspectives on Politics,* 12 (2014): 564-81.

[48]Noam Chomsky and Edward S. Herman, *Manufacturing Consent: The Political Economy*

of the Mass Media (New York: Pantheon, 2002); see also William Domhoff, Who Rules America? 5th ed. (New York: McGraw-Hill, 2005).

[49]James Druckman and Lawrence Jacobs, Who Governs? Presidents, Public Opinion, and Manipulation (Chicago: University of Chicago Press, 2015).

[50]Scott McClellan, What Happened: Inside the Bush White House and Washington's Culture of Deception (New York: Public Affairs, 2008).

[51]See, for example, Daniel Kahneman, Amos Tversky, and Paul Slovic, Judgment Under Uncertainty: Heuristics & Biases (Cambridge, UK: Cambridge University Press, 1982); Daniel Kahneman, Thinking Fast and Slow (New York: Farrar, Straus and Giroux, 2013).

[52]Pew Research Center polls, July 2015 and August 2016.

[53]Bradley Jones, "Support for Free Trade Agreements Rebounds Modestly, but Wide Partisan Differences Remain," Pew Research Center, April 25, 2017, http://www.pewresearch.org/fact-tank/2017/04/25/support-for-free-trade-agreements-rebounds-modestly-but-wide-partisan-differences-remain/.

[54]V. O. Key Jr., Public Opinion and American Democracy (New York: Knopf, 1964).

[55]"Notes from the Editors," Monthly Review, 50 (1999), https://monthlyreview.org/1999/03/01/mr-050-10-1999-03_0/.

[56]Quoted in Anthony King, "Running Scared," The Atlantic, January 1997.

[57]David Mayhew, Congress: The Electoral Connection (New Haven, Conn.: Yale University Press, 2004), 5.

[58]Anthony King, Running Scared (New York: Free Press, 1999).

[59]David A. Fahrenthold, Rosalind S. Helderman, and Jenna Portnoy, "What Went Wrong for Eric Cantor," The Washington Post, June 11, 2014, https://www.washingtonpost.com/politics/what-went-wrong-for-eric-cantor/2014/06/11/0be7c02c-f180-11e3-914c-1fbd0614e2d4_story.html.

[60]See, for example, Benjamin I. Page and Robert Y. Shapiro, "Effects of Public Opinion on Policy," American Political Science Review, 77 (March 1983): 178; Richard Sobel, The Impact of Public Opinion on U.S. Foreign Policy (New York: Oxford University Press, 2001); James Stimson, Tides of Consent: How Public Opinion Shapes American Politics (New York: Cambridge University Press, 2004); Jeff Manza and Fay Lomax Cook, "A Democratic Polity: Three Views of Policy Responsiveness to Public Opinion in the United States," American Politics Research, 30 (2002): 630–67; John W. Kingdon, Agendas, Alternatives, and Public Policies, 2d ed. (New York: Longman, 2003), 148–49.

CHAPTER SEVEN

[1]Walter Lippmann, Public Opinion (New York: Free Press, 1965), 36.

[2]Quoted in Ralph Volney Harlow, The Growth of the United States (New York: Henry Holt, 1943), 312.

[3]Thomas E. Patterson, The Vanishing Voter (New York: Knopf, 2002), 134.

[4]Ibid.

[5]Russell Dalton, "The Myth of the Disengaged American," Web publication of the Comparative Study of Electoral Systems, October 2005, 2.

[6]Keesha Gaskins and Sundeep Iyer, "The Challenge of Obtaining Voter Identification," Brennan Center for Justice, July 18, 2012, www.brennancenter.org/publication/challenge-obtaining-voter-identification.

[7]Crawford et al. v. Marion County Election Board et al., No. 07-21 (2008).

[8]Sam Corbett-Davies, Tobias Konitzer, and David Rothschild, "Poll: 60% of Republicans Believe Illegal Immigrants Vote; 43% Believe People Vote Using Dead People's Names," The Washington Post, October 24, 2016, https://www.washingtonpost.com/news/monkey-cage/wp/2016/10/24/poll-60-of-republicans-believe-illegal-immigrants-vote-43-believe-people-vote-using-dead-peoples-names/.

[9]See, Benjamin Highton, "Voter Identification Laws and Turnout," Annual Review of Political Science 20(2017): 149–167, https://www.annualreviews.org/doi/abs/10.1146/annurev-polisci-0512 15-022822.

[10]Justin Levitt, "The Truth About Voter Fraud," Brennan Center for Justice, November 9, 2007, https://www.brennancenter.org/publication/truth-about-voter-fraud.

[11]Ibid.

[12]Emily Bazelon, "A Crusader Against Voter Fraud Fails to Prove His Case," New York Times, June 19, 2018, https://www.nytimes.com/20 18/06/19/opinion/a-crusader-against-voter-fraud-fails-to-prove-his-case.html.

[13]Ivor Crewe, "Electoral Participation," in David Butler, Howard R. Penniman, and Austin Ranney,

eds., *Democracy at the Polls* (Washington, D.C.: American Enterprise Institute, 1981), 251–53.

[14]Richard Boyd, "Decline of U.S. Voter Turnout," *American Politics Quarterly,* 9 (April 1981): 142.

[15]Patterson, *The Vanishing Voter,* 135.

[16]For an overview of minority-group voting in the 2016 election, see William H. Frey, "Census Shows Pervasive Decline in 2016 Minority Voter Turnout," Brookings Institution, May 18, 2017, https://www.brookings.edu/blog/the-avenue/2017/05/18/census-shows-pervasive-decline-in-2016-minority-voter-turnout/.

[17]Markus Prior, *Hooked: How Politics Captures People's Interest* (New York: Cambridge University Press, 2019).

[18]Russell J. Dalton, "The Myth of the Disengaged American," *CSES Report,* October 25, 2005.

[19]Nick Berning, "MoveOn Kicks Off $20 Million Effort to Win Progressive Governing Majority in Nov. Elections," MoveOn, February 7, 2020, https://front.moveon.org/moveon-launches-2020-election-program/.

[20]Robert Putnam, *Bowling Alone: The Collapse and Revival of American Community* (New York: Simon & Schuster, 2000).

[21]Dalton, "Myth of the Disengaged American," 2.

[22]U.S. Department of Labor statistics, 2016.

[23]See Benjamin Ginsberg, *The Consequences of Consent* (New York: Random House, 1982), ch. 2.

[24]See, for example, Charles J. Stewart, Craig Allen Smith, and Robert E. Denton Jr., *Persuasion and Social Movements,* 5th ed. (Long Grove, Ill.: Waveland Press, 2007).

[25]Sidney Tarrow, *Power in Movement* (New York: Cambridge University Press, 1998).

[26]William Watts and Lloyd A. Free, eds., *The State of the Nation* (New York: University Books, Potomac Associates, 1967), 97.

[27]Sidney Verba and Norman Nie, *Participation in America* (New York: Harper & Row, 1972), 131.

[28]Larry M. Bartels, *Unequal Democracy,* 2nd ed. (Princeton, N.J.: Princeton University Press, 2016).

CHAPTER EIGHT

[1]E. E. Schattschneider, *Party Government* (New York: Rinehart, 1942), 1.

[2]See John Aldrich, *Why Parties? The Origin and Transformation of Political Parties in America* (Chicago: University of Chicago Press, 1995);

L. Sandy Maisel, *American Political Parties and Elections* (New York: Oxford University Press, 2007).

[3]E. E. Schattschneider, *The Semisovereign People: A Realist's View of Democracy in America* (New York: Holt, Rinehart & Winston, 1961), 140.

[4]Thomas E. Patterson, *The Vanishing Voter* (New York: Knopf, 2002), ch. 2.

[5]See Richard P. McCormick, *The Second American Party System: Party Formation in the Jacksonian Era* (Chapel Hill: University of North Carolina Press, 1966).

[6]Aldrich, *Why Parties?* 151.

[7]Kristi Andersen, *The Creation of a Democratic Majority, 1928–1936* (Chicago: University of Chicago Press, 1979).

[8]See Kevin Phillips, *The Emerging Republican Majority* (New Rochelle, N.Y.: Arlington House, 1969).

[9]See Arthur C. Paulson, *Electoral Realignment and the Outlook for American Democracy* (Boston: Northeastern University Press, 2006).

[10]Richard M. Scammon and Ben J. Wattenberg, *The Real Majority* (New York: Coward-McCann, 1970).

[11]John Green, Mark Rozell, and William Clyde Wilcox, eds., *The Christian Right in American Politics* (Washington, D.C.: Georgetown University Press, 2003).

[12]Jacob S. Hacker and Paul Pierson, *Off Center: The Republican Revolution and the Erosion of American Democracy* (New Haven, Conn.: Yale University Press, 2006); James E. Campbell, *Polarized: Making Sense of a Divided America* (Princeton, N.J.: Princeton University Press, 2016).

[13]Everett Carll Ladd and Charles D. Hadley, *Transformations of the American Party System* (New York: W.W. Norton, 1975); Gary Miller and Norman Schofield, "The Transformation of the Republican and Democratic Party Coalitions in the U.S.," *Perspectives on Politics,* 6 (2008): 433–50; Thomas E. Patterson, *Is the Republican Party Destroying Itself?* (Seattle, Wash.: KDP, 2020).

[14]Pew Research Center polls, 1987 for the 1980s figures and various dates for the more recent figures.

[15]See Duncan Black, "On the Rationale of Group Decision-Making," *Journal of Political Economy,* 56 (1948): 23–24; Anthony Downs, *An Economic Theory of Democracy* (New York: HarperCollins, 1957).

[16]Jocelyn Kiley, "In Polarized Era, Fewer Americans Hold a Mix of Conservative and Liberal Views," Pew Research Center, October 27, 2017, http://www.pewresearch.org/fact-tank/2017/10/23/in-polarized-era-fewer-americans-hold-a-mix-of-conservative-and-liberal-views/?utm_source=Pew+Research+Center&utm_campaign=0abc6f17c9-EMAIL_CAMPAIGN_2017_10_26&utm_medium=email&utm_term=0_3e953b9b70-0abc6f17c9-400267813.

[17]Bill Bishop, *The Big Sort: Why the Clustering of Like-Minded America Is Tearing Us Apart* (New York: Houghton Mifflin, 2008); Alan A. Abramowitz, "U.S. Senate Elections in a Polarized Era," in Burdett A. Loomis, ed., *The U.S. Senate: From Deliberation to Dysfunction* (Washington, D.C.: CQ Press, 2011), 27–48.

[18]Presidential election exit polls, 1980–2020; see also Lois Duke Whitaker, ed., *Voting the Gender Gap* (Urbana: University of Illinois Press, 2008); Karen M. Kaufmann, "The Gender Gap," *PS: Political Science & Politics,* July 2006, 447–53.

[19]2020 election exit polls.

[20]Daniel Cox and Robert Jones, "America's Changing Religious Identity," *PRRI*, September 6, 2017, https://www.prri.org/research/american-religious-landscape-christian-religiously-unaffiliated/.

[21]American National Election Studies (ANES) surveys, 2000–2016 elections.

[22]See John B. Judis and Ruy Teixeira, *The Emerging Democratic Majority* (New York: Scribner, 2002).

[23]James G. Gimpel, "Latinos and the 2002 Election: Republicans Do Well When Latinos Stay Home," Center for Immigration Studies, University of Maryland, January 2003, https://cis.org/Latinos-and-2002-Election; see also Jorge Ramos, *The Latino Wave: How Hispanics Are Transforming Politics in America* (New York: Harper Paperbacks, 2005); F. Chris Garcia and Gabriel Sanchez, *Hispanics and the U.S. Political System: Moving into the Mainstream* (Upper Saddle River, N.J.: Prentice-Hall, 2007).

[24]Thomas E. Patterson, *Is the Republican Party Destroying Itself?* (Seattle, Wash.: KDP, 2020).

[25]Micah L. Sifrey, *Spoiling for a Fight: Third-Party Politics in America* (New York: Routledge, 2003).

[26]Daniel A. Mazmanian, *Third Parties in Presidential Elections* (Washington, D.C.: Brookings Institution, 1984), 143–44.

[27]Lewis L. Gould, *Four Hats in the Ring: The 1912 Election and the Birth of Modern American Politics* (Lawrence: University Press of Kansas, 2008).

[28]See Lawrence Goodwyn, *The Populist Movement* (New York: Oxford University Press, 1978).

[29]See, for example, Eli Watkins, "How Gary Johnson and Jill Stein Helped Elect Donald Trump," *CNN*, November 25, 2016, https://www.cnn.com/2016/11/10/politics/gary-johnson-jill-stein-spoiler/index.html.

[30]See Anthony King, *Running Scared* (New York: Free Press, 1997); but also see James E. Campbell, *The American Campaign: U.S. Presidential Campaigns and the National Vote* (College Station: Texas A&M Press, 2008).

[31]See Paul S. Herrnson and John C. Green, eds., *Responsible Partisanship* (Lawrence: University Press of Kansas, 2003).

[32]See Paul S. Herrnson, "The Roles of Party Organizations, Party-Connected Committees, and Party Allies in Elections," *The Journal of Politics,* 71 (2009): 1207–24.

[33]See Marjorie Randon Hershey, *Party Politics in America,* 17th ed. (New York: Routledge, 2017).

[34]Federal Election Commission, 2020.

[35]Kathleen Hall Jamieson, *Packaging the Presidency: A History and Criticism of Presidential Campaign Advertising*, 3rd ed. (New York: Oxford University Press, 1996).

[36]Darrell M. West, *Air Wars: Television Advertising in Election Campaigns, 1952-2004,* 6th ed. (Washington, D.C.: CQ Press, 2013).

[37]Brad Adgate, "The 2020 Elections Will Set (Another) Ad Spending Record," *Forbes*, September 3, 2019, https://www.forbes.com/sites/bradadgate/2019/09/03/the-2020-elections-will-set-another-ad-spending-record/#3d75bc101836.

[38]See R. Douglas Arnold, *Congress, the Press, and Political Accountability* (Princeton, N.J.: Princeton University Press, 2013).

[39]Andrew Prokopandrew, "Do presidential debates matter? Here's the political science evidence," *Vox*, September 26, 2016, https://www.vox.com/2016/9/12/12847632/debates-trump-clinton-polls-political-science.

[40]Jennifer Stromer-Galley, *Presidential Campaigning in the Internet Age* (New York: Oxford University Press, 2014).

[41]Joseph Napolitan, *The Election Game and How to Win It* (New York: Doubleday, 1972); For a contemporary look at the campaigning process, see D. Sunshine Hillygus and Todd G.

Shields, *The Persuadable Voter: Wedge Issues in Presidential Campaigns* (Princeton, N.J.: Princeton University Press, 2008).

[42]Thomas E. Patterson, "News Coverage of the 2016 General Election: How the Press Failed the Voters," Shorenstein Center on Media, Politics and Public Policy," Harvard Kennedy School, Harvard University, Cambridge, MA, December 7, 2016, https://shorensteincenter.org/news-coverage-2016-general-election/.

[43]Thomas E. Patterson, "News Coverage of Donald Trump's First 100 Days," Shorenstein Center on Media, Politics, and Public Policy, Harvard Kennedy School, May 18, 2017, https://shorensteincenter.org/news-coverage-donald-trumps-first-100-days/; Jeffrey E. Cohen, *The Presidency in the Era of 24-Hour News* (Princeton, N.J.: Princeton University Press, 2008), 33.

[44]"U.S. Media Coverage," Media Tenor, March 17, 2020. Data provided to author by Media Tenor.

[45]Quoted by Nancy Gibbs in her Theodore H. White Lecture, Harvard Kennedy School, November 15, 2017.

[46]Quoted in Andrew Gripp, "Is Television Ruining Our Political Discourse?" *IVN*, September 26, 2015, https://andrewgripp.wordpress.com/2015/09/26/is-television-ruining-our-political-discourse/.

[47]Federal Election Commission projection, 2020.

[48]Federal Election Commission, 2018.

[49]David B. Magelby, J. Quin Monson, and Kelly D. Patterson, eds., *Dancing Without Partners: How Candidates, Parties and Interest Groups Interact in the New Campaign Finance Environment* (Provo, Utah: Brigham Young University Press, 2005).

[50]Bill Allison, "The 2020 presidential race might be remembered as when the dam broke on money in U.S. politics," *Fortune*, February 13, 2020, https://fortune.com/2020/02/13/2020-election-campaign-spending-money/.

[51]Emmett H. Buell Jr. and Lee Sigelman, *Attack Politics: Negativity in Presidential Campaigns Since 1960* (Lawrence: University Press of Kansas, 2008). For opposing views on the effect of negative advertising, see Stephen Ansolabehere and Shanto Iyengar, *Going Negative* (New York: Free Press, 1995); and John Geer, *In Defense of Negativity* (Chicago: University of Chicago Press, 2006).

[52]Darrell M. West, *Air Wars: Television Advertising in Election Campaigns, 1952-2004*, 6th ed. (Washington, D.C.: CQ Press, 2013), 140–46.

[53]See, for example, Robert Farley, "Romney's Solar Flareout," *FactCheck.org*, June 1, 2012, http://factcheck.org/2012/06/romneys-solar-flareout/.

[54]Thomas E. Patterson, *Out of Order* (New York: Knopf, 1993.)

[55]John Sides and Lynn Vavreck, "What Really Decided the 2012 Election, in 10 Graphs," *The Washington Post*, October 14, 2013.

[56]Brad Lockerbie, *Do Voters Look to the Future?* (Albany: State University of New York Press, 2009).

[57]"The Perception Gap," More in Common, poll conducted in 2019, https://perceptiongap.us/.

CHAPTER NINE

[1]E. E. Schattschneider, *The Semisovereign People: A Realist's View of Democracy in America* (New York: Holt, Rinehart & Winston, 1960), 35.

[2]Megan R. Wilson, "Analysis: More Than 6,000 Lobbyists Have Worked on Taxes in 2017," *The Hill*, December 1, 2017, http://thehill.com/business-a-lobbying/business-a-lobbying/362796-analysis-more-than-6000-lobbyists-have-worked-on.

[3]Andrew Perez, Abigail Luke, and Tim Zelina, "Business Group Spending on Lobbying in Washington Is At Least Double What's Publicly Reported," *The Intercept*, August 6, 2019, https://theintercept.com/2019/08/06/business-group-spending-on-lobbying-in-washington-is-at-least-double-whats-publicly-reported/.

[4]Anthony J. Nownes, *Total Lobbying: What Lobbyists Want (and How They Try to Get It)* (New York: Cambridge University Press, 2006).

[5]See Matthew J. Burbank, Ronald J. Hrebenar, and Robert C. Benedict, *Parties, Interest Groups, and Political Campaigns* (Boulder, Colo.: Paradigm, 2008).

[6]Alexis de Tocqueville, *Democracy in America (1835-1840)*, eds. J. P. Mayer and A. P. Kerr (Garden City, N.Y.: Doubleday/Anchor, 1969), bk. 2, ch. 4.

[7]E. Pendleton Herring, *Group Representation Before Congress,* (Washington, D.C.: Brookings Institution, 1929), 78.

[8]U.S. Bureau of Labor Statistics, 2020.

[9]See Jack L. Walker, *Mobilizing Interest Groups in America* (Ann Arbor: University of Michigan Press, 1991).

[10]See Nownes, *Total Lobbying*. The author is indebted to Professor Anthony Nownes of the

University of Tennessee for the observations contained in this paragraph.

[11]Christopher J. Bosso, "The Color of Money: Environmental Groups and the Pathologies of Fund Raising," in Allan J. Cigler and Burdett Loomis, eds., *Interest Group Politics,* 4th ed. (Washington, D.C.: CQ Press, 1995), 101–3.

[12]Arbitron Radio Research and Corporation for Public Broadcasting Financial Reports, 2015.

[13]Mancur Olson, *The Logic of Collective Action,* rev. ed. (Cambridge, Mass.: Harvard University Press, 1971), 64.

[14]Theda Skocpol, *Diminished Democracy* (Norman: University of Oklahoma Press, 2003).

[15]Olson, *The Logic of Collective Action,* 147.

[16]Tyler O'Neil, "What the Left Doesn't Want You to Know About Trump's Tax Cuts," *PJMedia,* April 15, 2019, https://pjmedia.com/trending/what-the-left-doesnt-want-you-to-know-about-trumps-tax-cuts/; Dylan Matthews and Alexia Fernandez Campbell, "The Numbers Are in, and the House Republican Tax Bill Raises Taxes on over a Quarter of Americans," *Vox,* November 8, 2017. https://www.vox.com/policy-and-politics/2017/11/6/16614540/house-republican-tax-plan-paul-ryan-tax-policy-center.

[17]Ibid.

[18]Jeffrey N. Birnbaum, "Washington's Power 25: Which Pressure Groups Are Best at Manipulating the Laws We Live By?" *Fortune,* December 8, 1997.

[19]Frank R. Baumgartner, Jeffrey M. Berry, Marie Hojnacki, David C. Kimball, and Beth L. Leech, *Lobbying and Policy Change: Who Wins, Who Loses, and Why* (Chicago: University of Chicago Press, 2009).

[20]Norman J. Ornstein and Shirley Elder, *Interest Groups, Lobbying, and Policymaking* (Washington, D.C.: CQ Press, 1978), 82–86.

[21]See Paul S. Herrnson, Ronald G. Shaiko, and Clyde Wilcox, *The Interest Group Connection: Electioneering, Lobbying, and Policymaking in Washington,* 2nd ed. (Washington, D.C.: CQ Press, 2004).

[22]Quoted in a *National Journal* excerpt in Thomas E. Patterson, *The American Democracy,* 9th ed., (New York: McGraw-Hill, 2009), 245b.

[23]See John Mark Hansen, *Gaining Access* (Chicago: Chicago University Press, 1991); Bruce Wolpe and Bertram Levine, *Lobbying Congress* (Washington, D.C.: CQ Press, 1996).

[24]Center for Responsive Politics data, 2020, https://www.opensecrets.org/lobby/.

[25]Bara Vaida, "K-Street Paradox: $1.3 Million per Hour," *National Journal,* March 13, 2010.

[26]Quoted in Ornstein and Elder, *Interest Groups, Lobbying, and Policymaking,* 77.

[27]Steve Reinberg, "Debate Builds over Drug Companies' Fees to FDA," *The Washington Post,* April 13, 2007, www.washington-post.com/wp-dyn/content/article/2007/04/13/AR2007041301449.html.

[28]Paul J. Quirk, *Industry Influence in Federal Regulatory Agencies* (Princeton, N.J.: Princeton University Press, 1981); John E. Chubb, *Interest Groups and the Bureaucracy: The Politics of Energy* (Stanford, Calif.: Stanford University Press, 1983), 200–201.

[29]Lee Epstein and C. K. Rowland, "Interest Groups in the Courts," *American Political Science Review,* 85 (1991): 205–17.

[30]Richard Davis, *Electing Justice: Fixing the Supreme Court Nomination Process* (New York: Oxford University Press, 2005).

[31]OpenSecrets.org, 2020, https://www.opensecrets.org/industries/indus.php?Ind=D.

[32]Hugh Heclo, "Issue Networks and the Executive Establishment," in Anthony King, ed., *The New American Political System* (Washington, D.C.: American Enterprise Institute, 1978), 87–124.

[33]Norman J. Ornstein and Shirley Elder, *Interest Groups, Lobbying, and Policymaking* (Washington, D.C.: CQ Press, 1978), 88–93.

[34]See, for example, Gallup poll of January 2018.

[35]Christopher Ingraham, "Nobody Knows How Many Members the NRA Has, but Its Tax Returns Offer Some Clues," *The Washington Post,* February 26, 2016, https://www.washingtonpost.com/news/wonk/wp/2018/02/26/nobody-knows-how-many-members-the-nra-has-but-its-tax-returns-offer-some-clues/.

[36]Quoted in Mark Green, "Political PAC-Man," *The New Republic,* December 13, 1982, 20; see also Richard Skinner, *More Than Money: Interest Group Action in Congressional Elections* (Lanham, Md.: Rowman & Littlefield, 2006); Mark J. Rozell, Clyde Wilcox, and David Madland, *Interest Groups in American Campaigns,* 2nd ed. (Washington, D.C.: CQ Press, 2005).

[37]Jacob Pramuk, "AARP Warns Republicans It Has 'Strong Opposition' to Obamacare Replacement Bill," *CNBC,* May 25, 2017, https://www.cnbc.com/2017/05/25/aarp-has-strong-opposition-on-a-health-bill-that-slams-seniors.html.

[38]Federal Election Commission data, 2020.

[39]Ibid.

[40]Jennifer Babson and Kelly St. John, "Momentum Helps GOP Collect Record Amounts from PACs," *Congressional Quarterly Weekly Report,* December 3, 1994, 3456.

[41]*Citizens United v. Federal Election Commission,* 558 U.S. 50 (2010).

[42]Karl Evers-Hillstrom, "Super PACs Outmaneuver Outdated Rules to Leave Voters in the Dark," OpenSecrets.org, March 18, 2020, https://www.opensecrets.org/news/2020/03/sunshine-week-2020-super-pacs-loophole/.

[43]Bernie Sanders, "Overturn Citizens United," *U.S. News & World Report,* January 13, 2012, www.usnews.com/debate-club/are-super-pacs-harming-us-politics/overturn-citizens-united.

[44]Bradley Smith, "Super PACs Level the Playing Field," *U.S. News & World Report,* January 13, 2012, www.usnews.com/debate-club/are-super-pacs-harming-us-politics/super-pacs-level-the-playing-field.

[45]Jack L. Walker, *Mobilizing Interest Groups in America* (Ann Arbor: University of Michigan Press, 1991), 112.

[46]Theodore J. Lowi, *The End of Liberalism: The Second Republic of the United States* (New York: Norton, 1979).

[47]Larry Bartels, *Unequal Democracy: The Political Economy of the New Gilded Age* (Princeton, N.J.: Princeton University Press, 2008).

[48]Martin Gilens and Benjamin I. Page, "Testing Theories of American Politics: Elites, Interest Groups, and Average Citizens," *Perspectives on Politics,* 12 (2104): 564–81, http://citeseerx.ist.psu.edu/viewdoc/download;jsessionid=37EDA24D1D5DA87AEB950CEFE63883FF?doi=10.1.1.668.8647&rep=rep1&type=pdf.

[49]See, for example, James A. Stimson, *Tides of Consent: How Public Opinion Shapes American Politics* (New York: Cambridge University Press, 2004).

Chapter Ten

[1]Theodore H. White, *The Making of the President, 1972* (New York: Bantam Books, 1973), 327.

[2]See Bill Kovach and Tom Rosenstiel, *The Elements of Journalism* (New York: Three Rivers Press, 2001).

[3]See Rodger Streitmatter, *Mightier Than the Sword: How the News Media Have Shaped American History* (Westport, Conn.: Praeger, 2008).

[4]Frank Luther Mott, *American Journalism, a History: 1690-1960* (New York: Macmillan, 1962), 114–15; see also Si Sheppard, *The Partisan Press: A History of Media Bias in the United States* (Jefferson, N.C.: McFarland, 2007).

[5]Edwin Emery, *The Press and America: An Interpretive History of the Mass Media* (Englewood Cliffs, N.J.: Prentice-Hall, 1977), 350.

[6]Quoted in Mott, *American Journalism,* 529.

[7]Quoted in David Halberstam, *The Powers That Be* (New York: Knopf, 1979), 208–9.

[8]Nancy Kranich, "The Information Commons," Brennan Center for Justice, New York University School of Law, 2004, https://www.aaup.org/sites/default/files/files/InformationCommons.pdf.

[9]See, for example, Thomas E. Patterson and Robert D. McClure, *The Unseeing Eye* (New York: Putnam, 1976).

[10]Filipe R. Campante and Daniel Hojman, "Media and Polarization," Faculty Research Working Paper Series, Harvard Kennedy School, December 2009, https://projects.iq.harvard.edu/files/wcfia/files/rcampante_media_polarization.pdf.

[11]For reasons that are not fully understood, conservatives have a much stronger preference for partisan talk show. According to both polling and ratings data, conservative talk show hosts dominate the partisan talk show sector. They attract roughly 90 percent of the partisan talk show audience.

[12]Pew Research Center, "Audio and Podcasting Fact Sheet," June 16, 2017, http://www.journalism.org/fact-sheet/audio-and-podcasting/.

[13]William Cole, ed., *The Most of A. J. Liebling* (New York: Simon, 1963), 7.

[14]See, for example, J. Sonia Huang and Wei-Ching Wang, "Application of the Long Tail Economy to the Online News Market," *Journal of Media Economics,* 27 (2014): 158–76.

[15]Matthew Hindman, *The Myth of Digital Democracy* (Princeton, N.J.: Princeton University Press, 2009), 90–91.

[16]Douglas A. McIntyre, "Breitbart Audience Steady at 83 Million," *24/7 Wall Street,* September 30, 2017, https://247wallst.com/media/2017/09/30/breitbart-audience-steady-at-83-million/.

[17]Zach Exley, "Black Pigeon Speaks: The Anatomy of the Worldview of an Alt-Right YouTuber," Shorenstein Center on Media,

Politics, and Public Policy, Harvard Kennedy School, Harvard University, June 28, 2017, https://shorensteincenter.org/anatomy-of-alt-right-youtuber/.

[18]Meg Kelly and Elyse Samuels, "How Russia Weaponized Social Media, Got Caught, and Escaped Consequences," *The Washington Post*, November 18, 2019, https://www.washingtonpost.com/politics/2019/11/18/how-russia-weaponized-social-media-got-caught-escaped-consequences/.

[19]Nicholas Confessore and Daisuke Wakabayashi, "Russians Spun American Rage Into a Weapon," *The New York Times*, October 10, 2017.

[20]Kathleen Hall Jamieson and Karlyn Kohrs Campbell, *The Interplay of Influence,* rev. ed. (Boston: Wadsworth, 2005), 4.

[21]Donald Shaw and Maxwell McCombs, *The Emergence of American Political Issues: The Agenda-Setting Function of the Press* (St. Paul, Minn.: West, 1977).

[22]Bernard C. Cohen, *The Press and Foreign Policy* (Princeton, N.J.: Princeton University Press, 1963), 13.

[23]See Kathleen Hall Jamieson, *Eloquence in an Electronic Age* (New York: Oxford University Press, 1988), 42.

[24]Thomas E. Patterson, "News Coverage of Donald Trump's First 100 Days," Shorenstein Center on Media, Politics and Public Policy, Harvard Kennedy School, Harvard University, May 18, 2017, https://shorensteincenter.org/news-coverage-donald-trumps-first-100-days/.

[25]Greg Prince, "Trump's Tweets Are Seen by Less Than One Percent of His Followers, Social Media Expert Claims," *Newsweek,* January 3, 2018, http://www.newsweek.com/trump-tweets-one-percent-mainstream-media-769207.

[26]Stephen J. Farnsworth and S. Robert Lichter, *The Mediated Presidency: Television News and Presidential Governance* (Lanham, Md.: Rowman & Littlefield, 2006).

[27]Kiku Adatto, *Sound Bite Democracy,* Joan Shorenstein Center on the Press, Politics, and Public Policy, Research Paper R-2, Harvard University, June 1990.

[28]Center for Media and Public Affairs studies, available at www.cmpa.com/studies.

[29]Robert Entman, "Framing: Towards Clarification of a Fractured Paradigm," in Denis McQuail, ed., *McQuail's Reader in Mass Communication Theory* (London: Sage, 2002), 391–92.

[30]Thomas E. Patterson, *Out of Order* (New York: Knopf, 1993), 84.

[31]The classic study of priming is Shanto Iyengar, Mark Peters, and Donald Kinder, "Experimental Demonstrations of the "Not-So-Minimal" Consequences of Television News Programs," *The American Political Science Review,* 76 (1982): 848–58.

[32]Ibid.

[33]See, for example, Joseph N. Cappella and Kathleen Hall Jamieson, *Spiral of Cynicism* (New York: Oxford University Press, 1997), 159.

[34]Jay Rosen, *What Are Journalists For?* (New Haven, Conn.: Yale University Press, 1999), 295; Thomas E. Patterson, *How America Lost Its Mind* (Norman: Oklahoma University Press, 2019), 61–62.

[35]Sarah Sobieraj and Jeffrey M. Berry, "From Incivility to Outrage: Political Discourse in Blogs, Talk Radio, and Cable News," *Political Communication,* 28(2011): 27.

[36]Ibid, 27–28.

[37]Ibid, 30.

[38]Michael M. Grynbaum, "In Prime Time, Two Versions of Impeachment for a Divided Nation," *The New York Times,* November 21, 2019, https://www.nytimes.com/2019/11/16/business/media/impeachment-media-fox-msnbc.html.

[39]Quoted in Stephen Bates, *Realigning Journalism with Democracy: The Hutchins Commission, Its Times, and Ours* (Washington, D.C.: The Annenberg Washington Program of Northwestern University, 1995), 11.

[40]Thomas E. Patterson, "Doing Well and Doing Good," Joan Shorenstein Center on the Press, Politics, and Public Policy, Kennedy School of Government, Harvard University, December 2000, http://www.hks.harvard.edu/presspol/publications/reports/soft_news_and_critical_journalism_2000.pdf.

[41]Patterson, "Doing Well and Doing Good," 3–5; see also Michele Weldon, *Everyman News: The Changing American Front Page* (Columbus: University of Missouri Press, 2007), 37; Walter C. Dean and Atiba Pertilla, "I-Teams and 'Eye Candy': The Reality of Local TV News," in Tom Rosenstiel, Marion Just, Todd L. Belt, Atiba Pertilla, Walter Dean, and Dante Chinni, eds., *We Interrupt This Newscast* (New York: Cambridge University Press, 2007), 31–35; Matthew Robert Kerbel, *If It Bleeds It Leads* (New York: Basic Books, 2000).

[42]Douglas Mataconis, "Casey Anthony Trial Got More News Coverage than GOP Candidates," *Outside the Beltway,* July 6, 2011,

http://www.outsidethebeltway.com/casey-anthony-trial-got-more-news-coverage-than-gop-candidates/; "Casey Anthony Murder Trial Garners Extensive Media Coverage," *Los Angeles Times,* July 6, 2011, http://articles.latimes.com/2011/jul/06/entertainment/la-et-casey-anthony-trial-sidebar-20110706.

[43]Franklin Foer, *World Without Mind: The Existential Threat of Big Tech* (New York: Penguin Press, 2017), 147. Reference to the number of users is from CrowdTangle's website.

[44]Mark Thompson, *Enough Said: What's Gone Wrong with the Language of Politics* (New York: St. Martin's Press, 2016), 106.

[45]Foer, *World Without Mind,* 139.

[46]David Bauder, "Hear the One About Trump? You've Probably Heard a Lot," Associated Press, November 9, 2018, https://apnews.com/091e519ff65e48e2b58175b16d4bab3f; see also, Mehnaaz Momen, *Political Satire, Postmodern Reality, and the Trump Presidency* (Lanham, MD: Lexington Books, 2019).

[47]Marcus Prior, *Post-Broadcast Democracy* (New York: Cambridge University Press, 2007).

[48]Martin J. Wattenberg, *Is Voting for Young People?* (New York: Pearson Longman, 2008), 32.

[49]Editor and Publisher Yearbook data for 1975.

[50]Arbitron data for television news; Alliance for Audited Media data for newspapers.

[51]"Daily time spent reading newspapers per capita in the United States from 2010 to 2018 (in minutes)," Statista. Downloaded October 24, 2017: https://www.statista.com/statistics/186934/us-newspaper-reading-habits-since-2002/

[52]Ryan Chittum, "Print Newspapers Still Dominate Readers' Attention: Another Look at How Much Time Is Spent Reading Newspapers Online and in Print," *Columbia Journalism Review,* October 31, 2017, http://archives.cjr.org/the_audit/newspapers_time_spent.php.

[53]Steve Sternberg, "Will All TV Median Ages Soon Be over 50?" *MediaPost,* April 30, 2015, https://www.mediapost.com/publications/article/248728/will-all-tv-median-ages-soon-be-over-50.html?edition=.

[54]See, for example, Thomas E. Patterson, *The Mass Media Election* (New York: Praeger, 1980), 159–65.

[55]Filipe R. Campante and Daniel Hojman, "Media and Polarization," Faculty Research Working Paper Series, Harvard Kennedy School, December 2009, file:///C:/Users/tpatters/Downloads/RWP10-002-Campante-Hojman%20(1).pdf.

[56]Duncan J. Watts and David M. Rothschild, "Don't Blame the Election on Fake News. Blame It on the Media," *Columbia Journalism Review,* December 5, 2017, https://www.cjr.org/analysis/fake-news-media-election-trump.php.

[57]See, for example, Thomas E. Patterson, *Out of Order* (New York: Knopf, 1993), 53–93; Bruce Buchanan, *Renewing Presidential Politics* (Lanham, Md.: Rowman & Littlefield, 1996), 149; Regina G. Lawrence and Melody Rose, *Hillary Clinton's Race for the White House: Gender Politics and the Media on the Campaign Trail* (Boulder, Colo.: Lynne Rienner, 2009), 183.

[58]Thomas E. Patterson, "Of Polls, Mountains: U.S. Journalists and Their Use of Election Surveys," *Public Opinion Quarterly,* 69 (2005): 716–24.

[59]Tom Rosenstiel, Carl Gottlieb, and Lee Ann Brady, "Time of Peril for TV News," Project for Excellence in Journalism, 2000.

[60]Neil Postman, *Amusing Ourselves to Death: Public Discourse in the Age of Show Business* (New York: Viking, 1985), 106.

[61]Paul Starr, "Governing in the Age of Fox News," *The Atlantic,* January/February 2010, https://www.theatlantic.com/magazine/archive/2010/01/governing-in-the-age-of-fox-news/307838/; Natalie Jomini Stroud, "Media Use and Political Predispositions: Revisiting the Concept of Selective Exposure," *Political Behavior,* 30 (2008): 341–66.

[62]Pew Research Center polls, various dates.

[63]Jeffrey Gottfried, Michael Barthel, and Amy Mitchell, "Trump, Clinton Voters Divided in Their Main Source for Election News," Pew Research Center, January 18, 2017, http://www.journalism.org/2017/01/18/trump-clinton-voters-divided-in-their-main-source-for-election-news/.

[64]Ibid.

[65]Kathleen Hall Jamieson and Joseph N. Cappella, *Echo Chamber* (New York: Oxford University Press, 2008), 232; various Pew Research Center surveys.

[66]Ezra Klein, "Unpopular Mandate," *The New Yorker,* June 25, 2012, 33.

[67]"Partisanship and Political Animosity in 2016," Pew Research Center, June 2016, http://www.people-press.org/2016/06/22/partisanship-and-political-animosity-in-2016/.

[68]Diana Mutz, *In-Your-Face Politics* (Princeton, N.J.: Princeton University Press, 2015).

[69]Kathleen Hall Jamieson and Joseph N. Cappella, *Echo Chamber* (New York: Oxford University Press, 2010), 195–98.

[70]Carmen Stavrositu, "Selective Exposure," in Kerric Harvey, ed., *Encyclopedia of Social Media and Politics* (Thousand Oaks, Calif.: Sage, 2014): 1117–19.

[71]See, for example, Matthew Levendusky, *How Partisan Media Polarize America* (Chicago: University of Chicago Press, 2013).

[72]See David T. Z. Mindich, *Tuned Out: Why Americans under 40 Don't Follow the News* (New York: Oxford University Press, 2005).

[73]Thomas E. Patterson, "Young People and News," report of the Joan Shorenstein Center on the Press, Politics, and Public Policy, Kennedy School of Government, Harvard University, July 2007, http://www.hks.harvard.edu/presspol/research/carnegie-knight/young_people_and_news_2007.pdf.

[74]See, Kevin Arcenaux and Martin Johnson, *Changing Minds of Changing Channels: Partisan News in an Age of Choice* (Chicago: University of Chicago Press, 2013.)

[75]Wattenberg, Martin P., *Is Voting for Young People?,* (New York: Pearson Longman, 2008), 32.

[76]Kevin McSpadden, "You Now Have a Shorter Attention Span Than a Goldfish," *Time,* May 14, 2015, http://time.com/3858309/attention-spans-goldfish/.

[77]Wattenberg, *Is Voting for Young People?*, 75–80.

[78]Thomas E. Patterson, *How America Lost Its Mind* (Norman, OK: University of Oklahoma Press, 2019), 31.

[79]Nielsen Company audience report, 2017.

[80]Herbert A. Simon, "Designing Organizations for an Information-Rich World," in Martin Greenberger, ed., *Computers, Communication, and the Public Interest* (Baltimore, Md.: Johns Hopkins University Press, 1971), 40–41.

[81]Quoted in Steve Lohr, "The Smartphone's Rapid Rise from Gadget to Tool to Necessity," *The New York Times,* June 10, 2009, B1.

[82]Kenneth Burke, "How Many Texts Do People Send Every Day?" *Text Request,* May 18, 2016, https://www.textrequest.com/blog/many-texts-people-send-per-day/.

Chapter Eleven

[1]Roger H. Davidson and Walter J. Oleszek, *Congress and Its Members,* 10th ed. (Washington, D.C.: CQ Press, 2008), 4.

[2]See Paul S. Herrnson, *Congressional Elections: Campaigning at Home and in Washington,* 7th ed. (Washington, D.C.: CQ Press, 2012).

[3]See Gary C. Jacobson, *The Politics of Congressional Elections,* 8th ed. (New York: Longman, 2012).

[4]David Mayhew, *Congress: The Electoral Connection* (New Haven, Conn.: Yale University Press, 2004), 5.

[5]Bruce Cain, John Ferejohn, and Morris P. Fiorina, *The Personal Vote* (Cambridge, Mass.: Harvard University Press, 1987).

[6]Information provided by Clerk of the House.

[7]Lara E. Chausow, R. Eric Peterson, and Amber Hope Wilhelm, "Senate Staff Levels in Member, Committee, Leadership, and Other Offices, 1977–2014," Congressional Research Service, March 19, 2015, https://www.scribd.com/doc/315590129/Senate-Staff-Levels-in-Member-Committee-Leadership-And-Other-Offices-1977-2014.

[8]"Total Number of MPs, Peers and Staff," House of Commons Library, October 3, 2016. House of Commons members who hold leadership positions have larger staffs than the three people of the typical member.

[9]Edward Sidlow, *Challenging the Incumbent: An Underdog's Undertaking* (Washington, D.C.: CQ Press, 2003); David C. W. Parker, *The Power of Money in Congressional Campaigns, 1880–2006* (Norman: University of Oklahoma Press, 2008). See also Marian Currinder, *Money in the House: Campaign Funds and Congressional Party Politics* (Boulder, Colo.: Westview Press, 2008).

[10]Federal Election Commission data.

[11]OpenSecrets.org data, 2018.

[12]Federal Election Commission data, 2020.

[13]*Rucho v. Common Cause,* No. 18-422 (2019).

[14]Bill Bishop, *The Big Sort: Why the Clustering of Like-Minded America Is Tearing Us Apart* (New York: Houghton Mifflin, 2008).

[15]Jesse Sussell and James A. Thomson, "Are Changing Constituencies Driving Rising Polarization in the U.S. House of Representatives," Rand Corporation, 2015, https://www.rand.org/pubs/research_reports/RR896.html. See also Thomas E. Mann, "Polarizing the House of Representatives: How Much Does Gerrymandering Matter?" in Pietro S. Nivola and David W. Brady, eds., *Red and Blue Nation? Characteristics and Causes of America's Polarized Politics,* Vol. 1 (Washington, D.C.: Brookings Institution Press, 2006).

[16]Quoted in "A Tale of Myths and Measures: Who Is Truly Vulnerable?" *Congressional Quarterly Weekly Report,* December 4, 1993, 7; see also Dennis F. Thompson, *Ethics in Congress* (Washington, D.C.: Brookings Institution, 1995).

[17]James E. Campbell, *The Presidential Pulse of Congressional Elections* (Lexington: University Press of Kentucky, 1993).

[18]Robert Erikson, "The Puzzle of Midterm Losses," *Journal of Politics,* 50 (November 1988): 1011–29.

[19]Exit polls, 2018.

[20]See Eric D. Lawrence, Forrest Maltzman, and Steven S. Smith, "Who Wins? Party Effects in Legislative Voting," *Legislative Studies Quarterly,* 31 (2006): 33–69; Elaine C. Kamarck, "Increasing Turnout in Congressional Primaries," Brookings Institution, July 2014, 10, https://www.brookings.edu/wp-content/uploads/2016/06/KamarckIncreasing-Turnout-in-Congressional-Primaries72614.pdf.

[21]Elaine C. Kamarck and James Wallner, "Anticipating Trouble: Congressional Primaries and Incumbent Behavior," Brookings Institution, October 2018, https://www.brookings.edu/wp-content/uploads/2018/10/GS_10292018_Primaries-and-Incumbent-Behavior.pdf; Sean M. Theriault, *Party Polarization in Congress* (New York: Cambridge University Press, 2008); Barry C. Burden, "Candidate Positions in U.S. Congressional Elections," *British Journal of Political Science,* 34 (2004): 211–27.

[22]Eliana Johnson, "Ingraham's Insurrection," *National Review,* June 12, 2014, www.nationalreview.com/2014/06/ingrahams-insurrection-eliana-johnson.

[23]Linda L. Fowler and Robert D. McClure, *Political Ambition* (New Haven, Conn.: Yale University Press, 1989).

[24]See, for example, Avery Anapol, "Poll: Dems Lead by 15 Points on Generic House Ballot," *The Hill,* March 1, 2018, http://thehill.com/homenews/house/376272-poll-dems-lead-by-15-points-on-generic-house-ballot.

[25]Jo Mannies, "Outside money played outsized role in McCaskill-Hawley Senate race," St. Louis Public Radio, December 4, 2018, https://news.stlpublicradio.org/post/outside-money-played-outsized-role-mccaskill-hawley-senate-race#stream/0.

[26]*Congressional Quarterly Weekly Report,* various dates.

[27]Cited in Ryan Lizza, "The Obama Memos," *The New Yorker,* January 30, 2012, 36.

[28]Steven Smith, *Party Influence in Congress* (New York: Cambridge University Press, 2007); Barbara Sinclair, *Party Wars: Polarization and the Politics of National Policy Making* (Norman: University of Oklahoma Press, 2006).

[29]Danielle Thomsen, *Opting Out of Congress* (New York: Cambridge University Press, 2017).

[30]Elaina Plott, "Paul Ryan Pledges: No Immigration Reform Under Obama," *National Review,* October 27, 2015, https://www.nationalreview.com/2015/10/paul-ryan-promises-no-immigration-reform-obama-administration/.

[31]Quoted in Stephen E. Frantzich and Claude Berube, *Congress: Games and Strategies* (Lanham, Md.: Rowman & Littlefield, 2009), 159.

[32]Quoted in Jonathan Rauch, "How American Politics Went Insane," *The Atlantic,* July/August 2016, https://www.theatlantic.com/magazine/archive/2016/07/how-american-politics-went-insane/485570/.

[33]Randall Strahan, *Leading Representatives: The Agency of Leaders in the Politics of the U.S. House* (Baltimore, Md.: Johns Hopkins University Press, 2007); David King, *Turf Wars* (Chicago: University of Chicago Press, 1997).

[34]See Stephen E. Frantzich and Steven E. Schier, *Congress: Games and Strategies* (Dubuque, Iowa: Brown & Benchmark, 1995), 127.

[35]See Gerald S. Strom, *The Logic of Lawmaking* (Baltimore, Md.: Johns Hopkins University Press, 1990).

[36]See Barbara Sinclair, *Unorthodox Lawmaking: New Legislative Processes in the U.S. Congress,* 3rd ed. (Washington, D.C.: CQ Press, 2007).

[37]See Jon R. Bond and Richard Fleisher, eds., *Polarized Politics: Congress and the President in a Partisan Era* (Washington, D.C.: CQ Press, 2000).

[38]See Gary Orfield, *Congressional Power: Congress and Social Change* (New York: Harcourt Brace Jovanovich, 1975).

[39]James L. Sundquist, "Congress and the President: Enemies or Partners?" in Lawrence C. Dodd and Bruce I. Oppenheimer, eds., *Congress Reconsidered* (New York: Praeger, 1977), 240.

[40]Kelly Dittmar, Kira Sanbonmatsu, Susan J. Carroll, Debbie Walsh, and Catherine Wineinger, "Representation Matters: Women in the U.S. Congress," Center for American Women and Politics, Eagleton Institute of Politics, Rutgers University, 2017, https://cawp.rutgers.edu/sites/default/files/resources/representationmatters.pdf.

[41]Sarah F. Anzia and Christopher R. Berry, "The Jackie (and Jill) Robinson Effect: Why Do Congresswomen Outperform Congressmen?" *American Journal of Political Science,* 55 (2011): 478–93, https://onlinelibrary.wiley.com/doi/abs/10.1111/j.1540-5907.2011.00512.x.

[42]Craig Volden, Alan E. Wiseman, and Dana E. Wittmer, "Women's Issues and Their Fates in the US Congress," *Political Science Research & Methods*, 40 (2018): 679–96, https://www.cambridge.org/core/journals/political-science-research-and-methods/article/womens-issues-and-their-fates-in-the-us-congress/817B6C136C6CC03F4A13514A93E4AAEA.

[43]Brian Frederick, "Are Female House Member Still More Liberal in a Polarized Era," *Congress & the Presidency*, 36 (2009): 181–202, https://www.tandfonline.com/doi/abs/10.1080/07343460902948097.

[44]Judith Warner, "104 Women in Congress. Does It Matter?," *Politico Magazine*, January/February 2015, https://www.politico.com/magazine/story/2015/01/104-women-in-congress-does-it-matter-113903.

[45]Barry C. Burden, *Personal Roots of Representation* (Princeton, N.J.: Princeton University Press, 2007).

[46]Keith Krehbiel, "Are Congressional Committees Composed of Preference Outliers?" *American Political Science Review*, 84 (1990): 149–64; Richard L. Hall and Bernard Grofman, "The Committee Assignment Process and the Conditional Nature of Committee Bias," *American Political Science Review*, 84 (1990): 1149–66.

[47]See, for example, Alan Abramowitz, *The Disappearing Center: Engaged Citizens, Polarization and American Democracy* (New Haven, Conn.: Yale University Press, 2011).

[48]Fareed Zakaria, "Why Political Polarization Has Gone Wild in America (and What to Do About It)," *CNN World*, July 24, 2011; Frances E. Lee, *Beyond Ideology: Politics, Principles, and Partisanship in the U.S. Senate* (Chicago: University of Chicago Press, 2009).

[49]Frances E. Lee, *Insecure Majorities: Congress and the Perpetual Campaign* (Chicago: University of Chicago Press, 2016), 200–3.

[50]Ibid, 139.

[51]Joel A. Aberbach and Mark A. Peterson, eds., *The Executive Branch* (New York: Oxford University Press, 2005), 534–35.

[52]Joel Aberback, *Keeping a Watchful Eye* (Washington, D.C.: Brookings Institution, 1990); David Rosenbloom, *Building a Congress Centered Public Administration* (Tuscaloosa: University of Alabama Press, 2001).

[53]Lauren Carroll," *PolitiFact*, July 6, 2017, http://www.politifact.com/truth-o-meter/article/2017/jul/06/17-intelligence-organizations-or-four-either-way-r/.

[54]Pew Research Center, "Beyond Distrust: How Americans View Their Government," November 23, 2015, http://www.people-press.org/2015/11/23/beyond-distrust-how-americans-view-their-government/.

[55]John R. Hibbing and Elizabeth Theiss-Morse, *Stealth Democracy: Americans' Belief About How Government Should Work* (New York: Cambridge University Press, 2002).

CHAPTER TWELVE

[1]Jeffrey Goldberg, "James Mattis Denounces President Trump, Describes Him as a Threat to the Constitution," *The Atlantic*, June 3, 2020, https://www.theatlantic.com/politics/archive/2020/06/james-mattis-denounces-trump-protests-militarization/612640/.

[2]James W. Davis, *The American Presidency* (New York: Harper & Row, 1987), 13; Sidney Milkis and Michael Nelson, *The American Presidency: Origins and Development, 1790-2007*, 7th ed. (Washington, D.C.: CQ Press, 2015); see also Bruce Ackerman, *The Failure of the Founding Fathers* (Cambridge, Mass.: Belknap Press of Harvard University Press, 2005).

[3]See, for example, Barry M. Blechman and Stephen S. Kaplan, *Force Without War* (Washington, D.C.: Brookings Institution, 1978); Arthur M. Schlesinger Jr., *War and the American Presidency* (New York: Norton, 2004).

[4]James Bryce, *The American Commonwealth* (New York: Commonwealth Edition, 1908), 230.

[5]Quoted in Wilfred E. Binkley, *President and Congress*, 3rd ed. (New York: Vintage, 1962), 142.

[6]Peri E. Arnold, *Remaking the Presidency* (Lawrence: University Press of Kansas, 2009).

[7]Theodore Roosevelt, *An Autobiography* (New York: Scribner, 1931), 383.

[8]See Richard M. Pious, *The American Presidency* (New York: Basic Books, 1979), 83.

[9]Harry S. Truman, *Years of Trial and Hope* (New York: Signet, 1956), 535.

[10]Erwin C. Hargrove, *The Effective Presidency: Lessons on Leadership from John F. Kennedy to George W. Bush* (Boulder, Colo.: Paradigm, 2007).

[11]Quoted in Richard J. Ellis, *The Development of the American Presidency* (New York: Routledge, 2015), 194.

[12]See Thomas S. Langston, *The Cold War Presidency: A Documentary History* (Washington, D.C.: CQ Press, 2006).

[13]See Garry Wills, *Bomb Power: The Modern Presidency and the National Security State* (New York: Penguin Press, 2010).

[14]Quoted in Duncan Watts, *The American Presidency* (Edinburgh, Scotland: University of Edinburgh Press, 2009), 104.

[15]See James W. Ceaser, *Presidential Election: Theory and Development* (Princeton, N.J.: Princeton University Press, 1969).

[16]"It's the Media, Stupid, Not Advertising," Media Tenor, March 1, 2020, data provided to author by Media Tenor.

[17]John P. Burke, *The Institutionalized Presidency* (Baltimore, Md.: Johns Hopkins University Press, 1992); Charles E. Walcott and Karen M. Hult, *Governing the White House* (Lawrence: University Press of Kansas, 1995).

[18]Quoted in Stephen J. Wayne, *Road to the White House* (New York: St. Martin's Press, 1992), 143; but see Jody C. Baumgartner, *The American Vice Presidency Reconsidered* (Westport, Conn.: Praeger, 2006).

[19]See Jeffrey E. Cohen, *The Politics of the United States Cabinet* (Pittsburgh, Pa.: University of Pittsburgh Press, 1988); Shirley Anne Warshaw, *Powersharing: White House–Cabinet Relations in the Modern Presidency* (Albany: State University of New York Press, 1995).

[20]State Department data as of 2020.

[21]James Pfiffner, *The Modern Presidency* (New York: St. Martin's Press, 1994), 123; James Pfiffner, "Recruiting Executive Branch Leaders: The Office of Presidential Personnel," Brookings Institution, Spring 2001, www.brookings.edu/research/articles/2001/03/spring-governance-pfiffner.

[22]Quoted in James MacGregor Burns, "Our Super-Government—Can We Control It?" *The New York Times,* April 24, 1949, 32.

[23]See Paul C. Light, *Thickening Government: Federal Hierarchy and the Diffusion of Accountability* (Washington, D.C.: Brookings Institution, 1995).

[24]Peter Baker, Katie Benner, and Michael D. Shear, "Jeff Sessions Is Forced Out as Attorney General as Trump Installs Loyalist," *The New York Times,* November 7, 2018, https://www.nytimes.com/2018/11/07/us/politics/sessions-resigns.html.

[25]John P. Burke, *Presidential Power: Theories and Dilemmas* (Boulder, Colo.: Westview Press, 2016).

[26]Quoted in Lori Cox Han, *New Directions in the American Presidency* (New York: Routledge, 2010).

[27]Matthew Eshbaugh-Soha, *Breaking Through the Noise: Presidential Leadership, Public Opinion, and the News Media* (Palo Alto, CA: Stanford University Press, 2011), p. 16: Jeffrey E. Cohen, "The Presidency and the Mass Media," *The Oxford Handbook of the American Presidency* (New York: Oxford University Press, 2009).

[28]Michael D. Shear, Maggie Haberman, Nicholas Confessore, Karen Yourish, Larry Buchanan, and Keith Collins, "How Trump Reshaped the Presidency in over 11,000 Tweets," *The New York Times,* November 2, 2019, https://www.nytimes.com/interactive/2019/11/02/us/politics/trump-twitter-presidency.html.

[29]Ibid.

[30]Thomas E. Patterson, *Out of Order* (New York: Knopf, 1993); Center for Media & Public Affairs, Pew Research Center, and Media Tenor data for Clinton through Obama; Amy Mitchell, Jeffrey Gottfried, Galen Stocking, Katerina Eva Matsa, and Elizabeth Grieco, "Covering President Trump in a Polarized Media Environment," Pew Research Center, October 2, 2017, http://www.journalism.org/2017/10/02/covering-president-trump-in-a-polarized-media-environment/.

[31]Greg Prince, "Trump's Tweets Are Seen by Less Than One Percent of His Followers," *Newsweek,* January 3, 2018, http://www.newsweek.com/trump-tweets-one-percent-mainstream-media-769207.

[32]Bernard Goldberg, *Bias: A CBS Insider Exposes How the Media Distort News* (New York: Harper Paperbacks, 2003).

[33]David D'Alessio and Mike Allen, "Media Bias in Presidential Elections: A Meta-Analysis," *Journal of Communication,* 50 (2000): 133–56.

[34]Thomas E. Patterson, "News Coverage of the 2016 General Election: How the Press Failed the Voters," Shorenstein Center on Media, Politics and Public Policy, Harvard Kennedy School, Harvard University, Cambridge, MA, December 7, 2016, https://shorensteincenter.org/news-coverage-2016-general-election/.

[35]Thomas E. Patterson, *The Vanishing Voter* (New York: Knopf, 2002), 73–76.

[36]Michael Robinson, "Public Affairs Television and the Growth of Political Malaise," *American Political Science Review,* 70 (1976): 409–32.

[37]Mark Rozell, "Press Coverage of Congress," in Thomas Mann and Norman Ornstein, eds., *Congress, the Press, and the Public* (Washington, D.C.: American Enterprise Institute and Brookings Institution, 1994), 109.

[38]Robinson, "Public Affairs Television and the Growth of Political Malaise."

[39]The press's negativity and sensationalism have had another effect as well. They have damaged the press's credibility. According to a 2007 survey conducted by the Center for Public Leadership at Harvard University's John F. Kennedy School of Government, the press has the lowest public confidence rating of any major U.S. institution.

[40]Charles O. Jones, *The President in a Separated System* (Washington, DC: Brookings Institution Press, 2005), p. 173.

[41]Sidney Blumenthal, *The Permanent Campaign* (Boston: Beacon Press, 1980); Brendan J. Doherty, *The Rise of the President's Permanent Campaign* (Lawrence, KS: University of Kansas Press, 2012).

[42]Thomas E. Patterson, *The Mass Media Election* (New York: Praeger, 1980).

[43]Quoted in Joe Klein, "The Perils of the Permanent Campaign," *Time*, October 5, 2005, http://content.time.com/time/magazine/article/0,9171,1124332,00.html.

[44]Samuel Kernell, *Going Public: New Strategies of Presidential Leadership,* 3rd ed. (Washington, D.C.: CQ Press, 1997), 1; see also Robert M. Eisinger, *The Evolution of Presidential Polling* (New York: Cambridge University Press, 2003); Stephen J. Farnsworth and S. Robert Lichter, *Mediated Presidency: Television News & Presidential Governance* (Lanham, Md.: Rowman & Littlefield, 2005).

[45]Anthony Corrado and Kathryn Dunn Tenpas, "Permanent Campaign Brushes Aside Tradition," Brookings Institution, March 30, 2004, https://www.brookings.edu/opinions/permanent-campaign-brushes-aside-tradition/.

[46]Thomas E. Patterson, "News Coverage of Donald Trump's First 100 Days," Shorenstein Center on Media, Politics and Public Policy, Harvard Kennedy School, Harvard University, Cambridge, MA, May 18, 2017, https://shorensteincenter.org/news-coverage-donald-trumps-first-100-days/; Michael Wolff, *Fire and Fury: Inside the Trump White House* (New York: Henry Holt, 2018); Julia Carrie Wong, "'Way Ahead of the Field': Inside Trump's Unprecedented Social Media Campaign," *The Guardian*, July 3, 2019, https://www.theguardian.com/us-news/2019/jul/02/way-ahead-of-the-field-inside-the-trump-campaigns-unprecedented-social-media-campaign.

[47]David A. Graham, "Trump Never Stopped Campaigning Long Enough to Govern," *The Atlantic*, June 18, 2019, https://www.theatlantic.com/ideas/archive/2019/06/trump-cant-relaunch-a-campaign-that-never-stopped/591949/.

[48]Thomas P. (Tip) O'Neill, with William Novak, *Man of the House: The Life and Political Memoirs of Speaker Tip O'Neill* (New York: Random House, 1987), 297.

[49]Ibid., 33.

[50]Richard E. Neustadt, *Presidential Power and the Modern Presidents* (New York: Free Press, 1990), 71–72.

[51]Julie Hirschfeld Davis and Michael D. Shear, "Trump Signs Spending Bill, Reversing Veto Threat and Avoiding Government Shutdown," *The New York Times*, March 23, 2018, https://www.nytimes.com/2018/03/23/us/politics/trump-veto-spending-bill.html.

[52]Charles O. Jones, *The Presidency in a Separated System* (Washington, D.C.: Brookings Institution, 2005).

[53]Quoted in Ryan Lizza, "The Obama Memos," *The New Yorker,* January 30, 2012, 44.

[54]Sanford Levinson and Jack M. Balkin, *Democracy and Dysfunction* (Chicago, IL: University of Chicago Press, 2019).

[55]This figure includes formal presidential memorandums, which have the same legal status as executive orders but take a somewhat different form.

[56]*United States v. Belmont,* 57 U.S. 758 (1937).

[57]Robert DiClerico, *The American President,* 6th ed. (Englewood Cliffs, N.J.: Prentice-Hall, 1999), 47.

[58]Quoted in Antonio Thompson and Christos Frentzos, *The Routledge Handbook of American Military and Diplomatic History* (New York: Routledge, 2013), 301.

[59]Matt Compton, "We Can't Wait: President Obama in Nevada," The White House, October 24, 2011, ://obamawhitehouse.archives.gov/blog/2011/10/24/we-cant-wait-president-obama-nevada.

[60]Quoted in Emmet John Hughes, *The Ordeal of Power: A Political Memoir of the Eisenhower Years* (New York: Athenaeum 1963), 124.

[61]David Goetsch, *Effective Leadership* (Upper Saddle River, N.J.: Prentice-Hall, 2004).

[62]Stephen Skowronek, *Presidential Leadership in Political Time* (Lawrence: University of Kansas Press, 2008).

[63]Stephen Skowronek, *The Politics Presidents Make* (Cambridge, Mass.: Belknap Press of Harvard University, 1997).

[64]Erwin Hargrove, *The Power of the Modern Presidency* (New York: Knopf, 1974); see also John H. Kessel, *Presidents, the Presidency, and the Political Environment* (Washington, D.C.: CQ Press, 2001); Skowronek, *Presidential Leadership in Political Time.*

[65]John E. Mueller, "Presidential Popularity from Truman to Johnson," *American Political Science Review,* 64 (March 1970): 18–34; Kathleen Frankovic, "Public Opinion in the 1992 Campaign," in Gerald M. Pomper, ed., *The Election of 1992* (Chatham, N.J.: Chatham House, 1993); Chris J. Dolan, *The Presidency and Economic Policy* (Lanham, Md.: Rowman & Littlefield, 2007).

[66]Paul Light, *Presidents' Agenda* (Baltimore, Md.: Johns Hopkins University Press, 1999).

[67]James P. Pfiffner, *The Strategic Presidency: Hitting the Ground Running,* 2nd ed. (Chicago: Dorsey Press, 1996).

[68]Aaron Wildavsky, "The Two Presidencies," *Trans-Action,* December 1966, 7.

[69]Pfiffner, *Modern Presidency,* ch. 6.

[70]Quoted in Jonathan Masters, "U.S. Foreign Policy Powers: Congress and the President," Council on Foreign Relations, March 2, 2017, https://www.cfr.org/backgrounder/us-foreign-policy-powers-congress-and-president.

[71]Susan Decker, "Trump's 25% Steel Import Tariffs Upheld by U.S. Appeals Court," *Bloomberg News,* February 28, 2020, https://www.bloomberg.com/news/articles/2020-02-28/trump-s-25-steel-import-tariffs-upheld-by-u-s-appeals-court.

[72]John T. Bennett, "Trump's Winning Pattern with Legislation Might Become a Thing of the Past: CQ Vote Studies," *Roll Call,* February 28, 2019, https://www.rollcall.com/2019/02/28/trumps-winning-pattern-with-legislation-might-become-a-thing-of-the-past-cq-vote-studies/.

[73]"Tracking Congress in the Age of Trump," *FiveThirtyEight,* https://projects.fivethirtyeight.com/congress-trump-score/votes/.

[74]Quoted in Lizza, "The Obama Memos," 49.

[75]Glenn Kessler and Meg Kelly, "President Trump Made 2,140 False or Misleading Claims in His First Year," *The Washington Post,* January 20, 2018, https://www.washingtonpost.com/news/fact-checker/wp/2018/01/20/president-trump-made-2140-false-or-misleading-claims-in-his-first-year/?utm_term=.c2f5bab7d97f.

[76]Hugh Heclo, "Introduction: The Presidential Illusion," in Hugh Heclo and Lester M. Salamon, eds., *The Illusion of Presidential Government* (Boulder, Colo.: Westview Press, 1981), 2.

CHAPTER THIRTEEN

[1]Max Weber, *Economy and Society* (New York: Bedminster Press, 1968), 223. Translated and edited by Guenther Roth and Claus Wittich. Originally published in 1921.

[2]Michael Laris, Ian Duncan, and Lori Aratani, "FAA's Lax Oversight Played Part in Boeing 737 Max Crashes, but Agency Is Pushing to Become More Industry-Friendly," *The Washington Post,* October 28, 2019, https://www.washingtonpost.com/local/trafficandcommuting/faas-lax-oversight-played-part-in-boeing-737-max-crashes-but-agency-is-pushing-to-become-more-industry-friendly/2019/10/27/bc0bf184-f4e1-11e9-ad8b-85e2aa00b5ce_story.html.

[3]Reason-Rupe poll, July 2014.

[4]Charles T. Goodsell, *The Case for Bureaucracy,* 2d ed., (Chatham, N.J.: Chatham House, 1985), 55–60.

[5]Paul C. Light, "Cascade of Failures: Why Government Fails, and How to Stop It," Brookings Institution, July 2014, https://www.brookings.edu/wp-content/uploads/2016/06/Light_Cascade-of-Failures_Why-Govt-Fails.pdf.

[6]Ed Pilkington and Tom McCarthy, "The Missing Six Weeks," *The Guardian,* March 28, 2020, https://www.theguardian.com/us-news/2020/mar/28/trump-coronavirus-politics-us-health-disaster

[7]Weber, *Economy and Society,* 23.

[8]Paul Light, *A Government Ill-Executed* (Cambridge, Mass.: Harvard University Press, 2009); "The True Size of Government," Volker Alliance, September 29, 2017), https://www.volckeralliance.org/true-size-government.

[9]See Mark Sauter and James Carafano, *Homeland Security* (New York: McGraw-Hill, 2005).

[10]Office of Personnel Management data, 2016.

[11]Gregory A. Huber, *The Craft of Bureaucratic Neutrality: Interests and Influence in Governmental Regulation of Occupational Safety* (New York: Cambridge University Press, 2007); Herbert Kaufman, "Emerging Conflicts in the Doctrine of Public Administration," *American Political Science Review* 50 (December 1956): 1060.

[12]See Allen Schick, *The Federal Budget: Politics, Policy, Process,* 3rd ed. (Washington, D.C.: Brookings Institution, 2007).

[13]Zeeshan Aleem, "Trump Wants to Gut the State Department by 25 Percent," *Vox,* February 12, 2018, https://www.vox.com/policy-and-politics/2018/2/12/17004372/trump-budget-state-department-defense-cuts.

[14]See Cornelius M. Kerwin, *Rulemaking,* 3rd ed. (Washington, D.C.: CQ Press, 2003); Daniel E. Hall, *Administrative Law: Bureaucracy in a Democracy* (Upper Saddle River, N.J.: Prentice-Hall, 2005).

[15]See Hugh Heclo, *A Government of Strangers* (Washington, D.C.: Brookings Institution, 1977), 117–18.

[16]Quoted in Aaron Wildavsky, *The Politics of the Budgetary Process,* 4th ed. (Boston: Little, Brown, 1984), 19; see also Dennis D. Riley, *Bureaucracy and the Policy Process: Keeping the Promises* (Lanham, Md.: Rowman & Littlefield, 2005).

[17]Joel D. Aberbach and Bert A. Rockman, "Clashing Beliefs Within the Executive Branch," *American Political Science Review,* 70 (June 1976): 461.

[18]Norton E. Long, "Power and Administration," *Public Administration Review,* 10 (Autumn 1949): 269; Joel D. Aberbach and Bert A. Rockman, *In the Web of Politics* (Washington, D.C.: Brookings Institution, 2000).

[19]See B. Guy Peters, *The Politics of Bureaucracy,* 5th ed. (New York: Routledge, 2001).

[20]See B. Dan Wood and Richard W. Waterman, *Bureaucratic Dynamics* (Boulder, Colo.: Westview Press, 1994); Edward C. Page and Bill Jenkins, *Policy Bureaucracy: Government with a Cast of Thousands* (New York: Oxford University Press, 2005).

[21]See, for example, Ed Blazina, "Transit Leaders Lobby Congress to Restore Federal Grants for New Projects," *Pittsburgh Post-Gazette,* March 19, 2018, http://www.post-gazette.com/news/transportation/2018/03/19/American-Public-Transportation-Association-federal-grants-cut-by-Trump-lobby-Congress-bus-rapid-transit/stories/201803190141.

[22]Long, "Power and Administration," 269; see also John Mark Hansen, *Gaining Access* (Chicago: University of Chicago Press, 1991).

[23]Ibid, 118.

[24]William T. Gormley Jr. and Steven J. Balla, *Bureaucracy and Democracy* (Washington, D.C.: CQ Press, 2003); Kevin B. Smith, *Public Administration: Power and Politics in the Fourth Branch of Government* (New York: Oxford University Press, 2006).

[25]James P. Pfiffner, "The National Performance Review in Perspective," working paper 94-4, Institute of Public Policy, George Mason University, 1994, 2.

[26]*Seila Law LLC v. Consumer Financial Protection Bureau,* No. 19-7 (2020).

[27]Ibid., 12.

[28]Kaufman, "Emerging Conflicts," 1062.

[29]Environmental Integrity Project data, February 2018, http://www.environmentalintegrity.org/news/civil-penalties-decline-under-trump-administration/.

[30]Heclo, *Government of Strangers,* 104.

[31]William F. West, "The Administrative Presidency as Reactive Oversight: Implications for Positive and Normative Theory," *Public Administration Review,* 75 (2015): 523–33.

[32]Ibid., 225.

[33]See Joel D. Aberbach, *Keeping a Watchful Eye* (Washington, D.C.: Brookings Institution, 1990).

[34]Douglas A. Van Belle and Kenneth M. Mash, *A Novel Approach to Politics* (Washington, D.C.: CQ Press, 2006).

[35]See Donald Kettl, *Deficit Politics* (New York: Macmillan, 1992).

[36]David Rosenbloom, "The Evolution of the Administrative State, and Transformations of Administrative Law," in David Rosenbloom and Richard Schwartz, eds., *Handbook of Regulation and Administrative Law* (New York: Marcel Dekker, 1994), 3–36.

[37]*Pigeford v. Veneman,* U.S. District Court for the District of Columbia, Civil Action No. 97-1978 (1999).

[38]See *Vermont Yankee Nuclear Power Corp. v. National Resources Defense Council, Inc.,* 435 U.S. 519 (1978); *Chevron v. National Resources Defense Council,* 467 U.S. 837 (1984); *Heckler v. Chaney,* 470 U.S. 821 (1985); but see *FDA v. Brown & Williamson Tobacco Co.,* 529 U.S. 120 (2000).

[39]See Mark W. Huddleston, "The Carter Civil Service Reforms," *Political Science Quarterly,* (Winter 1981–82): 607–22.

[40]Ed O'Keefe, "Senior Executive Service Needs Overhaul, Outside Study Finds," *The Washington Post,* August 20, 2009.

[41]Jordain Carney, "Rand Paul Reads Alleged Whistleblower's Name on Senate Floor," *The*

Hill, February 4, 2020, https://thehill.com/homenews/senate/481417-rand-paul-reads-alleged-whistleblowers-name-on-senate-floor.

[42]See Brian J. Cook, *Bureaucracy and Self-Government* (Baltimore, Md.: Johns Hopkins University Press, 1996).

CHAPTER FOURTEEN

[1]*Marbury v. Madison,* 5 U.S. 137 (1803).

[2]*Obergefell v. Hodges,* No 14–556 (2015).

[3]*South Carolina v. North Carolina* 558 U.S. 256 (2010).

[4]Steven G. Calabresi and James Lindgren, "Term Limits for the Supreme Court: Life Tenure Reconsidered," in Roger C. Cramton and Paul D. Carrington, eds, *Reforming the Court: Term Limits for Supreme Court Justices* (Durham, N.C.: Carolina Academic Press, 2006).

[5]Supreme Court of the United States data. https://www.supremecourt.gov/about/justicecaseload.aspx.

[6]Henry Glick, *Courts, Politics, and Justice,* 3rd ed. (New York: McGraw-Hill, 1993), 120.

[7]For the content of this paragraph, the author is indebted to Professor Tony Wiley of Dodge City Community College.

[8]Timothy R. Johnson, Paul Wahlbeck, and James Spriggs, "The Influence of Oral Arguments on the U.S. Supreme Court," *American Political Science Review,* 100 (2006): 99–113.

[9]Lawrence Baum, *The Supreme Court,* 8th ed. (Washington, D.C.: CQ Press, 2003), 120.

[10]From a letter to the author by Frank Schwartz of Beaver College; this section reflects substantially Professor Schwartz's recommendations to the author, as does the later section that addresses the federal court myth.

[11]*Hutto v. Davis,* 370 U.S. 256 (1982).

[12]See Richard Davis, *Electing Justices* (New York: Oxford University Press, 2005).

[13]Robert Scigliano, *The Supreme Court and the Presidency* (New York: Free Press, 1971), 146; see also Lee Epstein and Jack Knight, *The Choices Justices Make* (Washington, D.C.: CQ Press, 1998); Stefanie A. Lundquist, David A. Yalof, and John A. Clark, "The Impact of Presidential Appointments to the Supreme Court: Cohesive and Divisive Voting Within Presidential Blocs," *Political Research Quarterly,* 53 (2000): 795–814.

[14]Quoted in Baum, *Supreme Court,* 37.

[15]Quoted in Kermit L. Hall and Kevin T. McGuire, *The Judicial Branch* (New York: Oxford University Press, 2005), 77.

[16]See Virginia A. Hettinger et al., *Judging on a Collegial Court: Influences on Federal Appellate Decision Making* (Charlottesville: University of Virginia Press, 2006).

[17]John Gottschall, "Reagan's Appointments to the U.S. Courts of Appeals," *Judicature,* 48 (1986): 54.

[18]See, for example, "Politicization in the Federal Judiciary and Its Effect on the Federal Judicial Function," *New York University Journal of Legislation & Public Policy,* 19 (2017), https://papers.ssrn.com/sol3/papers.cfm?abstract_id=2995008.

[19]Quoted in Louis Fisher, *American Constitutional Law* (New York: McGraw-Hill, 1990), 5.

[20]Quoted in Charles P. Curtis, *Law and Large as Life* (New York: Simon & Schuster, 1959), 156–57.

[21]See Lee Epstein and Jack Knight, *The Choices Justices Make* (New York: Longman, 1995); Thomas G. Hansford and James F. Spriggs II, *The Politics of Precedent on the Supreme Court* (Princeton, N.J.: Princeton University Press, 2006).

[22]*Bostock v. Clayton County,* No. 16-1817 (2020).

[23]John Schmidhauser, *The Supreme Court* (New York: Holt, Rinehart & Winston, 1964), 6.

[24]*McConnell v. Federal Election Commission,* 540 U.S. 93 (2003).

[25]*Citizens United v. Federal Election Commission,* 558 U.S. 310 (2010).

[26]Alma Cohen and Crystal S. Yang, "Judicial Politics and Sentencing Decisions," *American Economic Journal,* 11 (2019): 160–91.

[27]Neal Devins and Lawrence Baum, *The Company They Keep: How Partisan Divisions Came to the Supreme Court* (New York: Oxford University Press, 2019).

[28]Jeffrey A. Segal and Harold J. Spaeth, *The Supreme Court and the Attitudinal Model Revisited* (New York: Cambridge University Press, 2002), 404.

[29]Devins and Baum, *The Company They Keep.*

[30]Brian Lamb, Susan Swain, and Mark Farkas, *The Supreme Court* (New York: Public Affairs, 2010), 6.

[31]Stephen L. Wasby, *The Supreme Court in the Federal Judicial System,* 4th ed. (Chicago: Nelson-Hall, 1993), 53.

[32]*District of Columbia v. Heller,* 554 U.S. 570 (2008).

[33]Rob Arthur, "Trump's Justice Department Isn't Enforcing Civil Rights," *Vice News*, February 23, 2018, https://news.vice.com/en_us/article/wj44y4/trumps-justice-department-isnt-enforcing-civil-rights.

[34]*Gonzales v. Raich*, 545 U.S. 1 (2005).

[35]Richard Davis, *Electing Justices* (New York: Oxford University Press, 2005).

[36]Eyder Peralta, "NSA's Bulk Collection Of Americans' Phone Data Is Illegal, Appeals Court Rules," National Public Radio, May 7, 2019, https://www.npr.org/sections/thetwo-way/2015/05/07/404898259/federal-court-bulk-collection-of-phone-metadata-is-illegal.

[37]See Antonin Scalia, *A Matter of Interpretation* (Princeton, N.J.: Princeton University Press, 1997).

[38]See Stephen Breyer, "Our Democratic Constitution," James Madison Lecture, New York University Law School, New York, October 22, 2001.

[39]Henry J. Abraham, "The Judicial Function Under the Constitution," *News for Teachers of Political Science,* 41 (Spring 1984): 14.

[40]*National Federation of Independent Business v. Sebelius,* No. 11-393 (2012).

[41]Frank H. Easterbrook, "Do Liberals and Conservatives Differ in Judicial Activism," *University of Colorado Law Review,* 73 (2002): 1401.

Chapter Fifteen

[1]Marc Allen Eisner, Jeffrey Worsham, and Evan J. Rinquist, *Contemporary Regulatory Policy* (Boulder, Colo.: Lynne Rienner, 2006).

[2]This section relies substantially on Alan Stone, *Regulation and Its Alternatives* (Washington, D.C.: CQ Press, 1982).

[3]See Marc Allen Eisner, *Regulatory Politics in Transition,* 2nd ed. (Baltimore, Md.: Johns Hopkins University Press, 2000).

[4]See Richard A. Harris and Sidney M. Milkis, *The Politics of Regulatory Change* (New York: Oxford University Press, 1996).

[5]Lawrence E. Mitchell, *Corporate Irresponsibility* (New Haven, Conn.: Yale University Press, 2003).

[6]H. Peyton Young, *Equity: In Theory and Practice* (Princeton, N.J.: Princeton University Press, 1995).

[7]Michael Greenwood, "8 Million Lives Saved Since Surgeon General's Tobacco Warning 50 Years Ago," *YaleNews*, January 7, 2014, http://news.yale.edu/2014/01/07/8-million-lives-saved-surgeon-general-s-tobacco-warning-50-years-ago.

[8]Ann E. Marimow, "FDA Can Regulate E-cigarettes Just Like Conventional Cigarettes, Appeals Court Says," *The Washington Post,* December 10, 2019, https://www.washingtonpost.com/local/legal-issues/fda-can-regulate-e-cigarettes-just-like-conventional-cigarettes-appeals-court-says/2019/12/10/e4c28836-cffc-11e9-b29b-a528dc82154a_story.html.

[9]Board on Population Health and Public Health Practice, *The Future of Drug Safety: Promoting and Protecting the Health of the Public* (Washington, D.C.: National Academies Press, 2007).

[10]Rachel Carson, *Silent Spring* (Boston: Houghton Mifflin, 1962); see also Lester R. Brown, *Plan B2.0: Rescuing a Planet Under Stress and a Civilization in Trouble* (New York: Norton, 2006).

[11]See Walter A. Rosenbaum, *Environmental Politics and Policy,* 10th ed. (Washington, D.C.: CQ Press, 2016); Norman J. Vig and Michael E. Kraft, eds., *Environmental Policy: New Directions for the Twenty-First Century* (Washington, D.C.: CQ Press, 2003).

[12]"Global Climate Report—Annual 2019," National Oceanic and Atmospheric Administration, https://www.ncdc.noaa.gov/sotc/global/201913.

[13]*Janus v. American Federation of State, County and Municipal Employees,* No. 16-1466 (2018).

[14]Elliot A. Rosen, *Roosevelt, the Great Depression, and the Economics of Recovery* (Charlottesville: University of Virginia Press, 2007).

[15]See Robert Lekachman, *The Age of Keynes* (New York: Random House, 1966); see also Richard Kopke, Geoffrey M. B. Tootell, and Robert K. Trist, eds., *The Macroeconomics of Fiscal Policy* (Cambridge, Mass.: MIT Press, 2006).

[16]See Bruce Bartlett, *Reaganomics: Supply-Side Economics* (Westport, Conn.: Arlington House, 1981).

[17]Paul Krugman, "Hey, Lucky Duckies," *The New York Times,* December 3, 2002, A31.

[18]"The Cost of Rising Interest Rates," Committee for a Responsible Federal Budget, December 14, 2016, http://www.crfb.org/papers/cost-rising-interest-rates.

[19] Alan O. Ebenstein, *Milton Friedman: A Biography* (New York: Palgrave Macmillan, 2007).

[20] Edward Hadas and Hugh Dixon, "Quantitative Easing: A Therapy of Last Resort," *The New York Times,* January 1, 2009, www.nytimes.com/2009/01/11/business/worldbusiness/11iht-views12.1.19248009.html.

[21] Martin Mayer, *FED: The Inside Story of How the World's Most Powerful Financial Institution Drives the Markets* (New York: Free Press, 2001).

[22] See, for example, Megan Leonhardt, "Banks May Soon Offer Americans More Loan Options—Here's What Experts Say You Need to Know Before Borrowing," CNBC, March 27, 2020, https://www.cnbc.com/2020/03/27/americans-may-soon-have-more-loan-options-heres-what-to-know.html.

CHAPTER SIXTEEN

[1] *Federalist* No. 10.

[2] Chad Stone, Danilo Trisi, Arloc Sherman, and Roderick Taylor, "A Guide to Statistical Trends in Income Inequality," Center on Budget & Policy Priorities, August 29, 2018, https://www.cbpp.org/research/poverty-and-inequality/a-guide-to-statistics-on-historicaltrends-in-income-inequality.

[3] U.S. Census Bureau, 2020.

[4] Emmanuel Saez and Thomas Piketty, "Income Inequality in the United States: 1913–1998," *Quarterly Journal of Economics,* 118 (2003): 1–39.

[5] Paul Krugman, *The Conscience of a Liberal* (New York: Norton, 2007), 7–8.

[6] David Kocieniewski, "Since 1980s, the Kindest of Tax Cuts for the Rich," *The New York Times,* January 18, 2012.

[7] Andrew Flowers, "The Top 1 Percent Earns a Lot from Cashing In on Investments," *FiveThirtyEight,* January 20, 2015, http://fivethirtyeight.com/datalab/the-top-1-percent-earns-a-lot-from-cashing-in-on-investments/.

[8] Kathleen Elkins, "80% of Americans Own an Unbelievably Small Portion of the Country's Wealth," *Business Insider,* June 15, 2015, www.businessinsider.com/inequality-in-the-us-is-much-more-extreme-than-you-think-2015-6.

[9] Adam Looney and Kevin B. Moore, "Changes in the Distribution of After-Tax Wealth: Has Income Tax Policy Increased Wealth Inequality?" Federal Reserve Board, Washington, D.C., 2015.

[10] Thomas L. Hungerford, "Changes in the Distribution of Income Among Tax Filers Between 1996 and 2006: The Role of Labor Income, Capital Income, and Tax Policy," Congressional Research Service, December 29, 2011, Washington, D.C.

[11] Lawrence Mishel, "Unions, Inequality, and Faltering Middle-Class Wages," Economic Policy Institute, August 29, 2012, www.epi.org/publication/ib342-unions-inequality-faltering-middle-class/.

[12] Katie Sanders, "Rattner: Manufacturing Wages Today in America Lower Than Average Wages in the Economy as a Whole,'" *Punditfact,* March 30, 2014, www.politifact.com/punditfact/statements/2014/mar/30/steven-rattner/rattner-manufacturing-wages-today-america-lower-av/.

[13] Stephen Gold, "The Competitive Edge: Manufacturing's Multiplier Effect—It's Bigger Than You Think," *Industry Week,* September 2, 2014, www.industryweek.com/global-economy/competitive-edge-manufacturings-multiplier-effect-its-bigger-you-think.

[14] Kenneth P. Vogel and Jim Tankersley, "With Billions at Stake in Tax Debate, Lobbyists Played Hardball," *The New York Times,* December 15, 2017, https://www.nytimes.com/2017/12/15/us/politics/lobbyists-tax-overhaul-congress.html?mtrref=www.google.com&auth=login-email.

[15] Ben Brody, "Business Groups Spent Big on Lobbying During the Tax Overhaul," *Bloomberg News,* January 23, 2018, https://www.bloomberg.com/news/articles/2018-01-23/tax-bill-prompts-business-to-pay-heavily-for-lobbying-campaigns.

[16] "Census Shows 1 in 2 People Are Poor or Low-Income," *USA Today,* December 15, 2011, http://usatoday30.usatoday.com/news/nation/story/2011-12-15/poor-census-low-income/51944034/1.

[17] Phil Harvey and Lisa Conyers, *The Human Cost of Welfare* (Westport, Conn.: Praeger, 2016).

[18] See Felicia Ann Kornbluh, *The Battle for Welfare Rights: Politics and Poverty in Modern America* (Philadelphia: University of Pennsylvania Press, 2007).

[19] V. O. Key Jr., *The Responsible Electorate* (Cambridge, Mass.: Belknap Press of Harvard University, 1966), 43.

[20] Everett Carll Ladd, *American Political Parties* (New York: Norton, 1970), 205.

[21]See Jason DeParle, *American Dream: Three Women, Ten Kids, and a Nation's Drive to End Welfare* (New York: Penguin, 2005).

[22]Alberto Alesina and Edward Glaeser, *Fighting Poverty in the U.S. and Europe* (New York: Oxford University Press, 2006).

[23]Kaiser Family Foundation, "A Primer on Medicare Financing," January 31, 2011, http://kff.org/health-reform/issue-brief/a-primer-on-medicare-financing/.

[24]Emily Ekins, "Poll: 77% Say Government Efforts to Fight Poverty Have Been 'Ineffective,'" Cato Institute, September 26, 2019, https://www.cato.org/blog/poll-77-say-government-efforts-fight-poverty-have-been-ineffective;

[25]Charles Murray, *Losing Ground: American Social Policy, 1950-1980* (New York: Basic Books, 1984).

[26]Signe-Mary McKernan and Caroline Ratcliffe, "Events That Trigger Poverty Entries and Exits," *Social Science Quarterly,* 86 (2005): 1146-69.

[27]Ibid.

[28]See Christopher Howard, *The Welfare State Nobody Knows* (Princeton, N.J.: Princeton University Press, 2006).

[29]Mark Byrnes, "U.S. Spending on Social Welfare Programs Is Way Up, but Far Less of It Goes to the Poorest," *CityLab,* May 19, 2014, https://www.citylab.com/equity/2014/05/us-spending-on-social-welfare-programs-is-way-up-but-far-less-of-it-goes-to-the-poorest/371124/.

[30]Said of George H. W. Bush at the 1988 Democratic Convention. The quote is variously attributed to Ann Richards or Jim Hightower.

[31]For a history of public education, see Joel H. Spring, *The American School 1642-2004* (New York: McGraw-Hill, 2008).

[32]*San Antonio Independent School District v Rodriguez,* 411 U.S. 1 (1973).

[33]*The 2012 Kids Count Data Book: State Trends in Child Well-Being,* a report of the Annie E. Casey Foundation, July 25, 2012, www.aecf.org/resources/the-2012-kids-count-data-book/.

[34]Sean F. Reardon, Rachel A. Valentino, Demetra Kalogrides, Kenneth A. Shores, and Erica H. Greenberg, "Patterns and Trends in Racial Academic Achievement Gaps Among States, 1999-2011," Stanford University Graduate School of Education, August, 2013, https://cepa.stanford.edu/sites/default/files/reardon%20et%20al%20state%20achievement%20gaps%20aug2013.pdf.

[35]Based on Organization for Economic Cooperation and Development (OECD) data, 2006; see Douglas S. Reed, *On Equal Terms: The Constitutional Politics of Educational Opportunity* (Princeton, N.J.: Princeton University Press, 2003).

[36]U.S. Department of Education data, 2019.

[37]Stanley Feldman and John Zaller, "The Political Culture of Ambivalence: Ideological Responses to the Welfare State," *American Journal of Political Science,* 36 (1992): 268-307.

[38]Robert E. Lane, "Market Justice, Political Justice," *American Political Science Review,* 80 (June 1986): 383-402.

CHAPTER SEVENTEEN

[1]See, for example, Peter Trubowitz, *Defining the National Interest* (Chicago: University of Chicago Press, 1997).

[2]See Douglas T. Stuart, *Creating the National Security State* (Princeton, N.J.: Princeton University Press, 2008).

[3]See Mr. X. (George Kennan), "The Sources of Soviet Conduct," *Foreign Affairs,* 25 (July 1947): 566-82.

[4]David M. Barrett, *Uncertain Warriors: Lyndon Johnson and His Vietnam Advisors* (Lawrence: University Press of Kansas, 1993); see also Stanley Karnow, *Vietnam: A History* (New York: Penguin, 1983).

[5]See Dag Henriksen, *NATO's Gamble* (Annapolis, Md.: Naval Institute Press, 2007).

[6]See Ron Susskind, *The One-Percent Solution* (New York: Simon & Schuster, 2007).

[7]West Point speech, June 1, 2002; for an opposing view, see Gary Hart, *The Shield and the Cloak: The Security of the Commons* (New York: Oxford University Press, 2006).

[8]Nick Ritchie, *The Political Road to War with Iraq: Bush, 9/11 and the Drive to Overthrow Saddam* (New York: Routledge, 2007).

[9]Pew Research Center for the People and the Press, "Public Attitudes Toward the War in Iraq: 2003-2008," March 19, 2008, http://pewresearch.org/pubs/770/iraq-war-five-year-anniversary.

[10]Brian Michael Jenkins, "Fifteen Years On, Where Are We in the 'War on Terror'?" *Counter Terrorism Center Sentinel,* 9 (2016), https://ctc.usma.edu/fifteen-years-on-where-are-we-in-the-war-on-terror/.

[11]Quoted in Jeffrey A. Engel, "Putin Wants to Make Russia Great Again," *DallasNews*, October 5, 2017, https://www.dallasnews.com/opinion/commentary/2017/10/05/putin-wants-make-russia-great.

[12]Cristina Maza, "Russia and China Are Closer Than Ever Before, Beijing Says," *Newsweek*, April 6, 2018, http://www.newsweek.com/russia-and-china-are-closer-ever-beijing-says-it-launches-trade-war-trump-875304.

[13]Remarks of Nicholas Burns, World Affairs Council, Washington, D.C., June 23, 2011.

[14]"Military Expenditures," Stockholm International Peace Research Institute, 2020, https://www.sipri.org/research/armament-and-disarmament/arms-and-military-expenditure/military-expenditure.

[15]Statement of the U.S. Secretary of Defense, Leon Panetta, January 26, 2012.

[16]Thomas Rid and Thomas A. Keaney, eds., *Understanding Counterinsurgency Warfare* (New York: Routledge, 2010).

[17]See Richard Pearlstein, *Fatal Torture? Transnational Terrorism and the New Global Disorder* (Austin: University of Texas Press, 2004), 15–23.

[18]John Mueller, "Trends in Popular Support for the Wars in Korea and Vietnam," *American Political Science Review*, 65 (June 1971): 358–75; see also John Mueller, "The Iraq Syndrome," *Foreign Affairs* (November/December 2005).

[19]George C. Wilson, *This War Really Matters: Inside the Fight for Defense Dollars* (Washington, D.C.: CQ Press, 2000).

[20]Anthony H. Cordesman, "The Mattis Resignation and the U.S. FY2020 Defense Budget and Strategy Crisis," Center for Strategic & International Studies, January 3, 2019, https://www.csis.org/analysis/mattis-resignation-and-us-fy2020-defense-budget-and-strategy-crisis.

[21]*The World Competitiveness Yearbook* (Lausanne, Switzerland: International Institute for Management Development, 2008).

[22]U.S. government data, various agencies, 2020.

[23]William H. Branson, *Trends in U.S. International Trade and Investment Since World War II*, NBER Working Paper No. 469 (Cambridge, Mass.: National Bureau of Economic Research, April 1980).

[24]Robert Whaples, "Do Economists Agree on Anything? Yes!," *The Economists' Voice*, 3 (2006): 1–6.

[25]Ana Swanson and Alan Rappeport, "Trump Signs China Trade Deal, Putting Economic Conflict on Pause," *The New York Times*, January 15, 2020, https://www.nytimes.com/2020/01/15/business/economy/china-trade-deal.html.

[26]David Steven Jacoby, *Trump, Trade, and the End of Globalization* (Westport, Conn.: Praeger, 2018).

[27]Bianca DiJulio, Jamie Firth, and Mollyann Brodie, "Data Note: Americans' Views on the U.S. Role in Global Health," *Kaiser Family Foundation*, January 23, 2015, http://www.kff.org/global-health-policy/poll-finding/data-note-americans-views-on-the-u-s-role-in-global-health/; "As Sequester Deadline Looms, Little Support for Cutting Most Programs," Pew Research Center, February 22, 2013, http://www.people-press.org/2013/02/22/as-sequester-deadline-looms-little-support-for-cutting-most-programs/.

[28]Organization for Economic Co-operation and Development (OECD) data, 2020.

[29]Paola Subacchi and Stephen Pickford, *Legitimacy vs. Effectiveness for the G20: A Dynamic Approach to Global Economic Governance* (London, UK: Royal Institute of International Affairs, October 2011), 2.

INDEX

AARP (American Association of Retired Persons), 197, 256–257, 264, 490
ABC, 280, 291, 292, 295, 385
abolition, 9, 12
abortion
  partial-birth abortion, 109
  party polarization, 110
  presidential authority, 346
  right of privacy, 109–110
  undue burden standard, 109
absolute immunity, 48
accommodation doctrine, 105
accountability, 399–409
accused persons, 111–121
  appeal rights, 120
  arrest phase, 112, 115
  civil liberties overview, 111
  due process, 94–95, 111, 112
  fair-trial rights, 93, 115–118
  illegally obtained evidence, 116–117
  Miranda warning, 115, 116, 120
  racial profiling, 120
  search and seizure, 92–93, 111–115, 117, 123
  sentencing phase, 118
  suspicion phase, 111–115
  trial phase, 115–118
ACLU (American Civil Liberties Union), 261, 435
Act of Toleration, 104
Adams, John, 29, 47, 51, 98, 213, 431
Adarand v. Pena (1995), 139
administrative agencies. *See* federal bureaucracy
administrative law, 430
administrative law judges, 406–407
advertisement, negative, 238
affirmative action, 137–140
Affordable Care Act (2010), 2, 87, 106, 483
  federalism and passage of, 87
  free-exercise clause, 106
  party polarization, 87
Afghanistan invasion (1979), 505, 506
Afghanistan War, 507, 510, 516
AFL-CIO, 249, 259
African Americans
  bureaucrats, 408
  civil rights movement, 12, 136, 137, 201, 217, 218, 371
  COVID-19 pandemic and, 155
  discrimination, 128
  in elective office, 141. *See also* Obama, Barack
  family, 141

  group orientation, 174–178
  Jim Crow, 9, 130
  judicial appointees, 427
  lynchings, 10
  population (1790), 34
  poverty among, 10, 141
  racial profiling, 120
  school segregation, 130–132
  "separate but equal" ruling, 74, 129
  slavery. *See* slavery
  state-by-state population, 34, 149
  Supreme Court justices, 424–425
  voting rights, 136, 188–189
age
  age discrimination, 153
  Congressional service requirements, 309
  entitlement programs, 488
  group orientation, 178
  public opinion, 178
  voter turnout, 195
  voting rights, 190
Age Discrimination Act (1975), 153
Age Discrimination in Employment Act (1967), 153
agency capture, 260
agency point of view, 394–396
agenda setting, 284
agenda setter, president as, 358
agents of socialization, 167–169
agricultural conservation programs, 182
agricultural groups, 250, 261
Aid for Families with Dependent Children (AFDC), 483, 484, 486
Ailes, Roger, 237, 280
air wars, 233
Airline Deregulation Act (1978), 404, 448
al Qaeda, 507, 510, 511, 517
Alaska Natives. *See* Native Americans
Albanian, 506
alienation, 195
Alito, Samuel, Jr., 417, 428, 431, 433, 440
America. *See* United States
American Association of University Professors (AAUP), 251
American Bar Association (ABA), 251
American Civil Liberties Union (ACLU), 261, 435
American Conservative Union (ACU), 251
American Dilemma, An (Myrdal), 155
American Federation of Teachers, 249
American Independent Party, 226
American Medical Association (AMA), 251